Business Law

Denis Keenan LLB (Hons) FCIS DMA Cert. Ed.

Of the Middle Temple, Barrister-at-Law
Formerly Head of Department
of Business Studies and Law,
Mid-Essex Technical College and School of Art
(now Chelmer Essex Institute of Higher Education)

Sarah Riches LLB (Hons) PGCE

Lecturer in Law,
Bolton Institute of of Higher Education

Pitman

PITMAN PUBLISHING
128 Long Acre, London WC2E 9AN

First published in Great Britain 1987
Reprinted 1988

British Library Cataloguing in Publication Data
Keenan, Denis
  Business law.
  1. Corporation law—England
  I. Title   II. Riches, Sarah
  344.206'65   KD2057
  ISBN 0–273–02415–9

Printed and bound in Great Britain at The Bath Press, Avon

Contents

NINA.

Preface

This book has been written mainly for those students taking the BTEC National Option Unit Business Law (U252P). We have followed closely the revised specifications for this unit which take effect from September 1987. Our intention is to provide a textbook in keeping with the aims of the new Business Law Unit while covering the indicative content fully. Nevertheless, we feel that the book will have a wider appeal, particularly to those taking examinations in business law who find the study of law to be somewhat of a linguistic challenge.

We have assumed that the reader has no previous knowledge of English law; our starting point is basic principles and when specialist legal terms are used we have given clear 'jargon free' explanations. The book is designed to provide the reader with an understanding of the changing legal framework within which modern business organizations must operate. The emphasis is on law in its business context. Thus a range of business documents have been included enabling the reader to relate the principles of business law to the real world of business.

In this connection our thanks are due to the Consumer Credit Trade Association, The Road Haulage Association and HMSO for giving us their kind permission to reproduce certain of these documents. The reader should appreciate that the versions of these documents and forms appearing in our text are reduced in size and also that the copyright in them must be respected. This extends also to any alteration or variation in them without the authorization of the owner of the copyright.

The implementation strategy of the revised Business Law Unit stresses the development of a variety of learning activities. At the end of each chapter we have provided a selection of questions and activities related specifically to the material introduced in that chapter. We have also devised sample assignments which draw on the general themes of each section of the text. The suggested assignments are designed to enable the students to achieve the principal objectives and develop the skills particularly relevant to the unit: communicating, information gathering and identifying and tackling problems.

One of the main themes of the new unit is legal change. It is appropriate, therefore, to record some of the major developments which have occurred since the typescript was submitted.

Chapter 2: The changing law

The *European Communities (Amendment) Act 1986* ratifies the Single European Act (SEA) which was approved by the European Council in December 1985 and signed in February 1986. The main features of the SEA are –

The European Council (meetings of the Heads of State of the Member States and the Commission's President) becomes a formal part of the institutional framework of the European Community.

The Council must meet at least twice a year.

The Council is given the power to create a new Court of First Instance, attached to the European Court of Justice.

A new decision-making procedure (*co-operation procedure*) is established involving the Council, Commission and Parliament.

The role of the Parliament in the legislative process is strengthened.

The provisions for qualified majority voting in the Council are extended to help the Community meet the 1992 target for the completion of the internal market.

The Community's competence is widened to cover co-operation in economic and monetary policy, social policy, economic and social cohesion, research and technological development and the environment.

The European Assembly is to be known formally as the European Parliament.

Chapter 8: Introduction to the law of contract

The Minors' Contracts Act 1986 which received the Royal Assent on 11 April 1987 implements the recommendations of the Law Commission contained in their 1984 Report. It will allow a minor on reaching 18 to ratify a contract or loan made when he or she was a minor. It will also make any guarantee supporting a loan to a minor enforceable against the adult guarantor (reversing *Coutts & Co v Browne-Lecky* (1946)). A court will be able to order the return of non-necessary goods (or the proceeds of their sale) acquired under a contract later repudiated by the minor.

Chapter 11: Sale of goods

The High Court in *Bernstein v Pamsons Motors (Golders Green) Ltd* (1986) *The Times* October 25 considered how long a buyer may keep goods without prejudicing his right to reject them for a breach of condition under s.11 of the Sale of Goods Act 1979.

Mr Bernstein bought a new car from Pamsons in January 1985. After three weeks of use (and 142 miles on the clock) the engine seized up. The car was repaired under the warranty but Mr Bernstein refused to take the car back. Rougier J held that Pamsons were in breach of the implied conditions under s.14, but Mr Bernstein was deemed to have accepted the goods under s.35 and thereby had lost his right to treat the contract as repudiated and reject the car.

Chapter 13: Manufacturer's liability

The *Consumer Safety (Amendment) Act 1986*, which came into force on 8 August 1986 strengthens the powers of customs officers and trading standards officers to deal with the problem of unsafe goods.

The *Consumer Protection Act 1987* which received the Royal Assent on 15 May 1987 aims to remedy three areas of weakness in consumer protection law: product liability, safety of goods and misleading price indications.

(1) *Product liability*. Part 1 of the Bill implements the European Community's Directive on Product Liability. It will impose strict liability on manufacturers, importers (into the Community) and 'own-branders' in respect of products which are defective or unsafe. Liability is limited to death or personal injury or loss or damage to property provided the damages would be more than £275. Unprocessed food is exempted and a 'development risks' defence has been included.

(2) *Safety of Goods*. It will be a criminal offence to supply consumer goods which are not reasonably safe having regard to all the circumstances.

(3) *Misleading prices*. Section 11 of the Trade Descriptions Act 1968 and the Price Marking (Bargain Offers) Order 1979 will be repealed and replaced by a new general criminal offence of giving a misleading price indication. The Act will not be brought into force immediately.

In conclusion Sarah Riches extends her thanks to Teri Carrigan who typed her chapters and to her husband Brian McCaughey who was supportive throughout and provided helpful comments and criticisms.

In the preparation of the book the authors and their publishers have received the invaluable assistance of Mary Keenan in terms of the preparation and initial editing of the typescript and proofs, together with the index of statutes and of cases.

Our thanks go also to those at Pitmans who were closely involved, in particular David Carpenter, the Managing Editor, who was with us from the beginning, and more recently Simon Lake, Business Management Publisher and, of course, the printers for their assistance in processing a rather complex typescript and the proofs. For the errors and omissions we are, of course, solely responsible.

June 1987   Denis Keenan
Sarah Riches

Index of statutes

Index of cases

Introduction to Law

The nature of law

The law affects every aspect of our lives; it governs our conduct from the cradle to the grave and its influence even extends from before our birth to after our death. We live in a society which has developed a complex body of rules to control the activities of its members. There are laws which govern working conditions (e.g. by laying down minimum standards of health and safety), laws which regulate leisure pursuits (e.g. by banning the sale of alcohol at football matches), and laws which control personal relationships (e.g. by prohibiting marriage between close relatives).

In this book we are concerned with one specific area of law: the rules which affect the business world. We shall consider such matters as the requirements that must be observed to start a business venture, the rights and duties which arise from business transactions and the consequences of business failure. In order to understand the legal implications of business activities, it is first necessary to examine some basic features of our English legal system. It is important to remember that English law refers to the law as it applies to England and Wales. Scotland and Northern Ireland have their own distinct legal systems.

Classification of law

There are a number of ways in which the law may be classified; the most important are as follows –

(1) *Public and private law*. The distinction between public and private law is illustrated in Fig. 1.1.

(*a*) *Public law*. Public law is concerned with the relationship between the State and its citizens. This comprises several specialist areas such as –

(*i*) *Constitutional law*. Constitutional law is concerned with the workings of the British constitution. It covers such matters as the position of the Crown, the composition and procedures of Parliament, the functioning of central and local government, citizenship and the civil liberties of individual citizens.

(*ii*) *Administrative law*. There has been a dramatic increase in the activities of government during the last hundred years. Schemes have been introduced to help ensure a minimum standard of living for everybody. Government agencies are involved,

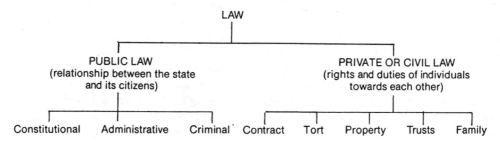

Fig. 1.1 The distinction between public and private law.

for example, in the provision of a state retirement pension, supplementary benefit and child benefit. A large number of disputes arise from the administration of these schemes and a body of law, administrative law, has developed to deal with the complaints of individuals against the decisions of the administering agency.

(*iii*) *Criminal law*. Certain kinds of wrongdoing pose such a serious threat to the good order of society that they are considered crimes against the whole community. The criminal law makes such anti-social behaviour an offence against the state and offenders are liable to punishment. The state accepts responsibility for the detection, prosecution and punishment of offenders.

(*b*) *Private law*. Private law is primarily concerned with the rights and duties of individuals towards each other. The state's involvement in this area of law is confined to providing a civilized method of resolving the dispute that has arisen. Thus the legal process is begun by the aggrieved citizen and not by the state. Private law is also called civil law and is often contrasted with criminal law.

(2) *Criminal and civil law*. Legal rules are generally divided into two categories: criminal and civil. It is important to understand the nature of the division because there are fundamental differences in the purpose, procedure and terminology of each branch of law.

(*a*) *Criminal law*. The criminal law is concerned with forbidding certain forms of wrongful conduct and punishing those who engage in the prohibited acts. Criminal proceedings are normally brought in the name of the Crown and are called *prosecutions*. (It should be noted that prosecutions may also be undertaken by various public bodies, such as the trading standards department of the local authority, and by private individuals: e.g. a store detective prosecuting a shoplifter.) You have a *prosecutor* who *prosecutes* a *defendant* in the *criminal courts*. The consequences of being found guilty are so serious that the standard of proof is higher than in civil cases: the allegations of criminal conduct must be proved beyond a reasonable doubt. If the prosecution is successful, the defendant is found *guilty* (*convicted*) and may be *punished* by the courts. The punishments available to the court include imprison-

ment, fines, probation or perhaps community service. If the prosecution is unsuccessful the defendant is found *not guilty* (*acquitted*). A businessman may find himself in breach of the criminal law under such enactments as the Trade Descriptions Act 1968, the Consumer Safety Act 1978 and the Companies Act 1985.

(*b*) *Civil law*. The civil law deals with the private rights and obligations which arise between individuals. The purpose of the action is to remedy the wrong that has been suffered. Enforcement of the civil law is the responsibility of the individual who has been wronged; the state's role is to provide the procedure and the courts necessary to resolve the dispute. In civil proceedings a *plaintiff* sues a *defendant* in the *civil courts*. The plaintiff will be successful if he can prove his case on the balance of probabilities, i.e. the evidence weighs more in favour of the plaintiff than of the defendant. If the plaintiff wins his action the defendant is said to be *liable* and the court will order an appropriate remedy such as damages (financial compensation) or an injunction (an order to do or not do something). If the plaintiff is not successful the defendant is found *not liable*. Many of the laws affecting the businessman are part of the civil law, especially contract, tort and property law. (The basic features of the different branches of civil law will be examined in greater detail later in this chapter.) The main differences between civil and criminal law are illustrated in Fig. 1.2.

The distinction between the criminal and civil law does not depend on the nature of the wrongful act, because the same act may give rise to both civil and criminal proceedings. Consider the consequences of a typical motor accident. Julie is crossing the road at a zebra crossing when she is struck by a car driven by Gordon. An ambulance takes Julie to a local hospital where it is discovered that she has sustained a broken leg. Meanwhile the police have arrived at the scene of the accident and they breathalyse Gordon. The result is positive and Gordon is charged with the criminal offence of driving with excess alcohol. He appears before the local magistrates' court and is convicted. He is disqualified from driving for 18 months and fined £400. The fine is paid to the court; it does not go to compensate the victim of the criminal act. However, a criminal court now has a limited power to order an offender to pay compensation for any 'personal injury, loss or damage' caused to the victim of his offence. Julie will be able to pursue a civil action against Gordon to remedy the personal wrong she has suffered. She sues Gordon under the tort of negligence, seeking damages for the injuries she has sustained. The case is heard in the High Court where Gordon is found liable. He is ordered to pay £6000 in damages.

back to 1066 when William of Normandy gained the Crown of England by defeating King Harold at the Battle of Hastings.

Before the arrival of the Normans in 1066 there really was no such thing as English law. The Anglo-Saxon legal system was based on the local community. Each area had its own courts in which local customs were applied. The Norman Conquest did not have an

	Criminal law	Civil law
Concerns	Offences against the state	Disputes between private individuals
Purpose of the action	To preserve order in the community by punishing offenders and deterring others	To remedy the wrong which has been suffered
The parties	A prosecutor prosecutes a defendant	A plaintiff sues a defendant
Where the action is heard	The criminal courts i.e. magistrates' court or Crown Court	The civil courts i.e. county court or High Court
Standard of proof	The prosecutor must prove his case beyond a reasonable doubt	The plaintiff must establish his case on the balance of probabilities
Decision	A defendant may be convicted if he is guilty and acquitted if he is innocent	A defendant may be found liable or not liable
Sanctions	Imprisonment, fine, probation, community service	Damages, injunction, specific performance, rescission
Examples	Murder, theft, drunken driving, using a false trade description	Contract, tort, trusts, property law

Fig. 1.2 The differences between criminal and civil law.

(3) *Common law and equity.* Legal rules may also be classified according to whether they form part of the common law or equity. The distinction between these two systems of law is rooted in history and can only be understood properly by examining the origins of English law. English legal development can be traced

immediate effect on English law; indeed, William promised the English that they could keep their customary laws. The Normans were great administrators and they soon embarked on a process of centralization, which created the right climate for the evolution of a uniform system of law for the whole country.

The common law

The Norman kings ruled with the help of the most important and powerful men in the land who formed a body known as the Curia Regis (King's Council). This assembly carried out a number of functions: it acted as a primitive legislature, performed administrative tasks and exercised certain judicial powers. The meetings of the Curia Regis came to be of two types: occasional assemblies attended by the barons and more frequent but smaller meetings of royal officials. These officials began to specialize in certain types of work and departments were formed. This trend eventually led to the development of courts to hear cases of a particular kind. The courts which had emerged by the end of the thirteenth century became known as the Courts of Common Law and they sat at Westminster. The first to appear was the Court of Exchequer. It dealt with taxation disputes but later extended its jurisdiction to other civil cases. The Court of Common Pleas was the next court to be established. It heard disputes of a civil nature between one citizen and another. The Court of King's Bench, the last court to appear, became the most important of the three courts because of its close association with the king. Its jurisdiction included civil and criminal cases and it developed a supervisory function over the activities of the inferior courts.

The Normans exercised central control by sending representatives of the king from Westminster to all parts of the country to check up on the local administration. At first these royal commissioners exercised a number of tasks: they made records of land and wealth, collected taxes and adjudicated in disputes brought before them. The judicial powers gradually became more important than the others. To begin with, these commissioners (or justices) applied local customary law at the hearings, but in time local customs were replaced by a body of rules applying to the whole country.

When they had completed their travels round the country, the justices returned to Westminster where they discussed the customs they had encountered. By a gradual process of sifting these customs, rejecting those which were unreasonable and accepting those which were not, they formed a uniform pattern of law throughout England. Thus by selecting certain customs and applying them in all future similar cases, the *common law* of England was created.

A civil action at common law was begun with the issue of a writ which was purchased from the offices of the Chancery, a department of the Curia Regis under the control of the Chancellor. Different kinds of action were covered by different writs. The procedural rules and type of trial varied with the nature of the writ. It was essential that the correct writ was chosen, otherwise the plaintiff would not be allowed to proceed with his action.

Equity

Over a period of time the common law became a very rigid system of law and in many cases it was impossible to obtain justice from the courts. The main defects of the common law were as follows –

(*a*) The common law failed to keep pace with the needs of an increasingly complex society. The writ system was slow to respond to new types of action. If a suitable writ was not available, an injured party could not obtain a remedy, no matter how just his claim.

(*b*) The writ system was very complicated, but trivial mistakes could defeat a claim.

(*c*) The only remedy available in the common law courts was an award of damages. This was not always a suitable or adequate remedy.

(*d*) Men of wealth and power could overawe a court and there were complaints of bribery and intimidation of jurors.

It became the practice of aggrieved citizens to petition the king for assistance. As the volume of petitions increased, the king passed them to the Curia Regis and a committee was set up to hear the petitions. The hearings were presided over by the Chancellor and in time petitions were addressed to him alone. By the fifteenth century the Chancellor had started to hear petitions on his own and the Court of Chancery was established. The body of rules applied by the court was called *Equity*.

The early chancellors were drawn from the ranks of the clergy and their decisions reflected their ecclesiastical background. They examined the consciences of the parties and then ordered what was fair and just. At first, each chancellor acted as he thought best. Decisions varied from chancellor to chancellor and this resulted in a great deal of uncertainty for petitioners. Eventually chancellors began to follow previous decisions and a large body of fixed rules grew up.

The decisions of the Court of Chancery were often at odds with those made in the common law courts. This proved a source of conflict until the start of the seventeenth century when James I ruled that, in cases of conflict, equity was to prevail. For several centuries the English legal system continued to develop with two distinct sets of rules administered in separate courts. Equity is not a complete system of law. Equitable principles were formulated to remedy specific defects in the common law. They were designed to complement the common law rules and not replace them. Equity has made an important contribution to the development of English law, particularly in the following areas –

(1) *Recognition of new rights.* The common law did not recognize the concept of the trust. A trust arises where a settlor (S) conveys property to a trustee (T) to hold on trust for a beneficiary (B). The common law treated T as if he were the owner of the property and B's claims were ignored. The Court of Chancery, however, would require T to act according to his conscience and administer the trust on B's behalf. Thus equity recognized and enforced the rights of a beneficiary under a trust. The Court of Chancery also came to the aid of borrowers who had mortgaged their property as security for a loan. If the loan was not repaid by the agreed date, the common law position was that the lender (mortgagee) became the owner of the property and the borrower (mortgager) was still required to repay the outstanding balance. Equity gave the mortgagor the right to pay off the loan and recover his property even though the repayment date had passed. This equitable principle is known as the equity of redemption. It will be considered in more detail in Chapter 17.

(2) *Introduction of new remedies.* The new equitable rights were enforced by means of new equitable remedies. In the field of contract law, the Court of Chancery developed such remedies as the injunction, specific performance, rescission and rectification, which will be examined in Chapter 8. These remedies were not available as of right like common law remedies: they were discretionary. The Court of Chancery could refuse to grant an equitable remedy if, for example, the plaintiff had himself acted unfairly.

By the nineteenth century the administration of justice had reached an unhappy state of affairs and was heavily criticized. The existence of separate courts for the administration of common law and equity meant that someone who wanted help from both the common law and equity had to bring two separate cases in two separate courts. If a person started an action in the wrong court he could not get a remedy until he brought his case to the right court. The proceedings in the Court of Chancery had become notorious for their length and expense. (Charles Dickens satirized the delays of Chancery in his novel *Bleak House*.) Comprehensive reform of the many deficiencies of the English legal system was effected by several statutes in the nineteenth century, culminating in the Judicature Acts 1873–1875. The separate common law courts and Court of Chancery were replaced by a Supreme Court of Judicature which comprised the Court of Appeal and High Court. Every judge was empowered henceforth to administer both common law and equity in his court. Thus a plaintiff seeking a common law remedy and an equitable remedy need only pursue one action in one court. The Acts also confirmed that where common law and equity conflict equity should prevail. These reforms did not have the effect of removing the distinction between the two sets of rules: common law and equity are still two separate but complementary systems of law today. A judge may draw upon both sets of rules to decide a case. See, for example, the decision of Denning, J., in the *High Trees Case* (p. 167).

Some basic principles of liability

Before we consider the specific areas of law governing the activities of business organizations, we must first of all study the branches of law which are most likely to affect businessmen and certain basic principles of liability.

Law of contract

A contract is an agreement between two or more persons which is legally enforceable. The law is concerned with determining which agreements are binding, the nature and extent of the obligations freely undertaken by the parties and the legal consequences of breaking contractual promises. Every type of business transaction, from buying and selling goods and services, to employing staff, is governed by the law of contract. The legal framework of business contracts for the supply of goods and services is the theme of Section C of this book.

Law of torts

A tort is a civil wrong. Unlike the obligations voluntarily accepted by the parties to a contract, a tort consists of the breach of a duty imposed by the law. The law of torts seeks to compensate the victims of certain forms of harmful conduct. Examples of torts include the following.

Negligence

The tort of negligence is concerned with certain kinds of careless conduct (or statements) which cause damage or loss to others. It consists of three essential elements: a duty of care, a breach of that duty, and damage caused to the plaintiff as a result of the breach of duty. The aim of an action in negligence is to recover compensation for the following kinds of damage –

(1) *Personal injuries including death, disablement, physical injury or nervous shock:* e.g. the manufacturers of a pair of woollen underpants from which a chemical had not been properly removed were required to compensate the wearer who contracted dermatitis. (*Grant* v *Australian Knitting Mills Ltd* (1936).) (See p. 211 and Chap. 13.)

(2) *Damage to property:* e.g. the Home Office was held liable for damage caused to a yacht by escaping Borstal boys. (*Home Office* v *Dorset Yacht Ltd* (1970).)

(3) *Financial loss:* e.g. a petrol company was required to compensate a tenant of one of its petrol stations in respect of the financial loss he suffered in taking the lease on the strength of negligent representations about the estimated sales of petrol made by the company's representatives (*Esso Petroleum Co. Ltd* v *Mardon* (1976).)

The tort of negligence will be studied in more detail in Chaps. 13 and 14.

Trespass

The tort of trespass is one of the oldest torts. It takes three forms: trespass to the person, trespass to goods and trespass to land.

(1) *Trespass to the person* comprises three separate actions: battery, assault and false imprisonment. Battery is a direct and intentional application of force against the person. The slightest touch can amount to a battery. Assault includes putting a person in fear of a battery. Examples include swinging a punch, even when it does not connect, or pointing a gun at somebody. False imprisonment consists of unlawfully restraining a person from going wherever he wants, e.g. unlawful detention by a store detective who mistakenly believes that a customer has been shoplifting.

(2) *Trespass to goods* is the wrongful interference with a person's possession of goods. This tort may be committed by destroying another's goods, stealing them or simply moving them from one place to another.

(3) *Trespass to land* can be defined as unlawful interference with the possession of someone's land. Straying off a footpath is an example of trespass to land.

Nuisance

There are two kinds of nuisance: public and private. Public nuisance (an act or omission which causes discomfort or inconvenience to a class of Her Majesty's subjects) is essentially a crime. However, individuals who have been particularly affected by the nuisance may bring an action in tort. Polluting a river could amount to a public nuisance. Private nuisance consists of unreasonable interference with a person's use or enjoyment of land, in the shape of such things as smoke, smell or noise.

Conversion

The tort of conversion involves doing some act in relation to another's goods which is inconsistent with the other's rights to the goods. The wrongful act must constitute a challenge to, or a denial of, the plaintiff's title to the goods. Examples of conversion include stealing goods and re-selling them, wrongfully retaining goods or destroying them. Conversion is one aspect of the tort of trespass to goods; both are examples of wrongful interference with goods, which has been the subject of legislation in the shape of the Torts (Interference with Goods) Act 1977.

Liability in tort is essentially 'fault based'. This means that a plaintiff must prove that the defendant acted intentionally or negligently and was, therefore, blameworthy. There are, however, two situations where liability may be imposed even though the defendant is not at fault.

(1) *Torts of strict liability*. These are torts where the plaintiff can recover compensation for loss or damage without having to prove fault or intention on the part of the defendant. Breach of statutory duty (see later p. 292) and conversion are examples of torts imposing strict liability.

(2) *Vicarious liability*. In certain situations one person may be held liable for the torts of another. This type of liability is known as vicarious liability. An employer, for example, is vicariously liable for the torts of his employees committed during the course of employment. Vicarious liability may also arise between partners and between a principal and his agent. Vicarious liability will be studied in more detail in Chapter 18.

Law of property

The law of property is concerned with the rights which may arise in relation to anything that can be owned. Thus, 'property' covers land, goods and intangible rights such as debts, copyrights or the goodwill of a business. The legal implications of acquiring, using and disposing of business property will be studied in depth in Section D. In order fully to understand other principles of business law which you will encounter before Section D, it is necessary to consider the relationships which may arise between persons and property; namely the rights of ownership and possession.

(1) *Ownership*. Ownership describes the greatest rights that a person can have in relation to property. An owner enjoys the fullest powers of use and disposal over the property allowed by law. The owner of this book, for example, has the right to read it, lend it to a friend, hire it out, pledge it as security for a loan, or even tear it into shreds. An owner does not enjoy absolute rights; restrictions may be imposed to protect the rights of other members of the community. Thus ownership of a house does not entitle the occupants to hold frequent wild parties to the annoyance of neighbours.

(2) *Possession*. Possession consists of two elements: physical control and the intention to exclude others. For example, you have possession of the watch you are wearing, the clothes in your wardrobe at home and

your car which is parked while you are at work. Ownership and possession often go hand in hand, but may be divorced. The viewer of a hired TV enjoys possession of the set, but ownership remains with the TV rental firm. If your house is burgled, you remain the owner of the stolen property, but the burglar obtains (unlawful) possession.

Criminal law

As we have seen already, a crime is an offence against the state. The consequences of a criminal conviction are not confined to the punishment inflicted by the court. For example, if a person is convicted for theft, his name will probably appear in the local papers causing shame and embarrassment and he may even lose his job. The sanctions are so severe that the criminal law normally requires an element of moral fault on the part of the offender. Thus, the prosecution must establish two essential elements: *actus reus* (prohibited act) and *mens rea* (guilty mind). For most criminal offences, both elements must be present to create criminal liability. If you pick up someone else's umbrella thinking that it is your own, you cannot be guilty of theft because of the absence of a guilty mind.

There are, however, some statutory offences where Parliament has dispensed with the requirement of mens rea. Performance of the wrongful act alone makes the offender liable. These are known as crimes of strict liability. Selling food which is unfit for human consumption contrary to the Food Act 1984 is an example of an offence of strict liability. The prosecutor is not required to show that the seller knew that the food was unfit. He will secure a conviction merely by establishing that the food was unfit and that it was sold.

Questions/activities

1. What is law and why is it necessary?

2. What is the 'common law' and how was it created?

3. Why did equity develop and how did it differ from the common law? What is the present relationship between the two systems.

4. Consider the following legal actions and indicate whether civil or criminal proceedings would result:

(a) Ann decides to divorce her husband, Barry, after ten years of marriage.

(b) Colin is given a parking ticket by a traffic warden for parking on double yellow lines.

(c) Diane returns a faulty steam iron to the shop where she bought it, but the shop refuse to give her a refund.

(d) Eamonn drives at 50 mph on a stretch of road where there is a 30 mph limit. He fails to see Fiona who is crossing the road. She is knocked down and sustains severe injuries.

(e) Graham takes a copy of 'Business Law' from the reference section of the library, with the intention of returning it when he has finished his first assignment. He finds the book so valuable that he decides to keep it.

(f) Hazel returns to England after working abroad for three years. Whilst abroad, she rented her flat to Ian. She now gives him notice to quit but he refuses to move out.

2

The changing law

Over nine hundred years of history have helped shape the institutions, procedures and body of rules which make up our modern English legal system. The law is a living creation that reflects the aims and needs of the society it serves, each generation leaving its mark on the law.

The rate of legal change has varied greatly down the centuries. English law developed at a relatively gentle pace up until the end of the eighteenth century, but as Britain moved into the industrial age, the pace of legal change quickened. Life in the 1980s is fast-moving and the rate of legal change is just as hectic. The law does not stand still for long today.

Ideally, business requires a stable environment within which to operate. Yet the framework of law which governs business activities is subject to constant change. The burden of keeping up to date may be eased slightly by making use of professional people such as an accountant or solicitor to advise on the latest development in such areas as tax or company law. Nevertheless the businessman will still need to keep himself informed of general legal changes which will affect his day-to-day running of the business. If he employs others in his business, he will need to keep up to date on such matters as health and safety at work, the rights of his employees and his duties as an employer. If he sells goods direct to the consumer, he must be aware of changes in consumer protection law. Almost every aspect of his business will be subject to legal regulation and the law could always change.

In this chapter we will explore why the law changes and the mechanism by which change takes place. We will also examine a recent legal change, the Data Protection Act 1984, and consider its implications for business activities, practices and procedures.

Causes of legal change

Legal changes can be divided into two broad catagories according to their causes. The first type of legal change is caused by the law responding to changes taking place in society. Political, social and economic changes, technological advancements and changing moral beliefs all lead eventually to changes in the law. Indeed, the law must be responsive to new circumstances and attitudes if it is to enjoy continued respect. The second type of legal change arises from the need to keep the law in good working order. Like any piece of sophisticated machinery, the law machine must be kept in a neat and tidy condition, maintained on a regular basis and essential repairs undertaken when necessary.

We will now examine these two types of legal change in more detail.

Legal change and the changing world

Think about the changes that have taken place in our world over the past 100 years. The first to come to mind are probably the spectacular scientific and technological achievements of the past century – motor vehicles, aircraft, the telephone, radio and TV, computers and exploration of space. Each new development creates its own demand for legal change. Consider, for example, the vast body of law which has grown up around the motor vehicle: there are regulations governing such matters as the construction and maintenance of motor vehicles, the conduct of drivers on the road and even where vehicles may be parked. Indeed, over half of the criminal cases tried by magistrates' courts are directly related to the use of motor vehicles. The increasing volume of traffic on the roads and the resulting inexorable rise in traffic accidents has also led to developments in the civil law, especially in the areas of the law of tort and insurance. More dramatic changes to the system of compensating the victims of motor accidents have been canvassed in recent years, principally by the Royal Commission on Civil Liability in 1978. Its recommendation of a 'no fault' system of compensation financed by a levy on petrol sales still awaits implementation.

While science and technology have been taking great leaps forward over the last century, other less dramatic changes have been taking place. The role and functions of the elected government, for example, have altered quite considerably. Nineteenth-century government was characterized by the *laissez-faire* philosophy of minimum interference in the lives of individuals. The government's limited role was to defend the country from external threats, to promote Britain's interests abroad and maintain internal order. In the twentieth century, governments have taken increasing responsibility for the social and economic well-being of citizens. Naturally, the political parties have their own conflicting ideas about how to cure the country's ills. New tactics are tried with each change of government. The law is used as the means of achieving the desired political, economic and social changes. The development of law on certain contentious issues can often resemble a swinging pendulum as successive governments pursue their opposing political objectives. The changes in the law relating to trade union rights and privileges over the past fifteen years are a perfect illustration of the pendulum effect. The Conservative Government of 1970–74 sought to curb what they saw as the damaging power of the unions by subjecting them to greater legal regulation. The experiment was not a success. One of the first tasks of the Labour Government which was elected in 1974 was to dismantle the Industrial Relations Act 1971 and restore the unions to their privileged legal position. When the Conservatives were returned to power in 1979, they tried again and succeeded in implementing more effective legal control of union activities.

One of the more controversial changes of recent times was the United Kingdom's entry into the Common Market in 1973. The government's motives were clearly directed at the economic and social benefits which it was expected would be derived from joining the European Communities. But membership also brought great legal changes in its wake: the traditional sovereignty of the Westminster Parliament has been called into question, our courts are now subject to the rulings of the European Court of Justice and parts of our substantive law have been re-modelled to conform to European specifications, e.g. on company law.

Changing moral beliefs and social attitudes are potent causes of legal change. In the past twenty years or so, great changes have taken place in the laws governing personal morality: the laws against homosexuality have been relaxed, abortion has been legalized and divorce is more freely obtainable. Society's view of the role of women has altered greatly over the past century. The rights of women have been advanced, not only by Parliament in measures like the Sex Discrimination Act 1975, but also by the courts in their approach to such matters as rights to the matrimonial home when a marriage breaks down.

The law is an adaptable creature responsive to the complex changes taking place around it. But sometimes in the midst of all this change, the more technical parts of the law, sometimes known as 'lawyers' law', can be ignored. A programme of reform is necessary to ensure that these vitally important, if less glamorous, areas of law do not fall into a state of disrepair.

Law reform

'Lawyers' law' consists largely of the body of rules developed over many years by judges deciding cases according to principles laid down in past cases. One of the great strengths of the system of judge-made law is its flexibility: judges can adapt or re-work the rules of common law or equity to meet changing circumstances. Although modern judges have shown themselves willing to take a bold approach to the task of keeping case law in tune with the times, there is a limit to what can be achieved. Judicial law reform is likely to lead to haphazard, unsystematic changes in the law. Legal change becomes dependent on the chance of an appropriate case cropping up in a court which can effect change. Furthermore, our adversarial trial system is not the best vehicle for investigating the likely consequences of changing the law. Judges cannot commission independent research or consult interested bodies to gauge the effect of the proposed change. The limitations of a system of judge-led law reform led to the setting up of official law reform agencies, which, along with other methods of effecting change in the law, will be considered below.

The sources of legal change

Ideas for changing the law flow from many sources –

(1) *Official law reform agencies.* The main agent of law reform in England and Wales is the *Law Commission* which was established by the Law Commissions Act 1965. Its job is to keep the law as a whole under review, with a view to its systematic development and reform. The Commission has overall responsibility for planning and co-ordinating the activities of the various law reform agencies, as well as undertaking its own projects. A Law Commission project starts life by appearing as an item in its programme of work which is approved by the Lord Chancellor. The Commission's full-time staff of lawyers then prepare a working paper containing alternative proposals for reform. Following consultations with the legal profession, government departments and other interested bodies, the Commission submits a final report on a firm proposal for reform accompanied by a draft bill.

The Law Commission's programme is devised in consultation with the chairmen of the *Law Reform Committee* and the *Criminal Law Revision Committee* and specific items may be referred to them for consideration. These part-time standing committees of lawyers, the Lord Chancellor's Law Reform Committee and the Home Secretary's Criminal Law Revision Committee, deal with civil and criminal law reform matters, respectively.

(2) *Government departments.* Each government department is responsible for keeping the law in its own field of interest under constant review. Where issues involving policy consideration rather than technical law reform arise, ministers may prefer to set up a *departmental committee* to investigate the subject, rather than leave it to the Law Commission. Particularly important or controversial matters may lead to the setting up of a Royal Commission by the Crown on the advice of a minister. The dozen or so members of a Royal Commission usually reflect a balance of expert,

professional and lay opinion. They work on a part-time basis, often taking several years to investigate a problem thoroughly and make recommendations. Examples of recent Royal Commissions include the Benson Commission on Legal Services and the Philips Commission on Criminal Procedure.

(3) *Political parties and pressure groups.* At election time, the political parties compete for our votes on the basis of a package of social and economic reforms which they promise to carry out if elected. The successful party is assumed to have a mandate to implement the proposals outlined in its election manifesto. Manifesto commitments, however, form only part of a government's legislative programme. Other competing claims to parliamentary time must be accommodated. For example, legislation may be required in connection with our membership of the Common Market, or to give effect to a proposal from the Law Commission or a Royal Commission, or simply to deal with an unforeseen emergency. Government claims on Parliament's time will alter during its period in office, as policy changes are made in response to pressures from within Westminster or in the country at large. One of the most significant extra-parliamentary influences on the formulation and execution of government policies is pressure group activity.

Pressure groups are organized groups of people seeking to influence or change government policy without themselves wishing to form a government. Some pressure groups represent sectional interests in the community. The CBI, for example, represents business interests, while other pressure groups are formed to campaign on a single issue. CND, for example, is concerned solely with the cause of nuclear disarmament. Pressure groups use a variety of techniques to promote their causes, from holding public demonstrations to more direct attempts to gain the support of MPs. Pressure group activity may be negative in the sense of mobilizing opposition to a proposed government measure, or positive, in seeking to persuade the government to adopt a specific proposal in its legislative programme or to win over a backbench MP, hoping that he will be successful in the ballot for private members' Bills.

Law-making processes

So far we have considered the main causes of legal

change. We will now examine the mechanics of change. The expression 'sources of law' is often used to refer to the various ways in which law can come into being. The main sources of law today are legislation (Acts of Parliament), case law (judicial precedent) and European Community Law.

Legislation

Legislation is law enacted by the Queen in Parliament in the form of Acts of Parliament or statutes. Parliament is made up of two chambers: the House of Commons and the House of Lords. The Commons consists of 650 elected Members of Parliament (MPs) who represent an area of the country called a *constituency*. The political party which can command a majority of votes in the Commons forms the Government and its leader becomes the *Prime Minister*. Ministers are appointed by the Prime Minister to take charge of the various government departments. The most important ministers form the *Cabinet*, which is responsible for formulating government policy. The House of Lords, in contrast, is not an elected body. It is made up of a large number of hereditary peers, a smaller but more active set of life peers (non-hereditary peers), spiritual peers (the Archbishops of Canterbury and York and twenty-four bishops of the Church of England) and law lords. Constitutionally, Parliament is the supreme lawmaker. The supremacy of Parliament in the legislative sphere is known as the doctrine of parliamentary sovereignty. It means that Parliament can make any laws it pleases, no matter how perverse or unfair; Parliament may repeal the enactments of an earlier Parliament; it may delegate its legislative powers to other bodies or individuals. The courts are bound to apply the law enacted by Parliament; the judiciary cannot challenge the validity of an Act of Parliament, however absurd or unconstitutional it may appear to be.

The making of an Act of Parliament

The procedure by which a legislative proposal is translated into an Act of Parliament is long and complicated. Until all the stages in the process have been completed the embryonic Act is known as a Bill. There are different types of Bill –

(1) *Public Bills* change general law or affect the whole of the country. It is assumed that the bill extends to all of the United Kingdom unless there is a specific provision to the contrary. For example, the Supply of Goods and Services Act 1982 applies to England, Wales and Northern Ireland but not to Scotland.

(2) *Private Bills* do not alter the law for the whole community but deal with matters of concern in a particular locality or to a private firm or even individuals. Private Bills are mainly promoted by local authorities seeking additional powers to those granted by general legislation.

(3) *Government Bills* are introduced by a minister with the backing of the government and are almost certain to become law. Some of the bills are designed to implement the government's political policies, but others may be introduced to deal with an emergency which has arisen, or to amend or consolidate earlier legislation.

(4) *Private Members' Bills* are introduced by an individual MP or private peer (in the House of Lords) without guaranteed government backing. They usually deal with moral or legal questions rather than with purely party political matters. A private members' Bill is unlikely to become law unless the government lends its support. Some important law reform measures started life as private members' Bills, including the Murder (Abolition of the Death Penalty) Act 1965 and the Abortion Act 1967.

A Bill must pass through several stages receiving the consent of the Commons and Lords before it is presented for the Royal Assent.

A Bill may generally start life in either the Commons or the Lords and then pass to the other House, but in practice most public Bills start in the Commons and then proceed to the Lords: certain kinds of Bill such as Money Bills must originate in the Commons. The procedure for a Bill which is introduced in the Commons is illustrated in Fig. 2.1.

Delegated legislation

The activities of modern government are so varied, the problems which it deals with so complex and technical, that Parliament does not have sufficient time to deal personally with every piece of legislation required. This difficulty is overcome by passing an enabling Act of Parliament which sets out the basic structure of the legislation but allows other bodies or people to draw up

Procedure	Comment
House of Commons	
First Reading	The title of the Bill is formally read out. It is then printed and published.
Second Reading	The Minister (or MP) in charge explains the purpose of the Bill and a debate on its general principles follows. Provided the Bill survives any vote, it passes to the Committee stage.
Committee Stage	The Bill is discussed in detail by a Standing Committee (20–50 MPs chosen according to party strengths) or the whole House sitting as a Committee. The Bill is examined clause by clause and any amendments are voted on.
Report Stage	The Bill is formally reported to the House and amendments made in Committee are considered.
Third Reading	The Bill is debated again in general terms. Only minor verbal amendments can be made. If there is a majority in favour, the Bill proceeds to the other House.
House of Lords	The Bill passes through a similar procedure in the Lords. As a non-elected body they do not have an absolute right of veto, but they may delay the progress of a Bill.
Royal Assent	This is something of a formality as the Queen's approval is never refused these days. The Bill is now an Act of Parliament.

Fig. 2.1 The legislative process.

the detailed rules necessary. Rules made in this way are known as delegated legislation. The main forms of delegated legislation are as follows –

(1) *Orders in Council* are rules made under the authority of an Act by the Queen acting on the advice of the Privy Council (an honorary body descended from the old Curia Regis). In practice, the power to make orders is exercised by the cabinet, whose members are all privy councillors. The Queen's assent is a pure formality.

(2) *Rules and regulations* are made by a minister in respect of the area of government for which he is responsible; e.g. the power of the Secretary of State for Social Services to make detailed regulations about the supplementary benefits scheme. (Most orders, rules and regulations are collectively referred to as statutory instruments).

(3) *Byelaws* are made by local authorities and certain other public bodies, such as the boards of nationalized industries, to regulate their particular spheres of activity. This form of delegated legislation requires the consent of the appropriate minister.

Legislation and the judiciary

A Bill which successfully passes through the House of Commons and the House of Lords and has received the Royal Assent becomes an Act of Parliament. The sovereign law-making powers of the Queen in Parliament mean that the validity of a statute cannot be questioned by the courts. Nevertheless, the courts can exercise considerable influence over how the enacted law is applied in practical problems. Sooner or later, every Act of Parliament will be analysed by the judges in the course of cases which appear before them. It is the task of the judge to interpret and construe the words used by Parliament and thereby ascertain the intention of the legislature. The rules of interpretation followed by the judges may be classified according to their origin as either statutory rules or common law rules.

Statutory rules

(1) Modern Acts usually contain an interpretation section which defines certain key words used in that Act; e.g. s. 61(1) of the Sale of Goods Act 1979 contains definitions of words and phrases used throughout the Act.

(2) The Interpretation Act 1978 lays down certain basic rules of interpretation for all Acts; e.g. unless the contrary intention is indicated 'words in the singular shall include the plural and words in the plural shall include the singular' (s. 6 of the Interpretation Act 1978).

(3) Certain elements of the Act itself may prove useful. These are known as internal or intrinsic aids. The courts may look at the long title of the Act and its preamble (only found in Private Acts and older Public Acts). Headings, side notes and punctuation may also be considered but only to help clarify the meaning of ambiguous words.

Common law rules

Apart from the limited help provided by Parliament, the judges have been left to develop their own methods of statutory interpretation. A number of approaches to the task of interpretation have emerged, with the judges free to decide which approach is most appropriate to the case in hand. The most important rules of interpretation and various presumptions are explained below.

(1) *Literal rule.* According to the literal rule, if the words of the statute are clear and unambiguous, the court must give them their ordinary plain meaning, regardless of the result. Where a literal interpretation produces an absurd or perverse decision, it is up to Parliament to put matters right, and not the job of non-elected judges. For example, in the case of *Fisher* v *Bell* (1961) it was held that a shopkeeper who had flick knives in his shop window could not be guilty of the offence of offering for sale a flick knife contrary to the Restriction of Offensive Weapons Act 1959, even though it was precisely this kind of conduct that Parliament had intended to outlaw. It is an established principle of contract law that displaying goods in a shop window is not an offer to sell but merely an invitation to treat. The defendant had not offered to sell the flick knives and so could not be guilty of the offence. Parliament closed the loophole by passing amending legislation in 1961.

(2) *Golden rule.* Under the golden rule, where the words of a statute are capable of two or more meanings, the judge must adopt the interpretation which produces the least absurd result. Some judges even argue that the golden rule can be applied where the words have only one meaning, but a literal interpretation would lead to an absurdity. For example, in *Re Sigsworth* (1935) it was held that a man who murdered his mother could not inherit the property even though he appeared to be entitled on a literal interpretation of the Administration of Estates Act 1925. There is a basic legal principle that a person should not profit from his wrongdoing.

(3) *Mischief rule (rule in Heydon's Case).* This rule which derives from *Heydon's Case* (1584) lays down that the court must look at the Act to see what 'mischief' or defect in the common law the Act was passed to remedy, and then interpret the words of the Act in the light of this knowledge. In *Gardiner* v *Sevenoaks RDC* (1950), for example, Gardiner claimed that he was not bound by an Act which laid down regulations about the storage of films in premises because he kept his film in a cave. It was held that the cave should be classed as premises, because the purpose of the Act was to secure the safety of those working in the place of storage or living close by. The mischief rule is closely associated with the modern purposive approach to interpretation which says that a judge should adopt the construction which will promote the general aims or purposes underlying the provision.

(4) *Ejusdem generis rule.* Where general words follow particular words, the court should interpret the general words as meaning persons or things of the same class or genus; e.g. if the Act referred to 'cats, dogs or other animals', the general words, 'other animals', should be construed in the light of the particular words, 'cats, dogs', as meaning other kinds of domesticated animals and not wild animals.

(5) *Expressio unius est exclusio alterius rule.* Under this rule, the express mention of one or more things, implies the exclusion of others; e.g. if the Act simply mentioned 'dogs and cats', other kinds of domesticated animals are excluded.

(6) *The Presumptions.* Unless there are clear words to the contrary, the court will make a number of assumptions; for example, that the Act applies to the entire UK, it does not bind the Crown and is not retrospective (i.e. backdating the change in the law).

Case law (judicial precedent)

Despite the enormous volume of legislation produced by parliaments down the ages, statute law remains an incomplete system of law. Large parts of our law still derive from the decisions of judges. This judge-made law is based on a rule known as the *doctrine of binding judicial precedent*. The principle underlying the doctrine is that a decision made by a court in a case involving a particular set of circumstances is binding on other courts in later cases, where the relevant facts are the same or similar. The idea of the judges making use of previously decided cases dates back to the formation of the common law by the royal justices out of English customary law. But it was not until the nineteenth century that the general principle of judicial consistency in decision-making developed into a more rigid system of binding precedents. The necessary conditions for such a system did not exist until the standard of law reporting was improved by the creation of the Council of Law Reporting in 1865 and a hierarchy of courts was established by the Judicature Acts 1873–5 and the Appellate Jurisdiction Act 1876.

Precedent in action

Whenever a judge decides a case he makes a speech, which may last a few minutes in a simple matter but may run to many pages in the Law Reports in a complicated case before the House of Lords. Every judgment contains the following elements:

(1) The judge records his findings as to the relevant facts of the case, established from evidence presented in court.

(2) He discusses the law which relates to the facts as found; this may involve an examination of the provisions of an Act of Parliament and/or previous judicial decisions.

(3) He explains the reasons for his decision; i.e. the rule of law on which his decision is based. This is known as the *ratio decidendi* of a case. It is this part of the judgment which forms a precedent for future similar cases. Other comments by the judge which do not form part of the reasoning necessary to make the decision are referred to as *obiter dicta* (things said by the way); they do not have binding force.

(4) The judge concludes his speech by announcing the decision between the parties; e.g. 'I give judgment for the plaintiff for the amount claimed', or 'I would dismiss this appeal'.

Precedents may be either binding or persuasive. A binding precedent is one which a court must follow, while a persuasive precedent is one to which respect is paid but is not binding. Whether a court is bound by a particular precedent depends on its position in the hierarchy of courts relative to the court which established the precedent. The general rule is that the decisions of superior courts are binding on lower courts. You should refer to Chap. 3 for an outline of the structure of the civil and criminal courts before considering the position of the principal courts which follows.

European Court of Justice

Since joining the European Communities in 1973 all English courts have been bound by the decisions of the European Court of Justice in matters of European Law. The European Court tends to follow its own decisions but is not strictly bound to do so.

House of Lords

As the highest court of appeal in respect of our domestic law, the decisions of the House of Lords are binding on all other English courts. The House of Lords used to be bound by its own previous decisions. In 1966, however, the Lord Chancellor announced by way of a Practice Statement that the House would no longer regard itself absolutely bound by its own precedents. This freedom to depart from previous precedents has not been exercised very often.

Court of Appeal

The Civil Division of the Court of Appeal is bound by the decisions of the House of Lords and most judges accept that it is bound by its own previous decisions. Court of Appeal decisions are binding on lower civil courts, such as the High Court and county court. The Criminal Division of the Court of Appeal is bound by House of Lords' decisions and normally by its own decisions but, since it deals with questions of individual liberty, there appears to be greater freedom to depart from its own precedents. Decisions of the Criminal Division of the Court of Appeal are binding on lower criminal courts; e.g. the Crown Court and magistrates' court.

Divisional Courts

A Divisional Court is bound by the decisions of the House of Lords, the Court of Appeal and its own previous decisions, on the same lines as the Court of Appeal. Its decisions are binding on High Court judges sitting alone and lower courts such as the magistrates' court.

High Court

A High Court judge is bound by the decisions of the House of Lords, Court of Appeal and Divisional Courts, but is not bound by another High Court judge.

Other Courts

Magistrates' courts and county courts are bound by the decisions of higher courts but their own decisions have no binding force on other courts at the same level.

At first sight, the system of precedent seems to consist of a very rigid set of rules, which have the effect of restricting possible growth in the law. It is certainly true that a court can find itself bound by a bad precedent, the application of which causes great injustice in the particular case before it. However, the system is more flexible in practice. Since 1966, the House of Lords has not been bound by its own precedents, thus creating limited opportunities for the development of new legal principles. Moreover, any court can use a variety of techniques to avoid following an apparently binding precedent. There may be material differences between the facts of the case before the court and the facts of the case setting the precedent; and so the earlier case can be distinguished. It is by avoiding precedents in this way that the judges make law and contribute to the enormous wealth of detailed rules which characterize case law.

European Community law

On 1 January 1973 the United Kingdom became a member of the European Communities and thereby subject to a new source of law. Before we examine the nature of Community law and its impact on the English legal system, it is important to understand how the Communities have developed and how they function today.

Historical background

On 18 April 1951 ministers representing France, West Germany, Italy, Belgium, The Netherlands and Luxembourg took the first step towards the creation of the European Community which the United Kingdom finally joined in 1973. They signed the Treaty of Paris establishing the European Coal and Steel Community (ECSC) with the aim of placing coal and steel production under international control. The same six founding member states came together again in March 1957 to sign the two Treaties of Rome which set up the European Economic Community (EEC) and the European Atomic Energy Community (Euratom). The EEC is by far the most important of the three communities because its aim is the creation of a common market and harmonization of the economic policies of member states. For these purposes, the EEC has concerned itself with ensuring freedom of movement within the Community for persons, capital and services, devising common agricultural and transport policies and ensuring that competition within the EEC is not restricted or distorted. The constitution of each Community is to be found in the Treaty which established it. Since the Merger Treaty of 1965 the three Communities have shared common institutions.

In January 1972 four more European countries agreed to join the European Communities by signing the Treaty of Accession in Brussels. Only the United Kingdom, the Republic of Ireland and Denmark took their places from 1 January 1973: Norway failed to ratify the Treaty following a negative vote by the Norwegian electorate in a national referendum. In 1981, the nine became ten with the accession of Greece and membership was increased again when Spain and Portugal joined the Communities on 1 January 1986.

Community institutions

The aims and objectives of the Community are put into effect by four main institutions: the Council of Ministers, the Commission, the Parliament and the Court of Justice.

The Council of Ministers

The Council is made up of one minister from each member state chosen on the basis of the subject under discussion. Thus meetings of the Council may be attended by the foreign ministers of each country, but if, say, the common transport policy is under discussion, the Transport Ministers of each member state will attend.

The Council is the supreme law-maker for the Communities, but this power is restricted by the fact that in most cases it can only legislate in respect of proposals put forward by the Commission. Although few decisions require the approval of all member states, the Council has adopted the practice of unanimity for decisions where vital national interests are at stake. Other decisions may be taken on a simple majority vote or on a qualified majority vote, where larger countries such as the United Kingdom have more votes.

The Commission

The Commission is composed of seventeen members; the larger countries, France, West Germany, Italy, the United Kingdom and Spain are entitled to appoint two commissioners each, while the seven smaller countries may appoint one commissioner each. Commissioners are appointed for a period of four years by mutual agreement between the twelve member states. Once appointed, commissioners must act with complete independence in the interests of the Communities.

The Commission plays an important part in the legislative process of the Communities. It formulates community policy, drafts proposed legislation to be laid before the Council and it can exercise a limited legislative power of its own. The Commission is also responsible for implementing community legislation and ensuring that treaty obligations are being observed by member states.

Parliament

Originally, Members of the European Parliament (MEPs) were nominated by national parliaments from amongst their own members, but since 1979 MEPs have been directly elected by the citizens of member states. Elections are held every five years. There are at present 518 MEPs who tend to sit and vote according to political rather than national allegiances.

Despite its name, the European Parliament is an advisory or consultative body rather than a legislative one. It is consulted by the Council and Commission before certain decisions are taken: it can offer advice and opinions, it monitors the activities of the Commission and Council and has the power to dismiss the full Commission. It plays an important part in drawing up the Community Budget and can reject the entire budget.

Court of Justice

The Court of Justice, which sits in Luxembourg, is composed of thirteen judges drawn from each member state. They are assisted by several Advocates-General, whose function is to present an unbiased opinion of the case to the court. Judicial personnel are appointed by unanimous agreement between the governments of member states for terms of six years, which may be renewed.

The Court of Justice exercises judicial power within the Community. Its jurisdiction covers the following areas –

(1) *Preliminary rulings.* Under Art. 177 of the Treaty of Rome, any court or tribunal in a member state may ask the Court to give a preliminary ruling concerning the interpretation of the treaties or community legislation enacted under the treaties. If such a question is raised in a court against whose decision there is no further right of appeal, the ruling of the Court of Justice must be sought. References to the Court of Justice under Art. 177 are not appeals as such. The proceedings of the national court are suspended while the point of European law is determined by the European Court. The case then resumes in the national court, where the ruling is applied to the facts of the case.

(2) *Actions against member states.* Proceedings may be taken against member states either by the Commission or by another member state in respect of violations of the treaties or community legislation. If a case is established the Court will make a declaratory order relying on political pressure from member states to secure compliance with its judgment.

(3) *Actions against community institutions.* Actions may be brought against community institutions by other institutions, member states or, in certain circumstances, by corporate bodies and individuals. Such proceedings may be used to annul the acts of the Council and the Commission, to obtain a declaration that the Council or Commission has failed to act as

required by the treaties, to obtain compensation for damage caused by the unlawful actions of community institutions and their servants and to review penalties imposed by the Commission.

(4) *Community employment cases.* The Court also deals with disputes between the Communities and their employees.

Sources of Community law

The main sources of Community law are as follows –

(1) *The Treaties.* The Treaties are the primary source of European Community law. The foundations of the community legal system were laid in the original Treaties of Paris and Rome and have been added to by further Treaties, such as the Treaty of Accession. Some Treaty provisions are so specific that they take direct effect in member states and give rise to enforceable community rights. Other Treaty provisions, however, are less explicit and therefore not directly applicable. Member states are expected to give effect to such provisions by enacting specific legislation in their own parliaments.

(2) *Secondary law.* The Treaties empower the Council and Commission to make three types of legislation:

(*a*) *Regulations* are designed to achieve uniformity of law among the member states. They are of general application and have direct force of law in all member states without the need for further legislation.

(*b*) *Directives* seek to harmonize the law of member states. They are instructions to member states to bring their laws into line by a certain date. The states themselves are free to choose the methods by which the changes are implemented, e.g. by Act of Parliament or statutory instrument.

(*c*) *Decisions* may be addressed to a state, a company or an individual and are binding on the addressee.

(3) *Decisions of the Court of Justice.* Judgments of the Court of Justice on matters of European law are binding on courts within the member states.

Impact of Community membership on English law

Britain's application to join the European Communi-

ties was formally accepted and signified on 22 January 1972 when ministers of the United Kingdom Government signed the Treaty of Accession in Brussels. A treaty is an agreement between sovereign states, which is binding in international law only. Treaty obligations undertaken by the United Kingdom do not become law in this country unless and until they are embodied in legislation enacted by Parliament. Membership of the European Communities involved the acceptance of Community law as part of English law. This could only be achieved by passing an Act of Parliament: the European Communities Act 1972.

Section 2(1) of the 1972 Act provides that Community law which is intended to take direct effect within member states (i.e. provisions of the Treaties and regulations) shall automatically form part of the law of the United Kingdom. Under s. 2(2), community legislation which requires some act of implementation by member states (i.e. directives) may be brought into force by Orders in Council or ministerial regulations. Certain measures, such as the creation of major criminal offences, must be implemented by Act of Parliament. English courts are required by s. 3 to take note of the Treaties and the decisions of the European Court. The supremacy of Community law over English law is illustrated by the following case.

Macarthys Ltd v Smith (1980)
Mrs Smith was employed by Macarthys Ltd as a stockroom manager. She claimed that she was entitled to the same pay as her male predecessor in the job. The Court of Appeal held that the provisions of the Equal Pay Act 1970 only applied to comparisons between men and women employed by the same employer at the same time. However, Art. 119 of the Treaty of Rome provides that 'men and women should receive equal pay for equal work'. Mrs Smith's case was referred to the European Court of Justice, which ruled that Art. 119 applied to cases of a woman following a man in a job. The provisions of Art. 119 took priority over the Equal Pay Act 1970 by virtue of the European Communities Act 1972. Mrs Smith succeeded in her action for equal pay.

By enacting the European Communities Act 1972, the United Kingdom Parliament has relinquished part of its sovereignty. Certain forms of Community law automatically take precedence over English law without reference to Parliament. Nevertheless, the 1972 Act is a statute like any other and could be repealed by a future Parliament and full sovereignty would be restored.

The changing law – A case study: Implementing the Data Protection Act

It is an unfortunate fact of business life today that the legal environment in which business operates is subject to constant change. The implications of each new Act of Parliament, EEC regulation or judicial pronouncement must be assessed and business practices and procedures adjusted accordingly. The Data Protection Act 1984 (DPA) is an example of a change in the law which will have a significant impact on business. We will explore how business responds to legal change in general by examining the provisions of the DPA and considering its implications. But first, why was the DPA necessary?

Background to the Act

There are two main reasons why the government decided to take action to regulate the use of computers to process personal information: first, concern had been growing since the 1960s that the widespread use of increasingly sophisticated computers posed a considerable threat to the right to privacy. Computers not only had the ability to process large quantities of information at high speed, but could also transfer data quickly from one system to another, and combine information from different systems in ways which had not been possible before. Existing laws were inadequate to deal with this new threat to our civil liberties.

The second and main reason why the government introduced legislation was to avoid commercial isolation. In 1981, the UK became a signatory to the Council of Europe Convention on Data Protection. The Convention, which comes into force when ratified by five states, permits ratifying countries to prohibit the transfer of personal data to countries without comparable data protection legislation. Failure to introduce such legislation in this country would have led to some British firms with international interests facing a boycott.

The government's first attempt at legislation fell victim to the 1983 general election. The Bill was re-introduced by the returning Conservative Government;

it received the Royal Assent on 12 July 1984. The DPA did not come into force immediately: its provisions are being phased in gradually and will be fully operational only after 11 November 1987. A timetable of key dates in the implementation process is set out below in Fig. 2.2.

12 July 1984	Royal assent – the Bill becomes an Act of Parliament.
September 1984	Mr Eric Howe, formerly of the National Computing Centre, becomes the first Data Protection Registrar.
12 September 1984	Individual right to compensation for loss or unauthorized disclosure of data. Court may order erasure of data if there is a risk of further disclosure.
11 November 1985	Data Protection Registrar receives first applications for registration.
11 May 1986	End of registration period. It is now an offence to obtain, hold, disclose or transfer unregistered personal data. Individual right to compensation for inaccurate data. The court may order rectification or erasure of inaccurate data.
11 November 1987	Data Protection Registrar acquires full powers. He may • refuse applications for registration; • serve effective enforcement, de-registration and transfer of data prohibition notices; • apply to circuit judge for warrant to enter and search premises. Data Subjects have right of access to personal data.

Fig. 2.2 Timetable for implementing the Data Protection Act.

The Act itself

The DPA establishes a legal framework to regulate the use of computers to process personal information. Most persons who process, or have processed for them, personal information will be affected by the legislation. At the centre of the new scheme is the Data Protection Registrar. He is responsible for establishing a public register of those involved in processing personal information, promoting observance of certain data protection principles and generally disseminating information about the DPA. Individuals acquire new rights under the DPA, including a right to obtain details of information held about them and a right to obtain compensation for damage suffered in connection with inaccurate information or the loss or unauthorized destruction or disclosure of personal information.

The DPA does not establish blanket regulation of data which is automatically processed: there are exemptions from some or all of its provisions. The types of data which are completely exempt include data held solely for payroll, pensions or accounting purposes and data held for domestic purposes. Other kinds of data are exempt from certain parts of the DPA: for example, the subject access requirements do not apply to data held for preparing statistics and carrying out research. The nature and extent of each exemption is a complex matter and the Registrar's *Guideline Number One* should be consulted.

Terminology

The DPA introduces a new set of terms –

(1) *Data* refers to information which can be processed automatically. Thus, the DPA applies to information processed by computer but does not cover information stored or processed manually.

(2) *Personal data* are items of information about a living individual who may be identified either directly (e.g. by name) or indirectly from other information (e.g. payroll number). 'Personal data' includes expressions of opinion about an individual but not an indication of the intentions of the data user in respect of that individual.

(3) *A data user* is a person (an individual or an organization) who holds and controls the contents and use of a collection of personal data processed or intended to be processed automatically.

(4) *A computer bureau* is an organization or individual who processes personal data on behalf of data users or allows data users to process personal data on his equipment.

(5) *A data subject* is an individual who is the subject of personal data. Information about corporate bodies is not covered.

The Data Protection Principles

An unusual feature of the DPA is the enactment of a set of very general 'data protection principles' which must be complied with. The first seven principles apply only to data users; the eighth principle applies both to data users and computer bureaux. The principles are as follows –

(1) *The information to be contained in personal data shall be obtained and personal data shall be processed fairly and lawfully.* Data users should obtain and process personal data in accordance with the provisions of the DPA and other rules of common or statute law. The provider of data may not be misled or deceived about the purpose for which the data is to be held, used or disclosed.

(2) *Personal data shall be held only for one or more specified and lawful purposes.* Data users are required to register the purposes for which personal data are used. Care must be taken to ensure that the data are not used for an unregistered purpose.

(3) *Personal data held for any purpose or purposes shall not be used or disclosed in any manner incompatible with that purpose or those purposes.* Personal data should be disclosed only to persons who are detailed in the data user's entry in the Register. Data subjects have the right to claim compensation for damage caused by unauthorized disclosure of data.

(4) *Personal data held for any purpose or purposes shall be adequate, relevant and not excessive in relation to that purpose or those purposes.* Data users must be selective about the data held: it must relate directly to the purposes which have been registered.

(5) *Personal data shall be accurate, and, where necessary, kept up to date.* Data users should take steps to check the accuracy of information. Data subjects have the right to compensation for damage caused by inaccurate data. Files should be reviewed from time to time to update the information.

(6) *Personal data held for any purpose or purposes shall not be kept for longer than is necessary for that purpose or those purposes.* Once the specific purpose for which the data was collected has been achieved, the data should be destroyed.

(7) *An individual shall be entitled – (a) at reasonable intervals and without undue delay or expense: (i) to be informed by any data user whether he holds personal data of which that individual is the subject, and (ii) to access to any such data held by a data user, and (b) where appropriate, to have such data corrected or erased.* Data subjects acquire new rights of access to the computerized information held on them. Data users must establish procedures to deal with requests for access.

(8) *Appropriate security measures shall be taken against unauthorized access to or alteration, disclosure or destruction of personal data.* Data users and computer bureaux must take steps to secure the personal data they hold. The level of security will depend on the nature of the personal data and the damage likely to be caused by a breach of the principle and the measures necessary to ensure security.

Registration requirements

The DPA establishes a Data Protection Registrar who is responsible for setting up and maintaining a register of data users and computer bureaux, which will be open to public inspection.

Applications for registration must be made on form DPR.1 and accompanied by a fee of £22.50. Successful registrations are valid for up to three years. Entries in the Register in respect of data users consist of the following information –

(1) name and address of the data user,
(2) nature of data held and the purposes for which the data are kept and used,
(3) sources from which the data are obtained,
(4) persons to whom the data might be disclosed,
(5) transfer of data overseas, and
(6) one or more addresses for the receipt of requests from data subjects for access to data.

Computer bureaux are required only to provide details of name and address. Since 11 May 1985 it has been an offence for a data user to obtain, hold, disclose or transfer overseas unregistered data.

The Registrar may refuse an application for registration on the grounds that insufficient information has been provided by the applicant or because the Registrar believes that the data user is unlikely to observe the data protection principles. There is a right of appeal to the Data Protection Tribunal.

The first task facing a business organization is to decide exactly who will take responsibility for ensuring that the organization complies with the requirements of the DPA. The duties of such a data protection officer must be defined and lines of responsibility established. Initially, the data protection officer will be occupied with the applications for registration but the registration must be kept up to date and this includes devising a system to monitor any changes taking place so that they can be recorded on the register.

Data Protection Registrar

In addition to maintaining the Register, the Registrar is charged with ensuring that data users and computer bureaux comply with the data protection principles. For this purpose the Registrar has the power to issue the following notices:

(1) *An enforcement notice* requires a registered person to observe the data protection principles.

(2) *A de-registration notice* empowers the Registrar to remove all or some of the particulars relating to an entry on the Register, where an enforcement notice has proved ineffective or is likely to prove ineffective.

(3) *A transfer prohibition notice* prohibits the proposed transfer of data abroad, to a country which, for example, is not a party to the Convention or does not have adequate data protection legislation.

Each notice must include details of rights of appeal to the Data Protection Tribunal.

Rights of data subjects

The DPA creates a number of rights for data subjects. The corresponding duties of data users may give rise to claims for compensation. Business organizations should consider the possibility of obtaining insurance cover against such risks. The new rights are as follows –

(1) *Access to personal data.* A data subject is entitled to be informed whether a data user holds any

data about him and to be supplied with a copy of any such data in an intelligible form. The data user may insist on receiving a written request, checking the data subject's identity and the payment of a fee (subject to a maximum). The information must be made available within forty days. Clearly, business organizations must establish a clear procedure for dealing with requests for access to data.

(2) *Compensation for inaccuracy.* A data subject who suffers damage as a result of the inaccuracy of personal data held is entitled to compensation from the data user for any damage or distress caused by reason of the loss, destruction, disclosure or access. Two defences are open to data users –

(a) that reasonable care was taken to ensure the accuracy of the data;

(b) where data has been obtained from the data subject or a third party, that either of two markers appear with the data indicating that (i) the data was received in that form by the data user, or (ii) the data subject regards the data as inaccurate.

A data subject may apply to the court for an order to rectify or erase the inaccurate data.

(3) *Compensation for loss or unauthorized disclosure.* A data subject who suffers damage as a result of the loss, destruction or unauthorized disclosure of data is entitled to bring an action for compensation. It is a defence to prove that reasonable care was taken in all the circumstances to prevent the loss, destruction, disclosure or unauthorized access. The rules about non-disclosure do not apply in the following circumstances –

(a) the disclosure is made to the data subject or his agent;

(b) the data subject has assented to disclosure;

(c) the data user discloses the data to relevant employees;

(d) the data is disclosed in an emergency to prevent injury or damage to health;

(e) the disclosure is required by law.

Questions/activities

1. Every year the government announces its programme for legislation by way of the Queen's Speech at the State Opening of Parliament in October or November. Select one proposal for legislation. Find out why this legal change is being proposed. Keep a diary to record its progress through the legislative procedure. What changes are made to a Bill during its passage through Parliament?

2. Describe the relationship between Parliament and the judiciary in respect of Acts of Parliament.

3. What are the advantages and disadvantages of the doctrine of judicial precedent?

4. How has Britain's membership of the European Communities affected the English legal system?

5. Explain the differences between the following pairs:

(a) MP and MEP

(b) *ratio decidendi* and *obiter dicta*;

(c) a Bill and a statute;

(d) ECSC and EEC;

(e) the Law Commission and the Law Reform Committee;

(f) Orders in Council and bye laws;

(g) a binding precedent and persuasive precedent;

(h) the golden rule and the mischief rule;

(i) the Council of Ministers and the Commission;

(j) a regulation and a directive.

Legal services and dispute settlement

Every facet of modern business life is governed by the law. Today's businessman needs to be alert to the legal implications of his activities. He will require a basic understanding of the principles of business law so that legal considerations can be built into the planning and decision-making process. At some stage, however, professional legal advice and help is likely to be needed – to advise on the implications of a recent change in the law or to draft a legal document or to assist in resolving a dispute. In this chapter we will consider the sources of legal advice and information available to business and the various methods of settling business disputes.

Sources of legal advice and information

The legal profession

The legal profession in this country is divided into two distinct branches: barristers and solicitors. These two types of lawyer fulfil different functions, although there is a certain amount of overlap in their activities.

Solicitors are the general practitioners of the legal profession, providing an all-round legal service. Solicitors may practise alone but usually they operate in partnership with other solicitors. (They are not allowed to form companies nor to form partnerships with other professions, such as accountants.) Solicitors' offices normally occupy convenient locations, close to the commercial centres of our towns and cities.

The solicitor is often the first port of call for anyone with a legal problem; consequently, his work is enormously varied. The workload associated with personal or private clients includes drafting wills, conveyancing (the legal formalities of buying and selling a house), winding up a deceased person's estate, dealing with claims for compensation arising from accidents or matrimonial problems. Business clients generate a different kind of work; for example, forming companies or drafting partnership agreements, applying for licences, drawing up contracts, advising on tax changes or new legal obligations in respect of employees. When the legal problem involves court proceedings, the solicitor deals with the preparatory stages, such as gathering evidence and interviewing witnesses. He is also entitled to appear on behalf of his client in the magistrates' court, the county court and in front of tribunals. If the case necessitates an appearance in a higher court, then the services of a barrister must be engaged.

Most firms of solicitors employ staff who are not qualified as lawyers to deal with some of the more routine work of the legal office, such as conveyancing. Legal executives, as they are known, have only recently achieved professional recognition with the establishment of the Institute of Legal Executives in 1963. Unadmitted clerks may now qualify for membership by combining practical experience with success in the Institute's examinations.

If solicitors are the GPs of the legal world, the barristers are the consultant specialists. Barristers are regarded as specialists in advocacy (i.e. representing a client in court); they have a right to appear in any court, enjoying a monopoly on rights of audience in the higher courts. A barrister's work, however, is not confined to advocacy. Indeed, some barristers spend most of their time on paperwork – writing opinions on specialized and difficult areas of law for solicitors or drafting documents.

There are two types of barrister: QCs (Queen's Counsel) and juniors. After 15–20 years successful practice, a barrister may apply to become a QC or 'take silk'. Queen's Counsel (or 'silks') are appointed by the Queen on the advice of the Lord Chancellor. They represent the top 10 per cent of the barristers' profession. There are a number of advantages to taking silk: QCs enjoy a higher status, they command higher fees and can concentrate on advocacy and giving opinions rather than poorly remunerated 'paperwork'. They are known as 'leaders' because they normally only appear in court accompanied by a junior barrister.

Unlike solicitors, barristers are not allowed to form partnerships: they must practise on their own account. Nevertheless, groups of barristers share chambers (rooms in an office) and collectively employ a barristers' clerk who acts as their office manager.

Together, the two branches of the legal profession provide a comprehensive legal service. A person with a legal problem must first consult a solicitor and, in so doing, will enter into a contract for legal services. The solicitor will be competent to deal with most of the matters brought to him but in some cases he will need to retain the services of a barrister. The barrister's brief may be to give an opinion on a difficult point of law or to represent the client in court. A solicitor may approach any barrister to undertake the brief and, according to the 'cab-rank' principle, the barrister must accept the work subject to his availability and the negotiation of an appropriate fee. A barrister does not stand in a contractual relationship with the solicitor who instructs him. The fee is regarded as an 'honorarium'; consequently barristers cannot sue solicitors who are reluctant to pay, although the same solicitors may bring an action against recalcitrant clients. Both solicitors and barristers are immune from actions in negligence arising from the conduct of a case in court or work immediately preparatory to such a case, but they may be liable in respect of other aspects of their work, e.g. giving legal advice. The most important point to remember about the relationship between the two branches of the legal profession is that barristers depend on solicitors for work. Barristers may be instructed only by a solicitor. Clients cannot gain direct access to a barrister's services.

Lawyers in industry, commerce and public service

The vast majority of qualified lawyers work in private practice providing legal services to a wide range of clients. A growing number of organizations, however, are setting up their own legal departments staffed by solicitors and barristers. The functions of these 'house' lawyers depend on the type of organization they work for. Banks, insurance companies, building societies employ lawyers to fulfil their specialist legal requirements. Central government departments, local authorities, nationalized industries all employ their own lawyers to help them discharge their statutory function. The legal department of an industrial company undertakes legal work of a more general nature: conveyancing, drawing up contracts, providing advice on employment matters, company administration and so on.

Other sources of information and advice

The legal profession is not the only source of information and advice on legal matters which a businessman can turn to.

Accountants are well versed in the intricacies of tax laws and the complex requirements of company law. Some of the large firms of accountants have established business and management consultancy services.

Government departments are a fruitful source of information for the businessman; e.g. the Department of Employment on employment legislation, the Inland Revenue on tax, Customs and Excise on VAT regulations. There are also a large number of government-sponsored organizations providing information and advice; the Equal Opportunities Commission, the Commission for Racial Equality, the Health and Safety Commission, the Office of Fair Trading, the Small Firms Advisory Service, to name a few.

A businessman may also benefit from joining a trade association. The Consumer Credit Trade Association, for example, produces a quarterly journal which reports changes in the law. It also runs a Legal Advisory Bureau for its members.

Professional associations (e.g. the Institute of Personnel Management) perform a similar service for individuals employed in business.

Methods of dispute settlement: the courts

The courts are the focal point of our legal system. They provide a formal setting for the final settlement of many of the disputes that occur in our society. The conflict may be between individuals or, where a breach of the criminal law has been alleged, between the state and one of its citizens. It is the function of the court to establish the facts of the case, identify the legal rules to be applied and to formulate a solution. The decision of the court not only has an immediate impact on the parties concerned, but it also affects similar cases which may arise in the future as a result of the operation of the doctrine of judicial precedent.

Our present day system of courts and tribunals can be classified in a number of different ways:

(1) *Civil and criminal courts.* Some courts deal exclusively with either civil or criminal matters, but the majority hear both civil and criminal cases, e.g. magistrates' courts.

(2) *First instance and appeal courts.* A court which hears a case for the first time is known as a first instance court or a court of original jurisdiction. These courts can make mistakes, so there is provision for cases to be reheard by an appeal court. Some courts hear cases both at first instance and on appeal, e.g. the High Court.

(3) *Courts and tribunals.* In addition to the ordinary courts, Parliament has created a large number of special courts and tribunals to administer various aspects of social and welfare legislation. Social Security Appeal Tribunals, for example, deal with disputed claims to supplementary benefit.

In this chapter we will consider an outline of the existing criminal and civil court systems. We will also briefly explain the role of tribunals and arbitration as means of resolving disputes.

Classification of criminal offences

If a person is charged with a criminal offence he will be tried by either the magistrates' court or Crown Court. Cases are distributed between these two courts according to principles laid down in the Magistrates' Courts Act 1980. The seriousness of the offence determines the kind of trial a person receives. Minor offences, for example, most motoring offences, are tried summarily in the magistrates' court, while more serious offences, such as murder and robbery, are tried on indictment by a judge and jury in the Crown Court. The system of appeals from the decisions of these two courts is illustrated in Fig. 3.1 (less serious offences) and 3.2 (more serious offences).

Criminal courts

Magistrates' courts

Magistrates' courts have been part of the legal scene for over six hundred years. Today their importance lies in the fact that not only do all criminal prosecutions begin life in this court, but 97 per cent end there in summary trial.

There are two kinds of magistrate, or justice of the peace, as they are also known. *Lay magistrates* are part-time, unpaid amateur judges. They are appointed by the Lord Chancellor on the recommendation of local committees from among the 'great and good' of a local community. (In Greater Manchester, Lancashire and Merseyside, appointments are made by the Chancellor of the Duchy of Lancaster.) Since legal knowledge is not a qualification for the position, a new magistrate must undergo an initial course of training. In court, the justices are given guidance on points of law by a legally qualified *justices' clerk*. A minimum of two lay magistrates is required to try a case, but usually three sit together. *Stipendiary magistrates* are full-time, paid, professional judges appointed from the ranks of barristers or solicitors. They work in London and other big cities such as Birmingham and Manchester and sit alone to try a case.

Jurisdiction

As well as their civil jurisdiction, which will be discussed later in this chapter, the magistrates deal with the following criminal matters:

(1) *Trial of minor offences.* The magistrates are responsible for deciding both the verdict and the sentence. Their sentencing powers are limited to six months' imprisonment or a £2000 fine in respect of any one offence. The maximum sentence they can impose is twelve months' imprisonment, where a person is convicted of two or more offences. However, in some cases they have the power to send a convicted person to the Crown Court for sentencing.

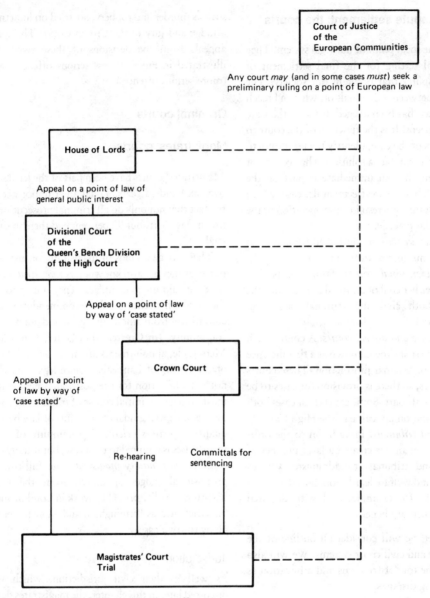

Fig. 3.1 Criminal courts dealing with minor offences.

(2) *Committal proceedings.* A person cannot be tried by the Crown Court unless he is first brought before the magistrates' court so that the justices can assess whether the prosecution has a good enough case to justify a trial. One magistrate may sit alone for this purpose.

(3) *Juvenile courts.* If a child (aged 10 to 13) or young person (aged 14 to 16) commits a criminal offence they can be brought before a specially selected group of magistrates sitting as a juvenile court. The court has a wide range of sentences at its disposal, including custodial measures. Juveniles are protected from the potentially damaging effects of a court appearance in a number of ways. The less formal proceedings must be held separately from an adult court, the public are not admitted and there are strict controls on what the press can report.

(4) *Criminal administration.* Magistrates issue summonses, warrants of arrest and search and grant bail to people awaiting trial.

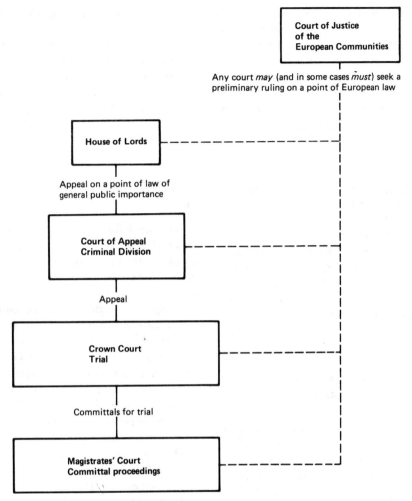

Fig. 3.2 Criminal courts dealing with serious offences.

Crown Courts

Crown Courts were established in 1972 by the Courts Act 1971 to replace the long established system of quarter sessions and assize courts.

Trial on indictment in the Crown Court is by a judge assisted by a jury of twelve. The most serious cases, such as murder, must be heard by a High Court Judge, while less serious matters may be dealt with by either a circuit judge or a recorder (a part-time judge).

The jury comprises men and women between the ages of eighteen and sixty-five, drawn at random from the electoral roll. The functions of the judge and jury are quite distinct. The judge is responsible for the conduct of the trial. He rules on points of law and sums up the case for the jury. The jury must consider all the evidence to decide whether the accused is guilty or innocent. If they convict, the judge plays the final part in the proceedings by passing sentence.

When the Crown Court is hearing an appeal, or where it is dealing with a person committed for sentencing from the magistrates, there is no jury. The judge sits with between two and four lay magistrates.

Jurisdiction

The Crown Court has the power to deal with the following criminal matters:

(1) *Trial of serious offences.*

(2) *Committals for sentencing* from the magistrates' courts.

(3) *Appeals from magistrates' courts.* The defend-

ant (but not the prosecution) may appeal against conviction and/or sentence. The appeal takes the form of a complete rehearing of the case. The Crown Court can confirm or reverse or vary the decision of the magistrates or return the case to them with an expression of its opinion. The court can impose any sentence which the magistrates' court could have passed. This means that the defendant faces the danger that he may receive a more severe sentence on appeal.

Divisional Court of the Queen's Bench Division of the High Court

The High Court is split into three divisions: Queen's Bench, Family and Chancery. When the court is hearing an appeal or, in the case of the Queen's Bench Division, exercising its supervisory jurisdiction, a minimum of two High Court Judges sit together and it becomes known as a 'Divisional Court'.

Jurisdiction
The jurisdiction of the Divisional Court of the Queen's Bench in criminal matters is as follows:

(1) *Appeals from magistrates' courts.* An appeal may be made by way of *case stated* by either the prosecution or the defence, but only on a point of law. This form of appeal requires the magistrates to provide a 'case' for the opinion of the High Court. The 'case' consists of a statement containing the magistrates' findings of fact, the arguments put forward by the parties, the decision and the reasons for it. The Divisional Court has the power to confirm, reverse or amend the decision of the magistrates' court or it can send the case back with an expression of its opinion.

(2) *Appeals from Crown Court.* The Divisional Court also hears appeals by way of case stated from the Crown Court, in respect of all criminal cases dealt with by that court other than trials on indictment.

(3) *Judicial Review.* The Divisional Court of the Queen's Bench plays an important role in monitoring abuse of power when it deals with applications for judicial review. As part of this general supervisory power, it can quash the decision of a magistrates' court which has exceeded its powers or failed to observe the rules of natural justice.

Court of Appeal (Criminal Division)

The Court of Appeal consists of two Divisions. The *Criminal Division* is composed of the Lord Chief Justice, a maximum of 23 Lords Justices of Appeal and any High Court judge who is asked to sit. Normally, three judges sit to hear a case, but if a difficult or important point of law is involved, a court of five or seven may be convened.

Jurisdiction
The Court of Appeal deals with the following criminal cases:

(1) *Appeals from trials on indictment in the Crown Court.* The defence (but not the prosecution) may appeal against the conviction and/or sentence. In an appeal against conviction, the court may confirm or quash the conviction, or order a new trial. Where there is an appeal against the sentence, the court may confirm or reduce the sentence or substitute one form of sentence for another.

(2) *References by the Attorney-General.* Where a person has been acquitted following trial on indictment in the Crown Court, the Attorney-General may refer any point of law which has arisen in the case to the Court of Appeal for its opinion. The decision of the court does not affect the outcome of the original trial.

(3) *References by the Home Secretary.* The Home Secretary has the power to refer a case or a point arising in a case after a person has been convicted on indictment to the Court of Appeal for its consideration.

House of Lords

The House of Lords is not only the second chamber of our Parliament, but also acts as a final court of appeal in both civil and criminal matters for both England and Northern Ireland, and in civil matters for Scotland. The judges are drawn from the Lord Chancellor, Lords of Appeal in Ordinary (*Law Lords*) and peers who have held or are holding high judicial office. A minimum of three is required, but in practice five normally sit to hear an appeal. Decisions are by majority judgment.

Jurisdiction
The House of Lords hears the following criminal appeals:

(1) *Appeals from the Court of Appeal (Criminal Division).*

(2) *Appeals from the Divisional Court of the Queen's Bench Division.*

In both cases, either the prosecution or defence may

appeal, provided a point of law of general public importance is involved. Permission must be obtained from either the House of Lords or the Court of Appeal or the Divisional Court, as appropriate.

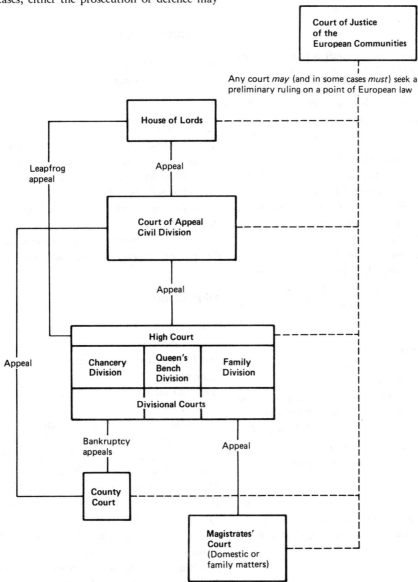

Fig. 3.3 Civil courts.

Civil Courts

County courts

County courts were established in 1846 to provide a

cheap and speedy method for the settlement of small civil disputes. Today, over 90 per cent of civil proceedings are brought in these local courts.

The county courts are staffed by circuit judges. They usually sit alone to hear a case, but a jury of eight may be called where, for example, fraud has been alleged. The judge is assisted by a registrar, who must be a solicitor of at least seven years' standing. He also has limited jurisdiction to try cases where the claim does not exceed £500 or, with the consent of the parties, any action within the general jurisdiction of the court.

Jurisdiction

The jurisdiction of the county court is limited in two ways: geographically and, in most cases, financially. Actions must be brought in the court for the district where either the defendant lives or carries on business, or where the reason for the action arose. The types of action which the court can deal with are as follows:

(1) *Actions in contract and tort* (except defamation, which is dealt with by the High Court) where the amount claimed does not exceed £5000.

(2) *Actions for the recovery of land* or concerning the title or rights over land where the rateable value does not exceed £1000.

(3) *Actions in equity* where the amount involved does not exceed £30 000. This category includes proceedings involving mortgages and trusts.

(4) *Bankruptcies.* The jurisdiction is unlimited in amount, but not all county courts have bankruptcy jurisdiction.

(5) *Company winding-ups* where the paid up share capital of the company does not exceed £120 000. The court must have bankruptcy jurisdiction.

(6) *Probate proceedings* where the amount of the deceased person's estate does not exceed £30 000.

(7) *Family matters*, e.g. undefended divorce. The court must have divorce jurisdiction.

(8) *Consumer credit*, landlord and tenant and racial discrimination cases.

Actions which exceed the limits of the county court are normally heard by the High Court. However, the parties may agree to such an action being dealt with by the lower court.

Small claims

In 1973, the Lord Chancellor introduced a special scheme for small claims in the county court. This was a response to the criticism that people were discouraged from pursuing actions because county court justice was likely to cost more than the amount in dispute. At present, if the amount claimed does not exceed £500,

the dispute will be dealt with by means of 'arbitration'. The parties are encouraged to do without legal representation. The hearing is in private, in an informal atmosphere. Strict rules of procedure and evidence are dispensed with and each side pays its own costs.

Magistrates' courts

The overwhelming majority of cases heard by the magistrates are criminal, but they also have a limited civil jurisdiction.

Jurisdiction

(1) *Domestic proceedings*, e.g. matrimonial proceedings, for maintenance or custody of children.

(2) *Recovery of certain civil debts*, e.g. income tax, electricity and water charges.

(3) *Licensing matters*, e.g. public houses and betting shops.

(4) *Juvenile courts* deal with proceedings to take children into the care of a local authority.

High Court

The High Court has its headquarters in London at the Royal Courts of Justice in the Strand, but there are a number of district registries in the larger cities in England and Wales. Each Division of the High Court is presided over by a senior judge: the Lord Chief Justice is head of the Queen's Bench Division, the Lord Chancellor is the nominal President of the Chancery Division (in practice the job is done by the Vice-Chancellor) and there is a President of the Family Division. They are assisted by a maximum of eighty High Court judges, who are distributed between the divisions, the largest number being attached to the Queen's Bench. When the High Court is operating as a court of first instance, trial is usually by judge alone. However, a jury of twelve may be called in cases involving defamation, malicious prosecution, false imprisonment and fraud. The Divisional Courts consist of two or three judges.

Jurisdiction

All three Divisions are equally competent to hear any case but in practice specific matters are allocated to each Division.

(1) *Queen's Bench Division*. The jurisdiction of this division covers civil and criminal matters, cases at first instance and on appeal. In addition, it exercises an extremely important supervisory function.

The Queen's Bench Division sitting as an ordinary court hears the following cases:

(*a*) *Actions in contract and tort* where the amount claimed is more than £5000.

(*b*) *A Commercial Court* deals with disputes concerning insurance, banking and the interpretation of commercial documents.

(*c*) *An Admiralty Court* deals with admiralty actions arising out of, for example, collisions at sea and salvage.

The Divisional Court of the Queen's Bench Division hears the following matters:

(*a*) *Civil appeals* (other than in matrimonial proceedings) by way of case stated from magistrates and from the Crown Court.

(*b*) *Judicial review* of the actions of inferior courts, tribunals and administrative bodies. For this purpose, the court may make orders of *mandamus*, *prohibition* and *certiorari*. If someone has been unlawfully detained, for example in a mental hospital, they may apply to the Divisional Court for a writ of 'habeas corpus'.

(2) *Chancery Division*. The Chancery Division hears the following actions:

(*a*) *Equity matters*, which were dealt with by the old Court of Chancery before 1875 and other cases allocated to it since then. These include actions involving trusts, mortgages, partnerships, specific performance of contracts, rectification of deeds, companies, bankruptcies and taxation.

(*b*) *A Court of Protection* deals with actions involving the management of the property and affairs of mental patients.

(*c*) *A Patents Court* deals with patents and related matters.

(*d*) *Appeals* from the Commissioners of Inland Revenue on income tax matters.

The Divisional Court of the Chancery Division hears appeals from the county courts in bankruptcy matters.

(3) *Family Division*. The first instance jurisdiction of the Family Division includes:

(*a*) *Matrimonial matters*, e.g. defended divorces.

(*b*) *Actions involving children*, e.g. adoption and legitimacy.

The Divisional Court of the Family Division hears appeals from magistrates' courts, county courts and the Crown Court in matters relating to the family.

Crown Court

Like the magistrates' courts, the Crown Court is mainly a criminal court, but it too has a civil jurisdiction, hearing appeals from the magistrates' in affiliation and licensing matters.

Court of Appeal (Civil Division)

The Civil Division of the Court of Appeal is headed by the Master of the Rolls, who is assisted by the Lord Justices of Appeal. Normally three judges sit to hear an appeal, although in important cases a full court of five may be assembled. Since 1982, some cases have been heard by two judges, in an attempt to reduce the waiting time for hearings. Decisions are made by a simple majority.

Jurisdiction

The court hears appeals from the High Court, county courts (except in bankruptcy cases) and various tribunals, such as the Lands Tribunal and the Employment Appeal Tribunal. It may uphold or reverse the decision of the lower court, or change the award of damages. In certain situations, it may order a new trial.

House of Lords

The House of Lords is the final court of appeal in civil matters. Its composition was discussed earlier in this chapter.

Jurisdiction

The Law Lords hear civil appeals from the following sources:

(1) *The Court of Appeal*, with the permission of the Court of Appeal or the House of Lords.

(2) *The High Court*, under the 'leapfrog' procedure introduced by the Administration of Justice Act 1969. This form of appeal goes straight to the House of Lords, 'leapfrogging' the Court of Appeal. The trial judge must certify that the case is suitable for an appeal direct to the House of Lords because it involves a point

of law of general public importance relating wholly or mainly to a statute or statutory instrument (often concerned with taxation); the House must grant leave to appeal and the parties must consent.

Other important courts

Court of Justice of the European Communities

On joining the European Communities in 1973, the United Kingdom agreed to accept the rulings of the European Court of Justice in matters of European law (see further p. 19). The House of Lords continues to be the final court of appeal in respect of purely domestic law, but where a dispute has a European element, any English court or tribunal *may* seek (and in some cases *must*) seek the opinion of the European Court in Luxembourg on the point of European law in question.

Judicial Committee of the Privy Council

The Judicial Committee of the Privy Council is not a formal part of our court structure, yet it has had a considerable influence on the development of English law. The Committee advises the Queen on criminal and civil appeals from the Isle of Man, the Channel Islands, British Colonies and Protectorates and from certain independent Commonwealth countries. The Committee's decisions are very influential because cases are usually heard by the Lord Chancellor and Lords of Appeal in Ordinary with the addition of senior Commonwealth judges, where appropriate.

Tribunals

The work of the ordinary courts is supplemented by a large number of tribunals set up by Act of Parliament to hear and decide upon disputes in specialized areas. As the lives of ordinary people have been affected more and more by the activities of government, particularly since the advent of the welfare state, so there has been a considerable growth in the number and jurisdiction of tribunals. They deal with a wide range of subjects, such as social security, employment, mental health, agriculture, land, rents and transport.

The attraction of tribunals is that they operate cheaply and quickly with a minimum of formalities. Although the chairman is usually legally qualified, other members are drawn from lay experts in the subject under consideration. Legal representation is discouraged as generally legal aid is not available and costs are not awarded.

The work of tribunals is subject to scrutiny by the courts. An appeal from the decision of a tribunal can normally be made to the ordinary courts on a point of law, but not on the facts. The Divisional Court of the Queen's Bench Division ensures that a tribunal acts fairly according to its powers.

One of the best known tribunals is the *industrial tribunal*. When it was established in 1964, it had a very limited jurisdiction, but now it is one of the busiest tribunals. It sits locally to hear complaints by employees about contracts of employment, unfair dismissal, redundancy, sex and race discrimination in employment and equal pay. The tribunal consists of a legally qualified chairman aided by two lay members, one representing employers and the other representing employees. The proceedings are fairly informal, especially as the strict rules of evidence are relaxed. Employees are not entitled to legal aid for a tribunal hearing but they can be represented by a trade union official or a friend. Normally each side pays its own costs. The tribunal's powers include being able to make awards of compensation totalling thousands of pounds. An appeal lies to the Employment Appeal Tribunal and from there to the Court of Appeal.

Arbitration

A court appearance can be a very costly and public way of resolving a dispute. Many in the commercial world seek to avoid the possibility by agreeing at the outset that any dispute will be referred to arbitration. Such clauses are often contained in contracts of insurance and partnership. Arbitration schemes have also been set up by trade bodies, such as the Association of British Travel Agents, to deal with complaints involving their members. Arbitration allows the parties to present their arguments to an arbitrator of their choice, in private and at their own convenience. The arbitrator may be legally qualified but usually he has special knowledge or experience of the subject matter. Both sides agree to be bound by the decision of the arbitrator, which can be enforced as if it were the judgment of a court.

Conciliation

In this chapter we have examined formal methods of settling disputes by means of legal action in a court or tribunal. In practice, only a relatively small number of disputes are resolved in this way. The vast majority are settled by more informal means before they reach the door of the court. There are many good reasons why the parties may prefer an 'out of court' compromise to courtroom conflict: e.g. fear of spoiling an otherwise satisfactory relationship, the cost of legal action, the amount of money at stake, difficulty in predicting the outcome of the case, the likelihood of bad publicity. The drawbacks of pursuing a court action act as a powerful incentive for the parties to settle out of court.

In some cases, however, the initiative for a settlement comes not from the parties themselves, but from an outside agency; for example, the Advisory, Conciliation and Arbitration Service (ACAS) tries to resolve both collective and individual disputes between employers and employees by means of conciliation. ACAS receives a copy of all industrial tribunal applications. A conciliation officer will then offer his services to the parties to help them reach a settlement. Many claims are settled at this stage with the parties avoiding the ordeal of a tribunal hearing.

Questions/activities

1. For each of the actions listed below state:

(*a*) which court or tribunal would hear the case?
(*b*) what type of lawyer could represent the parties?
(*c*) who would try the action?
(*d*) to which court or tribunal would an appeal lie?

(*i*) a prosecution for murder;
(*ii*) an undefended divorce;
(*iii*) a claim for damages of £15 000 for negligence;
(*iv*) an application for a late extension by the licensee of a public house;
(*v*) a claim by an employee that he has been unfairly dismissed;
(*vi*) a bankruptcy petition where the debts are £20 000;
(*vii*) a claim by a ratepayer that his local authority has failed to produce accounts for public inspection as required by law;
(*viii*) a prosecution for drunken driving;
(*ix*) a claim for damages of £200 for breach of contract;
(*x*) an application by a Social Services Department to take a child into care.

2. What part do laymen take in the administration of the legal system? Should they be replaced by professionals?

3. Our legal system often allows for two levels of appeal. Is this a wasteful use of resources?

4. What are the advantages and disadvantages of using tribunals rather than the ordinary courts to decide disputes?

Business Organizations

4

Classification and survey of types of business organizations

Classification of business organizations

The private sector

A business can be run in what is called the private sector of commerce and industry through any one of THREE types of business organization. These are given below.

The sole trader
This means going it alone with a one-person business. You can take all the profits of the business but suffer all its losses and have all the problems and worries.

The partnership
You can share the losses (if any) and the problems and worries with a partner or partners but of course the profits must also be shared. It is normally necessary for the partners to make a contract called a partnership agreement which is often in writing because it then provides a good record of what was agreed about the business. However, writing is not necessary; a verbal agreement will do and, ind~ed, a partnership can in some cases be inferred from conduct.

The company
A business may be incorporated *as a registered company*. This is created by following a registration procedure carried out through the Registrar of Companies in Cardiff. He is an official of a government department called the Department of Trade and Industry.

A registered company can be formed by two or more people who become its shareholders. Directors must be appointed to manage the company and act as its agents. A company secretary must also be appointed either from the shareholders or from among those advising the business, such as an accountant (provided he is not also the company's auditor, who cannot hold an office of profit within the company) or solicitor.

In the past trading companies were incorporated by *Royal Charter*. However, incorporation by registration was set up in 1844 by the Joint Stock Companies Act of that year, and it is most unlikely that incorporation by Royal Charter would be used today to incorporate a commercial business. Charters are still used to incorporate certain organizations such as professional bodies which control the professions, e.g. the Chartered Institute of Secretaries and Administrators, and for incorporating certain bodies in the public sector, such as the British Broadcasting Corporation.

As to how you get a charter, the organization wanting one sends what is called a petition to the Privy Council. The Privy Council consists of members of the current Cabinet who become members of the Council when they first take office, former members of the Cabinet, and others appointed by the Queen on the recommendation of the Prime Minister as an honour for service in some branch of public affairs at home or overseas. The petition asks for the grant of a charter and sets out the powers required. If the Privy Council considers that it is appropriate to grant a charter the Crown will be advised to do so.

The public sector

If it is thought to be right for an organization to be put

into, or brought into, the public sector, as in the case of organizations providing goods or services to the public on a national basis with a complete or partial monopoly, e.g. coal, it is usual to create a public corporation to manage the industry. These corporations are financed by the government and not from private resources, such as share capital. They are formed by Act of Parliament or Royal Charter. Examples are British Coal, which was developed when the coal industry was nationalized by the Coal Industry Nationalization Act 1946, and the BBC, which was incorporated by Royal Charter in 1926.

These corporations are not run by a government department but have a minister who accounts to Parliament for their conduct. There are two types of public corporations –

(1) *Commercial public corporations.* These run an industry on commercial lines under the broad control of a minister. Thus British Coal is under the broad control of the Energy Secretary.

(2) *Social services corporations.* These run a social service for the government. An example is the Health and Safety Executive which was set up by the Health and Safety at Work, etc., Act 1974 to supervise and enforce health and safety in industry through inspectors.

Public ownership can also be achieved by the government acquiring the share capital of a registered company. The Rolls-Royce (Purchase) Act 1971 achieved this in the case of Rolls-Royce Ltd. People nominated by the government then go on to the board of directors.

The public corporation has a separate legal personality and its objects and powers are in the Act of Parliament which sets it up. If they take over an existing industry being run by a registered company, the shareholders whose assets are taken over must be compensated.

Natural and juristic persons

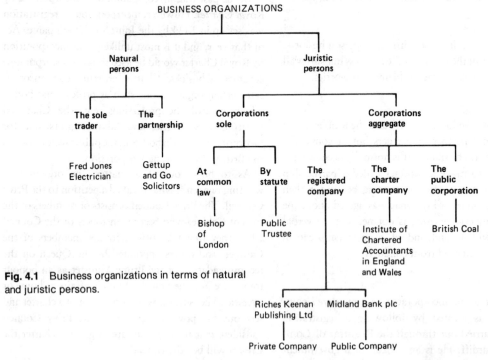

Fig. 4.1 Business organizations in terms of natural and juristic persons.

Natural persons

These are human beings who are known to the law as natural persons. An adult human being has in general terms the full range of legal rights and a full range of legal duties. Thus, if A makes a contract with B and B fails to perform it, A has a *right* to damages because B failed to perform a *duty*. A similar situation would occur if A failed in his *duty* to perform the contract thus denying B his *right* to have it performed.

However, the law distinguishes between certain classes of human beings and gives them a *status* which means that they have more limited rights and duties than are given to other persons. Examples are minors (persons under the age of 18), and persons of unsound mind.

Some contracts of minors are not binding on them and they cannot be sued if they fail to perform them. Persons of unsound mind can refuse to perform their contracts where the other party was aware of the mental state when the contract was made. These matters are more fully dealt with in Chapter 8.

Non-human creatures are not legal persons and do not have those rights and duties which a human being gets at birth. However, animals may be protected by the law for certain purposes, such as conservation. For example, s. 9 of the Wildlife and Countryside Act 1981 protects certain wild animals by making it a criminal offence for a person intentionally to kill, injure, or take any animal included in Sch. 5 to that Act, e.g. bats.

Juristic persons

Legal personality is not given only to human beings. Persons can form a corporation, that corporation having a legal personality with similar rights and duties to human beings. As we have seen, these corporations are formed by Royal Charter, Act of Parliament, or by registration under the Companies Act 1985 or previous Acts. There are also corporations sole, which were introduced by lawyers under common law.

Charter companies and those formed by Act of Parliament have their own legal personalities and act through human agents. This is also true of the registered company, which is allowed by law through the agency of its directors to make contracts, hold property, and carry on business on its own account, regardless of the particular persons who may happen at the particular time to hold its shares.

Thus if A and B form a registered company, AB Ltd, the separate legal personality of AB Ltd is created on formation. A and B can now make contracts on behalf of AB Ltd as its agents. The rights and duties under those contracts will belong to AB Ltd and not to A and B as individuals. The rule of corporate personality is illustrated by the case set out below.

Salomon v Salomon & Co. (1897)

Mr Salomon carried on business as a leather merchant and boot manufacturer. In 1892 he formed a limited company to take over the business. Mr Salomon was the major shareholder. His wife, daughter and four sons were also shareholders. They had only one share each. The company gave Mr Salomon 20 000 shares of £1 each in payment for the business and he said that a further £10 000 of the purchase price could be regarded as a loan to the company which it could repay later. Meantime the loan was secured on the assets of the company. This charge on the assets made Mr Salomon a secured creditor who, under the rules of company law, would get his money before unsecured (or trade) creditors if the company was wound up. The company fell on hard times and a liquidator was appointed. The debts of the unsecured creditors amounted to nearly £8000 and the company's assets were approximately £6000. The unsecured creditors claimed all the remaining assets on the grounds that Mr Salomon and the company were one. Thus he could not lend money to himself or give himself a security over his own assets. Eventually, the House of Lords held that the company was a separate and distinct person. The loan and the security were valid transactions between separate individuals, i.e. Mr Salomon and the company and therefore Mr Salomon was entitled to the remaining assets in part-payment of the secured loan.

Comment. The creditors of Mr Salomon's original business had been paid off. The unsecured creditors were creditors of the company and the House of Lords said that they must be deemed to know that they were dealing with a limited company whose members, provided they had paid for their shares in full, could not be obliged to meet its debts.

Looking behind the corporate personality

This idea of corporate personality can lead to abuse and where, for example, it has been used to avoid legal obligations, the courts have been prepared to ignore the separate personality of the company (or draw aside the corporate veil or curtain) and treat the business as if it was being run by its individual members. An illustration of this appears below.

Gilford Motor Co. Ltd v Horne (1933)

Mr Horne had been employed by Gilford. He had agreed to a restraint of trade in his contract under which he would not approach the company's customers to try to get them to transfer their custom to any similar business which Mr Horne might run himself.

Mr Horne left his job with Gilford and set up a similar business using a registered company structure. He then began to send out circulars to the customers of Gilford inviting them to do business with his company.

Gilford asked the court for an injunction to stop Mr Horne's activities and he said that he was not competing but his company was and that the company had not agreed to a restraint of trade. An injunction was granted against both Mr Horne and his company to stop the circularization of Gilford's customers. The corporate structure could not be used by Mr Horne to evade his legal contractual duties.

Corporations sole

All the forms of corporation which have been discussed so far have one feature in common which is that they are corporations aggregate, having more than one member. However, English law also recognizes the idea of the corporation sole which is a corporation having only one member.

A number of such corporations were created by the common lawyers in early times because they were concerned that land did not always have an owner and that there could be a break, however slight, in ownership.

Church lands, for example, were vested in the vicar of the particular area and at higher levels in other church dignitaries, such as the bishop of the diocese. When such persons died, the land had no legal owner until a successor was appointed to the job so the common lawyers created the concept of the corporation sole under which the office of vicar or bishop was a corporation and the present vicar or bishop the sole member of that corporation. The land was then transferred to the corporation and the death of the particular vicar or bishop had thereafter no effect on the landholding because the corporation did not die and continued to own the land. The Bishop of London is a corporation sole and the present holder of the office is the sole member of the corporation. The Crown is also a corporation sole.

It does not seem likely that any further corporations of this sort will be created by the common law but they can still be created by Act of Parliament. For example, the Public Trustee Act 1906 sets up the office of Public Trustee as a corporation sole. The Public Trustee will act as an executor to administer a person's estate when that person dies, or as a trustee, to look after property for beneficiaries such as young children, and a lot of property is put into his ownership for the benefit of others from time to time. It would be very difficult to transfer all this property to the new holder of the office on the death or retirement of the civil servant who is in fact the Public Trustee. So the person who holds the office of Public Trustee is the sole member of a corporation called the Public Trustee and the property over which he has control is transferred to that corporation and not to the individual who is the holder of the office.

Survey of types of business organizations: advantages and disadvantages

The major advantages and disadvantages of the various forms of business organizations in the private sector will now be looked at under the headings set out below.

Commencement of business

Sole traders and partnerships

These organizations can commence business merely by opening the doors of the premises. It is usual to register for Value Added Tax and of course the premises which are being used must under planning and other regulations be available for business purposes.

If the organization is not using the name of its proprietor(s), but using a business name, as where Freda Green trades as 'London Fashions' (the business name), or Fred and Freda Brown trade as 'Paris Fashions' (the business name), then the organization must comply with the requirements of the Business Names Act 1985. This will be dealt with in more detail in a later chapter, but it contains provisions restricting the choice of the business name. For example, a name must not be chosen which suggests a connection with central and local government. This is to prevent the public getting a possibly false sense of security because these government authorities get a regular and safe income from taxes and rates. There are also requirements regarding disclosure of the name during the lifetime of the business.

Companies

A private company cannot trade until its application for registration has been dealt with by the Registrar of Companies and he has given the company a certificate of incorporation.

The Companies Act 1985 requires public companies to have an issued share capital of at least £50 000 in nominal value, of which at least one-quarter has been paid plus the whole of any premium. This is essential so that the company can trade and/or borrow.

If, therefore, a public company does have an authorized capital of £50 000 and the shares are £1 each but are sold for £1.50, that is at a premium of 50p, the company must have a paid up share capital of £37 500 before it can trade and/or borrow.

All business is carried out in the name of the company which will normally register for VAT. The choice of the corporate name and a business name, if the company uses one, is controlled by the Companies Act 1985 and the Business Names Act 1985, and these Acts provide also for publicity to be given to the name. These matters will be dealt with in a later chapter.

Capital

Sole traders and partnerships

All businesses need money to begin trading; some kind of start-up finance. Sole traders must either put in enough of their own money if they have it or put in what they have and try to borrow the rest. Partners are in the same position. Certainly, a bank will not lend 100 per cent of the finance.

Usually the best place to try for a loan is one of the large banks. The bank will want some security for its money and this may mean giving the bank a mortgage on the house of the sole trader, or houses of the partners.

Interest rates can differ according to the deal given by the bank. Interest may be variable and change with the base rate, as is the case where the bank allows the organization to overdraw a bank account up to a certain amount. The alternative is a loan at a fixed rate of interest. These are usually more expensive but may be better than an overdraft facility if the loan is taken at a time of low interest rates.

A partnership can, of course, attract more capital by admitting new partners. There is, however, a limit to this because the Companies Act 1985 restricts a partnership to a maximum of twenty people; but some professions, e.g. accountants and solicitors, are exempt and can have partnerships of unlimited size.

Companies

Here the capital structure is more complicated. If two people wishing to form a private company and be its directors contribute £10 000 each to form the company, which has what is called a nominal (or authorized) capital of £40 000, each of the two members taking 20 000 shares of £1 each, then –

(1) all the company's capital is *issued*;
(2) the £20 000 cash received by the company is its *paid-up capital*;
(3) the balance of £20 000 remaining is the *uncalled capital*. This can be called up for payment at any time in accordance with what is said in the company's articles as to the length of notice to be given.

A company may also raise money by borrowing, often from a bank, either by way of a loan at fixed interest, or more commonly, by the granting of an overdraft facility.

The lender does not become a member of the company and if the company falls on hard times and is wound up the lender, being a creditor, is entitled to recover his loan before the shareholders get anything for their shares.

A lending bank will take a security (called a debenture) over the company's assets for its loan and will usually ask the directors to give another security by guaranteeing the loan so that if the company does not repay it they will have to. This takes away some of the advantages of limited liability.

There is no limit on the number of shareholders which a company may have and so it can raise as much capital as it wishes if it can sell its shares to outsiders. A public company can offer its shares to the public, but a private company must negotiate personally with outsiders who might buy its shares.

Liability of the proprietors

Sole traders

A sole trader is liable for the debts of the business to the extent of everything he owns. Even his private possessions may be ordered to be sold to pay the debts of the business. There is no such thing as limited liability. A sole trader can make a free transfer of personal assets to a husband or wife (spouse) or other relative, but the transfer can be set aside and the assets returned to the sole trader and then used to pay the business creditors if the court is satisfied the transfer was to defeat creditors. Also, if property is transferred to a spouse it is lost to the sole trader if the marriage ends in divorce and the spouse refuses to give it up.

Partnerships

Partners are jointly and severally liable for the debts of the firm. They can be sued together by a creditor who has not been paid. They can also be sued individually (or severally). Thus, if A, B and C are partners and the firm owes X £3000 but this cannot be paid from the partnership funds, then, for example, X may sue A for the whole £3000 and A may then try to get a contribution of £1000 from B and £1000 from C. If they are insolvent he will not get the contribution, or at least not all of it.

The liability extends to the private assets of the partners. Even the estate of a deceased partner is liable for the debts of the firm incurred while he was a partner if there is anything left in his estate after paying his private debts.

There is also liability for the debts of the firm incurred after retirement unless the firm's existing customers are informed of the retirement and public notice of retirement is given in the *London Gazette*, which is a daily publication obtainable from Her Majesty's Stationery Office.

There may be a limited partnership and those who want to put a limit on their liability for the debts of a partnership firm may become limited partners. This is provided for by the Limited Partnerships Act 1907.

However, at least one partner must have unlimited liability for all the debts of the firm. A limited partner is not liable for the debts of the firm, though if the firm fails and is dissolved his capital may be used to pay its debts as far as required before any of it is returned to him.

A limited partnership is, however, unsatisfactory because the limited partner has no right to take part in the management of the firm. If he does he becomes liable with the other partners for the debts and liabilities of the firm during the period for which he was involved in management.

Companies

The rule of limited liability which says that a shareholder in a company who has once paid for his shares in full cannot be required to pay any more money into the company even if it cannot pay its debts, does allow the shareholders in a company to leave the company's creditors unpaid.

However, directors and members may have personal liability if they have continued to trade and incur debts when the company was unable to pay its existing debts. These matters will be dealt with further in Chapter 7.

Also, company directors are, as we have seen, often asked to give their personal guarantees of certain debts of the company, for example, a bank overdraft. This makes limited liability a bit of an illusion for them since, if the company does not pay, they can be required to do so.

Continuity
Sole traders

The death of a sole trader brings the organization to an end and the executors who are in charge of the sole trader's affairs will either have to sell the business as a going concern to someone else or sell the assets one by one to other businesses.

If a sole trader becomes bankrupt there is no way in which he can legally continue in business because if he obtains credit beyond a prescribed amount (currently £250) either alone or jointly with someone else, without telling the person who gives the credit that he is an undischarged bankrupt, he commits a criminal offence.

Partnerships

The death, bankruptcy, or retirement of a partner can lead to the firm closing down business but it is usual for the partnership agreement to provide that the business shall continue under the remaining partner or partners. However, the continuing partners or sole partner (as he is perhaps strangely called) will have to find the money to buy out the share of the deceased, bankrupt or retiring partner. Unless the firm has provided for this it can cause difficulties in terms of raising the necessary funds.

Companies

A company has what is called perpetual succession. Thus if A and B are the members of AB Ltd and A dies or becomes bankrupt, the executors or trustee in bankruptcy, as the case may be, must sell A's shares to a purchaser if they wish to realize the cash paid for them. The company's capital is unaffected and the company is not dissolved. A company can purchase its own shares under the Companies Act 1985 but it is not forced to do so.

Publicity and external control of the undertaking

Sole traders and partnerships

Little, if any, publicity, attaches by law to the affairs of these organizations. Their paperwork and administration is a matter for them to decide, subject, in a partnership, to anything that the partnership agreement may say about this. These organizations can keep their accounts on scraps of paper in a shoebox if they wish to, though obviously they should keep proper accounts. However, subject to satisfying the Revenue as to the genuineness of their accounts, usually through an independent accountant, there are no legal formalities and no filing of documents or accounts for the public to see.

Companies

A considerable amount of publicity attaches to companies – even small private ones.

Unless the members of the company have unlimited liability – which is a possible form of corporate organization – the company must file its accounts annually together with the reports of its directors and auditors. These items are kept by the Registrar and are available for inspection by the public on request from Companies House.

The 1985 Act requires all companies, public and private, to appoint auditors. This is an expense which is not forced upon sole traders or partners, though, as we have seen, the services of an accountant are often required to prepare the accounts and submit them to the Revenue.

The Companies Act 1985 allows *small companies* to avoid certain publicity in regard to the accounts. A small company is one which has satisfied two of the following conditions for the current financial year and the one before –

(1) *Turnover*, i.e. gross income before deducting the expenses of running the business, not exceeding £2 million;
(2) *Balance sheet total*, which is in effect the total assets, not exceeding £975 000;
(3) *Employees*, not exceeding 50 as an average throughout the year.

A small company is allowed to file modified accounts with the Registrar instead of a copy of the full accounts required by the Companies Act 1985. The members of the company, however, are entitled to a copy of the full accounts. In particular, the modified accounts do not have to show details of the salaries of directors and higher-paid employees, nor is it necessary to file a directors' report or a profit and loss account.

The directors must state in the accounts that the company satisfies the conditions for a small company and this must be supported by a report by the auditors giving an opinion confirming this. The auditors' report on the full accounts must accompany the modified accounts, even though the full accounts are not sent to the Registrar.

All companies must file with the Registrar of Companies an annual return showing, for example, who the company's directors and its secretary are and the interests of the directors as directors in other companies. The return also shows the changes in the company's membership over the year and a full list of members must be given every three years.

In addition, formal company meetings, called annual general meetings, must be held by a company at specified intervals so that shareholders are kept informed of corporate activities.

In conclusion, therefore, those who run companies will have to spend some time in ensuring that the business is carried on in such a way as to comply with company legislation. The sole trader and partner have a much less complicated legal environment which can be to their advantage.

Questions/activities

1. Which of the following business organizations have been formed by registration –

(*a*) Wilkinson-Brown & Co., Chartered Accountants;

(*b*) Mammoth plc;

(*c*) The United Kingdom Atomic Energy Authority;

(*d*) Small Ltd.

2. 'A registered company is a juristic or legal person and is therefore a legal entity distinct from its members'.

Explain this statement and state two advantages of incorporation showing how these advantages depend upon corporate personality.

3. 'The court will not allow the theory of corporate personality to be used as a means of fraud or sharp practice – the judge has the power to draw aside the corporate veil'.

Explain what happens when the court does draw aside the veil and describe a situation in which the court has exercised its power.

4. In relation to a company what is –

(*a*) its authorized share capital;

(*b*) its issued share capital;

(*c*) its paid up capital;

(*d*) its uncalled capital?

5. A and B are partners. The firm is insolvent. A creditor, Joe, has successfully sued A for a debt of £2000. What rights, if any, has A against B?

6. A, B, C and D wish to form a partnership in which all of them will be limited partners. Advise them.

7. What is the maximum number of employees allowed to a company which wishes to qualify as a 'small' company?

5

The sole trader

Having introduced the various business organizations, we will now consider, in more detail, the legal environment in which sole traders, partnerships, and companies operate. In this chapter we deal with the sole trader.

Formation of the business

Name of the organization

Business names

(*a*) *Generally.* As we have seen, the main formality facing the sole trader on commencement of business is the Business Names Act 1985. Even this does not apply if he trades in his own name. If, however, a business name is chosen, then the 1985 Act must be complied with. A business name occurs where the organization is run in a name which does not consist *only* of the surname of the sole trader. Forenames or initials are allowed in addition.

Therefore, if Charlie Brown is in business as 'Brown', or 'C Brown', or 'Charlie Brown', the name of the organization is not affected by the Act. The names are not business names. Recognized abbreviations may also be used, such as 'Chas Brown', and still the name is not a business name.

However, if Charlie Brown is in business as 'High Road Garage', or 'Chas Brown & Co', 'C Brown & Co', 'Brown & Co', he is using a business name and the 1985 Act must be complied with as regards choice of the name and disclosure of the name of the true owner.

The rules regarding disclosure do not apply where the only addition to the name of the sole trader is an indication that the business is being carried on in succession to a former owner.

Often a sole trader will want to use the name of the previous owner of the business so that he can use the goodwill attached to it. Goodwill is the probability that customers will continue to use the old business for their requirements. It may also be a *reputation* for a certain class of article, such as a Dunhill pipe. If Charlie Brown bought a business called 'The Village Stores' from Harry Lime, the new business could be called 'Charlie [Chas or C] Brown (formerly Harry Lime's)' and would not be affected by the Act. However, if Charlie Brown went further than merely including his own name and that of the previous owner as if he traded as 'Charlie ['Chas' or 'C'] Brown Village Stores (formerly Harry Lime's)' or 'Village Stores', he would have a business name and would have to comply with the Act.

(*b*) *Restriction on choice of business name.* As we have seen, the *main* controls are that a sole trader's business must not be carried on in Great Britain –

(*i*) under a name which leads people to believe that it is connected with a central or local government authority unless the Department of Trade and Industry agrees. This is to prevent a possibly false sense of security in the public who deal with the business because these authorities get regular income from the enforced payment of taxes and rates.

(*ii*) Under a sensitive name unless the relevant body agrees. These are set out in regulations issued by the Department of Trade and Industry. Examples are that if the word 'bank' is to be used the permission of the Bank of England is required and if the word

'Royal' is to be used the Home Office must agree.

(*c*) *Disclosure of true owner's name: what must be disclosed?* A user of a business name must disclose his or her name together with a business or other address in Great Britain. This is to enable documents such as writs to commence a legal claim to be served at that address.

(*d*) *Where must the information be disclosed?*

(*i*) In a clear and readable way on all business letters, written orders for the supply of goods or services, invoices and receipts issued by the business, and written demands for the payment of money owed to the business.

(*ii*) Prominently, so that it can be easily seen and read in any premises where the business is carried on, but only if customers or suppliers of goods or services go on to those premises.

(*iii*) Disclosure must also be made immediately and in writing to anybody with whom business is being done or discussed if the person concerned asks for the information. This would mean, for example, giving the information on, say a business card, to a salesman to whom an order was being given or discussed if the salesman asks for the names of the owners of the business.

(*e*) *What happens if an owner does not comply with the law?* A sole trader who does not obey the law commits a *criminal offence* and is liable to a fine. On the *civil side* he may not be able to enforce his contracts; for example, to sue successfully for debts owed to him. This will be so where, for example, the other party to the contract can show if he is sued that he has been unable to bring a claim against the business because of lack of knowledge of the name and address of the owner.

Suppose that Freda Green trades as 'Paris Fashions' in Lancashire and supplies Jane Brown with dresses for her boutique in Yorkshire, but without giving Jane Brown any idea that she, Freda Green, owns Paris Fashions. Suppose, further, that Freda moves her business to Kent and Jane Brown finds that the dresses are sub-standard and wants to return them, but cannot because she does not know where 'Paris Fashions' has gone. If Jane is sued for non-payment by Freda, the court may refuse Freda's claim, though the judge has a discretion to enforce it if in the circumstances he thinks it is just and equitable to do so.

Passing off

A sole trader must not run his business under a name which is so like that of an existing concern that the public will confuse the two businesses. Similarity of name is not enough; usually the two concerns must also carry on the same or a similar business.

If this does happen the sole trader will be liable to a civil action for the tort of passing off and the existing concern can ask the court for an injunction to stop the use of its name. If it is successful in getting the injunction and the new organization still carries on business under the confusing name its owner is in contempt of court and may be fined or imprisoned until he complies and changes the name of his business.

However, a sole trader may do business in his own name even if this does cause confusion, provided that he does not go further and advertise or manufacture his goods in such a way as to confuse his products with those of the existing concern.

Dissolution

Our sole trader, whom we shall call Fred Smith, may decide at any time to retire from the business and dissolve it by selling off the assets of the business to other tradespeople. Alternatively, the business may be sold as a going concern to another trader and continue under him.

Apart from the legal formalities involved in selling and transferring assets, for example, conveying shop premises to a new owner, there are no special legal difficulties provided all the debts of the business are paid in full. However, if Fred cannot pay his debts he may be forced to dissolve his business by his creditors under a process called bankruptcy.

Bankruptcy procedure: generally

Bankruptcy procedure is set out in the Insolvency Act 1986. Bankruptcy proceedings, which involve asking the court for a bankruptcy order, may be taken against Fred by creditors. Fred may also take proceedings to make himself bankrupt if he cannot pay his debts. His affairs will then be taken over by an insolvency practitioner, who is usually an accountant.

This may be a great relief to Fred if, as is likely, he is being pressed and harrassed to pay debts he cannot

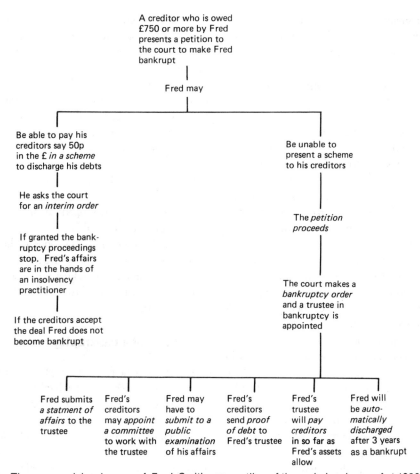

A creditor who is owed £750 or more by Fred presents a petition to the court to make Fred bankrupt

Fred may

Be able to pay his creditors say 50p in the £ *in a scheme* to discharge his debts

He asks the court for an *interim order*

If granted the bankruptcy proceedings stop. Fred's affairs are in the hands of an insolvency practitioner

If the creditors accept the deal Fred does not become bankrupt

Be unable to present a scheme to his creditors

The *petition proceeds*

The court makes a *bankruptcy order* and a trustee in bankruptcy is appointed

Fred submits *a statment of affairs* to the trustee

Fred's creditors may *appoint a committee* to work with the trustee

Fred may have to *submit to a public examination* of his affairs

Fred's creditors send *proof of debt* to Fred's trustee

Fred's trustee will *pay creditors* in so far as Fred's assets allow

Fred will be *automatically discharged* after 3 years as a bankrupt

Fig. 5.1 The personal insolvency of Fred Smith: an outline of the main Insolvency Act 1986 procedures.

meet. On bankruptcy his creditors will have to press the insolvency practitioner to pay. He is, of course, an independent person and a lot of the nastiness goes out of the situation once he takes over from Fred.

The petition

A petition to the court for a bankruptcy order may be presented by a creditor or creditors only if –

(1) The creditor presenting it is owed £750 or more (called the bankruptcy level) by Fred. Two or more creditors (none of whom is individually owed £750) may present a *joint petition* if together they are owed £750 or more by Fred, as where A is owed £280 and B £600.

(2) The debt is defined as a debt *now due* which Fred appears to be unable to pay, or a *future debt* which

Fred has no reasonable prospect of being able to pay.

(3) To show that this is so the creditor(s) if the debt is now due must send Fred a further demand asking for payment. If the demand is not complied with within three weeks the court will accept that Fred cannot pay the debt.

(4) If the debt is a *future debt*, such as a loan repayable in the future, the creditor(s) must send Fred a demand asking him to give evidence that he will be able to pay it. If Fred does not provide satisfactory evidence within three weeks of the demand that he will be able to meet the debt when it is due the court will accept that there is no reasonable prospect that it will be paid.

(5) It is also necessary that the debt is not secured, as by a charge on Fred's property. A secured creditor cannot present a petition unless he is, for example, prepared to give up his security. In any case, secured creditors, such as banks who have taken a security in

return, say, for giving Fred an overdraft facility, will normally get their money by selling that property of Fred's over which they have a charge.

Schemes of arrangement under the Deeds of Arrangement Act 1914

(1) Fred may wish to put a proposal to his creditors under which he will hand over his business to a trustee for the benefit of his creditors. The trustee will be an independent person such as an accountant who may be able to deal more expertly with the sale of Fred's business or the running of it and so pay the creditors off. If the creditors are willing to go along with this Fred will not be made bankrupt.

(2) Alternatively, Fred may wish to put up a scheme of arrangement by way of compromise of his debts. This would involve the creditors accepting final payment of (say) 50p in the £, which they may feel will be a better deal than bankruptcy, particularly if the cost of the bankruptcy proceedings is likely to be high.

(3) These schemes need the consent of a majority in number and value of the creditors. For example, if there are 100 creditors and A is owed £901 and the other 99 are owed £1 each, the rest cannot force a scheme on A because he has the majority in value, although the others have a majority in number. Equally, A plus forty-nine of the rest cannot force the scheme on the others. A plus forty-nine creditors have a majority in value but not in number. However, A plus fifty of the rest could force the scheme on the others; they have a majority in number of 51 per cent and a clear majority in value.

The interim order under the Insolvency Act 1986

(1) It would, of course, be difficult for Fred to make proposals for a scheme if a particular creditor (or creditors) had presented a petition to bankrupt him and was proceeding with it.

(2) Therefore, if Fred wants breathing space to try a scheme to prevent his bankruptcy, he may, when a creditor presents a petition (or, indeed, if he thinks a scheme might be acceptable after he has presented a petition against himself) apply to the court to make what is called an interim order.

(3) This protects his property and stops the proceed-ings for a bankruptcy order from carrying on. Also secured creditors are prevented from selling that property of Fred's on which the security has been taken, though any scheme which is accepted cannot take away the rights of secured creditors to be paid before unsecured creditors. Still, an interim order will keep Fred's property together while a scheme is considered.

(4) As part of obtaining an interim order Fred must give the name of a qualified insolvency practitioner (called a 'nominee') who is willing to act as a supervisor for the proposed scheme. The court must be satisfied that –

(a) the nominee is properly qualified as an insolvency practitioner; and

(b) Fred has not made a previous application for an interim order in the last twelve months. Obviously, a debtor cannot keep asking for these orders so as, perhaps artificially, to put off bankruptcy proceedings.

The effect of a bankruptcy order

(1) If a scheme is either not put forward, or, if put forward, not accepted, the bankruptcy proceedings will, if successful, end in the court making a bankruptcy order.

(2) Once the order is made and Fred becomes bankrupt his property is automatically transferred to the control of the Official Receiver. He is a civil servant dealing with bankruptcy with the aid of a staff of suitably qualified people. If Fred had put up a scheme of arrangement which had failed to get acceptance the 'supervisor' of that scheme could have been appointed as trustee to Fred instead of the Official Receiver.

(3) The transfer of Fred's property to the control of the Official Receiver does not apply to such tools, books, vehicles, and other items of equipment as are necessary to Fred to be used personally by him in his job as in the case of a sole trader plumber. Nor does it apply to such clothing, bedding, furniture, household equipment, and provisions as are necessary for the domestic needs of Fred and his family. These items are retained in Fred's ownership and control.

(4) Fred is required to submit a statement of affairs to the Official Receiver within twenty-one days of becoming bankrupt, i.e. twenty-one days from the day on which the bankruptcy order was made. This statement is the starting point of the taking over of

Fred's affairs by someone else. The statement will help in this.

(5) The main contents of the statement of affairs are –

(*a*) particulars of Fred's assets and liabilities;

(*b*) the names, residences, and occupations of his creditors;

(*c*) the securities, if any, held by them, plus the dates on which these securities were given.

Committee of creditors

(1) If someone other than the Official Receiver is appointed as Fred's trustee the creditors may at a general meeting set up a committee of creditors to keep an eye on the way in which the trustee deals with the assets. The trustee must take into account any directions given to him by the committee or of a general meeting of creditors. If there is a difference of view between the committee and the general meeting, the general meeting decision is followed.

(2) The trustee is not bound to set up a committee of creditors. However, it can be helpful to the trustee because the creditors, or some of them, may well have experience in Fred's area of trade.

(3) If one of the creditors who is supported by at least one half in value of the others gives notice to the trustee requiring him to set up a committee of creditors, he must do so. Thus if Fred's debts are £50 000 a creditor, or more likely creditors, owed at least £25 000 must want a committee of creditors.

The public examination

(1) Once a bankruptcy order has been made against Fred the Official Receiver (even if he is not the trustee) may apply to the court for the public examination of Fred. One half in value of Fred's creditors may require the Official Receiver to make the application to the court for a public examination.

(2) At the public examination Fred can be questioned by the Official Receiver or the trustee (where this is a different person from the Official Receiver), or by any creditor on the subject of his business affairs and dealings in property and the causes of business failure.

(3) The main purpose of the public examination is to help the Official Receiver to find out why Fred's business failed and whether he has been guilty of some

misconduct which could lead to his prosecution for a criminal offence, e.g. fraud.

The family home

(1) Fred's trustee may ask the court to make an order imposing a charge on Fred's main residence. This gives the trustee a first right to sell it and protects that right should Fred sell the home himself. The reason for this is that on bankruptcy the family home is exempt property in that it does not pass to the trustee, though the trustee can ask the court for an order for sale. This protects Fred's family from possible immediate eviction. However, until such time as it is sold, if it has to be, the trustee has a charge on it for Fred's share in it to protect the interests of the creditors. If the house is sold, it is sold subject to the trustee's charge.

(2) These special provisions exist because although the family home may be a most valuable asset, there may be problems in selling it. For example, Fred's house may be jointly owned with his wife who is not bankrupt. Here the court has a discretion under the Law of Property Act 1925 to let the wife and children, if any, live on in the house for a period of time and so prevent a sale straight away. The charge protects Fred's creditors in regard to his share in the house until it is sold and, indeed, afterwards in regard to the proceeds of sale.

Proof of debt

(1) Fred's creditors will send details of their debts to Fred's trustee. These details may be unsworn claims or may be sworn claims, which means that the creditor has gone to a solicitor and said to him on oath that the debt is really due.

(2) Both unsworn and sworn claims are called proofs of debt. The trustee will normally accept an unsworn claim unless he is doubtful about it and is going to challenge it, possibly before the court. If this is so he would probably ask the creditor to submit a sworn claim.

Mutual dealings: set off

(1) Any mutual dealings between Fred and any of his creditors are important. Say Fred is owed £20 by a customer, Sid, but Fred owes Sid £10. The trustee will

ask Sid to pay the £20 to him but Sid will be able to set off (as it is called) the £10 Fred owes him against the £20 he owes the trustee, and pay only £10 to Fred's trustee.

(2) This way Sid gets in fact a dividend of £1 in £1 on the debt Fred owes him. If there was no law allowing set off Sid would have to pay £20 to Fred's trustee and then prove for his debt of £10 in Fred's bankruptcy. If Fred's trustee had only sufficient assets from Fred's business to pay Fred's creditors 50p in the £1, then Sid would have had to pay £20 but would have got only £5 back. As it is he has had the whole £10 in value.

Carrying on the business and disclaimer

(1) Fred's trustee may, with the permission of the committee of creditors or the court, carry on Fred's business for a while (but not for too long) if it will bring more money in for the creditors.

(2) As we have seen, when the court makes the bankruptcy order Fred's property comes into the ownership and control of his trustee for the benefit of his creditors. One result of this is that in the case of an interest in land, such as a lease, say for twenty years, the trustee becomes in effect the owner of the lease and the landlord can ask the trustee, quite legally, to pay the rent. If, as is likely, the trustee is an accountant with a good practice, he will obviously be in a position to pay the rent and cannot really defend himself if he does not do so. The trustee may find, additionally, that the lease has repairing clauses which Fred has not carried out and the landlord may call upon the trustee to put the premises in good order.

(3) The trustee will therefore write to the landlord *disclaiming the property*. He then has no personal liability; nor has Fred any personal liability. The landlord is left to prove for his lost rent and perhaps the fact that Fred has not kept the premises in good order as damages in the bankruptcy. The landlord will get such payment as Fred's assets will allow. He is therefore by disclaimer put in the same position as the other creditors in the bankruptcy and loses any personal claim he may have made against the trustee or Fred.

Transactions at an undervalue and preferences

(1) Fred's trustee may swell the amount of assets available to the creditors by using those provisions of the Insolvency Act 1986 which deal with two problems –

(*a*) Cases where Fred might have decided not to give his property to his wife and risk the gift being set aside by a court order but to sell it to her at less than its real value so that his creditors would not be able to get it. This is called a sale at an undervalue.

(*b*) Cases where Fred has decided to pay certain of his creditors in full and prefer them to others. He might, for example, have decided to pay in full a debt to a person who had been particularly helpful to him in business or a debt which he owed a relative. This is not a transaction at undervalue because the person concerned is paid in full but it is a preference.

(2) Fred's trustee can recover property or money passing in a transaction at undervalue or as a preference as follows –

(*a*) transactions at an undervalue can be set aside by Fred's trustee and the property recovered for the benefit of creditors at any time within five years of the presentation of Fred's bankruptcy petition (this is before he was actually made bankrupt by the bankruptcy order);

(*b*) preferences may be set aside within six months of the petition; up to two years is allowed if the preference was to an *associate*, as where Fred paid a debt in full to his wife or other relative, or a partner in another business.

Payment of the creditors – preferential payments

(1) As the trustee gets in money from Fred's business, either as income or from the sale of assets, he will pay Fred's creditors in a set order of priority laid down in Sch. 6 of the Insolvency Act 1986 after providing money for his own fees and expenses.

(2) The main preferential debts are –

(*a*) income tax and capital gains tax for one year. If Fred owes more than one year's taxes the Crown may choose which year it wishes to be preferential but may have only one year.

(*b*) PAYE deductions which were made or ought to have been made in the twelve months before the bankruptcy;

(*c*) value added tax and car tax for six months and twelve months respectively before the bankruptcy;

(d) sums due in respect of general betting duty, gaming licence duty, or bingo duty within twelve months before the bankruptcy;

(e) wages or salaries of employees due within four months before the bankruptcy up to a maximum of £800 for each employee;

(f) all accrued holiday pay of employees;

(g) social security contributions not paid in the twelve months before the bankruptcy.

If the above debts come in total to £5000 and Fred's assets raise only £2500 each claimant will get half of what is claimed and other creditors will get nothing.

Protection of employees

(1) Under the Employment Protection (Consolidation) Act 1978 an employee who loses his job when his employer (in this case Fred) becomes bankrupt can claim through the Department of Employment the arrears of wages, holiday pay, and certain other payments which are owed to him rather than rely on the preferential payments procedure.

(2) Any payments made must be authorized by the Department of Employment and the right to recover the sums payable are transferred to the Department of Employment so that it can try to recover from the assets of the bankrupt employer the costs of any payments made, but only up to the preferential rights the actual employees would have had. What can be recovered from the Department of Employment may, in fact, be a higher sum than the preferential payments in bankruptcy allow.

(3) Major debts covered are as follows –

(a) arrears of pay for a period not exceeding eight weeks up to a rate prescribed annually by statutory instrument and currently £158 per week. Persons who earn more than £158 per week can only claim up to £158;

(b) pay in respect of holidays which has not been paid in respect of holidays actually taken and holidays due but not taken up to a rate again of £158 per week with a limit of six weeks;

(c) payments promised to an employee instead of giving him notice but not paid at a rate not exceeding £158 per week;

(d) any payment which Fred may not have made in regard to an award by an industrial tribunal of compensation to an employee for unfair dismissal.

(4) Claims on the Department of Employment will not normally be allowed if the trustee can satisfy the Department that the preferential payments will be paid from funds available in the bankruptcy and without undue delay.

Trade creditors

If all the preferential creditors have been paid in full payments can then be made to the ordinary unsecured or trade creditors. If these claims come in total to, say, £12 000 and the trustee has only £4000, each trade creditor will get one-third of what is claimed and the deferred creditors will get nothing.

Deferred creditors

If all the unsecured creditors can be paid, the deferred creditors come next. These are, for example, debts owed by Fred to (say) his wife. They are not paid until all other creditors have received payment in full.

Discharge of the bankrupt

(1) Fred will be automatically discharged three years after he became bankrupt unless the Official Receiver satisfies the court that Fred is not complying with his obligations, as where he is concealing assets.

(2) Any money owed by Fred which has not been paid at the date of discharge is no longer payable at law. Fred can then go back into business legally free of his old debts and with no restrictions on obtaining credit.

Questions/activities

1. Joseph David Soap wishes to set up in business on his own as a carpenter, having acquired a small business connection from John Smith. Which of the following trading names, if any, would require Joe to comply with the provisions of the Business Names Act 1985.

(a) David Soap

(b) J D Soap & Co.

(c) Joe Soap

(d) Joe Soap Carpentry (formerly John Smith's)

(e) J D Soap

(f) Chipaway

(g) Dave Soap

2. Your friend, Fred, intends to go into business on

his own as a timber merchant under the name of 'County Council Supplies'. What could happen to Fred if he does this?

3. Old John Brown has been in business as a furniture remover in Barchester since 1965. Last year young John Brown moved to Barchester and has started up a furniture removal business in his own name. Can old John Brown stop him?

4. Divide your class into four groups as near as you can. Without reference to a textbook each group should discuss the following problem. One member of the group should note up the group's advice and then compare this with the other groups so that a unified position in terms of advice for the whole class is obtained.

Adam Smith, a grocer, comes to you for advice on his finances. What advice would you give him in terms of each of the following questions which he asks you.

(a) 'Times have been very hard for me lately. I owe so many people so much money. I could probably pay my creditors say, half of what I owe them but no more. Is there a way of doing this given that I understand that a builder to whom I owe £1000 appears to have gone to court to make me bankrupt?'

(b) 'Anyway, I have tried to make my family safe. Last week I gave my wife the family home and on the same day sold her two terraced houses in Barchester worth £40 000 for £500. Yesterday I also paid my brother off. I owed him £1000 from when I started up so he should have it. My creditors can't upset these deals, I take it.'

(e) 'I have not paid John, my driver, for a month and I doubt whether I can now. I wish I could have helped him but I guess he will have to go down with all the other creditors. That's the position isn't it?'

(d) 'Of course, even if they make me bankrupt I shall rent another shop and go on trading. Nothing can be done about that, can it?'

6

The partnership

Definition and nature of a partnership

The Partnership Act 1890 sets out the basic rules which apply to this type of business organization. All section references in this chapter are to that Act unless there is a reference to some other Act.

Definition

A partnership is defined as 'The relation which subsists between persons carrying on a business in common with a view of profit'. (S. 1).

Explanation and consequences of the definition

(1) *The relation which subsists is one of contract.* A partnership agreement is a contract. However, it is not enough just to agree to be partners; you must also be *in a business which has started.*

Thus if Jane and John decide that they *will* run a shop as partners, they are not partners in the eyes of the law until the shop is actually operating.

While they are preparing to open, as by ordering goods and starting a bank account, they are not partners and contracts in the 'preparing' stage are not partnership contracts. If they are made they are made only by the person who actually enters into them.

Spicer (Keith) Ltd v Mansell (1970)

Mr Mansell (M) and Mr Bishop (B) lost their jobs. They agreed to go into business together and form a limited company to run a restaurant. While they were forming the company and before it had received its certificate of incorporation from the Registrar, Mr B ordered some goods from Spicer's for the business. They also opened a bank account in the name of the company.

The company was eventually formed but was not bound by the contract which Mr B had made because it was not in existence at the time. It was a pre-incorporation contract. These contracts do not bind the company when it comes into being.

Mr B went bankrupt before Spicer's had been paid. So, rather than prove in a bankruptcy, Spicer's sued M on the basis that he was a partner of Mr B and since partners are jointly and severally liable for the debts of the firm, M, they said, should pay and then get a contribution from B (though it was not too likely that he would).

The Court of Appeal decided that B and M were not partners. They were not carrying on a business together in partnership. They were preparing to carry on a business as a company as soon as they could. They were company promoters, not partners.

Comment. The case illustrates the importance of the relationship of partners and, indeed, its possible terrible consequences. Each partner makes the other his agent for the purpose of making contracts for him and, provided those contracts were within the scope of the partnership business, he is liable to perform all such contracts as if he had made them himself. Fortunately, for Mr Mansell in this case the Court did not accept that the parties were partners so that Mr Bishop was liable on his own for the debt to Spicer's.

(2) *A partnership is 'between persons'*, but a company, being a legal person, can be a partner with a

human person. The company may have limited liability while the human person has not. Two or more limited companies can be in partnership, forming a consortium as an alternative to merging one with the other.

(3) *Partners must be carrying on a business*, and for this reason a group of people who run a social club would not be a partnership.

Under s. 45 a business includes 'every trade, occupation, or profession', but this does not prevent a particular profession from having rules forbidding members to be in partnership; e.g. a barrister is not allowed to be in partnership with another barrister, at least for the purpose of practice at the Bar.

The importance of being in business together as partners is also shown by *Spicer* v *Mansell* (1970).

(4) *Partners must act in common*, and the most important result of this is that unless the agreement says something different, every general partner must be allowed to have a say in management, as s. 24(5) also provides. A partner who is kept out of management has a ground to dissolve the firm unless there is something in the agreement which limits the right to manage.

The specimen partnership agreement which appears at p. 77 should be looked at to see how management rights have been dealt with.

(5) *There must be a view of profit*, and so it is unlikely that those groups of persons who have got together to run railway preservation societies are partnerships.

(6) *The sharing of gross returns*, by A and B will not normally indicate a partnership between A and B. Partners share net profits, i.e. turnover less the outgoings of the business. Section 2 says that the sharing of gross returns does not, of itself, provide evidence of partnership as the following case shows.

Cox *v* Coulson (1916)

Mr Coulson had a lease of a theatre. A Mr Mill was the employer/manager of a theatre company. Mr Coulson and Mr Mill agreed to present a play called 'In time of war'. Mr Coulson was to provide the theatre and pay for the lighting and advertising and get 60 per cent of the money which came in at the box office - the gross takings. Mr Mill paid those taking part in the play and provided the scenery and the play itself and got 40 per cent of the gross takings.

Mrs Cox paid to see the play. As part of the performance an actor had to fire a revolver with a blank round in it. Because of alleged negligence a defective cartridge was put in the revolver and when the actor fired it Mrs Cox, who was sitting in the dress circle, was shot and injured. She wanted to succeed in a claim for damages against Mr Coulson. He had more money than Mr Mill. However, the actor was employed by Mr Mill and he alone was liable vicariously for the actor's negligence unless Mrs Cox could convince the court that Mill and Coulson were partners. The court decided that they were not; they were merely sharing the gross returns. Only the actor and Mr Mill were liable.

Comment. (*i*) The sharing or profits suggests a partnerlike concern with the expenses of the business and its general welfare. Sharing gross returns does not produce an *implied agreement* of partnership.

(*ii*) If there is an *express agreement*, oral or written, and in it the partners agree to share gross returns, then there would be a partnership.

(7) *Joint ownership* according to s. 2 does not of itself make the co-owners partners. That means that there is no joint and several liability for debt between the co-owners, say A and B. So if A and B are joint owners of 12 Acacia Avenue and A cannot pay a debt, say for a carpet which he has had fitted in his bedroom, B cannot be made liable as a partner. Co-owners are not agents one of the other as partners are.

(8) *Formalities*, that is, writing, is not required for a partnership agreement. However, to make quite sure what has been agreed by the partners there should be a written agreement.

A specimen agreement is set out on p. 77. This shows what is normally dealt with by such agreements.

The sharing of profits as evidence of partnership

At one time the sharing of profits was almost conclusive evidence of partnership. During this period a number of everyday business transactions could give rise to a partnership, though the parties did not want this because of the possibility of incurring liability for another's debts. The position was eventually clarified in regard to the business transactions set out below by s. 2(3) of the Act of 1890.

(*a*) *Partners can pay off a creditor by instalments out of the profits of the business.*

This comes from the following case which was decided before the 1890 Act.

Cox v Hickman (1860)

A trader had got into debt and his creditors decided that instead of making him bankrupt and getting only a proportion of what he owed them, they would let him keep the business but supervise him in the running of it and take a share of the profits each year until their debts were paid in full.

An attempt was made in this case to make one of the supervising creditor/trustees liable for the trader's debts as a partner. But was he a partner? The court said he was not. He was a creditor being paid off by a share of profits.

Comment. (*i*) There was, in addition, no mutual participation in trade here, but a mere supervision of the business. Of course, if creditors assume an active role in management they may well become partners.

(*ii*) The more modern approach would be for the creditors to ask the court for the appointment of a receiver to run the business. Obviously, he would not be regarded as a partner.

(*b*) *Partners can pay their employees or agents by a share of profits.* It has long been the practice of some organizations to pay employees in part by some profit-sharing scheme. The Act makes this possible without putting the employees at risk of being regarded as partners and liable for the debts of the firm if the true partners run into money trouble.

The provision is also important to the true partners because the giving of labour is sufficient to form a partnership: the putting in of money by way of capital is not essential. So this provision makes sure that the employees themselves cannot claim to be partners just because they are sharing profits under an employees' scheme.

(*c*) *Partners can pay an annuity (which is a sum of money paid at intervals during the lifetime of the person who is due to receive it) by a share of profits to the widow or child of a deceased partner.* These annuities are common in partnership agreements. This provision prevents those who receive these annuities from being regarded as partners by creditors of the firm merely because they have a share of profits. Once again, however, it is important that the persons receiving the annuity do not take part in the management of the firm.

Annuities payable to male widowers are covered.

(See s. 6(*b*) of the Interpretation Act 1978: 'Words importing female gender include masculine gender unless a contrary intention appears.') There is no contrary indication here.

(*d*) *Partners can pay interest on a loan by a share of net profits provided that the contract of loan is in writing and signed by all the parties to it.* This provision will protect a lender if a creditor tries to make him liable for the debts of the firm he has lent the money to, as where the creditor argues that the lender is really a dormant partner.

However, the lender must not take part in the running of the business. Remember also that the lender will not need the protection of this provision if he is paid a fixed rate of interest on his loan, e.g. 10 per cent per annum instead of 10 per cent per annum of the profit. If he is paid 10 per cent per annum interest he is clearly a creditor and not a partner.

Do not think that because there is no written contract that a lender will always be a partner. It is still a matter for the court to decide if it is argued that he is. Normally a properly drafted written contract should persuade the court that the lender is not a partner.

(*e*) *Partners can pay for goodwill by a share of profits.* If A sells his business to partners B and C, and B and C pay in cash for the tangible assets of A's business, e.g. the plant and machinery, A, B and C may agree that the goodwill of A's business should be paid for by giving A a share of the profits for a period of time. A will not be regarded as a partner unless, of course, he takes part in the management of the business.

The application of the section is illustrated by the case set out below.

Pratt v Strick (1932)

A doctor sold his practice, including goodwill, to another doctor, it being agreed that the selling doctor would, for three months, live in the house from which the practice was carried on and introduce his patients to the purchasing doctor, being entitled to half the profits and liable for half the expenses during that three months. Mr Strick, an inspector of taxes, raised an assessment on the selling doctor under the Finance Act 1929 under which the selling doctor was said to be liable to tax as a partner with the purchasing doctor on three-twelfths of the annual profit, not merely the profit he took in the three months he was introducing patients. The court said that there was no partnership and the practice was the purchasing doctor's from the date of sale. Mr Strick's assessment was not valid.

Comment. This provision recognizes that one way of paying for goodwill is out of the profits it is said to create. In addition, the contract is, of course, a contract of sale of a business so it is hardly likely that it could be regarded as a contract of partnership.

Deferred creditors – generally

Under s. 3 those receiving money from the firm under headings (d) and (e) above are deferred creditors if the partners go bankrupt during their lifetime or die insolvent.

Lenders and sellers of goodwill will not get any of the money owed to them until all other creditors have been paid £1 in the £.

Thus the lender of money and the seller of goodwill do not get the best of both worlds. Section 2 provides that they do not become partners and liable for debts but s. 3 makes them deferred creditors if the partners are insolvent.

Deferred creditors – lenders with security

A lender who becomes a deferred creditor because of the partner's insolvency is in a better position if he has taken a security over an asset or assets of the firm.

The court decided in *Re Lonergan, ex p. Sheil* (1877) that a deferred lender can enforce a security by selling the asset or assets taken as security because the first right to claim the debt (which is deferred by s. 3) and the second right to enforce the security are independent rights, and the second right is not deferred by s. 3.

Types of partners

Partners are of different types in law as set out below.

The general partner

This is the usual type of partner who, under s. 24, has the right to take part in the management of the business unless there is an agreement between himself and the other partner(s) that he should not. For example, the partnership agreement may say that some junior partners are not to order goods or sign cheques. We shall see, however, that in spite of restrictions of this kind, if a junior partner ordered goods on behalf of the firm, though he had no authority to do so, the contract

would be good and the seller could sue the partners for the price if they did not pay.

However, by ignoring the partnership agreement and making unauthorized contracts in this way, the junior partner could give his co-partners grounds to dissolve the firm and exclude him from their future business operations.

The dormant partner

The 1890 Act does not mention this type of partner but in fact he is a partner who puts money (capital) into the firm but takes no active part in the management of the business. If he does take part in management he would cease to be a dormant partner and become a general partner.

The salaried partner

It is quite common today, at least in professional practices of, for example, solicitors and accountants, to offer a young assistant a salaried partnership without the assistant putting any money into the firm as the general partners do.

Normally, these salaried partners are paid a salary just as an employee is with tax and national insurance being deducted from it. They are not partners for the purpose of dissolving the firm. If they want to leave they do so by serving out their notice or getting paid instead.

However, because they usually appear on the firm's letterheading as partners, they could, according to the decision in *Stekel* v *Ellice* (1973), be liable to pay the debts of the firm as a partner by estoppel (see below).

Because of this case a salaried partner should get a full indemnity, as it is called, from the general partners in case he is made to pay the firm's debts. In practice this will not happen unless the firm has not paid its debts. Liability as a partner is joint and several so that if A is a full partner and B a salaried partner, and the debt £2000, either A or B could be made to pay it all and then claim only a contribution, which would often be one half, from the other partner. Thus if B pays the £2000 he is entitled to £1000 from A. However, if B gets an indemnity from A, then if B has to pay the £2000, he can recover *all* of it from A.

The partner by holding out (or by estoppel)

The usual way in which this happens in practice is where a person allows his or her name to appear on the firm's letterheading, whether that person is or is not a full partner. (See *Stekel* v *Ellice* (1973).) It can also happen on the retirement of a partner if the partner retiring does not get his name off the letterheading.

Under s. 14 everyone who by words, spoken or written, or by conduct, represents himself, or knowingly allows himself to be represented as a partner in a particular firm, is liable as a partner to anyone who has, because of that, given credit to the firm.

Thus, although such a person is not truly a partner, he may be sued by a creditor who was led to believe that in fact he was a partner.

However, to become a partner by holding out (or estoppel, as it is also called) the person held out must *know* that he is being held out as a partner. The following case is an example.

Tower Cabinet Co. Ltd v Ingram (1949)

In January 1946 Ingram and a person named Christmas began to carry on business in partnership as household furnishers under the name of 'Merry's' at Silver Street, Edmonton, London. The partnership lasted until April 1947 when it was brought to an end by mutual agreement. After the dissolution of the firm Christmas continued to run 'Merry's' and had new notepaper printed on which Ingram's name did not appear. In January 1948 Christmas was approached by a representative of Tower Cabinet and eventually ordered some furniture from them. The order was confirmed on letterheading which had been in use before the original partnership was dissolved and Ingram's name was on it, as well as that of Christmas. Ingram had no knowledge of this and it was contrary to an agreement which had been made between him and Christmas that the old letterheading was not to be used. Tower Cabinet obtained a judgment for the price of the goods against 'Merry's' and then tried to enforce that judgment against Ingram as a member of the firm. The court decided that since Ingram had not knowingly allowed himself to be represented as a partner in 'Merry's' within s. 14 of the Partnership Act 1890, he was not liable as a partner by holding out (or estoppel).

Comment. As the case shows, a partner who has retired will not be liable if after retirement his name appears on the firm's letterheading if the other partners agree before he retires that the stock of old letterheading will be destroyed, or that his name will be crossed out. If old notepaper is used in spite of the agreement, the ex-partner is not liable: there is no duty in law to stop people telling lies! However, something should be done to show lack of consent if it is known that old letterheading is being used. This could be, for example, a recorded delivery letter to the continuing partners expressing dissent.

A partner who intends to work with the firm, perhaps part-time, after retirement, can avoid the above problems by describing himself on the firm's letterheading as a 'consultant'.

The person who is held out is liable to a creditor who has relied on him being a partner. That is all s. 14 says. However, in *Hudgell Yeates & Co.* v *Watson* (1978), the court said that the true or actual partners could also be liable to such a creditor if they themselves were responsible for the holding out or knowingly allowed holding out to take place.

Finally s. 14 provides that the continued use of a deceased partner's name will not make his estate (that is, the property he has left on death) liable for the debts of the firm.

Membership of the firm

As we have seen, for most partnerships, the maximum number of partners allowed is twenty but this limit does not apply, for example, to partnerships of solicitors, accountants, and members of The Stock Exchange, where there may be partnerships of unlimited size. We have seen, also, that practising barristers cannot be in partnership.

These are negative rules but there are some positive provisions to try to help people become partners in the Sex Discrimination Act 1975 and the Race Relations Act 1976. The sex discrimination and the race discrimination provisions are extended to partnerships but in the case of race discrimination only if there are six or more partners, as regards failure to offer a person a partnership on sex or race grounds, or to offer it but on worse terms, or to refuse or give inferior benefits, facilities, and services to a partner on the grounds of sex or race. For example, to refuse a cheap loan for house purchase or the use of a firm's car.

The restrictions on race discrimination to firms with

six or more partners does in fact allow race discrimination in the smaller firms, but not, for example in the major accounting or law firms.

A minor may become a member of a partnership (*Lovell and Christmas* v *Beauchamp* (1894)) but can avoid (get out of) the contract at any time while he is under eighteen or for a reasonable period of time afterwards.

The law in practice prohibits a partnership with a person of unsound mind who does not understand the nature of the partnership arrangement he has made. These capacity problems are also dealt with in Chapter 8.

The firm and the firm name

Generally

In English law the partnership firm is not an artificial person separate from the partners. In other words, it is not a person (or *persona*) at law as a company is.

If there are ten partners in 'Snooks, Twitchett & Co', then the firm name, that is, 'Snooks, Twitchett & Co', is only a convenient short form for (or a collective designation of) all the partners. It saves reeling off all their names when business is done. Thus a contract can be made in the firm name.

If the firm wishes to sue, or if it is sued by a creditor, the Rules of the Supreme Court (which are rules made by the judges to deal with procedure in court) do give a sort of personality to the firm in that they allow –

(*a*) actions by and against outsiders in the firm name; 'Snooks, Twitchett & Co' can sue or be sued in that name;

(*b*) enforcement of judgments and orders is allowed against the assets of the firm, as by taking and selling those assets to pay the judgment creditor.

A judgment against the firm can also be enforced in the same way against the private property of any partner if the assets of the firm are not enough.

So, although in legal theory a partnership firm is not a *persona* at law, yet for some practical purposes, e.g. contracting, suing and being sued, the firm is regarded as a sort of independent entity.

Choice of name

Restrictions on the name chosen for the firm are set out below.

Passing off at common law

As far as the common law is concerned, partners, say A and B, can trade in any name that suits them so long as the name does not suggest that their business is the same as that of a competitor. It must not deceive or confuse the customers of some other person or persons, say, C and D.

If it does the court will, if asked, give an injunction and/or damages against A and B to protect the business of C and D.

However, people can carry on business in their *own names*, even if there is some confusion with other person's business, unless it is part of a scheme deliberately to deceive the public as the following case shows.

Croft v Day (1843)

A firm called Day & Martin were well-known makers of boot polish. The original Mr Day and Mr Martin had been dead for some time but Mr Croft had bought the business and carried it on in the 'Day & Martin' name. A real Mr Day and a real Mr Martin went into the manufacture of boot polish and adopted the Day & Martin name for the fraudulent purpose of representing to the public that they were the old and widely-known firm of that name. Mr Croft went to court and was given an injunction to stop the real Mr Day and the real Mr Martin trading in their own names in the circumstances of this case.

Business names and company legislation

Under the Business Names Act 1985 the names of all the members of a partnership and their addresses in Great Britain where documents can be served must be stated in a notice which must be prominently displayed so that it can be easily read at all the firm's business premises. The names must also be stated in readable form on all business letters and documents. However, this requirement is relaxed in the case of a firm which has more than twenty partners. If there are more than twenty partners, none of the partners' names need appear on business letters and documents (except in the text or by way of signature) but there must be a statement on the business letters and documents of the firm's principal place of business with an indication that a list of partners' names can be obtained and inspected there. The Act also requires every partnership to provide to anyone with whom it is doing or discussing business a note of the partners' names and addresses on such information being asked for by that person.

In some cases official approval is required for the use of certain partnership names. For example, the use of the word 'Royal' in a firm's name requires the approval of the Home Office, and the use of the word 'Bank' requires the approval of the Bank of England.

Under the Companies Act 1985 the use of the descriptions 'Company' or 'and Company' are allowed for partnerships even though they suggest that they are companies. However, the Companies Act 1985 makes it an offence to use a firm name which ends with the expression 'Limited' or 'Ltd' for associations such as partnerships, whether ordinary partnerships or limited partnerships. Failure to comply with this rule results in liability to a fine for every day it goes on.

The relationship between partners and outsiders

The power of a partner, including a salaried partner, to make himself and his other partners liable for transactions which he enters into *on behalf of the firm* (not on his own behalf) is based on the law of agency. Each partner is the agent of his co-partners.

Section 5 makes this clear. It says that every partner is the agent of the firm and of his co-partners for the purpose of the business of the partnership.

Partners' powers

A partner's authority to enter into transactions on behalf of the firm and his co-partners may be set out under the following headings.

Actual authority

If a partner is asked by his co-partners to buy a new van for the firm's use and makes a contract to purchase one, the firm is bound. Section 6 deals with authorized acts and says that the firm will be liable for the authorized acts of partners and also employees of the firm.

Apparent authority

If a partner enters into a transaction on behalf of the firm without authority, the person he deals with may, if he does not know of the lack of authority, hold the firm bound under the provisions of s. 5 which gives partners some apparent authority.

However, s. 5 says that *the transaction must be connected with the business.* If there is a dispute about this the court will decide what can be said to be 'connected', regardless of what the partnership agreement may say.

Mercantile Credit Co. Ltd *v* Garrod (1962)

Mr Parkin and Mr Garrod had entered into an agreement as partners for the letting of garages and the carrying out of motor repairs, but the agreement expressly excluded the buying and selling of cars. Parkin, without Garrod's knowledge sold a car to Mercantile for the sum of £700 but the owner of the car had not consented to the sale. The finance company did not, therefore, become owners of the car and wanted its money back. The court held that the firm was liable and that Mr Garrod was liable as a partner to repay what the firm owed to Mercantile. The judge dismissed the argument that the transaction did not bind the firm because the agreement excluded the buying and selling of cars. He looked at the matter instead from 'what was apparent to the outside world in general'. Parkin was doing an act of a like kind to the business carried on by persons trading as a garage.

Comment. The point of the case is that although the buying and selling of cars was expressly forbidden by the partnership agreement, the firm was bound. This is a correct application of s. 8, which provides that internal restrictions on the authority of partners will have effect only if the outsider deals with a partner, but with actual notice of the restrictions. In this case Mercantile had no such knowledge of the restrictions and, of course, there is no constructive notice of the contents of partnership agreements as there is of the objects of companies as set out in the memorandum. (See further p. 95.)

Also the transaction must be carried out *in the usual way of business.* In other words, it must be a *normal* transaction for the business.

An example can be seen in *Goldberg v Jenkins* (1889) where a partner borrowed money on behalf of the firm at 60 per cent interest per annum when money could be borrowed at between 6 per cent and 10 per cent per annum. He had no actual authority to enter into such a transaction and the court held that the firm was not bound to accept the loan. The firm did borrow money but it was not usual or normal to borrow at that high rate.

Finally, s. 5 says that *the outsider must know or believe that he is dealing with a partner in the firm.* Because of the requirements of the Business Names Act 1985 as regards the display of the names of the owners of the firm on various documents and in various places which we have already considered, a *dormant partner* is now more likely to be known as a partner to an outsider. So if a dormant partner makes an unauthorized contract in the ordinary course of business in the usual or normal way, the outsider should now be able to say that he knew or believed the dormant partner to be a partner. If so, a dormant partner can enter into an unauthorized transaction which will bind the firm under s. 5. If the outsider does not know the dormant partner is a member of the firm, as where the 1985 Act is not being complied with, then the firm will not be bound. A dormant partner would be since he made the contract.

Situations of apparent authority as laid down by case law

Section 5 does not say what acts are 'in the usual course of business'. However, the courts have, over the years, and sometimes in cases heard before the 1890 Act was passed codifying the law, decided that there are a number of definite areas in which a partner has apparent authority. These are set out below.

(*a*) *All partners in all businesses.* Here there is apparent authority to sell the goods (but not the land) of the firm, and to buy goods (but not land) on behalf of the firm; to receive money in payment of debts due to the firm and give valid receipts. So if A pays a debt due to the firm to B, a partner, who gives A a receipt then fails to put the money into the firm's funds, A is nevertheless discharged from payment of the debt. Partners can also employ workers, but once they are set on they are employees of *all* the partners so that one partner cannot discharge an employee without the consent of the others. Partners also have an insurable interest in the firm's property and can insure it. They may also employ a solicitor to defend the firm if an action is brought against it. The authority of an individual partner to employ a solicitor to bring an action on behalf of the firm seems to be restricted to actions to recover debts owing to the firm.

(*b*) *All partners in trading partnerships.* Partners in trading firms have powers *which are additional* to those set out in (*a*) above. Thus partners in a firm of grocers have more powers than partners in a professional practice, of, e.g. law or accountancy. There does not seem to be any good reason for this, but it has been confirmed by many cases in court and cannot be ignored.

In *Wheatley* v *Smithers* (1906) the judge said in regard to what was meant by the word 'trader': 'One important element in any definition of the term would be that trading implies buying or selling'. This was applied in *Higgins* v *Beauchamp* (1914) where it was decided that a partner in a business running a cinema had no implied power to borrow on behalf of the firm. The partnership agreement did not give power to borrow and because the firm did not trade in the *Wheatley* v *Smithers* sense, there was no implied power to borrow. If a firm is engaged in trade, the additional implied powers of the partners are:

(*a*) to draw, issue, accept, transfer, and indorse, promissory notes and bills of exchange, including cheques if connected with the business and in the usual way of business. *A partner in a non-trading business only has apparent authority to draw cheques in the firm's name on the firm's bankers.* If the cheque is stopped a payee, or someone he has indorsed it over to, can sue the firm on it;

(*b*) to borrow money on the credit of the firm even beyond any limit agreed on by the partners unless this limit is known to the lender. Borrowing includes overdrawing a bank account;

(*c*) to secure the loan, which means giving the lender a right to sell property belonging to the firm if the loan is not repaid. The procedure for giving a security in this way is dealt with in Chapter 17.

Situations of no apparent authority

No partner, whether in a trading firm or not, has apparent authority in the following situations –

(1) He cannot make the firm liable on a deed. He needs the authority of the other partners. This authority must be given by deed. In English law an agent who is to make contracts under seal must be appointed as an agent by a written document under seal.

(2) He cannot give a guarantee, e.g. of another

person's debt, on which the firm will be liable.

(3) He cannot accept payment of a debt at a discount by, e.g. accepting 75p instead of £1, nor can he take something for the debt which is not money. He cannot, therefore, take shares in a company in payment of a debt owed to the firm.

(4) He cannot bind the firm by agreeing to go to arbitration with a dispute. Going to arbitration with a dispute and having it heard by, say, an engineer, if the dispute relates, for example to the quality of engineering work done under a contract, is a sort of compromise of the right to go first to a court of law and have the case heard by a judge. A partner cannot compromise the legal rights of the firm.

(5) As we have seen, a partner has no apparent authority to convey or enter into a contract for the sale of partnership land.

A partner's liability for debt and breach of contract by the firm

If, because of actual or apparent authority, a partner (or for that matter another agent such as an employee) makes the firm liable to pay a debt or carry out a contract, as where goods are ordered and the firm refuses to take delivery, the usual procedure will be to sue the firm in the firm name. If the court gives the plaintiff a judgment and the firm does not have sufficient assets to meet it, the partners are liable to pay it from their private assets. Under s. 3 of the Civil Liability (Contribution) Act 1978 each partner is liable to pay the amount of the judgment in full. He will then have a right to what is called a contribution from his co-partners.

Before the 1978 Act contribution was equal. Thus if A paid a partnership debt of £300 he could ask his partners, B and C, for a contribution of £100 each.

This rule of equal contribution was taken away by s. 2 of the 1978 Act, which provides that the amount of any contribution which the court may give is to be what it thinks is 'just and equitable' so that it need not in all cases be equal, but most often will be.

The effect of the above rules is that a partner can be required to pay the firm's debts from his private assets. From this we can see that only if *all* the partners are unable to pay the firm's debts will the firm be truly insolvent.

Under s. 9 the estate of a deceased partner is also liable for the debts of the firm which were incurred while the deceased was a partner.

Other areas of liability

Torts

Under s. 10 the firm is liable for the torts of partners which they commit in the ordinary course of business but not where the partner acts outside the scope of the firm's usual activities.

Therefore a partner in an accountancy practice who prepares the financial statements of a company negligently in the course of the firm's business will not only be liable to the client and possibly to others who rely on those statements say, to invest in the company, but will also make his fellow-partners liable.

At common law the firm is also liable for the torts of its employees committed in the course of their employment. So if the firm's van driver injures a pedestrian by negligent driving, both he and the firm would be liable under the common law rule of vicarious liability.

The words of s. 10 make it clear that there is no action by one partner against the firm's assets for injuries caused by torts in the course of business. In *Mair* v *Wood* (1948) a partner who had been injured through the negligence of his co-partner who had not maintained the firm's ship properly, could not sue the firm because of s. 10 but must sue the partner personally.

Misapplication of property

Under s. 11 if a partner, when acting within the scope of his authority, receives money or property, say from a client, and uses it for his private purposes and then cannot repay it, the firm is liable to make good the loss to the client.

Breach of trust

Suppose that in a partnership between A, B and C A is a trustee of his own family trust in his private capacity but wrongfully brings some of the trust money into the firm, say to cover up the fact that he has drawn more than the agreed monthly allowance from the firm.

Under s. 13 B and C are not liable to make good that money to the trust unless they knew that the money A had brought in was trust money.

Liability of incoming and outgoing partners

Now we shall deal with the period during which the partner is liable for the firm's debts, or to put it in another way, from what date do his co-partners become his agents and when does that agency come to an end?

There are four things to look at as set out below.

(1) *Admission as a partner.* Under s. 17 a person does not simply by becoming a partner take on liability for debts incurred by the firm before he joined it. He can if he wishes take on this liability by a process called novation (see below).

(2) *Retirement as a partner.* Also under s. 17 a person does not, by retiring, cease to be liable for the debts and obligations of the firm incurred before he retired. The law is not likely to allow a partner to avoid his liabilities simply by retiring from the firm.

A retiring partner is not liable for future debts unless, as we have seen, he is held out under s. 14 or under s. 36 because he has not given proper notice of his retirement. (See below.)

The date on which the contract was made or order given decides the matter of liability. So in a contract for the sale of goods, A, a retired partner, will be liable if the contract or order was made or given when he was a partner, even if the goods were delivered after he had retired.

(3) *Novation and indemnity.* Under s. 17 a retiring partner may be discharged from liabilities incurred before retirement if an agreement to that effect, called a *novation*, is made with the following people as parties to it –

(a) the partners who are to continue the business;

(b) the creditor concerned; and

(c) the retiring partner.

The agreement releases the retiring partner from his liabilities and accepts in his place the liability of the continuing partners, either alone or with the addition of any new partners.

Creditors are not forced to accept or take part in novation and may continue to regard the retiring partner as liable for debts incurred while he was a partner.

If this is so, the retiring partner should get an *indemnity* from the continuing partners. This will not release him from liability to the creditors but if he does have to pay

a pre-retirement debt, he can recover what he has paid in full under the indemnity, and not just a contribution which is all he could recover without the indemnity.

The indemnity approach is much more common than the novation approach. In fact the indemnity is often found in the partnership agreement which may have a clause such as 'In the event of retirement the remaining partners shall take over the liabilities of the firm.'

(4) *Notifying retirement.* The law requires a retiring partner to notify his retirement. The reason for this is that people who deal with the firm are entitled, in all fairness, to assume when they do business with it that all the partners are the same unless there has been notice of a change.

The rules are set out in s. 36 which states, in effect, that if X who was a partner in Y & Co, leaves the firm and the firm contracts with Z who knew that X was a member of the firm, but does not know that he has left, X will be liable to Z (along with other partners of course) if the firm does not meet its obligations. To avoid this liability there must have been adequate notice of X's retirement.

In order to indicate what adequate notice is, the law divides creditors into three classes as follows –

(a) *Creditors who have previously dealt with the firm and who knew X was a partner.* In this case it is necessary to show that the creditor received *actual* notice of the retirement. This may be by a letter from the firm, or by receiving a letter from the firm on which X's name is deleted, or by seeing the notice of retirement in the *London Gazette* (see below), *but only if he actually reads the Gazette.*

(b) *Creditors who have not had previous dealings with the firm but who knew or believed X to be a partner before he retired.* As far as these people go, X will not be liable for post-retirement debts –

(i) If they had for some reason actual knowledge of X's retirement; or

(ii) X's retirement was published in *The London Gazette, whether it was seen or not.*

The London Gazette is published daily by HMSO and contains all sorts of public announcements, for example, bankruptcies, company liquidations and partnership dissolutions.

(c) *Creditors who have not had previous dealings with the firm and do not know that X was ever a present.* These people cannot hold X liable for post-retirement debts even if no notice has been received by them and even though no notice has been put in the *Gazette*. X could only be liable to these people if he was knowingly held out as a partner under s. 14.

In *Tower Cabinet Co. Ltd* v *Ingram* (1949), which was dealt with earlier in this chapter, no notice of Mr Ingram's retirement was put in the *Gazette*, but he was not liable to Tower Cabinet under s. 36 because they did not know or believe him to be a partner prior to his retirement. He was not liable either under s. 14 (holding out) for reasons already given.

Section 36 states that the estate of a deceased or bankrupt partner is not liable for debts incurred after death or bankruptcy, as the case may be, even if no advertisement or notice of any kind has been given.

Relationship of partners within the partnership

We shall now deal with the relation of partners to one another. It is governed by ss. 19–31 of the 1890 Act, the provisions of which are set out below.

The ability to change the partnership agreement

Section 19 states that partners can change the business of the firm but because of the provisions of s. 24 *all* the partners must be in agreement about this.

Partners can also change the provisions of the 1890 Act which the Act puts into partnership agreements unless the partners have dealt with the matter in the agreement themselves. For example, the Act provides in s. 24 that profits and losses are to be shared equally but the partners may provide for a different share, e.g. one-third/two-thirds, in their agreement.

The provisions of the Act which deal with the relationship of the partners and outsiders cannot be changed in this way. Section 8 says that internal restrictions on the authority of partners, for example in the partnership agreement, have no effect on an outsider unless he has *actual* notice of the restriction.

This was illustrated by the case of *Mercantile Credit Co. Ltd* v *Garrod* (1962) where the partnership agreement said that there was to be no buying or selling of cars. This did not prevent the sale of a car to Mercantile by a partner being good, since Mercantile had no knowledge of the restriction.

A written partnership agreement may be varied by attaching a written and signed indorsement to the original agreement. However, even where the original agreement is written (and obviously if it is oral) the partners may, either orally or by the way they deal with one another, vary the agreement. This is not surprising since the original agreement of partners does not have to be in writing.

The case which follows is an example of partners agreeing to one thing but sliding into a different way of going on. The books of the firm were kept and the accounts prepared from them in a way which was different from the original agreement.

Pilling v Pilling (1865)

A father took his two sons into partnership with him. The partnership agreement provided that the assets of the business were to remain the father's and that he and his sons should share profits and losses in thirds. Each son was to have, in addition to a one-third share of the profits, £150 a year out of the father's share of profit and repairs and expenses were to be paid out of profits. It was also agreed that the father *only* should have 4 per cent on his capital per annum and that the depreciation of the mill and machinery, i.e. the major assets, was to be deducted before the profit was calculated.

The partnership lasted for ten years and no depreciation was charged on the mill and machinery. The £150 per annum was paid to the sons but it was charged against the profits of the business and not against the father's share. Each partner was credited with interest on capital, not merely the father, but, as it happens, the profit was divided into thirds. Later on the court was asked to decide whether the assets of the business still belonged to the father or whether they belonged to the firm as partnership property. The court decided that the way in which the partners had dealt with each other was evidence of a new agreement. The assets were therefore partnership property, even though the articles had said that they were to continue to belong to the father.

Comment. The major change here was to allow each partner interest on capital and not only the father who had brought the capital in. From this the court presumed that the father's capital had become partnership property and had not remained his personal property, as was the original intention in the agreement.

Partnership property

Here we will deal with the partnership assets. Just because certain assets are used in the business does not mean that they are partnership assets; they may belong just to one partner. As we shall see, it is often a matter of vital importance to decide whether property is a firm's asset or the private asset of a partner.

Generally

Section 20 provides that all property originally brought into the firm or bought on account of the firm is partnership property unless there is some evidence to the contrary.

The section is no help in deciding what is or what is not partnership property because it does not say when property is brought into the firm or bought or acquired by the firm. Therefore the partnership agreement should define what assets are to be treated as partnership property.

If there is nothing about it in the partnership agreement, partnership property will normally be –

(a) *Property bought with the firm's money.* Section 21 says that property bought with money belonging to the firm is presumed to have been bought for the firm unless there is evidence that this was not the intention.

(b) *Property brought into the firm by a partner* who has the value of it credited to his capital account, thus clearly indicating that he brings it in.

(c) *Property which the partners treat as the property of the firm.* This point is illustrated by the facts of *Pilling* v *Pilling* (1887) (above) and by *Waterer* v *Waterer* (1873) (below).

Under s. 20 where partners buy property with the profits of land which does not belong to the firm but which they own jointly in a private capacity, the property bought is not partnership property but is also jointly owned by the partners but in a private capacity.

This is illustrated by the following case.

Davis v Davis (1894)

Two sons inherited their father's business under his will and also three freehold houses as joint owners. They let one of the houses and spent the rent on adapting one of the other two for partnership purposes. It was later decided by the court that the house adapted for business purposes was not partnership property. The money spent adapting it was the joint money of the two and not partnership funds. The property adapted was owned jointly by the partners in a private capacity. As we have seen, under s. 2, joint ownership does not of itself create partnership.

Also, the mere fact that property is used in the business is not enough to transfer that property to the firm. This statement is supported by the cases on the point, though one of them, *Waterer* v *Waterer* (1873) (below), says the opposite, partly, it is thought, because of the type of business that it was.

Miles v Clark (1953)

Mr Clark wished to start a photography business and he took a lease of premises for the purpose. He was not a skilled photographer and employed other people to do the photography work. The business made a loss but after some negotiations Mr Miles, who was a successful free-lance photographer, decided to join in with Mr Clark. Miles brought in his customers and there were a large number of these. The agreement made between Miles and Clark provided that the profits were to be shared equally and that Miles was to draw £153 per month on account of his profits. The business did well but Miles and Clark quarrelled and it had to be wound up. In this action the court was asked to decide the ownership of the assets and Miles was claiming a share in all the assets of the business. The court decided that there was no agreement except as to the way profits were to be divided and so the stock in trade of the firm and other consumable items, such as films, must be considered as part of the partnership assets, even though they were brought in by Clark. However, the lease and other plant and equipment should be treated as belonging to the partner who brought them in – that was Clark. The personal goodwill, i.e. customers, belonged to the person who brought them in, so Miles retained the value of his customers and Clark retained the value of his.

Waterer v Waterer (1873)

A nurseryman on his death left his land to his three sons, F, M, and J, as joint owners. The nursery business, which he also left to his sons, was operated on part of this land. The sons carried on the business and bought more land out of the money left by their father. This new land was also used in the business. F and J bought M's share of the land and the business and paid (i) out of money in their father's estate, and (ii) out of money borrowed on the security of land. F died and the question arose whether his share in the land was a share in partnership property or not. The court decided that both the land left by will and the land later purchased was partnership property.

Comment. One reason for the decision seems to have been that in a nursery gardening business it is impossible to separate the land from the business. The judge said that it was in fact, in nursery gardening, practically impossible to separate the use of the soil for the trees and shrubs from the trees and shrubs themselves which constitute the substantial stock-in-trade.

We have seen from the decision in *Miles* (above) that items of stock-in-trade are brought in by use in the business because they are either sold or consumed and it cannot be expected that the partner who brought them in can ever have thought he would take them out.

In addition it is basically a question of what the parties intended as to whether a particular piece of property did or did not become partnership property. As regards this, the son who sold his land and share in the business asked *one price* for both and this was also influential in leading the court to the view that he regarded the land as part of the business.

Nature of a partner's interest in partnership property

(a) *Land (or real property).* If land is to become partnership property a trust must be used. The firm has no separate personality (or *persona*) and cannot take ownership of the land.

The Law of Property Act 1925 says that it is not possible for more than four people to have the joint legal ownership of land. This is mainly to simplify conveyancing in that no more than four signatures are ever necessary when the land is sold.

However, it does mean that if land (which includes a lease of land) is transferred to a firm of more than four partners, the transfer must be made to two, three, or four of them. They then declare a trust over the land in favour of all the partners, including themselves. This must be in writing because the Law of Property Act 1925 requires this. A minimum of two human trustees is required for a trust over land otherwise it is difficult to sell the land. A receipt for the buyer's money must be given by at least two trustees, otherwise those who benefit under the trust still have an interest in the land

itself, which the purchaser would not want.

It is the general policy of the law of trusts to have two trustees so that breach of trust is made more difficult. This rule about trusts of land reinforces the two-trustee principle. If there are fewer than four partners all can take the conveyance and declare the trust as above.

Even if no trust is declared in the above cases a trust will still exist because s. 20 of the 1890 Act provides that when real property is brought into the firm it is automatically held on trust.

(b) *Personal property.* Property such as office equipment is co-owned by the partners. No partner has the ownership of any particular piece of property. His co-ownership just gives him the right to a share of any surplus assets which there would have been at a particular point in time if the assets were sold and debts and liabilities paid. This right can be enforced if the firm closes down or a partner retires without the need for a trust.

The commercial importance of identifying partnership property

The ability to identify partnership property is important in the business world –

(a) *To the partners themselves,* because any increase in value of partnership property belongs to the firm (i.e. all the partners) but if the property belongs to only one partner the increased value belongs to him alone. Also, a decrease in value is suffered by the firm if it is partnership property but if it belongs to only one partner all the loss is his.

(b) *To the creditors of the firm and the creditors of the partners individually,* since this affects what property is available to pay their debts if the business fails. If a firm goes out of business and all the partners are also insolvent, then the firm's creditors can have the firm's assets sold to pay their debts before the private creditors of the partners have access to those assets. Also, private creditors have first right to sell private assets before the firm's creditors have access to them.

(c) *Because dealings with partnership property must be only for partnership purposes in accordance with the partnership agreement.* If the property is owned personally by a partner he can do what he likes with it unless the firm has some contractual rights over it, as where the firm is renting it from the partner. Obviously, the contract must be complied with or an action for damages would be available to the firm against the partner.

Assignment of a share in a partnership

A partner may assign his share of the partnership –

(a) *by redeemable charge*, for example to give a security for a private debt. Such a charge can be released by paying the debt; or

(b) *absolutely*, as part, for example, of a separation agreement. (See *re Garwood's Trusts* (1903) (below).)

Section 31 of the Partnership Act 1890, which applies in the case of assignments, provides that the assignee –

(i) cannot interfere in the management of the firm, nor is he entitled to accounts or to inspect the books (*Re Garwood's Trusts* (1903) (below));

(ii) is entitled to receive the share of profit to which the assignor/partner would otherwise be entitled, though he must accept the share of profit agreed by the partners in the accounts.

Re Garwood's Trusts, Garwood v Paynter (1903)

Three partners carried on a colliery business, and the partnership articles provided that they should share profits equally. No provision was made for the payment of salaries to the partners. One of the partners, J T Garwood, separated from his wife and in February 1889 he made a settlement in connection with the separation under which he charged his share in the partnership business and assets with payment to the trustees of the settlement of £10 000, and he also agreed to pay to the trustees two-thirds of his annual share of the profits. After the settlement had been made, the partners began to take turns to supervise the loading of coal at the pithead because they suspected theft, and since this involved them in extra work they paid themselves salaries out of profits, thus reducing the share of the profit accruing to J T Garwood, and reducing, also, the amount of money going to his wife. The wife objected to the payment of salaries. The court decided, it having been proved that the partners had acted in good faith in the matter and did genuinely work for their salaries, the payment of such salaries was part of the management of administration of the business within s. 31 of the Partnership Act and was binding on the assignees under the settlement, namely the trustees of the settlement made on J T Garwood's separation.

If the firm is dissolved, the assignee is entitled –

(a) to the assignor/partner's share of assets, and

(b) to accounts at the date of dissolution and until final winding up and distribution to assist him in checking the accuracy of that share.

As regards the debts of the firm, the assignee is not personally liable. However, if the assignment is absolute he must indemnify the assignor/partner against liability to pay the firm's debts incurred before or after assignment.

As regards the right of the other partners to dissolve the firm on assignment, the Act of 1890 does not mention the assignment of a share as a cause of dissolution. This is not a difficulty where a partnership is at will, since it can be dissolved by notice at any time. Where a partnership is for a fixed term, e.g. joint lives, then assignment is a ground for dissolution if the agreement so provides, but the court does not seem to have power to dissolve on the 'just and equitable' ground if there is no express provision in the partnership agreement.

Implied financial terms

These are set out below.

Profits and losses

Section 24 says that unless there is some other agreement between the partners then all partners are to share equally in the capital and profits of the business and must contribute equally towards losses of capital, or otherwise.

This is regardless of capital contributed. If those who have contributed more capital are to get more of the profit, the partnership agreement must say so.

Interest on capital

Section 24 also says that unless the partners agree, no partner is to get interest on the capital he puts into the firm. In practice, where partners do not make equal contributions of capital it is often agreed that those who contributed more are to get interest on capital at an agreed rate per annum. This interest is taken away from profits before they are distributed to the partners.

Interest on advances (loans)

If a partner helps to finance the firm by making it a loan

on top of contributing capital, then s. 24 provides that he is entitled to 5 per cent per annum on the advance (or loan) from the date when it was made. There is no rule that an advance to a partner by the firm carries interest. This has to be specially provided for.

Indemnity

Section 24 also requires the firm to indemnify every partner who makes payments from his own funds in the ordinary conduct of the business. Thus, if while a partner is negotiating an insurance for the firm, he is told by the broker that a premium on an existing policy is due that day and pays it with his own private cheque, the firm must pay him back.

Implied management powers

Management powers are normally written out in the partnership agreement. If not, the following rules apply.

(a) *Under s. 24(5) every partner may take part in the management of the business.* This is not surprising because a partnership is defined as the carrying on of business 'in common'. The right is also a fair one because a partner may find himself saddled with the debts of a firm, and if this is so, he should at least have the chance of managing it.

Any unjustified exclusion of a partner from the management of the firm will almost certainly enable him to petition to dissolve the firm on the just and equitable ground in s. 35.

This right to manage concept has also been applied to small companies which are essentially partnerships in all but legal form. Cases illustrating this, such as *Ebrahimi* v *Westbourne Galleries* (1972) will be looked at in Chapter 7.

(b) *Section 24(6) says that a partner is not entitled to a salary.* Partners share profits, but if the firm has some partners who are more active in the business than others it is usual for the partnership agreement to provide for a salary for the active partners which is paid in addition to a share of profit.

Apart from that, a partner who has had to work harder than usual because his fellow partner has failed to work as he should in the business is entitled to an extra amount from the firm's assets, but only if it is dissolved. (*Airey* v *Borham* (1861).)

(c) *Under s. 24(7) and (8) no new partners can be brought in and no change may be made in the business of the firm unless all the partners consent.* It should be noted, however, that a retiring partner's consent is not required.

This is a fair provision. New partners ought not to be thrust upon the old partners by a majority vote. Mutual confidence is essential.

As regards what are called 'ordinary matters', these are to be settled by a majority of the partners regardless of capital contributed, provided the decisions are made in good faith and after proper consultation with all of the partners. The Act makes no attempt to define 'ordinary matters'. There is no case law to help us. Much will depend upon the circumstances of the case.

(d) *Under s. 24(9) every partner is entitled to access to, and may also inspect and copy the firm's books.* These books must be kept at the place where the business is run, or if there is more than one place, at the main place of business.

The court will make an order (an injunction) preventing a partner from exercising the above rights if he is, e.g. taking the names of customers from the books to try to get them to use his own separate business instead of that of the firm.

Inspection may be through an agent (*Bevan* v *Webb* (1901)), so that a partner who was not able himself to assess financial information could employ an accountant to inspect the books.

(e) *Although the 1890 Act says nothing about it, it is implied by law that every partner shall attend at, and work in, the business.* If he does not, the other partners have a ground to dissolve the firm. However, there is normally no claim for damages for breach of contract, these being a common law remedy and partnership, being based on equity, has no remedy of damages for breach of duty between partners.

Expulsion of a partner

Section 25 says that no majority of partners can expel any other partner unless a power to do so appears in the partnership agreement.

If an expulsion is challenged in the courts, then the judge will be most concerned to see that a majority expulsion clause has not been abused.

It must be shown –

(a) *That the complaint which is said to allow expulsion is covered by the expulsion clause.* For example, in *Snow* v *Milford* (1868) the court decided that the 'adultery of a banker all over Exeter' was not a ground for his expulsion because it was not within the wording of the expulsion clause. This dealt only with financial frauds which would discredit a banking business.

(b) *That the partner expelled was told what he had done wrong and given a chance to explain.* An illustration is to be found in *Barnes* v *Youngs* (1898) where a partner who was living with a woman to whom he was not married continued to do so after becoming a partner. There was nothing to show that this was damaging to the firm's business. Even so, he was expelled by his fellow partners who refused to tell him why they were doing so. The court held that his expulsion was unlawful and ineffective.

(c) *That those who exercised the power of expulsion did so in all good faith.* For example, in *Blisset* v *Daniel* (1853) a partner was expelled. He had done nothing wrong to hurt the firm, but the partnership agreement said that a majority of the partners could buy out another. The motive of the other partners was just to get a bigger share of the property and profits. The court said that the expulsion was not effective. It was done in bad faith.

However, if (a) to (c) above are satisfied the court will regard the expulsion as valid. For example, in *Greenaway* v *Greenaway* (1940), the partnership agreement provided for expulsion in the event of conduct contrary to the good faith required of partners or prejudicial to their general interest. After several years of quarrelling, one partner assaulted another. The offender was given notice of expulsion. The court later said that although quarrelling by itself was not enough, the assault was inexcusable. Another reason for the expulsion was the fact that the offending partner had made disapproving remarks about a fellow partner to the firm's employees. This was not in line with the good faith rule. The expulsion was valid.

Of course, the expelled partner is entitled to his share of the firm's assets, as he would be if he retired. However, provision is often made to pay him out over a period of time and not immediately so that he cannot demand his total share of the assets as soon as he is expelled.

Relationship of utmost good faith

It is a basic principle of partnership law that each partner must treat his co-partners with utmost fairness and good faith. Example of bad faith in this context is, as we have seen, *Blisset* v *Daniel* (1853).

The principle of utmost good faith is not set out as a general proposition in the 1890 Act. The Act does, however, set out certain areas to which the good faith principle is applied. They are as follows –

(a) *The duty to account.* Section 28 requires every partner to give true accounts and full information regarding all things affecting the firm to any partner.

This is a *positive duty* to disclose facts. It is not merely a *negative duty* not to misrepresent facts.

As the following case shows, silence can amount to misrepresentation as between partner and partner.

Law v Law (1905)
Two brothers, William Law and James Law, were partners in a woollen manufacturers' business in Halifax. William lived in London and did not take a very active part in the business and James offered to buy William's share for £10 000. After the sale William discovered that certain partnership assets, that is money lent on mortgage, had not been disclosed to him by James. William brought an action against James for misrepresentation. The court decided that there was a duty of disclosure in this sort of case and the action was settled by the payment of £3550 to William, which he accepted in discharge of all claims between him and his brother.

Under s. 29 each partner must also account to the firm for any benefit he has had without the consent of the other partners from any transaction concerning the firm or from any use by him of the partnership name or customer connection. An illustration is to be found in the following case.

Bentley v Craven (1853)
Mr Bentley carried on business in partnership with the defendants, Messrs Craven, Prest and Younge, as sugar refiners at Southampton. Craven was the firm's buyer and because of this he was able to buy sugar at a great advantage as to price. He bought supplies of sugar cheaply and sold it to the firm at the market price. The other partners did not realize that he was selling on his own account and Bentley, when he found out, brought this action, claiming for

the firm a profit of some £853 made by Craven. The court decided that the firm was entitled to it.

Comment. Those who wish to make comparisons with other fiduciaries will note that a partner, like a trustee, may not make a private gain out of his membership of the firm. There is also a comparison with directors' secret profits and benefits, which will be dealt with in Chapter 7.

(b) *Duty not to compete with the firm.* Section 30 provides that if a partner without the consent of his co-partners carries on any business of the same kind as his firm so as to compete with it, he must account for and pay over to the firm all the profits he has made from that competing business.

Section 30 is in fact no more than an extension of the duty to account because a partner cannot be prevented from competing by the use of s. 30. The section actually allows him to compete but requires him to hand over *all* the profits of the competing business.

A particular partnership agreement may expressly provide that there shall be no competing business. If this is so, the other partners can get an injunction from the court to stop the competing business from being carried on.

Dissolution

A partnership is usually dissolved without the help of the court, though sometimes the court is brought in.

Non-judicial dissolution

Any of the following events will normally bring about a dissolution of a partnership.

(a) *The ending of the period for which the partnership was to exist.* Section 32(a) states that a partnership for a fixed term is dissolved when the term expires. A partnership for the joint lives of A, B and C ends on the death of A or B or C.

(b) *The achievement of the purpose for which the partnership was formed.* By reason of s. 32(b) a partnership for a single undertaking is dissolved at the end of it. In *Winsor* v *Schroeder* (1979), S and W put up equal amounts of cash to buy a house, improve it, and then sell it at a profit which was to be divided equally. The court decided that they were partners under s. 32(b) and that the partnership would end when the land was sold and the profit, if any, divided.

If in partnerships of the types set out in (a) and (b) above, the firm continues in business after the period has expired, without any settlement of their affairs by the partners, an agreement not to dissolve will be implied. Unless there is a new agreement to cover the continuing partnership, it is a partnership at will. Section 27 applies to it so that the rights and duties of the partners are the same as before the original partnership ended. However, since it has now become a partnership at will, any partner can give notice to end it.

(c) *By the giving of notice.* Under s. 32(c) a partnership which is not entered into for a period of time or for a particular purpose can be dissolved by notice given by *any partner*, but not a limited partner.

The notice must be in writing if the partnership agreement is in the form of a deed. (S. 26(2).) If not, oral notice will do.

The notice takes effect when all the partners know of it or from any later date which the person giving the notice states as the date of dissolution. (S. 32(c).) No particular period of notice is required. Withdrawal of the notice requires the consent of *all* the partners (*Jones* v *Lloyd* (1874)), otherwise the dissolution goes ahead and the court will, if asked by a partner, order the other partners to wind up the firm with him. The court said in *Peyton* v *Mindham* (1972) that it could and would declare a dissolution notice to be of no effect if it was given in bad faith as where A and B dissolve a partnership with C by notice in order to exclude C from valuable future contracts.

Dissolution by notice depends on what the partnership agreement says. If, as in *Moss* v *Elphick* (1910), the partnership agreement says that dissolution is only to be by mutual consent of the partners, s. 32(c) does not apply.

(d) *Death of a partner.* Under s. 33(1) the death of a partner (but not a limited partner) dissolves the firm. The share of the partner who has died goes to his personal representatives who are usually appointed by his will. They have the rights of a partner in a dissolution. Partnership agreements usually provide that the firm shall continue after the death of a partner so that the dissolution is only a technical one. A deceased partner's share is paid out to his personal representatives, although partnership agreements do sometimes provide for repayment of capital by instalments, or by annuities, e.g. to a spouse or other dependant. Of course, there is bound to be a true dissolution of a two-partner firm when one partner dies since if the other carries on business, it is as a sole trader.

(e) *Bankruptcy of a partner.* By reason of s. 33(1) the bankruptcy of a partner (not a limited partner) dissolves the firm. The partnership agreement usually provides that the business shall continue under the non-bankrupt partners, which means that the dissolution is again only a technical one, and the bankrupt partner's share is paid out to his trustee in bankruptcy. The agreement to continue the business must be made before the partner becomes bankrupt. (*Whitmore v Mason* (1861).)

(f) *Illegality.* Under s. 34 a partnership *is in every case* dissolved by illegality. There can be no contracting-out in the partnership agreement.

There are two types of illegality –

(i) *Where the business is unlawful,* for example, where the objects are unlawful because, as in *Stevenson & Sons Ltd v AG für Cartonnagen Industrie* (1918) the English company, Stevenson, was in partnership with a German company as a sole agent to sell the German company's goods. This would obviously involve day-to-day trading with an enemy in wartime and the partnership was therefore dissolved on the grounds of illegality; and

(ii) *where the partners cannot legally form a partnership to carry on what is otherwise a legal business,* as in *Hudgell, Yeates & Co. v Watson* (1978) where a firm of solicitors was regarded as dissolved when one partner had made himself unqualified to practise as a solicitor by mistakenly failing to renew his annual practising certificate.

(g) *Charge.* Section 33(2) says that if a partner's share in the partnership (not a limited partner's share) is charged to pay a private debt, the firm may be dissolved, *not automatically,* but at the *option* of the other partners (including, this time, limited partners). There is no indication in the Act whether the option is exercisable by any partner or by a majority or by all unanimously. Since it seems similar to expulsion it may require the unanimous consent of the other partners.

The charge is a form of *involuntary assignment* of a partner's share. A private creditor of a partner who has been to court and got a judgment for debt cannot take the assets of the firm so as to pay it. He can, however, apply to the court under s. 23 for a charging order against the debtor-partner's share of the assets and profits of the firm.

The court may appoint a receiver under s. 23 to help the creditor to collect the share and under the same section the other partners can pay off the creditor and take over the charge which they can then enforce gradually against the partner, e.g. by taking some part only of his share of profit until he has paid off the debt.

Judicial dissolution

Dissolution by the court (normally the Chancery Division of the High Court) is necessary if there is a partnership for a fixed time or purpose and a partner wants to dissolve a firm before the time has expired or the purpose has been achieved *and* there is nothing in the partnership agreement which allows this to be done.

There must be grounds for dissolution. These are set out below.

(a) *Partner's mental incapability.* This a ground under the Mental Health Act 1983. The petition for dissolution is in this case heard by the Court of Protection which sits to look after the property of people who are of unsound mind or under some other disability. The partner concerned must be unable, because of mental disorder, of managing his property and affairs.

A petition may be presented on behalf of the partner who is under the disability or by any of the other partners.

(b) *Partner's physical incapacity.* This is a ground under s. 35(b). The incapacity must be permanent. In *Whitwell v Arthur* (1865) a partner was paralysed for some months. He had recovered when the court heard the petition and it would not grant a dissolution.

Partnership agreements often contain express clauses which allow dissolution after a stated period of incapacity. In *Peyton v Mindham* (1972) a clause allowing a fixed-term partnership to be dissolved after nine months' incapacity was enforced. (See the model partnership deed, clause 16(g) at p. 81.)

Section 35(b) states that the incapacitated partner cannot petition. It is up to his co-partners to do so otherwise he continues as a partner.

(c) *Conduct prejudicial to the business.* Section 35(c) provides for this. The conduct may relate to the business, as in *Essell v Hayward* (1860) where a solicitor/partner misappropriated trust money in the course of his duties as a partner. This was a ground for dissolving a partnership for a fixed term, i.e. the joint lives of the partners.

It may, of course, be outside conduct. This will usually justify a dissolution it if results in a criminal conviction for fraud or dishonesty.

Moral misconduct is not enough unless, in the view of the court, it is likely to affect the business. In *Snow* v *Milford* (1868) where the matter of dissolution was also considered, as well as the matter of expulsion, 'massive adultery all over Exeter' was not regarded by the court as sufficient grounds for dissolution under s. 35(c).

Section 35(c) forbids a petition by the partner in default.

(d) *Wilful or persistent breach of the agreement or conduct affecting the relationship.* This is covered by s. 35(d). It includes, for example, refusal to meet on business or keep accounts, continued quarrelling and very serious internal disagreements. However, as the court said in *Loscombe* v *Russell* (1830), the conduct must be 'serious'. Thus occasional rudeness or bad temper would not suffice.

'Wilful' means a serious breach inflicting damage on the firm. Less serious breaches are enough if 'persistent'. In *Cheesman* v *Price* (1865) a partner failed seventeen times to enter small amounts of money he had received in the firm's books. The court ordered dissolution. The essential trust between the partners had gone.

Again, s. 35(d) forbids a petition by the partner in default. *No partner can force a dissolution by his own default.*

(e) *The business can only be carried on at a loss.* This is provided for by s. 35(e). It is hardly surprising as a ground for dissolution in view of the fact that partners are in business together with a view of profit, as s. 1 states. Therefore they must have a means to release themselves from loss.

Section 35(e) is not available if the losses are temporary. In *Handyside* v *Campbell* (1901) a sound business was losing money because a senior managing partner was ill. He asked the court for a dissolution. The court would not grant it. The other partners could manage the firm back to financial prosperity.

The court will not, however, expect the partners to put in more capital. (*Jennings* v *Baddeley* (1856).)

Any partner may petition.

(f) *The just and equitable ground.* Under s. 35(f) the court may dissolve a partnership if it is just and equitable to do so. Although there is no direct authority on s. 35(f), it appears to give the court wide powers to hear petitions which could not be made under the other five heads that we have considered.

In *Harrison* v *Tennant* (1856) a judicial dissolution was ordered where a partner was involved in long and messy litigation which he refused to settle. A similar order was made in *Baring* v *Dix* (1786) where the objects of the firm could not be achieved.

It appears from *Re Yenidje Tobacco Co. Ltd* (1916), a company dissolution based upon the fact that the company was in reality a partnership, that deadlock between the partners is enough for dissolution, even though the business is prospering.

All partners may petition. The court is unlikely, however, to dissolve a firm on the petition of a partner committing misconduct unless the other partners are doing so as well.

Creditors cannot petition the court to dissolve a firm of fewer than eight partners. They must proceed against the partners individually under the bankruptcy laws if the firm is not paying its debts.

If there are eight or more partners the firm can be wound up as an unregistered company under the Companies Act 1985. Under the provisions of the 1985 Act creditors can petition on certain grounds which are available in a company winding up, for example, if the firm cannot pay its debts.

Effect of dissolution

(a) *Authority of partners during winding up.* Sections 37 and 38 in effect give the former partners authority to conduct the winding up. There is no need to employ a person such as a liquidator, as is the case in companies. Where a firm is dissolved a partner is not liable for debts incurred by his co-partners after the dissolution if notice is given to customers of the firm and in the *London Gazette*. Section 37 allows a partner who wishes to place a notice of dissolution in the *Gazette* to compel the other partners to concur in that exercise. Customers must be circularized if any partner requires it.

However, s. 38 allows the former partners to bind each other in transactions so far as it is necessary to wind up the firm and complete transactions begun, but unfinished at the time of the dissolution. Thus in *Re*

Bourne (1906) a partner was allowed to grant a security to secure the continuance of the firm's overdraft. A bankrupt partner has no such authority.

(*b*) *Profits after dissolution.* The process of winding up the firm takes time. Profits may be made during the period between dissolution and final account and repayment of capital. Section 42 protects a deceased partner's estate or any outgoing partner not involved in the winding up, as to the share of profit made during that period. The section provides that the outgoing partner or the personal representatives may choose 5 per cent per annum interest on capital, or such part of the profits as is regarded by the court to be attributable to the use of his share of the assets.

If, after dissolution, a surviving partner has carried on the business and produced profits, a proportion of which must go to an outgoing partner or to personal representatives under s. 42, he may deduct a managerial allowance from any amounts payable. (*Manley* v *Sartori* (1927).) It will be recalled that partners are not normally entitled to a salary or allowance, but only to profits. The *Manley* case provides an exception.

(*c*) *Realization and distribution of the assets.*

(*i*) *Realization.* If it is not intended to bring the business to an end (i.e. wind it up) following a dissolution by reason, e.g. of death or retirement, the partnership agreement usually provides that the deceased or retiring partner's share in the firm's assets shall go to the remaining partners and that they shall pay a price for it based on the last set of accounts.

If this is not to be done the assets of the firm will be sold on dissolution.

Section 39 gives each partner on dissolution the right to insist that the assets of the firm be used to pay creditors in full and that any surplus be paid to the partners according to their entitlement. For this purpose each partner has what is called a lien over the assets. It becomes effective only on dissolution. It is enforceable by the partner concerned applying to the court for the appointment of a receiver under his lien who will make the appropriate distribution.

(*ii*) *Sale of goodwill.* If the assets are sold one of them may well be goodwill. There are a number of definitions of goodwill, e.g. 'the probability of the old customers resorting to the old place' (Lord Eldon, a famous Lord Chancellor); 'the public approbation which has been won by the business' (Sir Arthur Underhill – an authority on partnership law), and 'the

benefit arising from connection and reputation' (Lord Lindley – one of our greatest equity lawyers, and later a judge who was the first author of the standard practitioners' work *Lindley on Partnership*).

Goodwill is in financial terms the excess of the price you pay for a business over the net tangible assets, such as plant and machinery, which you acquire.

When goodwill is sold the seller and buyer usually agree by the contract of sale to restrictions to stop the seller from, for example, setting up in the same business again next door to the one he has just sold and taking back the goodwill of that business.

If there is no agreement as to restrictions on the seller the position is as set out below.

- The purchaser may represent himself as continuing the business of the seller (*Churton* v *Douglas* (1859)), but he must not hold out the seller as still being in the business.
- The seller may, however, carry on a similar business and compete with the buyer (*Trego* v *Hunt* (1896)); this can decrease the value of partnership goodwill.
- The seller must not, however, compete under the name of the former firm or represent himself as continuing the same business.
- The seller may advertise his new business but may not actually circularize or otherwise canvass customers of his old firm.

(*iii*) *Final account.* When the firm is dissolved and the property sold there is a final account between the partners and then a distribution of the assets. This account is a record of transactions from the date of the last accounts to the date of the winding up.

(*iv*) *Distribution of assets.* Section 44 applies and if the assets when realized are sufficient to satisfy all claims payment is made first to outside creditors, both secured and unsecured. Then each partner is paid what is due to him as advances or loans, as distinct from capital. The costs of the winding up are then paid. (*Potter* v *Jackson* (1880).) Then each partner is paid the amount of capital due to him; any surplus is divided between the partners in the profit-sharing ratio.

If there are insufficient assets to pay outside creditors and the partners' entitlements, s. 44(*a*) applies and the partners have to make good the deficiency in the profit-sharing ratio.

If a partner cannot make such a payment the Partnership Act does not require the solvent partners to pay in their share. The solvent partners pay in their share of the loss in the profit-sharing ratio; since then there will be insufficient funds to repay all the partners' entitlement to capital such repayments will be made ratably, the effect being that the loss is borne in the ratio of contributed capital and not in the same ratio as profits were shared.

This comes from the case of *Garneer* v *Murray* (1904) where there were three partners, Garner, Murray and Wilkins, and they shared profits and losses equally. Their balance sheet, after paying off creditors and partners' advances, was as follows (there is some rounding off in the figures to make the illustration of principle more straightforward) –

of the firm as usual, but in practice the creditors will have to get their money from B. Therefore B will bear A's share of the firm's burden of debt as well as his own.

If both A and B are insolvent then different rules are applied. There are three sets of creditors –

(a) A's private creditors;
(b) B's private creditors; and
(c) the firm's creditors.

Groups (a) and (b) are called 'separate creditors', while those in (c) are called 'joint creditors'.

One insolvency practitioner is put in charge of the whole administration. The assets of the firm are

Balance Sheet

Capital Accounts	£		£
Garner	2400	Cash	1891
Murray	300	Firm's loss	660
		Debt owed to the firm by Wilkins	149
	2700		2700

The court decided –

(*i*) that the loss of £660 must be shared in the profit and loss sharing ratio, i.e. equally; but

(*ii*) since Wilkins was bankrupt and could not pay in his share of the loss (i.e. £220) and could not pay the debt owed to the firm, the whole of Wilkins' debt, i.e. £220 + £149 = £369, should be borne by the solvent partners in the ratio of their capitals, i.e. £2400 to £300, or 8:1. After deducting Garner's share of the loss (i.e. £328) he was entitled to £2400–£328 = £2072. After deducting Murray's share of the loss (i.e. £41) he was entitled to £300–£41 = £259. So together they were entitled to £2331 but, since there was only £1891 in cash, they could only get £2331 between them if they first paid in £220 each, that is, their share of the firm's loss – £1891 + £440 = £2331. Since there is no point in these cases in paying money in only to draw it out, they actually took £1681 (Garner) and £210 (Murray), thus sharing the loss in the capital ratio.

The insolvent partnership

If A and B are partners and A becomes bankrupt but B remains solvent, the partners will be liable for the debts

divided among the joint creditors and only if there is a surplus can the separate creditors seek payment from the assets of the firm, and only if there is a surplus on the separate accounts of A and B can the joint creditors seek payment from the separate estates of the partners.

The partners cannot compete with the firm's creditors. Thus, if A who is now bankrupt had made a loan to his insolvent firm, no claim can be made by him on the firm's assets until all outside creditors of the firm have received payment in full.

Limited partnerships

Generally

The Limited Partnerships Act 1907 provides for the formation of limited partnerships in which one or more of the partners has only limited liability for the firm's debts. These partnerships are not common because in most cases the objective of limited liability can be better achieved by incorporation as a private company.

A limited partnership is not a legal entity and must not have more than twenty members, though this provision does not apply to limited partnerships of solicitors, accountants, or stockbrokers, among others. There must also be one general partner whose liability for the debts of the firm is unlimited. A body corporate may be a limited partner.

Registration

Every limited partnership must be registered with the Registrar of Companies. The following particulars must be registered by means of a statement signed by the partners –

(a) the firm name;
(b) the general nature of the business;
(c) the principal place of business;
(d) the full name of each partner;
(e) the date of commencement of the term of the partnership, if any;
(f) a statement that it is a limited partnership;
(g) the particulars of each limited partner and the amount contributed by him, whether in cash or otherwise.

Any change in the above particulars or the fact that a general partner becomes a limited partner must be notified to the Registrar within seven days. Failure to register means that the limited partner is fully liable as a general partner. When a general partner becomes a limited partner, the fact must be advertised in the *London Gazette* if the transaction is to be effective in law.

The Register of Limited Partnerships is open to inspection by the public who may also obtain certified copies of, or extracts from, any registered statement.

Rights and duties of a limited partner

A limited partner is not liable for the debts of the firm beyond his capital, but he may not withdraw any part of his capital and, even if he were to do so, he would still be liable to the firm's creditors for the amount he originally subscribed.

A limited partner has no power to bind the firm and may not take part in its management. If he does manage the firm he becomes liable for all the liabilities incurred by the firm during that period. Nevertheless, he may give advice on management to the other partners and he may also inspect the books.

The death, bankruptcy or mental disorder of a limited partner does not dissolve the partnership and a limited partner cannot dissolve the partnership by notice.

Model form of partnership deed

MODEL FORM OF PARTNERSHIP DEED

(with explanatory comments)

AN AGREEMENT made this *2nd* day of *June* one thousand nine hundred and *eighty-six* between *John Jones* of *Bleak House, Barchester; Chartered Accountant* and *Jane James* of *12, Acacia Avenue, Barchester; Chartered Accountant* and *William Pitt* of *55 Low Terrace, Barchester; Chartered Accountant*

IT IS HEREBY AGREED AND DECLARED AS FOLLOWS:-

Duration and objects

1. The said *John Jones, Jane James and William Pitt* shall become and remain partners in the business of Chartered Accountants for a term of *five* years from the date of this deed if they shall so long live.

Comment .The period of five years ensures that it is not a partnership at will. We do not want a partnership at will because it can be terminated by notice at any time thus allowing a partner to leave the firm with ease so that years of work is brought to an end at the will of one partner.

2. Although the partnership constituted by this Deed is for a period of *five* years nevertheless it is the intention of the parties hereto to continue in partnership from *five* year period to *five* year period subject only to the incidence of death or retirement.

Comment . Since a fixed term has been agreed there should be provision for it to be continued upon the same terms on the expiry of the fixed term. It is better to include this in the deed so that there is no doubt what will happen at the end of each term of five years. In any case of course, s 27 would apply and the partnership would be at will but on the same terms as the fixed partnership which had just expired.

3. The death retirement expulsion or bankruptcy of a partner shall not determine the partnership between the partners but without prejudice to the generality of this clause the parties hereto shall review the provisions of this deed whenever the admission of a new profit-sharing partner into the partnership is being contemplated.

Comment . This clause is inserted to make sure, for example, that the death of a partner does not cause a dissolutuon as between those partners who remain and that the business continues under the remaining partners. If this clause was not included there would be an automatic dissolution under s 33(1) on the death of a partner.

Firm name

4. The partners shall practise in partnership under the firm name of *Jones, James, Pitt & Co.* (or such other name as the partners may hereafter agree).

Location 5.   The business of the partnership shall be carried on at
of   *10 Oak Buildings, Barchester*
practice   and/or such other place or places as the partners may from
time to time decide.

Bankers 6. (i) The bankers of the firm shall be the *Barchester*
and   Bank plc or such other bankers as the partners shall agree
application upon both for the moneys of clients for the time being in
of   the keeping of the partnership and for the moneys of the
partnership partnership.
money

(ii) All partnership money shall be paid to the bankers of
the partnership to the credit of the partnership and the
partners shall make such regulations as they may from time
to time see fit for opening operating or closing the bank
accounts of the partnership and for providing the money
required for current expenses.

(iii) All outgoings incurred for or in carrying on the
partnership business and all losses and damages which shall
happen or be incurred in relation to the business are to be
paid out of the moneys and profits of the partnership and if
there is a deficiency shall be contributed by the partners
in the shares in which they are for the time being respectively
entitled to the profits of the partnership.

Comment. Clause 6(ii) gives the partners power to make
regulations as to who may draw cheques in the name of the
firm. In many cases this will be each partner alone, though
where there are more than two partners it is usual to provide
that all cheques over a certain amount are to be signed by
at least two of the partners,.

Capital 7. (i) The initial capital of the partnership shall be a sum of
£30,000   to be contributed by the partners in equal
shares together with such further cash capital (if any) as
the partners may from time to time agree to be required (in
addition to any loan capital) for the purposes of the
partnership and which shall be provided (except as may from
time to time be otherwise agreed by the partners) in the
proportion in which the partners are for the time being
entitled to share in the profits of the partnership.

(ii) *Five thousand pounds (£5,000)* being the agreed value
of the goodwill of the business carried on at *10 Sandy Lane,*
Barchester
by the said *John Jones*   which will be taken
over by the said partnership and which shall be credited in
the books of the firm as part of the capital brought in by
the said *John Jones*

(iii) The said sum of *£30,000*   and any further
capital provided by the partners shall carry interest at the
rate of *twelve (12)* per cent per annum to be payable *half-*
yearly in arrear on 30th June and 31st December
or at such other rate and payable at such other times as the
partners shall from time to time decide.

Comment. Unless there is a specific provision such as the one
in (iii) above interest on capital is not payable.

Profits 8. The partners shall be entitled to the net profits arising from the business in *equal share* or such other shares as may from time to time be agreed by the partners. Such net profits shall be divided among the partners immediately after the settlement of the annual accounts in the manner hereafter provided.

Comment . Oddly enough, although the 1890 Act says that partners are in business with a view of profit it says nothing about dividing profit. This special provision makes the matter of division clear.

Management and control of the partnership 9. The control and management of the partnership shall remain in the hands of the partners and salaried partners (if any) shall not be entitled to take part therein.

Circulation of agendas and other information 10. All agendas and minutes of partners' meetings and balance sheets and profit and loss accounts shall be circulated to all partners.

Partnership accounts and partners' drawings 11. At the close of business on the *31st May* in the year one thousand nine hundred and *eighty-seven* and on the same day in each succeeding year the accounts of the partnership shall be made up.

Each partner may draw on account of his share of profit to such extent as may be decided by the partners from time to time.

Comment . The partners may agree, for example, that £1000 per month as a maximum be drawn. It is usually also provided that if on taking the annual account the sums drawn out by any of the partners are found to exceed the sum to which that partner is entitled as his share of the year's profits the excess shall be refunded immediately.

Conduct of the partnership business 12. Each partner shall diligently employ himself in the partnership business and carry on and conduct the same for the greatest advantage of the partnership.

Holidays 13. Each partner shall be entitled to *five* weeks holiday in aggregate in each year of the partnership.

Comment . It may sometimes be found that the agreement states that some or all of this holiday must be taken between certain dates in the year.

Restrictions

14. No partner shall without the previous consent of the others -

(a) hire or dismiss any employee or take any trainee;

(b) purchase goods in the name or on behalf of the firm to an amount exceeding *One thousand (£1,000) pounds*

(c) compound release or discharge any debt owing to the partnership without receiving the full amount therefor;

(d) be engaged or interested whether directly or indirectly in any business or occupation other than the partnership business;

(e) advance the moneys of or deliver on credit any goods belonging to the partnership;

(f) make any assignment either absolutely or by way of charge of his share in the partnership;

(g) give any security or undertaking for the payment of any debt or liability out of the moneys or property of the partnership;

(h) introduce or attempt to introduce another person into the business of the partnership;

(i) enter into any bond or become surety for any persons or do or knowingly permit to be done anything whereby the capital or property of the partnership may be seized attached or taken in execution.

Comment. This clause can be extended as required. However, since partners have considerable apparent authority under s.5 of the 1890 Act and case law the above prohibitions will in many cases not prevent an outsider who has no knowledge of them from claiming against the firm.

They do provide grounds for dissolution of the firm if a partner is in wilful or persistent breach of them or the partnership agreement in general.

It is generally unwise to have a very large number of prohibitions because this is likely to restrict the activities of the firm and its individual partners unduly.

Partners' debts and engagements 15. Every partner shall during the partnership pay his present and future separate debts and at all times indemnify the other partners and each of them and the capital and effects of the partnership against his said debts and engagements and against all actions suits claims and demands on account thereof.

Expulsion of partners 16. If any partner shall:

(a) by act or default commit any flagrant breach of his duties as a partner or of the agreements and stipulations herein contained; or

(b) fail to account and pay over or refund to the partnership any money for which he is accountable to the partnership within 14 days after being required so to do by a partner specifically so authorised by a decision of the partners; or

(c) act in any respect contrary to the good faith which ought to be observed between partners; or

(d) become subject to the bankruptcy laws; or

(e) enter into any composition or arrangement with or for the benefit of his creditors; or

(f) be or become permanently incapacited by mental disorder, ill-health, accident or otherwise from attending the partnership business; or

(g) except with the consent of the other partners absent himself from the said business for more than *six* calendar months in any one year or for more than *ninety* consecutive days (absence during the usual holidays or due to temporary illness or as agreed not being reckoned);

then and in any such case the other partners may by notice in writing given to him or (in the case of his being found incapable by reason of mental disorder of managing and administering his property and affairs for the purposes of Part VII of the Mental Health Act 1983) to his receiver or other appropriate person or left at the office of the partnership determine the partnership so far as he may be concerned and publish a notice of dissolution of the partnership in the name of and as against such partner whereupon the partnership will so far as regards such partner immediately cease and determine accordingly but without prejudice to the remedies of the other partners for any antecedent breach of any of the stipulations or agreements aforesaid and any question as to a case having arisen to authorise such notice shall be referred to arbitration.

Dissolution 17. Upon the dissolution of the partnership by the death of a partner or by a partner retiring, the other partners shall be entitled to purchase upon the terms hereinafter specified the share of the partner (including goodwill) so dying or retiring: provided that written notice of intention to purchase shall be given to the retiring partner or to the personal representatives of the deceased partner within *two* calendar months after the date of the dissolution.

18. The purchase money payable under clause 17 hereof shall be the net value of the share of the deceased or retiring partner as at the date of the dissolution after satisfying all outstanding liabilities of the partnership with interest at the rate of *ten* % per annum as from the date of dissolution: provided that if the value of the said share cannot be agreed upon the same shall be submitted to arbitration in the manner hereinafter provided.

The purchase money shall be paid by *six equal* instalments the first instalment to be paid at the end of *three months* after the date of the dissolution and thereafter at the end of each succeeding period of *three months* with interest at the rate of *ten* % per annum upon so much of the purchase money as shall remain unpaid for the time being and such purchase money shall if required be secured by the bond of the surviving partners with not fewer than two sureties.

Goodwill 19. For the purposes of the foregoing clauses the goodwill of the partnership shall be deemed to be valued at ~~three years'~~ purchase of the average net profits of the partnership for the preceding ~~five~~ years or the average of the whole period if the partnership shall have subsisted for less than ~~five~~ years.

Comment. Any other basis of assessment which the partners may decide upon could of course have been included or the matter of goodwill could have been omitted entirely.

20. In the event of one of the partners retiring and the other partners purchasing his share the retiring partner shall not during the unexpired residue of the term of the partnership carry on or be interested either directly or indirectly in any business similar to that of the said partnership and competing therewith within a radius of ~~one mile~~ of *10 Oak Buildings Barchester* or of any other place of business belonging to the partnership at the date of the notice of retirement.

21. Upon the determination of the partnership any partner or his personal representative shall have power to sign in the name of the firm notice of the dissolution for publication in the Gazette.

Arbitration 22. Should any doubt or difference arise at any time between the said partners or their personal representatives with regard to the interpretation or effect of this agreement or in respect of the rights duties and liabilities of any partner or his personal representatives whether in connection with the conduct or winding up of the affairs of the partnership, such doubt or difference shall be submitted to a single arbitrator to be appointed by the President for the time being of the Institute of Chartered Accountants in England a and Wales.

IN WITNESS whereof the parties hereto have hereunto set their hands and seals the day and year first above-mentioned.

Signed, sealed and delivered by the
above-named John Jones in the
presence of,   *John Jones*

George Blake,   *George Blake*
42 Hill Top,
Barchester.

Signed, sealed and delivered by the
above-named Jane James in the
presence of,

George Blake.   *George Blake*   *Jane James*

Signed, sealed and delivered by the
above-named William Pitt in the   *William Pitt* .
presence of,

George Blake.   *George Blake*

Note. Partnership deeds usually contain also complex provisions relating to life assurance for retirement; annuities for partners' dependants in the case of death, and annuities to partners in the event of permanent incapacity. There are often, also, much more complex provisions relating to payments to be made to any partner on death or retirement and the continuation of the partnership for tax purposes. However, these do not assist in the understanding of the Partnership Act 1890 and involve knowledge of matters not dealt with in this text. They have accordingly been omitted.

Questions/activities

1. Joe is a solicitor employed by Bloggs & Co. There are two partners, Harry and Ian. Ian is intending to retire and it has been decided that Joe should replace Ian as a partner with Harry carrying on as a partner.

Write a letter to each of Joe, Harry, and Ian explaining what steps each should take to protect himself as a result of the changeover.

2. Cliff has been asked by his friends, Don and Eric, to help them set up an antiques business. Don and Eric want Cliff to lend them £5000 and they say they will give Cliff one-third of the profits instead of interest on the loan.

What are the dangers to Cliff in such an arrangement and how can he overcome them?

3. Fred is a new partner in Gee & Co, a firm of surveyors. In discussion at a recent meeting of the partners Fred was told that the office building at which the firm is based is not partnership property. Fred asks you –

(a) What is meant by the expression 'partnership property'?

(b) What effect will it have on him if the office building is not partnership property?

(c) How can it be that an asset which is used in the firm's business is not in fact partnership property?

Assignment

You have been appointed as partnership secretary in the firm of Jones, James Pitt, Chartered Accountants. The partnership articles appear at pp. 78. The following problems emerge over a number of partners' meetings –

(i) John Jones soon became unhappy about his future prospects. He retired from the firm last month and has taken a partnership with Snooks & Co, Chartered Accountants, whose office is two doors way from the offices of Jones, James & Pitt. Jane James and William Pitt, the remaining partners, are anxious to stop John from competing with them.

(ii) Before he left, John Jones contracted to buy a micro-computer system for the practice from Scroggs Ltd, although at an earlier partners' meeting it was decided that the purchase should be deferred for one year. The system cost £5000. Jane and William have so far refused to take delivery of the system or pay for it.

(iii) Scroggs Ltd have written to the firm saying that unless the debt is paid they will petition the court to wind up the firm.

Having read the partnership articles thoroughly –

(a) prepare a memorandum for the next partners' meeting outlining the legal position of the firm in the three cases described above.

(b) If you think there is a claim under (i) above, draft a letter to the firm's solicitors, Weeks & Co, for the signature of the partners, stating what has happened and describing the relevant provisions of the partnership articles.

(c) Draft a letter to Scroggs Ltd to deal with whatever you think the legal position is under (ii) and (iii) above.

7

Companies

In Chapter 4 we made a general survey of the different types of business organization – the sole trader, the partnership, and the corporation. In particular we considered the role of the corporation as a business organization in the public and private sectors.

This chapter is concerned only with one type of corporation – the registered company, because this is the basic form of corporate business organization. The law relating to registered companies is to be found mainly in the Companies Act 1985 and case law. All section references in this chapter are to the Companies Act 1985 unless otherwise indicated.

Types of registered companies

Registered companies may be limited or unlimited and public or private.

Limited companies

Most registered companies are limited by shares. This means that the liability of the members of the company is limited. The company's liability is not limited. It must pay its debts so long as it has any funds from which to do so.

Where the liability of the members of the company is limited by shares it means that once the members have paid the full nominal value of their shares, plus any premium that may have been payable on them, they cannot be asked to pay any more even if the company is wound up and cannot pay its creditors in full from the funds that are left.

If, therefore, John Green owns 100 shares issued at £1 each by Boxo plc, then once he has paid £100 to Boxo plc for them neither he nor anyone else who buys them from him can be required to pay more. If the shares had been issued at a premium of 50p, then once John had paid £150 to Boxo, neither he nor anyone else who bought the shares from him could be required to pay more. If John transferred the shares before he had paid for them in full, then the person who bought them from him would have to pay the balance if called upon to do so by Boxo plc.

Companies may also be limited by guarantee. An example is the Associated Examining Board. In this case the members are liable only to the amount they have agreed upon in the memorandum. (A specimen memorandum appears at p. 131.) There is a separate clause in the memorandum of a guarantee company which might say, for example –

'Every member of the company undertakes to contribute such amount as may be required (not exceeding £100) to the company's assets if it should be wound up while he is a member or within one year after he ceased to be a member, for payment of the company's debts and liabilities contracted before he ceased to be a member and of the costs charges and expenses of winding up.'

Obviously, this liability arises only if the company is wound up. Guarantee companies cannot be registered with a share capital as well so they will normally get their income from members' subscriptions, as in the case of a club.

Unlimited companies

Companies may be registered in which the liability of members is unlimited. Not many of these exist because of the personal liability of their members which is unpopular. However, some organisations such as The Stock Exchange will not admit a stockbroking company to membership unless the members of the company are personally liable for its debts.

Also, there is some advantage over a partnership in that there is a separate company *persona* for making contracts and holding property plus perpetual succession so that, for example, the death of a member does not cause a dissolution.

The main advantage over the limited company is that unlimited companies do not have to file accounts with the Registrar so that the public has no access to their financial statements. However, the price of financial secrecy is unlimited liability.

The memorandum of an unlimited company does not contain any clause stating that the liability of its members is limited. This achieves the unlimited liability.

These companies may also have a share capital in which case the members must pay for their shares in full plus any premium and even then they have personal liability for the company's debts if it is wound up and does not have sufficient funds to pay its debts. These companies are always private companies. Public companies must be limited (normally by shares).

Public and private companies

The Companies Act 1985 defines a public company and leaves private companies largely undefined other than by the fact that they are companies which do not satisfy the public limited company (plc) definition, and, s. 170 of the Financial Services Act 1986 generally prohibits the issue by private companies of advertisements offering their securities.

A public company is a company limited by shares. Its memorandum of association has a separate clause stating that it is a public company.

Only two members are required for both the public and private company. Also, a public company cannot start trading or borrow money until it has received a certificate from the Registrar of Companies under s. 117.

This certificate will not be given unless the issued share capital of the company is at least £50 000 and not less than one-quarter of the nominal value of each share and the whole of any premium has been received by the company.

Therefore, at least £50 000 in nominal value of shares must have been purchased in the company and £12 500 paid up on them. If the shares were of a nominal value of £1 and issued at a premium of 50p, then a company would have had to receive £12 500 plus £25 000 = £37 500. This is to stop public companies starting up in business without enough capital and then possibly being wound up quickly leaving the creditors unpaid.

If a company does trade or borrow without an s. 117 certificate the company and its directors commit a criminal offence. However, transactions such as contracts for the supply of goods and loans can be enforced against the company. Also, if the company is asked to pay, say for goods supplied and does not do so within 21 days of the demand, the company's directors become jointly and severally liable to pay the debts.

Formation

A company, whether public or private, is formed (or incorporated) by applying for registration with the Registrar of Companies in Cardiff. The people who want the company to be formed (who are called the promoters) must send certain documents to the Registrar. The main ones are set out below.

(*a*) The memorandum of association;
(*b*) the articles of association.

These documents are dealt with in more detail on pp 92 and 97.

(*c*) Form G12 (see Fig. 7.1), being a statutory declaration of compliance with the requirements of the Companies Act 1985 as regards registration which is required by s. 12.

This declaration may be given by a solicitor who has been assisting in the formation of the company or by a person named as a director or the secretary of the company in Form G10 (see Fig. 7.2).

The declaration is usually made before a commissioner for oaths (a solicitor) and false statements made in the declaration could result in the person making them being prosecuted for the crime of perjury.

G

COMPANIES FORM No. 12

Statutory Declaration of compliance with requirements on application for registration of a company

12

Pursuant to section 12(3) of the Companies Act 1985

Please do not
write in
this margin

To the Registrar of Companies

For official use

For official use

Please complete
legibly, preferably
in black type, or
bold block lettering

Name of company

* insert full
name of Company

* RICHES, KEENAN PUBLISHING LIMITED

I, _Denis Keenan_

of _2, LOW STREET,_
BARCHESTER

† delete as
appropriate

do solemnly and sincerely declare that I am a [~~Solicitor engaged in the formation of the company~~]†
[person named as director or secretary of the company in the statement delivered to the registrar
under section 10(2)]† and that all the requirements of the above Act in respect of the registration of the
above company and of matters precedent and incidental to it have been complied with,

And I make this solemn declaration conscientiously believing the same to be true and by virtue of the
provisions of the Statutory Declarations Act 1835

Declared at _14 High Street,_
Barchester

Declarant to sign below

the _third_ day of _March_
One thousand nine hundred and _eighty six_
before me _H. Middleton._

DKeenan

A Commissioner for Oaths or Notary Public or Justice of
the Peace or Solicitor having the powers conferred on a
Commissioner for Oaths.

Presentor's name address and
reference (if any):

Dalton e Co.
Chartered
        Accountants
120, High Street
Barchester

For official Use

New Companies Section

Post room

Fig. 7.1 Company registration declaration.

G

COMPANIES FORM No. 10

Statement of first directors and secretary and intended situation of registered office

10

Pursuant to section 10 of the Companies Act 1985

Please do not
write in
this margin

To the Registrar of Companies

**Please complete
legibly, preferably
in black type, or
bold block lettering**

For official use

Name of company

* insert full name
  of company

* RICHES, KEENAN PUBLISHING LIMITED

The intended situation of the registered office of the company on incorporation is as stated below

140, HIGH STREET,
BARCHESTER

Postcode BB 26 OYE

If the memorandum is delivered by an agent for the subscribers of the memorandum please mark 'X' in the box opposite and insert the agent's name and address below

X

DALTON & CO,
CHARTERED ACCOUNTANTS,
120, HIGH STREET,
BARCHESTER

Postcode BB26 OYE

Number of continuation sheets attached (see note 1)

NIL

Presentor's name address and
reference (if any):

DALTON & CO.,
CHARTERED
         ACCOUNTANTS,
120 HIGH STREET
BARCHESTER

For official Use

General Section

Post room

Page 1

Fig. 7.2 Statement of first directors, secretary and intended situation of registered office. (*Continued on pp. 88–89*)

The name(s) and particulars of the person who is, or the persons who are, to be the first director or directors of the company (note 2) are as follows:

Name (note 3) RICHES, SARAH	Business occupation AUTHOR / LECTURER
Previous name(s) (note 3) —	Nationality BRITISH
Address (note 4) 1, HIGH STREET BARCHESTER	
Postcode BB26 OYE	Date of birth (where applicable) (note 6) —
Other directorships † DODGY TRAINING LIMITED	

I consent to act as director of the company named on page 1

Signature *Sarah Riches*   Date 3. March 1986

Name (note 3) KEENAN, DENIS, JOSEPH	Business occupation AUTHOR / LECTURER
Previous name(s) (note 3) —	Nationality BRITISH
Address (note 4) 2, LOW STREET BARCHESTER	
Postcode BB26 OBG	Date of birth (where applicable) (note 6) —
Other directorships † DODGY FINANCE LIMITED	

I consent to act as director of the company named on page 1

Signature *Denis Keenan*   Date 3 March 1986

Name (note 3)	Business occupation
Previous name(s) (note 3)	Nationality
Address (note 4)	
Postcode	Date of birth (where applicable) (note 6)
Other directorships †	

I consent to act as director of the company named on page 1

Signature   Date

Fig. 7.2 (*continued*).

Please do not
write in
this margin

Please complete
legibly, preferably
in black type, or
bold block lettering

The name(s) and particulars of the person who is, or the persons who are, to be the first secretary, or joint secretaries, of the company are as follows:

Name (notes 3 & 7)	WILLIAMS, JANE MARY

Previous name(s) (note 3)	—

Address (notes 4 & 7)	25, MIDDLE STREET
	BARCHESTER

	Postcode	BB26 9AM

I consent to act as secretary of the company named on page 1

Signature *JM Williams*   Date **3 March 1986**

Name (notes 3 & 7)	

Previous name(s) (note 3)	

Address (notes 4 & 7)	

	Postcode	

I consent to act as secretary of the company named on page 1

Signature   Date

delete if the form is
signed by the
subcribers

Signature of agent on behalf of subsribers   Date

delete if the form is
signed by an agent on
behalf of the
subscribers.

All the subscribers
must sign either
personally or by a
person or persons
authorised to sign
for them.

Signed	*Sarah Riches*	Date	3|3|86
Signed	*Denis Keenan*	Date	3|3|86
Signed		Date	
Signed		Date	
Signed		Date	
Signed		Date	

Fig. 7.2 (*continued*).

Notes

1 If the spaces on Page 2 are insufficient the names and particulars must be entered on the prescribed continuation sheet(s).

2 'Director' includes any person who occupies the position of a director, by whatever name called.

3. For an individual, his present christian name(s) and surname must be given, together with any previous christian name(s) or surname(s).

   "Christian name" includes a forename. In the case of a peer or person usually known by a title different from his surname, "surname" means that title. In the case of a corporation, its corporate name must be given.

   A previous christian name or surname need not be given if:—

   (a) in the case of a married woman, it was a name by which she was known before her marriage; or

   (b) it was changed or ceased to be used at least 20 years ago, or before the person who previously used it reached the age of 18; or

   (c) in the case of a peer or a person usually known by a British title different from his surname, it was a name by which he was known before he adopted the title or succeeded to it

4 Usual residential address must be given or, in the case of a corporation, the registered or principal office.

5 The names must be given of all bodies corporate incorporated in Great Britain of which the director is also a director, or has been a director at any time during the preceeding five years.

   However, a present or past directorship need not be disclosed if it is, or has been, held in a body corporate which, throughout that directorship, has been:—

   (a) a dormant company (which is a company which has had no transactions required to be entered in the company's accounting records, except any which may have arisen from the taking of shares in the company by a subscriber to the memorandum as such).

   (b) a body corporate of which the company making the return was a wholly-owned subsidiary;

   (c) a wholly-owned subsidiary of the company making the return; or

   (d) a wholly-owned subsidiary of a body corporate of which the company making the return was also a wholly owned subsidiary.

6. Dates of birth need only be given if the company making the return is:—

   (a) a public company;
   (b) the subsidiary of a public company; or
   (c) the subsidiary of a public company registered in Northern Ireland

7 Where all the partners in a firm are joint secretaries, only the name and principal office of the firm need be stated.

   Where the secretary or one of the joint secretaries is a Scottish firm the details required are the firm name and its principal office.

(*d*) Form G10 (see Fig. 7.2), which is a statement of the company's first directors and secretary required by s. 10.

Those persons named in the statement are just by being named in it appointed as the first directors and secretary of the company.

If the Registrar is satisfied with the contents of the above documents he will issue a certificate of incorporation. (See Fig. 7.3.)

Pre-incorporation contracts

Generally

A company cannot make contracts until it has been incorporated. This takes place on the first moment of the day of the date on its certificate of incorporation.

Transactions entered into by the company's promoters and others in connection with its business before that time are not binding on the company when it is incorporated and the company cannot adopt these contracts after its incorporation. Thus if the company's directors, who are its agents, were to write to a seller of goods and say that the company was now formed and would take over a pre-incorporation contract, the company would not be bound by it.

However, the company's promoters or other persons who may act for it at the pre-incorporation stage do incur personal liability to the other party to the contract under s. 36.

Phonogram Ltd *v* Lane 1981

Phonogram lent £6000 for the business of a company to be called Fragile Management Ltd. Mr

CERTIFICATE OF INCORPORATION

No. 1383617

I hereby certify that

RICHES KEENAN PUBLISHING LIMITED

is this day incorporated under the Companies Act 1985 **and that the** Company is Limited.

Given under my hand at Cardiff the 4th APRIL 1986

J. Bloggs

J. BLOGGS

Assistant Registrar of Companies

C.173

Fig. 7.3 Certificate of incorporation.

Lane, who was not a promoter of Fragile, signed 'for and on behalf of' the company a letter promising repayment by Fragile. The company was never formed and Phonogram sued Mr Lane personally for repayment of the sum of £6000 under what is now s. 36. The Court of Appeal decided that Mr Lane was personally liable.

Comment. The case shows that although s. 36 is usually discussed in the context of making promoters personally liable, anyone acting on the company's business at the pre-incorporation stage is covered by s. 36. Also, the section says that a person acting for the company can avoid personal liability by an express agreement in the pre-incorporation contract that he is not to be liable. This case decides that the words 'for and on behalf of' the company was not enough. They do not amount to a specific agreement to prevent personal liability.

Solutions to the problem of personal liability of promoters

A promoter or other person conducting the company's business prior to its incorporation can overcome the difficulties facing him as regards personal liability in the following ways.

(*a*) By incorporating the company before any business is done so that there are no pre-incorporation transactions.

(*b*) By agreeing a draft contract with the other party and making it an object of the company that the company shall enter into it on formation. Nevertheless, if the company does not in fact enter into it, through the agency of its directors, there is no binding agreement either on the promoter or on the other party or the company.

(*c*) By making a binding contract between the promoter and the other party and a draft contract on the same terms with the company. The binding contract must provide that once the company is formed and signs the draft contract through its agents, the promoter is released from the first contract which was binding on him.

This is a simple solution for most promoters who, after all, are usually promoting their own businesses as companies. They are normally in charge of the company and the board following incorporation and can easily arrange that the company signs through its agents

the draft contract, thus releasing the promoter from his first binding contract.

(*d*) By making a pre-incorporation contract with a specific clause saying that the promoter is not liable on it, as s. 36 allows. There would seem to be little point in a third party signing such a contract since neither the company nor the promoter would be bound.

The Memorandum of Association

We shall learn about this document by dealing with the clauses it must contain and in the context of the specimen memorandum which appears on pp. 131.

The company's name (Clause 1)

A company is only a legal person but, like a human being, it must have a name. The Companies Act 1985 and the Business Names Act 1985 together contain a system for controlling the names and business names of companies. The main rules are set out below.

On registration
The following rules apply.

(*a*) *The final words of the name – generally.* A private company, whether limited by shares or guarantee, must end its name with the word 'limited'. (S. 25.) A public company must end its name with the words 'public limited company'. (S. 25.) The short forms – 'Ltd' and 'plc' – are allowed by s. 27. These words, or their short forms, must not appear elsewhere in the name. (S. 26.) There are criminal penalties on the company and its officers for wrongful use under ss. 33 and 34.

(*b*) *The final words of the name – an exemption.* Section 30 allows private companies limited by guarantee to apply for exemption in the sense of leaving off the word 'limited' from the name. The section gives automatic exemption if the conditions are satisfied. The company simply sends to the Registrar of Companies what is called a statutory declaration, which is a statement made before a commissioner for oaths that certain facts are true. The declaration is signed by a director and the secretary of the company. The facts that it declares to be true are the ones which s. 30 requires for exemption, that is that

– the objects of the company are to promote

commerce, art, science, education, religion, charity, or any profession, and anything that would help that.

- the company's profits or income will be applied to the promotion of those objects.
- the payment of dividends is prohibited.
- all surplus assets on a winding up will be transferred to another body with similar or charitable objects.

If the company at any time does not satisfy the above requirements, the Registrar may direct it to include 'limited' in its name again.

The exemption is not fully effective because, although the company need not use the word limited in its name, s. 351 says that despite the exemption, all business letters and order forms of the company must include a statement that it is limited.

(*c*) *Same, similar, and offensive names.* Under s. 26 a name will not be accepted by the Registrar if it is the *same* as one already on the Index of Names which he is required to keep by s. 714. *Similar* names will be registered. So if there is a company called Widgets Ltd on the Index the Registrar would register a new company called Widgets (Holdings) Ltd.

However, a company may be required by the Trade Secretary to change its name within twelve months of registration if it is 'too like' that of a company already on the Index. (S. 28.) It is up to other companies to ascertain this, e.g. by purchasing daily extracts from the Register of the names of companies which have gone on it. There are firms which will supply these.

If a period of twelve months has passed the Trade Secretary can do nothing under s. 28 but Widgets Ltd could bring an action at common law for passing off. For example, in *Société Anonyme des Anciens Établissements Panhard et Lavassor* v *Levassor Motor Co. Ltd* (1901) (which we can call the *Panhard* case) the plaintiff was a French company whose cars were sold in England. The French company wished to set up an English company to act as an agent in England to improve the sales of their cars here.

To try to stop this the defendant English company was registered, the hope being that the French company could not then register an English company in their name in England because a company with that name would already be on the Register.

The court said that the name of the English company must be taken off the Register. The members of the English company were told that they must change the name of their company or wind it up.

Finally, a name will not be registered if it is in the opinion of the Trade Secretary offensive or the publication of which would be a criminal offence.

(*d*) *Connection with the government.* A name which is likely to suggest a connection with the government or a local authority, e.g. 'District Council Supplies Ltd' will be registered only if the Trade Secretary approves. (S. 26.)

(*e*) *Sensitive names.* A name which includes any word or expression which is to be found in regulations made by the Trade Secretary under s. 29 will not be registered as a company or business name unless the Trade Secretary approves.

The list of these sensitive names (which all imply some connection of prestige) also states the name of a government department or other organization which can object to the use of the name and which must be approached and say that it does not disapprove before the Trade Secretary can give his approval.

Examples under regulations already issued are that for the use of 'Prince', 'Princess', 'Queen', approval of the Home Office is required, and for 'Bank', 'Banking', approval of the Bank of England is necessary.

Change of name

A company can change its name and have one which is different from the name it was registered in.

(*a*) *Voluntary change.* A company may by special resolution change its name at any time.

A special resolution is an important form of resolution which will be looked at again later, but for now it will be enough to say that the meeting at which it is passed must be called by at least twenty-one days' notice and that the resolution must be passed by a majority of at least three-quarters of those present at the meeting in person or by proxy (i.e. by a person appointed to attend and vote for the shareholder) *and* voting. Thus if the company has members attending the meeting in person or by proxy who between them have 100 votes, then at least 75 votes must be cast for the resolution.

The new name must comply with the same requirements as on first registration which are listed above. The Registrar issues a new certificate of incorporation and the change does not take effect until that has been done.

(b) *Compulsory change.* The Trade Secretary may (as we have seen) within twelve months of registration direct a change if the name in which the company has been registered is too like (or the same) as one which appears on the Registrar's Index of Names. (S. 28(2).)

The Trade Secretary may also within five years of the date of registration direct a company to change its name if he believes that misleading information was provided at the time of its registration. (S. 28(3).) *There is no appeal to the court in this case.*

A company might, for example, have misled the Registrar as to the nature of its business in order to obtain registration in a particular name, as where a company called 'Prosperous Investments Trust' really intended after registration to manufacture cheap home computers and not engage in the investment trust business.

Furthermore, the Trade Secretary may direct a company to change its name *at any time* if the registered name gives so misleading an indication of its activities as to be likely to cause confusion and harm to the public. (S. 32.)

In this case the company may appeal to the court against the direction. Section 32 is aimed at much the same problem as s. 28(3) but can apply in a rather different situation, as where a company called 'Prosperous Investments Trust' went through a genuine form of registration but was later acquired and used for the making of cheap home computers. These companies are called 'shell' companies and what goes on behind the shell is deceptive in terms of the name of that shell.

Publication of name

Sections 348 and 349 provide that the company's full name must be shown in an obvious place and in readable form outside the registered office and all places of business, and on all business letters, notices, and official publications, and in all bills of exchange, cheques, promissory notes, orders for money or goods, receipts and invoices, signed or issued on its behalf.

Fines can be imposed on the company and its officers for failure to comply with the sections and also the officers of the company may incur personal liability for any amount due unless it is paid by the company. (S. 349(2), (3), and (4).) Thus in *Hendon* v *Adelman* (1973) a cheque signed on behalf of L & R Agencies Ltd omitted the ampersand (&) in the company's name, which appeared as L R Agencies Ltd. It was held

that the directors who had signed the cheque had not complied with what is now s. 349 and so they were personally liable on it.

Business names

If a company has a place of business in Great Britain and carries on business here in a name which is not the corporate name – for example, Boxo Ltd carrying on business as 'Paris Fashions' – then the business name (Paris Fashions) must not suggest a connection with government or a local authority or contain sensitive words without the approval of the Trade Secretary, and in the case of sensitive names, also the approval of the body listed in the Regulations referred to above. (Ss 2 and 3, Business Names Act 1985.)

A company which is using a business name has to state its corporate name in readable form on all business letters, orders for goods and services, invoices, receipts, and written demands for payment of business debts, and must also give an address in Great Britain where the service of documents will be effective. This is normally the registered office.

A notice giving the same information must be shown in a prominent place in any premises where the business is carried on and to which customers and suppliers have access. Furthermore, the corporate name and address for service of documents must be given straightaway and in writing on request to anyone who is doing or negotiating business with the company. (S. 4, Business Names Act 1985.)

The criminal sanction consists of default fines on the company if it does not comply and also on its directors and other officers such as a secretary. (S. 7, Business Names Act 1985.) The civil sanction is that the company may not be able to enforce its contracts. (S. 5, Business Names Act 1985.) The rules on this are the same as for partners and sole traders who are operating under a business name but have not followed the Business Names Act 1985. (The sanction is explained on p. 48.)

So far as our specimen memorandum is concerned, we have chosen to form our company in the personal names of the shareholders and directors. Those who form companies often have to do this because all the made up names they want, e.g. City Publishing Ltd, are already on the Index. If this is so, personal names will be registered even though a company with that name is already on the Register, provided that the names are those of directors of the business.

Registered office (Clause 2)

As will be seen from the specimen memorandum, there is only a statement that the registered office is situated in England. The actual address is not given but, as we have seen, it is filed with the Registrar when applying for registration. (See Form G10 at p. 87.)

The address can be changed within England and Wales (but not to Scotland) by a 51 per cent majority of the members (called an ordinary resolution), or by the directors if, as is usual, they are given this power by the articles.

If a company is to have its registered office in Scotland it must be registered in Edinburgh.

Objects (Clause 3)

Generally

This clause lists the things which the company can do. If it enters into a transaction which is not included in the clause, that transaction will be *ultra vires* (that is, beyond its powers) and void (that is, of no effect).

Ashbury Railway Carriage & Iron Co. v Riche (1875)

The company was formed for the purposes of making and selling railway waggons and other railway plant. It got a contract to build a railway system in Belgium and entered into an agreement under which Riche was to be a subcontractor in this exercise. The company later ran into difficulties and the directors told Riche that his contract was at an end. He sued for breach of that contract. The House of Lords decided that he had no claim because the contract which the company had made to construct the railway system and of which he was a subcontractor was *ultra vires* and void. On a proper reading of the objects the company had power to supply things for railways but had no power actually to make them.

By way of explanation of the decision of the above case, it should be said that the *ultra vires* rule was brought in by the courts to protect shareholders. It was thought that if a shareholder, X, bought shares in a company which had as its main object publishing and allied activities (see specimen memorandum clause

3(a)), then X would not want the directors of that company to start up a different kind of business because he wanted his money in publishing.

In more recent times it has been noted that shareholders are not so fussy about the kind of business the directors take the company into so long as it makes money to pay dividends and raises the price of the company's shares on the stock market.

The people most affected by the *ultra vires* rule today are creditors who have, say, supplied goods to the company which it had no power to buy. If the company is solvent no doubt the creditor will be paid, but if it goes into liquidation he will not even be able to put a claim in. The other creditors will get something on their debts if the company has any funds, but the *ultra vires* creditor will get nothing.

For this reason it has become usual to put in the objects clause a large number of objects and powers, as is the case with our specimen memorandum, and also to say, as the final paragraph of our clause 3 which follows 3(w) does, that each clause contains an independent main object which can be carried on separately from the others. The House of Lords decided in *Cotman* v *Brougham* (1918) that this type of clause was legal.

If this clause did not appear the court would regard our clause 3(a), which contains our main object, as our only business activity and say that all the other clauses contained only powers to be used to achieve the end of publishing.

Therefore, our power of investment set out in clause 3(b) would be restricted to investment in the activities set out in clause 3(a). However, we have an independent main objects clause and may therefore invest in other activities, for example, in the shares of oil companies.

Also the decision of the Court of Appeal in *Bell Houses Ltd* v *City Wall Properties Ltd* (1966) states that an objects clause can be drafted in such a way as to allow the company to carry on any additional business which the members or directors choose. Our clause 3(b) is an example and allows the members by ordinary resolution (not the directors, as in *Bell Houses*) to resolve to carry on another business in addition to publishing.

In this way the limitations which are placed on a company's business activities by the *ultra vires* rule have been much reduced, though, of course, the control over the activities of the directors by the members has also been lessened. In fact with a large number of clauses in the objects clause, as our typical memorandum has, together with an independent objects sub-clause as in *Cotman* and a type of *Bell Houses* clause, the modern company's contractual capacity approaches that of a natural person. The *ultra vires* rule as a method of controlling the activities of the board has been largely abandoned. However, as we shall see, the directors must exercise their powers, as agents, for a proper purpose and if they do not the transaction may be affected under the general rules of agency rather than the rules of *ultra vires*. This matter will be considered further when we deal with directors.

Companies Act 1985

Section 35 now represents the United Kingdom's response to Article 9 of the First Directive (No 68/151) issued by the European Economic Community for the harmonization of company law in the member states of the EEC.

It was intended considerably to reduce the effect of the *ultra vires* rule on the claims of creditors, but it has little relevance today since few transactions are likely to be *ultra vires* anyway.

However, on the assumption that the narrow scope of a particular company's memorandum may still allow for this, a few words about the section may be worthwhile.

The section provides that as regards a person who deals in good faith (which in general means that he has no *actual* notice of the company's lack of power) with a company, any transaction decided on by its directors shall be deemed (or regarded) to be within the capacity of the company to enter into validly and the other party to the transaction shall not be bound to enquire about the capacity of the company to engage in it and shall be presumed to have acted in good faith unless it is proved otherwise. The outsider has no constructive notice of the contents of the objects clause, as he has at common law. For example, if we take the *Ashbury* case, Mr Riche was regarded as *knowing* what Ashbury's objects clause contained and this is so at common law even though the outsider has not looked at the company's memorandum or articles.

Unfortunately, the section applies only if the transaction has been 'decided on by the directors'. This means that the board must have resolved to enter into the transaction or have resolved to ratify (or adopt) the

act of a director or executive who has entered into it for the company. However, the section applies to the acts of a sole effective director who is running the company with the whole-hearted consent of the rest of the board. This may sometimes happen in a family company. For example in *International Sales and Agencies v Marcus* (1982) a Mr Munsey, who was in effect the managing director of International Sales, was being allowed to run the company by a Mrs Fancy and her son Ismat, who were the other two directors and also the wife and son respectively of a former major shareholder and director, Mr Fancy who had died. It was said by the court that acts by Mr Munsey which were *ultra vires* the company might nevertheless have been made good by what is now s. 35, even though that section does use the plural term 'decided on by the *directors*'.

In so far as it is still required, s. 35 will be more effective in private companies where even trivial matters are often decided by the board than in PLCs such as ICI, where many transactions never go to the board at all but are decided on by executives below board level.

Altering the objects clause

Under s. 4 the objects clause can be changed by a special resolution. This type of resolution has already been explained in dealing with changing the company's name.

In particular, s. 4(*d*) provides that a company may change its objects to carry on some business which can be conveniently or advantageously combined with the business of the company. This allows the company to carry on a new business, provided it does not conflict with the existing business.

Re Cyclists Touring Club (1907)

The company's memorandum contained the following objects –

(*i*) the protection of cyclists on the road;

(*ii*) to give legal aid to the same to enable them to enforce their rights;

(*iii*) to furnish road maps and routes for cyclists.

The company wanted to change its objects to add the following clause 'to assist and protect the pastime of touring by the use of all vehicles'. The Court decided that the alteration could not be allowed because protection of the interests of motorists could conflict with the existing object of protecting the interests of cyclists.. The company could not serve both masters properly.

Once a special resolution has been passed it stands unless within twenty-one days of it being passed the holder(s) of 15 per cent of the company's issued share capital or, if the company's share capital is divided into classes, say A ordinary and B ordinary, 15 per cent of the holders of any class, apply to the court to cancel it, as in *Cyclists Touring Club* (above). Those who apply must *not* have voted for the resolution.

The court need not cancel the resolution but may instead, under s. 5(5), order the purchase of the dissentients' shares *from the company's funds*, thus reducing its capital. Alternatively, the other members may buy the shares, in which case capital is not reduced.

Limitation of liability (Clause 4)

This, as can be seen from the specimen memorandum, simply states: 'The liability of the members is limited' – unless of course the company is unlimited, when this clause is not put in.

The clause cannot be altered so as to make the company an unlimited one. However, the company may be re-registered as unlimited under s. 49. All unlimited companies must be private companies and public companies cannot apply for re-registration under s. 49, but must convert to private companies first.

An unlimited company may re-register as a limited company under s. 51. This does not apply to a company which was previously a limited company but re-registered as an unlimited one. In this case there is no going back.

Capital (Clause 5)

This clause must state the amount of the company's authorized capital and its division into a fixed nominal (or par) value. In our case the authorized capital is £10 000 divided into 10 000 shares of £1 each.

The main result of this clause is that English companies cannot have what are called 'no par' value shares. In the case of no par shares, the company would decide to issue, say 100 shares and receive, say £200. This £200 would appear in the balance sheet as 'stated capital'. In this country if the shares had a nominal value of £1 each the balance sheet would have to show called up share capital as £100 and share premium account £100.

The share premium account is like capital and is a

rather clumsy way of indicating that the whole £200 the company has received is capital. With no par value shares this is obvious. The whole £200 is shown in the balance sheet as stated capital and it is clear what it is.

As we have already seen, the authorized share capital of a plc must be at least £50 000 divided into shares of a fixed nominal (or par) value.

Association clause

Finally, there is an association clause which states that the subscribers wish to be formed into a company and that they agree to take the shares opposite their names.

Articles of association

The second major document governing the company is the articles of association. A specimen set of articles appears on pp. 135. Reference will be made to these as required in the rest of this chapter.

Companies which do not wish to draft their own articles may adopt Table A of the Schedule to the Companies (Tables A–F) Regulations 1985, or they may have adopted earlier Tables A in previous company legislation.

We have not done this. Our articles have been specially drafted, largely to show that in dealing with companies we must always be prepared to find articles which are specially drafted and to note how they sometimes differ from Table A.

Those who learn Table A and assume that no other form of articles exist will be in some trouble in dealing with companies. It will be of interest to see, where appropriate, how our own articles differ from Table A.

For the moment it would be advisable for the reader to look at the major headings of our model and see in broad terms what the articles cover. As will be seen, they regulate the rights of the members of the company and the manner in which the business of the company shall be done.

The articles must be printed, divided into paragraphs numbered consecutively, and signed by each subscriber to the memorandum in the presence of at least one witness. (S. 7(3).)

Legal effect of the articles

The articles (together with the memorandum) when

registered are a contract which binds the company and the members as if signed and sealed by each member; so says s. 14(1).

It follows from this that –

(*a*) *The members are bound to the company by the provisions of the articles.* This is illustrated by the following case.

Hickman *v* Kent or Romney Marsh Sheep Breeders' Association (1915)

The articles of the Association provided that any dispute between a member and the company must be taken first to arbitration. H, a shareholder, who was complaining that he had been wrongfully expelled from the company, took his case first to the High Court. The court decided that the action could not continue in the High Court. H was contractually bound by the articles to take the dispute to arbitration first.

(*b*) *The company is also bound to the members in respect of their rights as members.* Again, the following case is an illustration of this point.

Pender *v* Lushington (1877)

The articles of the Direct United States Cable Co. gave its members voting rights but fixed a maximum amount of votes (100) which each member could cast no matter how many shares he held. The Globe Telegraph and Trust Co. held a large number of shares in Direct United and to evade the 100 votes rule and increase its voting power it transferred some of its shares to P who agreed to be a nominee of Globe and vote with it. L, who was the chairman of Direct United refused to allow P to cast his votes and a resolution supported by Globe and P was lost. P asked the court for an injunction to restrain the company and L from declaring that P's votes were bad. The court granted the injunction. P had a contractual right to vote given to him by the articles and he could enforce this right. His votes must be accepted.

(*c*) *Each member is bound to the other members.* this is illustrated by the following case.

Rayfield *v* Hands (1958)

A clause in the articles of a company provided that: 'Every member who intends to transfer shares shall inform the directors who will take the said shares equally between them at a fair value'. Rayfield, a

member, told the defendant directors that he wanted to transfer his shares. The directors refused to take and pay for them, saying that they had no liability to do so.

The court decided that the word 'will' indicated an obligation to take the shares and that the clause imposed a contractual obligation on the directors to take them. This was in the nature of a collateral contract. When a member bought shares he made a contract with the company but also a collateral contract with the other members to observe the provisions of the articles. Thus the members could sue each other and there was no need for the company, with whom the main contract was made, to be a party to the action.

Comment. Although the article placed the obligation to take shares *on the directors*, the judge construed this as an obligation falling upon the directors in their capacity as *members*. Otherwise the contractual aspect of the provision in the articles would not have applied. The articles are not a contract between the company and the directors who, in their capacity as directors, are outsiders for this purpose. (See below.)

(*d*) *Neither the company nor the members are bound to outsiders.* This is illustrated by the following case.

Eley *v* The Positive Government Security Life Assurance Co. Ltd (1876)

The articles of the company appointed Mr Eley as solicitor of the company for life. During the course of this employment he became a member of the company. Later he was dismissed and brought an action against the company for damages for breach of the contract which he said was contained in the articles. The court decided that his action failed. There was no contract between the company and Mr Eley. He was an outsider in his capacity as a solicitor. The articles gave him rights only in his capacity as a member.

Alteration of the articles

The company may alter or add to its articles by a special resolution (s. 9), subject to certain restrictions of which the following are the most important.

(1) The court will not allow an alteration to be enforced if it is not for the benefit of the members as a

whole, as where the company takes a power of expulsion of members for no particular reason.

Brown v British Abrasive Wheel Co. Ltd (1919)

The majority shareholders (98%) in a company agreed to provide more capital for the company on condition that the 2 per cent minority (who were not prepared to put more money in) would sell their shares to the majority. Negotiations having failed, the articles were altered to include a clause under which a shareholder was forced to transfer his shares to the other members at a fair value if requested to do so in writing. The court decided that the alteration could not be allowed. The clause could be used to deprive any minority shareholder of his shares without any reason being given and it was not for the benefit of the company (i.e. the members) as a whole that any one or more of their number should be expelled for no good reason.

However, expulsion is allowed if it does benefit the members as a whole as where the member expelled is competing with the company.

Sidebottom v Kershaw Leese & Co. Ltd (1920)

Mr Sidebottom, who was a minority shareholder in the company, carried on a business which competed with the company. Because of this the articles were altered to include a clause under which any shareholder who competed with the company had to transfer his shares at a fair value to persons nominated by the directors. The Court of Appeal decided that the alteration was valid. Although it only applied to a particular member at the time, it could be applied in the future to any member who competed with the company (but not of course to members who did not). This would always be for the benefit of the company in that its members would have power to exclude a competitor.

(2) A company cannot justify breach of a contract outside of the articles by showing that the breach resulted from an alteration of the articles.

Southern Foundries Ltd v Shirlaw (1940)

Mr Shirlaw, who was a director of Southern Foundries, was appointed managing director of that company for ten years by a contract outside the articles. The company was taken over by Federated Industries. With their voting power they altered the articles to provide that Federated Industries had power to remove any director of Southern Foundries and that the managing director of Southern Foundries must also be a director. Mr Shirlaw was subsequently removed from his directorship and therefore could no longer qualify as managing director and his contract was terminated while it still had some years to run. The House of Lords decided that the company was liable in damages. Although a company always had a legal right to change its articles, if by doing so it caused a breach of an outside contract then, while the alteration could not be prevented, the company was liable in damages if there was a breach of a contract outside of the articles as a result of the alteration.

(3) Shareholders' rights are contained in the articles. Obviously, these rights can be changed by a special resolution of the company in general meeting. However, if the company has more than one class of shares, e.g. A Ordinaries and B Ordinaries, then the special resolution is not enough.

Under s. 125 a special resolution is not effective unless holders of three-quarters of the issued shares of each class consent in writing, e.g. by returning a tear-off slip on a letter to indicate their agreement or not, or by means of an extraordinary resolution at a class meeting.

In addition, s. 127 applies; under this 15 per cent of the class who did not vote for the variation may apply to the court within twenty-one days of the resolution which altered the articles. Once such an application has been made the variation will not take effect unless and until it is confirmed by the court.

So if under our specimen Article 3 we had created shares of different classes all of which had one vote per share on a poll, as Article 52 provides, then any special resolution of the company in general meeting to change that article, e.g. to one vote per share to the holders of A Ordinaries, and one vote per two shares to the holders of B Ordinaries, would need also the approval of class meetings as required above, in particular the approval of the holders of shares in Class B.

The point of this is that those holding the A Ordinary shares may well be able to get a special resolution in general meeting and so weaken the position of the B Ordinary shareholders, but they cannot do so without the necessary class consent of the B Ordinary shareholders. The changes also need the consent of those holding A Ordinary shares but in the circumstances outlined above this consent would almost certainly be given.

Financing the company

We shall now deal with the raising of money for the company.

Share capital

The capital of a company may be divided into preference and ordinary shares. In addition, both of these classes of shares may, under s. 159, be issued as redeemable by the company at a future date.

Preference shares

These shares have the right to payment of a fixed dividend, e.g. 12 per cent of the nominal value, before any dividend is paid on the other shares. However, there is no right to such dividend unless the company has sufficient distributable profits to pay it. This is why preference shares differ from loan capital. Interest on loan capital must be paid whether the company has distributable profits or not. If it has no profits it must be paid from capital as by a sale of assets or the raising of a further loan.

Once the preference dividend has been paid in full the preference shareholders have no right to share in surplus profit with the ordinary shareholders unless, as is rare, the preference shares are participating preference shares. Preference shares may be cumulative or non-cumulative. If they are cumulative and in any one year there are insufficient profits to pay the preference dividend, it is carried forward and added to the dividend for the following year and is paid then if there are sufficient profits.

So if Eric is the holder of 100 Preference Shares of £1 each, carrying a preference dividend of 12 per cent, then if in year one the dividend cannot be paid, the £12 to which Eric is entitled is carried forward to year two and if there are sufficient profits in that year Eric will receive £24. If the shares are non-cumulative Eric would not receive the £12 lost in year one, but only £12 for year two and subsequently.

Ordinary (or equity) shares

These rank for dividend after the preference shares and sometimes also the terms of issue provide that the preference shares shall have a right to claim repayment of capital before the ordinary shares if the company is wound up.

Ordinary shares, therefore, carry most risk. Generally they have most of the voting rights in general meetings and therefore control the company, it being common to provide that the preference shares shall not have a vote at all unless their dividend is in arrear. Ordinary shares receive a fluctuating dividend which depends upon distributable profits left after the preference dividend has been paid.

Redeemable shares

Under s. 159 a company with a share capital may, if authorized by its articles, (as our company is in Article 3) issue redeemable shares, whether ordinary or preference. Commonly, redeemable shares are made redeemable between certain dates. The holder thus knows that his shares cannot be redeemed before the earlier of the two dates, which is usually a number of years after the issue of the shares in order to give him an investment which will last for a reasonable period. He also knows that the shares are bound to be redeemed by the later of the two dates mentioned.

The power to issue redeemable equity shares is useful in the expansion of the small business. Outside investors often like ordinary share capital with its greater potential returns in the way of dividend and capital gain, but the smaller businessman may wish to buy them out after the business has developed. He can do this by issuing redeemable ordinary shares. Redeemable preference shares are less attractive to the speculative investor. They are safe but carry only a fixed dividend no matter how high the profits.

Purchase of own shares

Sections 162–178 apply and any company may by following the procedures laid down in these sections purchase its own shares, including any redeemable shares – as where the date for redemption has not arrived. The shareholder(s) concerned must of course be willing to sell the shares and the company must want to buy them. The company cannot be forced to buy them, nor can a shareholder be forced to sell.

The important legal considerations are set out below.

(*i*) The company's articles must allow the purchase, as ours do (see Art. 4).

(*ii*) The shares must be fully paid. The Companies Act 1985 does not allow the purchase (or for that matter, redemption) of partly-paid shares.

(*iii*) The company must have at least two members after the purchase has taken place and one of those members at least must hold non-redeemable shares.

(*iv*) A public limited company must have allotted share capital of at least £50 000.

(*v*) The shares must be cancelled following purchase. The company cannot hold and therefore trade in its own shares.

Market purchase

Public companies may make a market purchase on The Stock Exchange or Unlisted Securities Market, or an off-market purchase from an individual shareholder.

Before a Stock Exchange purchase can be made by the directors the members must approve by ordinary resolution. The resolution must state the maximum number of shares which the directors can acquire and the maximum and minimum prices which they can pay. The minimum price is often specified, but the maximum price is usually according to a formula, for example one based upon the Daily Official List of The Stock Exchange on a day or days preceding the day on which the share is contracted to be purchased.

The duration of the authority to purchase must be stated in the resolution by stating the date on which it expires.

A copy of the resolution must be filed with the Registrar of Companies within fifteen days after it is passed.

Off-market purchase

These provisions are mainly for private companies but can be used, as we have seen, by PLCs whose shares are *not* listed on The Stock Exchange or quoted on the Unlisted Securities Market, which is regulated by the Stock Exchange for the smaller PLCs which cannot or who do not wish to comply with the conditions for a full listing on The Stock Exchange.

The procedure is as follows –

(*i*) A special resolution of the members is required before the contract is entered into. *The contract must therefore be approved in advance.* So far as PLCs are concerned (but not private companies) the resolution must specify the duration of authority to make the contract being a period not longer than eighteen months.

(*ii*) The special resolution is *not* effective unless the 'raft contract is made available for inspection by the members at the registered office during the fifteen days immediately preceding the meeting and at the meeting.

(*iii*) The special resolution is invalid if passed by the votes of the member whose shares are being purchased. Thus there must be sufficient other shareholders' votes to give the necessary majority of 75 per cent of those voting in person or by proxy. The member whose shares are being purchased can vote other shares he may have which are not being purchased on a poll but he cannot in any event vote on a show of hands.

Off-market contingent contracts

All companies may make contingent purchase contracts. These are contracts by the company to buy its own shares on the happening of a future event, for example, a contract to buy the shares of an employee on retirement. This is permitted if the procedures for an off-market purchase set out above are followed.

It should be noted that the company cannot assign its right to buy the shares to someone else. This is to prevent a market developing in contingent purchase contracts.

The company cannot release, i.e. give up, its right to buy except by authorization of a special resolution of the members.

Purchase of own shares: miscellaneous provisions

When a company has purchased its own shares it must within twenty-eight days disclose the fact to the Registrar, giving the number and nominal value of the shares purchased and the date they were delivered to the company. Furthermore, the contract of purchase must be kept at the registered office for ten years and can be inspected by members. In a PLC it can be inspected also by any other person without charge.

If a company fails to purchase the shares when it has agreed to do so there is no action by the member for damages. However, he can bring an action for specific performance but the court will not make such an order unless the company can pay for the shares from its distributable profits.

Purchase (or redemption) from capital – private companies only

This provision is intended for private companies who have some distributable profits *but these are not enough* to purchase or redeem the shares and the company is either unwilling or unable to raise money from a fresh issue of shares. In such a case it can purchase or redeem its shares partly from capital.

It is in effect an easier procedure for private companies to reduce their share capital or to satisfy the claims of a retiring member or the estate of a deceased member in respect of shares in the company which might not be easily saleable elsewhere.

As regards the conditions, the articles must authorize a purchase from capital, as ours do. (See Art. 4.) The 'permissible capital payment' (PCP) is the shortfall after taking into account distributable profits or the proceeds of a fresh issue of shares which the company must utilize first. If there are no distributable profits or proceeds of a fresh issue of shares there can be no purchase or redemption wholly from capital. This restricts the advantages of the section to some extent.

There must be a statutory declaration of solvency by the directors. This says that the company will be solvent immediately after making the purchase (or redemption) and for one year afterwards. The statutory declaration states the PCP and the declaration itself is based on accounts prepared within three months before the statutory declaration, taking into account any distributions which may have been made between the accounts and the statutory declaration.

A report by the auditors must be attached to the statutory declaration stating that the PCP has been properly calculated *and* that the directors' opinion as to solvency is reasonable in terms of the facts of which the auditors are aware.

A special resolution of the members is also required and the statutory declaration and auditors' report must be available for inspection *at the meeting*. The resolution must be passed within one week of the date of the statutory declaration. It is invalid if passed with the votes of the shares of the person whose shares are being bought. Such persons may vote other shares on a poll but not on a show of hands.

The capital payment must be made not earlier than five weeks (to allow for objections) and not later than seven weeks from the resolution. If an indefinite period was allowed for the capital payment the statutory declaration would be getting outdated, so seven weeks is the maximum time.

Publicity must be given in order to protect creditors. A notice in writing may be given to all the company's creditors stating the fact and the date of the special

resolution, the amount of the PCP, that the statutory declaration and auditors' report can be inspected at the registered office and that any creditor may seek to restrain the payment by applying to the court to cancel the special resolution during the period of five weeks from the special resolution. The statutory declaration and auditors' report must be kept at the registered office for inspection by any member or creditor until the end of the fifth week following the special resolution.

Alternatively, an advertisement may be put in *The London Gazette* and one national newspaper giving the same information as listed above.

At the date of the notice or advertisement copies of the statutory declaration and auditors' report must have been sent to the Registrar so that they are available for inspection by a company search.

Dissentient shareholders or creditors may also apply to the court, within five weeks of the resolution, to cancel it, for example if available profits have not been utilized. The court may order the purchase of the dissentient shares or the payment of creditors.

If the company goes into insolvent winding up within twelve months of a payment from capital, then the seller of the shares and the directors giving the statutory declaration are each liable to repay the money in full with a right of contribution against the others involved.

Loan capital

Trading companies have an implied power to borrow and charge their assets as security for a loan, i.e. to give the lender a right to appoint a receiver to sell the company's assets in order to repay the loan if the company does not otherwise repay it.

Even so the memorandum usually gives an express power to borrow and details of the extent to which the company can charge its assets as security. (See Clause 3(*j*) of the specimen memorandum at p. 132.)

Section 117 puts restrictions on borrowing by newly-formed PLCs. Such companies cannot commence business or borrow until they have received a certificate allowing them to do this from the Registrar of Companies.

The certificate will not be issued until at least £50 000-worth of the company's capital has been allotted (sold) and at least one-quarter of the nominal value of each share and the whole of any premium has been received by the company.

Debenture and debenture stock

When a lender makes a loan to a company he will obviously require some evidence of that fact. This is usually a written document under seal which is called a debenture, a term which has its origin in the latin word for 'owing'.

A *single debenture* evidences a loan from a person where the lender is in privity of contract with the company and is a creditor of it. Its modern use is to secure a loan or overdraft facility from a bank. In this context it is the document by which the company charges in favour of the bank all its assets and undertaking, thus giving the bank the right to appoint an administrative receiver if the company does not pay what it owes. The administrative receiver runs the company while he is realizing money from the company's assets to pay the bank. If the company is a going concern when he has done this – and often his management will have cured the company's ills – the running of the company is handed back to its board of directors. This is in contrast to a liquidator of a company in a winding up. He is really an undertaker and his job is to sell what assets the company has to pay the creditors as far as he can and then see that the company is removed from the Register.

Debenture stock is found where the loan is to come from the public, those who subscribe for the debenture stock receiving a stock certificate rather like a share certificate. The company keeps a register of debenture holders and the stock certificates can be transferred from one person to another in a similar way to shares. However, unlike shares, which cannot be issued at a discount (s. 100), debentures can be so issued. It would, for example, be unlawful to issue say, a £1 share at 75p, but this would be legal in the case of a debenture.

When debentures are issued for public subscription, the company enters into a trust deed with trustees for the debenture holders. The trustees are often an insurance company. The insurance company has the charge over the assets and the power to appoint a receiver and the trustees are the creditors of the company on trust for the individual stock holders who are not in privity of contract with the company.

From a commercial point of view this is necessary because the holders of debenture stock are widely dispersed and need some central authority, such as the trustees to look after their interests with the company.

Our company could not make an issue of debenture stock since, under the Financial Services Act 1986, a private company cannot offer its shares or debentures to the public. We could, however, issue a debenture to a bank for the purpose of securing an overdraft facility since this would not be a public issue.

Registration of charges

Under s. 396 a charge to secure a debenture or an issue of debentures must be registered with the Registrar of Companies. The object of this is to show those doing business with the company, who may inspect the Register, what charges there are affecting the company's property.

In addition, copies of the documents creating charges must be kept at the company's registered office and be available for inspection by members and creditors without charge. (Ss. 406 and 408.)

The company must also keep a register of charges affecting its property. (S. 407.) This may also be inspected by members and creditors without charge. (S. 408.)

Failure to register a charge

Failure to register a charge with the Registrar within twenty-one days of its creation means that the charge will be void if the company is wound up and a liquidator appointed, or if a receiver is appointed by another secured creditor. The lender would then become an unsecured creditor and lose his rights to appoint a receiver and his priority for payment in a liquidation.

It is because the security may be lost that the law allows a secured creditor to register the charge himself and to claim the costs from the company. (S. 399.)

However, in practice, banks, who commonly lend money or give overdraft facilities to companies on a secured debenture, get the signatures of the appropriate officers of the company on the document registering the charge and then post it to the Registrar in Cardiff themselves. Thus the company registers the charge but the bank ensures that this is done.

Failure to register the charge in the company's register leads to a default fine on the company's officers at fault, but the charge is still valid.

The issue of shares and debentures

Generally

Under s. 80 the directors of public and private companies cannot issue shares without the express authority of the members. This is usually given by the members by ordinary resolution at a general meeting of the company. The authority may be given for a particular allotment of shares or it may be a general power, though if it is it can be given only for a maximum period of five years and then it must be renewed. The authority once given may be taken away or varied by the members by ordinary resolution insofar as it has not been exercised.

Similar permission to allot debenture stock is not required unless the debentures can by the terms of issue be converted at some time in the future to shares.

Under s. 89, when public and private companies wish to offer shares where the members have given them power under s. 80, they must offer them to existing members first in proportion to their present holdings, e.g. one new for three existing shares, or whatever formula covers the number of shares being issued.

This requirement to issue to existing members may be excluded. A *private company* can add to its articles by a special resolution a clause stating that these pre-emption rights, as they are called, shall not apply to the company and this will last unless and until the articles are altered by special resolution or the company ceases to be a private company. It may in fact be permanent.

A *public company* (and a private company which does not adopt the above approach) can disapply the pre-emption rights only by special resolution of its members which may be for a particular issue or a general disapplication which can only be for five years and then must be renewed. Alternatively, a public company and a private company may disapply pre-emption rights temporarily by a provision in the articles, but this must be renewed every five years and is not the permanent alteration referred to above.

The provisions of ss. 80 and 89 prevent the directors from using the power of allotment to issue shares to persons favourable to themselves in order to keep their position on the board and thus their control of the company. This did happen in the past but now the consent of the members is required, both to allot the shares in the first place and then to issue them outside to persons other than existing members.

The prospectus

Generally

A private company cannot issue a prospectus because, as we have seen, it cannot offer its shares or debentures to the public. It must sell its securities by private negotiation with individuals interested.

However, a public company, provided it has the necessary member authority under s. 80 and the members have disapplied their pre-emption rights under s. 89, may issue shares by means of a prospectus. This is a document explaining the nature of the investments which a would be subscriber to the issue will be taking.

The company will want to make the prospectus as attractive as possible and to prevent the public from being misled the Companies Act 1985 applies the provisions of Sch. 3 to the prospectus of a PLC seeking funds on the Unlisted Securities Market (USM) while the Stock Exchange (Listing) Regulations 1984 (see now Financial Services Act 1986) apply to flotations by listed PLCs. The Act and the Regulations require certain disclosures of interest to would-be investors to be made in the prospectus. Sch. 3 is a little specialized and its contents are not included.

The disclosure requirements of the 1984 Regulations (which are technical and complex) have also been omitted as inappropriate to a text of this nature.

Offer for sale

A public company which intends to issue shares or debentures to the public could, in law, do so directly itself. However, such issues require considerable expertise and experience in those who make them and the method used is normally an offer for sale.

Under an offer for sale the securities (shares or debentures) are offered to the public by an issuing house instead of being offered by the company direct to the public. Just before the offer the issuing house will have agreed to buy the securities concerned and is, in effect, offering its own shares to the public. Nevertheless, the above legislation applies to the offer and the prospectus issued under the offer for sale must comply with Sch. 3 or the 1984 Regulations.

The issuing house is paid by the fact that it purchases the shares at one price from the company and offers them at a slightly higher price to the public.

Allotment of shares under a prospectus

The company must obtain one quarter of the nominal value of each share issued plus the whole of any premium on it before it can allot shares to those members of the public who want to take them. (S. 101.)

It is also most important in a contract to take shares in a public company that the shares shall be quoted on a recognized stock exchange. If they are not so quoted they have no market and there is some difficulty in selling them.

Consequently, if a prospectus states that application has been made for permission for the shares or debentures to be dealt with on The Stock Exchange, then any allotment on an application under that prospectus is void if the permission is refused.

If it is refused the company must immediately repay all the money received from applicants; if such money is not repaid within eight days of the refusal of a listing on The Stock Exchange, the directors are liable to repay the money.

Misleading prospectuses

A person who subscribes for shares or debentures under a misleading prospectus has certain remedies. The main ones are set out below. They depend to some extent upon whether the flotation is by a listed company or a company whose shares are quoted on the Unlisted Securities Market (USM). The aim of the Stock Exchange in setting up the USM was to encourage small and medium-sized businesses to get a public quotation for their shares. The costs of admission to the USM are much lower than for a full listing and the amount of Stock Exchange regulation is much less.

Rescission of the contract to take the shares (available in both listed and USM flotations)

If this remedy, which is dealt with in greater detail at p. 173, is successful, the person who has subscribed for the shares will get his money back and will cease to be a member. In other words, he gets out of the company.

An action for rescission may be brought for false statements by directors or experts, e.g. accountants who have given financial reports in a prospectus, or for failing to include material facts in the prospectus.

Coles v White City (Manchester) Greyhound Association Ltd (1929)

A prospectus stated that certain land was 'eminently suitable' for greyhound racing. This was true only if the local authority gave permission (a) to erect stands for the public, and (b) for kennels.

This permission had not been obtained and a shareholder brought this action to rescind the contract. The court decided that the omission, i.e. failure to reveal that the permission had not been obtained, made the prospectus misleading and the plaintiff got rescission.

However, rescission is a remedy which is easily lost. Rescission puts the parties in the position they were in before they made the contract. It totally unscrambles the contract as if it never existed. It is therefore a drastic remedy and is subject to restrictions as follows –

(i) *Delay*. The subscriber must bring his claim without delay. The general rule here is that it must be brought within a 'reasonable time', that being a matter of fact for the court to decide.

In the context of prospectuses, however, there is a more precise statement in *Heymann v European Central Rail Co.* (1868) where the court said that the remedy of rescission would be lost unless the action was commenced within three months of discovering that the prospectus was misleading.

(ii) *Affirmation*. The subscriber must not affirm the contract. So he must not, for example, take a dividend; attempt to sell the shares; attend meetings; vote at meetings, or pay more money on the shares if the company calls upon him to do so.

Remedies for damages against the directors and experts

These remedies will leave the subscriber as a shareholder in the company but he will get money compensation from the directors or experts if the shares are less valuable than they would have been if the prospectus had not been misleading.

There are two main areas of claim as follows –

(i) *Section 67, Companies Act 1985* (available only in USM flotations). This is an action for money compensation. It is similar to a claim under the Misrepresentation Act 1967 for negligent misrepresentation and under s. 68 the director or expert concerned will have a successful defence if he can show that he had reasonable grounds to believe that the statement was true. This will depend upon the degree to which he has tried to verify the statement.

Section 68, however, contains in addition certain special defences to a claim under s. 67 to fit the company situation. For example, an expert can prove that he did not consent to the inclusion of his report in the prospectus. A director may say that he did not consent to the issue of the prospectus but he must have given public notice of that fact. He can also say that the statement was contained in the report of an expert when of course the action is against the expert.

(*ii*) *The tort of negligence* (available in listed and USM flotations). This is a wider claim than that under s. 67 because it covers opinions, whereas s. 67, like all forms of contractual misrepresentation, covers only statements of existing fact. Thus negligent statements as to the company's future prospects would be covered here but not by s. 67.

Since experts are not employed by the company, nor are they its agents, the action is against the expert personally. The company is not vicariously liable.

The action against the directors is also a personal one since, although they are agents of the company, a main Stock Exchange and also a USM listing require the prospectus to state that the directors have taken all reasonable care to ensure that the prospectus is not misleading. Legal opinion on this is that the statement confines the action to the directors personally and that the company is not vicariously liable.

The Stock Exchange (Listing) Regulations 1984 – (listed company flotations only)

The Stock Exchange (Listing) Regulations 1984 (SI 1984/716) made a considerable impact on those requirements of English company law which relate to the breach of prospectus requirements. The Regulations, which came fully into force on 1 January 1985, implement EEC Directives 79/279 (conditions for admission to listing); 80/390 (listing particulars); 81/121 (regular information to be supplied by listed companies). The provisions are now in the Financial Services Act 1986. The Companies Act 1985 does not apply to issues by listed PLCs, but only to USM issues, until rules are made under the 1986 Act.

Listed securities

(*a*) *Exclusion of 1985 Act (Reg. 7)*. This provides that where an application has been made to the Council of The Stock Exchange for the admission of any securities to listing and the Council has approved listing particulars then:

(*i*) a form of application issued with a document which sets out the approved listing particulars or indicates where they can be obtained, need *not* have with it a prospectus otherwise required by the 1985 Act; and

(*ii*) in relation to an offer of any of those securities made by means of a document as referred to in (*i*) the provisions of the 1985 Act which would otherwise apply regarding liability do not apply.

Having excluded the 1985 Act, Reg. 3 substitutes the provisions of the Listing Particulars Directive (LPD) 80/390. This appears in Sch. 1 of the Regulations.

(*b*) *Liability (Art. 4 of the LPD)*. This states that the listing particulars in the prospectus shall contain the information which, according to the particular nature of the issuer and of the securities, is necessary to enable *investors and their investment advisors* to make an informed assessment of the assets and liabilities, financial position, profits and losses and prospects of the issuer and of the rights attaching to such securities.

The effect of this seems to be to give express liability to those responsible for the listing particulars for material mis-statements, material omissions, and misleading opinions. It replaces s. 67 of the 1985 Act (compensation for subscribers misled by statement in prospectus) with a new type of action. However, any liability, civil or criminal, which a person may incur under the general law (as distinct from the Companies Act 1985) continues to exist. Thus a plaintiff could still, e.g. sue for rescission or for a negligent mis-statement under *Hedley Byrne* v. *Heller* (1963) and of course under Art. 4.

(c) *Who is responsible? (Art. 4 of the LPD)*. This puts liability upon those responsible for the listing particulars as provided for in Heading 1.1 of Schedules A and B of the Directive. These are identical and say that a prospectus must state the name and function of natural persons and the name and registered office of legal persons responsible for the listing particulars or for certain parts of them with, in the latter case, an indication of which parts.

No further guidance is given, but The Stock Exchange seems to interpret this as applying only to directors by requiring a responsibility statement only from them to appear in the prospectus (now strictly speaking the listing particulars). However, responsibility will surely continue to be a matter of fact for the court. Before the Regulations came into force The Stock Exchange also required a statement only by directors, but it was never felt that this was a bar to an action against, e.g. professional persons also involved.

(d) *Defences (Reg. 5).* This provides that a person responsible for non-compliance with or a contravention of Art 4. (see (b) above) shall not be liable if

(i) he did not know of it; or

(ii) it was an honest mistake of fact on his part; or

(iii) it was in respect of a matter which in the opinion of the court was immaterial, or he ought, in any case, reasonably to be excused.

This seems wider than s. 68, Companies Act, 1985 because there is no need to prove reasonable grounds for believing a statement was true. The defence seems to apply whether lack of knowledge was reasonable or not. It seems to encourage directors and others to remain in ignorance.

(e) *Who can sue? (Art. 4 of the LPD).* This states that the duty is owed to 'investors and their investment advisors'. This would seem to include all subscribers, whether they have relied on the prospectus or not. Materiality appears to be the test and not reliance. So it seems a subscriber need not be aware of the error or even have seen the listing particulars.

(f) *Contents of the prospectus (Art. 5 of the LPD).* Schedule 3 of the 1985 Act does not apply. A prospectus must contain *at least* the items in Schedules A, B or C (depending on the type of security). These appear in full in the Regulations, which are too detailed to be included in a book of this nature. However, if you can get hold of a listed company's prospectus – they appear not infrequently in, for example, the *Financial Times*, *The Times*, or *The Daily Telegraph* – you will find it instructive to read what the regulations require.

Membership

Becoming a member

A person may become a member of a company –

(1) By *subscribing* the memorandum of association. Membership commences from the moment of subscription. On registration of the company the names of the subscribers must be entered in the register of members. (S. 22.) They are, however, members without such an entry.

(2) By *agreeing* to become a member and having his name entered on the register of members. Actual entry on the register is essential for membership, which commences only from the date of entry. A person may show *agreement* to become a member –

(a) by obtaining shares from the company, by applying for them as a result of a prospectus (public company), or following private negotiation (private company);

(b) by taking a transfer from an existing member following a purchase or a gift of the shares.

Minors

A minor may be a member unless the articles forbid this. The contract is voidable, which means that the minor can repudiate his shares at any time while a minor and for a reasonable time after becoming eighteeen. He cannot recover any money paid on the shares unless there has been total failure of consideration. Since being a member of a company appears in itself to be a benefit regardless of dividends, the minor is unlikely to be able to use this 'no consideration' rule.

Personal representatives

The personal representatives of a deceased member do not become members themselves unless they ask for and obtain registration. However, s. 187 gives them the right to transfer the shares.

Bankrupts

A bankrupt member can still exercise the rights of a member. He may, for example, vote or appoint a proxy to vote for him. However, he must exercise his rights and deal with any dividends he receives in the way in which his trustee in bankruptcy directs. The trustee in bankruptcy has the same right as a personal representative to ask for registration as the holder of the shares.

Shareholders' rights

The main rights given by law to a shareholder are as follows –

(1) *A right to transfer his shares.* This is subject to

any restrictions which may be found in the articles. Private companies may restrict the right to transfer shares, for example by giving the directors in the articles a right to refuse registration of the person to whom they have been transferred. Public companies listed on The Stock Exchange or the USM cannot have restrictions of this kind in their articles.

(2) *Meetings*. A member is entitled to receive notice of meetings and to attend and vote or appoint a proxy to attend and vote for him.

(3) *Dividends*. A shareholder's right to dividend depends on the company having sufficient distributable profits out of which to pay the dividend.

Although dividend is declared by the members in general meeting, the members cannot declare a dividend unless the directors recommend one. Furthermore, they can resolve to reduce the dividend recommended by the directors but cannot increase it.

(4) *Accounts*. A shareholder is entitled to a copy of the company's accounts within seven months of its accounting reference date (i.e. the end of its financial year) in the case of a public company and ten months in the case of a private company.

The matter of the alteration of shareholders' rights has already been considered (see p. 99).

Shareholders' duties

A shareholder is under a duty to pay for his shares when called upon to do so but is not in general liable for the company's debts beyond the amount (if any) outstanding on his shares. There are some exceptional cases; for example, where to the member's knowledge, the membership of the company falls below two and the company carries on business with that reduced number for more than six months, the liability of the existing member for debts incurred after the expiration of the six months is joint and several with the company. (S. 24.)

Thus the member is treated as if he were a partner with the company and if the debt is, say, £2000, the remaining member can be asked to pay the full amount and seek a contribution of £1000 from the company. The member is not, of course, likely to be sued unless the company is insolvent, in which case he has little chance of getting the contribution.

Cessation of membership

The most usual ways in practice that a person may cease to be a member of a company are by –

(1) Transfer of his shares to a purchaser or as a gift.

(2) Rescission of the contract under a misleading prospectus.

(3) Redemption or purchase of shares by the company.

(4) Death or bankruptcy.

(5) Winding up of the company.

Meetings and resolutions

Shareholders' meetings

There are two kinds of company general meeting: the annual general meeting and an extraordinary general meeting.

Annual general meeting
Section 366 states that an annual general meeting must be held in every calendar year and not more than fifteen months after the last one. So if a company held an annual general meeting on 31 March 1987 it must hold the next one in 1988 and on or before 30 June 1988.

However, if a company holds its first annual general meeting within eighteen months of its incorporation it need not hold one in its year of incorporation or the following year. Thus if a company was incorporated on 1 November 1986 it would have until 30 April 1988 to hold its first annual general meeting.

The notice of the meeting must say that it is the annual general meeting. A specimen notice appears below.

Extraordinary general meetings
All general meetings other than the annual general meeting are extraordinary general meetings. They may be called by the directors at any time.

Section 368 gives holders of not less than one-tenth of the paid up share capital on which all calls due have been paid the right to requisition an extraordinary general meeting. The requisition must state the objects of the meeting, be signed by the requisitionists, and deposited at the registered office of the company. If the directors do not call a meeting within twenty-one days

---

RICHES KEENAN PUBLISHING LIMITED

NOTICE IS HEREBY GIVEN THAT THE
FIRST ANNUAL GENERAL MEETING of
the company will be held at 140,
High Street, Barchester on the 6th
day of January 1987 at 10.30 a.m. to
transact the ordinary business of
the company.*
    A member entitled to attend and
vote at the meeting is entitled
to appoint a proxy to attend and
vote instead of him. A proxy need
not also be a member.
                    By order of the board

J. M. WILLIAMS
....

Secretary

140, High Street,
Barchester.

1 December 1986

---

* Article 44 of our articles states the
ordinary business of our AGM and no
notice of it is required. If the articles
do not include references to ordinary
business (and the current Table A does
not) the items of business set out in
our Art. 44 would have to be set out in
the notice.

---

of the date of depositing the requisition, the requisitionists, or the majority in value of them, may call the meeting within three months of the date of the deposit.

Section 368 is defective in the sense that although the directors are required to *call* the meeting, they need not call the meeting within any particular period of time. Thus, they would appear to be within the section if they call the meeting for, say, six months ahead, even though this might frustrate the purpose of the requisitionists.

However, our Article 41 requires that in our company the meeting be held not later than eight weeks after the deposit of the requisition.

Notice of meetings

This must be given in accordance with the provisions of the articles. Our Article 43 requires twenty-one clear days' notice (i.e. excluding the day of service of the notice and the day of the meeting) of the annual general meeting and for a meeting to pass a special resolution or appoint a director, and fourteen clear days in other cases.

The articles usually provide, as our Article 43 does, that a meeting shall not be invalid because a particular member does not receive notice.

In order to work out the clear days notice we also need a provision like the one in our Article 95 which says that notice is deemed (or assumed) to be served twenty-four hours after posting. Thus if we post the notice of an extraordinary general meeting on say, 1 February, it is deemed served on 2 February and we can hold the meeting on 17 February at the earliest.

Quorum at general meetings

Under our Article 45 no business may be validly done at a general meeting unless a quorum (i.e. minimum number) of members is present when the meeting begins. This means in effect that there need not be a quorum throughout the meeting so long as there is one at the beginning.

Article 45 also provides that two members *personally present* (not by proxy) shall be a quorum.

Voting

This may be by a show of hands in which case, obviously, each member has one vote, regardless of the number of shares or proxies he holds. However, the articles usually lay down that the chairman or a certain number of members may demand a poll; Table A and our Article 49 provide for two. If a poll is successfully demanded, each member has one vote per share and proxies can be used. (See our Article 52.)

Proxies

If the articles so provide, voting on a poll may be by proxy (see our Article 53). A proxy is a written authority given by the member to another person to vote for him at a specified meeting. The company may require these authorities to be deposited at the company's office before the meeting. However, under s. 372 the articles cannot require them to be deposited more than 48 hours before the meeting. Our Article 57 requires forty-eight hours.

Minutes

A company must keep minutes of the proceedings at its general and board meetings (see further p. 121). Members have a right to inspect the minutes of general meetings but not those of directors' meetings.

Resolutions

There are four main kinds of resolution as set out below.

(1) *An ordinary resolution*, which may be defined as 'a resolution passed by a majority (over 50 per cent) of persons present and voting in person or by proxy at a general meeting'.

Any business may be validly done by this type of resolution unless the articles or the Companies Acts provide for a special or extraordinary resolution for that particular business.

An example of the use of an ordinary resolution is for the members to give their permission for the directors to allot the company's unissued share capital under s. 80.

(2) *An extraordinary resolution*, which is one passed by a majority of not less than three-quarters of the members who, being entitled to vote, do so whether in person or by proxy at a general meeting of which notice has been given specifying the intention to propose a resolution as an extraordinary resolution. (S. 378(1).) Under s. 369 fourteen days' notice of the meeting must be given.

The company may resolve by an extraordinary resolution to wind up if it cannot by reason of its liabilities continue in business.

(3) *A special resolution*, which is one passed by the same majority as is required for an extraordinary resolution at a general meeting of which at least twenty-one days' notice has been given stating the intention to propose the resolution as a special resolution. (S. 378(2).)

The distinction between a special and extraordinary resolution lies, therefore, in the period of notice of the meeting. A special resolution requires twenty-one days, whereas an extraordinary resolution requires only fourteen. The majorities are the same.

A special resolution is required for example, to alter the objects clause, to change the company's name, or the articles, or for the company to approve in advance a contract to make an off-market purchase of its shares. Section 380 provides that within fifteen days of the passing of an extraordinary or special resolution a copy of the resolution must be forwarded to the Registrar of Companies. Some ordinary resolutions must be sent to the Registrar but by no means all. An example of one which requires filing is the ordinary resolution to allow the directors to exercise a power of allotment under s. 80.

The copy sent to the Registrar may be printed or be in any form approved by the Registrar. (S. 380.) He will accept a typewritten copy.

(4) *Ordinary resolutions after special notice.* Sec-

tion 379 requires that for certain ordinary resolutions, for example, one removing a director before his period of office is ended, special notice must be given.

Where special notice is required it must be given to the company secretary not less than twenty-eight days before the meeting at which the resolution is to be proposed and by the company to the members not less than twenty-one days before that meeting.

This means that if, for example, a member wishes to propose the removal of a director by this procedure under s. 303, then when he stands up at the meeting to propose that removal, the company secretary must have been on notice of his intention to do so for twenty-eight days at least and the members for twenty-one days at least.

The purpose of the notice of twenty-eight days is so that the company secretary can alert the director concerned to the possibility of his removal so that the director can circulate members with his reasons why he should not be removed or, that failing, prepare an oral statement to be given at the meeting at which his removal is proposed.

Before leaving the topic of resolutions passed at meetings, it should be noted that resolutions can be passed by a small number of members. For example, if a company has 5000 members but only thirty attend the meeting and seventy appoint proxies, a special, or extraordinary, or ordinary resolution can be validly passed by three-quarters or at least 51 per cent, as the case may be, taken from those present at the meeting and voting in person or by proxy.

Protection of minority interests

The rule in *Foss* v *Harbottle* (1843)

The rule in *Foss* is that the majority of the members, by which we mean those who can command more than 50 per cent of the votes in general meeting, will be able to get the company to do what they want it to do, even if this does not suit the other members. It is in other words a principle of majority rule.

In that sense it is very hard on the minority, so when we consider minority rights it is the *exceptions* to *Foss* that we are looking at. The rule has not been allowed to ride roughshod over all minority rights.

In addition, there are some situations of wrongs to the minority which *fall outside the rule* in *Foss* and to

which that decision does not apply.

Foss v Harbottle (1843)

The plaintiffs, Foss and Turton, were shareholders in a company called 'The Victoria Park Company' which was formed to buy land to use as a pleasure park. The defendants were the other directors and shareholders of the company. The plaintiffs alleged that the defendants had defrauded the company in various ways and, in particular, that certain of the defendants had sold land belonging to them to the company at a very high price without disclosing this to the members of the company. The plaintiffs now sued on behalf of the company and asked the court to order that the defendants make good the losses to the company. The court decided that since the members of the company had not been consulted and that since it was possible that a simple majority of them in general meeting might resolve to allow the defendants to keep the alleged profits, the court would not give a remedy to the company at the request of the minority.

The rule does not apply where the wrong is not to the company but to the member personally

One of the major cases which illustrates this has already been considered in the section on the articles. It is *Pender* v *Lushington* (1877) on p. 98. Mr Pender did not challenge the principle of majority rule but merely complained that an individual, the chairman of the company, was refusing to allow him to exercise his voting rights which were given to him in the articles. The court said that his votes must be accepted. There was no question of majority rule in this case. It was merely a claim for a personal wrong by an individual within the company. In such a situation *Foss* did not apply.

Exceptions to *Foss*

The main exceptions appear below.

(1) *Where the act of the majority is ultra vires.* As we have seen, those who can command a simple majority in general meeting cannot ratify an *ultra vires* transaction.

In the *Ashbury* case, the facts of which appear at p. 95, it was said by the court that not even *all* the members could agree to adopt an *ultra vires* act. They must alter the objects clause so that it covers the transaction and then let the company enter into it again.

So a member may ask the court to grant an injunction to stop the directors carrying out an *ultra vires* act and *Foss* will not prevent this. The majority cannot resolve to act *ultra vires* in any case.

(2) *Fraud on the minority.* This is a wide category and only the main examples can be given here. Fraud in this context means some sort of improper behaviour by the majority which amounts to an abuse of their voting control.

There are three main areas in which this rule is applied –

(*a*) *where the minority itself is defrauded.* Here we find cases of expulsion of members without reason. Thus in *Brown* v *British Abrasive Wheel Co. Ltd* (1919), the facts of which appear on p. 99, the rule in *Foss* did not prevent Brown going to court and complaining that the majority intended to insert a provision in the articles containing a power of expulsion without reason because the majority could not use their voting power in this improper fashion.

However, a power to expel members who compete against the company is not an improper use of voting power by the majority, as the decision in *Sidebottom* v *Kershaw Leese & Co. Ltd* (1920) (see p. 99) illustrates.

These cases are not examples of wrongs to members personally but to members of the company generally. The plaintiff represents not only himself, as in *Pender*, but also all other members who might in future be affected by the fraud, i.e. expelled without reason. *Foss* is potentially a bar here because a minority shareholder is challenging on behalf of himself and other shareholders in a representative action the right of the majority to rule the company in the future. In *Pender* the plaintiff was merely challenging the right of an individual, i.e. the chairman, to refuse him (and not other members) the right to cast his votes. However, as we have seen in *Brown*, *Foss* will not be a bar where the court finds that the majority are acting in an improper manner.

(*b*) *The proper purpose rule.* If the directors use, or propose to use, their powers, or those of the company, for an improper purpose, then a minority shareholder can bring a representative claim on behalf of himself and the other shareholders asking that the transaction

in question be set aside or stopped. Suppose that an hotel company is the subject of a take-over bid by a property developer who wishes to convert the hotels into offices. Suppose again that to keep themselves in control of the company and to keep it as an hotel company the directors lease the hotels to their pension trustees who in turn lease them back to the hotel company with the condition that the premises are only to be used as hotels.

This will frustrate the bid; the bidder will not go ahead and the change of use of the property from hotels to offices, which might have given a better dividend to the shareholders of the hotel company, will not take place.

In such a situation a member of the hotel company could bring a representative action on behalf of himself and the other shareholders to stop or set aside the leasing arrangements.

However, it is very important to note that the rule in *Foss* will prevent such a claim unless the plaintiff can show that the 'wrongdoers', i.e. the directors, are also in control of the voting in general meeting. If they are not then the action cannot proceed because a simple majority in general meeting can, and may, approve the action of the directors.

It is not necessary in (*a*) above for the plaintiff to show that the 'wrongdoers' are in control of the voting in general meeting because a simple majority cannot ratify an act which is a fraud on the minority anyway. A simple majority can ratify the acts of directors for an improper purpose short of fraud on the minority.

(*c*) *Where the company is defrauded.* Actions here are of an entirely different nature. The member sues here to put right *a wrong done to the company* and not (except indirectly) a wrong to its members. The action is not representative, but *derivative*. The plaintiff gets his right to sue from the company.

In these cases the company is never the plaintiff. A company can only be brought into court as a plaintiff by its directors or a simple majority of its members.

However, the company must appear in the action, otherwise the court cannot give it a remedy. This is done by the plaintiff bringing the company into court as a defendant, but it is only a nominal defendant; in reality it is the plaintiff in the case.

The decision in *Foss* will prevent a derivative action unless the plaintiff can show that the 'wrongdoers' are also in control of the voting in general meetings. If they are not the action cannot proceed because a simple majority can and may approve of the action of the directors and even if this is unlikely, in view of the circumstances of the case, the attitude of the majority must be tested.

An illustration is provided by the following case.

Cook v Deeks (1916)

The directors of a construction company negotiated for a construction contract on behalf of the company and then took the contract in their own names and for their own benefit. In other words, they misappropriated a corporate opportunity, which is a breach of duty by a director. A meeting of the company was called and the directors, by their votes as holders of three-quarters of the shares, passed a resolution declaring that the company had no interest in the contract. Mr Cook brought a derivative claim on behalf of the company against the directors and the court decided that the benefit of the contract belonged to the company and the directors must account to the company for any profits that they made on the contract.

Can damage by negligence be a fraud on the minority?

It would seem that a minority shareholder may bring a claim where the directors use their powers negligently and that negligent conduct causes loss to the company, at least so long as the negligence has resulted in a benefit to the wrongdoers. This sort of conduct can apparently be brought under the head of 'fraud on the minority'.

Daniels v Daniels (1978)

A husband and wife were two directors of a company and also its majority shareholders. They caused the company to sell to the wife (Mrs Beryl Daniels) some land owned by the company. Four years later she resold the land for over twenty-eight times what she paid for it. The plaintiffs, who were minority shareholders, sought a remedy for the company on the basis that the negligence of the defendants had caused the company loss because they had sold its property at an undervalue. No fraud was alleged.

The court was asked whether there was a claim in law on these facts and the court said that there was. In particular, the judge said that there would be a claim 'Where the directors used their powers, intentionally or unintentionally, fraudulently or negligently, in a manner which benefits themselves at the expense of the company'.

Comment. Whether such a claim can be brought for negligent mismanagement of the company causing loss, but without benefit to the wrongdoer, is not clear. In *Pavlides* v *Jensen* (1956) the court said that there was no claim for pure negligence without profit.

In such a case, however, it would appear that the minority can petition under s. 459 for 'unfair prejudice' (see below).

Once again, it is essential if a claim is to be brought for negligence with benefit that the wrongdoers are in control of the voting at general meetings. Negligence, with or without benefit to the wrongdoers, can be ratified by the members in general meeting, provided the wrongdoers are not in control of the voting.

Statutory protection of the minority

In addition to the protection available to the minority by reason of the *exceptions* to *Foss*, various minority rights are given by statute.

The most far-reaching is the right of a minority shareholder to petition the court for relief under s. 459 where the shareholder believes that his interests are being 'unfairly prejudiced' by the way in which the company's affairs are being carried on. This section will be looked at separately.

Other main examples of statutory protection are:

(*a*) the right given to 15 per cent to object to the court in regard to a proposed variation of class rights (see p. 99);

(*b*) the right given to 15 per cent to object to the court regarding a proposal to change the company's objects (see p. 97);

(*c*) the right given to any shareholder to apply to the court to cancel the special resolution under which a private company proposes to make a purchase of shares partly from capital (see p. 102);

(*d*) the right of a member of a solvent company to petition the court for a winding up order on the just and equitable ground (see p. 126);

(*e*) the right given to one-tenth to require the convening of an extraordinary general meeting (see p. 108);

(*f*) the right given to one-twentieth to get an item up for discussion at the AGM. (S. 376.)

Relief from unfair prejudice

Under s. 459 any member may petition the court on the grounds that the affairs of the company are being conducted in a manner which is unfairly prejudicial to the interests of some part of the members (including at least the petitioner himself) or that any actual or proposed act is so unfairly prejudicial.

There has been some case law on this section but insufficient at the time of writing to be able to say for certain what the precise meaning of the section might be. The following is a summary of what is known so far.

Unfair prejudice

The circumstances leading to 'unfair prejudice' according to the Jenkins' Committee, which was set up to consider company law reform and reported in 1962, were as follows:

(a) directors paying themselves excessive salaries, thus depriving the members of any dividends or of adequate dividends;

(b) refusal of the board to put the personal representatives of a deceased shareholder on the register, thus preventing the shares from being voted and leading sometimes to the personal representatives selling the shares to the directors at an inadequate price;

(c) the issue of shares to directors on advantageous terms;

(d) the refusal by the board to recommend payment of dividends on non-cumulative preference shares held by a minority.

It may also be that negligent mismanagement by the directors causing loss to the company is unfairly prejudicial conduct, though this is as yet uncertain in view of the absence of definitive case law.

No doubt a petition could be presented but negligent or inefficient management usually affects *all* the members and not *part* only, as the section requires.

In *Re Carrington Viyella* (1983) a petition to the court under what is now s. 459 that a service contract between the company and its chairman was not in the best interests of the company was turned down because if the petition was true it affected all the members and not merely part of the members. If this reasoning is applied to petitions alleging negligent mismanagement it would seem that they will fail.

According to the court in *Re a Company* (1983), it is not unfairly prejudicial for the directors to refuse to purchase the company's shares under s. 162. In that case the executors of a deceased shareholder in a private company wanted to cash in the shares to provide a trust fund for the education and maintenance of the deceased shareholder's minor children. This fund would have yielded more than the company was paying in dividends on the shares. In the event the directors would not buy the shares, though they were prepared to approve a sale to an outsider if one could be found. This conduct was not unfairly prejudicial, said the Court.

However, it seems that removal from the board as in *Ebrahimi* v *Westbourne Galleries* (1972), or other exclusion from management, is covered. The section talks about conduct unfairly prejudicial *to the interests* of some part of the members, and in a private company a substantial shareholder can expect to be a director: it is an interest of his membership.

The court said that this was the case in *re London School of Electronics* (1985) where a director was excluded from management. The court made an order for the purchase of his shares by the majority shareholders. Thus he got his capital out and could go into another business. It will be seen that this is a better remedy than *Westbourne*, i.e. winding up under the just and equitable ground. The person excluded from management gets his capital out without the need to wind up a solvent company when the directors have merely fallen out with each other.

Relief available

Section 461 gives the court a power to make any order it sees fit to relieve the unfair prejudice, including in particular an order to:

(a) *regulate the future conduct* of the company's affairs. This could include the making of a court order altering the articles as in the following case.

Re H R Harmer (1959)

Mr H, senior, formed a company through which to deal in stamps. He gave his two sons shares in the company but kept voting control himself. Mr H senior was 'governing director' and his sons were also directors. Mr H senior ignored resolutions of the board; he set up a branch abroad which the board had resolved should not be set up; he dismissed trusted employees; drew unauthorized expenses; and engaged a private detective to watch the staff, presumably because he thought they might steal valuable stamps (imagine the effect on industrial relations!).

Eventually the sons petitioned the court under a repealed section of the Companies Act 1948 which required proof of oppression of the minority.

The court found oppression (and would certainly have found unfair prejudice). In giving relief the court ordered Mr H senior to act in accordance with the decisions of the board and ordered that he should not interfere in the company's affairs otherwise than as the board decided. The company's articles were altered by the court order to this effect.

Comment. Once the articles have been altered by the court order a special resolution is not enough to change the articles affected by the court order. The court itself must give permission for the change.

(*b*) *to restrain the doing or continuance of any act* complained of by the petitioner. Under this the court could presumably make an order directing the reduction of directors remuneration found to be excessive and preventing the payment of dividends to the minority.

(*c*) *to authorize civil proceedings* to be brought in the name of the company by such persons and on such terms as the court directs. This provision is of particular interest in that the court may authorize the bringing of civil proceedings by the company, seemingly without any of the restrictions of *Foss* on derivative claims. It should be noted that the claim would not be derivative. The company would be the plaintiff under the court order and there would be no need for the nominal defendant procedure.

(*d*) *to provide for the purchase* of a member's shares by the company or its other members and if the former is chosen, reduce the company's share capital as required.

This provision was, of course, applied in *Re London School of Electronics* (1985) where the order was that the majority shareholders should buy the shares of the member/director who had been excluded from management.

Directors and secretary

The management of a company is usually entrusted to a small group of people called directors. The main control of the shareholders lies in their power to appoint or remove directors. The company secretary is an important officer of the company in terms of its day-to-day administration.

Every public company must have at least two directors and every private company at least one. (S. 282.) Every company must have a secretary and a sole director cannot also be the secretary. (S. 283.)

Appointment

The first directors are usually named in the articles. The first directors in our company were named in that way (see Article 60). If no appointment is made in the articles the subscribers of the memorandum, or a majority of them, may make the appointment in writing.

Neither of these methods of appointment is effective unless the person concerned is named and gives consent in the statement of first directors, etc. (Form G10, see p. 87) which is required by s. 10(2).

Subsequently directors are usually appointed by the members of the company in general meeting by ordinary resolution. The board of directors is normally allowed to fill casual vacancies (see our Article 72), that is, vacancies which come about because e.g. a director, dies or resigns his directorship before his term of office has come to an end, or to appoint additional directors up to the permitted maximum. Our maximum is five (see Article 59), and so if we have only two directors the board could appoint up to three more under our Article 72. Directors approved as additional or to fill casual vacancies usually hold office until the next AGM (see Article 72) when the members decide by ordinary resolution whether they are to continue in office.

Generally, one or more full-time directors is appointed a *managing director*. The articles must provide for the appointment (see our Article 77) and articles normally enable the board to confer on the managing director any of the powers exercisable by the board and to vary his powers. (See Article 77.)

Many of the provisions of company law, e.g. the rules relating to directors' loans and the disclosure of those loans in the accounts (see p. 116), apply to 'shadow directors'. These are, under s. 741, people in accordance with whose directions or instructions the board of the company is accustomed to act but excluding professional advisers such as lawyers and accountants who may give the board professional advice on which they usually act.

The above provisions are intended to stop the evasion of the law relating to directors by a major shareholder who can control the company without being on the board. Such a person cannot, for example, get around the law relating to directors' loans by resigning temporarily from the board in order to allow the company to make him a loan. He would be covered because he would be a 'shadow director'.

Remuneration

If a director is to receive remuneration his contract of service (if he is an employee, executive director (e.g. sales director), or the articles (in the case of a fee paid non-executive director) must provide for it. (See our Article 61.) As regards an executive director's service contract, s. 318 says that the company must keep a copy of it, normally at the registered office, and that this copy is to be open to the inspection of members. While this may be of general interest, it is vital where a member or members intends to try to remove a director from the board before his term of office has expired. A director who is removed in this way has a right to sue for damages if he has a contract which has still some time to run.

Members can look at the contract and see what their act in removing the director might cost the company.

The notes to the accounts of the company must under Sch. 4 disclose the salaries or fees of the directors and the chairman.

Enforcement of fair dealing by directors

Duration of contracts of employment

Under s. 319 contracts of employment with directors which are for a period of more than five years and cannot be terminated by the company by notice, must be approved by the members by ordinary resolution in general meeting. If this is not done the contract can be terminated by reasonable notice, which is not defined by the Act but which at common law would be at least three months. (*James* v *Kent & Co. Ltd* (1950).)

This provision is also useful to those who want to remove a director from office. In the past boards of directors have given themselves long contracts without consulting the members. This has made it difficult to remove them because the compensation payable under a long service contract which had been broken by removal of the director concerned was sometimes more than the company could afford.

Substantial property transactions

Section 320 requires the approval of the members by ordinary resolution in general meeting of any contract to transfer to, or receive from, a director (or connected person, see below) a non-cash asset, e.g. land, exceeding £50 000 or exceeding 10 per cent of the company's net assets, whichever is the lower. The section does not apply, however, to non-cash assets of *less* than £1000 in value.

Thus a company whose assets less its liabilities amounted to £200 000 would have to comply with s. 320 in respect of a transaction with a director for a non-cash asset worth £20 000 or more.

Section 320 is designed to prevent directors (at least without member approval) from buying assets from the company at less than their true value or transferring their own property to the company at more than market value.

Transfers to and from connected persons are regarded as transfers to and from a director himself. The main category of connected persons are a director's wife or husband and children under eighteen, plus companies in which the director, together with his connected persons, hold one-fifth or more interest in the equity share capital. A director's partner is also included. (S. 346.)

Loans, quasi-loans, and credit taken by directors

Sections 330–347 deal with the above matters. The rules are more strict for 'relevant' companies than they are for 'non-relevant' companies.

Relevant companies are all public companies and private companies which are part of a group containing at least one public company. Free-standing private companies, i.e. those which are not members of a group, are non-relevant companies. Our own company is therefore a non-relevant company and under this heading we shall consider fully only the restrictions on free-standing private companies, though some comparison will be made with the position in relevant companies.

First, a description of loans, quasi-loans, and credit.

(*a*) *Loans and quasi-loans.* Basically, a quasi-loan

occurs when a director incurs personal expenditure but the company pays the bill. The director pays the company back later. In a loan the company would put the director in funds; he would buy, e.g. personal goods, and then repay the loan.

Examples of quasi-loans are –

(*i*) the company buys a yearly railway season ticket for a director to get to work; he repays the company over twelve months;

(*ii*) a director uses a company credit card to pay for personal goods, e.g. a video. The company pays the credit card company and the director repays his company over an agreed period;

(*iii*) the company purchases an airline ticket for a director's wife who is accompanying him on a business trip at the director's expense. The director repays the company over an agreed period.

It should be noted that the director's own expenses for the trip which would be paid by the company are not affected. It is only *personal* and not business transactions which are controlled.

(*b*) *Credit*. Examples of credit are –

(*i*) A furniture company sells furniture to a director on terms that payment be deferred for twelve months;

(*ii*) the company services a director's personal car in its workshops and the director is given time to pay;

(*iii*) the company sells a Rolls-Royce to the wife of one of its directors under a hire purchase agreement.

Control over loans, quasi-loans and credit

The position is as follows –

(*i*) There is no restriction on quasi-loans and credit on the directors or connected persons of our non-relevant company. Just by way of comparison, in a relevant company quasi-loans to directors and connected persons would be restricted to £1000 outstanding at any one time and repayment to the company of any quasi-loan incurred must be made within two months. Credit to a director or connected person would be restricted to £5000 but there is no particular time for repayment.

(*ii*) There is no bar on transactions with connected persons in our non-relevant company. In a relevant company transactions with connected persons are controlled as if they were with the director himself;

(*iii*) loans to directors and shadow directors. In our non-relevant publishing company we can make a loan

to a director only if it would assist in his duties. There is no limit to the amount which we can lend but the loan must be approved by an ordinary resolution of the members at or before the AGM after it is lent. If the loan is by contract repayable within six months after the next AGM it is not necessary to have the approval of the members.

This is a very restrictive provision because we must be able to show that the loan was to assist in duties. If, for example, one of our directors was being moved to another part of the country to run a branch office, we could provide a bridging loan to finance the purchase of a house in the area while he was selling his present home. Unless we can do this we can only lend up to £2500 maximum. All companies can do this for any purpose whatsoever and without the approval of the members or repayment within six months of the next AGM.

If we were a relevant company we could again lend to assist in duties but this time the loan would be limited to £10 000.

Non-relevant money-lending companies are better of. They can lend to one of their directors for any purpose and without limit provided the loan is on ordinary commercial terms, e.g. no better rate of interest or repayment terms than a member of the public would get if he was of the same financial standing as the director concerned.

Moneylending companies can also lend money to a director for the purpose of the purchase or improvement of his principal residence up to a maximum of £50 000, provided it is on the same terms as are available to the company's employees for house purchase and improvement loans.

Disclosure in accounts

All transactions involving loans, quasi-loans and credit to directors and their connected persons in all companies, relevant and non-relevant, must be disclosed in notes to the company's accounts. There is an exemption in the case of credit, provided the credit did not at any time during the year in question exceed £5000.

Even though, as in our company, there is no control over quasi-loans and credit, if any such transaction is entered into with a director or his connected person during the period covered by the accounts it must be disclosed. Thus the credit transaction in (*b*)(*iii*) above is not controlled in a non-relevant company but must be disclosed in its accounts. The wife is a connected person and the credit for a Rolls-Royce is bound to exceed £5000.

Disclosure is done by stating in the note to the accounts the name of the director concerned and the opening position in regard to a loan, quasi-loan or credit, the highest point reached in the year covered by the accounts and the closing position. A loan up to a maximum of £2500 which can be made without restriction must nevertheless be disclosed in this way.

If the directors refuse to disclose these matters in the company's accounts the auditors *must* do so in their report.

Material interests

Material interests of directors and their connected persons must also be disclosed in a note to the accounts. A material interest could be, for example, a contract to build a new office block which the company had entered into with a building firm run by a director, or by the spouse of a director.

It might also be a loan to the brother of a director. A brother is not a connected person but the loan might be a material interest.

The Companies Act 1985 states that the board of directors will decide whether a transaction is material, though the auditors must disclose it in their report if the directors fail to disclose it in the accounts and the auditor thinks it is material.

There are exemptions from disclosure for material interests of £1000 or less. Material interests exceeding £5000 must always be disclosed. Between these two figures it depends on the net assets of the company. Disclosure is required if the value of a material interest exceeds 1 per cent of the net assets of the company. Thus a company with net assets of £400 000 would have to disclose material interests of £4000 and above.

Removal

Under the provisions of s. 303 every company has power to remove any director before the end of his period of office.

The removal is carried out by an ordinary resolution of the members in general meeting. Special notice of twenty-eight days must be given to the company secretary that the resolution will be moved. The meeting at which the removal of a director under s. 303 is to be considered must be called by at least twenty-one days' notice.

The director is entitled to have a written statement in his defence, as it were, sent with the notice of the meeting. That failing, he can make an oral statement at the meeting.

As we have seen, the removal of a director does not affect any right he may have to claim money compensation for the dismissal.

Retirement

The company's articles generally provide that a certain number of directors shall retire annually. This is called retirement by rotation. Our article provides for one-third to retire annually (see Article 67). Those retiring are usually eligible for re-election (see Article 68).

Resignation

The articles usually provide that a director vacates office when he notifies his resignation to the company (see Article 64).

Disqualification

The grounds for disqualification of directors in our company are set out in Article 64. This is a usual type of article which companies have.

In addition, the court may disqualify directors. For example, under s. 3 of the Company Directors (Disqualification) Act 1986 the court can disqualify a director following persistent default in filing returns, accounts, and other documents with the Registrar. Persistent default is conclusively proved by the fact that the director has had three convictions in a period of five years for this kind of offence. The maximum period of disqualification in this case is five years.

A register of disqualification orders made by the court is kept by the Registrar of Companies. The public can inspect that register and see the names of those currently disqualified from acting as directors. Obviously, the name is removed at the end of the period of disqualification.

Powers of directors

The Act requires certain powers to be exercised by the members, e.g. alteration of the memorandum and articles. Apart from this the distribution of powers between the board and the members depends entirely on the articles (see Articles 62 and 63).

Duties of directors

The relationship between a company and its directors is that of principal and agent and as agents the directors stand in a *fiduciary relationship* to their principal, the company. In addition, directors owe *a duty of care at common law not to act negligently* in managing the company's affairs.

Fiduciary duties

Examples of these duties are as follows –

(i) *Directors must use their powers for the proper purpose.* That is, for the benefit of the company. If they do not do so the transactions they have entered into can be avoided by the company *provided that the person with whom the directors dealt was aware of the improper use of the power.*

Rolled Steel Products (Holdings) Ltd v British Steel Corporation (1985)

A Mr Shenkman was a 50 per cent shareholder in Rolled Steel and held all the issued share capital in another company called Scottish Steel. Scottish Steel owed a lot of money to BSC and Mr Shenkman had given his personal guarantee of that debt. BSC wanted more security and Mr S caused Rolled Steel to enter into a guarantee of the Scottish Steel debt as well. There was no benefit to Rolled Steel in this and BSC knew there was not.

Rolled Steel went into liquidation, as did Scottish Steel, and the court was asked to decide whether BSC could prove in the liquidation of Rolled Steel on the guarantee.

Eventually the Court of Appeal decided that they could not. The transaction was not *ultra vires* Rolled Steel because the objects clause contained a paragraph giving an express power to enter into guarantees. Rolled Steel also had an independent objects clause, as in *Cotman v Brougham* (1918), so the giving of guarantees was an object of the company which it could exercise whether there was

any benefit to it or not. However, Mr S and the other directors of Rolled Steel had exercised a power to give guarantees for an improper purpose, i.e. a purpose which was of no benefit to the company. The guarantee could, therefore, be avoided by the liquidator of Rolled Steel provided that those to whom it was given were aware of the improper purpose. Since BSC knew that there was no benefit to Rolled Steel in the guarantee they could not enforce it and prove in the liquidation.

Comment. If BSC had not been on notice of the circumstances in which Rolled Steel had been made to enter into the guarantee, they could have claimed upon it in the liquidation.

(ii) *Directors must not take secret profits and benefits from the company.* This is illustrated by the following case.

Industrial Development Consultants Ltd v Cooley (1972)

Mr Cooley, an architect, was the managing director of Industrial Development Consultants Ltd which carried on business as building and development consultants. He represented the company in negotiations with the Eastern Gas Board which were intended to get contracts for the company to design four large depots for the EGB.

The Board did not give the contracts to the company but soon afterwards asked Mr C whether he would take on the contracts in his private capacity. He told the company he was suffering from a nervous breakdown and got released from his service contract and was then given the EGB contracts. The company sued him for the profit on the four contracts. The court decided that since Mr C got the chance to make the profit while he was managing director of the company he must account to the company for all the profit received on the four contracts.

Duty of skill and care, i.e. not to act negligently

There is nothing in the Companies Act which sets out the standard of skill and care which a director must bring to his work. We must therefore turn to case law where the position is as set out below.

(i) *Non-executive directors without business qualifications or experience,* e.g. a doctor of medicine who has recently joined the board of his family company which makes steel castings.

The standard of care here is by reason of the decision in *Re City Equitable Fire Insurance Co.* (1925) *subjective* in that the director is only required to do his best. He is bound only to show such skill and care in the conduct of the company's business as may be expected from a person of his actual knowledge or experience (or lack of it). Also, he is not required to give all his attention to the company's business, nor to attend all board meetings. He can rely on the advice of the company's officials unless he has reason to suspect their competence.

(*ii*) *Non-executive directors with relevant qualifications and/or experience in business.* The standard here is *objective*. This means that a director of, say, an insurance company who is not an employee/executive director but who is professionally qualified in the field of insurance or has experience in that area must exercise such reasonable skill and care as may be *expected* from a person of his professional standing and/or experience.

This was made clear in *Dorchester Finance* v *Stebbing* (1977) where a chartered accountant and a non-qualified, but experienced, accountant were held liable along with a chartered accountant executive director for loss to the company caused by the making of loans which could not be recovered by the company because they infringed what is now the Consumer Credit Act 1974.

The two non-executive directors had facilitated the illegal lending by signing blank cheques, but had acted with good faith throughout. They had, however, failed to attend board meetings, leaving the running of the company to the executive director, Mr S. The court said that non-executive directors who were qualified or experienced could not rely on the subjective standard in the *Re City Equitable* case. They must assist in the management of the company.

(*iii*) *Executive directors.* Directors such as finance directors are normally employed for their expertise in company matters and under contracts of service. Here the decision in *Lister v Romford Ice and Cold Storage Co. Ltd* (1957) applies. This states that there is an implied term in the contract of service that the director will exercise the reasonable skill and care which a person in his position *ought* to have. Thus the test is objective and the *City Equitable* case does not apply.

The above duties, both fiduciary and of skill and care, are owed to the company. If loss is caused it is the company which must sue and which will be compensated. The duties are not owed directly to individual shareholders, even though the price of their shares might have fallen as a result of the breach of duty. (*Prudential Assurance Co. Ltd* v *Newman Industries Ltd* (*No. 2*) (1982).)

Duties to employees

Until 1980 directors owed no duties to employees but this was provided for in the Companies Act 1980. The current provision is s. 309 of the Companies Act 1985, which states that the matters to which the directors of a company are to have regard in the performance of their duties is to include the interests of the company's employees in general as well as the interests of its members.

The duty cannot be enforced directly by the employees since it is owed to the company (or, in other words, the shareholders). It means that in, say, a scheme of reconstruction of the company, the directors would have to show that they had considered the position of employees who might be made redundant.

However, s. 309 would not allow the directors to put the interests of the employees entirely before those of the company. For example, s. 309 would provide a justification for directors (if challenged by the shareholders) who carried out a reconstruction in such a way as to save jobs. It would not be within s. 309 for the directors to carry on the company's business at a loss and put it at risk of liquidation in order to save jobs.

All s. 309 means is that the directors cannot be accused by the shareholders of being in breach of their duty if they consider the interests of the employees. There is no positive duty to do anything for them.

Section 719 provides that the powers of a company are to be assumed to include the power to make provisions for its own or its subsidiary's employees, or former employees, when the company or its subsidiary ceases to carry on the whole or part of its business or transfers the whole or part of its business to someone else. This means that redundancy payments on a scale more generous than the state requires can be paid in the liquidation, or on a transfer of the business to those who lose their jobs.

Unless there are different provisions in the memorandum or articles, an ordinary resolution of the members is required to approve the exercise of this section. Once such a resolution has been passed, the power can be exercised by a liquidator. However, the payment can only come from surplus assets which would otherwise have gone to shareholders. There must be no reduction in the funds available to creditors.

Directors' duties to outsiders

Directors' duties are not in general owed to outsiders, i.e. those who are not shareholders or employees. However, where the directors make a contract with an outsider on behalf of a company, the directors may be liable, as other agents are, for breach of warranty of authority. The basis of this action is that an agent warrants to the third party that his principal has the capacity to make the contract and that he, the agent is authorized to make it. Thus, if the contract is beyond the company's powers or those of the directors and does not bind the company, there may be an action against the directors for breach of warranty of authority. This will be for money compensation.

Directors' meetings

Notice of board meetings must be given to all directors unless they are out of the United Kingdom. Unless the articles otherwise provide any director can call a board meeting (see our Article 78).

Quorum

Table A provides that the quorum necessary for the valid transaction of business by the directors may be fixed by the directors themselves and unless it is so fixed then the quorum is two directors personally present (see our Article 78).

Voting

Unless the articles say differently, each director has one vote and resolutions of the board require a majority of only one. If there is an equality of votes the resolution is lost unless the chairman has and exercises a casting vote (see our Article 78).

Directors as agents

If the board acting together (or collectively) or one director acting on his own, has *actual authority* to make a particular contract on behalf of the company and that contract is within the company's powers, then

the contract when made will be binding on the company.

However, where the directors act together, or as individuals, beyond their powers the position is as set out below.

Collective acts of the board

There are the following possibilities.

(1) *Companies Act 1985*. Section 35 provides that if a company enters into a transaction 'decided on by the directors' which is beyond the powers of the directors (or for that matter, the company, as we have seen) under the memorandum and articles, the other party may treat the company as bound by it if he acted in good faith. If the requirements are met a transaction made by the board beyond its powers would bind the company.

(2) *The rule in Turquand's case*. This rule is best explained by looking straightaway at the facts of the case.

Royal British Bank v Turquand (1856)

The articles of the company gave the directors the power to exercise the company's borrowing powers if they first obtained approval of the members by ordinary resolution in general meeting.

The directors borrowed money for the company but did not get the ordinary resolution and the question whether the loan was valid or not arose.

The court said it was. The bank could sue the company to recover its loan even though the directors were not, as it happened, authorized to borrow. The bank was an outsider and was entitled to assume that an ordinary resolution in general meeting had been passed.

Comment. The rule exists because there is constructive notice of the memorandum and articles. The rule states that where a transaction has been entered into by the directors as agents of the company but without authority, then provided the board might have had authority under the provisions of the memorandum and articles, the outsider is entitled to assume that the authority exists. Furthermore, he is not required to make enquiries of management to see whether proper internal procedures had been carried out. He is not forced to go 'indoors the management'. In fact the rule is called the 'indoor management rule'.

Of course, there would have been constructive notice

of the failure to file a special resolution in terms that it would not have been present on the company's file at the Companies Registry, and then the rule in *Turquand* would not apply as, the following case shows.

Irvine v Union Bank of Australia (1877)

A company's articles provided that the directors could borrow only up to an amount equal to half the paid up capital of the company.

The bank to its knowledge lent more than this and then claimed that its loan was valid under *Turquand*. The court decided that *Turquand* did not apply. If the limit had been increased a special resolution would have had to have been passed to alter the articles and this would have been filed at the Companies Registry. The bank, therefore, had constructive notice of the absence of this resolution on the file and that the directors' powers had not been increased. There was no need to go indoors the management to find this out, so the indoor management rule did not apply.

(3) *Relationship between s. 35 and the rule in Turquand's case.* Section 35 gives the same protection as *Turquand* where correct internal procedures were not followed but is in some ways wider than *Turquand*. This is because a person dealing with the company in good faith is not, under s. 35, regarded as having constructive notice of the company's memorandum and articles and of its file at the Companies Registry, certainly so far as this is necessary to be regarded as having knowledge of resolutions changing the memorandum or articles.

Thus an outsider would be protected by s. 35 even if the company's constitution expressly forbade the transaction, as in *Irvine*. The bank in *Irvine* would have had an enforceable loan if it had been able to use s. 35.

On the other hand, *Turquand*'s case would appear to be wider in some respects than s. 35 because it was applied in *Mahoney v East Holyford Mining Co.* (1875) where the directors who made the transaction had never been appointed at all, and in *Davis v R. Bolton & Co.* (1894) where the directors made a transfer of shares without a quorum at the meeting. The transfer was held valid.

Although s. 35 has not been fully interpreted by the courts, it seems logical to suppose that it would not apply in the circumstances of *Mahoney* and *Davis* because the court will presumably expect that when an English statute says 'decided on by the directors' it means directors who are properly appointed and have a quorum at the relevant meeting.

(4) *The proper purpose rule.* As we have seen, directors must use their agency powers for the proper purpose, that is for the benefit of the company. If they do not do so, the transactions they have entered into, while not *ultra vires* themselves or the company, can be avoided by the company provided that the person with whom the directors dealt was aware of the improper use of the power. (See again the *Rolled Steel* case at p. 119.)

Acts of individual directors and other officers of the company

To what extent will a company be bound by a transaction entered into by an individual director or other officer, e.g. the company secretary, who has no actual authority to enter into it?

There are the following possibilities –

(1) *Companies Act 1985.* As we have seen from the decision in *International Sales and Agencies Ltd v Marcus* (1982) (see p. 96), the sole effective director of a company may overcome his own lack of authority and even lack of power in the company itself under s. 35 because his transactions may be regarded as 'decided on by the directors' for the purposes of s. 35.

(2) *The rules of agency law – usual authority.* Where a director or other officer of a company has no actual authority to enter into a transaction an outsider may be able to regard the company as bound by it if it is usual in the company context for a director or officer to be able to enter into a transaction of the kind in question. Since it is usual to delegate wide powers to a managing director, an outsider will normally be protected if he is dealing with a person who is managing director or who has been held out as such by the company.

Thus in *Freeman & Lockyer v Buckhurst Park Properties Ltd* (1964), a managing director without express authority of the board, but with their knowledge, employed on behalf of the company a firm of architects and surveyors for the submission of an application for planning permission which involved preparing plans and defining boundaries. It was held that the company was liable to pay their fees. The managing director had bound the company by his acts which were within the usual authority of a managing director.

Where, however, the outsider deals with some other director or officer, his position is much less secure. An ordinary director and other officers of the company have little usual authority to bind the company.

Once one gets below the director level the position becomes even more of a problem. There is little, if any, usual authority in the executive of a company to make contracts on its behalf without actual authority, though it would appear that a company secretary has authority to bind the company in contracts relating to day-to-day administration.

Thus in *Panorama Developments* v *Fidelis Furnishing Fabrics* (1971), the secretary of a company ordered cars from a car hire firm representing that they were required to meet the company's customers at London Airport. Instead he used the cars for his own purposes. The company did not pay the bill so the car hire firm claimed from the secretary's company. It was held that the company was liable for its secretary had usual authority to make contracts such as the present one which was concerned with the administrative side of the business.

The secretary

Every company must have a secretary and a sole director cannot also be the secretary. (S. 283.) A corporation may be a secretary to a company, but a company, X, cannot have as secretary a company, Y, if the sole director of company Y is also the sole director or secretary of company X. (S. 283.)

Section 284 provides that a provision requiring or authorizing a thing to be done by or to a director and the secretary shall not be satisfied by its being done by or to the same person acting both as director and secretary. By s. 288 the register of directors includes particulars of the secretary.

It is usual for the secretary to be appointed by the directors who may fix his term of office and the conditions upon which he is to hold office. Our Article 63(c) confers such a power upon the board. The secretary is an employee of the company. He is regarded as such for the purpose of preferential payments in a winding up. (See p. 317.)

As we have seen, the secretary enjoys the power to make contracts on behalf of the company even without

authority. This is, however, restricted to contracts in the administrative operations of the company, including the employment of office staff and the management of the office, together with the hiring of transport. (See the *Panorama* case.)

His authority is not unlimited. He cannot, without authority, borrow money on behalf of the company. (*Re Cleadon Trust Ltd* (1939).) He cannot, without authority, commence an action in the courts on the company's behalf. (*Daimler Co. Ltd* v *Continental Tyre and Rubber Co. Ltd* (1916).) He cannot summon a general meeting himself (*Re State of Wyoming Syndicate* (1901), nor register a transfer of shares without the board's approval (*Chida Mines Ltd* v *Anderson* (1905)). These are powers which are vested in the directors.

Certain duties are directly imposed on the secretary by statute. The most important of these includes the submission of the annual return. (See p. 149.)

Company insolvency

Types of insolvency practitioners

(1) *The administrator.* The administration procedure which was set up by the Insolvency Act 1985 but is now contained in the Insolvency Act 1986 is designed and intended –

(*a*) to promote the survival of companies as a going concern; and

(*b*) to secure the preservation of jobs.

An administrator is appointed by the court on the petition of the company or on the petition of the directors, or on the petition of any creditors. The debt need not be of any minimum value and unsecured creditors can petition. This is the major contrast with the appointment of an administrative receiver (see below).

The Insolvency Act 1986 gives an administrator full powers to manage the company, hopefully to the point at which he can make it viable again and vacate office in favour of a permanent management.

(2) *A receiver.* A receiver is a person who has a legal right to receive property belonging to another. If A has lent money to company B, say, on the security of its Manchester warehouse (a fixed charge), the debenture which contains the terms of the loan will usually give the lender a right to appoint a receiver if repayment of

the loan plus interest are not made within a stated period of time.

The receiver in this case does not *manage* the company but merely sells the warehouse and pays off the lender, returning any balance to the company. It is this which provides a contrast with the appointment of an administrator and an administrative receiver, both of whom have power to manage the company.

(3) *An administrative receiver*. This type of receiver is appointed most usually by a bank under a debenture to secure an overdraft facility or by trustees for debenture holders in the case of a public issue of debenture stock (see p. 103).

In these cases the debenture or trust deed creating the charge will usually give the administrative receiver power over the whole undertaking of the company (a floating charge), including the power to *manage* the assets and carry on the business. Where this is so his title is changed to administrative receiver to reflect the fact that he is not a mere receiver but can also administer or run the company.

He is not bound to do so. His main duty is still to get sufficient money to pay the person who appointed him, e.g. the bank. If he can do this better by trading with the company for a while, then, unlike a receiver he may do this. Many administrative receivers do trade successfully, at least with parts of a company, to the point where these parts can be sold off as going concerns and their business is preserved.

This is not the primary function of the administrative receiver, as it is of an administrator. The trading is only part of the duty to pay the person making the appointment.

Generally speaking, then, an administrative receiver is used to provide a machinery under which a secured creditor, such as a bank, may recover money lent on the security of the company's assets when the terms of the loan have been breached, e.g. where a company is not making payment of interest and/or capital properly, or a bank has called in an overdraft having lost faith in the company's ability to repay it.

(4) *A liquidator*. A liquidator is a person placed in charge of a process under which a company's assets are sold and the debts of the company paid from the proceeds, any balance being returned to the shareholders.

When this has been done the company has nothing left and it may be dissolved, its separate existence as a corporate entity being brought to an end.

The liquidator is therefore in some senses an undertaker whose object is to bury the company as soon as possible after selling its assets and distributing the proceeds among its creditors and shareholders in accordance with their legal interests and priorities.

However, although a liquidator cannot carry on the company's business for any length of time, as an administrator or administrative receiver can, he may carry on its trade for a period of time where that would help a steady and more profitable sale of the assets over a period of time. (*Re Great Eastern Electric Co. Ltd* (1941).)

Qualifications of insolvency practitioners

To safeguard the public by ensuring that those who take over companies in the capacity of insolvency practitioner of whatever kind are appropriately qualified, the Insolvency Act 1986 provides that they must be members of a recognized professional body, e.g. the Institute of Chartered Accountants in England and Wales, and be authorized to act as an insolvency practitioner by the rules of that body. The professional bodies concerned must have applied successfully to the Trade Secretary for recognition.

The Act also provides for an individual application to the Trade Secretary. This is intended for those who do not belong to recognized professional bodies.

In both cases the professional body and the Trade Secretary must be satisfied that the education, training and experience requirements for the office are complied with.

Authorization is for the period stated in the authorization, e.g. twelve months, and may be withdrawn. Insolvency practitioners must also show that they have made proper bonding arrangements with an insurance company to deal with any loss which might happen to the company because of their maladministration of its affairs.

Appointment of insolvency practitioners

We can now consider in more detail how the various insolvency practitioners are appointed.

Appointment of an administrator

Whereas the appointment of a receiver and an administrative receiver or a liquidator can in appropriate circumstances, as we shall see, be made without the aid of the court, an administrator can, under the Insolvency Act 1986, only be appointed by the court.

The court must be satisfied –

(*i*) that the company is (or is likely to become) insolvent; and

(*ii*) that the order is likely to secure the survival of the company; or

(*iii*) the sale of its assets will be more advantageous than under a liquidation.

The administrator may be given specific powers in the order to re-organize the company, including making compromises with its members and/or creditors in order to achieve (*ii*) above.

An administration order may be applied for –

(*i*) by the members by ordinary resolution; or

(*ii*) the directors following a board resolution; or

(*iii*) a creditor (or creditors).

All or any of these groups may apply together or separately.

There can be no application by an individual member or individual director, though presumably a sole effective director, such as we discussed in *International Sales and Agencies Ltd* v *Marcus* (1982) (see p. 96) could present a petition.

So far as creditors are concerned, the debt need not be of any minimum value (contract compulsory liquidation and individual insolvency), and unsecured creditors can petition. The appointment of a receiver is confined to those secured creditors with a fixed charge and the appointment of an administrative receiver to those secured creditors with a floating charge over the whole undertaking of the company.

The holder of a floating charge, such as a bank, can block the making of an administration order. If the bank has already appointed an administrative receiver it must consent to the making of the order. If it has not made such an appointment it must be informed that the petition has been presented and may make an appointment of an administrative receiver who may then carry out his functions and render the appointment of an administrator pointless.

Appointment of an administrative receiver

Administrative receivers are appointed by secured creditors under express powers in a debenture or a trust deed. The debenture holder or the trustees will have made sure that the debenture or trust deed gives details as to the fact situations in which an appointment can be made and the way of making it.

If the loan is for a fixed period of time, say three years, the following fact situations in which an administrative receiver may be appointed are normally included –

(*i*) if the company goes into liquidation;

(*ii*) if a judgment creditor or landlord is levying execution or distress. This means that a person to whom the company owes money has sued the company and got a judgment. The company has not paid it, so the creditor is putting the bailiffs in to take the company's property and sell it to pay the judgment debt. A landlord who is owed rent can also do this but when he does it is called 'distress';

(*iii*) if the company ceases to carry on business;

(*iv*) if the company is in breach of any condition of the charge; for example if it has not paid interest or repaid the loan in the time scale agreed;

(*v*) if someone else appoints a receiver. This could happen, for example, where several persons had fixed charges over specific assets of the company and one or more of them had appointed a receiver to sell the property to pay the debt.

If the loan is repayable on demand, as with a bank overdraft facility, then, although it is usual to include terms similar to those at (*i*) to (*v*) above, they are not really necessary, since in these circumstances it is enough to include in the debenture or trust deed a provision that an administrative receiver may be appointed if the money is not repaid following a formal demand from the lender, e.g. the bank.

Formalities for appointment: out of court

The formalities for appointment are set out in the debenture or trust deed. Appointment will be in writing and sometimes a deed may be required.

The Insolvency Act 1986 provides that an administrative receiver is the agent of the company and not of the debenture holder(s). This means that he can make contracts on behalf of the company.

However, the Insolvency Act 1986 provides that the receiver is personally liable on any contract which he makes unless the contract provides to the contrary. The

Act gives the receiver an indemnity (the right to reimburse himself in full) from the assets of the company should he have to meet a liability on a contract.

If the assets of the company are not sufficient the receiver must meet the liability in full or to the extent that the assets are not enough. He may, however, take an indemnity also from the debenture holder(s).

Formalities for appointment: by the court

The power to appoint receivers is given to the court by s. 37 of the Supreme Court Act 1981.

Sometimes a receiver may be appointed by the court, for example in the rare case where a secured creditor has not taken power in the debenture to appoint a receiver himself.

In addition, and more likely, the court will appoint a receiver even though the events in a debenture have not occurred so that an appointment out of court cannot be made. This could happen where the company has not stopped paying interest and/or capital and yet the assets of the company are at risk and a receiver is needed to protect the security. This was done, for example, in *Re London Pressed Hinge Co. Ltd* (1905) where unsecured creditors had got a judgment against the company and were about to levy execution – that is, to sell the company's property to pay their debts.

Notification of appointment

The person or persons who appoint an administrative receiver or get a court order appointing one must within seven days give notice of the appointment to the Registrar of Companies. The receiver should obtain confirmation from the persons involved that this has been done.

The administrative receiver must immediately give notice of his appointment to the company and notify all creditors within twenty-eight days, though the court can dispense with the notifying of creditors, e.g. where the assets are not valuable enough to warrant the expense.

Appointment of a liquidator

This depends upon the type of liquidation. There are two ways of winding up companies. These are set out below.

A compulsory winding up

(*a*) *Procedure.* The procedure is by way of petition to the Companies Court, which is part of the Chancery Division. A creditor is the most usual petitioner. The debt which the company owes to him (or to him and other creditors joining with him in the petition) must be at least £750.

There must also be a ground or grounds upon which to base the petition. These grounds, taken from the Insolvency Act 1986, are –

(1) a special resolution by the members to wind up. This would be extremely rare;

(2) failure of a newly-incorporated public company to obtain a certificate under s. 117 of the Companies Act 1985, allowing it to trade and borrow money, within one year of incorporation (see p. 85);

(3) failure to start business within one year of incorporation or suspending the business for a whole year;

(4) that the number of members has fallen below two;

(5) that the company is unable to pay its debts. This is assumed to be the case if a creditor for a sum *exceeding* £750 has served a demand in writing for payment and the company has failed to pay that sum or give a security for it within three weeks of serving the demand;

(6) that it is just and equitable that the company be wound up. A member will usually petition under this last heading and the petitions presented have been for a variety of reasons. In one case, *Re German Date Coffee Co.* (1882), two shareholders successfully petitioned for a winding up on the just and equitable ground where the company was formed to make coffee from dates by a German patent. It failed to get that patent and the court wound it up on the grounds that its principal object had failed. The company could not achieve the objects for which it was formed.

(*b*) *Commencement of liquidation.* If the court makes a winding up order the company is in liquidation but the date of the commencement of it is the earlier date on which the petition was presented to the court. If the directors have sold off the company's property between the time of presentation of the petition and the making of the winding up order, these sales are void so that if, for example, the directors had sold the company's assets off cheaply to other companies in which they had an interest, the liquidator could recover the property on taking over.

(c) *The Official Receiver.* When the order for compulsory liquidation is made a civil servant from the Official Receiver's office takes over as provisional liquidator. He is required to call separate meetings of members and creditors to see if a person other than someone from the Official Receiver's office should become liquidator, e.g. a chartered accountant from the private sector. The Official Receiver's representative is the chairman of the meetings and if the meetings decide on someone else the court will make the appointment. If there are different candidates the court decides which shall act. Most often the Official Receiver continues to act because these companies which are in compulsory liquidation are often heavily insolvent. If an accountant from the private sector is nominated it is by an ordinary resolution of the members and by a majority in number and value of the creditors.

Suppose the company has a hundred creditors. A is owed £1000, the other ninety-nine are owed £1 each. The others cannot make the nomination without A. They have the majority in number but not value. A plus forty-nine of the rest cannot make the nomination; they have the majority in value but not in number. However, A plus fifty of the rest can make the nomination; they now have a majority in number and value. It will be seen that creditors for small amounts cannot normally make the nomination of the liquidator.

If a liquidator from the private sector does act he may obtain assistance from a committee of creditors appointed at the meeting of creditors at which the liquidator was nominated. The committee is also required to authorize certain acts of a private sector liquidator, e.g. that he may carry on the business of the company so far as is necessary for a beneficial winding up.

Normally, however, the Official Receiver's representative continues to act and he does so without reference to any committee of creditors.

Voluntary winding up

(a) *Procedure.* In practice a company may be wound up voluntarily under the Insolvency Act 1986 in the following circumstances –

(i) if the members of the company resolve by special resolution that the company should be wound up voluntarily; or

(ii) if the members of the company resolve by extraordinary resolution to the effect that it cannot by reason of its liabilities continue its business and that it is advisable to wind up.

In (i) above the procedure will normally follow that laid down for a members' voluntary winding up but in (ii), in view of the company's financial problems, it would normally be a creditors' winding up.

(b) *Declaration of solvency.* In (i) above the directors will normally be able to give what is called a declaration of solvency. This states that the company is solvent and will be able to pay its debts within a stated period not exceeding twelve months from the commencement of the winding up.

The directors must make the declaration in the five weeks before the special resolution referred to in (i) above was passed or on that date but before the resolution was passed. A statement of the company's assets and liabilities must be given with the declaration and it must be filed with the Registrar of Companies.

If the directors make the declaration without reasonable grounds to believe that the company will be able to pay its debts, they are liable at the maximum to an unlimited fine and imprisonment for up to two years.

Also, if during a members' voluntary the liquidator appointed by the members is of the opinion that the company will not be able to pay its debts in line with the declaration of solvency, the Insolvency Act 1986 provides that he must call a meeting of creditors within twenty-eight days of reaching that opinion and put in front of the meeting a statement of the company's assets and liabilities.

As from the date when the liquidator calls the meeting of creditors, the company is in a creditors' voluntary winding-up and the creditors' meeting referred to above can appoint a liquidator to take over from the person appointed by the members and may also appoint a committee of creditors to assist the liquidator. In other words, the creditors are then in the driving seat.

(c) *Appointment of liquidator.* If a declaration of solvency can be given the winding up proceeds as a members' voluntary and the members appoint the liquidator by ordinary resolution. The court does not make the appointment as it does in a compulsory winding up following usually upon a nomination by creditors.

If a declaration of solvency cannot be given the members, by ordinary resolution, may nominate a liquidator. However, the creditors make the appointment and can appoint the members' nominee or someone else, subject to an appeal to the court by any director, member or creditor of the company. The creditors may also appoint a committee to act with the liquidator.

(*d*) *Commencement of winding up.* A voluntary winding up, whether a members' or creditors', commences on the passing of the relevant resolutions referred to in (*a*)(*i*) and (*ii*) above.

Legal effects of appointment of insolvency practitioners

Effect of appointment of administrator

(*a*) *Between the date of the petition for an administration order and the making of an order or the dismissal of the petition.* While the procedure for obtaining an administration order is being gone through the Insolvency Act 1986 provides that –

(*i*) no resolution can be passed or order made for winding up. A person can present a petition for compulsory winding up but the court cannot make a winding up order on it;

(*ii*) a person entitled to appoint an administrative receiver under a debenture, e.g. a bank, can do so and the administrative receiver may carry out his functions of, for example, realizing the company's assets to pay his debenture holders. This would in many cases make the petition for an administration order pointless and it would be better to withdraw it;

(*iii*) if an administrative receiver is in post when the petition for an administration order is made, he, too, can carry out his functions. Again, in many cases it would be pointless to petition for an administration order if an administrative receiver was already in post but the Insolvency Act of 1986 does allow it;

(*iv*) a person with a fixed charge cannot take any steps to enforce it by the appointment of a receiver. If a receiver is in post under a fixed charge he cannot continue with his functions;

(*v*) the owner of goods which the company is leasing, or has taken on hire purchase or purchased under retention arrangements in the contract of sale (see further p. 214) cannot legally take any steps to take them back;

(*vi*) no other legal proceedings may be commenced or continued, nor can the company's property be taken to be sold to pay an existing judgment debt.

It should be noted that the court may allow a person to exercise the rights denied him by (*iv*), (*v*) and (*vi*) above. These rights can also be exercised against an administrative receiver if one is in post even while the court is deciding whether to appoint an administrator, but not if the person who appointed the administrative receiver has consented to the making of an administration order.

In effect, therefore, the above provisions suspend the rights of existing unsecured creditors and secured creditors with a fixed charge. Those with a floating charge under which an administrative receiver has been or could be appointed must consent. Holders of a floating charge under which administrative receivers are appointed must be informed of the presentation of a petition for an administration order and so they will be alerted to it.

(*b*) *Effect of making an administration order.* Once the order is made the position is as follows –

(*i*) any petition for winding up is dismissed;

(*ii*) any administrative receiver in post vacates office;

(*iii*) a receiver of part only of the company's property, e.g. a receiver under a fixed charge on the company's land and buildings, vacates office if the administrator requests him to do so;

(*iv*) while the order is in force no resolution may be passed or order made for winding up;

(*v*) no administrative receiver may be appointed and also, unless the court or the administrator permits it, no steps may be taken to repossess goods as in (*a*)(*v*) above, and no other legal proceedings as in (*a*)(*vi*) above can be commenced or continued.

Administrator's powers

The Insolvency Act 1986 gives a general power to manage the company and sets out a list of specially mentioned powers. These cover everything an administrator is likely to want to do.

He acts as agent of the company so employees are not dismissed by his appointment, though he may of course dismiss them as agent of the company and they would then have a right to sue the company for redundancy or unfair dismissal.

Directors are not dismissed but their powers of

management cannot be exercised unless the administrator consents. However the administrator can remove directors and appoint new ones. He can thus assemble a new management team, which is particularly important where the object of the administration order is the survival of the company.

Effect of appointing an administrative receiver

The directors are not dismissed by the appointment of an administrative receiver but their powers to deal with the company's property are suspended during the receivership.

As regards employees, where the administrative receiver is appointed out of court, e.g. by a bank under powers in a debenture, contracts of employment will continue because under the Insolvency Act 1986 a receiver appointed out of court is an agent of the company. Although the appointment of an administrative receiver does not terminate contracts of employment, an administrative receiver may dismiss employees as an agent of the company and they would have a claim against the company for redundancy or unfair dismissal as the case may be. If an administrative receiver allows an employee to work for the company for more than fourteen days after the receivership commenced, he is regarded as having adopted the contract of service and is personally liable to pay wages, though he is able to get the money back from the assets of the company if it has any.

In most cases the contract of the managing director will be terminated by the appointment of an administrative receiver because the administrative receiver is going to manage the company and the two posts are inconsistent with each other. However, in *Griffiths v Secretary of State for Social Services* (1973) a managing director was held not to be dismissed when a receiver was appointed to his company, but only on a part-time basis.

A receiver who is appointed by the court is not an agent of the company but an officer of the court, and the main difference in this case is that employees of the company are automatically dismissed.

Effect of the appointment of a liquidator

(*a*) In a *compulsory winding up* the court order brings to an end contracts of employment with the company. The powers of the directors to act on the company's behalf are also ended. Employees are

therefore dismissed, though the liquidator may re-employ them where, for example, the business is to be continued for a while so that a better price might be obtained for the assets. Even so, employees can probably regard themselves as dismissed because the company has ceased to employ them, the new contract being with the liquidator.

(*b*) In a *voluntary winding up* the powers of the directors cease on the appointment of a liquidator. If the company's business ceases employees are dismissed. If the liquidator continues the business for a while the position is as in (*a*) above.

Major duties of insolvency practitioners

The administrator

The major duty of the administrator relates to his proposals for the administration. Within three months of his appointment, or a longer period if the court allows it, the administrator must lay his proposals for the company before a meeting of all the creditors. Copies of it go to all the members and to the Registrar.

The meeting of creditors may ask for modification of the proposals but the administrator is not required to accept these unless he approves of them. If no agreement can be reached with the creditors the court may discharge the administration order. There is no need for the court to approve the proposals; its function is limited to discharging the administration order if the proposals are not approved.

The meeting which approves the administrator's original proposals may establish a creditors' committee. This may call for information about the administrator's activities. Its consent is not required for anything he does.

The administrative receiver

An administrative receiver's first duty is to deal with the assets of the company, to satisfy, first, the claims of the preferential creditors, if any – for example, wages or salaries of employees due, but not paid within the four months before the appointment of the administrative receiver up to a maximum of £800 for each employee – and, second, the claim of the debenture holder(s) who appointed him.

His duty is to apply the proceeds of the assets which he realizes as follows:

(*i*) in paying his own expenses and remuneration;

(*ii*) in meeting the costs incurred by those who brought an action in court, if any, to secure his appointment;

(*iii*) in paying preferential creditors; and

(*iv*) in meeting the debenture debt with interest to the date of payment.

Any surplus will be paid over to the company or to the liquidator if the company is in the course of liquidation.

The liquidator

A liquidator is under a duty to get in and realize the company's property and pay out the proceeds in accordance with priorities established by law, i.e. –

(*i*) the costs of winding up;

(*ii*) the preferential debts;

(*iii*) creditors with a security over the company's property;

(*iv*) unsecured ordinary creditors; and

(*v*) the deferred debts.

These are, for example, sums due to members in their capacity as members, such as dividends which have been declared but not paid.

Any surplus will be distributed among members according to their rights under the articles or the terms of the issue of their shares.

Conclusion of insolvency procedures

Administration

If the business succeeds during the period of the administration the administrator will hand it back to the directors. If it fails, or is not sold, or its assets disposed of, then a winding up will normally follow. A liquidator must be appointed to wind up the company formally.

In addition the Insolvency Act 1986 provides that the administrator (and only he) may apply to the court for discharge of the administration order if he is of opinion that its purposes have been achieved or are impossible or if the creditors require him to do so.

An administrative receivership

As we have seen, when the administrative receiver has made all the necessary payments in the order in which the law requires, any surplus will be handed over to the company's directors or to the liquidator, if it is in the course of liquidation.

Liquidation

The final stages of a winding up are as follows –

(*a*) *compulsory winding up*. Once the liquidator has paid off the creditors and distributed the surplus assets (if any) and summoned a final meeting of the company's creditors he can vacate office. The company is dissolved at the end of three months from the receipt by the Registrar of the liquidator's notice that the final meeting of creditors has been held and that the liquidator has vacated office.

(*b*) *Voluntary winding up*. In a voluntary winding up the liquidator will call final meetings of the company and creditors for approval of his accounts. Within a week he will file with the Registrar his accounts and a return of the meeting and two months later the company is dissolved.

Whether it is a compulsory or voluntary winding up the court can restore the company to the Register within two years if, for example, further assets are discovered which should have been distributed to creditors.

Specimen Memorandum of Association

The Companies Act 1985

COMPANY LIMITED BY SHARES

Memorandum of Association of

RICHES, KEENAN PUBLISHING LIMITED

1. The name of the company is Riches, Keenan Publishing Ltd.
2. The registered office of the company will be situate in England
3. The objects for which the company is established are:

(a) To carry on business as authors, editors, proprietors, printers and publishers of newspapers, journals, pamphlets, circulars, magazines, books and other literary and advertising works and undertakings, and to carry on all or any of the businesses of printers, stationers, litho-graphers, stereotypers, electrotypers, photographic printers, chromo lithographers, photo lithographers, photo process, steel and copper plate engravers, die sinkers, typefounders, photographers, dealers in parchment, advertising agents, designers, draughtsmen, publishers and dealers in or manufacturers of any other articles or things of a character similar or analogous to the foregoing or any of them, or connected therewith and to establish and carry on, as may from time to time by the company be thought fit, a tutorial and lecturing system, college, school, or colleges and schools, where students may receive tuition in economics, sciences, arts, industry, languages, commerce, journalism, and all or any other branches of knowledge, or endeavour to provide for the giving and holding of lectures, scholarships, exhibitions, classes and photographic and recording disc and tape media for the promotion or advancement of education.

(b) To carry on any other business (whether manufacturing or otherwise) which may seem to the company capable of being conveniently carried on in connection with the above objects, or calculated directly or indirectly to enhance the value of or render more profitable any of the company's property.

(c) To purchase or by any other means acquire any freehold, leasehold, or other property for any estate or interest whatever, and any rights, privileges, or easements over or in respect of any property, and any buildings, offices, factories, mills, works, wharves, roads, railways, tramways, machinery, engines, rolling stock, vehicles, plant, live and dead stock, barges, vessels, or things, and any real or personal property or rights whatsoever which may be necessary for, or may be conveniently used with, or may enhance the value of any other property of the company.

(d) To build, construct, maintain, alter, enlarge, pull down, and remove or replace any buildings, offices, factories, mills, works, wharves, roads, railways, tramways, machinery, engines, walls, fences, banks, dams, sluices, or watercourses and to clear sites for the same, or to join with any person, firm, or company in doing any of the things aforesaid, and to work, manage, and control the same or join with others in so doing.

(e) To apply for, register, purchase, or by other means acquire and protect, prolong and renew, whether in the United Kingdom or elsewhere, any patents, patent rights, brevets d'invention, licences, trade marks, designs, protections, and concessions which may appear likely to be advantageous or useful to the company, and to use and turn to account and to manufacture under or grant licences or privileges in respect of the same, and to expend money in experimenting upon and testing and in improving or seeking to improve any patents, inventions, or rights which the company may acquire or propose to acquire.

(f) To acquire and undertake the whole or any part of the business, goodwill, and assets of any person, firm, or company carrying on or proposing to carry on any of the businesses which this company is authorized to carry on, and as part of the consideration for such acquisition to undertake all or any of the liabilities of such person, firm, or company, or to acquire an interest in, amalgamate with, or enter into partnership or into any arrangement for sharing profits, or for co-operation, or for limiting competition, or for mutual assistance with any such person, firm or company, or for subsidizing or otherwise assisting any such person, firm or company, and to give or accept, by way of consideration for any of the acts or things aforesaid or property acquired, any shares, debentures, debenture stock or securities that may be agreed upon, and to hold and retain, or sell, mortgage, and deal with any shares, debentures, debenture stock, or securities so received.

(*g*) To improve, manage, cultivate, develop, exchange, let on lease or otherwise, mortgage, charge, sell, dispose of, turn to account, grant rights and privileges in respect of, or otherwise deal with all or any part of the property and rights of the company.

(*h*) To invest and deal with the moneys of the company not immediately required in such shares or upon such securities and in such manner as may from time to time be determined.

(*i*) To lend and advance money or give credit to such persons, firms, or companies and on such terms as may seem expedient, and in particular to customers of and others having dealings with the company, and to give guarantees or become security for any such persons, firms, or companies.

(*j*) To borrow or raise money in such manner as the company shall think fit, and in particular by the issue of debentures or debenture stock (perpetual or otherwise), and to secure the repayment of any money borrowed, raised, or owing, by mortgage, charge, or lien upon the whole or any part of the company's property or assets (whether present or future), including its uncalled capital, and also by a similar mortgage, charge, or lien to secure and guarantee the performance by the company of any obligation or liability it may undertake.

(*k*) To draw, make, accept, endorse, discount, execute, and issue promissory notes, bills of exchange, bills of lading, warrants, debentures, and other negotiable or transferable instruments.

(*l*) To apply for, promote, and obtain any Act of Parliament, provisional order, or licence of the Department of Trade and Industry or other authority for enabling the company to carry any of its objects into effect, or for effecting any modification of the company's constitution, or for any other purpose which may seem expedient, and to oppose any proceedings or applications which may seem calculated directly or indirectly to prejudice the company's interests.

(*m*) To enter into any arrangements with any governments or authorities (supreme, municipal, local, or otherwise), or any companies, firms, or persons that may seem conducive to the attainment of the company's objects or any of them, and to obtain from any such government, authority, company, firm, or person any charters, contracts, decrees, rights, privileges, and concessions which the company may think desirable, and to carry out, exercise, and comply with any such charters, contracts, decrees, rights, privileges, and concessions.

(*n*) To subscribe for, take, purchase, or otherwise acquire and hold shares or other interests in or securities of any other company having objects altogether or in part similar to those of this company or carrying on any business capable of being carried on so as directly or indirectly to benefit this company.

(*o*) To act as agents or brokers and as trustees for any person, firm, or company, and to undertake and perform sub-contracts, and also to act in any of the businesses of the company through or by means of agents, brokers, sub-contractors, or others.

(*p*) To remunerate any person, firm, or company rendering services to this company, either by cash payment or by the allotment to him or them of shares or securities of the company credited as paid up in full or in part or otherwise as may be thought expedient.

(*q*) To pay all or any expenses incurred in connection with the promotion, formation, and incorporation of the company, or to contract with any person, firm or company to pay the same, and to pay commissions to brokers and others for underwriting, placing, selling, or guaranteeing the subscription of any shares, debentures, debenture stock or securities of this company.

(*r*) To support and subscribe to any charitable or public object, and any institution, society, or club which may be for the benefit of the company or its employees, or may be connected with any town or place where the company carries on business; to give or award pensions, annuities, gratuities, and superannuation or other allowances or benefits or charitable aid to any persons who are or have been directors of, or who are or have been employed by, or who are serving or have served the company, and to the wives, widows, children, and other relatives and dependants of such persons; to make payments towards insurance; and to set up, establish, support, and maintain superannuation and other funds or schemes (whether contributory or non-contributory) for the benefit of any such persons and of their wives, widows, children, and other relatives and dependants.

(*s*) To promote any other company for the purpose of acquiring the whole or any part of the business or property and undertaking any of the liabilities of this company, or of undertaking any business or operations which may appear likely to assist or benefit this company or to enhance the value of any property or business of this company, and to place or guarantee the placing of, underwrite, subscribe for, or otherwise acquire all or any part of the shares or securities of any such company as aforesaid.

(*t*) To sell or otherwise dispose of the whole or any part of the business or property of the company, either together or in portions, for such consideration as the company may think fit, and in particular for shares, debentures, or securities of any company purchasing the same.

(*u*) To distribute among the members of the company in kind any property of the company, and in particular any shares, debentures, or securities of other companies belonging to this company or of which this company may have the power of disposing.

(*v*) To procure the company to be registered or recognized in any part of the world.

(*w*) To do all such other things as may be deemed incidental or conducive to the attainment of the above objects or any of them.

It is hereby expressly declared that each sub-clause of this clause shall be construed independently of the other sub-clauses hereof, and that none of the objects mentioned in any sub-clause shall be deemed to be merely subsidiary to the objects mentioned in any other sub-clause.

4. The liability of the members is limited.

5. The share capital of the company is £10 000 divided into 10 000 shares of £1 each.

WE, the several persons whose names, addresses and descriptions are subscribed are desirous of being formed into a company in pursuance of this Memorandum of Association, and we respectively agree to take the number of shares in the capital of the company set opposite our respective names.

Names, addresses and descriptions of subscribers	Number of shares taken by each subscriber
SARAH RICHES 1 High Street, Barchester AUTHOR/LECTURER *Sarah Riches*	ONE
DENIS KEENAN 2 Low Street, Barchester AUTHOR/LECTURER *Denis Keenan*	ONE
Total Shares Taken	TWO

Dated the 3 March 1986
Witness to the above signatures:
    John Green
    3 Middle Street,
    Barchester

John Green

Specimen Articles of Association

The Companies Act 1985

COMPANY LIMITED BY SHARES

Articles of Association of

RICHES KEENAN PUBLISHING LIMITED

Preliminary

1. The Regulations contained in Table A in the Schedule to the Companies (Tables A-F) Regulations 1985, shall not apply to this Company.

2. In these Articles, unless the context otherwise requires –

'The Act' shall mean the Companies Act, 1985 and every other Act incorporated therewith, or any Act or Acts of Parliament substituted therefor; and in case of any such substitution the references in these presents to the provisions of non-existing Acts of Parliament shall be read as referring to the provisions substituted therefor in the new Act or Acts of Parliament.

'The Register' shall mean that Register of Members to be kept as required by Section 352 of The Companies Act 1985.

'Month' shall mean calendar month.

'Paid up' shall include 'credited as paid up.'

'Secretary' shall include any person appointed to perform the duties of Secretary temporarily.

'In writing' shall include printed, lithographed, and typewritten.

Words which have a special meaning assigned to them in the Act shall have the same meaning in these presents.

Words importing the singular number only shall include the plural, and the converse shall also apply.

Words importing males shall include females.

Words importing individuals shall include corporations.

Share capital

3. Subject to the provisions of the Act and without prejudice to any rights attached to any existing shares, any share may be issued with such rights or restrictions as the company may by ordinary resolution determine. Subject to the provisions of the Act shares may be issued which are to be redeemed or are to be liable to be redeemed at the option of the company or the holder on such terms and in such manner as may be provided by the terms of issue.

Shares and certificates

4. Subject to the provisions of the Act the company may purchase its own shares (including any redeemable shares) and make a payment in respect of the redemption or purchase of its own shares otherwise than out of distributable profits of the company or the proceeds of a fresh issue of shares.

5. The directors may make arrangements on the issue of shares for a difference between the holders of such shares in the amount of calls to be paid and in the time of payment of such calls.

6. The company shall be entitled to treat the person whose name appears upon the register in respect of any share as the absolute owner thereof, and shall not be under any obligation to recognize any trust or equity or equitable claim to or interest in such share, whether or not it shall have express or other notice thereof.

7. Every member shall be entitled without payment to one certificate under the common seal of the company, specifying the share or shares held by him, with the distinctive numbers thereof (if any) and the amount paid up thereon. Such certificate shall be delivered to the member within two months after the allotment or registration of the transfer, as the case may be, of such share or shares.

8. If any member shall require additional certificates he shall pay for each such additional certificate such reasonable sum, as the directors shall determine.

9. If any certificate be defaced, worn out, lost, or destroyed, it may be renewed on payment of such reasonable sum as the directors may prescribe, and the person requiring the new certificate shall surrender the defaced or worn-out certificate, or give such evidence of its loss or destruction and such indemnity to the company as the directors think fit.

Joint holders of shares

10. Where two or more persons are registered as the holders of any share they shall be deemed to hold the same as joint tenants with benefit of survivorship, subject to the provisions following –

(a) The company shall not be bound to register more than three persons as the holders of any share.

(b) The joint holders of any share shall be liable, severally as well as jointly, in respect of all payments which ought to be made in respect of such share.

(c) On the death of any one of such joint holders the survivor or survivors shall be the only person or persons recognized by the company as having any title to such share; but the directors may require such evidence of death as they may deem fit.

(d) Any one of such joint holders may give effectual receipts for any dividend, bonus or return of capital payable to such joint holders.

(e) Only the person whose name stands first in the register of members as one of the joint holders of any share shall be entitled to delivery of the certificate relating to such share, or to receive notices from the company, or to attend or vote at general meetings of the company, and any notice given to such person shall be deemed notice to all the joint holders; but any one of such joint holders may be appointed the proxy of the person entitled to vote on behalf of the said joint holders, and as such proxy to attend the vote at general meetings of the company.

Calls on shares

11. The directors may from time to time make calls upon the members in respect of all moneys unpaid on their shares, provided that no call shall be payable within one month after the date when the last instalment of the last preceding call shall have been made payable; and each member shall, subject to receiving fourteen days' notice at least, specifying the time and place for payment, pay the amount called on his shares to the persons and at the times and places appointed by the directors. A call may be made payable by instalments.

12. A call shall be deemed to have been made at the time when the resolution of the directors authorizing such call was passed.

13. If a call payable in respect of any share or any instalment of a call be not paid before or on the day appointed for payment thereof, the holder for the time being of such share shall be liable to pay interest for the same at such rate as the directors shall determine from the day appointed for the payment of such call or instalment to the time of actual payment; but the directors may if they shall think fit waive the payment of such interest or any part thereof.

14. If by the terms of the issue of any shares, or otherwise, any amount is made payable at any fixed time or by instalments at any fixed times, whether on account of the amount of the shares or by way of premium, every such amount or instalment shall be payable as if it were a call duly made by the directors, and of which due notice had been given; and all the provisions hereof with respect to the payment of calls and interest thereon, or to the forefeiture of shares

for nonpayment of calls, shall apply to every such amount or instalment and the shares in respect of which it is payable.

Transfer of shares

15. The instrument of transfer of any share in the company shall be in writing, and shall be executed by or on behalf of the transferor and unless the share is fully paid by or on behalf of the transferee, and the transferor shall be deemed to remain the holder of such share until the name of the transferee is entered in the register in respect thereof.

Transmission of shares

17. On the death of any member (not being one of several joint holders of a share) the executors or administrators of such deceased member shall be the ony persons recognized by the company as having any title to such share.

18. Any person becoming entitled to a share in consequence of the death or bankruptcy of a member shall, upon such evidence being produced as may from time to time be required by the directors, have the right either to be registered as a member in respect of the share or, instead of being registered himself, to make such transfer of the share as the deceased or bankrupt person could have made; but the directors shall in either case have the same right to decline or suspend registration as they would have had in the case of a transfer of the share by the deceased or bankrupt person before the death or bankruptcy.

19. Any person becoming entitled to a share by reason of the death or bankruptcy of the holder shall be entitled to the same dividends and other advantages to which he would be entitled if he were the registered holder of the share, except that he shall not, before being registered as a member in respect of the share, be entitled in respect of it to exercise any right conferred by membership in relation to meetings of the company.

Forfeiture of shares and lien

20. If any member fail to pay any call or instalment of a call on the day appointed for payment thereof the directors may, at any time thereafter during such time as any part of the call or instalment remains unpaid, serve a notice on him requiring him to pay so much of the call or instalment as is unpaid, together with interest accrued and any expenses incurred by reason of such nonpayment.

21. The notice shall name a further day (not being earlier than the expiration of fourteen days from the date of the notice) on or before which such call or instalment and all interest accrued and expenses incurred by reason of such nonpayment are to be paid, and it shall also name the place where payment is to be made, such place being either the registered office or some other place at which calls of the company are usually made payable. The notice shall also state that in the event of nonpayment at or before the time and at the place appointed the shares in respect of which such call or instalment is payable will be liable to forfeiture.

22. If the requisitions of any such notice as aforesaid be not complied with, any shares in respect of which such notice has been given may at any time thereafter, before payment of all calls or instalments, interest, and expenses due in respect thereof has been made, be forfeited by a resolution of the directors to that effect.

23. Any shares so forfeited shall be deemed to be the property of the company, and, subject to the provisions of the Act, may be sold or otherwise disposed of in such manner, either subject to or discharged from all calls made or instalments due prior to the forfeiture, as the directors think fit; or the directors may at any time before such shares are sold or otherwise disposed of, annul the forfeiture upon such terms as they may approve.

24. Any person whose shares have been forfeited shall cease to be a member in respect of the forfeited shares, but shall, notwithstanding, remain liable to pay to the company all moneys which at the date of the forfeiture were presently payable by him to the company in respect of

the shares, together with interest thereon at such rate as the directors shall appoint, down to the date of payment; but the directors may, if they shall think fit, remit the payment of such interest or any part thereof.

25. When any shares have been forfeited an entry shall forthwith be made in the register of members of the company recording the forfeiture and the date thereof, and so soon as the shares so forfeited have been disposed of an entry shall also be made of the manner and date of the disposal thereof.

26. The company shall have a first and paramount lien upon all shares (not fully paid up) held by any member of the company (whether alone or jointly with other persons) and upon all dividends and bonuses which may be declared in respect of such shares, for all debts, obligations, and liabilities of such member to the company: Provided always that if the company shall register a transfer of any shares upon which it has such a lien as aforesaid without giving to the transferee notice of its claim, the said shares shall be freed and discharged from the lien of the company.

27. The directors may, at any time after the date for the payment or satisfaction of such debts, obligations, or liabilities shall have arrived, serve upon any member who is indebted or under obligation to the company, or upon the person entitled to his shares by reason of the death or bankruptcy of such member, a notice requiring him to pay the amount due to the company or satisfy the said obligation, and stating that if payment is not made or the said obligation is not satisfied within a time (not being less than fourteen days) specified in such notice, the shares held by such member will be liable to be sold, and if such member or the person entitled to his shares as aforesaid shall not comply with such notice within the time aforesaid, the directors, may sell such shares without further notice.

28. Upon any sale being made by the directors of any shares to satisfy the lien of the company thereon the proceeds shall be applied: first, in the payment of all costs of such sale; next, in satisfaction of the debts or obligations of the member to the company; and the residue (if any) shall be paid to the person entitled to the shares at the date of the sale or as he shall in writing direct.

29. An entry in the minute book of the company of the forfeiture of any shares, or that any shares have been sold to satisfy a lien of the company, shall be sufficient evidence, as against all persons entitled to such shares, that the said shares were properly forfeited or sold; and such entry, and the receipt of the company for the price of such shares, shall constitute a good title to such shares, and the name of the purchaser shall be entered in the register as a member of the company, and he shall be entitled to a certificate of title to the shares, and shall not be bound to see to the application of the purchase money, nor shall his title to the said shares be affected by any irregularity or invalidity in the proceedings in reference to the forfeiture or sale. The remedy (if any) of the former holder of such shares, and of any person claiming under or through him, shall be against the company and in damages only.

Alteration of share capital

30. The directors may, with the sanction of an Ordinary resolution of the company previously given in general meeting, increase the capital by the issue of new shares, such aggregate increase to be of such amount and to be divided into shares of such respective amounts as the resolution shall prescribe.

31. Subject to the provisions of the Act the new shares shall be issued upon such terms and conditions and with such rights, priorities, or privileges as the resolution sanctioning the increase of capital shall prescribe.

32. Any capital raised by the creation of new shares shall, unless otherwise provided by the conditions of issue, be considered as part of the original capital, and shall be subject to the same provisions with reference to the payment of calls and the forfeiture of shares on nonpayment of calls, transfer and transmission of shares, lien, or otherwise, as if it had been part of the original capital.

33. The company may by ordinary resolution

(a) Subdivide its existing shares or any of them into shares of smaller amount than is fixed by the memorandum of association: Provided that in the subdivision of the existing shares the proportion between the amount paid and the amount (if any) unpaid on each share of reduced amount shall be the same as it was in the case of the existing share from which the share of reduced amount is derived;

(b) Reduce its capital subject to the provisions of the Act;

(c) consolidate and divide its capital into shares of larger amount than its existing shares;

(d) cancel any shares which, at the date of the passing of the resolution, have not been taken or agreed to be taken by any person.

Borrowing powers

34. The directors may, with the consent of the company in general meeting, raise or borrow for the purposes of the company's business such sum or sums of money as they think fit. The directors may secure the repayment of or raise any such sum or sums as aforesaid by mortgage or charge upon the whole or any part of the property and assets of the company, present and future, including its uncalled or unissued capital, or by the issue, at such price as they may think fit, of bonds or debentures, either charged upon the whole or any part of the property and assets of the company or not so charged, or in such other way as the directors may think expedient.

35. Any bonds, debentures, debenture stock or other securities issued or to be issued by the company shall, subject to the provisions of the Act, be under the control of the directors, who may issue them upon such terms and conditions and in such manner and for such consideration as they shall consider to be for the benefit of the company.

36. The company may, upon the issue of any bonds, debentures, debenture stock or other securities, confer on the creditors of the company holding the same, or on any trustees or other persons acting on their behalf, a voice in the management of the company, whether by giving to them the right of attending and voting at general meetings, or by empowering them to appoint one or more of the directors of the company, or otherwise as may be agreed.

37. If the directors or any of them, or any other person, shall become personally liable for the payment of any sum primarily due from the company, the directors may execute or cause to be executed any mortgage, charge, or security over or affecting the whole or any part of the assets of the company by way of indemnity to secure the directors or persons so becoming liable as aforesaid from any loss in respect of such liability.

38. The register of charges shall be open to inspection by any creditor or member of the company without payment, and by any other person on payment of such reasonable sum as the directors may determine.

39. A register of the holders of the debentures of the company shall be kept at the registered office of the company, and shall be open to the inspection of the registered holders of such debentures and of any member of the company, subject to such restrictions as the company in general meeting may from time to time impose. The directors may close the said register for such period or periods as they may think fit, not exceeding in the aggregate thirty days in each year.

General meetings

40. The annual general meeting of the company shall be held in the month of March in each year at such time and place as the directors shall appoint. In default of an annual meeting being so held an annual meeting may be convened, to be held at any time during the next succeeding month, by any three members in the same manner as nearly as possible as that in which meetings are to be convened by the directors.

41. The directors may whenever they think fit, and they shall upon a requisition made in

writing by members in accordance with the Act convene an extraordinary general meeting of the company for a date not later than eight weeks after receipt of the requisition. If at any time there shall not be present in England and capable of acting sufficient directors to form a quorum, the directors in England capable of acting, or if there shall be no such directors then any two members, may convene an extraordinary general meeting of the company in the same manner as nearly as possible as that in which meetings may be convened by the directors, and the company at such extraordinary general meeting shall have power to elect directors.

42. In the case of an extraordinary meeting called in pursuance of a requisition, unless such meeting shall have been called by the directors, no business other than that stated in the requisition as the objects of the meeting shall be transacted.

43. An annual general meeting and an extraordinary general meeting called for the passing of a special resolution or a resolution appointing a person as a director shall be called by at least twenty-one clear days' notice. All other extraordinary general meetings shall be called by at least fourteen clear days' notice but a General Meeting may be called by shorter notice if it is so agreed –

(*a*) in the case of an annual general meeting by all the members entitled to attend and vote thereat; and

(*b*) in the case of any other meetings by a majority in number of the members having a right to attend and vote being a majority together holding not less than ninety-five per cent in nominal value of the shares giving that right. The notice shall specify the time and place of the meeting and the general nature of the business to be transacted and in the case of an annual general meeting shall specify the meeting as such.

Subject to the provisions of the Articles and to any restrictions imposed on shares, the notice shall be given to all the members, to all persons entitled to a share in consequence of the death or bankruptcy of a member and to the directors and auditors.

Clear days in relation to the period of notice means that period excluding the day when the notice is given or deemed to be given and the day for which it is given or on which it is to take effect.

The accidental omission to give notice of a meeting to, or the non-receipt of notice of a meeting by, any person entitled to receive notice shall not invalidate the proceedings at that meeting.

Proceedings at general meetings

44. The business of an annual general meeting shall be to receive and consider the accounts and balance sheets and the reports of the directors and auditors, to elect directors in place of those retiring, to elect auditors and fix their remuneration, and to sanction a dividend. All other business transacted at an annual general meeting, and all business transacted at an extraordinary meeting, shall be deemed special.

45. No business shall be transacted at any general meeting except the declaration of a dividend or the adjournment of the meeting, unless a quorum of members is present at the time when the meeting proceeds to business; and such quorum shall consist of not less than two members personally present.

46. If within half an hour from the time appointed for the meeting a quorum be not present the meeting, if convened upon the requisition of members, shall be dissolved. In any other case it shall stand adjourned to the same day in the next week at the same time and place, and if at such adjourned meeting a quorum be not present, those members who are present shall be deemed to be a quorum, and may do all business which a full quorum might have done.

47. The chairman (if any) of the board of directors shall preside as chairman at every general meeting of the company. If there be no such chairman, or if at any meeting he be not present within fifteen minutes after the time appointed for holding the meeting, or is unwilling to act as chairman, the members present shall choose one of the directors present to be chairman; or if

no director be present and willing to take the chair the members present shall choose one of their number to be chairman.

48. The chairman may, with the consent of any meeting at which a quorum is present, adjourn the meeting from time to time and from place to place; but no business shall be transacted at any adjourned meeting other than the business left unfinished at the meeting from which the adjournment took place. When a meeting is adjourned for twenty-one days or more, notice of the adjourned meeting shall be given as in the case of an original meeting. Save as aforesaid, it shall not be necessary to give any notice of an adjournment or of the business to be transacted at an adjourned meeting.

49. At any general meeting every question shall be decided in the first instance by a show of hands; and unless a poll be (on or before the declaration of the result of the show of hands) demanded by at least two members entitled to vote, or directed by the chairman, a declaration by the chairman that a resolution has been carried or not carried, or carried or not carried by a particular majority, and an entry to that effect in the minutes of the meeting, shall be conclusive evidence of the facts, without proof of the number or proportion of the votes recorded in favour of or against such resolution.

50. If a poll be demanded or directed in the manner above mentioned it shall (subject to the provisions of the next succeeding article hereof) be taken at such time and in such manner as the chairman may appoint, and the result of such poll shall be deemed to be the resolution of the meeting at which the poll was so demanded. In the case of an equality of votes at any general meeting, whether upon a show of hands or on a poll, the chairman shall be entitled to a second or casting vote. In case of any dispute as to the admission or rejection of any vote the chairman shall determine the same, and such determination made in good faith shall be final and conclusive.

51. A poll demanded upon the election of a chairman or upon a question of adjournment shall be taken forthwith. Any business other than that upon which a poll has been demanded may be proceeded with pending the taking of the poll.

Votes of members

52. Upon a show of hands every member present in person shall have one vote only. Upon a poll every member present in person or by proxy shall have one vote for every share held by him.

53. A member in respect of whom an order has been made by any court having jurisdiction (whether in the United Kingdom or elsewhere) in matters concerning mental disorder may vote, whether on a show of hands or on a poll, by his receiver *curator bonis* or other person authorized in that behalf appointed by that court and any such receiver, *curator bonis* or other person may, on a poll, vote by proxy. Evidence to the satisfaction of the directors of the authority of the person claiming to exercise the right to vote shall be deposited at the office, or such other place as is specified in accordance with the Articles for the deposit of instruments of proxy, not less than forty-eight hours before the time appointed for holding the meeting or adjourned meeting at which the right to vote is to be exercised and in default the right to vote shall not be exercisable.

54. No member shall be entitled to vote at any general meeting unless all calls or other sums presently payable by him in respect of the shares held by him in the company have been paid, and no member shall be entitled to vote in respect of any shares that he has acquired by transfer at any meeting held after the expiration of three months from the incorporation of the company unless he has been possessed of the shares in respect of which he claims to vote for at least three months previous to the time of holding the meeting at which he proposes to vote.

55. On a poll votes may be given either personally or by proxy.

56. The instrument appointing a proxy shall be in writing under the hand of the appointer or of his attorney duly authorized in writing, or if such appointer be a corporation either under its

common seal or under the hand of an officer or attorney so authorized. Provided always that a corporation being a member of the company may appoint any one of its officers or any other person to be its proxy, and the person so appointed may attend and vote at any meeting and exercise the same functions on behalf of the corporation which he represents as if he were an individual shareholder.

57. The instrument appointing a proxy and the power of attorney or other authority (if any) under which it is signed, or a notarially certified copy of such power or authority, shall be deposited at the registered office of the company not less than forty-eight hours before the time fixed for holding the meeting at which the person named in such instrument is authorized to vote, and in default the instrument of proxy shall not be treated as valid.

58. An instrument appointing a proxy shall be in the following form, or in any other form of which the directors shall approve –

RICHES KEENAN PUBLISHING LIMITED

I,   , of   , being a member of Riches Keenan Publishing Limited hereby appoint   , of 13 Hughenden Green, Aylesbury, as my proxy to vote for me and on my behalf at the annual (*or* extraordinary, *as the case may be*) general meeting of the company to be held on the   day of   19   and at any adjournment thereof.
Signed on this   day of   19

Directors

59. The number of directors shall not be less than two nor more than five.
60. The following persons shall be the first directors of the company:

SARAH RICHES
DENIS KEENAN

61. The directors shall be entitled to such remuneration as the company may by ordinary resolution determine and unless the resolution provides otherwise, the remuneration shall be deemed to accrue from day to day.

Powers of directors

62. The business of the company shall be managed by the directors, who may pay all expenses incurred in the formation and registration of the company, and may exercise all such powers of the company as are not by the Act or by these Articles required to be exercised by the company in general meeting, subject, nevertheless, to any regulations of these Articles, to the provisions of the Act, and to such regulations, not being inconsistent with the aforesaid regulations or provisions, as may be prescribed by the company in General Meeting; but no regulation made by the company in General Meeting shall invalidate any prior act of the directors which would have been valid if such regulation had not been made.

63. Without prejudice to any of the powers by these Articles or by law conferred upon the directors, it is hereby declared that they shall have the following powers –

(*a*) To pay all the preliminary expenses incurred in or about the formation, promotion, and registration of the company and the procuring its capital to be subscribed.

(*b*) To purchase or otherwise acquire on behalf of the company any property, rights, or things which the company may purchase or acquire.

(*c*) To appoint, remove, or suspend any managers, secretaries, officers, clerks, agents, or servants, and to direct and control them, and fix and pay their remuneration.

(*d*) To enter into negotiations and agreements or contracts (preliminary, conditional, or final), and to give effect to, modify, vary, or rescind the same.

(*e*) To appoint agents and attorneys for the company in the United Kingdom or abroad, with such powers (including power to subdelegate) as may be thought fit, and to provide, if necessary, for the management of the affairs of the company by any other company or any firm or person.

(*f*) To enter into any arrangement with any company, firm, or person carrying on any business similar to that of this company for mutual concessions, or for any joint working or combination, or for any restriction upon competition, or for any pooling of business or profits that may seem desirable, and to carry the same into effect.

(*g*) To give, award, or allow any pension, gratuity, or compensation to any employee of the company, or his widow or children, that may appear to the directors just or proper, whether such employee, his widow or children, have or have not a legal claim upon the company.

(*h*) To commence and carry on, or defend, abandon, or compromise any legal proceedings whatsoever, including proceedings in bankruptcy, on behalf of the company, or to refer any claims or demands by or against the company to arbitration, and to observe and perform the awards, and to accept compositions from or give time to any debtor or contributory owing money or alleged to owe money to the company.

(*i*) To give receipts, releases, and discharges on behalf of the company.

(*j*) To invest and deal with any of the moneys of the company not immediately required for the purposes of its business in such manner as they may think fit, and to vary such investments or realize the amount invested therein.

(*k*) To give indemnities to any director or other person who has undertaken or is about to undertake any liability on behalf of the company, and to secure such director or other person against loss by giving him a mortgage or charge upon the whole or any of the property of the company by way of security.

(*l*) To remunerate any person rendering services to the company, whether in its regular employment or not, in such manner as may seem fit, whether by cash, salary, bonus, or shares or debentures, or by a commission or share of profits, either in any particular transaction or generally, or howsoever otherwise.

Disqualification of directors

64. The office of a director shall be vacated if –

(*a*) He ceased to be a director by virtue of any provision of the Act or he becomes prohibited by law from being a director; or

(*b*) he becomes bankrupt or makes any arrangement or composition with his creditors generally; or

(*c*) he is, or may be, suffering from mental disorder and either –

(*i*) he is admitted to hospital in pursuance of an application for treatment under the Mental Health Act 1983; or

(*ii*) an order is made by a court having jurisdiction (whether in the United Kingdom or elsewhere) in matters concerning mental disorder for his detention or the appointment of a receiver, *curator bonis* or other person to exercise powers with respect to his property or affairs;

(*d*) he resigns his office by notice to the company; or

(*e*) he shall for more than six consecutive months have been absent without permission of the directors from meetings of directors held during that period and the directors resolve that his office be vacated.

65. A director shall not be disqualified by his office from entering into contracts, arrangements, or dealings with the company, nor shall any contract, arrangement, or dealing with the company be voided, nor shall a director be liable to account to the company for any profit arising out of any contract, arrangement, or dealing with the company by reason of such director being a party to or interested in or deriving profit from any such contract, arrangement, or dealing, and being at the same time a director of the company, provided that such director

discloses to the board at or before the time when such contract, arrangement, or dealing is determined upon his interest therein, or, if his interest be subsequently acquired, provided that he on the first occasion possible discloses to the board the fact that he has acquired such interest. But, except in respect of any indemnity to a director under Article 63(k) hereof, no director shall vote as a director in regard to any contract, arrangement, or dealing in which he is interested, or upon any matter arising thereout, and if he shall so vote his vote shall not be counted, nor shall he be reckoned in estimating a quorum when any such contract, arrangement, or dealing is under consideration.

66. The continuing directors may act notwithstanding any vacancy in their body, but if and so long as the number of directors is reduced below the number fixed by or pursuant to the regulations of the company as the necessary quorum of directors, the continuing directors may act for the purpose of increasing the number of directors to that number, or of summoning a general meeting of the company, but for no other purpose.

Rotation of directors

67. At the first annual general meeting, and at the annual general meeting in every subsequent year, one third of the directors for the time being, or if their number is not three or a multiple of three then the number nearest to but not exceeding one third, shall retire from office, the directors to retire in each year being those who have been longest in office since their last election, but as between persons who became directors on the same day those to retire shall (unless they otherwise agree among themselves) be determined by lot.

68. A retiring director shall be eligible for re-election.

69. The company at the annual general meeting at which any director retires in manner aforesaid shall fill up the vacated office, and may fill up any other offices which may then be vacant, by electing the necessary number of persons, unless the company shall determine to reduce the number of directors. The company may also at any extraordinary general meeting, on notice duly given, fill up any vacancies in the office of director, or appoint additional directors, provided that the maximum hereinbefore mentioned be not exceeded.

70. If at any meeting at which an election of directors ought to take place the places of the vacating directors be not filled up, the vacating directors, or such of them as have not had their places filled up, shall continue in office until the annual general meeting in the next year, and so on from time to time until their places have been filled up.

71. The company may from time to time in general meeting increase or reduce the number of directors, and may also determine in what rotation such increased or reduced number is to go out of office.

72. The directors shall have power at any time and from time to time to appoint any other qualified person to be a director of the company either to fill a casual vacancy or as an addition to the board, but so that the total number of directors shall not at any time exceed the maximum number hereinbefore fixed. Any director so appointed shall hold office only until the next following annual general meeting, when he shall retire, but shall be eligible for re-election.

73. Seven days' previous notice in writing shall be given to the company of the intention of any member to propose any person other than a retiring director for election to the office of director: Provided always that, if the members present at a general meeting unanimously consent, the chairman of such meeting may waive the said notice, and may submit to the meeting the name of any person duly qualified.

Managing directors

74. The directors may from time to time appoint one or more of their body to be a managing director or manager of the company, and may fix his or their remuneration either by way of salary or commission or by conferring a right to participation in the profits of the company, or by a combination of two or more of those modes.

75. Every managing director or manager shall be liable to be dismissed or removed by the board of directors, and another person may be appointed in his place. The board may, however, subject to the provisions of the Act, enter into any agreement with any person who is or is about to become a managing director or manager with regard to the length and terms of his employment, but so that the remedy of any such person for any breach of such agreement shall be in damages only, and he shall have no right or claim to continue in such office contrary to the will of the directors or of the company in general meeting.

76. A managing director or manager shall not, while he continues to hold that office, be liable to retire by rotation, and he shall not be taken into account in determining the rotation in which the other directors shall retire (except for the purpose of fixing the number to retire in each year), but he shall be subject to the same provisions as regards removal and disqualification as the other directors, and if he cease to hold the office of director from any cause he shall *ipso facto* cease to be a managing director.

77. The directors may from time to time entrust to and confer upon the managing director or manager all or any of the powers of the directors that they may think fit. But the exercise of all powers by the managing director or manager shall be subject to such regulations and restrictions as the directors may from time to time make or impose, and the said powers may at any time be withdrawn, revoked, or varied.

Proceedings of directors

78. The directors may meet together for the dispatch of business, adjourn, and otherwise regulate their meetings as they think fit, and determine the quorum necessary for the transaction of business. Until otherwise determined two directors shall constitute a quorum. Questions arising at any meeting shall be decided by a majority of votes. In case of an equality of votes the chairman shall have a second or casting vote. A director may, and the secretary on the requisition of a director shall, at any time summon a meeting of the directors. Notice of every meeting of directors shall be given to every director who is in the United Kingdom.

79. The directors may elect a chairman of their meetings, and determine the period for which he is to hold office; but if no such chairman be elected, or if at any meeting the chairman be not present within five minutes after the time appointed for holding the same, the directors present shall choose some one of their number to be chairman of such meeting.

80. The directors may delegate any of their powers to committees, consisting of such member or members of their body as they think fit. Any committee so formed shall in the exercise of the powers so delegated conform to any regulations that may be imposed on him or them by the directors. The regulations herein contained for the meetings and proceedings of directors shall, so far as not altered by any regulations made by the directors, apply also to the meetings and proceedings of any committee.

81. All acts done by any meeting of the directors or of a committee of directors, or by any persons acting as directors, shall, notwithstanding that it be afterwards discovered that there was some defect in the appointment of any such directors or persons acting as aforesaid, or that they or any of them were disqualified, be as valid as if every such person had been duly appointed and was qualified to be a director.

Minutes

82. The directors shall cause minutes to be made in books provided for the purpose –
(a) of all appointments of officers made by the directors;
(b) of the names of the directors present at each meeting of the directors and of any committee of the directors;
(c) of all resolutions and proceedings at all meetings of the company and of the directors and of committees of directors.

The seal

83. The seal shall be used only by the authority of the directors or of a committee of directors authorized by the directors. The directors may determine who shall sign any instrument to which the seal is affixed and unless otherwise so determined it shall be signed by a director and by the secretary or by a second director.

Dividends

84. Subject to the provisions of the Act, the company may by ordinary resolution declare dividends in accordance with the respective rights of members, but no dividend shall exceed the amount recommended by the directors.

85. Subject to the provisions of the Act, the directors may pay interim dividends if it appears to them they are justified by the profits of the company available for distribution. If the share capital is divided into different classes, the directors may pay interim dividends on shares which confer deferred or non-preferred rights with regard to dividend as well as on shares which confer preferential rights with regard to dividend. No interim dividend shall be paid on shares carrying deferred or non-preferred rights if, at the time of payment, any preferential dividend is in arrear. The directors may also pay at intervals settled by them any dividend payable at a fixed rate if it appears to them that the profits available for distribution justify the payment. Provided the directors act in good faith they shall not incur any liability to the holders of shares conferring preferred rights for any loss they may suffer by the lawful payment of an interim dividend on any shares having deferred or non-preferred rights.

86. Except as otherwise provided by the rights attached to shares, all dividends shall be declared and paid according to the amounts paid up on the shares on which the dividend is paid. All dividends shall be apportioned and paid proportionately to the amounts paid up on the shares during any portion or portions of the period in respect of which the dividend is paid; but, if any share is issued on terms providing that it shall rank for dividend as from a particular date, that share shall rank for dividend accordingly.

87. A general meeting declaring a dividend may, upon the recommendation of the directors, direct that it shall be satisfied wholly or partly by the distribution of assets and, where any difficulty arises in regard to the distribution, the directors may settle the same and in particular may issue fractional certificates and fix the value for distribution of any assets and may determine that cash shall be paid to any member upon the footing of the value so fixed in order to adjust the rights of members and may vest any assets in trustees.

88. Any dividend or other moneys payable in respect of a share may be paid by cheque sent by post to the registered address of the person entitled or, if two or more persons are the holders of the share, or are jointly entitled to it by reason of the death or bankruptcy of the holder, to the registered address of that one of those persons who is first named in the register of members or to such person and to such address as the person or persons entitled may in writing direct. Every cheque shall be made payable to the order of the person or persons entitled or to such other person as the person or persons entitled may in writing direct and payment of the cheque shall be a good discharge to the company. Any joint holder or other person jointly entitled to a share as aforesaid may give receipts for any dividend or other moneys payable in respect of the share.

89. No dividend or other moneys payable in respect of a share shall bear interest against the company unless otherwise provided by the rights attached to the share.

90. Any dividend which has remained unclaimed for twelve years from the date when it became due for payment shall, if the directors so resolve, be forfeited and cease to remain owing by the company.

Accounts

91. No member shall (as such) have any right of inspecting any accounting records or other

book or document of the company except as conferred by statute or authorized by the directors or by ordinary resolution of the company.

Notices

92. A notice may be served by the company upon any member either personally or by sending it through the post addressed to such member at his registered address.

93. No member shall be entitled to have a notice served on him at any address not within the United Kingdom; and any member whose registered address is not within the United Kingdom may, by notice in writing, require the company to register an address within the United Kingdom, which, for the purpose of the service of notices, shall be deemed to be his registered address. Any member not having a registered address within the United Kingdom, and not having given notice as aforesaid, shall be deemed to have received in due course any notice which shall have been displayed in the company's office and shall remain there for the space of forty-eight hours, and such notice shall be deemed to have been received by such member at the expiration of twenty-four hours from the time when it shall have been so first displayed.

94. It shall not be necessary to give notice of general meetings to any person entitled to a share in consequence of the death or bankruptcy of a member unless such person shall have been duly registered as a member of the company.

95. Any notice if served by post shall be deemed to have been served at the expiration of twenty-four hours after it has been posted; and in proving such service it shall be sufficient to prove that the envelope containing the notice was properly addressed prepaid and posted.

Arbitration

96. If and whenever any difference shall arise between the company and any of the members or their respective representatives touching the construction of any of the Articles herein contained, or any act, matter, or thing made or done, or to be made or done, or omitted, or in regard to the rights and liabilities arising hereunder, or arising out of the relation existing between the parties by reason of these presents or of the Statutes, or any of them, such differences shall be forthwith referred to two arbitrators – one to be appointed by each party in difference – or to an umpire to be chosen by the arbitrators before entering on the consideration of the matters referred to them, and every such reference shall be conducted in accordance with the provisions of the Arbitration Acts.

Winding up

97. With the sanction of an extraordinary resolution of the members and any other sanction required by the Act any part of the assets of the company, including any shares in other companies, may be divided between the members of the company in specie, or may be vested in trustees for the benefit of such members, and the liquidation of the company may be closed and the company dissolved, but so that no member shall be compelled to accept any shares whereon there is any liability.

Names, Addresses and Descriptions

SARAH RICHES
1 High Street,
Barchester

Sarah Riches

AUTHOR/LECTURER

DENIS KEENAN
2 Low Street,
Barchester

Denis Keenan

AUTHOR/LECTURER

Dated the 3rd March 1986
Witness to the above signatures:
    John Green
    3 Middle Street,
    Barchester

John Green

A

COMPANIES FORM No. 363

Annual return of a company

Pursuant to sections 363 and 364 of the Companies Act 1985

363

Note The appropriate fee should accompany this form

To the Registrar of Companies

Please do not write in this margin

Please complete legibly, preferably in black type, or bold block lettering

* insert full name of company

† if the company has a share capital, this date must be the 14th day after the annual general meeting

For official use	Company number
[| | |]	1383617

Annual return of (note 1)

* RICHES KEENAN PUBLISHING LTD

The information in this return is as at

19 March   19 87   †.(The date of this return note 1)

Address of registered office of the company

140 HIGH STREET, BARCHESTER

	Postcode	BB26 0YE

Total amount of indebtedness of the company in respect of mortgages and charges (note 2).

£ 10,424.00

If different from the registered office, state address where the register of members or any register of debenture holders or any duplicate or part of any register of debentures is kept or may be inspected.

Register of members

/

Register of debenture holders

/

Particulars of the secretary

Name (notes 3 and 4)	WILLIAMS, JANE MARY
Previous name(s)(note 3)	
Address (notes 4 and 5)	25 MIDDLE STREET BARCHESTER

	Postcode	BB26 9AN

‡ only pages 1 and 2 need be completed in the case of a company without share capital

§ enter number of continuation sheets attached

We certify this return which comprises pages 1, 2, [3, 4, 5 and 6]‡ [plus§ _____ continuation sheets]

Signed J.J. Keenan   Director, and J.M. Williams   Secretary

Presenter's name address and reference (if any):

Riches Keenan Publishing Ltd

For official Use
General Section

Post room

Page 1

Particulars of the director(s) of the company (notes 6 and 7)

Name (note 3) RICHES, SARAH	**Business Occupation** AUTHOR/LECTURER
Previous name(s) (note 3)	**Nationality** BRITISH
Address (note 5) 1 HIGH STREET BARCHESTER Postcode BB26 OYE	**Date of birth** (note 9)
Other relevant past or present directorships* (note 8) DODGY TRAINING LIMITED	

Name (note 3) KEENAN, DENIS JOSEPH	**Business Occupation** AUTHOR/LECTURER
Previous name(s) (note 3)	**Nationality** BRITISH
Address (note 5) 2 LOW STREET BARCHESTER Postcode BB26 OBG	**Date of birth** (note 9)
Other relevant past or present directorships* (note 8) DODGY FINANCE LIMITED	

Name (note 3)	**Business Occupation**
Previous name(s) (note 3)	**Nationality**
Address (note 5) Postcode	**Date of birth** (note 9)
Other relevant past or present directorships* (note 8)	

Name (note 3)	**Business Occupation**
Previous name(s) (note 3)	**Nationality**
Address (note 5) Postcode	**Date of birth** (note 9)
Other relevant past or present directorships* (note 8)	

Summary of share capital and debentures

Nominal share capital   £ *10,000*

	Number of shares	Class	Nominal value of each share
divided into:- 1	10,000	ORDINARY	£
2			£
3			£

Issued share capital and debentures

		Number	Class
1.Number of shares of each class taken up to the date of this return.	1	10,000	ORDINARY
	2		
	3		
2.Number of shares of each class issued subject to payment wholly in cash	1	10,000	ORDINARY
	2		
	3		
3.Number of shares of each class issued as fully paid up for aconsideration other than cash	1		
	2		
	3		

		Amount per share	
4.Number of shares of each class issued as partly paid up for a consideration other than cash and extent to which each such share is so paid up	1	£	
	2	£	
	3	£	
5.Number of shares (if any) of each class issued at a discount	1		
	2		
	3		

Continued on page 4

LIST OF PAST

Folio in register ledger containing particulars	Names and Addresses	
1	RICHES, SARAH, 1 HIGH STREET, BARCHESTER	1
		2
2	KEENAN, DENIS JOSEPH, 2 LOW ST, BARCHESTER	3
		4
		5
		6
		7
		8
		9
		10
		11
		12
		13
		14
		15

Summary of share capital and debentures continued

	Amount	Number	Class	
6 Amount of discount on the issue of shares which has not been written off at the date of this return	£			
7 Amount per share called up on number of shares of each class	£ 1	10,000	ORDINARY	1
	£			2
	£			3
8 Total amount of calls received (note 10)	£ 10,000			
9 Total amount (if any) agreed to be considered as paid on number of shares of each class issued as fully paid up for a consideration other than cash	£			1
	£			2
	£			3
10 Total amount (if any) agreed to be considered as paid on number of shares of each class issued as partly paid up for a consideration other than cash	£			1
	£			2
	£			3
11 Total amount of calls unpaid	£			
12 Total amount of sums (if any) paid by way of commission in respect of any shares or debentures	£			
13 Total amount of the sums (if any) allowed by way of discount for any debentures since the date of the last return	£			
14 Total number of shares of each class forfeited				1
				2
				3
15 Total amount paid (if any) on shares forfeited	£			
16 Total amount of shares for which share warrants to bearer are outstanding	£			
17 Total amount of share warrants to bearer issued and ISSUED	£			
surrendered respectively since the date of the last return SURRENDERED	£			
18 Number of shares comprised in each share warrant to bearer, specifying in the case of warrants of different kinds, particulars of each kind				

AND PRESENT MEMBERS (notes 11 and 12)

	Account of Shares			
Number of shares or amount of stock held by existing members at date of return (note 11)	Particulars of shares transferred since the date of the last return,or,in the case of the first return,of the incorporation of the company,by (a) persons who are still members,and (b) persons who have ceased to be members (note 12)			Remarks
	Number	Date of Registration of transfer (a)	(b)	
5000					1
					2
5000					3
					4
					5
					6
					7
					8
					9
					10
					11
					12
					13
					14
					15

LIST OF PAST

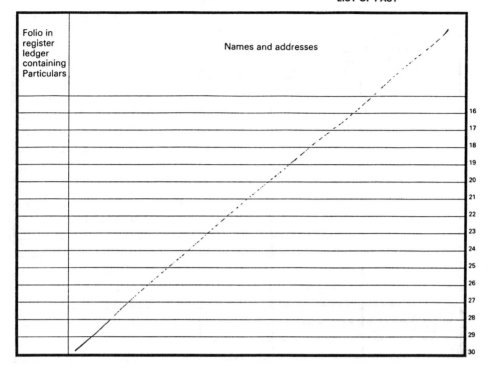

Folio in register ledger containing Particulars	Names and addresses	
		16
		17
		18
		19
		20
		21
		22
		23
		24
		25
		26
		27
		28
		29
		30

Notes

1. An annual return is required for every calendar year. If the company has a share capital the date of this return must be the 14th day after the date of the annual general meeting. If it does not have a share capital the date of this return must be a date not more than 42 days after the annual general meeting

2. This section should include only indebtedness in respect of charges (whenever created) of any description set out in section 396(1) of the Companies Act 1985 (in the case of English and Welsh companies) or section 410(4) of that Act (in the case of Scottish companies).

3. For an individual, his present christian name(s) and surname must be given, together with any previous christian name(s) or surname(s).

   "Christian name" includes a forename. In the case of a peer or person usually known by a title different from his surname, "surname" means that title. In the case of a corporation, its corporate name must be given.

   A previous christian name or surname need not be given if:—

   (a) in the case of a married woman, it was a name by which she was known before her marriage; or

   (b) it was changed or ceased to be used at least 20 years ago, or before the person who previously used it reached the age of 18; or

   (c) in the case of a peer or a person usually known by a British title different from his surname, it was a name by which he was known before he adopted the title or succeeded to it

4. Where all the partners in a firm are joint secretaries, only the firm name and its principal office need be given.

   Where the secretary or one of the joint secretaries is a Scottish firm, give only the firm name and its principal office.

5. Usual residential address must be given. In the case of a corporation, give the registered or principal office.

6. Director includes any person who occupies the position of a director, by whatever name called, and any person in accordance with whose directions or instructions the directors of the company are accustomed to act.

7. If the space provided for listing directors is inadequate, a prescribed continuation sheet must be used.

8. The names must be given of all bodies corporate incorporated in Great Britain of which the director is also a director, or has been a director at any time during the preceeding five years.

   However a present or past directorship need not be disclosed if it is, or has been, held in a body corporate which, throughout that directorship, has been:—

   (a) a dormant company (which is a company which has had no transactions required to be entered in the company's accounting records, except any which may have arisen from the taking of shares in the company by a subscriber to the memorandum as such).

   (b) a body corporate of which the company making the return was a wholly-owned subsidiary;

AND PRESENT MEMBERS Continued (notes 11 and 12)

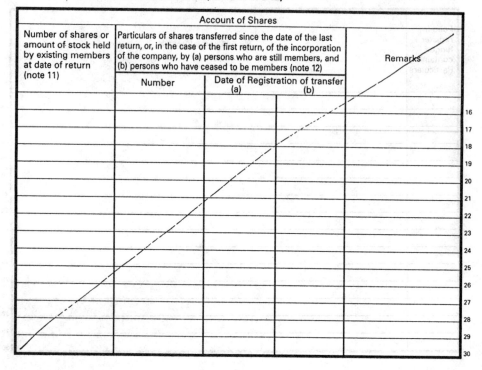

Number of shares or amount of stock held by existing members at date of return (note 11)	Particulars of shares transferred since the date of the last return, or, in the case of the first return, of the incorporation of the company, by (a) persons who are still members, and (b) persons who have ceased to be members (note 12)		Remarks
	Number	Date of Registration of transfer (a) (b)	

16
17
18
19
20
21
22
23
24
25
26
27
28
29
30

(c) a wholly-owned subsidiary of the company making the return; or

(d) a wholly-owned subsidiary of a body corporate of which the company making the return was also a wholly owned subsidiary.

9. Dates of birth need only be given if the company making the return is:—

    (a) a public company;
    (b) the subsidiary of a public company; or
    (c) the subsidiary of a public company registered in Northern Ireland

10. Include payments on application and allotment, and any sums received or shares forfeited.

11. Show all the persons currently holding shares or stock in the company at the date of the return, giving their names and addresses, the number of shares or amount of stock held, and details of all transfers since the last return or, if this is the first annual return of the company, all transfers since the company was incorporated. If more than one class of share is held please add more columns as appropriate.

Additionally, show all persons and their relevant details if they have ceased to be members since the last return was made, or if this is the first return, since the company was incorporated.

If the list of members is not in alphabetical order, an index which will enable any member to be readily located within the list must be attached to this return. If the space provided for listing members is inadequate, a prescribed continuation sheet is available.

If full details have been given on the return for either of the last two years, a company may, if it so wishes, only include in this section details relating to persons who since the date of the last return:
    (a) have become members;
    (b) have ceased to be members; or
    (c) are existing members whose holdings of stock or shares have changed.
If full details have been given on the return for either of the last two years and there have been no changes please state "No Change".

12. For consistency, it is suggested that particulars should be placed opposite the name of the transferor and not opposite that of the transferee, but the name of the transferee may be inserted in the remarks column opposite the particulars of each transfer.

Questions/activities

1. Able and Ben are the promoters of Wye Ltd and are the two subscribers to the memorandum. The documents required to be sent to the Registrar of Companies in order to obtain the incorporation of Wye Ltd are ready to go. One of Wye Ltd's objects is to acquire the business of John Wye. John is getting difficult and insists that a contract for the sale of his business shall be signed now or the deal is off.

Advise Able and Ben, who do not want to lose the opportunity to acquire John Wye's undertaking.

2. The articles of association of Trent Ltd state that Cyril and David are appointed until age sixty as Company Secretary and Chief Accountant respectively at salaries of £2000 per annum. Cyril and David took up their posts five years ago, when they were thirty-five and forty respectively.

(a) Cyril has received a letter from the Chairman of Trent Ltd discharging him from the post of Company Secretary. Cyril would like to retain the job;

(b) David has given his resignation to the Board of Trent Ltd but the Board will not accept it.

Advise Cyril and David.

3. Derwent Ltd has suffered declining profits for four years. The directors have not declared a dividend for three years and in order to avoid facing the shareholders did not call an AGM last year.

Eric, who holds shares in Derwent has got together with some of his fellow shareholders to form a group to see what can be done to get the company better managed.

Write a letter to Eric advising him and telling him how the group should proceed in practical terms.

4. Severn Ltd runs a very successful business and makes a good profit. However, over the past few years the controlling directors have increased their remuneration so that it absorbs all the profits. Jane, who is a minority shareholder not on the board, gets no dividends and wishes to do something about this state of affairs.

Explain to Jane what action she should take.

5. As Secretary of Ouse Ltd write a memorandum for the Board explaining the differences between raising finance –

(a) by an issue of shares;

(b) by an issue of unsecured loan stock;

(c) by an issue of debentures secured by a floating charge over the company's assets; and

(d) by an issue of preference shares.

6. (a) How is the voluntary winding up of a company brought about?

(b) What decides whether a voluntary winding up is controlled –

(i) by the members, or

(ii) by the creditors.

Assignment

You have recently been appointed secretary to Pottery Ltd, a company making china and run by a Stoke family. You discover that the board is currently facing two major problems as follows –

(a) in the early 1950s the former chairman, Arthur Stock, allowed certain retailers of the company's goods to buy a special class of preference share called the 'Preference B' share; 200 shares of £1 each were issued. The object was to give the retailers a sense of identity with Pottery Ltd but with the security of a voting preference share.

The present management, led by Arthur's son, Ronald, is willing to retain the Preference B shares provided the holders of those shares are willing to give up their voting rights and become non-voting preference shares. Some holders of the shares are apparently not willing to give up their voting rights.

(b) The board of Pottery Ltd has also discovered that one of its ordinary shareholders, Thomas Mugg, is running a competing business making china. It is concerned that Thomas is entitled by company law to receive documents of Pottery Ltd, such as accounts and directors' reports, and to obtain information from its registers and that this will assist Thomas in his competitive activities.

You are required to advise the board on the above matters.

NOTE: Each member of the group should prepare a package of materials to present to the board. This will include a memorandum setting out the legal position and possible solutions. It could also include advice on types of resolutions which may be required; types of meetings, and a draft of any necessary correspondence, e.g. to shareholders and others.

The group should then discuss each student package with a view to reaching a definitive position for the group as a whole as to the procedures to be followed.

Business Contracting

8

Introduction to the law of contract

Business contracting – generally

Once the businessman has decided on the particular
form of business organization that suits his needs he can
concentrate on his main purpose: establishing and
building up the business. This will involve acquiring
premises and equipment, taking on employees, buying
raw materials and stock, marketing the product or
service and meeting orders. Underpinning all these
business transactions is the presence of a contract.

Most people think that a contract is a formal written
document which has been signed by the parties,
independently witnessed and sealed, with great cerem-
ony, by affixing a red wax seal. If all contracts took this
form there would be little room for argument about
whether the parties had entered into a legally binding
agreement, the obligations they had undertaken or the
consequences of failing to carry out the terms of the
agreement. In practice, however, few contracts are like
this. The vast majority of contracts are entered into
without formalities. The parties may even be unaware
of the legal significance of their actions. Think about
the agreements you have made over the past week:

- buying a newspaper;
- taking the bus or train into work or college;
- agreeing to complete an assignment by a particular date;
- getting a cup of coffee at break-time;
- arranging to meet a friend for lunch.

Can all these transactions be classed as contracts?
You probably feel that some of them were never
intended to have legal consequences. So, what then is a
contract? When is a contract formed? What are the

obligations of the parties to a contract? What happens
if either party breaks the agreement? The answers to
these questions are provided by the law of contract.

The foundations of the present-day law of contract
were laid in the nineteenth century. This period in our
history saw the rapid expansion of trade and industry,
and, inevitably, an increase in the volume of commercial disputes. Businessmen turned to the courts for a
solution. Gradually, the judges developed a body of
settled rules which reflected both the commercial
background of the disputes from which they arose and
the prevailing beliefs of the time. The dominant
economic philosophy of the nineteenth century was
laissez-faire individualism – the view that the state
should not meddle in the affairs of business and that
individuals should be free to determine their own
destinies. This philosophy was mirrored in the law of
contract by two assumptions: freedom of contract and
equality of bargaining power. The judges assumed that
everyone was free to choose which contracts they
entered into and the terms on which they did so. If
negotiations could not produce an acceptable basis for
agreement, the parties were, in theory, free to take their
business elsewhere. The parties were deemed to be of
equal bargaining strength.

The judges' assumptions produced an acceptable
legal framework for the regulation of business transactions. Parliament, too, played its part by codifying
parts of the common law of particular relevance to the
businessman; e.g. the law relating to contracts for the
sale of goods became the Sale of Goods Act 1893 (now
the Sale of Goods Act 1979). However, the same basic
rules were applied in situations where one of the parties

was in a weak bargaining position. Employees, consumers and borrowers found themselves without adequate protection from the law. It has been necessary for Parliament to intervene to redress the balance between employers and employees, businessmen and consumers, lenders and borrowers. In these areas, the concept of freedom of contract has been modified.

This Section is concerned with 'Business Contracting': transactions between one businessman and another, and between the businessman and consumers. The emphasis is on the legal framework governing the supply of goods and services. In order to understand these specific areas of business law, it is necessary to look at the basic ground rules of the law of contract first.

Nature of a contract

A contract has been defined as a legally binding agreement or, in the words of Sir Frederick Pollock, 'A promise or set of promises which the law will enforce.' However, not all promises or agreements give rise to contracts. If you agreed to keep the house tidy while your parents were away on holiday, you would not expect to find yourself in the county court being sued for breach of contract if you failed to do so. So what kinds of agreements does the law recognize as creating enforceable rights and duties?

Types of contract

Contracts may be divided into two broad classes –

(1) *Specialty contracts*. These formal contracts are also known as contracts under seal or by deed. The contract must be in writing and 'signed, sealed and delivered'. Certain contracts, such as conveyances of land, must be made under seal, but these are relatively few in number.

(2) *Simple contracts*. Contracts which are not made under seal are known as simple contracts. They are informal contracts and may be made in any way – orally, in writing, or they may be implied from conduct.

Essentials of a valid contract

The essential ingredients of a contract are –

(1) *Agreement*. An agreement is formed when one party accepts the offer of another.

(2) *Consideration*. The parties must show that their agreement is part of a bargain; each side must promise to give or do something for the other.

(3) *Intention*. The law will not concern itself with purely domestic or social arrangements. The parties must have intended their agreement to have legal consequences.

(4) *Form*. In some cases, certain formalities (that is, writing) must be observed.

(5) *Capacity*. The parties must be legally capable of entering into a contract.

(6) *Genuineness of consent*. The agreement must have been entered into freely and involve a 'meeting of minds'.

(7) *Legality*. The purpose of the agreement must not be illegal or contrary to public policy.

A contract which possesses all these requirements is said to be valid. If one of the parties fails to live up to his promises he may be sued for a breach of contract. The absence of an essential element will render the contract either void, voidable or unenforceable.

(1) *Void contracts*. The term 'void contract' is a contradiction in terms since the whole transaction is regarded a nullity. It means that at no time has there been a contract between the parties. Any goods or money obtained under the agreement must be returned. Where items have been resold to a third party, they may be recovered by the original owner. A contract may be rendered void, for example, by some forms of mistake.

(2) *Voidable contracts*. Contracts founded on a misrepresentation and some agreements made by minors fall into this category. The contract may every respect respect as a valid contract unless and until one of the parties takes steps to avoid it. Anything obtained under the contract must be returned, insofar as this is possible. If goods have been resold before the contract was avoided, the original owner will not be able to reclaim them.

(3) *Unenforceable contracts*. An unenforceable contract is a valid contract but it cannot be enforced in the courts if one of the parties refuses to carry out its terms. Items received under the contract cannot be reclaimed. Agreements for the sale of land are unenforceable unless evidenced in writing.

The essential elements of a valid contract will now be considered in more detail. Remember – just as a dwelling must have sound foundations, walls and a roof, so must a contract have all its essentials to be valid.

Agreement *things needed*

The first requisite of any contract is an agreement. At least two parties are required; one of them, the offeror, makes an offer which the other, the offeree, accepts.

Offer

An offer is a proposal made on certain terms by the offeror together with a promise to be bound by that proposal if the offeree accepts the stated terms. An offer may be made expressly – for example, when an employer writes to a prospective employee to offer him a job – or impliedly, by conduct – for example, bidding at an auction.

The offer may be made to a specific person, in which case it can only be accepted by that person. If an offer is made to a group of people, it may be accepted by any member of the group. An offer can even be made to the whole world, such as where someone offers a reward for the return of a lost dog. The offer can be accepted by anyone who knows about it, and finds the dog.

Carlill v Carbolic Smoke Ball Co. (1893)

The defendants inserted advertisements in a number of newspapers stating that they would pay £100 to anyone who caught 'flu after using their smoke balls as directed for 14 days. They further stated that to show their sincerity in the matter they had deposited £1000 at the Alliance Bank to meet possible claims. Mrs Carlill bought one of the smoke balls, used it as directed but still caught 'flu. She claimed the £100 reward but was refused, so she sued the defendants in contract. One of the defences put forward was that the defendants had attempted to contract with the whole world, which was clearly impossible. The Court of Appeal held that the defendants had made an offer to the whole world and they would be liable to anyone who came forward and performed the required conditions. Mrs Carlill recovered the £100.

It is important to identify when a true offer has been made because once it is accepted the parties are bound.

If the words and actions of one party do not amount to an offer, however, the other person cannot by saying. 'I accept,' create a contract. A genuine offer must, therefore, be distinguished from what is known as an 'invitation to treat'.

An invitation to treat

This is where a person holds himself out as ready to receive offers, which he may then either accept or reject. The following are examples of invitations to treat:

(1) *The display of goods with a price ticket attached in a shop window or on a supermarket shelf*. This is not an offer to sell but an invitation for customers to make an offer to buy.

Fisher v Bell (1961)

A shopkeeper had a flick-knife on display in his shop window. He was charged with offering for sale an offensive weapon contrary to the provisions of the Restriction of Offensive Weapons Act 1959. He was acquitted on appeal. The Divisional Court of the Queen's Bench Division held that the display of goods with a price ticket attached in a shop window is an invitation to treat and not an offer to sell. (The Restriction of Offensive Weapons Act 1961 was passed soon after this case to close the loophole in the law.)

Thus, it is a clearly established principle of civil law that if a piece of merchandise is displayed for sale with an incorrect price ticket attached to it, the retailer is not obliged to sell at that price. Under the criminal law, however, the retailer may find himself facing a prosecution for a breach of the provisions of the Trade Descriptions Act 1968.

(2) *Advertisements, catalogues and brochures.* Many businesses make use of the press, TV and commercial radio to sell their products direct to the public. Even if the word 'offer' is used, the advertisement is still an invitation to treat. The customer makes the offer, which may be accepted or rejected by the mail order firm. There are, however, some situations where the advertisement may be regarded as a definite offer, e.g. as in *Carlill* v *Carbolic Smoke Ball Co.* (1893).

(3) *Company prospectuses.* When a company wishes to raise capital by selling shares to the public, it must issue a prospectus (an invitation to treat). Potential investors apply for shares (the offer) and the

directors then decide who to allot shares to (the acceptance).

(4) *Auctions*. At an auction sale the call for bids by an auctioneer is an invitation to treat. The bids are offers. The auctioneer selects the highest bid and acceptance is completed by the fall of the hammer.

(5) *Tenders*. Large undertakings, such as public authorities, often place contracts inviting interested firms to tender (offer) for the business. The acceptance of a tender has different legal consequences, depending on the wording of the original invitation to tender. There are two possibilities –

(a) *Example 1*. The Metropolitan Borough of Newtown invites tenders for the supply of 100 tons of potatoes for the use of the School Meals Service in the Borough from 1 January to 31 December. The acceptance of a tender creates a legally binding contract. The successful supplier must deliver 100 tons of potatoes which the Borough must pay for.

(b) *Example 2*. The Metropolitan Borough of Newtown invites tenders for the supply of potatoes, not exceeding 100 tons, for the period 1 January to 31 December as and when required by the School Meals Service. The acceptance of a tender in this situation has the effect of creating a standing offer on the part of the supplier to deliver potatoes if and when orders are placed by the School Meals Service. This form of tender does not prevent the supplier giving notice that he will not supply potatoes in the future or the School Meals Service from not placing orders, if they decide to cut potatoes from the school dinner menu.

(6) *Statements of price in negotiations for the sale of land*. Where the subject matter of a proposed sale is land, the courts are reluctant to find a definite offer to sell unless very clearly stated.

Clifton v Palumbo (1944)

In the course of negotiations for the sale of a large estate, the plaintiff wrote to the defendant: 'I am prepared to offer my Lytham estate for £600 000. I also agree that sufficient time shall be given to you to complete a schedule of completion.' The Court of Appeal held that these words did not amount to a firm offer to sell, but rather a preliminary statement as to price.

Termination of the offer

An offer can end in a number of ways:

(1) *By acceptance*. An offer which has been accepted, constitutes a contract. That offer is no longer available for acceptance.

(2) *By rejection*. An offer is rejected if –

(a) the offeree notifies the offerer that he does not wish to accept the offer;

(b) the offeree attempts to accept the offer but subject to certain conditions;

(c) the offeree makes a counter-offer.

Hyde v Wrench (1840)

Wrench offered to sell his farm to Hyde for £1000. Hyde replied with a 'counter offer' of £950, which was refused. Hyde then said that he was prepared to meet the original offer of £1000. It was held that no contract had been formed. The 'counter-offer' of £950 had the effect of rejecting Wrench's original offer.

Sometimes it is difficult to decide whether the offeree is making a counter-offer or simply asking for more information about the offer. A request for more information will not reject the offer.

Stevenson v McLean (1880)

The defendant offered to sell a quantity of iron to the plaintiffs for cash. The plaintiffs asked whether they could have credit terms. When no reply to their inquiry was forthcoming, the plaintiffs accepted the terms of the original offer. Meanwhile, the defendant had sold the iron elsewhere. It was held that the inquiry was a request for more information, not a rejection of the offer. The defendant was liable for breach of contract.

(3) *By revocation before acceptance*. An offer may be revoked (withdrawn) at any time before acceptance but it will only be effective when the offeree learns about it. It is not necessary that the offeror himself should tell the offeree; the information may be conveyed by a reliable third party.

Dickinson v Dodds (1876)

The defendant, on Wednesday, offered to sell some property to the plaintiff, the offer to be left open until 9 a.m., Friday. On Thursday, the plaintiff heard from a Mr Berry that the defendant had sold the property to someone else. Nevertheless the plaintiff wrote a letter of acceptance which was handed to the defendant at 7 a.m. on the Friday morning. The Court of Appeal held that as the plaintiff had heard about the revocation from Berry, who was a reliable source, the offer was no longer available for acceptance. No contract had been formed.

In *Dickinson* v *Dodds* the offer was expressed to be open until Friday at 9 a.m. Such an offer may be revoked before the end of the time limit, unless it has already been accepted or the offeree has given some consideration, for example, paying £1 to keep the offer open.

(4) *If the offer lapses*. The offeror may stipulate that the offer is only open for a limited period of time. Once the time limit has passed, any acceptance will be invalid. Even if no time limit is mentioned, the offer will not remain open indefinitely. It must be accepted within a reasonable time.

Ramsgate Victoria Hotel Co v Montefiore (1866)

The defendant offered to buy shares in the plaintiff's company in June. The shares were eventually allotted in November. The defendant refused to take them up. The Court of Exchequer held that the defendant's offer to take shares had lapsed through an unreasonable delay in acceptance.

What is a reasonable time will vary with the type of contract.

(5) *Death*. If the offeror dies after having made an offer and the offeree is notified of the death, any acceptance will be invalid. However, where the offeree accepts in ignorance of what has happened, the fate of the offer seems to depend on the nature of the contract. An offer which involves the personal service of the offeror clearly cannot be enforced, but other offers may survive, be accepted and carried out by the deceased's personal representatives. If the offeree dies, there can be no acceptance. The offer was made to that person and no one else can accept.

Acceptance

Once the presence of a valid offer has been established, the next stage in the formation of an agreement is to find an acceptance of that offer. The acceptance must be made while the offer is still open. It must be absolute and unqualified.

Unconditional acceptance

If the offeree attempts to vary the terms offered, this will be treated as a counter-offer. As we have already

seen in *Hyde* v *Wrench* (p. 162) this has the effect of rejecting the original offer. A similar problem exists in 'battle of forms' cases. This is where the offeror makes an offer on his own pre-printed standard form which contains certain terms, and the offeree accepts on his own standard form which contains conflicting terms.

Butler Machine Tool Co. v Ex-Cell-O Corp (England) (1979)

The plaintiffs offered to supply a machine tool to the defendants for £75 535. However, the quotation included a term which would entitle the sellers to increase this price (price-variation clause). The defendants accepted the offer on their own standard terms which did not provide for any variation of their quoted price. The plaintiffs acknowledged the order. When the machine was delivered, the plaintiffs claimed an extra £2892 which the defendants refused to pay. The Court of Appeal held that the defendants had not unconditionally accepted the original offer. They had made a counter-offer which had been accepted by the plaintiffs. The defendants' terms governed the contract. The plaintiffs' action to recover the increase in price, therefore, failed.

One form of conditional acceptance is the use of the phrase 'subject to contract' in negotiations involving the sale of land. These words mean that the parties do not intend to be bound at that stage.

Method of acceptance

An acceptance may take any form. It can be given verbally, or in writing but mental acceptance is not enough.

Felthouse v Bindley (1862)

The plaintiff had been negotiating to buy his nephew's horse. He eventually wrote to his nephew: 'If I hear no more about him, I shall consider the horse is mine at £30 15s.' The nephew did not reply to this letter but he did ask the auctioneer, who had been engaged to sell all his farming stock, to keep the horse out of the sale as he had sold it to his uncle. The auctioneer by mistake included the horse in the sale and was sued by the uncle in the tort of conversion. The basis of the uncle's claim was that the auctioneer had sold his property. The court held that the uncle had no claim. Although the nephew had mentally accepted the offer, some form of positive action was required for a valid acceptance. Since there was no contract between the uncle and nephew, ownership of the horse had not passed to the uncle.

Comment. This case established the principle that the offeree's silence or failure to act cannot constitute a valid acceptance. The rule has a particularly useful application to the problem of 'inertia selling'. This is where a trader sends unsolicited goods to a person's home, stipulating that if he does not receive a reply within a specified time, he will assume that his offer to sell the goods has been accepted and the indicated price is payable. The *Felthouse* rule makes it clear that a recipient of goods in these circumstances is not obliged to pay, because his silence or inaction cannot amount to an acceptance. Many people, however, have paid up in ignorance of the law.

More effective control of 'inertia selling' was introduced in the form of the Unsolicited Goods and Services Act 1971. Under this Act, unsolicited goods become the property of a private recipient if the sender fails to collect them within six months. The recipient can cut short the six month period by giving written notice to the sender, who then has thirty days to collect the goods. It is an offence for a trader to demand payment for, or threaten proceedings in respect of, goods which have not been ordered.

Felthouse v *Bindley* would seem to suggest that only an oral or written acceptance will be valid. However, acceptance may be implied from a person's conduct, such as returning a lost dog in a reward case, or using a smoke ball in the prescribed manner in *Carlill* v *Carbolic Smoke Ball Co.* (see p. 161).

The offeror may state that the acceptance must be in a particular form. It follows that the offeror's wishes should be respected. So if he asks for an acceptance in writing, a verbal acceptance by telephone will not be valid. Sometimes the offeror may say 'reply by return post', when he really means 'reply quickly' and a telephone call would be acceptable. Provided the chosen method of acceptance fulfils the intentions of the offeror it will be binding.

Yates Building Co. Ltd *v* R J Pulleyn & Sons (York) Ltd (1975)
The vendors of a piece of land stated that an option to buy it should be exercised by 'notice in writing ... to be sent registered or recorded delivery'. The acceptance was sent by ordinary post. The Court of Appeal held that the vendor's intention was to ensure that they received written notification of acceptance. The requirement to use registered or recorded delivery was more in the nature of a helpful suggestion than a condition of acceptance.

Communication of acceptance
The general rule is that an acceptance must be communicated to the offeror, either by the offeree himself or by someone authorized by the offeree. The contract is formed at the time and place the acceptance is received by the offeror. If the post, however, is the proper method of communication between the parties, then acceptance is effective immediately the letter of acceptance is posted. Provided the letter is properly stamped, addressed and posted, the contract is formed on posting, even if the letter is delayed or never reaches its destination.

Household Fire Insurance Co. *v* Grant (1879)
Grant applied for shares in the plaintiff company. A letter of allotment was posted but Grant never received it. When the company went into liquidation Grant was asked, as a shareholder, to contribute the amount still outstanding on the shares he held. The Court of Appeal held that Grant was a shareholder of the company. The contract to buy shares was formed when the letter of allotment (acceptance) was posted.

The 'postal rules' have been applied to acceptances by telegram but not to more instantaneous methods of communication such as telex and telephone.

Clearly, the 'postal rules' are a potential problem for an offeror: if the letter of acceptance is lost in the post, he may be unaware that a binding contract has been formed. An offeror can protect himself by specifically stating that the acceptance is only complete when received on or before a certain date.

Holwell Securities Ltd *v* Hughes (1973)
Dr Hughes had agreed to grant Holwell Securities Ltd an option to buy his premises. The option, which would constitute the acceptance, was exercisable 'by notice in writing' to the doctor within six months. The Company posted a letter of acceptance but it was never delivered. The Court of Appeal held that no contract had been formed. Since Dr Hughes had stipulated actual 'notice' of the acceptance the postal rules did not apply. The acceptance would only be effective when received by the doctor.

Note that the postal rules only apply to the communication of acceptances: offers and revocations of offers must be communicated to be effective.

Consideration

On the previous pages we have seen how an agreement is formed – the requirements of offer and acceptance. But the mere fact of an agreement alone does not make a contract. The law concerns itself with bargains. This means that each side must promise to give or do something for the other. The element of exchange is known as 'consideration' and is an essential element of every valid simple contract. A promise of a gift will not be binding unless made in the form of a specialty contract (see p. 160).

Consideration can take two forms: executed or executory. What is the difference between them?

Executed consideration is where one party promises to do something in return for the act of another, e.g. reward cases.

PROMISE	ACT
£10 reward offered for the return of 'Lucky' – black and white cat Ring Mrs Smith (215–8793)	David sees the advert in the local paper. He finds the cat, returns it to Mrs Smith and claims the reward

'Cash with order' terms are an example of executed consideration.

Executory consideration is where the parties exchange promises to perform acts in the future, e.g. 'cash on delivery' terms.

PROMISE	PROMISE
Jones & Co. Ltd promises to pay £550 when a new electronic typewriter is delivered.	Fastype Ltd promise to deliver the typewriter within six weeks.

Rules governing consideration

(1) *Consideration must not be in the past*. If one party voluntarily performs an act, and the other party then makes a promise, the consideration for the promise is said to be in the past. Past consideration is regarded as no consideration at all.

ACT	PROMISE
John gives Susan a lift home in his car after work.	On arrival Susan offers John £1 towards the petrol but finding that she has not got any change says she will give him the money next day at work.

In this example, John cannot enforce Susan's promise to pay £1 because the consideration for the promise (giving the lift) is in the past. John would have given Susan the lift home without expecting payment and so there was no bargain between the parties.

Re McArdle (1951)

Mr McArdle died leaving a house to his wife for her life-time and then to his children. While Mrs McArdle was still alive one of the children and his wife moved into the house. The wife made a number of improvements to the house costing £488. After the work had been completed, all the children signed a document in which they promised to reimburse the wife when their father's estate was finally distributed. The Court of Appeal held that this was a case of past consideration. The promise to pay £488 to the wife was made after the improvements had been completed and was, therefore, not binding.

The rule about past consideration is not strictly followed. If, for example, a person is asked to perform a service, which he duly carries out, and later a promise to pay is made, the promise will be binding.

Re Casey's Patents, Stewart v Casey (1892)

Casey agreed to promote certain patents which had been granted to Stewart and another. (A patent gives the holder exclusive rights to profit from an invention). Two years later Stewart wrote to Casey giving him a one-third share of the patents 'in consideration' of Casey's efforts. It was held that Stewart's original request raised an implication that Casey's work would be paid for. The later letter merely fixed the amount of the payment.

(2) *Consideration must move from the promisee.* An action for breach of contract can only be brought by someone who has himself given consideration. A stranger to the consideration cannot take advantage of the contract, even though it may have been made for his benefit.

Tweddle v Atkinson (1861)

John Tweddle and William Guy agreed that they would pay a sum of money to Tweddle's son, William, who had married Guy's daughter. William Guy died without paying his share and William Tweddle sued his late father-in-law's executor (Atkinson). His claim failed because he had not provided any consideration for the promise to pay.

This rule is closely related to the doctrine of privity of contract. This states that a person cannot be bound by, or take advantage of, a contract to which he was not a party.

(3) *Consideration must not be illegal.* The courts will not entertain an action where the consideration is contrary to a rule of law or is immoral. The question of legality will be considered in more detail on p. 174.

(4) *Consideration must be sufficient but need not be adequate.* It must be possible to attach some value to the consideration but there is no requirement for the bargain to be strictly commercial. If a man is prepared to sell his Jaguar car for £1, the contract will not fail for lack of consideration. The courts will not help someone who complains of making a bad bargain. The following are examples of cases where the consideration was of little value, but, nevertheless, it was held to be sufficient.

Thomas v Thomas (1842)

After the death of her husband Mrs Thomas agreed to pay rent of £1 a year in order to continue living in the same house. It was held that the payment of £1 was valid consideration.

Chappell & Co Ltd v Nestlé Co. Ltd (1959)

Nestlé's were running a special offer whereby members of the public could obtain a copy of the record 'Rockin' Shoes' by sending off three wrappers from Nestlé's sixpenny chocolate bars, plus 1s 6d. The records had been made by Hardy & Co. but the copyright was owned by Chappell & Co. Ltd, who claimed that there had been breaches of their copyright. The case turned round whether the three wrappers were part of the consideration. The House of Lords held that they were – even though they were thrown away when received. In the words of Lord Somervell, 'A peppercorn does not cease to be good consideration if it is established that the promisee does not like pepper and will throw away the corn'.

A person who promises to carry out a duty which he is already obliged to perform is in reality offering nothing of value. The 'consideration' will be insufficient. However, if a person does more than he is bound to do, there may be sufficient consideration. The promise may involve a public duty imposed by law.

Collins v Godefroy (1831)

Collins was subpoenaed to give evidence in a case in which Godefroy was a party. (A subpoena is a court order which compels a person's attendance at court). Godefroy promised to pay 6 gns for Collins' loss of time. Collins' action to recover this money failed because he was already under a legal duty to appear in court. He hadn't done anything extra.

Glasbrook Bros. Ltd v Glamorgan County Council (1925)

Glasbrook Bros were the owners of a strike-hit mine. They asked for police protection for the safety men whose presence was necessary to prevent the mine flooding. They were unhappy with the arrangements originally offered by the local police. Eventually it was agreed that seventy policemen would be stationed in the colliery and that Glasbrook Bros would pay for this extra security. The House of Lords held that, since the police had provided more protection than they thought necessary, this constituted consideration. They were entitled to payment.

Similar principles apply where a person is bound by a pre-existing contractual duty.

Stilk v Myrick (1809)

During the course of a voyage from London to the Baltic and back, two of a ship's crew deserted. The captain promised to share the wages of the deserters amongst the remaining crew. It was held that this promise was not binding as the sailors were already contractually bound to meet such emergencies of the voyage. They had not provided consideration.

Hartley v Ponsonby (1857)

When almost half of the crew of a ship deserted, the captain offered those remaining £40 extra to complete the voyage. In this case, the ship was so seriously undermanned that the rest of the journey had become extremely hazardous. It was held that this fact discharged the sailors from their existing contract and left them free to enter into a new contract for the rest of the voyage.

A slightly different problem arises where a person agrees to accept a smaller sum of money as full payment under a contract to pay a larger amount. For example, what is the legal position if Derek owes Graham £100, but Graham says that he will accept £90 in full settlement? Can Graham change his mind and sue for the outstanding £10? The long-established common law rule is that an agreement to accept a lesser sum is not binding unless supported by fresh consideration.

Foakes v Beer (1884)

Mrs Beer had obtained judgment for a debt against Dr Foakes. She agreed that she would take no further action in the matter provided that Foakes paid £500 immediately and the rest by half-yearly instalments of £150. Foakes duly kept to his side of the agreement. Judgment debts, however, carry interest. The House of Lords held that Mrs Beer was entitled to the £360 interest which had accrued. Foakes had not 'bought' her promise to take no further action on the judgment. He had not provided any consideration.

There are a number of exceptions to the rule. If the smaller payment is made, at the creditor's request –

(*a*) at an earlier time, or
(*b*) at a different place, or
(*c*) with an additional item, or
(*d*) by a different method –

Consideration has been shown. (*Note* that since the decision in *D & C Builders Ltd v Rees* (1965), payment by cheque rather than by cash does not release a debtor from his obligation to pay the full amount.) The rule does not apply to a composition agreement. This is where a debtor agrees with all his creditors to pay so much in the £ of what he owes. Provided the debtor honours the agreement, a creditor cannot sue for any outstanding sum.

The final exception is provided by equity. You will remember from Chap. 1 that equity is a system of law based on the idea of fairness and doing right according to your conscience. The rule about part-payment would seem an ideal candidate for intervention by equity. It seems very unfair that a court will support a person who has gone back on his word especially where the agreement to accept a lesser amount has been relied upon. The equitable rule of promissory estoppel which was developed by Denning, J, in the *High Trees Case* may provide some assistance.

Central London Property Trust Ltd v High Trees House Ltd (1947)

In 1937 the plaintiffs granted a 99-year lease on a block of flats in London to the defendants at an annual rent of £2500. Owing to the outbreak of war in 1939, the defendants found it very difficult to get tenants for the flats and so in 1940 it was agreed that the rent should be reduced to £1250. By 1945 the flats were full again and the plaintiffs sued to recover the arrears of rent as fixed by the 1937 agreement for the last two quarters of 1945. Denning, J, held that they were entitled to recover this money, but if they had sued for the arrears from 1940–45, the 1940 agreement would have defeated their claim. The defendants had relied upon the reduction in rent and equity would require the plaintiffs to honour the promises contained in the 1940 agreement.

Thus it seems that if a person promises that he will not insist on his strict legal rights, and the promise is acted upon, then the law will require the promise to be honoured even though it is not supported by consideration. The following points should be noted about promissory estoppel:

(1) The rule can only be used as a defence.
(2) The promise must have been relied upon, i.e. the money saved committed to something else.
(3) Whoever seeks the help of equity must himself have acted equitably or fairly.
(4) The rule does not as yet extinguish rights: it only suspends the rights of the promisor. So if the promise refers to a particular period of time or a state of affairs (e.g. war conditions), the promisor can revert to the original position at the end of the stated time or when conditions change by giving notice to the promisee.

Intention

So far we have established two requirements for a binding contract: agreement and consideration. The law demands, in addition, that the parties intended to enter into a legal relationship. After all, if you invite a friend round for a social evening at your house, you wouldn't expect legal action to follow if the occasion has to be cancelled. So how does the law decide what the parties intended? For the purpose of establishing the intention of the parties, agreements are divided into two categories: social/domestic and business/commercial agreements.

Business/commercial agreements

In the case of a business agreement, it is automatically presumed that the parties intended to make a legally enforceable contract. It is possible, however, to remove the intention by the inclusion of an express statement to that effect in the agreement.

Rose and Frank Co. v Crompton (J R) & Brothers Ltd (1925)

The defendants, English paper tissue manufacturers, entered into an agreement with the plaintiffs, an American firm, whereby the plaintiffs were to act as sole agents for the sale of the defendants' tissues in the US. The written agreement contained the following 'Honourable Pledge Clause'.

'This arrangement is not entered into … as a formal or legal agreement and shall not be subject to legal jurisdiction in the law courts … but it is only a definite expression and record of the purpose and intention of the parties concerned to which they honourably pledge themselves that it will be carried through with mutual loyalty and friendly co-operation'.

The plaintiffs placed orders for tissues which were accepted by the defendants. Before the orders were sent, the defendants terminated the agency agreement and refused to send the tissues. The House of Lords held that the sole agency agreement was not binding owing to the inclusion of the 'honourable pledge clause'. Insofar as orders had been placed and accepted, however, contracts had been created and the defendants, in failing to execute them, were in breach of contract.

When the parties enter into an agreement 'subject to contract' they are expressly stating that they will not be bound unless and until a formal contract is drawn up.

There are situations where it would appear at first sight that the parties had entered into a commercial arrangement, but, nevertheless, a contract is not created.

(1) *Collective agreements.* Employers and trade unions regularly enter into collective agreements about rates of pay and conditions of employment. Section 18 of the Trade Union and Labour Relations Act 1974 provides that such agreements are not intended to be legally enforceable unless they are in writing and expressly affirm that they are intended to be binding.

(2) *Advertisements.* Generally speaking, vague promises or guarantees given in the course of promoting a product are not intended to be taken seriously. By contrast, more specific pledges such as, 'If you can find the same holiday at a lower price in a different brochure, we will refund you the difference', are likely to be binding. (See *Carlill v Carbolic Smoke Ball Co.* on p. 161.)

(3) *Public bodies.* Where one of the parties is a public body which is bound by Act of Parliament to supply a particular service, there is no intention to enter into a contract with customers. For example, if you post a letter by ordinary first class mail and it is delayed or lost, you cannot sue the Post Office for breach of contract.

Social/domestic arrangements

Social arrangements between friends do not usually amount to contracts because the parties never intend their agreement to be legally binding. You might agree to meet someone for lunch or accept an invitation to a party, but in neither case have you entered into a contract. If it can be shown, however, that the transaction had a commercial flavour, the court may be prepared to find the necessary intention for a contract.

Simpkins v Pays (1955)

The plaintiff, Simpkins, lodged with the defendant, Mrs Pays and her granddaughter. Each week all three ladies jointly completed a competition run by a Sunday newspaper. The entries were sent off in the defendant's name. One entry won a prize of £750 which the defendant refused to share with the plaintiff. It was held that the parties had embarked on a joint enterprise, expecting to share any prize money. There was an intention to enter into a legal relationship and the plaintiff was entitled to one-third of the winnings.

Most domestic arrangements within families are not intended to be legally binding. An agreement between husband and wife or parent and child does not normally give rise to a contract. That is not to say that there can never be business contracts between members of a family. Many family businesses are run as partnerships; a wife can be employed by her husband.

If the husband and wife are living apart, they can make a binding separation agreement.

Merritt v Merritt (1969)

Mr Merritt had left his wife to live with another woman. He agreed that if his wife completed the mortgage repayments on the matrimonial home, he would transfer the house to her. Mrs Merritt duly completed the repayments but her husband refused to convey the house to her. The Court of Appeal held that, as the parties were living apart, the agreement was enforceable.

Form

If you ask someone what a contract is, you will probably be told that it is a written document. Some contracts are indeed in writing but the majority are created much more informally, either orally or implied from conduct.

Generally, the law does not require complex formalities to be observed to form a contract. There are, however, some types of contract which are exceptions to this rule.

(1) *Contracts which must be under seal.* Certain transactions involving land require the execution of a deed, i.e. conveyances, legal mortgages and leases for more than three years. A promise of a gift is not binding unless in this form.

(2) *Contracts which must be in writing.* Under the Bills of Exchange Act 1882, bills of exchange, cheques and promissory notes must be in writing. Similarly the transfer of shares in a limited company must be in writing. Regulations introduced under the Consumer Credit Act 1974 lay down requirements about the form and content of regulated consumer credit and hire agreements. The Employment Protection (Consolidation) Act 1978 requires that employees are given a written statement of the terms and conditions of employment within thirteen weeks of starting work. Failure to provide a written statement does not affect the validity of a contract of employment, although it does entitle an employee to refer the matter to an industrial tribunal. The tribunal can decide on the particulars which should have been included in the written statement. (See also p. 273.) An example of a possible form of written statement may be seen on p. 276.

(3) *Contracts which must be evidenced in writing.* In two cases the courts will not enforce the contract unless there is written evidence of its main terms contained in a note or memorandum. They are:

(*a*) *Contracts of guarantee.* If you borrow money or buy goods on credit you may be asked to find someone who will guarantee the debt. This means that if you do not or cannot repay the money, the guarantor will pay your debt for you. A more detailed discussion of guarantees appears on p. 263.

(*b*) *Contracts for the sale or other disposition of land or any interest in land.* The note or memorandum must identify the parties, the subject matter of the contract and contain the signature or initials of the person against whom action is to be taken. In the case of land, the consideration must also be stated.

The requirement of written evidence does not affect the formation of such contracts. The absence of writing does not make the agreement void; so if any money or property has changed hands it can be kept. However, if one of the parties wishes to enforce the contract in the courts, the necessary note or memorandum must be produced, unless the equitable principle of part performance applies. This means that the court may grant specific performance of the contract provided the following conditions are met:

(1) It must be the kind of contract for which specific performance can be granted. In practice, this means contracts involving land.

(2) The plaintiff must have carried out acts of part performance.

(3) A reasonable explanation of the acts of part performance must be the existence of a contract between the parties.

(4) There must be sufficient oral evidence of the terms of the contract.

(5) It must be almost in the nature of fraud for the defendant to rely on the lack of written evidence.

Wakeham v Mackenzie (1968)

Mrs Wakeham, a widow, made an oral agreement with an elderly widower, whereby she would look after him for the rest of his life and in return she should get his house and its contents on his death. It was also agreed that Mrs Wakeham would pay for her board and her own coal. The widower died but he had not kept his promise to leave her the house. The widower's executor argued that Mrs Wakeham was not entitled to the property because of the absence of any written evidence. It was held that her acts of part performance in giving up her flat to move in with the widower were sufficient to justify an order of specific performance to carry out the terms of the oral agreement.

Capacity

'If there is one thing which more than another public policy requires it is that men of full age and competent understanding shall have the utmost liberty of contracting and their contracts when entered into freely and voluntarily shall be held sacred and shall be enforced by courts of justice' (Sir George Jessel, 1875).

This classic statement of freedom of contract by a nineteenth-century Master of the Rolls still essentially holds good today – it is assumed that everyone is capable of entering into a contract. There are, however, some groups of people who are in need of the law's protection either because of their age or inability to appreciate their own actions. The groups which are covered by special rules are those under the age of 18 (minors), mental patients and drunks.

Minors

Before 1970 anyone under the age of twenty-one was known as an infant. The age of majority was lowered to eighteen on 1 January 1970 and 'infants' were renamed 'minors'. The rules relating to contractual capacity are designed to protect the minor from exploitation by adults. A minor is free to enter into contracts and enforce his rights against an adult. The adult's rights will depend on whether the contract is valid, voidable or void.

(a) *Valid contracts.* There are two types of contract which will bind a minor: contracts for necessary goods and services and beneficial contracts of service.

A minor must pay a reasonable price for 'necessaries' sold and delivered to him. Section 3 of the Sale of Goods Act 1979 defines 'necessaries' as 'goods suitable to the condition in life of the minor and to his actual requirements at the time of sale and delivery'. Clearly, luxury goods are excluded. Expensive but useful items may be necessaries provided they are appropriate to the social background and financial circumstances of the minor. If the minor is already adequately supplied, the goods will not be classed as necessaries.

Nash v Inman (1908)

A Savile Row tailor sued an infant Cambridge student for the price of clothes (including eleven fancy waistcoats) he had supplied. The tailor failed in his action because the student was already adequately supplied with clothes.

A minor is also bound by contracts of employment, apprenticeship and education, which, taken as a whole, are for his benefit.

Roberts v Gray (1913)

The infant defendant had agreed to go on a world tour with the plaintiff, a professional billiards player. After the plaintiff had spent much time and some money organizing the tour, the infant changed his mind and refused to go. The plaintiff sued for breach of contract. The Court of Appeal held that this was essentially a contract to receive instruction. Since this was for the infant's benefit the contract was valid. The plaintiff was awarded £1500 damages.

If the minor sets himself up in business, he will not be bound by his trading contracts, even though they are for his benefit. The minor can, nonetheless, sue on these contracts.

Cowern v Nield (1912)

Nield was an infant hay and straw dealer. He refused to deliver a quantity of hay which had been paid for by Cowern. It was held that, provided the infant had not acted fraudulently, he was not liable to repay Cowern.

(b) *Voidable contracts.* There are three kinds of contract which are voidable: leases of land, partnerships and the purchase of shares. Voidable means that the contract is binding on the minor until he decides to reject it. He must repudiate the contract before becoming eighteen or within a reasonable time of reaching eighteen. The main effect of repudiation is to relieve the minor of all future liabilities, but he can be sued for liabilities which have already accrued, such as arrears of rent.

(c) *Void contracts.* Section 1 of the Infants Relief Act 1874 provides that certain minors' contracts are 'absolutely void'. They are contracts for the repayment of money lent or to be lent, or for the supply of non-necessary goods and all accounts stated. Normally, if a contract is void, neither party can sue on it and any money or property which has been transferred can be recovered. In practice, 'absolutely void' has been taken to mean that the contract cannot be enforced against the minor. The minor, however, can still acquire rights by these contracts and sue for breach.

Coutts & Co. v Browne-Lecky (1946)

A bank allowed an infant customer to overdraw his account. The overdraft had been guaranteed by two adults. When the overdraft was not cleared, the bank sought to make the adult guarantors liable for the debt. It was held that, as the loan was void under s. 1 of the Infants Relief Act 1874, there was no debt. Since the essence of a guarantee is to answer for the debt of another, it followed that the adult guarantors could not be liable either. The bank's action failed.

There are two situations where an adult may be able to seek some redress against a minor. If money is lent to a minor to enable him to buy necessaries, the lender can recover that part of the loan which is actually spent on necessaries at a reasonable price. Secondly, where the minor has acted fraudulently, by lying about his age for example, he can be made to return the goods or money which he still has in his possession. If he has parted with the goods or the precise notes and coins, the adult cannot get them back.

Drunks and mental patients

Section 3 of the Sale of Goods Act 1979 provides that they are required to pay a reasonable price for necessaries in the same way as minors. Other kinds of contract are governed by common law. If a person is suffering from mental disability or drunkenness at the time of making the contract he will be able to avoid his liabilities provided he can show that he did not understand what the agreement was about and the other person was aware of his disability.

The judges of the Court of Protection may exercise wide powers over the property and affairs of mental patients placed in their care under the Mental Health Act 1983. They can make contracts on behalf of the patient and carry out contracts already made by him.

Genuineness of consent

The most basic requirement of a contract is the presence of an agreement. It must have been entered into voluntarily and involved 'a genuine meeting of minds'. The agreement may be invalidated by a number of factors – mistake, misrepresentation, duress and undue influence.

Mistake

The general rule of common law is that a mistake does not affect the validity of a contract. The guiding principle is *caveat emptor*, which means 'let the buyer beware'. So if a person agrees to pay £1000 for a car, when in reality it is only worth £500, the contract is valid and he must stand the loss.

Leaf v International Galleries (1950)

Mr Leaf bought a painting of 'Salisbury Cathedral' from International Galleries for £85. The Gallery attributed the painting to John Constable. When Leaf tried to sell the painting five years later, he was informed that it was not by Constable. Both the buyer and seller had made a mistake about the quality and value of the painting but this did not affect the validity of the contract.

It should be noted that a mistake of law will not invalidate a contract, since everyone is presumed to know the law.

There are, however, some kinds of mistake which so undermine the agreement that the contract is void. If this is the case, no rights of ownership can pass and any goods which have changed hands can be recovered. A mistake will invalidate the contract in the following situations –

(1) *Mistakes as to the subject-matter of the contract.* The parties may be mistaken as to the identity of the subject matter. If a seller makes an offer in respect of one thing and the buyer accepts, but is thinking of something else, the parties are clearly talking at cross-purposes and there is no contract.

Raffles v Wichelhaus (1864)

The defendant agreed to buy cotton which was described as 'arriving on the Peerless from Bombay'. There were two ships called the Peerless sailing from Bombay: one in October and the other in December. It was held that there was no binding contract between the parties as the defendant meant one ship and the plaintiff the other.

When the parties contract in the mistaken belief that a particular thing is in existence, but in fact it has ceased to exist, the contract is void.

Couturier v Hastie (1856)

A contract was made for the sale of Indian corn which the parties believed to be on board a ship bound for the UK. Unknown to the parties, the corn had overheated during the voyage and been landed at the nearest port and sold. The House of Lords held that the agreement was void.

(2) *Mistake as to the identity of one of the parties.* If one party makes a mistake about the identity of the person he is contracting with, this may invalidate the contract. Where the identity of the party contracted with is material to the contract, a mistake will result in the contract being void.

Cundy v Lindsay (1878)

Lindsay & Co, Belfast linen manufacturers, received an order for a large quantity of handkerchiefs from a rogue called Blenkarn. The rogue had signed his name in such a way that it looked like 'Blenkiron & Co.', a well-known, respectable firm. Lindsay & Co despatched the goods on credit to Blenkarn who resold 250 dozen to Cundy. Blenkarn did not pay for the goods and was later convicted of obtaining goods by false pretences. Lindsay & Co. sued Cundy for conversion. The House of Lords held that the contract between Lindsay & Co. and Blenkarn was void for mistake. Lindsay & Co. intended to deal with Blenkiron & Co., not the rogue, Blenkarn. Cundy was liable in conversion.

Where the identity of the other party is not material, the contract will be valid until the mistaken party realizes that he has been misled and avoids the contract for misrepresentation.

Lewis v Averay (1971)

Lewis sold his car to a man who claimed he was Richard Greene, the star of a popular television series, 'Robin Hood'. The man paid by cheque, producing a pass to Pinewood Studios as proof of his identity. He resold the car to Averay. The cheque had been taken from a stolen cheque book and was later dishonoured. Lewis sued Averay in the tort of conversion. The Court of Appeal held that Lewis intended to deal with the man actually in front of him despite his fraudulent claim to be Richard Greene. The contract between Lewis and the rogue was not void for mistake, but rather voidable for a fraudulent misrepresentation. Since Lewis had not avoided the contract by the time the rogue sold the car to

Averay, Averay acquired good rights of ownership. He was not liable in conversion.

(3) *Mistaken signing of a written document.* As a general rule, a person who signs a document is assumed to have read, understood and agreed to its contents. Exceptionally, a person may be able to plead *non est factum* – 'It is not my deed'. Three elements must be present if the contract is to be avoided: the signature must have been induced by fraud, the document signed must be fundamentally different from that thought to be signed, and the signer must not have acted negligently.

Mistake in equity

At common law, mistake only rarely invalidates a contract. It may, nevertheless, be possible for the court to apply equitable principles to achieve a measure of justice in the case. A court may grant the following forms of equitable relief.

(1) *Rescission on terms.* The court may be prepared to set aside an agreement, provided the parties accept the conditions imposed by the court for a fairer solution to the problem.

Grist v Bailey (1966)

Bailey agreed to sell a house to Grist for £850. The price was based on both parties' belief that the house had a sitting tenant. The value of the house with vacant possession would have been about £2250. Unknown to the parties, the tenants had died and their son did not stay on in the property. The judge held that the contract was not void at common law but he was prepared to set the contract aside provided Bailey offered to sell the property to Grist for the proper market price of £2250.

(2) *Rectification.* If a mistake is made in reducing an oral agreement into writing, the court may rectify the document so that it expresses the true intention of the parties.

(3) *Specific performance.* A court may refuse to grant an order of specific performance against a party who made a mistake, if it would be unfair to enforce the contract against him.

Misrepresentation

The formation of a contract is often preceded by a series

of negotiations between the parties. Some of the statements made may later turn out to be false. The nature of the statement will determine whether a remedy is available and, if it is, the type of remedy.

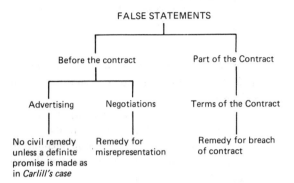

Fig. 8.1 Remedies for false statements

A false statement, which is not incorporated into the contract, is known as a misrepresentation. A misrepresentation is a false statement made by one party which induces the other to enter into a contract. As a general rule, a positive statement must be made; keeping quiet about something does not normally amount to misrepresentation. Gestures, smiles and nods can amount to a statement and there are certain situations where a failure to speak will amount to an actionable misrepresentation, e.g.:

(1) where there is a relationship of good faith between the parties, e.g. between partners (see further p. 70);

(2) where the contract is one of utmost good faith, e.g. proposals for insurance cover;

(3) where a half truth is offered (in one case a solicitor stated that he was not aware of any restrictive covenants on a piece of land, which was literally true, but if he had bothered to read relevant documents he would have discovered that there were indeed restrictive covenants);

(4) where there has been a change in circumstances between the time of the negotiations and the conclusion of the contract.

The misrepresentation must involve a statement of fact and not a statement of law, opinion or intention.

Bissett v Wilkinson (1927)

During the course of negotiations for the sale of a farm in New Zealand to Wilkinson, Bissett stated that the land would support 2000 sheep. The farm had not previously been used for grazing sheep and Wilkinson knew this. It was held that Bissett was merely expressing his opinion. There was no misrepresentation.

It must be shown that the statement has induced the person to whom it was made to enter into the contract. If the person attempts to check the truth of what has been said, he clearly has not relied on the statement.

Kinds of misrepresentation and their effects

There are three kinds of misrepresentation: fraudulent, negligent or innocent. In each case, the contract is voidable.

(1) *Fraudulent misrepresentation.* If the person making the statement knows that what he has said is false, he will be liable for fraud. The injured party may rescind the contract and also sue for damages for the tort of deceit.

(2) *Negligent misrepresentation.* This is where the person making the false statement has no reasonable grounds for believing the statement to be true. Damages may be awarded either for the tort of negligence or under s. 2(1) of the Misrepresentation Act 1967. The injured party is more likely to be successful under the Act, because it reverses the normal burden of proof. Thus the defendant will only escape liability if he can prove that the statement was made innocently. The judge may also award rescission as well as damages.

(3) *Innocent misrepresentation.* An innocent misrepresentation is a false statement made by a person who had reasonable grounds to believe that it was true, not only when it was made, but also when the contract was entered into. The basic remedy is rescission of the contract: under s. 2(2) of the Misrepresentation Act 1967, the court may in its discretion award damages instead.

Rescission

Rescission aims to restore the parties to their pre-contractual positions. Money or goods which have changed hands must be returned. Like all equitable remedies it is not available as of right. In particular, the court may refuse to award rescission in the following circumstances:

(*a*) *Where the injured party has received some benefit under the contract or has in some way affirmed it*. A long delay in taking legal action is taken as evidence of affirmation.

(*b*) *Where the parties cannot be restored to their original positions* because, for example, goods have been destroyed or they have been sold to a third party.

Duress and undue influence

The general rule of law is that a contract will be valid only if the parties entered into it freely and voluntarily. At common law, where a party to a contract or his family is subjected to violence or threats of violence, the contract may be avoided on the grounds of duress.

Equity, in addition, recognizes a more subtle form of pressure: undue influence. The relationship between the parties may be such that one occupies a position of dominance and influence over the other. There are several relationships, such as doctor and patient, solicitor and client, parent and child, where it is automatically assumed that undue influence has been at work. The contract will be set aside unless the dominant person can show that the complainant had independent advice. Where there is no special relationship between the parties, the plaintiff must prove that pressure was applied.

Legality

The principle of freedom of contract is subject to a basic rule that the courts will not uphold an agreement which is illegal or contrary to public policy. Where the contract involves some kind of moral wrongdoing, it will be illegal. If, however, the conduct is neither immoral nor blameworthy, but simply undesirable, the contract will be void. A court may object to an agreement either because of a rule of common law or because it is contrary to statute.

(1) *Contracts illegal at common law*. The following agreements come into this category:

(*a*) *Contracts to commit crimes or civil wrongs*; e.g. a contract to assassinate someone or to defraud the Inland Revenue.

(*b*) *Contracts involving sexual immorality*; e.g. an agreement to pay an allowance to a mistress or any contract with an immoral purpose.

Pearce v Brooks (1866)

Pearce let a coach out on hire to a prostitute (Brooks) knowing that it would be used by her to ply her trade. The coach was returned in a damaged state. Pearce was unable to recover the hire charges or for the damage as the court refused to help him enforce a contract for an immoral purpose.

(*c*) *Contracts tending to promote corruption in public life*; e.g. a contract to bribe an official or to procure a title.

(*d*) *Contracts of trading with an enemy in wartime*.

(*e*) *Contracts directed against the welfare of a friendly foreign state*; e.g. a partnership intending to import whisky into America during Prohibition (*Foster v Driscoll* (1929)).

(*f*) *Contracts prejudicial to the administration of justice*; e.g. a contract not to prosecute a person for an offence concerning the public.

Consequences of illegality

A contract which is illegal from the start will be void and unenforceable. Money or property transferred under the contract is not usually recoverable. This general rule is subject to three exceptions:

(1) A party can recover money or property if he can establish his case without relying on the illegal contract, e.g. by suing in tort.

(2) If the parties are not equally at fault, the less guilty party may be allowed to recover.

(3) A party may recover if he repents before the contract has been substantially performed.

Some contracts are quite innocent at the outset, but become illegal, because of the intention of one of the parties, e.g. a landlord lets out a flat, unaware of the tenant's intention to install his mistress in it. In this situation, one of the parties is innocent. The guilty party cannot sue on the contract or succeed in any way against the innocent party. The innocent party will protect his rights if he repudiates the contract as soon as he is aware of the illegality.

Contracts void at common law

There are three types of contract in this category:

(*a*) *Contracts to oust the jurisdiction of the courts*.

A clause which seeks to prevent the courts trying an issue is void. This rule does not affect 'binding in honour only' clauses by which the parties agree not to create a contract (p. 168).

(b) *Contracts prejudicial to the status of marriage.* This includes a contract to restrain a person from marrying at all or except for one person. Contracts not to marry a person of a particular religious faith or nationality may be upheld if they are reasonable.

A contract which provides for a possible future separation of husband and wife will be void, but if the marriage is breaking up, they may make a contract to provide for their immediate separation. Contracts to introduce men and women with a view to their subsequent marriage are void. These are known as marriage-brokage contracts.

(c) *Contracts in restraint of trade.* These are contracts which restrict the future liberty of a person to carry on his business, trade or profession in any way he chooses. There are four main types of restraint:

(1) A term in a contract of employment which restricts the employee's freedom to work after the contract has terminated.

EXAMPLE

The Top Knot Salon employs Jane as a hairdresser, on the terms that Jane will not set up her own hairdressing business within a three mile radius of the Top Knot Salon for two years after leaving their employ.

(2) A 'sales' agreement by which a trader agrees to restrict his orders to one supplier.

(3) A contract for the sale of a business by which the seller agrees not to compete with the buyer.

(4) Contracts between traders and businessmen to regulate prices or output. This branch of the law is now largely covered by the Restrictive Trade Practices Acts 1976 and 1977 and the Resale Prices Act 1976.

A contract in restraint of trade is contrary to public policy and void unless it is shown to be reasonable. The restraint must be reasonable as between the parties and from the point of view of the community. A restraint will be reasonable if it is designed to protect legitimate interests, such as lists of customers or trade secrets. A restraint which is excessive as regards its area, time of operation or the trades which it forbids will be void.

Esso Petroleum Co. Ltd v Harper's Garage (Stourport) Ltd (1967)

Harper's owned two garages. They entered into a 'solus' agreement with Esso by which they agreed to buy all their motor fuel from Esso, to keep the garages open at all reasonable hours and not to sell the garages without ensuring that the purchaser entered into a similar agreement with Esso. In return, Esso allowed a rebate on all fuels bought. The agreement was to last for four and a half years in respect of one garage and twenty-one years for the other. The latter garage was mortgaged to Esso for a loan of £7000 repayable over twenty-one years and not earlier. The House of Lords held that the agreements were in restraint of trade and, therefore, void, unless they could be justified as reasonable. The agreement which lasted for four and a half years was reasonable but the other, which lasted for twenty-one years, was not.

Consequences

A clause which is in restraint of trade is void and unenforceable. It may be possible, however, to separate out the void parts of the contract. The lawful main part can then be enforced by the court. Any money paid, or property transferred, is recoverable.

Contracts illegal by statute

Some statutes expressly prohibit a certain type of contract. For example, under Part I of the Resale Prices Act 1976, collective agreements by two or more persons regulating the price at which goods may be resold are unlawful. The provision outlaws the practice of 'blacklisting' retailers who sell goods below a minimum resale price fixed by suppliers.

Not all statutes are quite so specific. Some contracts may incidentally infringe the provisions of an Act of Parliament because, for example, one of the parties is trading without a licence, or statutory requirements have not been observed. It seems that the contract will be illegal if it was Parliament's intention in passing the Act to preserve public order or protect the public.

Cope v Rowlands (1836)

A court refused to enforce a contract on behalf of an unlicensed broker because the purpose of the licensing requirements was to protect the public.

The contract will be valid if it appears that the statutory provision was imposed for an administrative purpose

Smith v Mawhood (1895)

A tobacconist was able to sue on a contract for the sale of tobacco even though he did not have a licence as required by statute. The sole aim of the statute was to raise revenue, not to prohibit contracts made by unlicensed tobacconists.

Consequences

The effects of the illegality on the contract are the same as for contracts which are illegal at common law.

Contracts void by statute

Two of the more important examples of these are gaming and wagering contracts and restrictive practices contracts.

(*a*) *Gaming and wagering contracts*. Gaming is defined by the Betting, Gaming and Lotteries Act 1963 as 'the playing of a game of chance for winning in money or money's worth'. All the players must have an equal chance of winning. Wagering is where two opposing parties stake something on the result of a future uncertain event or the facts of a past or present event. The parties must not have a special interest in the event and it must be possible for one to win and the other to lose.

The Gaming Act 1845 provides that all contracts by way of 'gaming or wagering shall be null and void'. The contract cannot be enforced in the courts and any money or property transferred cannot be recovered.

(*b*) *Restrictive practices contracts*. Under the Restrictive Trade Practices Act 1976 agreements between persons carrying on businesses which are designed to fix prices or regulate the supply of goods must be registered with the Director General of Fair Trading. The agreements are presumed void unless the parties can prove to the Restrictive Practices Court that the agreement is in the public interest. Failure to register an agreement renders the restriction void.

Under Part II of the Resale Prices Act 1976 a term in a contract for the sale of goods between a supplier and a dealer which imposes a minimum price for the resale of those goods is void. The Restrictive Practices Court may exempt certain goods provided this is in the public interest. Only two exemptions have been made by the Court so far – in relation to books and medicaments.

Since joining the European Economic Community, the United Kingdom has been subject to Community law on competition; in particular Art. 85 of the Treaty of Rome. This provides that agreements which affect trade between the member states by preventing, restricting or distorting competition within the common market are void.

Discharge of contracts

The contract may come to an end and the parties discharged from their contractual obligations in four ways: by performance, agreement, frustration and breach.

Performance

The general rule is that the parties must carry out precisely what they agreed under their contract. If one of the parties does something less than, or different from, that which he agreed to do, he is not discharged from the contract and, moreover, cannot sue on the contract.

Cutter v Powell (1795)

Cutter agreed to serve on a ship sailing from Jamaica to Liverpool. He was to be paid 30 guineas on arrival at Liverpool. The ship sailed on 2 August, arriving in Liverpool on 9 October. But Cutter died at sea on 20 September. It was held that his widow could not recover anything for the work he had done before he died. Cutter was obliged to complete the voyage before he was entitled to payment.

Bolton v Mahadeva (1972)

Bolton installed a central heating system in Mahadeva's house for an agreed price of £560. The work was carried out defectively and it was estimated that it would cost £179 to put matters right. The Court of Appeal held that since Bolton had not performed his side of the contract, he could recover nothing for the work he had done.

In each of these cases, one party has profited from the failure of the other to provide complete performance. A strict application of rule about precise performance would frequently lead to injustice. It is not surprising, therefore, that certain exceptions to the rule have developed.

(1) *Doctrine of substantial performance*. If the court decides that the plaintiff has substantially carried

out the terms of the contract, he may recover for the work he has done. The defendant can counterclaim for any defects in performance.

Hoenig v Isaacs (1952)

The plaintiff agreed to decorate the defendant's flat and fit a bookcase and wardrobe for £750. On completion of the work the defendant paid £400 but he complained about faulty workmanship and refused to pay the balance of £350. The Court of Appeal held that the contract had been substantially performed. The plaintiff was entitled to the outstanding £350, less the cost of remedying the defects, which was estimated at £55 18s 2d.

(2) *Acceptance of partial performance.* If one of the parties only partially carries out his side of the contract, but the other party, exercising a genuine choice, accepts the benefit of the partial performance, the court will infer a promise to pay for the benefit received.

(3) *Performance prevented by the promisee.* A person who is prevented from carrying out his side of the bargain by the other party can bring an action to recover for the work he has done.

Planché v Colburn (1831)

The plaintiff agreed to write a book on 'Costume and Ancient Armour', on completion of which he was to receive £100. After he had done the necessary research and written part of the book, the publishers abandoned the project. He recovered 50 guineas for the work he had done.

(4) *Divisible contracts.* Some contracts are said to be 'entire'. This means that a party is not entitled to payment until he has completely performed his part of the contract, e.g. *Cutter* v *Powell* (1795). Other contracts may be divisible, i.e. the obligations can be split up into stages or parts. Payment can be claimed for each completed stage. A contract to build a house usually provides for payment to be made in three stages: after the foundations have been laid, when the roof goes on and on completion of the house.

Agreement

The parties may have agreed in their original contract that it should end automatically with the happening of some event or after a fixed period of time. The agreement may have included a term allowing either party to terminate the contract by giving notice. A contract of employment, for example, can be brought to an end by either the employer or employee giving reasonable notice to the other. The Employment Protection (Consolidation) Act 1978 lays down statutory minimum periods of notice. Employers must also consider the rules about unfair dismissal and redundancy.

A contract may be discharged by the execution of a separate agreement. The new agreement will only discharge the old contract if it possesses all the characteristics of a valid contract; in particular, consideration must be present. When neither party has yet performed his side of the contract, there is no difficulty. Both sides, by waiving their rights, are providing something of value which constitutes consideration. The situation is different where one side has already completely performed his obligations and the other party wishes to be released. The legal position has already been explained on p. 167. The person seeking release must either provide fresh consideration or the agreement must be drawn up in the form of a deed.

Frustration

[handwritten: Something which makes the contract impossible to happen]

An agreement which is impossible of performance from the outset will be void for mistake, as in *Couturier* v *Hastie* (1856). But what is the legal position, where initially it is perfectly possible to carry out the contract, and then a change in circumstances occurs making it impossible to carry out the agreement?

Until the last century, the rule was that the parties were under an absolute duty to perform their contractual obligations. A person was not excused simply because outside events had made performance impossible.

Paradine v Jane (1647)

During the course of the English Civil War, a tenant was evicted from certain property by Prince Rupert and his army. In an action by the landlord to recover three years' arrears of rent, it was held that the tenant was not relieved from the obligation to pay rent simply because he had been unable to enjoy the property.

Starting with the case of *Taylor* v *Caldwell* (1863), the courts recognized an exception to the rule about absolute contracts under the doctrine of frustration: if further performance of the contract is prevented because of events beyond the control of the parties, the contract is terminated and the parties discharged from their obligations. The doctrine will apply in the following circumstances:

(1) *Physical impossibility*. This is where something or someone necessary to carry out the contract ceases to be available.

Taylor v Caldwell (1863)

The plaintiff had hired the Surrey Gardens and Music Hall for a series of concerts. However, after making the agreement and before the date of the first performance, the hall was destroyed by fire. It was held that the contract was discharged and the parties released from their obligations.

If the presence of a particular person is necessary for the execution of the contract, the death of that person will clearly discharge the contract. Frustration may also apply if a party is unavailable because of illness, internment or imprisonment.

Hare v Murphy Bros (1974)

Hare was sentenced to twelve months' imprisonment for unlawful wounding and was, therefore, unavailable to carry out his responsibilities as a foreman. It was held that this frustrated his contract of employment.

(2) *Supervening illegality*. A subsequent change in the law or in circumstances may make performance of the contract illegal. An export contract will be discharged if war breaks out with the country of destination.

(3) *Foundation of the contract destroyed*. The parties may have made their contract on the basis of some forthcoming event. If the event fails to take place and, as a result, the main purpose of the contract cannot be achieved, the doctrine of frustration will apply.

Krell v Henry (1903)

Henry hired a room overlooking the route of Edward VII's coronation procession. The procession was cancelled owing to the King's serious illness. Although it would have been possible to come and sit in the room, the main purpose of the contract, to view the procession, had been destroyed. The Court of Appeal held that the contract had been frustrated.

A contract will only be frustrated if the change in circumstances has had a substantial effect on the main purpose of the contract. The fact that it has become more difficult or expensive to carry out the contract will not excuse the parties.

Tsakiroglou & Co. Ltd v Noblee and Thorl GmbH (1961)

In October 1956 sellers agreed to deliver ground nuts from Port Sudan to buyers in Hamburg, shipment to take place during November/December 1956. On 2 November, the Suez Canal was closed to traffic. The sellers failed to deliver and, when sued for breach of contract, argued that the contract had been frustrated. Clearly, it had not become impossible to carry out the contract: shipment could have been made via the Cape of Good Hope – a longer and much more expensive operation. The House of Lords held that this was not sufficient to discharge the contract for frustration.

The doctrine of frustration will not apply in the following situations –

(*a*) where the parties have foreseen the likelihood of such an event occurring and have made express provision for it in the contract;

(*b*) where one of the parties is responsible for the frustrating event.

The consequences of frustration

At common law, a frustrating event has the effect of bringing the contract to an immediate end. The rights and liabilities of the parties are frozen at the moment of frustration. The rule was that money payable before frustration remained payable and money paid before frustration could not be recovered. Any money which did not become payable until after frustration ceased to be payable. The harsh consequences of this rule were modified by the House of Lords in the *Fibrosa Case* (1943) and wider changes were introduced under the Law Reform (Frustrated Contracts) Act 1943.

The Act made two important changes:

(1) Money payable before frustration ceases to be payable and money paid before frustration can be recovered. The court may in its discretion allow the payee to recover or retain all or part of the sums to cover any expenses incurred.

(2) A party who has carried out acts of part performance can recover compensation for any valuable benefit (other than a payment of money) conferred on the other party.

The Act does not apply to (*a*) contracts for the carriage of goods by sea, (*b*) insurance contracts, and (*c*) contracts for the sale of specific goods, which are covered by s. 7 of the Sale of Goods Act 1979. The parties may exclude the effect of the Act by express agreement.

Breach

A breach of contract may occur in a number of ways. It may be an anticipatory or an actual breach.

Anticipatory breach
This is where a party states in advance that he does not intend to carry out his side of the contract or puts himself in a position whereby he will be unable to perform. The injured party may sue immediately for breach of contract or, alternatively, wait for the time for performance to arrive to see whether the other party is prepared to carry out the contract.

Hochster v **De la Tour (1853)**
The plaintiff was engaged by the defendant in April 1852 to act as a courier for travel in Europe from 1 June 1852. On 11 May the defendant wrote to the plaintiff to inform him that his services were no longer required. The plaintiff started an action for breach of contract on 22 May. Although the date for performance had not yet arrived, it was held that the defendant's letter constituted an actionable breach of contract.

It can be dangerous to wait for the time for performance. The injured party may lose the right to sue for breach of contract, if, in the meantime, the contract is discharged for frustration.

Actual breach
One party may fail completely to perform his side of the bargain or he may fail to carry out one or some of his obligations. Not every breach of contract has the effect of discharging the parties from their contractual obligations. The terms of a contract may be divided into those terms which are important (conditions) and the less important terms (warranties). The distinction

will be considered in more detail in Chap. 10. A breach of condition does not automatically terminate the contract. The injured party has a choice: he may wish to be discharged from the contract or he may prefer to carry on with the contract and claim damages for the breach. A breach of warranty only entitles the injured party to sue for damages.

Remedies

So far we have looked at essential elements of a valid contract, the factors which may affect the validity of an agreement and the way in which a contract may come to an end. We now turn to the remedies available to the injured party when a term of the contract has been broken. Every breach of contract will give the injured party the common law right to recover damages (financial compensation). Other remedies, such as specific performance and injunction, may be granted at the discretion of the court as part of its equitable jurisdiction.

Damages

In the business world it is quite common for the parties to agree in advance the damages that will be payable in the event of a breach of contract. These are known as liquidated damages. If there is no prior agreement as to the sum to be paid, the amount of damages is said to be unliquidated.

Liquidated damages
It makes commercial common sense for the parties to establish at the outset of their relationship the financial consequences of failing to live up to their bargain. Provided the parties have made a genuine attempt to estimate the likely loss, the courts will accept the relevant figure as the damages payable. In practice, knowing the likely outcome of any legal action, the party at fault will simply pay up, without argument. An example of liquidated damages are the charges imposed for cancelling a holiday. (See Fig. 8.2.)

Of course, there is a temptation for a party with stronger bargaining power to try to impose a penalty clause, which is really designed as a threat to secure performance. The distinction between liquidated damages and penalty clauses is illustrated by the following cases:

Sunkist Tours – Cancellation charges

Cancellation notified	Charges
Over 6 weeks prior to departure	Loss of deposit
within 4 to 6 weeks of departure	30% of holiday cost
within 2 to 4 weeks of departure	45% of holiday cost
within 1 day to 2 weeks of departure	60% of holiday cost
on or after the day of departure	100% of holiday cost

Fig. 8.2 A sample of a cancellation charges notice.

Dunlop Pneumatic Tyre Co. Ltd *v* **New Garage & Motor Co. Ltd (1915)**
Dunlop supplied tyres to New Garage under an agreement by which, in return for a trade discount, New Garage agreed to pay £5 by way of 'liquidated damages' for every item sold below list prices. The House of Lords held that since the sum was not extravagant, it was a genuine attempt by the parties to estimate the damage which price undercutting would cause Dunlop. The £5 was liquidated damages.

Ford Motor Co. *v* **Armstrong (1915)**
Armstrong, a retailer, agreed to pay £250 for each Ford car sold below the manufacturer's list price. The Court of Appeal held that the clause was void as a penalty.

If the court holds that the sum is liquidated damages, it will be enforced irrespective of whether the actual loss is greater or smaller.

Cellulose Acetate Silk Co. Ltd *v* **Widnes Foundry Ltd (1933)**
Widnes Foundry agreed to pay £20 for every week of delay in completing a plant for the Silk Co. The work was completed 30 weeks late. The Silk Co. claimed that their actual losses amounted to nearly £6000. It was held that Widnes Foundry were only liable to pay £20 a week (i.e. £600) as agreed.

Unliquidated damages
The aim of unliquidated damages is to put the injured party in the position he would have been in if the

contract had been carried out properly. Damages are designed to compensate for loss. If no loss has been suffered, the court will only award nominal damages: a small sum to mark the fact that there had been a breach of contract. The courts observe the following guidelines when awarding damages:

(1) *The damages can include sums for financial loss, damage to property, personal injuries and distress, disappointment and upset caused to the plaintiff.*

Jarvis *v* **Swan's Tours (1973)**
Jarvis, a solicitor, paid £63.45 for a two-week winter sports holiday in Switzerland. The Swan's Tours brochure promised a 'house party' atmosphere at the hotel, a bar which would be open several evenings a week and a host who spoke English. The holiday was a considerable disappointment: in the second week, he was the only guest in the hotel and no one else could speak English. The bar was only open one evening and the ski-ing was disappointing. The Court of Appeal awarded him £125 to compensate for 'the loss of entertainment and enjoyment which he was promised'.

Exemplary or punitive damages which are designed to punish the party in breach are not normally awarded in contract.

(2) *The injured party cannot necessarily recover damages for every kind of loss which he has suffered.* The breach might have caused a chain reaction of events to occur. Clearly there is a point beyond which the damage becomes too remote from the original breach.

The rules relating to remoteness of damage were laid down in *Hadley* v *Baxendale* (1854). The injured party may recover damages for –

(*a*) loss which has resulted naturally and in the ordinary course of events from the defendant's breach, and

(*b*) the loss which, although not a natural consequence of the defendant's breach, was in the minds of the parties when the contract was made.

The practical application of these rules can be seen in the following cases.

Victoria Laundry (Windsor) Ltd *v* Newman Industries Ltd (1949)

The plaintiffs, a firm of launderers and dyers, wished to expand their business and, for this purpose, had ordered a new boiler from the defendants. The boiler was damaged during the course of its removal and as a result there was a five-month delay in delivery. The plaintiff claimed:

(a) damages of £16 per week for the loss of profits they would have made on the planned expansion of their laundry business; and

(b) damages of £262 a week for loss of profits they would have made on extremely lucrative dyeing contracts.

The Court of Appeal held that they were entitled to recover for the normal loss of profits on both cleaning and dyeing contracts, but they could not recover for the especially profitable dyeing contracts of which the defendants were ignorant.

Simpson *v* London and North Western Rail Co. (1876)

Simpson entrusted samples of his products to the defendants for delivery to Newcastle, for exhibition at an agricultural show. The goods were marked 'must be at Newcastle on Monday certain'. They failed to arrive in time. The defendants were held liable for Simpson's prospective loss of profit arising from his inability to exhibit at Newcastle. They had agreed to carry the goods knowing of the special instructions of the customer.

(3) *Provided the loss is not too remote, the next matter to consider is how much is payable by way of damages.* As we have already seen, the object is to put the injured party in the same position as if the contract had been performed. The precise sum will vary according to the subject matter of the contract and the nature and extent of the breach. Breaches of contract for the sale of goods are subject to the rules laid down in the Sale of Goods Act 1979. They will be considered in more detail in Chapter 11.

(4) *Once a breach of contract has occurred, the innocent party is under a duty to mitigate (minimize) his loss.* He cannot stand back and allow the loss to get worse. A seller whose goods have been rejected, for example, must attempt to get the best possible price for them elsewhere. The plaintiff will not be able to recover for that part of the loss which has resulted from his failure to mitigate.

Brace *v* Calder (1895)

The plaintiff was dismissed by his employers but offered immediate re-engagement on the same terms and conditions as before. He refused the offer and instead sued to recover the salary he would have received for the remaining nineteen months of his two year contract. It was held that the plaintiff should have mitigated the loss by accepting the employer's reasonable offer of re-employment. He was entitled to nominal damages only.

Equitable remedies

The normal remedy for a breach of contract is an award of damages at common law. There are some situations, however, where damages would be neither adequate nor appropriate. Equity developed other forms of relief to ensure that justice is done. The more important of these equitable remedies are specific performance and injunction.

Specific performance

A decree of specific performance is an order of the court requiring the party in breach to carry out his contractual obligations. Failure to comply with the directions of the court, lays the defendant open to the imposition of penalties for contempt of court.

Like all equitable remedies, the grant of specific performance is discretionary. It may be withheld in the following circumstances:

(1) *Damages adequate.* An order for specific performance will not be made if damages would be an adequate remedy. Most breaches of contract can be remedied by an award of monetary compensation. If it is a contract for the sale of a unique item, however, no

sum of money can compensate the disappointed buyer for his lost opportunity, and specific performance will be granted. Each piece of land is regarded as being unique and thus the remedy is available in contract for the sale of land.

(2) *Mutuality*. Equity requires mutuality as regards its remedies. This means that both parties must potentially be able to seek an order of specific performance. An adult cannot obtain such an order against a minor, so a minor will not be awarded specific performance either.

(3) *Supervision*. An order will not be made unless the court can adequately supervise its enforcement. It is for this reason that specific performance will not be awarded to enforce building contracts, because the court cannot supervise on the day-to-day basis which would be necessary. Similar principles apply to employment contracts.

(4) *Discretion*. The court may refuse specific performance where it is felt that it would not be just and equitable to grant it.

Injunction

This is an order of the court requiring the party at fault not to break the contract. Its main use is to enforce the negative promises that can occasionally be found in employment contracts (and see p. 175). The employee may agree, for example, not to work in a similar capacity for a rival employer during the period of his contract.

Warner Bros v Nelson (1936)
The film actress, Bette Davis, had agreed not to work as an actress for anyone else during the period of her contract with Warner Bros. In breach of this agreement she left the USA and entered into a contract with a third party in this country. The court held that Warner Bros were entitled to an injunction to prevent the star breaking the negative provision in the contract.

It should be noted that an injunction cannot be used as a back door method of enforcing a contract of employment for which specific performance is not available. Warner Bros could prevent Miss Davis working as an actress for anyone else. They could not have obtained a decree of specific performance to force her to return to their studio.

Limitation of actions

The right to sue does not last indefinitely. The Limitation Act 1980 imposes time limits within which an action for breach of contract must be brought. They are:

(1) *an action on a simple contract* must be brought within six years of the date when the cause of action accrued;

(2) *an action on a contract made under seal* will be statute barred after twelve years from the date when the cause of action accrued.

These time limits may be extended as follows:

(*a*) where fraud or mistake is alleged time does not start to run until 'the plaintiff has discovered the fraud, concealment or mistake or could with reasonable diligence have discovered it';

(*b*) if the plaintiff is under a disability, such as minority or mental incapacity the time limits do not start to operate until the disability is removed, i.e. in the case of a minor on reaching eighteen;

(*c*) where the claim is for a debt or the liquidated sum, and the defendant acknowledges the claim or makes part-payment, time will run from the date of acknowledgement or part-payment.

The rules about limitation of actions do not apply to the equitable remedies. Nevertheless, the equitable maxim 'delay defeats equity' will apply to defeat a plaintiff who waits too long before taking legal action.

Questions/activities

1. Make a list of all the agreements you made (*a*) today, and (*b*) yesterday. Identify which agreements are contracts and explain why they are legally binding.

2. Are these statements true or false?

(*a*) Most of the law of contract can be found in Acts of Parliament.

(*b*) All contracts must be in writing.

(*c*) Conveyances of land must be in the form of a specialty contract.

(*d*) The absence of an essential element will always render a contract void.

3. Analyse the following transactions in terms of offer and acceptance:

(*a*) filling a job vacancy;

(*b*) parking a car in a multi-storey car park;

(c) taking a bus ride;

(d) buying a cup of coffee from an automatic vending machine;

(e) buying a packet of soap powder from a supermarket.

4. On 13 September, Fiona, a newly qualified dentist, receives the following note from her uncle:

10 Park Street
LONDON W1 A54

Dear Fiona

We talked some time ago about your buying some of my dental equipment when I retire from my London practice at the end of this month. I am prepared to let you have everything for £15 000. Let me know fairly quickly if you're interested because I've already had a very good offer from one of my colleagues.
Your affectionate uncle
Arnold

Fiona is keen to take advantage of her uncle's offer but is unsure whether she can raise such a large amount of money by the end of September. She phones her uncle to find out whether she can have until after Christmas to pay. Her uncle is away at a conference and so Fiona leaves a message with his secretary.

Two weeks pass by and, as Fiona has not heard from her uncle, she arranges a loan with her bank. On 28 September she writes to her uncle, accepting his offer and enclosing a cheque for £15 000.

On September, her uncle phones to say that he has already sold the equipment to someone else.

Advise Fiona.

5. Lynx Cars Ltd, the manufacturers of a revolutionary fuel-efficient small car, enter into a five-year dealership agreement with Roadstar Ltd, a northern-based firm of car dealers, in November 1985. A clause in the agreement states: 'This agreement is not intended to be legally binding but the parties honourably pledge that they will carry out its terms.' Roadstar Ltd place an initial order for 2000 cars to be delivered by the end of 1986, which is accepted by the manufacturers. One month after the successful launch of the car at the Motor Show, Lynx Cars Ltd write to Roadstar Ltd informing them that, owing to production difficulties, they estimate that they will be able to deliver only 200 cars by the end of 1986. They further state that they will be withdrawing from the dealership agreement

from the end of 1986 so that they can concentrate their resources on their south of England car dealers.

Advise Roadstar Ltd.

6. Mrs Harris, the owner of three rented houses in Extown, asks her next door neighbour, Ted, to collect rent from the tenants for her while she is abroad on business. Ted collects the rents and when Mrs Harris returns she says to him, 'I'll give you £50 for your work'. Can Ted enforce the promise?

7. John, a plumber, installs a new bathroom for Mr and Mrs Bolton for an agreed price of £500. Five weeks after sending the bill John still has not received payment. He rings the Boltons and speaks to Mrs Bolton. She says that she is unhappy about the quality of John's work which she claims is only worth £350 at most. She also tells John that her husband has just lost his job and they can only afford to pay £100. John reluctantly agrees to accept a cheque for this amount 'in full settlement'. Three months later John hears that Mr Bolton is back in employment and he wonders whether he can recover the outstanding money.

8. What formalities, if any, must be completed for the following contracts:

(a) a guarantee for a bank overdraft;

(b) the sale of a second-hand car;

(c) a contract of employment;

(d) the lease of a house for twenty-one years;

(e) a promise to pay £50 a year for the next five years to a charity.

9. Kathy, aged seventeen, decides to leave home because she does not get on with her parents. Over the next three weeks she enters into the following agreements:

(a) She borrows £500 from her older brother to tide her over until she can find a job.

(b) She takes a two-year lease on a bed-sit, paying three months' rent in advance.

(c) By pretending to be twenty-one, she orders a £700 suite of furniture from Palatial Pads Ltd on twelve months' interest-free credit.

(d) She sets up a home catering business and immediately agrees to cater for a hundred people attending a twenty-first birthday party for a price of £300. She insists on £100 deposit. As the day for the party approaches she finds that she has taken on too much work for one person so she rings her customers on the afternoon of the party to say that she won't be able to do the catering after all.

Discuss the legal effects of these transactions.

10. Arthur, the manager of Lookout Cars Ltd, asks his young assistant, Terry, to look after the business while he is away on holiday. It is an eventful week for Terry.

(a) Early Monday morning Terry sells a second-hand Mini to Doris. The car had been advertised in the local press as follows:

> 83 (Y) Mini Mayfair 14 000 miles, Blue £3095

Doris returns on Wednesday to tell Terry that the Mini's clock has been turned back and that it has actually done 60 000 miles.

(b) On Tuesday, Terry finalises a part-exchange deal with Mr Walker. Unknown to either of them, Mrs Walker was involved, earlier in the day, in a serious car crash while driving the old car. The car is a 'write-off'.

(c) On Wednesday, a man calls into the showrooms introducing himself, falsely, as James Dean MP. He agrees to buy a new Orion car, but when he pulls out a cheque book, Terry says that he is reluctant to accept a cheque. The man then produces a pass to the House of Commons as proof of his identity. Terry accepts the cheque and the man drives off in the car. Terry has just learned from the bank that the cheque has been dishonoured. The man sold the car to Pete, a university student.

(d) On Thursday, Daisy, Lookout Ltd's secretary, puts a number of letters in front of Terry for his signature. Terry is busy talking to the workshop manager at the time and signs his name without reading each one. He has now discovered that one of the letters was an undertaking to act as a guarantor for a £5000 loan to Daisy by the Midshires Bank PLC.

Explain to Terry the legal position in each situation.

11. George is the owner of a confectioner's shop in Chorley which is world famous for its unique Chorley Chocolate Bar. The secret recipe for the chocolate bar has been handed down four generations of George's family. George himself is a bachelor and with no one to carry on the business, he decides to retire and sell the shop. After much careful vetting, George agrees to sell the shop, including the goodwill and the secret recipe, to Maria. As part of the contract George agrees that:

(a) he will not engage in any form of sweet making in the whole of the United Kingdom for the next twenty years, and,

(b) he will not reveal the secret formula for the chocolate bar to anyone else.

Maria bought the business with the aid of a twenty-year mortgage from the Castletown Cocoa Co. Ltd. Maria has further agreed to obtain all her supplies of cocoa from this company for the next twenty years.

After three very successful years in Chorley, Maria hears that George is supplying Chorley Chocolate Bars to shops near to his retirement home in Bournemouth. About the same time, Maria is approached by Cocoa Suppliers Ltd who offer to supply all her cocoa needs at cheaper prices than she is currently paying Castletown Cocoa Co. Ltd.

Advise Maria.

12. Kevin is the owner of a small Hull-based firm, which specializes in office removals. He operates with two vans and three employees. He contracts to remove two partners in a firm of accountants, who are moving from their main office in Hull to establish a branch office in Scunthorpe. To minimize the disruption to office routine, the move is to take place on a Sunday.

What is the legal position in the following situations –

(a) The Humber bridge is closed because of high winds (the only alternative route is a much longer and more expensive journey via Goole).

(b) As a conservation measure, the government imposes regulations banning business traffic from the roads on Sundays.

(c) Kevin takes on a house removal for the same day. One of the vans fails its MOT on the Friday and Kevin decides to use the only one available for the house removal.

(d) Kevin and his three employees are taken ill with influenza and are not well enough to carry out the move.

(e) Kevin completes the removal except for one filing cabinet which he didn't have room for. He refuses to make a special journey for it because, 'it would cost too much in petrol'.

13. Wholesome Foods Ltd decided to build an extension to their Newtown bakery to cope with increased demand for their wholemeal bread. The contract is awarded to Bettabuilders Co. Ltd who agree to complete the work by 1 May. On the strength of the planned increased capacity at the bakery, Wholesome Foods Ltd conclude an extremely profitable contract with the Newtown Council to supply all the bread to

local schools from 4 May. Owing to extreme bad weather in February and March, Bettabuilders Co. Ltd complete the extension ten weeks late. Wholesome Foods Ltd estimate their losses as:

(1) £100 a week for the profits they would have made on the expected general increase in bread sales; and

(2) £400 a week for the profits they would have made on the schools contract.

(*a*) What damages will Wholesome Foods Ltd recover?

(*b*) How would your answer differ if Bettabuilders Co. Ltd had agreed to pay £50 for every week of delay in completing the extension?

14. Wreckless Eric, a rock concert promoter, pulls off one of the sensations of the rock world by getting the American Rock star, Tex Toucan, to come to Britain to give a six-concert tour to coincide with the release of his latest album. Tex agrees to give his exclusive services to Eric and promises that he 'will not sing, perform as a musician or act as an entertainer' for anyone else during the period of his stay.

After completing the first sell-out concert in Dagenham, Tex is approached by Crispin Green, a rival promoter, who persuades Tex to break his contract with Eric and appear instead at alternative venues arranged by Crispin.

Eric, who has made a considerable investment in this tour, wants to know what remedies are available to him.

Types of business contract

In this chapter we move away from studying basic principles of general application to all contracts to look at specific kinds of contracts in common use in the business world. The fundamentals of the law of contract are still largely governed by the common law. Over the past one hundred years, however, business transactions have increasingly become subject to statutory provisions. Parliament's original aim was to translate established common law rules into a format which would be more accessible and understandable to businessmen. As the years passed so the legislators' motives changed. Parliamentary interest in commercial law in the twentieth century has been prompted mainly by the need to regulate and control unfair business practices.

It is important that you can distinguish between different kinds of business transactions because different legal principles apply to each. The rights and duties of the parties will be determined by the nature of their contract and the legal rules which govern that particular kind of agreement. For example, contracts for the sale of goods are covered by the Sale of Goods Act 1979, while contracts for the sale of land are governed by the Law of Property Act 1925.

This chapter is designed to provide you with a brief guide to the different kinds of business contracts and the source of any legal rules which regulate them. The most important contracts will be considered in more detail in later chapters.

Contracts for the supply of goods

Sale of goods

The most common form of transaction in the business world is a contract for the sale of goods. Whenever you buy goods, whether from a supermarket, market stall, doorstep salesman, or by mail order, you have entered into a contract for the sale of goods. As we have already mentioned, the rights and duties of the parties to this type of contract are set out in the Sale of Goods Act 1979. The Act applies to all contracts for the sale of goods, from buying a sandwich at lunchtime to a multi-million pound deal to supply new aircraft to an airline company.

A contract for the sale of goods is defined in s. 2(1) of the Sale of Goods Act 1979 as:

'A contract by which the seller transfers or agrees to transfer the property in goods to the buyer for a money consideration called the price'.

This definition is extremely important because only those contracts which fall within it will be covered by the provisions of the 1979 Act. A closer look at the definition will help you distinguish a contract for the sale of goods from other similar kinds of contracts in which goods change hands.

Section 2(1) covers two possibilities: an actual sale and an agreement to sell at some future time. The essence of the transaction is the transfer of property in goods from the seller to the buyer. ('Property' in this context means ownership of the goods.) Goods include all tangible items of personal property such as food, clothes and furniture: land and money are excluded from the definition.

The consideration for the goods must be money, although a part-exchange deal in which goods are exchanged for other goods plus money will be covered by the Act because some money has changed hands.

The law relating to sale of goods contracts will be examined in more detail in Chapter 11.

Exchange or barter

No money changes hands in this type of contract. Instead there is a straight exchange of goods between the parties. The absence of money from the consideration means that the Sale of Goods Act 1979 does not apply to these contracts. The obligations of the parties have been governed by the common law, although the Supply of Goods and Services Act 1982 does now impose certain statutory duties on the supplier of goods under a contract of exchange.

Work and materials

Another way in which you can acquire goods is in consequence of a contract whose main purpose is the provision of services. If you take your car to be serviced by a garage, the main substance of the contract is the skill and labour of the mechanic in checking the car. The supply of such items as brake fluid and the renewal of spark plugs is an ancillary part of the contract.

The distinction between a contract of sale and a contract of work and materials is often a fine one.

Robinson v Graves (1935)

Robinson, an artist, was commissioned to paint a portrait for 250 guineas. The Court of Appeal held that this was a contract for Robinson's skill as an artist and not a contract for the sale of goods, i.e., the finished portrait.

However, a contract to buy a painting from an art gallery would be a sale of goods contract.

Contracts for work and materials are now subject to the Supply of Goods and Services Act 1982. The provisions of this Act will be discussed in Chapter 12.

Supply of goods on credit

There are a bewildering number of ways in which goods can be acquired and then paid for over a period of time. Hire purchase, 'interest free' credit, credit cards and bank loans are all readily available, enticing us to buy more than we can probably afford.

Consumer credit – credit if granted to an individual, sole trader or partnership not exceeding £15 000 – is strictly regulated by the Consumer Credit Act 1974. This Act is examined in detail in Chapter 15.

The more important forms of consumer credit agreement are described below:

(1) *Hire Purchase (HP)*. This is one of the best known ways of buying goods on credit. HP is essentially an agreement for the hire of goods, at the end of which the hirer may exercise an option to purchase them from the owner. The hirer obtains the immediate use and enjoyment of the goods, but he does not become the owner unless and until all the instalments are paid.

There is a subtle distinction between HP and a contract for the sale of goods. You will remember that the definition of a sale of goods includes agreements to transfer the ownership in goods at some time in the future. An HP agreement, however, does not bind the hirer to buy. He may choose to pay for the hire of the goods and then decline to purchase them.

(2) *Conditional sale*. A conditional sale is very similar to HP. The customer obtains immediate possession of the goods in return for the payment of regular instalments. The transfer of ownership is delayed until some specified condition is fulfilled. The difference between the two agreements is that the buyer under a conditional sale agreement is committed to buy from the outset. Thus a conditional sale is really a type of sale of goods contract.

(3) *Credit sale*. This is another way of buying goods and paying for them later. Unlike HP and conditional sale agreements, ownership of the goods passes to the buyer at the start of the agreement.

Contracts of bailment

A contract of bailment arises when the owner of goods (the bailor) entrusts possession of them into the care of another (the bailee). Examples of bailment include placing important documents in safe custody at a bank, taking clothes to be dry-cleaned, hiring a TV set.

The bailee's main duties are –

(1) to take reasonable care of the goods whilst they are in his possession, and

(2) to return them to the bailor, at the end of an agreed period or when requested.

Hiring is a particular example of a contract of bailment.

Fig. 9.1 A typical hire agreement form. Copyright © Consumer Credit Trade Association. (Original size A4)

RA
(b)
Hire Agreement *regulated by the Consumer Credit Act 1974*
No right of cancellation — minimum hire period not more than 17 months.

Agreement No. _____

Original

This agreement sets out the terms on which we (the owners) agree to let on hire the goods described below to you (the hirer) for the rental payments and on the terms set out below and overleaf.

The Owners _____
Name and address
_____

The Hirer _____
Full names please

Address _____
_____

Particulars of Goods and Period of Hire	Rentals (including VAT)	£	p
Description _____ _____	**A. Advance Rental** (rent for the first_____months of the hiring)		
Maker's Name _____	**Rentals (for the remainder of the hiring)**		
Model No. _____	For each of the next_____months		
Serial No._____	For each of the next_____months		
Accessories_____	For each of the next_____months		
Minimum Hire Period_____months commencing on the date of this agreement	For each month thereafter		

First monthly rental payable on_____19____
Subsequent rentals on the same day of each succeeding month.
We may at our discretion vary the rentals payable after the minimum hire period by one month's notice in writing.
We may vary the rentals if the VAT rate alters.
See Clause 4 overleaf for further details.

Maintenance of the Goods

Maintenance by the Owner   YES/NO

IMPORTANT — YOU SHOULD READ THIS CAREFULLY

YOUR RIGHTS

The Consumer Credit Act 1974 covers this agreement and lays down certain requirements for your protection which must be satisfied when the agreement is made. If they are not, we cannot enforce the agreement against you without a court order.

If you would like to know more about the protection and remedies provided under the Act, you should contact either your local Trading Standards Department or your nearest Citizens' Advice Bureau.

Witness: Signature _____

Name _____
Block letters please

Address_____

_____

Witness: Signature _____
Second witness required in Scotland only

Name _____
Block letters please

Address_____

DECLARATION BY HIRER

By signing this agreement you are declaring that:
★ Your particulars given above are correct
★ All the information you have given us is correct
★ You realise that we rely on that information when deciding whether to enter into this agreement.

> This is a Hire Agreement regulated by the Consumer Credit Act 1974. Sign it only if you want to be legally bound by its terms.
>
> Signature(s)
> of Hirer(s)_____
>
> Under this agreement the goods do not become your property and you must not sell them.

Signature of (or on behalf of) Owners _____

_____

Date of Owners' Signature (Date of Agreement)

RA(b)
Original

TERMS OF THE AGREEMENT

1 Ownership of the goods

This is a hire agreement. The goods will remain our property at all times and can never become yours. You must not sell or dispose of them.

2 Period of hire

You agree to hire the goods until the end of the minimum hire period stated overleaf or until the expiry of notice given under Clause 11, whichever is the later.

3 Payment

Before signing this agreement you must have paid the advance rental shown. By signing this agreement you agree to pay the rentals set out overleaf by their specified dates to us at the address stated overleaf or to any person or address notified by us in writing. Punctual payment is essential. If you pay by post you do so at your own risk.

4 Variation of rentals

We have the right to vary the rentals payable after the end of the minimum hire period by giving you one month's notice in writing expiring at or after the end of that period.

We may vary the rentals at any time to take account of a change in the rate of VAT.

5 Failure to pay on time

We have the right to charge interest at the rate of 10% per annum on all overdue amounts. This interest will be calculated on a daily basis from the date the amount falls due until it is received and will run both before and after any judgment.

6 Place where goods are kept

You must keep the goods safely at your address stated overleaf and may not move them elsewhere without first obtaining our written consent.

7 Care of the goods

You must use the goods in a careful and proper manner and (apart from any arrangements for maintenance under Clause 9) keep them in good working order, and replace batteries in remote control units, at your own expense. However you may not interfere with the internal working parts of the goods or attempt to clean tape heads, which only our representative may do.

8 Insurance against loss or damage

You are responsible for all loss or damage to the goods (except fair wear and tear) even if caused by acts or events outside your control. You must therefore insure the goods against loss or damage.

9 Maintenance

Where the agreement shows that we are to maintain the goods, you must notify us when the goods require maintenance or adjustment. We or our authorised representative will then carry this out.

If at any time we decide that it is no longer practicable to keep the goods in working order or, in the case of a radio or television set, if the transmission is unsatisfactory, we may either:

(a) replace the goods by other goods as similar as possible to those replaced or

(b) end this agreement by giving you seven days' notice in writing.

If we end this agreement under paragraph (b) you must let us collect the goods. You will not be liable for rentals falling due after such termination and will be entitled to recover any rental paid in advance in respect of the period after termination. This clause will not affect your statutory rights.

10 Licences

You must keep the goods properly licensed and produce the licence or payment receipt to us at our request.

11 Right to end the agreement

You or we may end this agreement by giving one month's notice in writing expiring at or after the end of the minimum hire period. You must then return the goods or make them available for collection by us.

12 Our further right to end the aggreement

We may end this agreement and take back the goods, after giving you written notice, if at any time:

(a) you fail to pay any amount within 14 days of its due date or commit any other breach of your obligations;

(b) you commit any act of bankruptcy or have a receiving, interim or bankruptcy order made against you or you petition for your own bankruptcy, or are served with a creditor's demand under the Insolvency Act 1986 or the Bankruptcy (Scotland) Act 1985, or make a formal composition or scheme with your creditors, or call a meeting of them; .

(c) execution is levied or attempted against any of your assets or income or, in Scotland, your assets are poinded or your wages arrested;

(d) the landlord of the premises where the goods are kept threatens or takes any step to distrain on the goods or, in Scotland, exercises his right of hypothec over the goods;

(e) you have given false information in connection with your entry into this agreement;

(f) the goods are destroyed or the insurers treat a claim under the policy for the goods on a total loss basis.

13 Your liability if we end the agreement

If we end this agreement you must pay us all rentals up to the date when this agreement comes to an end.

If we end this agreement under Clause 12 before the expiry of the minimum hire period you must also pay us a sum equal to the rentals for the period remaining to the end of the minimum hire period less any rentals obtained by us during this period by re-letting the goods and any other deduction which we may consider reasonable.

14 Expenses

You must repay on demand our expenses and legal costs for:

(a) finding your address if you change address without first informing us or finding the goods if they are not at the address given by you;

(b) taking steps, including court action, to recover the goods or to obtain payment for them.

15 TV transmissions

If the goods comprise a television set we undertake only, that it will receive those transmissions which are received when it is installed.

16 General provisions

(a) The word 'goods' includes any replacements, renewals or additions made to them by us or by you with our prior written consent.

(b) No relaxation or indulgence which we may grant to you shall affect our strict rights under this agreement.

(c) Where two or more of you are named as the hirer, you jointly and severally accept the obligations under this agreement. This means that each of you can be held fully responsible under this agreement.

(d) We may transfer our rights under this agreement.

17 When this agreement takes effect

This agreement will only take effect if and when it is signed by us or our authorised representative.

Hire

Under a hire agreement, the owner of goods allows someone else (the hirer) to make use of them in return for regular rental payments. The hirer obtains possession of the goods but ownership never passes to him and at the end of the agreement, the goods must be returned to the owner.

Most people are familiar with hire contracts in the context of TV and video rentals. A typical rental agreement can be seen in Fig. 9.1. Consumer hire agreements are covered by the provision of the Consumer Credit Act 1974.

Businesses also take advantage of hire as a method of obtaining the use of equipment which they require. (Hire in this context is usually referred to as 'leasing', the owner being known as the 'lessor' and the hirer as the 'lessee'.) The leasing agreement often includes an undertaking by the lessor to service the equipment regularly and effect repairs when necessary. Equipment leasing has allowed businesses to take advantage of the opportunities created by the rapidly changing new technology in the field of computing and word processing.

Goods supplied under hire contracts are subject to Part I of the Supply of Goods and Services Act 1982. (See Chap. 12.)

Employment contracts

There are two ways in which a person's services may be acquired. He may be engaged either as an employee under a contract of service or as an independent contractor under a contract for services.

(1) *Contract of service*. This type of contract creates the relationship of employer and employee between the parties. An employee provides his labour for his employer in return for wages. The employer exercises control over the way in which an employee carries out his work.

(2) *Contract for services*. A self-employed person is engaged under a contract for services. He is an independent contractor, agreeing to do work or provide services as and when he wishes. He enjoys considerable independence from the person who employs him.

Thus a chauffeur has a contract of service, whereas a taxi driver transports his 'fares' under a contract for services.

The distinction between employees and independent contractors is important for the following reasons:

(1) An employer is vicariously liable only for the torts of employees, not for those committed by independent contractors.

(2) Only employees are entitled to claim the benefit of various employment rights contained principally in the Employment Protection (Consolidation) Act 1978. These include protections in respect of unfair dismissal, redundancy, sex and race discrimination, maternity pay and leave, minimum periods of notice, and so on. A self-employed person cannot claim any of these rights. The law relating to the contract of employment will be examined in more detail in Chapter 18.

Contract of agency

An agent is someone who is employed by a principal to make contracts on his behalf with third parties. An employee who makes contracts on behalf of his employer is acting as an agent. A shop assistant, for example, is in this category. Alternatively, an agent may be an independent contractor who is engaged for his specialist skills and knowledge. A person who wishes to sell shares will usually employ the services of a stockbroker to arrange the sale for him.

Agents are given a number of names: the most common being 'broker', 'representative', or 'factor'.

Contracts concerning land

Every businessman must consider where he will locate his operations. A sole trader, such as a painter and decorator, may find that he can work successfully from home. In many cases, however, the nature of the business or the size of the operation will mean that separate premises have to be found. One of the decisions that must be taken is whether to buy or rent.

Transactions relating to land are governed primarily by the Law of Property Act 1925. This subject will be examined in detail in Chapter 16.

Mortgages

A mortgage is a method of borrowing money on the security of some property. The borrower (mortgagor) transfers an interest in the property to the lender (mortgagee): the lender may realize this interest if the loan is not repaid. Any kind of property (land, goods, insurance policies) may be the subject of a mortgage but, in practice, most mortgage advances are secured on land.

Contracts for financial services

Banking contracts

Banks provide a wide range of financial services to the commercial customer from current accounts, loan and overdraft facilities, to specialist services for those involved in foreign trade.

The relationship between a bank and its customers is contractual. The rights and duties of the parties to this contract have been developed over many years from the practice of merchants. Some aspects of banking law are contained in statutes, such as the Bills of Exchange Act 1882 and the Cheques Act 1957.

Insurance contracts

A prudent businessman will always assess the risks that might befall his business: he may fall ill, his premises might be destroyed by fire, or his stock stolen. These risks may be minimized by insurance.

A contract of insurance is an agreement whereby an insurance company undertakes to compensate a person, called the insured, if the risk insured against does in fact occur. The insured will be required to complete a proposal form. The contract is formed when the insurer accepts the proposal.

Insurance contracts are contracts of utmost good faith (*uberrimae fidei*). This means that the insured must voluntarily disclose all relevant information which may affect the insurer's decision to insure or the premium that will be charged. Failure to do so, however innocent, will allow the insurer to avoid the contract.

Standard form contracts

Whatever the nature of a contract, the law is based on the assumption that the terms of an individual contract are the result of bargaining between equals. It has long been the case, however, that businesses contract on the basis of standard terms contained in a pre-printed document known as a standard form contract. The terms are not usually open to negotiation: the customer must either accept them in their entirety as part and parcel of the deal, or take his business elsewhere.

The use of standard form contracts has several clear advantages for the businessman:

(1) If the terms of the contract are contained in a written document, the parties will be quite clear about what they have agreed to and this is likely to minimize the possibility of disputes at a later stage.

(2) It would be very time consuming to negotiate individual terms with every customer, especially where a fairly standard service is offered to a large number of people. For example, British Rail would soon come to a standstill if every intending passenger had to negotiate an individual contract before setting out on a journey.

(3) Once an organization has adopted standard terms of business the formation of a contract becomes a relatively routine matter which can be delegated to junior staff.

(4) Businessmen are constantly seeking ways to minimize their potential risks. A standard form contract can be used to 'dictate' terms which will be favourable to the businessman. He may include, for example, limitation or exclusion clauses which seek to limit or exempt him completely from liabilities which might otherwise be his responsibility.

The use of standard form contracts may be convenient and economical for the businessman, but it puts his customers at a considerable disadvantage. The drawbacks are as follows:

(1) Standard terms of business are often expressed in language which is virtually unintelligible to most people. A consumer may find himself bound by a contract even though he did not properly understand what had been 'agreed'. In some cases, the document may be so awe-inspiring, that it is not read at all.

(2) The concept of freedom of contract on which the law of contract is founded would seem to suggest that if the terms contained in a standard form contract are unacceptable, the customer can simply 'shop around' for a better deal. This may well happen in a competitive market where the parties possess equal bargaining powers; but in practice the parties rarely contract as equals. Consumers, in particular, have

found themselves in a weak bargaining position, victims of very one-sided contracts. In recent years, Parliament has stepped in to redress the balance in such measures as the Unfair Contract Terms Act 1977. We will return to this subject in the next chapter.

An example of a standard form contract appears in Fig. 9.2.

Questions/activities

For each of the examples given below identify –
(*a*) the different kinds of contracts described, and
(*b*) any statutes which apply to them.

1. Fixit Ltd agrees to install gas central heating in Jim Frost's bungalow for a price of £1200. £400 is to be paid in advance, with the balance due on completion of the work. *Conditional*

2. James buys a new Ford Sierra from Smiths Motors by trading in his A-reg Capri, topped up by £3000 in cash. *Exchange (Part)*

3. Kelly, Murphy & Co., Solicitors, enter into a two-year agreement with Copytech Ltd for the use of a photocopier. Copytech Ltd agree to keep the equipment 'in good repair'. *Bailment* *Contract of service*

4. Newtown Industrials plc employ Lorna Doone as a Sales Representative for the South Western region.

5. Bill Archer orders 10 cwt of fertilizer for use on his farm from Greener Fields Ltd. Payment is to be made within one month of delivery. *Credit Sale*

6. Kate buys a bottle of lemonade from her corner shop for 60p, plus 5p on the bottle.

7. Jack and Jill, up and coming young fashion designers, buy shop premises in Bath, with the aid of a loan secured on the property from their bank, West Country Bank plc.

8. You are a partner in a newly-formed firm of removers, Lift and Shift. Consider the arguments for and against drawing up a standard form of contract for your business. What terms might you include in such a document?

Road Haulage Association Limited

Fig. 9.2. A standard form of contract.

CONDITIONS OF CARRIAGE 1982

(hereinafter referred to as "the Carrier") is not a common carrier and accepts goods for carriage only upon that condition and the Conditions set out below. No servant or agent of the Carrier is permitted to alter or vary these Conditions in any way unless expressly authorized to do so.

1. Definitions

In these Conditions:

"*Trader*" means the customer who contracts for the services of the Carrier.

"*Contract*" means the contract of carriage between the Trader and the Carrier.

"*Consignment*" means goods in bulk or contained in one parcel, package or container, as the case may be, or any number of separate parcels, packages or containers sent at one time in one load by or for the Trader from one address to one address.

"*Dangerous Goods*" means:

(a) goods which are specified in the special classification of dangerous goods issued by the British Railways Board or which, although not specified therein, are not acceptable to the British Railways Board for conveyance on the ground of their dangerous or hazardous nature, or

(b) goods which, although not included in (a) above, are of a similar kind.

2. Parties and Sub-Contracting

(1) The Trader warrants that he is either the owner of the goods in any Consignment or is authorized by such owner to accept these Conditions on such owner's behalf.

(2) The Carrier and any other carrier employed by the Carrier may employ the services of any other carrier for the purpose of fulfilling the Contract in whole or in part and the name of every such other carrier shall be provided to the Trader on request.

(3) The Carrier contracts for itself and as agent of and trustee for its servants and agents and all other carriers referred to in (2) above and such other carrier's servants and agents and every reference in Conditions 3–17 inclusive hereof to "The Carrier" shall be redeemed to include every such other carrier, servant and agent with the intention that they shall have the benefit of the Contract and collectively and together with the Carrier be under no greater liability to the Trader or any other party than is the Carrier hereunder.

3. Dangerous Goods

If the Carrier agrees to accept Dangerous Goods for carriage such goods must be accompanied by a full declaration of their nature and contents and be properly and safely packed and labelled in accordance with any statutory regulations for the time being in force for carriage by road.

4. Loading and Unloading

(1) When collection or delivery takes place at the Trader's premises the Carrier shall not be under any obligation to provide any plant, power, or labour in addition to the Carrier's carmen, required for loading or unloading at such premises.

(2) The Carrier shall not be required to provide service beyond the usual place of collection or delivery but if any such service is given by the Carrier it shall be at the sole risk of the Trader who shall indemnify the Carrier against all claims and demands whatever which could not have been made if such service had not been given.

(3) (a) Goods requiring special appliances for unloading from the vehicle by which they are carried are accepted for carriage only on condition that such appliances are made available by the Trader at destination.

(b) When the Carrier is, without prior arrangement in writing with the Trader, called upon to load or unload goods requiring special appliances for loading or unloading, the Carrier shall be under no liability whatever to the Trader for any damage whatever, however caused, arising out of such loading or unloading and the Trader shall indemnify the Carrier against all claims and demands whatever which could not have been made if such assistance had not been given.

5. Consignment Notes

The Carrier shall, if so required, sign a document prepared by the sender acknowledging the receipt of the Consignment but no such document shall be evidence of the condition or of the correctness of the declared nature, quantity, or weight of the Consignment at the time it is received by the Carrier.

6. Transit

(1) Transit shall commence when the Carrier takes possession of the Consignment whether at the point of collection or at the Carrier's premises.

(2) Transit shall (unless otherwise previously determined) end when the Consignment is tendered at the usual place of delivery at the consignee's address within the customary cartage hours of the district. Provided that:

(a) if no safe and adequate access or no adequate unloading facilities there exist then transit shall be deemed to end at the expiry of one clear day after notice in writing (or by telephone if so previously agreed in writing) of the arrival of the Consignment at the Carrier's premises has been sent to the consignee; and

(b) when for any other reason whatever a Consignment cannot be delivered or when a Consignment is held by the Carrier 'to await order' or 'to be kept till called for' or upon any like instructions and such instructions are not given or the Consignment is not called for and removed, within a reasonable time, then transit shall be deemed to end.

7. Undelivered or Unclaimed Goods

Where the Carrier is unable for any reason to deliver a Consignment to the consignee or as he may order, or where by virtue of the proviso to Condition 6(2) hereof transit is deemed to be at an end, the Carrier may sell the goods and payment or tender of the proceeds after deduction of all proper charges and expenses in relation thereto and of all outstanding charges in relation to the carriage and storage of the goods shall (without prejudice to any claim or right which the Trader may have against the Carrier otherwise arising under these Conditions) discharge the Carrier from all liability in respect of such goods, their carriage and storage.

Provided that:

(a) the Carrier shall do what is reasonable to obtain the value of the Consignment and

(b) the power of sale shall not be exercised where the name and address of the sender or of the consignee is known unless the Carrier shall have done what is reasonable in the circumstances to give notice to the sender or, if the name and address of the sender is not known, to the consignee that the goods will be sold unless within the time specified in such notice, being a reasonable time in the circumstances from the giving of such notice, the goods are taken away or instructions are given for their disposal.

8. Carrier's Charges

(1) The Carrier's charges shall be payable by the Trader without prejudice to the Carrier's rights against the consignee or any other person. Provided that when goods are consigned 'carriage forward' the Trader shall not be required to pay such charges unless the consignee fails to pay after a reasonable demand has been made by the Carrier for payment thereof.

(2) Except where a quotation states otherwise all quotations based on a tonnage rate shall apply to the gross weight unless:

(a) the goods exceed 2.25 cubic metres in measurement per tonne, in which case the tonnage rate shall be computed upon and apply to each measurement of 2.25 cubic metres or any part thereof, or

(b) the size or shape of a Consignment necessitates the use of a vehicle of greater carrying capacity than the weight of the consignment would otherwise require, in which case the tonnage rate shall be computed upon and apply to the carrying capacity of such vehicle as is reasonably required.

(3) Charges shall be payable on the expiry of any time limit previously stipulated and the Carrier shall be entitled to interest at the average of the overdraft interest rates being charged at Lloyds Bank Limited and Barclays Bank Limited current at this time, calculated on a daily basis on all amounts overdue to the Carrier.

(Continued overleaf)

Liability for Loss and Damage

(1) The Trader shall be deemed to have elected to accept the terms set out in (2) of this Condition unless, before the transit commences, the Trader has agreed in writing that the Carrier shall not be liable for any loss or misdelivery of or damage to goods however or whenever caused and whether or not caused or contributed to directly or indirectly by any act, omission, neglect, default or other wrongdoing on the part of the Carrier.

(2) Subject to these Conditions the Carrier shall be liable for:

   (i) loss or misdelivery of or damage to livestock, bullion, money, securities, stamps, precious metals or precious stones only if

      (a) the Carrier has specifically agreed in writing to carry any such items and

      (b) the Trader has agreed in writing to reimburse the Carrier in respect of all additional costs which result from the carrying of the said items and

      (c) the loss, misdelivery or damage is occasioned during transit and results from negligent act or omission by the Carrier;

   (ii) any loss or misdelivery of or damage to any other goods occasioned during transit unless the same has arisen from, and the Carrier has used reasonable care to minimize the effects of,

      (a) act of God;

      (b) any consequences of war, invasion, act of foreign enemy, hostilities (whether war or not), civil war, rebellion, insurrection, military or usurped power or confiscation, requisition, or destruction of or damage to property by or under the order of any government or public or local authority;

      (c) seizure or forfeiture under legal process;

      (d) error, act, omission, mis-statement or misrepresentation by the Trader or other owner of the goods or by servants or agents of either of them;

      (e) inherent liability to wastage in bulk or weight, latent defect or inherent defect, vice or natural deterioration of the goods;

      (f) insufficient or improper packing;

      (g) insufficient or improper labelling or addressing;

      (h) riot, civil commotion, strike, lockout, general or partial stoppage or restraint of labour from whatever cause;

      (i) consignee not taking or accepting delivery within a reasonable time after the Consignment has been tendered.

(3) The Carrier shall not in any circumstances be liable for loss of or damage to goods after transit of such goods is deemed to have ended within the meaning of Condition 6(2) hereof, whether or not caused or contributed to directly or indirectly by any act, omission, neglect, default or other wrongdoing on the part of the Carrier.

10. Fraud

The Carrier shall not in any circumstances be liable in respect of a Consignment where there has been fraud on the part of the Trader or the owner of the goods or the servants or agents of either in respect of that Consignment, unless the fraud has been contributed by the complicity of the Carrier or of any servant of the Carrier acting in the course of his employment.

11. Limitation of Liability

(1) Except as otherwise provided in these Conditions the liability of the Carrier in respect of loss or mis-delivery of or damage to goods shall in all circumstances be limited as follows:

   (a) where loss, misdelivery or damage, however sustained, is in respect of the whole of the Consignment, to a sum calculated at the rate of £800 per tonne on either the gross weight of the Consignment or, where applicable, the tonnage computed in accordance with Condition 8(2)(a) or (b) hereof;

   (b) where loss, misdelivery or damage, however sustained, is in respect of part of the Consignment, to the proportion of the sum ascertained in accordance with (1)(a) of this Condition which the actual value of that part of the Consignment bears to the actual value of the whole of the Consignment.

Provided that:

   (i) nothing in this Condition shall limit the liability of the Carrier to less than the sum of £10;

   (ii) the Carrier shall be entitled to require proof of the value of the whole of the Consignment and of any part thereof lost, misdelivered or damaged;

   (iii) the Trader shall be entitled at any time prior to commencement of transit to give seven days' written notice to the Carrier requiring that the aforementioned £800 per tonne limit be increased but not so as to exceed the value of the Consignment and in the event of such notice being given the Trader shall within the said seven days agree with the Carrier an increase in the carriage charges in consideration of the said increased limit.

(2) Notwithstanding condition 11(1), the liability of the Carrier in respect of the indirect or consequential loss or damage, however arising and including loss of market, shall not exceed the amount of the carriage charges in respect of the Consignment or the amount of the claimant's proved loss, whichever is the smaller, unless,

   (a) at the time of entering into the Contract with the Carrier the Trader declares to the Carrier a special interest in delivery in the case of loss or damage or of an agreed time limit being exceeded and agrees to pay a surcharge calculated on the amount of that interest, and

   (b) prior to the commencement of transit the Trader has delivered to the Carrier written confirmation of the special interest, agreed time limit and amount of the interest.

12. Indemnity to the Carrier

The Trader shall indemnify the Carrier against:

(1) all consequences suffered by the Carrier (including but not limited to claims, demands, proceedings, fines, penalties, damages, costs, expenses, and loss of or damage to the carrying vehicle and to other goods carried) of any error, omission, mis-statement or misrepresentation by the Trader or other owner of the goods or by any servant or agent of either of them, insufficient or improper packing, labelling or addressing of the goods or fraud as in Condition 10;

(2) all claims and demands whatever by whoever made in excess of the liability of the Carrier under these Conditions;

(3) all losses suffered by and claims made against the Carrier in consequence of loss of or damage to property caused by or arising out of the carriage by the Carrier of Dangerous Goods whether or not declared by the Trader as such;

(4) all claims made upon the Carrier by H.M. Customs and Excise in respect of dutiable goods consigned in bond whether or not transit has ended or been suspended.

13. Time Limits for Claims

The Carrier shall not be liable for:

(1) loss from a parcel, package or container or from an unpacked Consignment or for damage to a Consignment or any part of a Consignment unless he is advised thereof in writing otherwise than upon a consignment note or delivery document within three days, and the claim is made in writing within seven days, after the termination of transit;

(2) loss, misdelivery or non-delivery of the whole of a Consignment or of any separate parcel, package or container forming part of a Consignment unless he is advised of the loss, misdelivery or non-delivery in writing otherwise than upon a consignment note or delivery document within twenty-eight days, and the claim is made in writing within forty-two days, after the commencement of transit.

Provided that if the Trader proves that:

   (a) it was not reasonably possible for the Trader to advise the Carrier or make a claim in writing within the time limit applicable and

   (b) such advice or claim was given or made within a reasonable time, the Carrier shall not have the benefit of the exclusion of liability afforded by this Condition.

14. General Lien

The Carrier shall have a general lien against the owner of the goods for any monies whatever due from the Trader or such other owner to the Carrier. If any such lien is not satisfied within a reasonable time the Carrier may at his absolute discretion sell the goods, or part thereof, as agent for the owner and apply the proceeds towards the monies due and the expenses of the retention, insurance and sale of the goods and shall, upon accounting to the Trader for any balance remaining, be discharged from all liability whatever in respect of the goods.

15. Unreasonable Detention

The Trader shall be liable for the cost of unreasonable detention of any vehicle, trailer, container or sheet but the rights of the Carrier against any other person in respect thereof shall remain unaffected.

16. Computation of Time

In the computation of time where any period provided by these Conditions is seven days or less, Saturdays, Sundays and all statutory public holidays shall be excluded.

17. Impossibility of Performance

The Carrier shall be relieved of its obligation to perform the Contract to the extent that the performance thereof is prevented by failure of the Trader, fire, weather conditions, industrial dispute, labour disturbance or cause beyond the reasonable control of the Carrier.

©Road Haulage Association Limited 1982

Registered with Office of Fair Trading, Ref. No. S/91

The terms of business contracts

As we have already seen, a contract comprises a set of promises which the law will enforce. The obligations undertaken by the parties are known as the *terms of the contract*. If a dispute arises the terms will become the object of intense scrutiny as the parties seek to justify their positions. The first task for any court is to establish exactly what was agreed by the parties. This may appear to be a relatively simple matter where the details of the agreement have been enshrined in a written contract, but even then problems can arise. The parties may have failed to express their intentions clearly or unambiguously; they may have omitted to mention a particular matter which later assumes great importance; the written document may contradict what was said during the course of oral negotiations. Where the contract is made wholly by word of mouth, the job of ascertaining the contents of the contract becomes even more difficult.

The terms of a contract are essentially a matter of express agreement between the parties. It should be noted, however, that additional terms can be implied into an agreement, even against the wishes of the parties, and certain terms which have been clearly stated, such as exclusion clauses, can be rendered completely ineffective by operation of the law.

In this chapter we examine the basic requirement of certainty of terms for the creation of a contract, how the contents of a contract are determined and the relative importance that may be attached to the duties and obligations undertaken by the parties. Finally, we will consider the effect of clauses which purport to exclude or limit the liability of one of the parties.

Certainty of terms

The terms of an agreement may be so vague and indefinite that in reality there is no contract in existence at all.

Bushwall Properties Ltd v Vortex Properties Ltd (1976)

The parties concluded an agreement for the sale of 51½ acres of land at £500000 to be paid in three instalments. The first payment of £250000 was to be followed in twelve months by a second payment of £125000 with the balance to be paid after a further twelve months, and 'on the occasion of each completion a proportionate part of the land' should be released to the buyers. The Court of Appeal held that as the parties had failed to provide a mechanism for allocating 'the proportionate part of the land', the entire agreement failed for uncertainty.

The presence of a vague term will not prove fatal in every case. Various devices exist for ascertaining the meaning of terms.

(1) The contract itself may provide the machinery whereby any disputes about the operation of the agreement can be resolved.

Foley v Classique Coaches Ltd (1934)

Foley sold part of his land to a coach company for use as a coach station, on condition that the company would buy all their petrol from him 'at a price to be agreed between the parties'. It was also agreed that any dispute arising from the contract should be submitted to arbitration. The parties failed to agree a price and the company refused to buy petrol from Foley.

The agreement to buy petrol was held to be binding despite the failure to agree a price because the parties had agreed a method by which the price could be ascertained, i.e., by arbitration.

(2) A court can ascertain the terms of a contract by reference to a trade custom or a course of previous dealings between the parties.

Hillas & Co Ltd *v* Arcos Ltd (1932)

The parties concluded a contract for the sale of a certain quantity of softwood timber 'of fair specification' over the 1930 season. The agreement also contained an option to buy further quantities in 1931, but no details were given as to the kind or size of the timber or the date of shipment. The 1930 agreement was carried out without difficulty but when the buyers tried to exercise the option for 1931, the sellers refused to supply the wood, claiming that they had only agreed to negotiate a further contract for 1931.

The House of Lords held that the sellers were bound to carry out the 1931 option. The terms of the contract could be ascertained by reference to the previous course of dealings between the parties.

(3) A meaningless term which is subsidiary to the main agreement can be ignored and the rest of the contract enforced.

Nicolene Ltd *v* Simmonds (1953)

The plaintiffs placed an order with the defendant for the supply of 3000 tons of steel reinforcing bars. The defendant wrote to the plaintiffs to accept the order, adding that 'we are in agreement that the usual conditions of acceptance apply'. There were no usual conditions of acceptance, so the words were meaningless.

The Court of Appeal held that as the rest of the contract made sense, the meaningless clause could be ignored.

Puffs, representations and terms

The first step in determining the terms of a contract is to establish what the parties said or wrote. That is not to say that all statements made during the course of negotiations will automatically be incorporated in the resulting contract. The statement may be a trader's puff, a representation or a term and if it turns out to be wrong, the plaintiff's remedy will depend on how the statement is classified. The differences are as follows –

(1) *Trader's puff.* If a car is described as 'totally immaculate' and 'incredible value' this is nothing more than typical advertising exaggeration. We are not expected to take such sales talk seriously and, consequently, there is no civil remedy if the statement turns out to be untrue.

(2) *Representation.* This is a statement of fact made by one party which induces the other to enter into the contract. As we have already seen in Chapter 8, the remedy for a misrepresentation is determined by the type of misrepresentation. You can refresh your memory by referring to Fig. 10.1.

(3) *Term.* Breach of a term of the contract entitles the injured party to claim damages and, if he has been deprived of substantially what he bargained for, he will also be able to repudiate the contract.

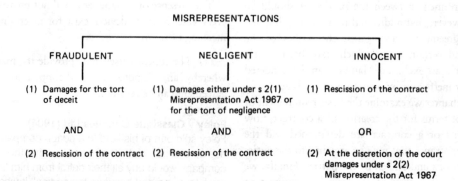

Fig. 10.1 Remedies for misrepresentation.

The distinction between a mere representation and a statement which becomes a term of the contract used to be very important. Before 1967 damages were not available for a misrepresentation unless it was made fraudulently, and the only remedy, rescission, could be easily lost. The injured party, therefore, would be keen to establish that the statement had been incorporated into the contract, so that he could claim damages for a breach of a contractual term. This generated a considerable body of complex case law. The Misrepresentation Act 1967, however, opened the way for an award of damages for non-fraudulent misrepresentation and, as a result, the distinction between terms and representations has become much less important.

It should be noted that the civil remedies in respect of false statements are complemented by criminal sanctions for breaches of the Trade Descriptions Acts 1968 and 1972. The Acts prohibit the use of certain false or misleading trade descriptions by a person acting in the course of a trade or business. The main offences are as follows –

(1) Applying a false trade description to any goods or supplying or offering to supply any goods to which a false trade description is applied, e.g. selling a car which indicates a false reading on the odometer (mileage recorder).

(2) Making misleading statements as to the price of goods, e.g. suggesting that the price of goods has been reduced.

(3) Knowingly or recklessly making a false statement in respect of the provision of services, accommodation or facilities, e.g. falsely describing a hotel's location as 'five minutes walk from the beach'.

The Acts are enforced by the local authority trading standards officers. A trader can be fined or imprisoned if convicted. The court also has the power to order the trader to compensate anyone who has suffered as a result of the offence.

Types of contractual terms

The terms of a contract delineate the obligations of the parties and these may vary greatly in importance. Traditionally, terms have been divided into two categories: conditions and warranties.

(1) *Conditions.* A condition is a major term which is vital to the main purpose of the contract. A breach of condition will entitle the injured party to repudiate the contract and claim damages. The breach does not automatically end the contract and the injured party may choose to go on with the contract, despite the breach, and recover damages instead.

(2) *Warranties.* A warranty is a less important term: it does not go to the root of the contract. A breach of warranty will only give the injured party the right to claim damages; he cannot repudiate the contract.

The difference between a condition and a warranty is illustrated by the following cases –

Poussard v Spiers (1876)

Madame Poussard was engaged to appear in an operetta from the start of its London run. Owing to illness, she was not available until a week after the show had opened and the producers were forced to engage a substitute. They now refused Madame Poussard's offer to take up her part.

It was held that the obligation to perform from the first night was a condition of the contract. Failure to carry out this term entitled the producers to repudiate Madame Poussard's contract.

Bettini v Gye (1876)

Bettini, an opera singer, was engaged by Gye to appear in a season of concerts. He undertook to be in London at least six days before the first concert for the purpose of rehearsals. He arrived three days late and Gye refused to accept his services.

It was held that the promise to appear for rehearsals was a less important term of the contract. Gye could claim compensation for a breach of warranty but he could not repudiate Bettini's contract.

The division of terms into conditions and warranties was included in the original Sale of Goods Act 1893, (now the Sale of Goods Act 1979). In s. 11(3) a condition is described as a stipulation 'the breach of which may give rise to a right to treat the contract as repudiated', while a warranty is a stipulation 'the breach of which may give rise to a claim for damages but not a right to reject the goods and treat the contract as repudiated'.

In recent years, the courts have recognized that it may be impossible to classify a term neatly in advance as either a condition or a warranty. Some undertakings may occupy an intermediate position, in that the term can be assessed only in the light of the consequences of a breach. If a breach of the term results in severe loss and damage, the injured party will be entitled to repudiate the contract; where the breach only involves minor loss, the injured party's remedies will be restricted to damages. These intermediate terms have become known as *innominate terms*.

Cehave N V v Bremer Handelsgesellschaft mbH (*The Hansa Nord*) (1975)

A clause in a contract for the sale of citrus pulp pellets stipulated that shipment was 'to be made in good condition'. Part of one consignment arrived in Rotterdam in a damaged condition and the buyers rejected the whole cargo. The defects were not particularly serious because some time later the buyers bought the very same cargo at a considerably reduced price, which they then proceeded to use for their original purpose.

The Court of Appeal held that the clause in question was an intermediate term. The breach was not so serious that it entitled the buyers to reject the whole cargo. It could be dealt with by an award of damages.

Express and implied terms

Another way in which the contents of a contract can be classified is according to whether the terms are express or implied.

Express terms

Express terms are the details of a contract which have been specifically agreed between the parties. They may be contained wholly in a written document or ascertained entirely from what the parties said to each other. In some cases, the terms may be partly written and partly verbal.

Harling v Eddy (1951)

A heifer was put up for sale by auction at Ashford Cattle Market. The sale was subject to the auctioneer's printed conditions of sale which stated that the auctioneer did not guarantee the condition of the animals sold. The appearance of this particular heifer was so poor when she entered the auction ring that no one was prepared to make a bid for her. The auctioneer then stated that there was nothing wrong with her and he would guarantee her in every respect. The heifer was sold to the plaintiff but was dead from tuberculosis within three months. The plaintiff successfully sued the auctioneer for damages.

The Court of Appeal held that the auctioneer was bound by his oral guarantee despite the contents of the written conditions of sale.

Types of express terms

The most common types of express terms, which are often a particular feature of standard form contracts, are exemption clauses, liquidated damage clauses and price variation clauses.

Exemption clause – generally

This term is used to describe an express term in a contract or a statement in a notice or sign which seeks to exclude or limit the responsibilities that might otherwise belong to a party.

Example 1 (estate agent's particulars)
'NOTICE. Messrs X, Y, Z & Co for themselves and for the vendors of this property whose agents they are, give notice that: ... (2). All statements contained in these particulars as to this property are made without responsibility on the part of Messrs X, Y, Z & Co. or the vendor. (3) None of the statements contained in these particulars as to this property are to be relied on as statements or representations of fact. (4) Any intending purchaser must satisfy himself by inspection or otherwise as to the correctness of each of the statements contained in these particulars. (5) The vendor does not make or give and neither Messrs X, Y, Z & Co. nor any person in their employment has any authority to make or give, any representation or warranty whatever in relation to this property.'

Example 2 (car park ticket)
'Entry to or use of this car park is subject to the current terms and conditions of the company. These conditions contain limited exemption clauses affecting all persons who enter or use the car park. Entry to and use of this car park is at your own risk.'

The legal effect of exemption clauses will be examined in detail later in this chapter.

Liquidated damages clause

This is a term in a contract which lays down the amount of damages that will be payable in the event of a breach of contract. A typical example may be seen on p. 180.

Price variation clause

Calculating a contract price in a period of inflation can be a very hit and miss operation. A contractor may find himself bound by a fixed price which has failed to take sufficient account of increases in the cost of raw materials, wages or overheads, such as rates. One solution to this problem is to insert a term in a contract which allows a variation in the contract price under certain circumstances.

Example 1 (holiday brochure)
'We will send you a final invoice 8 to 10 weeks before departure showing the balance you owe us and any surcharge we are forced to make because of increased costs to us.

We guarantee that any surcharges will be limited to £10 per person.

Only governmental action will alter this firm commitment. Any increase in costs which occurs after the issue of the final invoice will be borne by Sunkist Tours Ltd. In exchange for this firm promise and the risk to us, we will not make any refunds, or reduce any increases in other costs by any credit for favourable currency movements.'

Example 2 (building contract)
'Unless otherwise stated the contract price is based on the cost of labour, materials and all necessary services at the date of the quotation and increases or decreases in any such costs shall be a net addition to . or deduction from the contract price.'

Implied terms

In general, the contents of a contract are determined by agreement between the parties. Nevertheless, there are various circumstances in which additional terms may be implied into the agreement.

(1) *By custom*. A contract must always be examined in the light of its surrounding commercial context. The terms of a contract may have been negotiated against the background of the customs of a particular locality or trade. The parties automatically assume that their contract will be subject to such customs and so do not deal specifically with the matter in their contract.

Hutton v Warren (1836)

The tenant of a farm was given six months' notice to quit. His landlord insisted that he continue to cultivate the land during the notice period in keeping with custom. The tenant successfully argued that the same custom entitled him to a fair allowance for the seeds and labour he used on the land.

(2) *By the common law*. The courts will be prepared to imply a term into a contract in order to give effect to the obvious intentions of the parties. Sometimes the point at issue has been overlooked or the parties have failed to express their intention clearly. In these circumstances, the court will supply a term in the interests of 'business efficacy' so that the contract makes commercial common sense.

The Moorcock (1889)

The owner of a wharf agreed to provide mooring facilities for 'The Moorcock'. The ship was damaged when it hit a ridge of rock at low tide. The court implied an undertaking on the part of the wharf owner that it was a reasonably safe place to moor the ship. The wharf owner had broken his implied undertaking and was, therefore, liable in damages to the ship owner.

Certain standard terms have been implied by the common law in a number of business contracts. The courts will imply a term into a lease of a furnished house that it will be reasonably fit for habitation at the start of the tenancy. A contract of employment is subject to a number of implied terms. An employer is under a common law duty to provide a safe system of work for his employees, while an employee is under common law duties to obey legitimate orders and show good faith towards his employer.

By implying a term into the contract, the court is imposing reasonable obligations which the parties would have no doubt included in their agreement if they had troubled to think about the matter. These implied terms may be excluded by express agreement between the parties.

(3) *By statute*. A term may be implied in a contract

by Act of Parliament. In many cases, these implied terms began life among the customs of merchants, were recognized by the courts and then included in the statute which codified the common law rules. The best example of this process is provided by the law relating to the sale of goods. The original Sale of Goods Act 1893 was a codification of the common law rules which had been developed by the courts during the nineteenth century. The present Sale of Goods Act 1979 re-enacts the 1893 Act incorporating the changes made in the intervening years.

A number of terms are implied into a contract for the sale of goods under the Sale of Goods Act 1979. The best known are contained in ss. 12–15.

(*a*) *Section 12* (*title*). There is an implied condition in every contract for the sale of goods that the seller has the right to sell the goods and that he will transfer good title to the buyer. The seller will break this term, for example, if it transpires that the goods were stolen.

(*b*) *Section 13* (*description*). Where there is a sale of goods by description there is an implied condition that the goods will correspond with the description. A shirt described as 100 per cent cotton, for example, should not contain man-made fibres.

(*c*) *Section 14* (*quality and suitability*). Although this section preserves the well-established principle *caveat emptor* (Let the buyer beware), it does impose two duties on a seller who sells in the course of a business. First, there is an implied condition that the

goods are of merchantable quality. This means that if you buy a washing machine, it should actually work when you get it home. Second, where the buyer expressly or impliedly makes known any particular purpose for which the goods are required, there is an implied condition that the goods will be fit for that purpose. If you ask the salesman to recommend a heavy duty carpet which would be suitable for a lounge, it should not be threadbare after a couple of months.

(*d*) *Section 15* (*sample*). In sales by sample, there is an implied condition that the bulk will correspond with the sample. This means that if you have curtains made up for you, the quality of the material should match the sample that you examined in the shop.

Similar terms are implied into contracts for the supply of goods by way of hire purchase, hire, barter, or under work and materials contracts. The sources of these implied terms are summarized in Fig. 10.2.

Exemption clauses – the law

Exemption clauses are a common feature of business contracts. They are express terms which seek to exclude or limit the liability that might belong to one party in the event of a breach of contract. Such clauses are perfectly fair where they are the result of free negotiations between equals, but, all too often, they are

	Goods supplied by way of			
	Sale of goods	Hire purchase	Barter, work and materials	Hire
	Sale of Goods Act 1979	Supply of Goods (Implied Terms) Act 1973	Supply of Goods and Services Act 1982	Supply of Goods and Services Act 1982
Implied terms Title	s. 12	s. 8	s. 2	s. 7
Description	s. 13	s. 9	s. 3	s. 8
Quality and suitability	s. 14	s. 10	s. 4	s. 9
Sample	s. 15	s. 11	s. 5	s. 10

Fig. 10.2 The sources of statutory implied terms in contracts for the supply of goods.

imposed on a weaker party by a stronger party. This abuse of freedom of contract was most commonly practised against consumers. The courts attempted to deal with the problem, but the common law ultimately proved unequal to the ingenuity of those who sought the protection of the exemption. Over the years, Parliament stepped in to control the use of unfair exemption clauses in particular kinds of contracts and now the overwhelming majority of these clauses are covered by the provisions of the Unfair Contract Terms Act 1977. Statutory control of exemption clauses has been grafted on to the pre-existing common law rules. It is still necessary, therefore, to examine the attitude of the courts to these clauses. After we have done this, we will consider how Parliament has dealt with the problem.

Judicial control

The judges based their attack on exemption clauses on two main fronts: incorporation and interpretation.

Incorporation
The person wishing to rely on the exclusion clauses must show that it formed part of the contract. In this connection note the following rules –

(a) *Signed documents*. Where the exemption clause is contained in a document which has been signed, it will automatically form part of the contract. The signer is presumed to have read and understood the significance of all the terms contained in the document.

L'Estrange v Graucob (1934)
Miss L'Estrange bought an automatic cigarette vending machine for use in her café. She signed a 'sales agreement' which provided that 'Any express or implied condition, statement or warranty, statutory or otherwise, not stated herein is hereby excluded'. She did not read this document and was completely unaware of the sweeping exclusion clause hidden in the small print. The machine did not work properly but it was held that she was still bound to pay for it because by signing the agreement she had effectively signed her rights away.

This general rule will not apply where the signer can plead *non est factum* (see p. 172) or if the other party has misrepresented the terms of the agreement.

Curtis v Chemical Cleaning and Dyeing Co. (1951)
Mrs Curtis took a wedding dress to be cleaned by the defendants. She signed a piece of paper headed 'Receipt' after being told by the assistant that it exempted the cleaners from liability for damage to beads and sequins. The 'Receipt' in fact contained a clause excluding liability 'for any damage howsoever arising'. When the dress was returned it was badly stained. It was held that the cleaners could not escape liability for damage to the material of the dress by relying on the exemption clause because its scope had been misrepresented by the defendant's assistant.

(b) *Unsigned documents*. The exemption clause may be contained in an unsigned document such as a ticket or a notice. The clause will only form part of the contract if two conditions are met. First, the document must be regarded by a reasonable man as contractual in nature and as such likely to contain exemption clauses.

Chapelton v Barry Urban District Council (1940)
Mr Chapelton hired two deck chairs for three hours from the defendant council. He received two tickets which he put into his pocket without reading. Each ticket contained a clause exempting the defendants from liability for 'any accident or damage arising from the hire of the chair'. Mr Chapelton was injured when the chair he sat on collapsed. He successfully sued the council.

The Court of Appeal held that a reasonable man would assume that the ticket was a mere receipt and not a contractual document which might contain conditions. The defendants had not succeeded in incorporating the exemption into their contract with Mr Chapelton.

Even if the document may be regarded as contractual, the person seeking to rely on the exemption clause must show that reasonable steps have been taken either before the contract was made or at the time the contract was made to give notice of the clause to the other contracting party.

Olley v Marlborough Court Ltd (1949)
Mr and Mrs Olley booked in for a week's stay at the defendants' hotel. There was a notice in the bedroom which stated that 'the proprietors will not hold themselves responsible for articles lost or

stolen unless handed to the manageress for safe custody.' A stranger gained access to the Olley's room and stole Mrs Olley's furs.

The Court of Appeal held that the defendants were liable. The Olleys saw the notice only after the contract had been concluded at the reception desk. The exclusion clause could not protect the defendants because it had not been incorporated into the contract with the Olleys.

(c) *Previous course of dealings.* An exclusion clause may be binding even though it has not been included in the contract in question, if a previous course of dealings between the parties on the basis of such terms can be established. This principle has been accepted more readily in commercial contracts than in consumer transactions.

J Spurling v Bradshaw (1956)
The defendant delivered eight barrels of orange juice to the plaintiffs who were warehousemen. A few days later the defendant received a document from the plaintiffs which acknowledged receipt of the barrels. It also contained a clause exempting the plaintiffs from liability for loss or damage 'occasioned by the negligence, wrongful act or default' caused by themselves, their employees or agents. When the defendant collected the barrels some were empty, and some contained dirty water. He refused to pay the storage charges and was sued by the plaintiffs. Although the defendants did not receive the document containing the exclusion clause until after the conclusion of the contract, the clause had been incorporated into the contract as a result of a regular course of dealings between the parties over the years. The defendant had received similar documents on previous occasions and he was now bound by the terms contained in them.

Hollier v Rambler Motors (AMC) Ltd (1972)
Mr Hollier entered into an oral contract with the defendant garage to have his car repaired. While the car was in the garage it was damaged in a fire caused by the defendants' negligence. Mr Hollier had had his car repaired by the defendants on three or four occasions in the previous five years. In the past he had been asked to sign a form which stated that 'The company is not responsible for damage caused by fire to customers' cars on the premises' but he did not sign such a form on this occasion. The defendants argued that the exemption clause had been incorporated into the oral contract by a previous course of dealings.

The Court of Appeal rejected this argument and held that the defendants were liable. Three or four transactions over five years did not constitute a regular course of dealings.

(d) *Privity of contract.* According to the doctrine of privity of contract a person who is not a party to a contract can neither benefit from the contract nor be made liable under it. So while a duly incorporated exemption clause may protect a party to a contract it will not protect his servants or agents. They are strangers to the contract and so cannot take advantage of an exclusion or limitation clause.

Scruttons Ltd v Midland Silicones Ltd (1962)
A shipping company (the carrier) agreed to ship a drum of chemicals belonging to the plaintiffs from New York to London. The contract of carriage limited the liability of the carrier for damage to $500 (£179) per package. The drum was damaged by the negligence of the defendants, a firm of stevedores, who had been engaged by the carriers to unload the ship. The plaintiffs sued the defendants in tort for the full extent of the damage, which amounted to £593. The defendants claimed the protection of the limitation clause.

The House of Lords held in favour of the plaintiffs. The defendants were not parties to the contract of carriage and so they could not take advantage of the limitation clause.

Comment. During the course of his speech in the House of Lords Lord Reid suggested a way in which the benefit of an exemption could be made available to a third party, such as the firm of stevedores in this case. He said that four conditions must be fulfilled: (1) a contract of carriage must specifically state that the stevedore is intended to be protected by the exemption clause; (2) the carrier must make it clear that he is contracting both on his own behalf and as agent for the stevedores; (3) the carrier has authority from the stevedore to act in this way; and (4) there is some consideration moving from the stevedore. Legal draughtsmen duly took notice of the formula and it received the approval of the Privy Council in the *New Zealand Shipping Co. Ltd v A. M. Satterthwaite & Co. Ltd* (1974).

Interpretation
Where a clause is duly incorporated into a contract, the

courts will proceed to examine the words used to see if the clause covers the breach and loss which has actually occurred. The main rules of interpretation used by the courts are as follows –

(a) *Strict interpretation.* An exemption clause will be effective only if it expressly covers the kind of liability which has in fact arisen. A clause, for example, which excludes liability for a breach of warranty will not provide protection against liability for a breach of condition.

Baldry v Marshall (1925)

The plaintiff asked the defendants, who were motor dealers, to supply a car that would be suitable for touring purposes. The defendants recommended a Bugatti, which the plaintiff bought. The written contract excluded the defendant's liability for any 'guarantee or warranty, statutory or otherwise'. The car turned out to be unsuitable for the plaintiff's purposes, so he rejected it and sued to recover what he had paid.

The Court of Appeal held that the requirement that the car be suitable for touring was a condition. Since the clause did not exclude liability for breach of a condition, the plaintiff was not bound by it.

(b) *Contra proferentem.* If there is any ambiguity or doubt as to the meaning of an exemption clause the court will construe it *contra proferentem*, i.e. against the party who inserted it in the contract. Very clear words must be used before a party will be held exempt from liability in negligence.

White v John Warwick & Co. Ltd (1953)

The plaintiff hired a tradesman's cycle from the defendants. The written hire agreement stated that 'Nothing in this agreement shall render the owners liable for any personal injury'. While the plaintiff was riding the cycle, the saddle tilted forward and he was injured. The defendants might have been liable in tort (for negligence) as well as in contract.

The Court of Appeal held that the ambiguous wording of the exclusion clause would effectively protect the defendants from their strict contractual liability, but it would not exempt them from liability in negligence.

(c) *Repugnancy.* Under this rule, a court can strike out an exemption clause which is inconsistent with or repugnant to the main purpose of the contract.

J Evans & Sons (Portsmouth) Ltd v Andrea Merzario Ltd (1976)

The plaintiffs had imported machines from Italy for many years and for this purpose they used the services of the defendants, who were forwarding agents. When the defendants changed over to containers the plaintiffs were orally promised by the defendants that their goods would continue to be stowed below deck. On one occasion, the plaintiffs' container was stored on deck and it was lost when it slid overboard.

The Court of Appeal held that the defendants could not rely on an exemption clause contained in the standard conditions of the forwarding trade, on which the parties had contracted, because it was repugnant to the oral promise that had been given.

The doctrine of fundamental breach

The doctrine of fundamental breach was developed particularly by Lord Denning MR in the Court of Appeal, as an additional weapon in the judiciary's fight against exclusion clauses which had been properly incorporated into a contract. According to the doctrine no exemption clause, however clear and unambiguous, could, as a matter of law, protect a party from liability for a serious or fundamental breach of contract. This line of argument was rejected by the House of Lords in the *Suisse Case* (1966) but was then revived by the Court of Appeal. The House of Lords re-established their authority and finally demolished the doctrine in *Photo Productions Ltd v Securicor Transport Ltd* (1980).

Photo Productions Ltd v Securicor Transport Ltd (1980)

The defendants, a security company, agreed to provide a visiting patrol service at nights and weekends for the plaintiffs' factory. One night, the defendants' patrolman lit a fire inside the factory. The fire got out of control and the factory and its contents, worth a total of £615000, were completely destroyed. The defendants relied on an exclusion clause in their contract which stated that they would not be responsible 'For any injurious act or default by any employee ... unless such act or default could have been foreseen and avoided by the exercise of due diligence' by the defendants. The plaintiffs did not allege that the defendants had been negligent in employing the man who lit the fire.

The House of Lords held that the defendants were

protected by the exemption clause. Although a breach of contract with serious consequences had taken place, the exclusion clause, as a matter of construction, was clear and unambiguous and it covered even the 'fundamental' breach that had taken place.

The contract in the *Photo Productions* case was entered into before 1 February 1978 and so the House of Lords could not apply the provisions of the Unfair Contract Terms Act 1977. Nevertheless, their Lordships' decision was greatly influenced by the principles contained in the Act. In the words of Lord Wilberforce, 'After this Act, in commercial matters generally, when the parties are not of unequal bargaining power, and when risks are normally borne by insurance, there is everything to be said for leaving the parties free to apportion the risks as they think fit and for respecting their decision'. In this case the parties had contracted as equals and were clearly in the best position to decide how to allocate the risk of the factory being damaged or destroyed.

Statutory control

At first, Parliament intervened on a piecemeal basis to control the use of exemption clauses in specific types of contract. Section 43(7) of the Transport Act 1962 (repealed in 1977), for example, declared that any clause which purports to exclude or limit the liability of the British Railways Board in respect of injury or death to a passenger 'Shall be void and of no effect'. Other examples of statutory control of exemption clauses include the Occupiers' Liability Act 1957, the Carriage of Goods by Sea Act 1971, and the Defective Premises Act 1972. Parliamentary interest in exemption clauses culminated in the enactment of the Unfair Contract Terms Act 1977, which lays down rules of general application to most contracts.

Unfair Contract Terms Act 1977

Preliminary matters

(1) The Act came into force on 1 February 1978. It does not apply to contracts before that date.

(2) The title of the Act is misleading in two respects. First, it affects the law of tort as well as contract law

because it covers non-contractual notices and signs. Secondly, it does not deal with all unfair terms in contracts, only unfair exemption clauses.

(3) Most of the provisions of the Act apply only to 'business liability', i.e. liability for things done in the course of business or from the occupation of premises used for business purposes. A business includes a profession and the activities of any government department or local or public authority.

(4) The Act does not apply to international supply contracts and ss. 2–4 do not apply to certain contracts listed in Schedule 1, which includes –

(*a*) contracts of insurance;

(*b*) contracts in relation to land.

(5) The Act affords the greatest protection to consumers: under s. 12(1) a person 'deals as a consumer if –

(*a*) he neither makes the contract in the course of a business nor holds himself out as doing so, and –

(*b*) the other party does make the contract in the course of a business, and

(*c*) if it involves a contract for the supply of goods, that are of a type ordinarily supplied for private use or consumption.

The possibilities are summarized in Fig. 10.3.

The parties	Type of transaction
Businessman/private person –	Consumer transaction*
Businessman/businessman –	Non-consumer transaction
Private person/private person –	Non-consumer transaction

* If goods are supplied, they must be of a type ordinarily supplied for private use or consumption for the contract to be classed as a consumer transaction.

Fig. 10.3. Consumer and non-consumer transactions under the Unfair Contract Terms Act 1977.

(6) Exemption clauses are regulated by the Act in

two ways. They are either rendered void and completely ineffective or they are made subject to a test of reasonableness. Although the application of the 'reasonableness test' is a matter for the court to decide in the light of all the circumstances of a particular case, the Act lays down some guiding principles for the judges.

(*a*) Reasonableness must be judged in the case of a contractual term in the light of circumstances at the time when the contract was made and in the case of a non-contractual notice or sign, when the liability arose.

(*b*) It is up to the person who claims that a term or notice is reasonable to show that it is.

(*c*) Where the exemption clause appears in any kind of contract under which goods are supplied, its reasonableness may be judged according to the criteria contained in Schedule 2, which are as follows –

(*i*) The bargaining strengths of the parties relative to each other and the availability of alternative supplies. A monopoly supplier, for example, will find it difficult to justify a wide exclusion clause.

(*ii*) Whether the customer received an inducement to agree to the term. The supplier may have offered the customer a choice: a lower price but subject to an exemption clause or a higher price without the exemption. Provided a real choice is available, the supplier will probably be able to show that the exemption clause was reasonable.

(*iii*) Whether the customer knew or ought reasonably to have known of the existence and extent of the term. If the customer goes into the contract with his eyes wide open, he may have to accept the exemption clause.

(*iv*) Where the term excludes or restricts any relevant liability if some condition is not complied with, whether it was reasonable at the time of the contract to expect that compliance with that condition would be practicable. A supplier, for example, may limit his liability to defects which are brought to his attention within a certain time, e.g. three days. The court will consider whether compliance with such a time limit is practicable.

(*iv*) Whether the goods were manufactured, processed or adapted to the special order of the customer. An exemption clause may well be reasonable if the customer has insisted on the supplier complying with detailed specifications.

The reasonableness of exemption clauses in contracts

other than for the sale or supply of goods must be judged without the benefit of these criteria.

Exemption of liability for negligence (s. 2)

Under s. 2(1) no one acting in the course of a business can exclude or restrict his liability in negligence for death or personal injury by means of a term in a contract or by way of a notice. Liability in negligence for any other kind of loss or damage can be excluded provided the term or notice satisfies the 'reasonableness test' (s. 2(2)).

Exemption of liability for breach of contract (s. 3)

Section 3 applies to two types of contract made by businessmen:

(*a*) where the other party deals as a consumer; and

(*b*) where the businessman contracts on his own written standard terms of business.

In both cases, the businessman cannot exclude or limit his liability for breach of contract, non-performance of the contract or different performance of the contract unless the exemption clause satisfies the requirement of reasonableness.

Unreasonable indemnity clauses (s. 4)

An indemnity clause is a term in a contract between two parties (A and B) in which B agrees to indemnify A for any liability that A may be under. A may incur liability in respect of a third party (C) in which case B must compensate A for any claim which is made by C against A. A builder, for example, may get the owner of a house to agree to indemnify him for any injury or damage that his work on the house might cause to third parties. So if the builder negligently demolishes a wall and injures a next door neighbour, the builder can call on the house owner to make good any award of damages. In some cases, B is required to indemnify A in respect of a liability that A may be under to B himself. Such an indemnity clause has the same effect as an exclusion clause.

Under s. 4 indemnity clauses in contracts where one of the parties deals as a consumer are unenforceable unless they satisfy the requirement of reasonableness.

Guarantees of consumer goods (s. 5)

At one time, it was common practice for guarantees given with goods to contain a clause exempting the manufacturer from liability in negligence if the product proved defective. Under s. 5 a manufacturer or distributor cannot exclude or restrict his liability in negligence for loss arising from defects in goods ordinarily supplied for private use or consumption by means of a term or notice contained in a guarantee. (Manufacturers' guarantees will be examined in Chapter 13.)

Exemption of implied terms in contracts of sale and hire purchase (s. 6)

The original Sale of Goods Act 1893 gave the parties complete freedom to exclude the implied terms contained in ss. 12–15. Retailers often used the opportunity to deprive consumers of their rights by getting

customers to sign an order form, which included an exemption clause hidden in the small print or by displaying suitably worded notices at the point of sale. The Molony Committee on Consumer Protection which reported in 1962 identified the ease with which the implied terms could be excluded as a major defect in the Act and in 1969 the Law Commission made firm proposals for reform. The changes were effected by the Supply of Goods (Implied Terms) Act 1973 and incorporated into the revised Sale of Goods Act 1979.

The implied obligations as to the title contained in s. 12 of the Sale of Goods Act 1979 (sale of goods) and s. 8 of the Supply of Goods (Implied Terms) Act 1973 (hire purchase) cannot be excluded or restricted by any contract term.

The implied terms as to description, quality, etc. contained in ss. 13–15 of the Sale of Goods Act 1979 (sale of goods) and ss. 9–11 of the Supply of Goods (Implied Terms) Act 1973 (hire purchase) cannot be excluded or restricted by any contract term against a

		Exemption clauses in contracts for the supply of goods by way of –			
		Sale, HP, exchange and work + materials		Hire	
		Consumer transaction	Non-consumer transaction	Consumer transaction	Non-consumer transaction
	Title	Void	Void	Subject to reasonableness test	Subject to reasonableness test
Implied Terms	Description	Void	Subject to reasonableness test	Void	Subject to reasonableness test
	Quality and suitability	Void	Subject to reasonableness test	Void	Subject to reasonableness
	Sample	Void	Subject to reasonableness test	Void	Subject to reasonableness test

Fig. 10.4 Exemption of statutory implied terms in contracts for the supply of goods.

person dealing as a consumer. Where the person is not dealing as a consumer, the exemption clause is subject to the 'reasonableness test'.

Exemption of implied terms in other contracts for the supply of goods (s. 7)

Terms as to title, description, merchantability, fitness for purpose and sample are now included in contracts for the supply of goods by way of hire, exchange or work and materials contracts by virtue of the Supply of Goods and Services Act 1982. The implied obligation as to title contained in s. 2 of the 1982 Act (contracts of exchange or work and materials) cannot be excluded or restricted. Exclusion clauses relating to title in contracts of hire, contained in s. 7 are subject to the reasonableness test. The other implied terms cannot be excluded or restricted at all in consumer contracts but in other transactions the exemption is subject to the reasonableness test.

The complicated provisions of the Unfair Contract Terms Act 1977 in relation to the exclusion of statutory implied terms are summarized in Fig. 10.4.

Exemption of liability for misrepresentation (s. 8)

Section 3 of the Misrepresentation Act 1967, as amended by s. 8 of the Unfair Contract Terms Act 1977, provides that any clause which excludes or restricts liability for misrepresentation is ineffective unless it satisfies the requirement of reasonableness.

Cases decided under the Unfair Contract Terms Act 1977

Lally and Weller v George Bird (1980)
The defendant agreed to undertake a house removal for the plaintiffs for £100.80. The contract contained exemption clauses which limited the defendant's liability for losses or breakages to £10 per article and excluded all liability unless claims were made within three days. It was held that these clauses were unreasonable.

Waldron-Kelly v British Railways Board (1981)
The plaintiff placed a suitcase in the care of BR at Stockport railway station for delivery to Haverford West railway station. BR's General Conditions of Carriage limited their liability for non-delivery to an amount assessed by reference to the weight of the goods. The suitcase disappeared and the plaintiff claimed £320.32 as the full value of the suitcase. BR sought to rely on their Conditions which limited their liability to £27.

It was held that BR could not rely on the exemption clause because it did not satisfy the requirement of reasonableness. The plaintiff was awarded £320.32.

Fair Trading Act 1973

Parliament chose to focus the fight against exemption clauses by changing the civil law. The most offensive exemptions from liability, though void, were not illegal. Retailers continued to display notices such as 'No Refunds' or to include exclusion clauses in sales agreements. In many cases, the consumer was 'conned' into believing that he had been deprived of his rights.

The Fair Trading Act 1973, however, opened the way for such unfair consumer trade practices to be made illegal. The Consumer Transactions (Restrictions on Statements) Order 1976 (as amended) makes it a criminal offence for a trader to continue to use exclusion clauses rendered void by ss. 6 and 7 of the Unfair Contract Terms Act 1977. This outlaws the use of 'No money refunded' notices.

Questions/activities

1. (a) Explain what is meant by the following saying: 'The terms of a contract must be certain or capable of being made certain'.

(b) Consider the legal position in each of the situations given below –

(i) Sally, an actress, accepts an offer to play Ophelia in a new London production of Hamlet 'at a West End salary to be mutually agreed'. Sally and the producers cannot agree on an appropriate salary.

(ii) Gary agrees to buy a motorcycle from Speedy Garages Ltd 'on usual HP terms'. Gary has now learnt that he will be required to pay a 50 per cent deposit. He has not saved up enough money.

(iii) After lengthy negotiations for the sale of a flat, Anne, the purchaser, writes to the vendors, 'I accept your offer to sell 12A Sea Terrace, Sandy Bar, for £15 000, subject to the usual conditions of acceptance appropriate to this kind of sale'. Anne has been offered a job a hundred miles away and now wishes to withdraw from the purchase.

(*iv*) Mercurial Property Co Ltd grant a five-year lease on shop premises to Frosted Foods Ltd at a rent of £3000 a year. It is agreed that Frosted Foods Ltd will be able to extend the lease by a further three years, 'at such rent as may be agreed between the parties,' and that any dispute should be referred to arbitration. The parties have failed to agree the rent for the extension of the lease.

2. Paul is looking for a second-hand car when he sees an advertisement in his local evening paper which reads:

SLICK CAR SALES LTD

Hundreds of used car bargains. Lowest prices you've ever seen.

Definitely the lowest prices in Britain
* All cars purchased this month will include Road Fund Tax, Radio, Stereo and a full tank of petrol*

Paul visits the showrooms of Slick Cars and selects a car priced £3900 which the salesman tells him is a 1984 Fiesta which has done 16 000 miles and has had only one owner. Paul signs a sales agreement which describes the car as '1984 Ford Fiesta. Polar Grey, Registration Number B931 AJU'.

(*a*) From the facts given above, identify an example of each of the following: traders' puff, a representation, a condition and a warranty.

(*b*) What remedies will be available to Paul if any of the statements you identified in your answer to (*a*) turns out to be false.

(*c*) Identify three terms which will be implied into the contract.

3. Whilst on holiday at the seaside, Jim agrees to take his family to a 'Fun Park'. He pays £1 to park his car on a car park run by the Strand Council. A notice at the entrance of the car park, which has been partly obscured by overgrown shrubs, states, 'Cars parked entirely at owner's risk'.

Jim pays £7 for a family admission ticket to the 'Fun Park' which is managed by Leisure Ltd. The back of the ticket contains the following clause, 'The company does not accept liability for death or personal injury to visitors, howsoever caused'. Jim and his wife are watching their children on the 'waltzer' when a metal bar flies off, injuring Jim. After receiving hospital treatment Jim returns to his car to discover that it has been damaged by a Strand Council refuse van.

Advise Jim.

4. Angela buys an 'Onion' personal computer from Future Computers Ltd. She signs a sales note in the shop which states, 'Any express or implied condition, statement or warranty, statutory or otherwise is hereby excluded.' After a week's satisfactory use, the 'Onion' refuses to work. What is the legal position if –

(*a*) Angela bought the 'Onion' for her own personal use?

(*b*) Angela bought the 'Onion' to help in her work as an accountant?

Sale of goods

The law relating to contracts for the sale of goods is contained in the Sale of Goods Act 1979. This Act replaces the original Sale of Goods Act 1893 and includes all the amendments that had been made in the intervening years. It provides a framework for the relationship between the buyer and seller and covers such matters as the rights and duties of the parties and their remedies in the event of a breach.

It would be wrong to think that the Act governs every aspect of a sale of goods contract. Many of the general principles of contract law, which we studied in Chapter 8 still apply. A valid contract for the sale of goods, just like any other contract, must possess all the essential elements. The rules relating to the requirements of offer and acceptance, intention, consideration, etc. are largely untouched by the Act. The other important thing to remember is that the Act, in general, does not stop the parties from making their own tailor-made agreement. In many situations, the rules contained in the Act only apply where the parties have failed to make express arrangements as to their obligations.

We will now look at some of the more important provisions of the Sale of Goods Act 1979. For the rest of this chapter, section references are to the 1979 Act, unless otherwise indicated.

Definition

A contract of sale of goods is defined by s. 2(1) as 'a contract by which the seller transfers or agrees to transfer the property in goods to the buyer for a money consideration called the price'.

You should refer back to Chapter 9 for a detailed explanation of the key elements of this definition. The provisions of the Act only apply to those transactions which fall within the definition.

Formation

It is not necessary to observe complex formalities to create a contract for the sale of goods; it may be in writing or by word of mouth, or partly in writing and partly by word of mouth, or even implied from the conduct of the parties. Capacity to enter into a binding sale of goods contract is governed by the general law of contract, which we have already considered in Chapter 8.

The implied terms

The parties are generally free to agree between themselves the details of their contract. However, the Act also automatically includes a number of conditions and warranties in every contract for the sale of goods. These are known as the implied terms and they can be found in ss. 12–15.

Title (s. 12)

There is an implied condition on the part of the seller that in the case of a sale he has a right to sell the goods, and in the case of an agreement to sell he will have the right to sell when the property is to pass (s. 12(1)). If the seller cannot pass good title (rights of ownership) to the buyer, he will be liable for breach of a condition.

e stolen property

(handwritten marginalia: P did not buy ownership)

Rowland v Divall (1923)

Rowland bought a car from Divall for £334 and used it for 4 months. It later transpired that Divall had bought the car from someone who had stolen it and it had to be returned to the true owner. Rowland sued Divall to recover the full purchase price that he had paid. The Court of Appeal held that Divall was in breach of s. 12. Rowland had paid £334 to become the owner of the car. Since he had not received what he had contracted for, there was a total failure of consideration entitling him to a full refund.

Section 12(2) implies two warranties into sale of goods contracts:

(a) that the goods are free from any charges or encumbrances (third party rights) not made known to the buyer before the contract; and

(b) that the buyer will enjoy quiet possession of the goods.

Section 12(3)–(5) provides for a situation where the seller is unsure about his title to goods. He can sell them on the basis that he is transferring only such rights of ownership as he may have. If he does this there is no implied condition that he has the right to sell the goods, but the sale is subject to implied warranties relating to freedom from third party rights and quiet possession.

Description (s. 13)

Where there is a contract for the sale of goods by description, there is an implied condition that the goods will correspond with the description (s. 13(1)). If the buyer does not see the goods before he buys them (e.g. from a mail order catalogue), there has clearly been a sale by description. Even where the buyer has seen the goods and, perhaps, selected them himself, it may still be a sale by description, provided he has relied to some extent on a description.

Beale v Taylor (1967)

The defendant advertised a car for sale as a 1961 Triumph Herald. The plaintiff inspected the car before he bought it. He later discovered that the vehicle consisted of a rear half of a 1961 Herald which had been welded to the front half of an earlier model. The Court of Appeal held that the plaintiff was entitled to damages for breach of s. 13 even though he had seen and inspected the car. He had relied to some extent on the description contained in the advertisement.

The description of the goods may cover such matters as size, quantity, weight, ingredients, origin or even how they are to be packed. The slightest departure from the specifications will entitle the buyer to reject the goods for breach of a condition of the contract.

Re Moore & Co and Landauer & Co. (1921)

The plaintiffs agreed to supply 3000 tins of Australian canned fruit, packed in cases containing thirty tins each. When the goods were delivered, it was discovered that about half of the consignment was packed in cases containing twenty-four tins. Although the correct quantity had been delivered, the defendants decided to reject the whole consignment. It was held that this was a sale by description under s. 13 and, since the goods did not correspond with that description, the defendants were entitled to repudiate the contract.

Comment. This decision seems to be at odds with a well-established principle that the law does not concern itself with trifling matters. Lord Wilberforce in *Reardon Smith Line* v *Yngvar Hanson-Tangen* (1976) cast doubt on the correctness of the *Moore and Landauer* decision and suggested that it should be re-examined by the House of Lords.

A seller may ensure that the transaction is not a sale by description by including such phrases as, 'Bought as seen' or 'Sold as seen' in the contract (*Cavendish-Woodhouse Ltd* v *Manley* (1984)).

Quality and suitability (s. 14)

Section 14 starts by stating that there is no implied condition or warranty as to quality or fitness for a particular purpose except as provided by ss. 14 and 15. This preserves the idea of *caveat emptor* – let the buyer beware. Both of the conditions implied by s. 14 apply only 'where the seller sells goods in the course of a business'; not to sales by private individuals. So if you buy something privately, and it is defective or unsuitable, you cannot complain under s. 14.

Section 14 implies two conditions into every sale by a trader; that the goods are of merchantable quality and that they are fit for a particular purpose.

Merchantable quality

Section 14(2) provides that where the seller sells goods in the course of a business, there is an implied condition that the goods supplied are of merchantable quality, except to the extent of defects which are brought specifically to the buyer's attention before the contract is made or ought to have been noticed by the buyer if he has examined the goods.

Goods are of 'merchantable quality' according to s. 14(6), 'if they are as fit for the purpose(s) for which goods of that kind are commonly bought as it is reasonable to expect having regard to any description applied to them, the price (if relevant) and all other relevant circumstances'. This means that a brand new washing machine should wash your clothes properly, new shoes should not fall apart on their first outing, a meat pie bought for your lunch should not make you ill. The goods do not have to measure up to an absolute standard of quality. If you buy goods second-hand or very cheaply, you cannot expect perfection.

Bartlett v Sidney Marcus Ltd (1965)

The plaintiff bought a second-hand car from the defendants who were car dealers. The plaintiff was warned that the clutch was defective and he agreed to a reduction in the price of the car to take account of this. The defect turned out to be more serious and, therefore, more costly to repair, than he expected. He claimed that the defendants were in breach of s. 14(2).

The Court of Appeal held that in all the circumstances the car was of merchantable quality. As Lord Denning MR pointed out, 'A buyer should realize that when he buys a second-hand car defects may appear sooner or later.'

A buyer is not obliged to examine goods before he buys them and if he chooses not to do so he will still be entitled to full protection under s. 14(2). The buyer can lose his right to complain in two situations: first, where the seller specifically points out that the goods are faulty and, second, where he decides to check the goods, but fails to spot an obvious defect.

Fitness for a particular purpose

Section 14(3) provides that where the seller sells goods in the course of a business and the buyer, expressly or by implication, makes known to the seller any particular purpose for which the goods are being bought, there is an implied condition that the goods supplied are reasonably fit for that purpose, except where it can be shown that the buyer has not relied or that it would be

unreasonable for him to rely on the seller's skill and judgment.

If the buyer specifies the particular purpose for which he requires the goods (e.g. shoes suitable for running a marathon in) the goods must be suitable for the stated purpose. Where the buyer purchases goods with only one normal purpose, he makes his purpose known by implication. Food must be fit for eating and clothes fit for wearing.

Grant v Australian Knitting Mills Ltd (1936)

Dr Grant bought a pair of woollen underpants from a shop. The manufacturers neglected to remove properly a chemical which was used in the manufacturing process. Dr Grant developed a skin rash which turned into dermatitis. It was held that the underpants were not of merchantable quality or reasonably fit for the purpose. Although Dr Grant had not specifically stated the purpose for which he required the underpants, it was clear by implication that he intended to wear them.

If the buyer has any special requirements these must be made known to the seller.

Griffiths v Peter Conway Ltd (1939)

The plaintiff purchased a Harris tweed coat from the defendants. After wearing the coat for a short period of time, she contracted dermatitis. She failed in her claim for damages under s. 14(3). It was shown that the coat would not have affected someone with a normal skin. The plaintiff had not made known to the defendants the fact that she had an abnormally sensitive skin.

In order to be successful under s. 14(3), the buyer must show that he relied on the seller's skill and judgment. Reliance will normally be assumed from the fact that the buyer has taken his custom to that particular shop. However, if a buyer asks for an item under its brand name or lays down detailed specifications as to what he wants, he will find it difficult to show that he has relied on the seller's skill and judgment.

Sample (s. 15)

Section 15 provides that in a contract of sale by sample there is an implied condition –

'(a) that the bulk will correspond with the sample in quality;

(b) that the buyer will have a reasonable opportunity of comparing the bulk with the sample;

(c) that the goods will be free from any defect rendering them unmerchantable, which would not be apparent on reasonable examination of the sample.'

This section, like s. 13, applies to both business and private sales. The application of s. 15 can be illustrated by the following case –

Godley v Perry (1960)

The plaintiff, a six-year old boy, bought a plastic toy catapult for 6d from a newsagent's shop run by Perry, the first defendant. The catapult broke while in use and the plaintiff lost an eye. He sued Perry for breach of the implied conditions in s. 14(2) and (3). Perry had bought the catapults by sample from a wholesaler. He had tested the sample catapult by pulling back the elastic, but no defect had been revealed. Perry now brought the wholesaler into the action claiming a breach of the conditions in s. 15. The wholesaler had bought his supply of catapults by sample from another wholesaler who had obtained the catapults from Hong Kong. The first wholesaler brought the second wholesaler into the action alleging a similar breach of s. 15.

It was held that (1) the plaintiff could recover damages from the first defendant for breach of s. 14: the catapult was not of merchantable quality or fit for the purpose for which it had been bought; and (2) the first defendant could recover damages from the first wholesaler who in turn could recover damages from the second wholesaler, in both cases because there had been a breach of s. 15 which was implied in the relevant contract.

Transfer of property in the goods

The essence of a contract for the sale of goods is the transfer of property (ownership) in goods from the seller to the buyer. It is important to ascertain exactly when the property in goods passes from the seller to the buyer for the following reasons –

(1) If the goods are accidentally destroyed, it is necessary to know who bears the loss. Section 20 provides that risk normally passes with ownership.

(2) If either the seller or the buyer becomes bankrupt or, in the case of a company, goes into liquidation, it is necessary to discover who owns the goods.

(3) The remedy of an unpaid seller against a buyer will depend on whether ownership has been transferred. If property has passed to the buyer, he can be sued for the price of the goods. If property has not passed to the buyer, the seller can only sue for non-acceptance. (Remedies under the Sale of Goods Act 1979 will be discussed later in this chapter.)

The rules relating to the transfer of ownership depend on whether the goods are classified as specific goods or unascertained goods. Specific goods are 'goods identified and agreed on at the time a contract of sale is made'. This includes contracts such as purchasing groceries from a supermarket or buying a sheepskin coat from a market trader. Unascertained goods are those goods which are not identified and agreed on when the contract is made. An order for 10 cwt of coal to be delivered in three days' time involves unascertained goods, because it is impossible to identify which specific lumps of coal lying in the coal merchant's yard will make up the order. As soon as the 10 cwt of coal is set aside to fulfil this order, the goods are said to be ascertained.

Specific goods

Section 17 provides that the property in specific goods passes when the parties intend it to pass and to ascertain the intention of the parties 'regard shall be had to the terms of the contract, the conduct of the parties and the circumstances of the case'. If the parties do not indicate, expressly or impliedly, when they want ownership to pass, s. 18 sets out various rules to ascertain their presumed intention.

'Rule 1 – where there is an unconditional contract for the sale of specific goods in a deliverable state, the property in the goods passes to the buyer when the contract is made, and it is immaterial whether the time of payment or the time of delivery, or both, be postponed.' This means that a buyer can become the owner of goods even though he has not paid for them yet and they are still in the seller's possession.

Tarling v Baxter (1827)

A haystack was sold but before the buyer had taken it away, it was burned down. It was held that the buyer was still liable to pay the price because he became the owner of the haystack when the contract was made. It was immaterial that he had not yet taken delivery of the goods.

'Rule 2 – where there is contract for the sale of specific goods and the seller is bound to do something to the goods for the purpose of putting them into a deliverable state, the property does not pass until the thing is done and the buyer has notice that it has been done.' Where the seller agrees to alter the goods in some way for the buyer, ownership will pass when the alterations are completed and the buyer has been informed.

'Rule 3 – where there is a contract for the sale of specific goods in a deliverable state but the seller is bound to weigh, measure, test or do some other act or thing with reference to the goods for the purpose of ascertaining the price, the property does not pass until the act or thing is done and the buyer has notice that it has been done.' If, for example, you agree to buy a particular bag of potatoes, at a price of 10p a pound, you will not become the owner of the potatoes until the seller has weighed the bag and informed you of the price payable. If, however, it is agreed that the buyer will do the weighing, measuring or testing, ownership of the goods will pass in accordance with Rule 1, i.e. when the contract is made.

'Rule 4 – when goods are delivered to the buyer on approval or on sale or return ... the property in the goods passes to the buyer –

(a) when he signifies his approval or acceptance to the seller or does any other act adopting the transaction;

(b) if he does not signify his approval or acceptance to the seller but retains the goods without giving notice of rejection, then, if a time has been fixed for the return of the goods, on the expiration of that time, and, if no time has been fixed, on the expiration of a reasonable time'. Property in goods delivered on approval, will pass under part (a) of this rule either when the buyer informs the seller that he wishes to buy them or he 'adopts' the transaction, for example, by re-selling the goods. Part (b) of the rule is illustrated by the following case –

Elphick v Barnes (1880)
The seller handed a horse over to a prospective buyer on approval for eight days. Unfortunately, the horse died on the third day. It was held that

ownership of the horse had not passed to the buyer and, therefore, the seller would have to bear the loss.

Unascertained goods

In a sale of unascertained goods, the property passes to the buyer only when the goods have been ascertained (s. 16). If the parties then fail to mention when they intend ownership to pass, s. 18, Rule 5 will apply.

'Rule 5 – (1) where there is a contract for the sale of unascertained or future goods by description, and goods of that description and in a deliverable state are unconditionally appropriated to the contract, either by the seller with the assent of the buyer or by the buyer with the assent of the seller, the property in the goods then passes to the buyer; and the assent may be express or implied and may be given either before or after the appropriation is made.' Goods are 'unconditionally appropriated' to the contract, when they are separated from the bulk and earmarked for a particular buyer. Delivery to a carrier will amount to an 'appropriation' provided the buyer's goods can be clearly identified.

Healy v Howlett & Sons (1917)
The plaintiff agreed to sell twenty boxes of mackerel to the defendant. He despatched 190 boxes of mackerel by rail for delivery to various customers but the boxes were not labelled for particular customers. Employees of the railway company were entrusted with the task of allocating the correct number of boxes to each destination. The train was delayed and the fish deteriorated before twenty boxes could be set aside for the defendant.

It was held that the property in the goods had not passed to the buyer because the defendant's boxes had not been appropriated to the contract.

Reserving a right of disposal

The seller's overriding concern is to ensure that he receives payment in full for his goods. Clearly, this presents no problem to a retailer: he can insist on payment in cash or near cash (i.e. by cheque guaranteed with a cheque card, or a recognized credit card) before he releases the goods. In the business world, however, sellers are expected to do business on credit terms. If ownership of the goods passes to the buyer before he pays for them and he subsequently becomes bankrupt, or, in the case of a company, goes into liquidation, the seller will be treated as an ordinary trade creditor. As such, the seller is unlikely to recover what he is owed. He can protect himself from these considerable risks, by stating that the property in the goods shall not pass to the buyer until the contract price has been paid. Section 19 provides that where the seller has reserved the right of disposal of the goods until some condition is fulfilled, ownership of the goods will not pass to the buyer until that condition is met. The inclusion of such a reservation of title clause in the contract of sale will enable a seller to retrieve his goods and re-sell them if the buyer goes bankrupt or into receivership or liquidation before paying for them.

The position becomes much more complicated in the following situations –

(1) where the buyer has re-sold the goods, and
(2) where the buyer has mixed them with other goods during a manufacturing process and then sold the manufactured product.

Clearly, the seller cannot simply reclaim 'his' goods. However, he may be able to protect himself in relation to (1) by including a carefully worded clause in the contract, allowing him to trace the goods and claim the proceeds of sale. These terms are known as *Romalpa* clauses, after the name of the case in which they achieved prominence.

Aluminium Industrie Vaassen BV v Romalpa Aluminium Ltd (1976)

AIV, a Dutch company, sold aluminium foil to RA, an English company. A clause in the contract provided that (1) ownership of the foil would not pass to RA until it was paid for; (2) if the foil became mixed with other items during a manufacturing process, AIV would become the owner of the finished product and property would not pass until RA had paid for the foil; (3) unmixed foil and finished products should be stored separately; (4) RA were authorized to sell the finished product on condition that AIV were entitled to the proceeds of the sale. RA became insolvent and a receiver was appointed.

The Court of Appeal held that AIV were entitled to recover a quantity of unmixed foil and the proceeds of re-sale of some unmixed foil.

The sellers in the *Romalpa* case confined their claim to unmixed goods and so the Court of Appeal did not give a decision as to the position in relation to mixed goods. Later cases suggest that a *Romalpa* clause will be

effective in respect of mixed goods, only if it is registered with the Registrar of Companies as a charge over the assets of the buying company.

The effect on retention clauses of the appointment of an administrator to an insolvent company was examined in Chapter 7.

Sale by a person who is not the owner

As a general rule, a buyer cannot acquire ownership from someone who himself has neither ownership nor the owner's authority to sell. This rule, which is known as the *nemo dat* rule from the phrase *nemo dat quod non habet* – no one can give what he has not got – is embodied in s. 21: 'Where goods are sold by a person who is not their owner, and who does not sell them under the authority or with the consent of the owner, the buyer acquires no better title to the goods than the seller had ...'

In these circumstances, the buyer will be required to return the goods to their true owner. The buyer's only remedy is to sue the person who sold him the item for breach of s. 12. In most of these cases, however, the seller is a rogue who disappears before the buyer can take action against him. The unsuspecting buyer is left to bear the full brunt of the rogue's misdeeds. It is not surprising, therefore, that exceptions to the *nemo dat* rule have developed. The exceptions are as follows –

Estoppel (s. 21)

If the true owner by his conduct allows the innocent buyer to believe that the seller has the right to sell the goods, ownership of the goods will pass to the buyer because the true owner will be prevented (estopped) from denying that the seller had the right to sell.

Eastern Distributors Ltd v Goldring (1957)

Murphy was the owner of a van. He wanted to buy a car from Coker, a dealer, but he could not raise enough money for a deposit. Murphy and Coker then devised a scheme to generate the necessary finance. Coker would pretend that he owned the van: he would then sell the van and the car to a finance company, who would let both vehicles out on HP to Murphy. The proceeds of the sale of the van would raise sufficient money to finance the required HP deposits. Unfortunately, the finance company accepted the proposal for the van but turned the car down. Unknown to Murphy, Coker proceeded to sell the van to the finance company.

It was held that the finance company had become the owner of the van, because the original owner (Murphy) by his conduct had allowed the buyers (the finance company) to believe that the seller (Coker) had a right to sell the goods.

Agency (s. 21(2))

The law of agency applies to contracts for the sale of goods. An agent who sells his principal's goods in accordance with the principal's instructions passes a good title to the buyer because he is selling the goods with the authority and consent of the owner. The buyer may even acquire a good title to the goods where the agent has exceeded his actual authority, provided the agent is acting within the scope of his apparent or ostensible authority and the buyer is unaware of the agent's lack of authority.

Section 21(2) expressly preserves the rules contained in the Factors Act 1889 which enables the apparent owner of goods to dispose of them as if he were their true owner. A factor is an independent mercantile agent who buys and sells goods on behalf of other people, but does so in his own name. A factor can pass good title to a buyer if the following conditions are met –

(*a*) the goods being sold were in the possession of the factor with the consent of the true owner;

(*b*) the factor, in selling the goods, was acting in the ordinary course of business, and

(*c*) the buyer was unaware of any lack of authority on the part of the factor.

Sale under a common law or statutory power (s. 21(2))

Certain persons have the power under common law or statute to sell goods that belong to another. A pawnbroker, for example, has the right to sell goods which have been pledged with him, where the loan has not been repaid. The purchaser will acquire a good title to the goods.

Sale in market overt (s. 22)

A purchaser of goods sold in market overt obtains a good title to them provided that he buys them in good faith and without notice of any defect in the title of the seller. The term 'market overt' means every shop in the City of London and every public market which is legally constituted by Royal Charter, statute or custom.

Before a sale can be recognized as a sale in market overt, the following conditions must be observed –

(*a*) the sale must be public and open;

(*b*) the sale must take place in accordance with usual market practice;

(*c*) the goods must be of a kind which are normally dealt within the market;

(*d*) the goods themselves must be openly displayed for sale;

(*e*) the sale must be by the shopkeeper and not to him; and

(*f*) the sale must take place between sunrise and sunset.

Reid *v* Commissioner of Police of the Metropolis (1973)

A pair of Adam candelabra were stolen from Mr Reid's house. Some three months later they appeared on a stall at the New Caledonian Market in Southwark, where they were bought by a Mr Cocks early in the morning before the sun had risen. It was held that Mr Cocks had not acquired a good title to the candelabra because the sale took place before sunrise. The goods were returned to Mr Reid

Sale by a person with a voidable title (s. 23)

A person may obtain possession of goods under a contract which is void (e.g. for mistake). A void contract is, in fact, no contract at all. A purchaser in these circumstances does not acquire title to the goods and, therefore, cannot pass good title on to anyone else. The original owner will be able to maintain an action in the tort of conversion to recover the goods or their value from a third party who bought them in good faith. This is what happened in *Cundy* v *Lindsay* (1878) (see p. 172).

A person may also acquire goods under a contract which is voidable (e.g. for misrepresentation). In this case, the contract is valid unless and until it is avoided. Section 23 provides that where goods are re-sold before the contract has been avoided, the buyer acquires a good title to them provided he buys them in good faith and without notice of the seller's defect of title (see *Lewis* v *Averay* (1971), p. 172). If the original owner acts quickly to rescind the contract and then the goods are re-sold, the seller may be prevented from passing a good title to a purchaser (but see *Newtons of Wembley Ltd* v *Williams* (1964) overleaf).

Sale by a seller in possession of the goods (s. 24)

Where a seller sells goods but remains in possession of them, or any documents of title relating to them, any re-sale to a second buyer, who actually takes physical delivery of the goods or the documents of title, will pass a good title to the second buyer. The disappointed first buyer may sue the seller for non-delivery of the goods. The remedies of a buyer will be considered later in this chapter.

Re-sale by a buyer in possession of the goods with the consent of the seller (s. 25)

Where a person who has bought or agreed to buy goods obtains possession of the goods with the consent of the seller, any re-sale to a person, who takes the goods in good faith and without notice of the rights of the original seller has the same effect as if the person making the delivery or transfer were a mercantile agent in possession of the goods ... with the consent of the owner'. This exception to the *nemo dat* rule can be illustrated by the following case –

Newtons of Wembley Ltd *v* **Williams (1964)**
The plaintiffs sold a car to a rogue, who paid for it by a cheque which was later dishonoured. The plaintiffs took immediate steps to rescind their contract with the rogue (by informing the police). Some time later, the rogue re-sold the car in Warren Street in London, a well-established street market in used cars. The buyer then sold the car to the defendant.

The Court of Appeal held that the defendant acquired a good title to the car. When the rogue sold the car at Warren Street, he was a buyer in possession with the owner's consent and he acted in the same way as a mercantile agent (or dealer) would have done. He passed a good title to the purchaser who in turn passed title to the defendant.

Sale of motor vehicles on hire purchase (Hire Purchase Act 1964, Part III)

If a vehicle which is subject to a hire purchase (HP) agreement is sold by the hirer to a private person who buys in good faith and without notice of the HP agreement, the buyer acquires a good title to the vehicle, even as against the owner. Motor dealers and finance companies cannot claim the benefit of this provision and so they will not acquire good title to a vehicle which is already subject to an HP agreement.

The majority of finance companies are members of Hire Purchase Information Ltd (HPI). This organization maintains a register where finance companies can register their HP agreements.

When a car dealer is offered a car for sale, he can check with HPI to see if it is already subject to an HP agreement.

Performance of the contract

It is the duty of the seller to deliver the goods and the buyer's duty to accept and pay for them. The parties are free to make their own arrangements about the time and place of delivery and payment. The Act sets out the obligations of the seller and buyer, when they have not dealt with these matters specifically in their agreement.

Section 28 provides: 'Unless otherwise agreed, delivery of the goods and payment of the price are concurrent conditions ...'. This means that the seller can hold on to the goods until the buyer has paid for them.

Delivery

Delivery in the context of the Act means the voluntary transfer of possession from one person to another. The delivery may consist of –

(1) physically handing over the goods;

(2) handing over the means of control of the goods, e.g. the keys to the premises where they are stored;

(3) transferring documents of title; or

(4) where the goods are in possession of a third party, an acknowledgement by the third party that he is holding the goods on behalf of the buyer.

Place of delivery
In the absence of any agreement to the contrary, the place of delivery is the seller's place of business; it is up to the buyer to come and collect the goods (s. 29(2)). If, however, the seller agrees to send the goods and engages a carrier for this purpose, s. 32 provides that delivery to the carrier is deemed to be delivery to the buyer. The seller must make the best possible contract with the carrier on behalf of the buyer to ensure the safe arrival of the goods.

Time of delivery

The parties may have fixed a delivery date. Failure to make delivery by that date is a breach of condition, which entitles the buyer to repudiate the contract and sue for non-delivery (see later p. 219).

Where the seller agrees to send the goods and no time for sending them has been agreed, he must despatch them within a reasonable time (s. 29(3)). A demand for delivery by the buyer or an offer of delivery by the seller will not be valid unless made at a reasonable hour (s. 29(3)). What is reasonable is a question of fact.

If the seller is ready and willing to deliver the goods and he requests the buyer to take delivery, but the buyer does not comply with the request within a reasonable time, then the buyer will be liable for any resulting loss and a reasonable charge for the care and custody of the goods (s. 37).

Delivery of the wrong quantity (s. 30)

If the seller delivers a smaller quantity than ordered, the buyer may reject the consignment, but if he decides to accept the goods, he must pay for them at the contract rate.

If the seller sends a larger quantity than agreed, the buyer has the following choices –

(1) he may accept the goods he ordered and reject the rest;

(2) he may reject the lot;

(3) he may accept the whole consignment, paying for the extra goods at the contract rate.

If the seller delivers the contract goods but they are mixed with other goods, which have not been ordered, the buyer may either accept the contract goods and reject the rest, or reject the whole lot.

It should be noted that a buyer will not be entitled to reject a consignment where the discrepancy is minute.

Shipton, Anderson & Co. Ltd v Weil Bros & Co. Ltd (1912)

The sellers agreed to deliver 4950 tons of wheat They in fact delivered 4950 tons 55 lb. It was held that the difference was so trifling that it did not entitle the buyers to reject the whole consignment.

Delivery by instalments

Unless otherwise agreed, the buyer is not bound to accept delivery by instalments (s. 31(1)). The parties may, of course, agree that the goods are to be delivered in stated instalments. A breach of contract may occur in respect of one or more instalments (e.g., the seller may deliver goods which are unmerchantable or the buyer may refuse to take delivery of an instalment). Clearly, the injured party will be able to sue for damages, but the question then arises whether he is also entitled to repudiate the contract. The answer depends on whether the contract is indivisible or severable. A contract is usually treated as being severable if each instalment is to be separately paid for.

(1) *Indivisible contracts* (s. 11(4)). A breach of condition in respect of the first instalment will entitle the injured party to repudiate the whole contract. Breaches of condition in relation to the second and subsequent instalments must be treated as breaches of warranty for which the only remedy is an action in damages.

(2) *Severable contracts* (s. 31(2)). Whether a breach in relation to one or more instalments will entitle the injured party to repudiate the whole contract, depends 'on the terms of the contract and the circumstances of the case'. If the contract is silent on the matter, the courts apply two main tests:

(*a*) the size of the breach in relation to the whole contract, and

(*b*) the likelihood that the breach will be repeated.

Maple Flock Co. Ltd v Universal Furniture Products (Wembley) Ltd (1933)

The sellers agreed to deliver 100 tons of flock by instalments. The first fifteen instalments were satisfactory but the sixteenth was not up to the required standard. The buyers then took delivery of four more satisfactory loads before refusing further deliveries.

The court held that the buyers were not entitled to repudiate the contract. The defective flock constituted a small proportion of the total quantity delivered and there was little likelihood of the breach being repeated.

Acceptance

The buyer is bound to accept the goods which the seller delivers in accordance with the contract. Acceptance is deemed to have taken place under s. 35(1) when –

(1) the buyer tells the seller that he has accepted the goods; or

(2) he does anything to the goods which is inconsistent with the ownership of the seller (e.g. he re-sells them); or

(3) he retains the goods after the lapse of a reasonable time without telling the seller that he has rejected them.

Section 34 provides that the buyer is not deemed to have accepted the goods until he has had a reasonable opportunity to examine them to check that they are in accordance with the terms of the contract.

If the buyer exercises his right to reject the goods for breach of a condition, he must inform the seller of his refusal to accept them but he is not obliged to return them to the seller (s. 36).

Payment

The price is such a fundamental part of the transaction, that it will normally be fixed by the contract. However, it may be ascertained by the course of dealing between the parties or the contract may provide a mechanism for fixing the price e.g., by arbitration.

The parties may make their own agreement as to the time of payment. The seller may insist on payment in advance of delivery or, he may be prepared to extend a period of credit. In the absence of such express agreement, payment is due when the goods are delivered.

Remedies

Seller's remedies

Two sets of remedies are open to the seller. He can pursue *personal remedies* against the buyer himself and *real remedies* against the goods.

Personal remedies

The seller can sue the buyer for the contract price or for damages for non-acceptance.

(1) *Action for the price* (s. 49). The seller can bring an action for the contract price in two situations: where the property in the goods has passed to the buyer or where the buyer has failed to pay by a specified date, irrespective of whether ownership has passed to the buyer.

(2) *Damages for non-acceptance* (s. 50). If the property in the goods has not passed and the buyer will not accept the goods, the seller can sue for non-acceptance. The measure of damages is the estimated loss directly and naturally resulting in the ordinary course of events from the buyer's breach of contract (s. 50(2)). If the buyer wrongfully refuses to accept and pay for the goods, the seller is expected to mitigate his loss and sell them elsewhere for the best possible price. Section 50(3) provides guidance as to the measure of damages where there is an available market for the goods. If the market price is less than the contract price, the seller can recover the difference by way of damages. Where the market price is the same or even higher than the contract price, the seller will be entitled to nominal damages only. (The market price is calculated at the time when the goods ought to have been accepted.)

The following cases illustrate how s. 50 is applied in practice by the courts.

Thompson W L Ltd v Robinson (Gunmakers) Ltd (1955)

The defendants ordered a new Vanguard car from the plaintiff car dealers, but then refused to accept it. The defendants argued that they were only liable to pay nominal damages, since the contract price and the market price were the same.

It was held that there was no 'available market' for Vanguard cars because supply exceeded demand and, therefore, s. 50(3) did not apply. The dealers had sold one car less and under s. 50(2) they were entitled to their loss of profit on the sale.

Charter v Sullivan (1957)

A buyer refused to accept a new Hillman Minx car which he had ordered from a dealer. In contrast to the previous case, the demand for Hillman Minx cars exceeded supply and the dealer would have no difficulty in finding another buyer.

It was held that the dealer was entitled to nominal damages only. The buyer's breach would not affect the total number of cars that he would sell over a period of time.

Real remedies

The unpaid seller has three possible remedies in respect of the goods even though the property in the goods has passed to the buyer. They are lien, stoppage in transit and re-sale.

(1) *Lien* (ss. 41–43). A lien is a right to retain

possession of goods (but not to re-sell them) until the contract price has been paid. It is available in any of the following circumstances –

(*a*) where the goods have been sold without any mention of credit;

(*b*) where the goods have been sold on credit but the period of credit has expired;

(*c*) where the buyer becomes insolvent.

The seller will lose his right of lien if the price is paid or tendered or the buyer obtains possession of the goods. The seller cannot exercise this right to retain the goods if he has handed the goods to a carrier for transportation to the buyer without reserving the right of disposal of the goods or where he has given up the right.

(2) *Stoppage in transit (ss. 44–46)*. This is the right of the seller to stop goods in transit to the buyer, regain possession of them and retain them until payment has been received. The seller can exercise his right to stoppage in transit in only one situation – where the buyer has become insolvent.

(3) *Right of re-sale (ss. 47 and 48)*. The rights of lien and stoppage in transit by themselves do not give the seller any right to re-sell the goods. He is allowed, however, to re-sell the goods in the following circumstances –

(*a*) where the goods are of a perishable nature;

(*b*) where the seller gives notice to the buyer of his intention to re-sell and the buyer does not pay or tender the price within a reasonable time;

(*c*) where the seller expressly reserves the right of re-sale in the event of the buyer defaulting.

The seller can exercise the right of re-sale and also recover damages for any loss sustained by the buyer's breach of contract. The original contract of sale is rescinded and the new buyer acquires a good title to the goods as against the original buyer.

Buyer's remedies

Various remedies are available to the buyer, where the seller is in breach of contract.

Rejection of the goods (s. 11)

The buyer may repudiate the contract and reject the goods where the seller is in breach of a condition of the contract. Most of the implied terms contained in ss.

12–15 are conditions, so if the goods are not of merchantable quality or fit for a particular purpose, the buyer is entitled to reject them. This right will be lost as soon as the goods have been accepted (see p. 217): the buyer must treat the breach of condition as a breach of warranty which limits his remedy to a claim for damages.

An action for damages

(1) *Non-delivery (s. 51)*. The buyer can sue for non-delivery when the seller wrongfully neglects or refuses to deliver the goods. The measure of damages is the estimated loss directly and naturally resulting in the ordinary course of events from the seller's breach of contract. Where there is an available market for the goods, the measure of damages is usually the difference between the contract price and the higher price of obtaining similar goods elsewhere.

If the buyer has paid in advance and the goods are not delivered, he can recover the amount paid (s. 54) because there has been a total failure of consideration.

(2) *Breach of warranty (s. 53)*. The buyer can sue for damages under s. 53 in the following circumstances –

(*a*) where the seller is in breach of warranty;

(*b*) where the seller is in breach of a condition, but the buyer has chosen to carry on with the contract and claim damages instead;

(*c*) where the seller is in breach of a condition, but the buyer has lost the right to reject the goods (because he has accepted them).

The measure of damages is the estimated loss directly and naturally resulting from the breach. This is usually the difference in value between the goods actually delivered and goods fulfilling the warranty.

Specific performance (s. 52)

The buyer may sue for specific performance but only in cases where the goods are specific or ascertained and where monetary damages would not be an adequate remedy. A court is unlikely to make such an order if similar goods are available elsewhere.

Questions/activities

1. Sandra, who runs a flourishing florist's shop, decides to replace the van which she uses for making deliveries. She attends a long-established street market

in used cars, where she sees a van with a notice in the front window which reads: 'For Sale. 1976 Bedford van'. After a thorough inspection and a test drive she enters into a contract to buy the van from Mark. What is her legal position in the following circumstances –

(*a*) Sandra discovers that the vehicle is made up of two Bedford vans. The front half of a 1973 model has been welded to the rear half of a 1976 model and, as a result, the van is in a dangerous condition.

(*b*) During the test drive, Sandra noticed that the clutch was defective. Mark said that he was prepared to do the repairs himself or he would drop the price by £75. Sandra agreed to the reduction in price but her local garage has now told her that it will cost £150 to put the defect right.

(*c*) She has now been informed by the police that the van was stolen six months previously and that it must be returned to its true owner.

2. Greenacres, a firm of estate agents, decide to give their image a face-lift by refurbishing their reception area. They place the contract with a local company, Office Style Ltd, who agree to supply the following items –

(*a*) Six easy chairs and matching coffee table selected from Office Style's existing stock by Greenacres senior partner;

(*b*) a new carpet which has to be ordered direct from the manufacturer;

(*c*) a set of free-standing display units, already in stock, which Office Style agrees to adapt to hold the particulars of houses for sale.

The night before the re-fitting is due to take place, Office Style's warehouse, containing all the items for the Greenacres' job, is completely destroyed by fire.

Advise Greenacres.

3. Luigi owns an Italian restaurant. He has experienced a few problems with recent deliveries from his suppliers and he seeks your advice.

(*a*) He orders 500 tins of Italian tomatoes. The supplier delivers 400 tins of Italian tomatoes and 100 tins of Greek tomatoes.

(*b*) He orders 10 lb of parmesan cheese but the supplier delivers only 2 lb.

(*c*) He orders 50 lb of spaghetti. The supplier delivers 100 lb.

(*d*) He has a regular order with a local baker for 100 bread rolls to be delivered by 11 a.m. every day. On one occasion the rolls do not arrive until 2 p.m.

4. Jim agrees to supply 300 turkeys to a London butcher's shop during a three-week period prior to Christmas. What are Jim's remedies in each of the following situations?

(*a*) The butcher rings up at the end of November to cancel the order, because he has found a cheaper supplier.

(*b*) While the second consignment of 100 turkeys is being transported by rail to London, Jim hears from a neighbouring farmer that the butcher is having difficulty paying his debts.

Supply of goods and services

In the last chapter we looked at the statutory framework which regulates contracts for the sale of goods. The provisions of the Sale of Goods Act 1979, including the protection afforded the buyer by the implied terms contained in ss. 12–15, apply only to contracts where goods are sold for a *money consideration*. The sale of goods legislation did not cover other methods of obtaining goods (e.g. by HP, hire, barter or work and materials contracts), although the need for protection was just as great; nor did it have anything to say about the provision of services.

Implied terms as to title, description, quality, fitness for purpose and correspondence with sample, similar to those in the Sale of Goods Act, were put on a statutory basis first in respect of goods supplied on HP and later in relation to goods acquired using trading stamps. In 1979, the Law Commission recommended that the protection of statutory implied terms should be extended to all contracts for the supply of goods. This was achieved by the Supply of Goods and Services Act 1982. The Act also places on a statutory footing certain terms which had hitherto been implied by the common law in contracts for services.

The Supply of Goods and Services Act 1982 is divided into two main parts: Part I deals with implied terms in contracts for the supply of goods, while Part II covers implied terms in contracts for services. In this chapter, section references are to the 1982 Act unless otherwise indicated. We will now examine the provisions of the Act in more detail.

Implied terms in contracts for the supply of goods (Part I)

This Part of the Act was based on the recommendations

of the Law Commission contained in its Report on Implied Terms in Contracts for the Supply of Goods (Law. Com. No. 95), which had been published in 1979. The provisions of Part I, which came into force in January 1983, consist of two sets of implied terms. The first set applies to contracts for the transfer of property in goods and the second set applies to contracts of hire.

Contracts for the transfer of property in goods

The first set of terms, detailed in ss. 2–5 (see below), are implied into contracts for work and materials and barter, under which a person acquires ownership of goods. The terms, which were previously implied into these contracts by the common law, follow the pattern established by ss. 12–15 of the Sale of Goods Act 1979, in relation to contracts for the sale of goods.

Section 2 contains an implied *condition* that the transferor has the right to transfer the property and implied *warranties* that the goods are free from undisclosed third party rights and that the buyer will enjoy quiet possession of the goods. Where there is a contract for the transfer of goods by description, under s. 3 there is an implied *condition* that the goods will correspond to the description. Section 4 provides that where goods are transferred in the course of a business, there are implied *conditions* that the goods are of merchantable quality and reasonably fit for the purpose. According to s. 5, where there is a transfer of goods by reference to a sample, there is an implied *condition* that the bulk will correspond with the sample.

These implied terms apply in exactly the same way

as the terms implied by ss. 12–15 of the Sale of Goods Act 1979 (see pp. 209). Similarly, attempts to exclude the obligations contained in ss. 2–5 of the 1982 Act are subject to control on the 'Sale of Goods' model. The implied terms as to title (s. 2) cannot be excluded or restricted by any contract term. Sections 3–5 cannot be excluded or restricted where the transferee is dealing as a consumer; if the transferee is not dealing as a consumer, the exemption is subject to the reasonableness test, as laid down in the Unfair Contract Terms Act 1977 (see p. 205).

Contracts for the hire of goods

The second set of implied terms in Part I can be found in ss. 7–10. They apply to contracts under which 'one person bails or agrees to bail goods to another by way of hire' (s. 6). This includes both consumer and commercial hire agreements, but HP agreements are expressly excluded.

The terms implied in hire contracts by ss. 7–10 match as far as is possible the implied terms in contracts for the sale of goods. Section 7 provides that there is an implied *condition* that the bailor has a right to transfer possession of the goods to the bailee and that the bailee will enjoy quiet possession of the goods during the period of hire. By s. 8, where there is a contract for the hire of goods by description, there is an implied *condition* that the goods will correspond with the description. Section 9 provides that where goods are hired in the course of a business, there are implied *conditions* that the goods are of merchantable quality and reasonably fit for the purpose. Section 10 covers implied *conditions* in relation to contracts for the hire of goods by reference to a sample.

The implied terms contained in s. 7 (right to transfer and quiet possession) can be excluded or restricted provided that the exemption satisfies the reasonableness test. The implied terms as to description, quality and sample cannot be excluded or restricted as against a person dealing as a consumer; in a non-consumer transaction, these implied terms can be excluded subject to the requirement of reasonableness.

Implied terms in contracts for the supply of services (Part II)

Recent years have witnessed a dramatic growth in the service industry which has been matched by a corresponding increase in customer dissatisfaction. The National Consumer Council (NCC) highlighted the problems in its Report, 'Services Please' which was published in 1981. Part II of the Supply of Goods and Services Act 1982, which deals with contracts for services, is based largely on the recommendations put forward by the NCC. This part of the Act came into force on 4 July 1983.

A contract for the supply of services is one 'under which a person ("the supplier") agrees to carry out a service' (s. 12). This covers agreements where the supplier simply provides a service and nothing more, such as dry-cleaning or hairdressing. It also includes contracts where the provision of a service also involves the transfer of goods (e.g. installing central heating or repairing a car). The Act does not apply to contracts of service (employment) or apprenticeship.

The terms implied into a contract for services by this part of the Act are as follows.

Care and skill (s. 13)

Section 13 provides that where the supplier is acting in the course of a business, there is an implied term that the supplier will carry out the service with reasonable care and skill. So if you take your raincoat to be dry-cleaned and it is returned with a large tear in the fabric, clearly the cleaning process has not been carried out with reasonable care and skill.

Time for performance (s. 14)

Under s. 14, where the supplier is acting in the course of a business and the time for performance cannot be determined from the contract or ascertained by a course of dealing between the parties, there is an implied term that the supplier will carry out the service within a reasonable time. What is a reasonable time is a matter of fact. If you take your car into a garage for minor repairs, it is reasonable to allow a few days and, if spare parts have to be ordered, possibly a couple of weeks for the repairs to be completed. If the car is still in the garage six months later, the repairers will be in breach of s. 14.

Consideration (s. 15)

Section 15 provides that where the consideration

cannot be determined from the contract or by a course of dealing between the parties, there is an implied term that the customer will pay a reasonable charge for the service. If you call a plumber out to mend a burst pipe and no reference is made to his charges, he is entitled to a *reasonable* amount for his services on completion of the job.

You should note the following points about Part II of the Act –

(1) *Sections 13–15 imply 'terms' into contracts for services.* This means that the remedy available to the injured party will depend on the circumstances of the breach. If the breach goes to the root of the contract, it will be treated as a breach of a *condition* and the customer can repudiate the contract and claim damages – where the breach is slight, it will be regarded as a breach of *warranty* and the customer can recover damages only.

(2) *The Secretary of State has the power to exempt certain contracts for services from the effects of one or more of the sections in Part II.* An order has been made, for example, excluding s. 13 from applying to

(*a*) the services of an advocate in a court or tribunal, e.g. a solicitor appearing in a magistrates' court, and

(*b*) the services of company director.

(3) *Under s. 16 the rights, duties and liabilities imposed by ss. 12–15 may be excluded or limited subject to the provisions of the Unfair Contract Terms Act 1977.* The implied term contained in s. 13 (care and skill) is, therefore, subject to s. 2 of the 1977 Act (see p. 205), while the implied terms in ss. 14 and 15 (time for performance and consideration) seem to be covered by s. 3 of the 1977 Act (see p. 205).

Questions/activities

1. Fred recently obtained a '24″ remote control colour TV set'. What are Fred's rights and the source of these rights in the following circumstances –

(*a*) Just as he is sitting down to watch 'Match of the Day' there is a flash and a puff of smoke from the back of the TV and the screen goes blank. Fred bought the set new from a local department store. He paid for it in cash.

(*b*) Fred obtained the TV from his brother-in-law, Tom, by swapping his music centre. Fred was assured by Tom that it was a colour TV but so far he has only got a black and white picture.

(*c*) Fred is an American football enthusiast. He told the salesman at TV World Ltd, a local electrical shop, that he wanted a TV that would receive Channel 4 broadcasts. Fred, who is buying the TV on HP, has now discovered that he cannot get Channel 4 with this particular model.

(*d*) The remote control unit refuses to work. Fred acquired the TV on hire from a local TV rental firm.

2. Mr and Mrs Carter decide to install double-glazing in their house. They get three firms to provide 'estimates' for the job, the cheapest (£400) being submitted by Kozee Ltd, whom they ask to do the work. The Carters sign a contract but the document does not mention the price payable for the work or how long it will take to complete. The workmen start the job in July, but the work proceeds in fits and starts and is finished finally in December. The Carters are very unhappy with the workmanship; the house is still very draughty and there has been no noticeable saving in their fuel bills. They have now received a bill from Kozee Ltd for £900 and they seek your advice.

Manufacturer's liability

Hitherto, we have examined the rights and responsibilities of the parties to a contract, concentrating especially on the duties of a supplier of goods and services. In this chapter we turn our attention to the person who produces the goods. What exactly are the responsibilities of a manufacturer who puts defective products into circulation?

A striking feature of modern life is the constant bombardment we receive from expensive advertising or promotions conducted by manufacturers who are trying to persuade us to buy their products. It is hardly surprising, therefore, that if anything goes wrong with the product, the majority of people think that the manufacturer is responsible in law to put matters right. Certainly, most retailers do little to dispel this belief. It is true that if the manufacturer supplies goods directly to the customer, the customer is entitled to sue him on the contract for breach of the terms which are implied now in all contracts for the supply of goods. Very often, however, goods are not sold straight to the customer, but are distributed through a wholesaler, who sells them to a retailer, who in turn supplies them to the ultimate consumer. If the goods are faulty, the consumer's rights lie against the *retailer*, not against the person who created the problem in the first place.

The primary responsibility for compensating the consumer in respect of defective products is placed by the law of contract on the person who sold or supplied the goods; he is liable irrespective of whether he was at fault. Thus the law imposes what is known as 'strict liability' on retailers in respect of faulty goods. A good example of this principle is the case of *Godley* v *Perry* (1960) which was discussed in Chapter 11. The action

involved a young boy who lost an eye when his toy catapult broke. The boy had purchased the catapult three days earlier from a newsagent's shop. The newsagent had taken reasonable care to ensure that the catapults he sold were safe. Nevertheless, under the Sale of Goods Act, he was held strictly liable for the injuries caused to the boy.

The law of contract provides the main avenue for redress in respect of faulty goods. However, a contractual solution to the problem of defective goods has its limitations.

(1) The doctrine of privity of contract (see p. 166) means that the rights and duties created by a contract are confined to the parties. Only the purchaser can take an action in contract in respect of a defective product. For example, if in *Godley* v *Perry* the boy had received the catapult as a Christmas present from his parents, he would not have been able to sue the newsagent for compensation for his injuries under the Sale of Goods Act because of the absence of a contract between himself and the newsagent.

(2) The doctrine of privity also means that the consumer's rights in contract are restricted to an action against the person who sold or supplied him with the goods. Such 'rights' may prove illusory. The retailer may not have the means to pay compensation or he may have ceased trading because of insolvency.

(3) The retailer is required to bear the brunt of claims for compensation from aggrieved customers, even though he may be completely blameless. Of course, the retailer can sue his immediate supplier in contract for breach of the implied terms in the Sale of

Goods Act 1979. The supplier can sue the next person in the chain of contracts, which ultimately ends with the manufacturer. This chain of responsibility is illustrated in Fig. 13.1. Thus the manufacturer is required, albeit in a roundabout way, to accept responsibility for his defective products. However, this chain of responsibility may be broken, where, for example, there are reasonable exemption clauses in the contract between the retailer and wholesaler. If this is the case, the manufacturer will escape liability and the innocent retailer must absorb the cost of compensation.

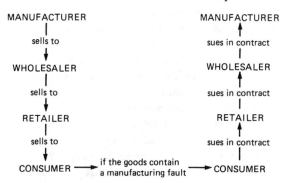

Fig. 13.1 The chain of responsibility for a defective product.

There is a case for a consumer, irrespective of whether he purchased the defective item, being able to take direct action against the manufacturer, but there are limited circumstances in which the manufacturer can be sued. These are

(1) under a collateral contract between the manufacturer and the consumer;

(2) in the tort of negligence; and

(3) under the Consumer Safety Act 1978.

Collateral contract

A manufacturer would soon go out of business if he directed all his energies to producing his goods as cheaply as possible. He must also develop a successful marketing strategy, to ensure that potential customers know about his products and are encouraged to buy them. This can be achieved, for example, by an advertising campaign, special promotions, personal visits by salesmen or the inclusion of a 'guarantee' or 'warranty' with the goods. Such activities may result in the manufacturer being directly liable *in contract* to the consumer, even though the consumer buys the goods

from a retailer. In this situation, there is clearly a contract of sale between the consumer and the retailer, to which the manufacturer is not a party, but there may also be another contract between the consumer and the manufacturer. This second, less obvious contract is known as a *collateral contract*; it is, in effect, an implied contract between the manufacturer and the consumer. A collateral contract may arise in two situations:

(a) from advertising and sales talk; and

(b) under a manufacturer's guarantee or warranty.

Advertising and sales talk

The classic example of a manufacturer being held to account for extravagant claims in an advertising campaign is the case of *Carlill v Carbolic Smoke Ball Co.* (1893) (see p. 161). You will recall that the company promised in an advertisement to pay £100 to anyone who contracted 'flu after using their smoke ball three times daily for two weeks. Mrs Carlill saw this advertisement, bought a smoke ball from a chemist, used it as directed but still caught 'flu. Even though Mrs Carlill had not bought the smoke ball directly from the company, it was held that there was a contract between them. The essential requirement of offer, acceptance and consideration were all present. The company had made Mrs Carlill an offer in their advertisement, which she had accepted by purchasing a smoke ball. The company's promise was supported by consideration from Mrs Carlill because she had bought a smoke ball from a retail chemist.

The same principle applies where the manufacturer's salesman calls on the consumer and makes promises about the performance of a product. If the consumer acts on the sales talk by obtaining the product from his own supplier and not directly from the manufacturer, the consumer will be able to hold the manufacturer to his promises under a collateral contract.

Shanklin Pier Ltd v Detel Products Ltd (1951)

Shanklin Pier Ltd engaged a firm of painting contractors to paint their pier at Shanklin on the Isle of Wight, specifying that they should use a paint called DMU, which was manufactured by Detel Products Ltd. A director of Detel Products had called previously on the managing director of the pier company and recommended DMU for the job, saying that it would last seven to ten years. In fact, the paint lasted only three months. The pier company could not sue the manufacturer for breach of a condition implied under the Sale of Goods Act, that the paint would be reasonably fit for the stated purpose, because they had not bought the paint themselves. Nor could they sue the painters, who, after all, had only followed the instructions they were given. So the pier company sued Detel Products for breach of their promise that the paint would last seven to ten years.

It was held that in addition to the contract for the sale of the paint (between the manufacturer and the painters) and the contract to paint the pier (between the painters and the pier owners) there was also a collateral contract between the pier company and the manufacturers. The bargain was that the manufacturer guaranteed the suitability of DMU and in return the pier company specified in their contract with the painters that DMU paint should be used.

Manufacturer's guarantees and warranties

Sometimes the manufacturer's confidence in his product is expressed formally in the shape of a written guarantee or warranty which accompanies the goods. A manufacturer's guarantee has become an expected standard feature of the sale of 'consumer durables' such as washing machines, TVs and cars. The 'guarantee' usually consists of an undertaking by the manufacturer to repair or replace faulty goods within a certain period of time. A typical guarantee can be seen below.

GUARANTEE

This appliance has been manufactured to exacting standards and the company guarantees that should any defect in materials or workmanship occur within 12 months of the date of purchase we will repair or, at our option, replace the defective part free of charge for labour or materials – always provided that the appliance has been used for normal domestic purposes in the United Kingdom and has been operated on an electricity supply which matches that shown on the rating table.

This guarantee in no way diminishes the buyer's statutory or legal rights, but it does not cover damage caused by misuse, negligence or damage in transit.

The question arises whether a manufacturer is bound to honour the promises contained in his guarantee. In other words, can the guarantee form the basis of a contract between the consumer and the manufacturer? Unfortunately, the legal position is far from clear. If the consumer can show that he knew about the guarantee before he bought the goods, he should be able to establish the existence of a collateral contract with the manufacturer by applying the reasoning employed in *Carlill*'s case. The liability of the manufacturer of defective goods which are under guarantee can be established in another way. The guarantee often takes the form of a postcard which the consumer must complete and send off to the manufacturer within a certain period of time. The inconvenience that this entails may be sufficient consideration to support the manufacturer's promises.

In the past, guarantees often contained an exemption clause which deprived the consumer of the rights he might otherwise have had against the manufacturer. Section 5 of the Unfair Contract Terms Act 1977 now prevents this practice by providing that any clause in a manufacturer's or distributor's guarantee purporting to exclude or restrict liability in negligence for loss or damage will be unenforceable against a consumer provided the following conditions are met –

(1) the goods are of a type ordinarily supplied for private use or consumption;

(2) the goods have proved defective while in consumer use; and

(3) the manufacturer or distributor did not sell the goods directly to the consumer.

Since 1 November 1978 manufacturers have been required to include a statement in their guarantees to the effect that the consumer's statutory rights were unaffected by the terms of the guarantee. Failure to make such a statement is a criminal offence by virtue of Orders made under the Fair Trading Act 1973.

Negligence

A manufacturer may be liable to a consumer for loss and damage caused by his defective products under the tort of negligence. The foundations of the modern law of negligence were laid in one of the best known cases in English law – *Donoghue* v *Stevenson* (1932)

Donoghue v Stevenson (1932)

Mrs Donoghue and a friend visited a cafe in Paisley run by a Mr Minchella. The friend bought a bottle of ginger beer for Mrs Donoghue. Mr Minchella opened the bottle, which was made of dark opaque glass, and poured some of the ginger beer into a tumbler. Unsuspecting, Mrs Donoghue drank the contents, but when her friend refilled the tumbler, the remains of a decomposing snail floated out. Mrs Donoghue suffered shock and severe gastro-enteritis as a result. She could not sue Mr Minchella for compensation for her injuries, because she had not bought the ginger beer himself. So she brought an action against the manufacturer of the ginger beer, Stevenson, arguing that he had been negligent.

The House of Lords held that, provided Mrs Donoghue could prove her allegations, she would be entitled to succeed. We shall never know whether there was in fact a snail in the bottle because the case was settled out of court for £100.

In order to establish negligence, a plaintiff must prove that –

(a) the defendant owed him a legal duty of care;

(b) the defendant was in breach of this duty; and

(c) the plaintiff suffered injury or loss as a result of the breach.

All three elements are essential to a successful action in negligence. We shall look at each requirement in more detail.

Duty of care

In *Donoghue v Stevenson* the House of Lords established the principle that a manufacturer owes a duty of care to all persons who are likely to come into contact with his goods. Lord Atkin explained the legal responsibilities of a manufacturer in the following way: '... a manufacturer of products, which he sells in such a form as to show that he intends them to reach the ultimate consumer in the form in which they left him with no reasonable possibility of intermediate examination, and with the knowledge that the absence of reasonable care in the preparation or putting up of the products will result in an injury to the consumer's life or property, owes a duty to the consumer to take that reasonable care.' There is no limit to the type of goods covered by this rule: cases have involved goods as diverse

as cars, a pair of underpants and a hot water bottle. Since 1932 the rule has been extended from manufacturers to cover anyone who does some work on the goods; for example, a repairer. The word 'consumer' has been given a wide interpretation to cover anyone who is likely to be injured by the lack of care.

Stennet v Hancock and Peters (1939)

Mrs Stennet was walking along a pavement when she was struck and injured by a piece of a wheel which had come off a passing lorry. She received damages from the owner of the garage where the wheel had been negligently repaired shortly before the accident.

Breach of duty

Probably the most difficult problem for a plaintiff to overcome is to establish a breach of duty of care. This means that a consumer must be able to prove that the manufacturer failed to act reasonably in all the circumstances. Liability in negligence is fault-based and the onus of proving that the manufacturer was at fault is on the consumer. This can be a very difficult task as usually the consumer has no means of knowing exactly what went wrong in the manufacturing process. Sometimes, however, the only reasonable explanation for the defect is that someone acted negligently: buns, for example, don't usually have stones in the middle of them. In this kind of situation, the consumer may be able to plead '*res-ipsa loquitur*' – 'the facts speak for themselves'. This has the effect of reversing the normal burden of proof; the manufacturer is presumed to have acted negligently unless he can prove that he took all reasonable care.

Steer v Durable Rubber Manufacturing Co. Ltd (1958)

A girl aged six was scalded when her three-month-old hot water bottle burst. She could not prove exactly how the defect had occurred, but she did establish that hot water bottles are expected to last three years.

The Court of Appeal held that in the circumstances it was up to the manufacturers to show that they had not been negligent. Since they could not do this, they were liable.

Damage resulting from the breach

Finally, the consumer must be able to prove that he has suffered loss or damage as a result of the manufacturer's breach of duty. If the damage is caused by some other factor, the manufacturer will not be liable. A car manufacturer, for example, cannot be held responsible for producing a car with defective steering if the occupants are injured in an accident caused by driving too fast in fog. Even if the consumer can establish a causal link between the breach of duty and the damage, he cannot necessarily recover damages for all the consequences of the manufacturer's negligence. The damage must not be too remote. A manufacturer is liable only for loss or damage which is reasonably foreseeable.

It is well established that a consumer can recover damages if the defective product causes personal injury or damage to the property. For example, if a gas cooker explodes, the consumer can recover for the damage caused to the kitchen in addition to the compensation he will receive for any personal injuries. However, the position is far from clear where the defect does not result in physical injury or damage to other property. Until fairly recently, it was a settled point of law that a consumer could not recover damages for pure financial loss, unless caused by a negligent mis-statement. So if a product simply ceased to work because of a manufacturing defect, the consumer could not sue the manufacturer in negligence for the cost of repair or replacement. The recent decision of the House of Lords in the *Junior Books* case suggests that in limited circumstances it may be possible to recover damages for economic or financial loss.

Junior Books Ltd v Veitchi Co. Ltd (1982)

Junior Books entered into a contract with a building firm for the construction of a new factory. Under this contract, the architects acting for Junior Books were entitled to nominate which sub-contractor was to be employed by the building firm to lay the flooring. The architects nominated Veitchi. The floor proved defective and Junior Books brought an action in negligence against Veitchi. Even though there was no suggestion that the floor was dangerous, Junior Books claimed damages for the cost of re-laying the floor and the consequential financial loss that this would involve (i.e. the factory would have to be closed down to enable the floor to be replaced).

The House of Lords held that Junior Books were entitled to recover damages from Veitchi. The relationship between the parties was so close that it gave rise to a duty to avoid careless work which would inevitably cause financial loss.

Although this decision represents a significant extension of the general principle laid down by Lord Atkin in *Donoghue v Stevenson*, it does not mean that a manufacturer is now liable to a consumer in respect of financial loss caused by a defective product. Their Lordships stressed that their decision was based on the very close proximity between the parties which fell just short of a direct contractual relationship. A manufacturer does not normally have such a close relationship with the consumers of his products.

Even if the consumer manages to overcome all the difficulties involved in proving negligence, the manufacturer may still be able to defeat the claim or secure a reduction in damages by showing that the accident was caused wholly or partly by the consumer's own negligence. The defence of contributory negligence may apply where, for example, the consumer had ignored operating instructions or continued to use a product knowing that it was defective. Under the Law Reform (Contributory Negligence) Act 1945, contributory negligence on the part of the consumer has the effect of reducing the damages awarded to the extent that the plaintiff was to blame for the accident. For example, if a court assesses the plaintiff's damages at £10 000, but finds that he was 50 per cent to blame for what happened, his damages will be reduced by 50 per cent and he will receive £5000.

Consumer Safety Act 1978

The Consumer Safety Act 1978 repealed the Consumer Protection Acts of 1961 and 1971 and replaces them with an improved legal framework to protect the public from the hazards of unsafe goods. This aim is achieved in the following ways.

Criminal liability

The Secretary of State is empowered to make safety regulations in respect of specific types of goods. The regulations may cover such matters as the composition, design, packaging or labelling of goods. They may require goods to conform to a particular standard or that appropriate warnings or instructions are given with the goods. The regulations made so far cover a wide range of products and include nightdresses, oil heaters, babies' dummies, toys, electric blankets, electrical equipment, cosmetics and prams. Failure to comply with the regulations is a criminal offence. The local trading standards department is responsible for enforcing the legislation and they can prosecute anyone involved in the supply of the unsafe goods, whether manufacturer, importer, wholesaler or retailer.

The Act also enables the Secretary of State to take quick action in respect of unsafe goods already on the market. He can issue a *prohibition order* to prevent the supply by any trader of a specific type of product. He can also serve a *prohibition notice* on a particular trader, requiring him to cease supplying unsafe goods. Finally, a *notice to warn* can be issued requiring a manufacturer or distributor to warn the public about the dangers of a product which is in circulation. It is a criminal offence to contravene these instructions.

Civil liability

The Act also provides a civil remedy for an individual consumer who has suffered loss or damage as a result of a trader's failure to comply with the safety regulations or a prohibition order or notice. For example, a child who is injured by a toy which contravenes the safety regulations will be able to sue the manufacturer for breach of statutory duty. There are two advantages to this kind of action: the child can claim compensation even if he received the toy as a gift and he does not have to prove that the manufacturer acted negligently. Thus, the Act imposes strict liability on a manufacturer, but only in respect of goods which are subject to an order by the Secretary of State.

Recent developments in product liability

Recent years have witnessed a growing interest in the subject of 'product liability'. This American term is used to describe liability for injury or loss caused by a defective product. Our law on this subject has grown up in a piecemeal fashion and, as a result, it is complicated and confusing.

The question of product liability has been considered by no less than four bodies in recent years: the Law Commission, the Council of Europe, the Royal Commission on Civil Liability (chaired by Lord Pearson) and the EEC. In every single case, the recommendations of these bodies involved imposing strict liability on the manufacturer of defective products. On 25 July 1985, the EEC Council of Ministers adopted a Directive on product liability and, consequently, the British Government were committed to implementing changes to our law within three years. (See now Consumer Protection Act 1987 in the Preface.)

Questions/activities

1. 'Death, injury and loss from manufacture is a commonplace in our society, but compensation for it is pure roulette ...': *Sunday Times*, 27 June 1976.

Discuss with reference to the law as it stands at present. How will implementation of the Consumer Protection Act 1987 improve the rights of consumers in respect of faulty goods?

2. Percy Brown's grandchildren club together to buy him a 'fully guaranteed' Warmglo Deluxe electric blanket for his eightieth birthday. As the winter evenings draw in, Percy decides that he would be warmer in bed with his new electric blanket than in his draughty sitting room. He establishes a routine – he puts the blanket on thirty minutes before he goes to bed and, despite warnings in the operating instructions, he keeps the blanket switched on at the highest setting, while he reads in bed. One particularly cold January night, the electric blanket catches fire (as a result of faulty wiring) just as Percy is about to go to sleep. He suffers slight burns to his leg, but the fire causes extensive damage to his bed.

Advise Percy.

Professional negligence

In the last chapter we examined the scope of a manufacturer's liability for the defective products he puts into circulation and the difficulties facing a consumer who is obliged to take direct action against a manufacturer. In the absence of a contract between the parties, individual rights of redress are confined largely to pursuing an action in negligence.

The law of negligence also has an important application to the provision of services. It opens up a remedy to those who are strangers to the contract for services but nevertheless have suffered a loss as a result of the contractor's negligence. Thus the principle established in *Donoghue* v *Stevenson* (1932) (see p. 227) applies not just to manufacturers but also to repairers who carry out their work carelessly. If a person is contracted to maintain and repair a lift, for example, he owes a legal duty, quite separate from his contractual obligations, to those using the lift to exercise reasonable care in his work.

Liability for physical injury or damage caused by a negligent act is well established. But what is the position of a person whose job involves giving professional advice? Clearly, he owes a duty to the person who has engaged his services, but does it extend to others who may have acted on his statements? In the last twenty years or so, the courts have developed the *Donoghue* v *Stevenson* principle to encompass negligent statements which cause financial loss. Professional groups, such as solicitors, accountants, bankers and surveyors, have felt the full impact of the change in judicial attitudes in this area of negligence liability. In this chapter, we will consider the fast developing area of law referred to as professional negligence.

Prior to 1963, it was generally accepted that in the absence of fraud, liability for making careless statements which caused financial loss depended on the existence of a contractual or fiduciary relationship between the parties. If the statement was made fraudulently, the injured party could recover damages for the tort of deceit. This view of the limited scope of a professional person's liability for careless statements is illustrated by the following case.

Candler v Crane, Christmas & Co. (1951)

The defendants, a firm of accountants, prepared a company's balance sheet and accounts, knowing that they were going to be used by the managing director to persuade the plaintiff, Candler, to invest money in the company. Relying on the accounts, the plaintiff invested £2000 which he lost when the company was wound up a year later. The plaintiff sued the defendants in negligence, alleging that the accounts had been prepared carelessly and did not accurately represent the true state of the company's affairs.

The Court of Appeal held (Denning, L. J. dissenting) that the defendants were not liable to the plaintiff because, in the absence of any contractual or fiduciary relationship, they did not owe him a duty of care.

In a powerful dissenting judgment, Denning, L. J., argued that the defendants did owe the plaintiff a duty of care. In his opinion, 'Accountants owe a duty of care not only to their own clients but also to all those whom they know will rely on their accounts in the transactions for which those accounts are prepared.' The duty of care arose from the close relationship between the parties and it followed, therefore, that no duty would be owed to complete strangers. Denning, L. J., had to wait twelve years for his arguments to be accepted.

The new judicial approach to negligent statements was heralded in a case involving bankers' references.

Hedley Byrne & Co. Ltd v Heller and Partners Ltd (1963)

Hedley Byrne were a firm of advertising agents and Easipower Ltd one of their clients. Before placing advertising contracts on behalf of Easipower, in circumstances which involved giving credit, Hedley Byrne instituted inquiries about Easipower's creditworthiness. Hedley Byrne asked their own bank, the National Provincial Bank Ltd, to obtain a reference from Easipower's bankers, Heller and Partners. Heller's reference, which was headed 'without responsibility on the part of the bank or its officials,' stated that Easipower was 'a respectably constituted company, considered good for its ordinary business engagements.' Relying on this satisfactory reply, Hedley Byrne executed advertising contracts for Easipower but they lost £17 000 when Easipower went into liquidation. Hedley Byrne sued Heller for the amount of the financial loss they had suffered as a result of the negligent preparation of the banker's reference.

The House of Lords held that Hellers were protected by the disclaimer of liability. Their Lordships then considered (*obiter dicta*) what the legal position would have been if the disclaimer had not been used. They all agreed that there could be liability for negligent mis-statement causing financial loss, even in the absence of a contractual or fiduciary relationship (the decision in *Candler* v *Crane, Christmas & Co.* was disapproved and the dissenting judgment of Denning, L. J. approved).

In the *Hedley Byrne* case, the House of Lords recognized a new type of liability: they indicated that damages could be received for careless statements. However, they were careful to avoid unleashing a Pandora's box of litigation. Their Lordships ruled that the existence of a duty of care in respect of negligent mis-statements was dependent on a 'special relationship' between the parties. Lord Morris described the relationship in the following terms –

'If someone possessed of a special skill undertakes, quite irrespective of contract, to apply that skill for the assistance of another person who relies on such skill, a duty of care will arise. Furthermore, if, in a sphere in which a person is so placed that others could reasonably rely on his judgement or his skill, or on his ability to make careful inquiry, a person takes it on himself to give information or advice to, or allows his information or advice to be passed on to, another person who, as he knows or should know, will place reliance on it, then a duty of care will arise.'

Although the *Hedley Byrne* case involved a banker, it is clear that the rule applies equally to the advice given by other professionals. We shall examine how the *Hedley Byrne* rule has been developed in relation to three particular professional groups: lawyers, accountants and valuers.

Lawyers

The liability of a legal adviser depends on the nature of the work he is engaged on. The decision of the House of Lords in *Rondel* v *Worsley* (1967) established that a barrister owes no duty of care to clients for whom he acts as advocate. In *Saif Ali* v *Sydney Mitchell & Co.* (1978) the House extended the immunity from legal action in two directions: to cover pre-trial work closely associated with the conduct of a trial and to protect solicitors acting as advocates. When it comes to work outside of court, however, both branches of the legal profession can be held accountable in the tort of negligence. The duties owed by a solicitor to third parties is illustrated by the following case.

Ross v Caunters (1980)

Mrs Ross was an intended beneficiary under a will drawn up on the testator's behalf by Caunters, a firm of solicitors. Caunters failed to advise the testator that attestation by a beneficiary or a beneficiary's spouse invalidates the gift. Mr Ross witnessed the will, and when the testator died the legacy to Mrs Ross was declared invalid.

The court held that a solicitor owes a duty of care not just to his client (in this case the testator) but also to third parties, such as Mrs Ross, who were intended to be benefited by his work. Mrs Ross succeeded in her action.

Accountants

The extent of an accountant's liability to non-clients was the subject of Lord Denning's influential judgment in *Candler* v *Crane, Christmas & Co.* (1951). He expressed the opinion that a duty of care was owed only to third parties of whom they had knowledge; it did not extend to strangers. This view is echoed in the 'special relationship' restriction on liability laid down in the Hedley Byrne case. But in a subsequent case involving accountants, Woolf, J., broadened the scope of liability to include persons of whom the accountants had no prior knowledge.

J E B Fasteners Ltd v Marks, Bloom & Co. (1981)

The defendants, a firm of accountants, prepared the accounts of a client company called B G Fasteners. The audit report inflated the value of the company's stock and, as a result, a misleading picture of the company's financial health was given. The accounts were shown to the plaintiffs who later took over the company. The plaintiffs sued the defendants to recover the money they had spent in keeping the ailing company afloat.

Woolf, J., found that the plaintiffs had taken over the company in order to secure the services of its directors. They would have bought the company even if they had been aware of its true financial position. The defendants were not liable because their negligence was not the cause of the plaintiff's loss.

Comment. This case is important because the judge accepted that an accountant could owe a duty of care to a person of whom he had no actual knowledge but where it was reasonably foreseeable that such a person would see the accounts and rely on them.

Valuers and surveyors

The potential scope and liability for negligent re-instatement was scrutinized again in the following case –

Yianni v Edwin Evans & Sons (1981)

The plaintiffs agreed to buy a house for £15 000 with the aid of a £12 000 mortgage from the Halifax Building Society. The building society instructed the defendants, a firm of surveyors and valuers, to value the house for them. Although the plaintiffs had to pay for the valuation, the contract was actually between the building society and the valuers. The building society made it clear that they did not accept responsibility for the valuers' report and that prospective purchasers were advised to have an independent survey carried out. The defendant's valuation report indicated that the house was satisfactory security for a £12 000 mortgage. After the plaintiffs had purchased the property, they discovered structural defects which would cost £18 000 to put right. The plaintiffs successfully sued the defendants in negligence. Despite the standard building society warning, only 10–15 per cent of purchasers have independent surveys carried out. It was reasonable, therefore, that the defendants should have the plaintiffs in contemplation as persons who were likely to rely on their valuation. The relationship between the parties gave rise to a duty of care. Accordingly, the valuers were held liable.

Questions/activities

1. Steven, an accountant, returning from his office, calls into a pub for a relaxing drink. He bumps into Paul, an old school friend, whom he has not seen for many years. During the course of the conversation over a number of pints, it emerges that Paul has recently inherited a substantial sum of money and is interested in investing in local businesses. Steven mentions that one of his clients, Precarious Ltd, is seeking financial backing and would make an attractive investment. By chance he has a copy of the company's accounts in his briefcase which he gives to Paul. Relying on these accounts, Paul invests £10 000 in Precarious Ltd but loses everything when Precarious goes into liquidation six months later. In fact, the accounts had been prepared negligently and did not reflect the parlous state of the company's affairs. Advise Paul.

2. Devise practical steps that might be taken by a person wishing to avoid liability for professional negligence.

Credit

At some time or another everyone makes use of credit. It may be a mortgage from a building society to buy your own home or hire purchase arranged by a car dealer to help you afford the latest model. When the monthly finances do not work out right, you will probably run up an overdraft at the bank. Even if it is just paying the milkman at the end of the week, you have made use of credit. People in business also rely on credit. A loan may be needed to translate a good idea into a marketable product. Established companies often have to look outside their own resources to finance expansion plans. Most businesses give and expect to receive a period of time in which to pay their trade bills.

Credit consists of either buying something and being given time to pay for it or borrowing money and paying it back later. The person giving the credit (the creditor) is providing a service, which the borrower (the debtor) is usually required to pay for, the price being a certain rate of interest.

Credit is not a new idea. Moneylenders have been around for centuries. However, the present century has witnessed a dramatic increase in its use, particularly to finance private house purchase and consumer spending on such items as cars, electrical goods and furniture. Despite the cautionary proverb, 'Neither a borrower nor a lender be', credit has several clear advantages. Most people lack the self-discipline to save up for expensive items. Credit allows them to enjoy the benefit of goods and services sooner than they otherwise would. In a period of inflation there is even the prospect of getting them more cheaply. To the producer and retailer credit means increased sales.

But the easy availability of credit can bring dangers to both sides. The problems facing the consumer are neatly summarized in a comment attributed to a county court judge: being persuaded by a man you don't know to sign an agreement you haven't read to buy furniture you don't need with money you haven't got. Since creditors face the risk that they may not be repaid they have channelled their energies into finding an effective way of securing their financial interests. Occasionally this has led to the imposition of unreasonably severe terms on borrowers. At first it was left to the judges to intervene to redress the balance; thus from medieval times Equity and the Court of Chancery came to the aid of mortgagors of land. With the passing of time, Parliament felt it necessary to impose piecemeal controls on credit agreements.

In the 1960s, concern about the inadequacies of our credit laws led the Labour government to set up a Committee on Consumer Credit under the chairmanship of Lord Crowther. The Committee reported in 1971 and some of its recommendations were enacted by the Consumer Credit Act 1974. The process of implementing the major overhaul of our credit laws has been a gradual one. The provisions of the Act have been brought into force by means of statutory instrument supplemented by ministerial regulation. The outstanding sections came into force on 19 May 1985 – eleven years after the Act was passed by Parliament.

This chapter will examine the various types of credit available and how they are regulated by the law, particularly the Consumer Credit Act 1974.

HPA **Hire-Purchase Agreement** *regulated by the Consumer Credit Act 1974*   Original
(c)   No right of cancellation

Agreement No. _____

This Hire-Purchase Agreement sets out below and overleaf the terms on which we (the owners) agree to let and you (the customer) agree to hire the goods described below:

The Owners _____
Name and address

_____

The Customer _____
Full names please

Address _____

_____

Particulars of Goods		Cash Price Incl. VAT	
Qty.	Description	£	p
	Identification Nos:		
	Total Cash Price (incl. VAT)		

Financial Details and Payments	£	p
Total Cash Price		
Less: Deposit (a)		
= Credit Extended		
Add: Charges		
= Balance Payable (b)		
Total Amount Payable (a) + (b)		
A.P.R.	____ %	
Number of monthly payments		
Commencing		
Subsequent payments on same day of each succeeding month		
Amount of each payment		
Amount of final payment (if different)		

TERMINATION: YOUR RIGHTS

You have a right to end this agreement. If you wish to do so, you should write to the person authorised to receive your payments. We will then be entitled to the return of the goods and to half the total amount payable under this agreement, that is £ _____ .[1] If you have already paid at least this amount plus any overdue instalments, you will not have to pay any more, provided you have taken reasonable care of the goods.

[1] Insert one-half of the total amount payable.

Witness: Signature _____

Name _____
Block letters please

Address _____

_____

Witness: Signature _____
Second witness required in Scotland only

Name _____
Block letters please

Address _____

_____

Signature of (or on behalf of) Owners

_____

Date of Owners' Signature (Date of Agreement)

REPOSSESSION: YOUR RIGHTS

If you fail to keep to your side of this agreement but you have paid at least one third of the total amount payable under this agreement, that is £ _____ ,[2] we may not take back the goods against your wishes unless we get a court order. (In Scotland, we may need to get a court order at any time.) If we do take them without your consent or a court order, you have the right to get back all the money you have paid under the agreement.

[2] Insert one third of the total amount payable.

DECLARATION BY CUSTOMER

By signing this agreement you are declaring that:

★ Your particulars given above are correct

★ All the information you have given us is correct

★ You realise that we rely on that information when deciding whether to enter into this agreement.

This is a Hire-Purchase Agreement regulated by the Consumer Credit Act 1974. Sign it only if you want to be legally bound by its terms.

Signature(s) of Customer(s) _____

The goods will not become your property until you have made all the payments. You must not sell them before then.

HPA
(c)
Original

TERMS OF THE AGREEMENT

1 Payment

Before signing this agreement you must have paid the deposit shown overleaf. By signing this agreement you agree to pay the Balance Payable by making the payments set out overleaf, by their specified dates, to us at the address given overleaf or to any person or address notified by us in writing. Punctual payment is essential. If you pay by post you do so at your own risk.

2 Failure to pay on time

We have the right to charge interest at the annual percentage rate shown overleaf on all overdue amounts. This interest will be calculated on a daily basis from the date the amount falls due until it is received and will run both before and after any judgment.

3 Ownership of the goods

You will become the owner of the goods only after we have received all amounts payable under this agreement including under Clauses 2 and 11. Until then the goods remain our property and your rights are solely those of a hirer.

4 Selling or disposing of the goods

You must keep the goods safely at your address and you may not sell or dispose of them or transfer your rights under this agreement. You may only part with the goods to have them repaired. You may not use the goods as security for any of your obligations.

5 Repair of the goods

You must keep the goods in good condition and repair at your own expense. You are responsible for all loss of or damage to them (except fair wear and tear) even if caused by acts or events outside your control. You must not allow a repairer or any other person to obtain a lien on or a right to retain the goods.

6 Change of address

You must immediately notify us in writing of any change of your address.

7 Inspection

You must allow us or our representative to inspect and test the goods at all reasonable times.

8 Insurance

You must keep the goods insured under a fully comprehensive policy of insurance at your own expense. You must notify us of loss of or damage to the goods and hold any monies payable under the policy in trust for us. You irrevocably authorise us to collect the monies from the insurers. If a claim is made against the insurers we may at our absolute discretion conduct any negotiations and effect any settlement with the insurers and you agree to abide by such settlement.

9 Your right to end the agreement

You have the right to end this agreement as set out in the notice 'Termination: Your Rights' overleaf. You must then at your own expense return the goods to us.

10 Our right to end the agreement

We may end this agreement, after giving you written notice, if:
(a) you fail to keep to any of the terms of this agreement;
(b) you commit any act of bankruptcy or have a receiving, interim or bankruptcy order made against you or you petition for your own bankruptcy, or are served with a creditor's demand under the Insolvency Act 1986 or the Bankruptcy (Scotland) Act 1985, or make a formal composition or scheme with your creditors, or call a meeting of them.
(c) you make a formal composition with or call a meeting of your creditors;
(d) execution is levied or attempted against any of your assets or income or, in Scotland, your possessions are poinded or your wages arrested;

(e) the landlord of the premises where the goods are kept threatens or takes any step to distrain on the goods or, in Scotland, exercises his right of hypothec over them;
(f) where you are a partnership, the partnership is dissolved;
(g) you have given false information in connection with your entry into this agreement;
(h) the goods are destroyed or the insurers treat a claim under the above policy on a total loss basis.

If we end this agreement then, subject to your rights as set out in the notice 'Repossession: Your Rights' overleaf, we may retake the goods. You will also then have to pay to us all overdue payments, and such further amount as is required to make up one half of the Total Amount Payable under this agreement. If you have failed to take reasonable care of the goods you may have to compensate us for this.

11 Expenses

You must repay on demand our expenses and legal costs for:
(a) finding your address if you change address without immediately informing us or finding the goods if they are not at the address given by you;
(b) taking steps, including court action, to recover the goods or to obtain payment for them.

12 Exclusion

(a) If you are dealing as consumer (as defined in the Unfair Contract Terms Act 1977) nothing in this agreement will affect your rights under the Supply of Goods (Implied Terms) Act 1973.
(b) In all other cases:
  (i) you rely on your own skill and judgement as to the quality of the goods and their fitness for their intended purpose:
  (ii) we will not be responsible for their quality, their fitness for any purpose or their correspondence with any description or specification.

13 General provisions

(a) The word 'goods' includes replacements, renewals and additions which we or you may make to them with our consent.
(b) No relaxation or indulgence which we may extend to you shall affect our strict rights under this agreement.
(c) Where two or more persons are named as the customer, you jointly and severally accept the obligations under this agreement. This means that each of you can be held fully responsible under this agreement.
(d) We may transfer our rights under this agreement.

14 When this agreement takes effect

This agreement will only take effect if and when it is signed by us or our authorised representative.

IMPORTANT — YOU SHOULD READ THIS CAREFULLY
YOUR RIGHTS

The Consumer Credit Act 1974 covers this agreement and lays down certain requirements for your protection which must be satisfied when the agreement is made. If they are not, we cannot enforce the agreement against you without a court order.

The Act also gives you a number of rights. You have a right to settle this agreement at any time by giving notice in writing and paying off all amounts payable under the agreement which may be reduced by a rebate.

If you would like to know more about the protection and remedies provided under the Act, you should contact either your local Trading Standards Department or your nearest Citizens' Advice Bureau.

Fig. 15.1 A typical hire purchase agreement form. Copyright © Consumer Credit Trade Association. (Original size A4)

Types of credit

Hire purchase

Hire purchase (HP) is probably the best known method of buying on the 'never-never'. From the legal point of view it is something of an 'odd man out' since the customer pays regular amounts for the *hire* of goods, only becoming the owner if he exercises an option to buy.

HP developed in the latter half of the nineteenth century. The traders of that time were looking for a form of credit to boost their sales which combined security for the creditor with a minimum of legal regulation. The chattel mortgage might have been a possibility, but the Bills of Sale Acts 1878 and 1882 provided for strict controls on mortgages of goods. Other ideas were tried and finally the right formula was found and judicially approved in *Helby* v *Matthews* (1895)

Helby v Matthews (1895)

Helby, a dealer, agreed to let a piano on HP to Brewster in return for thirty-six instalments of 10/6d per month. The agreement stated that Brewster would become the owner of the piano on payment of the final instalment. However, he could end the agreement at any time and return the piano to Helby, his only liability being to pay any arrears of rent. Four months after the start of the agreement, Brewster pledged the piano with a pawnbroker (Matthews).

It was held by the House of Lords that Helby was entitled to recover the piano from the pawnbroker. Brewster was merely the hirer of the piano and, as such, he could not pass title to the pawnbroker under s. 9 of the Factors Act 1889.

Comment. This is an application of the *nemo dat* rule, which we examined on p. 214.

The popularity of HP was guaranteed after this case. The advantages of this form of credit to traders were twofold: if the hirer failed to pay an instalment the owner could repossess the goods and if the goods fell into the hands of an innocent third party, the owner could recover them.

A modern HP agreement usually requires the customer to pay an initial deposit followed by equal weekly/monthly instalments for the hire of the goods. At the end of the agreement the hirer may exercise an option to buy for a relatively small sum. A specimen HP agreement is illustrated on pp. 234–5. The owner may be the supplier of the goods but today it is more likely to be a specialist finance company introduced by the supplier. If this is the case, the HP arrangements will involve two transactions, as explained in Fig. 15.2.

Conditional sale

Like HP, conditional sale gives the customer immediate possession of the goods, payment is by regular instalments and ownership only passes to the buyer when all the payments have been made. The important difference is that with HP the hirer may choose whether he wishes to buy the goods, while under a conditional sale agreement the customer is under an obligation to buy. The transfer of ownership is delayed until the buyer meets the condition specified in the agreement (usually payment of the final instalment).

Conditional sale has never been popular in this country and today its use is mainly confined to the purchase of industrial plant and equipment. It was one of the formulas considered by Victorian traders prior to the case of *Helby* v *Matthews* (1895). However, the decision of the Court of Appeal in *Lee* v *Butler* (1893) showed that since the customer had agreed to buy the goods he could pass good title to a third party under the Factors Act 1889, leaving the creditor without the security he required. Conditional sale was treated as a contract for the sale of goods, although in reality it has more in common with HP. The Hire Purchase Act 1964 (followed by the Consumer Credit Act 1974) resolved this difficulty by equating conditional sale with HP for most purposes.

Credit sale

This is a contract for the sale of goods whereby ownership and possession of the goods passes immediately to the buyer, but he is given time to pay. Since the purchaser becomes the owner of the goods straight away, he can re-sell them before the end of the agreement, provided he pays off what he owes, and if he defaults on his repayments, the seller cannot repossess the goods. This is in marked contrast to the position under an HP agreement. A specimen credit sale agreement is reproduced on pp. 238–9. This form of credit is used, for example, in purchases from mail order catalogues.

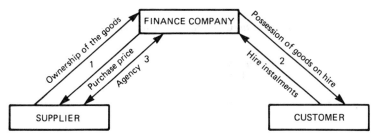

Fig. 15.2 A typical hire purchase arrangement.

NOTES

(1) Contract for the sale of goods between the supplier and the finance company covered by the Sale of Goods Act 1979.

(2) HP contract between the finance company and the customer. The agreement will be regulated by the Consumer Credit Act 1974, if the amount of the credit does not exceed £15 000 for agreements made after 19 May 1985 and the customer is not a company. If the Act does not cover the agreement, the common law applies.

(3) If the HP agreement is a regulated agreement under the Consumer Credit Act 1974, the dealer is regarded as an agent of the finance company. The finance company is equally responsible with the supplier for any misrepresentation or breach of contract.

Bank loans

There are various ways of borrowing from a bank.

(1) *Overdraft.* An overdraft may arise in one of two ways: either the customer makes an arrangement with the bank to overdraw his current account up to an agreed amount or, without prior agreement, he simply writes cheques for an amount greater than in his account. A variable rate of interest is charged on the amount drawn by the customer, calculated on a daily basis and bank charges usually become payable. Security may be needed for large sums. The bank can insist on repayment in full at any time. An overdraft is usually the cheapest way of borrowing from a bank.

(2) *Ordinary loan.* This type of loan is extended to bank customers and for a particular purpose – to buy a car, for example. A specific sum of money is borrowed for an agreed period of time. A separate loan account is opened by the bank into which the instalments are paid, usually by means of a standing order from the customer's current account. Variable interest is charged and security may be required.

(3) *Personal loan.* The loan is available to anyone, customer and non-customer alike, usually for a particular purpose. The period of the loan and interest are fixed when the credit is arranged. Again security may be asked for. It is usually a more expensive way of borrowing than either the overdraft or ordinary loan.

(4) *Budget account.* A budget account is used to help spread the payment of bills over the year. The customer calculates his annual outgoings on such items as gas, electricity and rates. The bank adds to this its service charge for operating the account. The total is divided by twelve and a standing order for this amount is placed to the credit of the budget account. The bills can then be paid with confidence as and when they arrive.

Credit cards

A credit card allows the holder to pay (usually up to a limit) for goods and services or to obtain a cash advance by producing a plastic personalized card. There are three main kinds of credit card:

(1) *Bank credit cards (Access and Visa).* Although these cards are linked to particular banks, an application may be made to any bank for its card. The holder is given a personal credit limit and he can use the card to buy goods and services or obtain a cash advance wherever the card is accepted, up to this limit. Traders involved in the scheme send details of purchases to the credit card company and are then reimbursed after a charge of between 2½ per cent and 5 per cent has been deducted. At the end of each month, the holder receives an account of his spending and details of the minimum

CSC **Credit Agreement** *regulated by the Consumer Credit Act 1974*   Original
(b)   With right of cancellation

Agreement No. _____

This credit sale agreement sets out below and overleaf the terms on which you (the customer) agree to buy the goods described below from us (the sellers).

The Sellers _____
Name and address

_____

The Customer _____
Full names please

Address _____

_____

Particulars of Goods		Cash Price Incl. VAT	
Qty.	Description	£	p
Total Cash Price (incl. VAT)			

Financial Details and Payments	£	p	
Total Cash Price			
Less Deposit: Cash £____ Pt. Ex. £____			(a)
= Amount of credit			
Add: Charges			
= Balance Payable			(b)
Total Amount Payable (a) + (b)			
A.P.R.		____%	
Number of monthly payments			
Commencing _____			
Subsequent payments on same day of each succeeding month			
Amount of each payment			
Amount of final payment (if different)			

Witness: Signature _____

Name _____
Block letters please

Address _____

_____

Witness: Signature _____
Second witness required in Scotland only

Name _____
Block letters please

Address _____

Signature of (or on behalf of) Sellers

_____

Date of Sellers' Signature (Date of Agreement)

_____

DECLARATION BY CUSTOMER
By signing this agreement you are declaring that:

★ Your particulars given above are correct

★ All the information you have given us is correct

★ You realise that we rely on that information when deciding whether to enter into this agreement.

This is a Credit Agreement regulated by the Consumer Credit Act 1974. Sign it only if you want to be legally bound by its terms.

Signature(s)
of Customer(s) _____

Date(s) of signature(s) _____

YOUR RIGHT TO CANCEL
Once you have signed this agreement, you will have for a short time a right to cancel it. Exact details of how and when you can do this will be sent to you by post by us.

✂ -

CANCELLATION FORM
(Complete and return this form ONLY IF YOU WISH TO CANCEL THE AGREEMENT).
To: _____ 1

I/We* hereby give notice that I/we* wish to cancel

agreement _____ 2

Signed _____

Date _____

Name _____

Address _____

Notes for cancellation form:
1 Sellers to insert name and address.
2 Sellers to insert reference number, code or other identification details
* Delete inapplicable word

CSC
(b)
Original

TERMS OF THE AGREEMENT

1 Payment

Before signing this agreement you must have paid the deposit shown overleaf. By signing this agreement you agree to pay the Balance Payable by making the payments set out overleaf, by their specified dates, to us at the address stated overleaf or to any person or address notified by us in writing. Punctual payment is essential. If you pay by post you do so at your own risk.

2 Right to demand earlier payment

If any amount is overdue for more than fourteen days we have the right, by sending you a notice of default, to require you to bring your payments up to date within seven days after service of the notice. If you do not do so, the whole of the balance remaining unpaid on the agreement shall then become due and payable immediately.

3 Earlier payment by you

If you pay off the balance on this agreement before the date on which the final payment falls due you will usually be entitled to a rebate of part of the charges.

4 Interest on sums overdue

We have the right to charge interest at the annual percentage rate shown overleaf on any amount payable under this agreement and not received by us by the date on which the final payment falls due. This interest will be calculated on a daily basis from that date until it is received.

5 General provisions

(a) No relaxation or indulgence which we may extend to you shall affect our strict rights under this agreement.
(b) We may transfer our rights under this agreement.
(c) You must inform us in writing within seven days of any change of your address. If you fail to do so you must repay our reasonable costs in finding your new address.
(d) Where two or more of you are named as the customer you jointly and severally accept the obligations under this agreement. This means that each of you can be held fully responsible under the agreement.

6 When this agreement takes effect

This agreement will only take effect if and when it is signed by us or our authorised representative.

IMPORTANT — YOU SHOULD READ THIS CAREFULLY
YOUR RIGHTS

The Consumer Credit Act 1974 covers this agreement and lays down certain requirements for your protection which must be satisfied when the agreement is made. If they are not, we cannot enforce the agreement against you without a court order.

The Act also gives you a number of rights. You have a right to settle this agreement at any time by giving notice in writing and paying off all amounts payable under the agreement which may be reduced by a rebate.

If you would like to know more about the protection and remedies provided under the Act, you should contact either your local Trading Standards Department or your nearest Citizens' Advice Bureau.

Fig. 15.3 A typical credit agreement form. Copyright © Consumer Credit Trade Association. (Original size A4)

amount that must be paid that month, (£5 or 5 per cent whichever is the greater). If the holder pays the account in full by the stipulated date, he is not charged interest and so will have received interest-free credit for anything up to eight weeks. (This does not apply to cash advances, for which a service charge is made.) Alternatively, part-payment may be sent, in which case interest is charged.

(2) *Charge cards (American Express and Diners Club)*. These cards work in much the same way as bank credit cards, allowing the holder to pay for goods and services at home and abroad by producing his card. The main differences are:

(*a*) the card holder pays an initial joining fee plus an annual membership fee;

(*b*) there is no pre-set credit limit: and

(*c*) the companies insist that the account is paid in full each month.

(3) *Retailers' credit cards (e.g. Marks and Spencer Charge-card)*. Many chain stores, supermarkets and garages issue their own credit cards to regular customers for use in their own establishments. The period of credit is usually a few weeks between making the purchases and the presentation of the account.

Shop budget account

This form of credit is operated by many large stores. The customer decides how much he can afford to pay each month. He is then allowed a spending limit of, for example, twelve times the £15 agreed. This allows the customer to spend up to £180 but never more than this. As regular repayments are made, he can make more purchases provided he does not exceed the £180 limit. This is known as 'revolving credit' or 'running account credit'. Interest is usually charged on the amount owing at the end of a specified period (usually a month).

Trading checks and vouchers

The check trader issues a check or voucher for a specified amount to his customer. The checks can be spent in any shop which has already agreed to accept them. The shop receives payment from the check trader, less a discount. The customer repays the check trader by small regular instalments including interest. Check trading is more common in the North. It is a fairly expensive way to borrow.

Credit unions

These are a form of self-help organization which are particularly popular in North America and are now catching on in this country. Credit unions are formed by people with something in common; they may belong to the same club or work together. They agree to make regular savings to form a pool of money. If any of the members needs money unexpectedly they can borrow from the pool. They are governed by the Credit Unions Act 1979.

Insurance policy loan

This is a loan obtained from an insurance company based on the security of an insurance policy with a 'cash-in' value.

Finance company personal loan

Big stores, car dealers, gas and electricity boards often arrange these loans to finance large purchases. They are also advertised in local newspapers.

Moneylenders

Moneylenders are often used by people who cannot get credit from more traditional sources. They are usually prepared to lend without security and as a result their interest charges can be very high.

Pawnbroking

This is one of the oldest ways of lending money. A pawnbroker will advance money for a short period of time, and in return will take possession of goods (for example, jewellery) as security. If the loan and interest are repaid, the goods are returned to the borrower; if the pawn is not redeemed, the goods may be sold by the pawnbroker.

Mortgage

Building societies, banks and local authorities are willing to lend money to help people buy their own homes. The mortgage is the interest taken by the lender in the property which acts as security for the loan. Mortgages are discussed in more detail in Chapter 17.

Consumer Credit Act 1974

Background to the Act

The Crowther Committee which had been set up in 1965 to investigate consumer credit found that our credit laws were in a mess. The rules having developed in a piecemeal way were to be found in a large number of statutes and also in the common law. Different rules had been created for different kinds of credit and in some areas the consumer was inadequately protected.

The Committee recommended the passing of two pieces of legislation. The government rejected the need for a Lending and Security Act which would have, amongst other things, set up a security register. However, they accepted the argument for a Consumer Sale and Loan Act to extend and improve the protective rules which already existed in relation to HP. This proposal became the Consumer Credit Act 1974. It replaces most of the earlier credit legislation with the exception of the Bills of Sale Acts 1878 and 1882 and the Hire Purchase Act 1964, Part III.

For the rest of this chapter, section references are to the 1974 Act, unless otherwise indicated.

Terminology

The Act introduced a new set of terms, the most important of which are explained here:

(1) *Debtor-creditor-supplier agreement (DCSA) (s. 12) and debtor-creditor agreement (DCA) (s. 13).* A DCSA arises where there is a connection between the creditor and the transaction for which the finance is being provided. The creditor and supplier of the goods or services for which the credit is being made available may be the same person. Where they are different people, it will be a DCSA if there is an arrangement between the supplier and creditor. Examples include HP, credit cards and trading checks.

If there is no connection between the creditor and any supplier, it will be a DCA. An overdraft from the bank to be spent as the customer wishes would come into this category.

(2) *Restricted-use credit agreement and unrestricted-use credit agreement (s. 11).* If the debtor is free to use the credit as he pleases, e.g., an overdraft, it will be an unrestricted-use credit agreement. Where the credit is tied to a particular transaction it will be restricted-use credit. Examples include HP, credit sale, shops' budget account, check trading and the use of credit cards to obtain goods and services.

(3) *Fixed-sum credit and running-account credit (s. 10).* Fixed-sum credit is where the agreement is made for a specific amount of credit (e.g. HP, bank loan). Running-account credit is sometimes referred to as 'revolving credit'. It is where the debtor can receive cash, goods or services from time to time to an amount which does not exceed his credit limit (e.g. overdraft, shops' budget account).

(4) *Credit tokens (s. 14).* The definition of a credit token covers credit cards, trading checks and vouchers but not cheque guarantee cards.

(5) *APR.* The Act promotes its primary objective of 'truth in lending' by creating a standard measure of the true cost of borrowing, which is the annual percentage rate of charge (APR). This allows the consumer to make a fair comparison between different credit deals. The first step in calculating the APR is to work out the total charge for credit. This figure includes all the costs involved in borrowing the money, such as interest charges and all other costs associated with the credit transaction, e.g. arrangement fees or insurance. The total is then expressed as an annual percentage rate (APR), calculated according to complex regulations made under s. 20. The easiest way of finding the APR is to use the Consumer Credit Tables which are published by HMSO. They are designed to cover some of the most common types of credit transaction. An example of how to calculate the APR using the Tables is given below.

Example

Cheryl borrows £200 from Lonestar Ltd. The loan plus interest charges of £29.84 is to be repaid in 52 weekly instalments of £4.42. The first step is to calculate the total charge for credit. In this case it is simply the interest charges of £29.84. Next the charge per pound lent must be worked out according to the formula: $\frac{C}{P}$

where C = total charge for credit and P = amount of credit.

Here the charge per pound lent is: $\frac{29.84}{200} = 0.1492$

The charge per pound lent is converted to the APR by

referring to the appropriate part of the Consumer Credit Tables (Part 1 in this case). If there are 52 weekly instalments and the charge per pound lent is 0.1492, the ARP is 32.2 per cent.

Agreements covered by the Act

Most of the Act only applies to 'regulated agreements'. Some agreements are 'partially regulated' while other agreements are said to be 'exempt'.

Regulated agreements
Two types of agreements are regulated by the Act – consumer credit agreements and consumer hire agreements.

(1) *Regulated consumer credit agreement*. This is a personal credit agreement by which the creditor provides the debtor with credit not exceeding £15 000 (s. 8). It is personal credit if the borrower is an individual or partnership, but not a company. Credit is defined in s. 9 as a 'cash loan or any other form of financial accommodation'. This covers HP, conditional sale, credit sale, loans, overdrafts, credit cards, shops' budget accounts and trading checks.

The £15 000 limit refers to the credit given. It does not include any deposit or interest charges. The total price paid, therefore, may exceed £15 000 but the agreement could still be regulated as explained in the following example:

Cash price of the goods = £17 000 paid for by –

> £2500   deposit
> £14 500   credit
> £750   interest

Total credit price = £17 750

Although the debtor pays a total of £17 750, the credit obtained is only £14 500 and so the agreement will be regulated.

(2) *Regulated consumer hire agreement*. This is an agreement under which goods are hired, leased, rented or bailed to an individual, which is capable of lasting for more than three months and does not require the hirer to pay more than £15 000 in rentals (s. 15).

Partially regulated agreements
Two kinds of agreements are only partially regulated by the Act:

(1) *Small agreement*. A small agreement is either a regulated consumer credit agreement (other than an HP or conditional sale agreement) where the credit does not exceed £50 or a regulated consumer hire agreement which does not require the hirer to pay more than £50 in rentals (s. 17).

(2) *Non-commercial agreement*. This is a consumer credit or consumer hire agreement which is not made by the creditor or owner in the course of a business carried on by him (s. 189(1)).

Exempt Agreements (s. 16)
(1) *Exempt consumer credit agreements*. The main types of exemption are as follows.

(a) *Mortgage lending* – loans made by building societies, local authorities and other bodies to finance the buying or developing of land;

(b) *Low cost credit* – DCAs where the APR does not exceed the highest of the London and Scottish clearing banks' base rates plus 1 per cent, or 13 per cent, whichever is the higher;

(c) *Finance of foreign trade* – credit agreements made in connection with the export of goods and services outside of the UK or their import into this country;

(d) *Normal trade credit* – the exemption covers two situations: first, where traders advance credit to sell goods and services and require the bill to be paid in one instalment (e.g. the milk and paper bill). Second, a DCSA for fixed-sum credit where the number of repayments does not exceed four or, where it is for running-account credit, the credit is repayable in one amount (e.g. American Express and Diners' Club cards). The agreement will not qualify for exemption if it is an HP or conditional sale or secured by an article taken in pawn.

(2) *Exempt consumer hire agreements*. There are only two exemptions. The hire of meters or metering equipment from electricity, gas and water authorities and telecommunications equipment from British Telecom.

General provisions with wider application
Some parts of the Act apply to otherwise 'exempt' agreements. For example, the safeguards on extortionate credit affect all credit irrespective of the amount and from 1 September 1985 the regulations concerning advertisements and quotations apply to all

institutions engaged in house mortgage lending.

Licensing of credit and hire businesses

The Act set up a comprehensive licensing system to control the activities of those in the credit and hire business, administered by the Director General of Fair Trading, There are six categories of business activity which need a licence:

(1) Consumer credit business, e.g. banks, money-lenders, finance companies;

(2) Consumer hire business, e.g. TV and car rental companies;

(3) Credit brokerage, e.g. car dealers, estate agents;

(4) Debt adjusters and debt counselling, e.g. Citizens' Advice Bureaux, accountants;

(5) Debt collecting;

(6) Credit reference agencies.

The applicants must show that they are fit persons to be in this kind of business.

Anyone who carries on any of the activities listed above without a licence commits a criminal offence. Moreover, an agreement made by an unlicensed trader is enforceable only at the discretion of the Director General.

Seeking business

The Act controls three ways of attracting business: advertising, canvassing and giving quotations.

Advertising (ss. 43–47)

The Act requires the Secretary of State to make regulations about the form and content of advertisements to ensure that they convey a fair and reasonably comprehensive indication of the nature of the credit and hire facilities offered and their true cost. The aim is to promote 'truth in lending' and so encourage consumers to shop around for the best credit bargain.

The Consumer Credit (Advertisements) Regulations 1980 apply to advertisements published on or after 6 October 1980. They permit three types of advertising: simple, intermediate and full, each with their own set of rules about the contents. (See Fig. 15.4.) Advertisers can choose which rules they wish to advertise under.

A criminal offence is committed if the advertisement

LONESTAR LTD
Finance Company

(a) *Simple advertisement*

CASH LOANS!
£20–£200

LONESTAR LTD
Phone
786-9231
For written details
of our loan facilities

(b) *Intermediate advertisement*

LOW COST LOANS!
£500–£2500

Loans available to home owners and mortgage payers (sorry no tenants)

Typical example
Borrow £2000 and pay back 24 monthly instalments of £99.32. Total amount repayable £2383.68.
APR 18.8%
LONESTAR LTD
15 High St
Newtown

(c) *Full advertisement*

Fig. 15.4 Types of credit advertising.

---

fails to comply with the regulations or contains false or misleading information. It is also an offence to advertise goods or services on credit where the advertiser does not hold himself out as prepared to sell for cash.

Canvassing (ss. 48–51)

It is an offence to canvass a DCA off trade premises. This outlaws the practice of stopping people in the street or calling uninvited at their homes to persuade them to take a loan. Traders need a special licence to canvass off trade premises credit agreements linked to the supply of goods and services or the hire of goods.

It is an offence to send any document to a minor inviting him to borrow money, obtain goods or services on credit, or to apply for information or advice on borrowing. It is also an offence to give or send a person a credit token if he has not asked for it. This rule does not apply to the renewal of credit cards.

Quotations (ss. 52–54)

Regulations have been made by the Secretary of State to control the content of quotations given on or after 6 October 1980. Traders are required to give customers who ask, written information about the credit terms being offered, giving due prominence to the APR. Failure to comply with the regulations constitutes a criminal offence.

Signing credit or hire agreements

Creditors or owners must observe certain formalities if they wish to enforce any agreement. These rules do not apply to non-commercial agreements. Small DCSAs for restricted-use credit are only subject to the provisions about pre-contractual disclosure (see (1) below).

(1) *Before signing* (s. 55). The prospective debtor or hirer must be given full details of the agreement he is about to sign.

(2) *The agreement* (s. 61). The agreement must:

(a) be readily legible;

(b) contain all the terms of the agreement (other than implied terms);

(c) comply with the regulations as to its form and content;

(d) in the case of a 'cancellable' agreement, contain details of the debtor's rights to cancel;

(e) be signed personally by the debtor and by or on behalf of the creditor.

(3) *Copies* (ss. 62 and 63). The debtor or hirer must receive either one or two copies of the agreement, depending on the circumstances. He must always receive a copy at the time of signing. However, the agreement is not normally completed at this time, as it is usually sent away for acceptance by the creditor or owner. If this is the case, the debtor must receive a second copy within seven days of the agreement being concluded. If it is a 'cancellable' agreement (see below), the second copy must be sent by post.

Failure to comply with the requirements as to formalities renders the agreement 'improperly executed'. This means that it can be enforced against the debtor or hirer only by order of the court.

Cancellation

Sections 67–74 provide a limited right for debtors or hirers to change their minds and withdraw from an agreement they have signed. This 'cooling-off' period applies to regulated agreements signed off trade premises where there has been some personal contact between the debtor or hirer and the salesman.

The debtor or hirer may serve notice of cancellation at any time between signing the agreement and five clear days after receiving the second copy of the agreement. If this right is exercised, the parties are returned to the position they were in before the agreement was signed. Any money received must be repaid, and if the debtor or hirer has acquired any goods, they must be made available for return.

Credit reference agencies

These organizations collect information about people's creditworthiness. It is normal practice for traders in the credit business to use the services of such an agency to vet the suitability of applicants for credit. Sections 157–159 give consumers the right to obtain the name and address of any agency used and, for a £1 fee, a copy of any file held. If the information is wrong, the consumer can add a correction to the file.

Liability of the supplier and creditor

A supplier of goods and services will be liable for any false statements he makes which persuade a customer to enter into an agreement (see p. 173). In addition, certain terms are implied into contracts for the supply of goods and services. If the supplier does not live up to his obligations, he may be sued by the customer for breach of contract (see Chapter 10).

If credit is involved in the purchase, the situation may be complicated by the fact that the creditor and supplier are not the same person. For example, a credit card may have been used to buy the goods. The Act contains two provisions which have the effect of making the credit grantor equally responsible for any misrepresentation or breach of contract by the supplier.

Section 56

In the case of regulated agreements, the dealer is deemed to be acting as the creditor's agent. The creditor is, therefore, responsible for the negotiations conducted on his behalf.

Section 75

This makes the creditor equally responsible with the supplier for any misrepresentation or breach of contract. However, the section only applies if the agreement meets the following conditions:

(a) it is a 'regulated' credit agreement;

(b) the cash price of the item is between £100 and £30 000;

(c) the credit is granted under an arrangement between the creditor and supplier.

Equal liability does not apply to non-commercial agreements or where the customer has arranged his own credit, such as a bank overdraft or a cash advance from a credit card company.

Extortionate terms

Sections 137–140 introduce sweeping new powers for the courts to re-open extortionate credit bargains so as to do justice between the parties. The provisions apply to all credit, irrespective of the amount involved. They allow an individual debtor or surety (a person who has given security for the credit) to bring the credit bargain to the attention of the court, either in a specific action or during the course of the proceedings relating to the agreement. A credit bargain is extortionate if it requires the debtor or his relatives to make payments which are grossly exorbitant or otherwise contravene ordinary principles of fair dealing.

The Act is not precise about what should be regarded as an extortionate rate of interest. Instead, it mentions general factors which should be taken into account by the court, such as:

(1) prevailing interest rates;

(2) the age, experience, business capacity and state of health of the debtor;

(3) the degree of financial pressure put on the debtor and the nature of that pressure;

(4) the degree of risk accepted by the creditor;

(5) the creditor's relationship with the debtor;

(6) whether the cash price quoted for the goods was true or 'colourable', i.e. inflated to make the credit charges appear more reasonable.

In *Barcabe* v *Edwards* (1983) the court held that a loan with an APR of 319 per cent was, prima facie, extortionate. It re-opened the agreement and substituted a flat rate of interest of 40 per cent which is equivalent to an APR of 92 per cent! In *A Ketley Ltd* v *Scott* (1981), a bridging loan with an estimated APR of 57.35 per cent was held not to be extortionate. The court took into account the high degree of risk taken by the creditors and the business experience of the debtor.

If the court finds that the credit bargain is extortionate, it may –

(1) direct a state of account between the two parties to be taken to establish, for example, how much money has been paid by the debtor and the amount still outstanding;

(2) set aside any obligation under the agreement;

(3) require the creditor to re-pay all or part of any sum paid under the agreement;

(4) direct the return of any property provided as security; or

(5) alter the terms of the credit bargain.

Termination and default

Both debtor and creditor may have reasons why they want their relationship to end. The debtor could have come into some money and wish to pay his debts off. Alternatively, he may have lost his job and no longer be able to afford the repayments. The creditor will want to take action against people who have not lived up to the agreements they have made.

Early settlement (ss. 94–97)

The debtor under a regulated consumer credit agreement is entitled to pay off what he owes at any time, on giving notice to the creditor of his intention to do so. This may entitle him to a rebate of interest.

Termination (ss. 98–101)

(1) *by the debtor*. The debtor under a regulated HP or conditional sale agreement may give notice to terminate the agreement at any time before the final

instalment is due. He must return the goods and pay off any arrears. In addition, he must pay the smallest of the following;

(*a*) a minimum amount specified in the agreement;

(*b*) half of the total purchase price; or

(*c*) an amount ordered by the court to compensate the creditor for his loss.

If the debtor has failed to take reasonable care of the goods, he must pay damages to the creditor.

(2) *By the creditor.* Usually the creditor will wish to terminate the agreement because the debtor has broken the agreement in some way. (This is dealt with below.) However, it should be noted that some agreements allow the creditor to terminate where there has been no default by the debtor. The agreement may specify that it can be terminated at any time or, if (for example) the creditor becomes unemployed or is convicted of a crime of dishonesty. If it is an agreement for a specified period which still has time to run, the creditor must give seven days' notice of his intention. The debtor may apply to the court for a 'time order' (see below).

Default (ss.87–89)

If the debtor has committed a breach of the agreement the creditor must serve a 'default notice' before he takes any of the following actions:

(1) to terminate the agreement;

(2) to demand earlier payment;

(3) to recover the possession of any goods or land;

(4) to treat any right conferred on the debtor by agreement as terminated, restricted or deferred; or

(5) to enforce any security.

The default notice must explain to the debtor the nature of his alleged breach, what he must do to put it right and by when, or, if the breach cannot be remedied, what must be paid by way of compensation. The time allowed for the debtor to remedy the breach must be at least seven days from service of the default notice. It must contain certain information about the consequences of failing to comply with the notice.

If the debtor carries out the requirements of the notice, the breach is treated as if it had never happened. Where the notice is not heeded, the creditor may pursue any remedies contained in the agreement, subject to the provisions of the Act. At this point, the debtor may seek the help of the court by applying for a time order.

Time orders (ss. 129–130)

A debtor may apply to the court for a time order where he has been served with either a default or non-default notice or in the course of an action by the creditor to enforce a regulated agreement. The court can allow the debtor time to remedy any breach or, where the breach consists of non-payment, time in which to pay the arrears. In the case of an HP or conditional sale agreement, the court may re-arrange the pattern of future instalments.

Repossession of the goods (ss. 90–92)

One of the attractions of HP to Victorian traders was that, if the hirer defaulted at any stage, the owner could recover the goods. Many HP agreements even gave creditors the right to enter the hirer's home for this purpose.

Debtors under regulated HP and conditional sale agreements now enjoy protection against the so-called 'snatch back':

(1) a creditor must obtain a court order before he enters any premises to repossess goods and

(2) if the debtor has paid at least one third of the total price and he has not terminated the agreement, the goods are 'protected'. The creditor cannot recover possession of 'protected goods' unless he obtains a court order. If a creditor ignores this requirement he faces severe penalties. The agreement terminates immediately, the debtor is released from all liabilities under the agreement and, in addition, can recover all money already paid.

Capital Finance Co. Ltd v Bray (1964)
Bray had paid over a third of the HP price of a car when he fell into arrears. A representative of the finance company took the car back without either Bray's consent or a court order. The company realized its mistake and returned the car to Bray. When the repayments were still not forthcoming, the company sued for possession of the car. This was granted by the court, which further held that Bray was entitled to recover everything that he had previously paid to the finance company.

Questions/activities

1. What kinds of credit are likely to be used by (*a*) a typical family (*b*) a sole trader and (*c*) a limited company?

2. What forms of credit would be available for the following purchases: (*a*) furniture (*b*) clothes (*c*) car, and (*d*) house? What kinds of institutions would provide the credit?

3. What are the current rates of interest for the following types of credit: (*a*) bank personal loan (*b*) shop budget account (*c*) building society mortgage (*d*) bank credit card (*e*) finance company personal loan (*f*) overdraft, and (*g*) HP?

4. What are the points of similarity between HP and credit sale? What are the differences?

5. Using the terminology of the Consumer Credit Act 1974 contained in List A, describe the credit transactions in List B.

List A: (*a*) DCSA; (*b*) DCA; (*c*) restricted-use credit; (*d*) unrestricted-use credit; (*e*) fixed-sum credit; (*f*) running account credit; (*g*) credit token agreement; (*h*) regulated consumer credit agreement; (*i*) regulated consumer hire agreement; (*j*) small agreement; (*k*) non-commercial agreement; (*l*) exempt agreement.

List B: (*a*) Arthur buys a suite of furniture from Matchstick Furniture PLC, paying twelve monthly instalments of £50 each. Ownership of the furniture passes to Arthur immediately.

(*b*) The Portland Bank PLC allows Beryl to overdraw her current account up to a limit of £1000.

(*c*) Colin sees a new car in the Showrooms of Rattle Cars Co. Ltd, which he wishes to buy. The company introduces him to Shady Finance Co. Ltd who agree to let Colin have the car on HP. Colin pays a deposit of £1500, and 24 monthly instalments of £20 each.

(*d*) Doris uses her Access credit card (on which she has a personal limit of £300) to buy a camera from Snapshot Ltd.

(*e*) Evan has *The Times* delivered to his home every day. He pays the bill at the end of each month.

(*f*) Freda buys and obtains possession of a coat and dress from Bondsman Mail Order Co. Ltd for £45. She pays this in 20 instalments of £2.25 each.

6. Gerald buys a new video. After two weeks' use the machine starts to mangle tapes. What are his rights, and against whom, if the purchase was financed in the following ways:

(*a*) cash payment direct to the retailers. Viewscene Ltd;

(*b*) bank credit card;

(*c*) HP arranged by Viewscene Ltd with Eazimoney Finance Co. Ltd;

(*d*) bank overdraft?

7. Harold agrees to take a car on HP from Tite Finance Co. Ltd for a total HP price of £3250, made up of a deposit of £850 plus 24 monthly payments of £100.

(*a*) the company receives a letter from Harold terminating the agreement because he has lost his job. What will Harold have to pay if he terminates in the following situations?

(*i*) After he has paid three instalments but before the fourth is due.

(*ii*) After he has paid four instalments and the fifth and sixth are still owing.

(*iii*) After he has paid twelve instalments and before the thirteenth is due, but the car was badly damaged in an accident.

(*b*) Harold does not terminate the agreement but fails to pay any instalments after the seventh instalment. What action can Tite Finance Co. Ltd take?

Suggested assignments

Assignment 1
A package holiday

Obtain a copy of a current package holiday brochure. Select a holiday which appeals to you. Read all the details relating to the holiday you have chosen (including the booking conditions and insurance cover). Complete the booking form for yourself and a friend. Now answer the following questions.

1. Identify the sequence of events in booking your holiday in terms of (*a*) invitation to treat; (*b*) offer; and (*c*) acceptance.

2. Can the offer be revoked? If so, when and how?

3. Identify the consideration.

4. Are there any restrictions on the under eighteens? If so, why?

5. Identify an example of each of the following types of clause –

(*a*) price variation clause

(*b*) liquidated damages clause

(*c*) exemption clause.

For each example, explain why the clause has been included in the brochure, its legal effect and whether it would be upheld by a court.

6. Using your brochure as a guide, explain what your rights are if any of the following events occur.

(*a*) You receive the final invoice nine weeks before departure. The balance due is considerably more than you expected to pay. The tour operator explains that the increases have become necessary because of 'currency fluctuations'. You work out that the price of your holiday has been increased by 15 per cent.

(*b*) Four days before departure, the tour operator informs you that your hotel is overbooked and it is necessary to transfer you to another resort, where you will be accommodated in a hotel of the same standard.

(*c*) Your outward flight is delayed by twelve hours because of industrial action by British air traffic controllers.

(*d*) Your hotel was described in the brochure as providing a twice-weekly cabaret, all rooms with sea views and the beach 200 yards away. The hotel proves to be a great disappointment: the beach is at least half a mile away, the sea can be glimpsed from your room but only by standing at one corner of the balcony and the cabaret never materializes.

(*e*) You and your friend hire a scooter. Your friend is badly injured in an accident and requires urgent expert medical attention.

7. (*a*) How can any complaints about your holiday be resolved?

(*b*) What are the advantages to the customer and tour operator of the following methods of settling unresolved disputes –

(1) ABTA arbitration scheme;

(2) Court action?

Assignment 2
A modern office
You work as a Personal Assistant to the Managing Director of H & J Co. Ltd, a small family-run light engineering company. Following a particularly successful financial year, the company decides to modernize its office equipment. The contract is awarded to A-Z Offices Ltd and includes the following features –

(1) the purchase of three electronic typewriters. Each machine carries a one year guarantee from the manufacturer, Hi-Tek Equipment Ltd, in respect of defective parts.

(2) a two-year leasing agreement for a photocopier. A-Z Offices Ltd agree to service the photocopier every three months for an additional annual charge of £100.

The morning after the first visit by a 'trainee' service engineer from A-Z Offices Ltd you are informed by Jane Smith, the office supervisor, that the photocopier will not work and that one of the typewriters has developed a fault – the 'a' key will not type. Jane contacted A-Z Offices Ltd and was informed that the typewriter was 'the manufacturer's responsibility' and that a charge would be made for a visit by a service engineer between normal quarterly service visits.

(1) Write a memo for your managing director outlining your company's legal position.

(2) Draft an appropriate letter to A-Z Offices Ltd ready for the managing director's signature.

Assignment 3
The golf club
You have recently been elected secretary of Oldbury Golf Club. At the last committee meeting, the treasurer announced that substantial increases in membership fees would be necessary unless alternative sources of income could be found. A committee member suggested that the clubhouse facilities could be hired out on a commercial basis to non-members for weddings, dinner dances, etc. The committee asks you to prepare a report for its next meeting on the legal implications of such a move.

Your report should cover the following matters –

(1) The question of drawing up a standard contract for the hire of the club rooms.

(2) The ways in which the club can minimize any possible liability it might have to members of the public attending functions at the clubhouse.

Assignment 4
Antiques
Oliver Twist decides to take early retirement from his civil service position so that he can indulge his interest in antiques. He buys an antiques shop in a small market town and also sets up a valuation service. He experiences a few setbacks in his first few weeks of trading and he seeks your advice on the problems that have arisen.

1. Oliver bought an attractive Victorian oil painting from a junk stall on the local market for the bargain price of £5. He sells the painting within a few days for £150 to a Mrs Bumble. A week later Mrs Bumble returns to the shop to reclaim the money she paid. She explains that the police called at her home and

identified the painting as stolen property. The police took the painting so that it could be returned to the original owner.

2. Oliver is asked to value a vase for a Mr Dombey. In his value report, Oliver states that, 'The vase is of no great interest and will only fetch between £80–£100 at auction'. Oliver charges £4 for this service. Acting on the report, Mr Dombey sells the vase privately for £90. He has now discovered that the vase is in fact worth £900 and is seeking compensation from Oliver.

3. Mr and Mrs Copperfield agree to buy a grand-father clock from Oliver for £1200. They leave a £20 deposit. Three days later the Copperfields inform Oliver that they have found a more attractive clock elsewhere and that they no longer wish to purchase the clock in his shop.

4. Oliver sells a chest of drawers to a Mr Pickwick. It is agreed that Oliver will mend one of the drawers which does not open smoothly. Oliver completes the work on the drawer, but before he had an opportunity to tell Mr Pickwick that the chest was ready for collection, there is a fire at his workshop and the chest of drawers is destroyed.

Assignment 5
Credit

You are employed by the Newtown Consumer Advice Centre as an advice worker specializing in consumer credit. While you were attending a conference, a number of people called in seeking your advice. The receptionist took down details of their queries. You find this information in your in-tray:

1. John and Tina Brown, a newly-wed couple, want to buy an £800 three piece suite from Discount Stores Ltd, the largest department store in Newtown. They are about to move in to a new house which means that they will not have enough spare cash to pay for the suite outright. They want to know what kinds of credit are available and from where. What are the differences between them? What are the advantages and disadvantages of each?

2. Jenny Jones – bought a new washing machine from Discount Stores Ltd on twelve months' credit provided by Dubious Finance Co. Ltd. Two weeks after the machine was installed it sprung a leak. The washing machine will not work at all now and Jenny's kitchen floor is ruined. She wants to know who is responsible.

3. Mr and Mrs Young – agreed to have double-glazing installed by Frame-up Co. Ltd. The company's representative told them that it would cost £900 if they paid cash, but they could spread the cost over twelve months for monthly payments of £140. The Youngs signed the agreement for the easy payment plan in their home. The representative took the documents away with him to be accepted by the company. The Youngs are now having second thoughts and they wonder what they can do.

4. Ted Loss – agreed to buy a car on HP from Knab Ltd; the total price was £3600. The car was delivered four months ago and Ted paid a deposit of £1200, agreeing to pay the balance by equal monthly instal-ments over two years. Ted has now lost his job and is behind with his payments. What is his best course of action?

Task

Prepare detailed notes to help you deal with these clients' problems ready for when they return. If you feel you have insufficient information, note down the questions you will need to ask.

Business Resources

Business property

Generally

English law divides property into real property and personal property. The assets of a business are usually made up of both sorts of property.

The distinction between the two sorts of property is mainly that real property cannot be moved but personal property can.

However, this is not the only test because some things which can be moved are regarded as real property and called fixtures, while other moveables are regarded as fittings which do not become part of the real property to which they are attached. A diagram showing the broad classification of property in English law appears at Fig. 16.1.

Fixtures and fittings

As we have seen, fixtures become part of the land itself; fittings do not. If a piece of personal property is securely attached to the ground it is probably a fixture but a second test needs to be applied in order to finally decide. If the piece of personal property was put on the land so that it could be better enjoyed for itself, it is not a fixture. However, if it is put on the land so that the land can be better enjoyed, then it is a fixture.

Leigh v Taylor (1902)
A person put some valuable tapestries on the wall of his house, the house being real property. He used tacks to fit them on a framework of wood and canvas which he then nailed to the wall. Upon his death the court had to decide whether the tapestries were real or personal property and it was decided

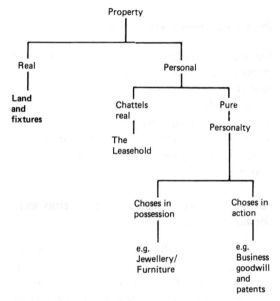

Fig. 16.1. The classification of property.

that they were still personal property. They had been fixed to the wall so that they could be better enjoyed for themselves.

Comment. A contrast is provided by *D'Eyncourt* v *Gregory* (1866) where certain statues, vases, and stone garden furniture standing on their own weight were decided to be real property because they formed part of the design of a landscaped garden. They were there for the better enjoyment of the land.

The importance of the idea of fixtures and fittings is that if you buy land and buildings, say as a business asset, then in the absence of a special provision in the conveyance to the contrary, the conveyance will pass the fixtures to the buyer and they cannot be removed by the seller. They are also regarded as included in the price. Fittings are not and can be removed by the seller in the absence of an agreement to the contrary.

The lease

A lease of land, e.g. office premises, is obviously an interest in land (or realty) but for historical reasons it is regarded as personal property and not real property.

This distinction has lost much of its importance in law, though still today if a person, T, were to leave by his will 'all my personal property to P and all my real property to R' P would get any leases which T had when he died.

Pure personalty and chattels real

The word personalty is another name for personal property. The word chattel is also used to describe personal property.

Although leaseholds are regarded as personalty they are over land and result in a person having use of land and so they are referred to as chattels real to distinguish them from pure personalty, such as a watch or a fountain pen.

Pure personalty – choses in possession and choses in action

Things such as jewellery and furniture which are tangible objects and have not only a money value but can also be enjoyed by the person who owns them *in a physical way* through the senses are called choses (or things) in possession.

Things which cannot be enjoyed by the person who owns them in a physical way, but which nevertheless are worth money, are called choses (or things) in action. Examples are patents, copyrights, trade marks, shares and cheques and the goodwill of a business. The value lies not in the thing itself but the legal right to money which it represents and the right to bring an action at law to enforce or protect that right should this become necessary.

Easements and profits

We have already dealt with a property right called a lease. This is a right to use another person's land for a period of time in return for the payment of rent. It is, however, also possible to have ownership of other rights over someone else's property.

Easements

A may have what is called an *easement* over B's land. This might be a *right of way* so that for example A could get goods and services into his business premises by bringing them across land belonging to another business.

An easement may also be a *right to light* which would prevent the owner of a neighbouring business from building on his own land but so close to A's premises that A was unable to use them without constant artificial light. A could stop such a building from being put up by asking the court for an injunction to protect his right of light.

An easement may also be a *right to support* from other buildings. Where a house or business premises are attached to other property, as with a semi-detached house, one property needs the support of the other.

Thus if B decides to pull down his semi-detached premises which will leave A's premises in danger of collapsing, A can, once again, ask the court for an injunction to prevent B from doing this.

The deeds of the various properties will usually reveal what easements exist between the landowners. Finally, it is important to note that an easement is a *private* right (a public right of way is a different matter with which we shall not deal), enjoyed by owners or occupiers of *land* over *neighbouring* land. You cannot by owning land in Essex have an easement over land in Yorkshire.

Profits

Sometimes the right which exists over someone else's land is to take something from the land. It may, for example, be a right to fish or cut wood.

These rights can be purchased over any land. Unlike an easement they are *not* restricted to rights over neighbouring land. You can, therefore, buy fishing rights over a river in Surrey even though you live in Lancashire and do not own any land at all in Surrey.

Securities

A person may raise a loan on the security of his property, whether real (say his house), or personal (say his shareholding in a company), and the lender has certain rights over the property so used as a security if the loan is not repaid. Securities are explained in Chapter 17.

A licence

An owner of property, A, may give another person, B, a contractual licence over his property, e.g. rent B a room in a guest house for six months. This is not a lease. It merely prevents B from being a trespasser on A's premises. B has no interest in the land as such but only his contractual rights. Buying a ticket for a football match is a form of contractual licence. We would all appreciate that such a transaction gave no rights in the football ground as such.

As regards the room B has rented, these days the law will usually require A to keep to his contract and issue an injunction to prevent A from evicting B after, say, three months only. However, since the licence is not a lease, a person with a licence has no Rent Act protection in terms, for example, of the amount of rent charged. Thus it is to the advantage of a landlord to give a licence rather than a lease.

Restrictive covenants

These covenants control the way in which a person uses his land. There is *public* control of the use of land through Town and Country Planning Acts and there are also building regulations to cover the way in which buildings are constructed. As well as *public* control, however there is also *private* control by means of restrictive covenants. If these are put into a lease of land the landlord can enforce them against the tenant because they are parties to the contract, in other words, there is privity of estate or contract between them.

However, it is often desirable that covenants (or agreements) restricting the use of land should be enforceable between those who own freehold properties. For example, when estates of private houses are built it is desirable in order to preserve the residential nature of the estate, that covenants, e.g. to use the premises for residential purposes only, should be complied with by the purchasers of the individual houses and also by those who buy from them and so on, and that these covenants should be enforceable by the house owners as between themselves.

The covenants are taken by the common seller of the property, e.g. the builder or developer (whoever owns the land), and then they can be enforced by the purchasers of the houses as between themselves. The builder or developer will not normally be able to enforce them because he will not usually own any land on the estate, having sold it all off for housing plots.

These covenants can be enforced between subsequent owners of the houses as an exception to the rule of privity of contract (see also p. 166). They are, however, void unless registered as a land charge at the Land Registry in London.

When a person buys a house a solicitor acting in the matter will get a search of the Land Register done and will find the restrictive covenants which exist over the property. If he does not find any, because they are not registered, then they are void.

Legal estates in land

There are only two legal estates in land – the fee simple absolute in possession (usually called a freehold) and the term of years absolute (usually called a leasehold).

The word estate is used because in theory at least the Queen owns all our land and we can only hold an estate, as it is called, from her. In other words, part of what she owns. However, the Queen has now no right to take back these estates from their owners.

The freehold

If we have an estate from the Queen then we want to know how long it will last. The fee simple absolute in possession (or freehold) lasts indefinitely and the word fee means that the land can be inherited, as where it is left by the owner to another person by a will. Simple means that it can be passed on to anyone. The word absolute means that it must not be what is called a modified fee, such as a life interest, which can only be an equitable interest behind a trust. (See below.)

There must also be possession of the land, though the freehold owner need not be living on the property; it is enough if he receives rent for it, as where he has let it on a lease to a tenant and is himself a landlord.

So, if freehold land is sold or left by will to X, then the freehold will belong to X and he can pass it on to another.

If, however, land is left 'to X for life and after his death to Y' then X does not take a legal estate of freehold, nor does Y. Y's interest is absolute but not yet in possession until X dies. X's interest is in possession but is not absolute because it is only for his life.

The above interests are equitable interests and can only be held on a trust. The trustees would have the freehold and when X died they could transfer the freehold to Y who would then by the absolute owner and the trust would come to an end.

The leasehold

A term of years absolute, usually called a lease, is an estate which lasts for a fixed time. It is usually given by a freehold owner to a tenant. It can be for a fixed period, e.g. twenty-one years, or on a periodic tenancy, e.g. weekly, monthly, or yearly.

A lease for a fixed term comes to an end when the term finishes. A periodic tenancy comes to an end when the appropriate period of notice expires, though in the case of some leases there may be statutory protection, e.g. the Rent Acts, which preserve the tenant's right to continue in occupation.

The rights and duties of an occupier of land

The main right of an occupier of land is to seek an injunction against persons who trespass on his land or, alternatively, sue the trespasser for damages. However, by the Civil Aviation Act 1982, aeroplanes have the right to fly over property at a reasonable height. In *Bernstein v Skyways and General Ltd* (1977) it was decided that the defendants were not liable for trespass when flying at approximately 630 feet over the plaintiff's house, the purpose being to take photographs and sell them to the plaintiff.

The duties of an occupier lie in the law of tort and are dealt with below.

Duties to those who are not on the premises

We must look separately at liability to persons on the road (or highway), if any, which is next to the premises. We must also consider liability to persons on premises which are next to the property.

1. *Liability to persons on the highway*. The occupier has a duty not to injure persons on the highway by allowing a harmful situation to develop on his land.

Holling v Yorkshire Traction Co. Ltd (1948)
Steam and smoke from the Traction Company's factory went across a road next to it and made it difficult to see. As a result two vehicles collided and this caused the death of Holling. The court said that the Traction Company were liable. It was negligent of the company not to post a man at each end of the affected area to warn of the danger.

2. *Liability to persons on adjoining premises*. An occupier has a duty not to injure persons on adjoining premises by allowing a harmful situation to develop on the land.

Taylor v Liverpool Corporation (1939)
The plaintiff was the daughter of the tenant of some flats owned by the Corporation. She was injured when a chimney stack from adjoining premises, also owned by the Corporation, fell into a yard. The Corporation had been negligent in that it had not maintained the chimney properly. The Corporation was liable in negligence and the plaintiff won her case.

Duties to persons on the premises

Under the Occupiers Liability Act 1957 an occupier of premises must take reasonable care to see that a visitor to his premises will be reasonably safe in using the premises for the purposes for which he is invited or permitted by the occupier to be on them.

Visitors – generally
The above duty is owed to all lawful visitors. These are individuals who enter the premises with the *express* permission of the occupier, as where A (an occupier) invites B (a plumber) to enter his home to repair a leaking pipe.

However, permission to enter premises is also *implied* by the law. So, for example, employees of the Electricity Board who enter premises to read meters are there by the implied permission of the occupier, as would also be a policeman with a search warrant, though in the last case it is unlikely that the occupier would expressly invite him on to the premises! The term visitor does not apply to trespassers.

Children

The 1957 Act provides that persons who occupy premises must take into account the fact that children may be less careful than adults and therefore the duty of care owed to children is higher.

An example of this is that things which constitute a trap or are especially alluring to children must be given special attention by an occupier, because he may be liable for any damage which such things cause, even if the child involved is a trespasser.

Glasgow Corporation *v* Taylor (1922)

A boy aged seven years died after he had eaten some poisonous berries which he picked from a tree in a park owned by the Corporation.

There was a notice in the park but the court decided that this was not adequate as a means of communicating the danger to young children. Also, the berries were within easy reach and were attractive to children. The Corporation was liable.

Visitors who are experts

The 1957 Act provides that persons who enter premises as part of their job, e.g. plumbers and electricians, ought to have a better appreciation of the risks which may arise while they are doing their work.

Roles *v* Nathan (1963)

N employed two chimney sweeps to clean out the flues of a heating system fuelled by coke. Although N warned the sweeps against it, they blocked off a ventilation hole while the coke fire was still alight. They were later killed by the escape of carbon monoxide fumes. This action, which was brought by the dependents of the sweeps, failed. The court decided that an occupier is entitled to assume that a chimney sweep will guard against such dangers.

Warnings

The 1957 Act states that if the occupier gives a warning of the danger it will free him from liability, but only if the warning makes the visitor safe.

It would not be enough, for example, for a cinema to give warning of a dangerous roof over what was the only approach to the ticket office. However, if customers in a shop are told not to go to the far end of it because builders have opened up a dangerous hole,

then the shopkeeper might well have no duty to a customer who defied his instruction and fell down the hole.

Exclusion of liability

The 1957 Act provides that an occupier may 'restrict or exclude his duty by agreement or otherwise'. However, because of the Unfair Contract Terms Act 1977 (see p. 205) there can be no exclusion of liability for death or personal injury on business premises. In regard to other loss, e.g. damage to the goods of a visitor, liability can be excluded only if it is reasonable to do so.

Faulty work of outside contractors

The 1957 Act allows an occupier to escape liability if the damage results from the faulty work of an outside contractor (called also an independent contractor) whose expertise is necessary to get the job done.

Cook *v* Broderip (1968)

The owner of a flat, Major Broderip, employed an apparently competent electrical contractor to fix a new socket. Mrs Cook, who was a cleaner, received an electric shock from the socket while she was working in the flat. This was because the contractor had failed to test it properly. The court decided that Major Broderip was not liable to Mrs Cook but the contractor was.

Trespassers

The position of trespassers is covered by the Occupiers' Liability Act 1984. The Act deals with the duty of an occupier to persons other than his visitors and this includes trespassers and persons entering land without the consent of the owner, but in the exercise of a private right of way or public access. In these cases the occupier owes a duty, if he is aware of the danger which exists, or has reasonable grounds to believe that it exists.

He must also know, or have reasonable grounds to believe, that the non-visitor concerned is in the vicinity of the danger – whether he has lawful authority to be in that vicinity or not.

Furthermore, the risk must be one which in all the circumstances of the case it is reasonable to expect the occupier to offer the non-visitor some protection against. The duty is to take such care as is reasonable in all the circumstances of the case to see that the non-visitor does not suffer injury because of the danger concerned. The duty may be discharged by giving warning of the danger or taking steps to discourage persons from incurring the risk.

Intellectual property and its protection

Generally

Intellectual property is a term used to refer to a product or a process which is marketable and profitable because it is unique.

This uniqueness is protected by *patent law*, which gives protection to technological inventions. The law relating to *registered designs* protects articles which are mass produced but distinguished from others by a registered design which appears upon them. The law of *copyright* protects, e.g. rights in literary, artistic, and musical works. The law of *trademarks* and *service marks* protects the use of a particular mark if it is used in trade.

The law also protects those in business from competitors who maliciously disparage their products or who pass off their own products as those of another business. There is also some protection in regard to the commercial use, e.g. by employees without permission, of confidential information.

Patents

The statutory law regarding patents is mostly to be found in the Patents Act 1977.

Application

An application for a patent can be made by or on behalf of the inventor and the grant of a patent will be made to the inventor himself or to any person who is entitled to it as where the inventor has sold the idea before patenting it.

What can be patented?

In order to be patented an invention must be new. For example a new system of double glazing. This will usually mean that it has not been disclosed publicly at any time anywhere in the world. Also it must be something which is invented so that those who are skilled in the field in which the invention has been made would not think of it as an obvious development. In addition, it must have an industrial, commercial or agricultural use.

If an application for a patent is refused by the Patent Office in London there is an appeal to the Patents Court, which is part of the Chancery Division of the High Court.

Registration

The Comptroller-General maintains at the Patent Office a register of patents and the date and entry gives priority over later inventions. A patent lasts for 20 years.

Employees' inventions

Under the 1977 Act an invention of an employee belongs to the employer if the employee arrives at it during his normal employment or during a specific job outside his normal duties. Other inventions, e.g. those made during the employee's spare time, belong to the employee.

Infringement

If another person, for example, makes the product without the owner's consent, then the owner can ask for an injunction or damages or for an account of the profits made from the use of the product.

Designs

Statute law relating to designs is to be found mainly in the Registered Designs Act 1949, the Copyright Act 1956, and the Design Copyright Act 1968.

What is meant by a design?

A design refers only to the features of shape, pattern or ornament applied to an article by an industrial process which appeals to, and is judged solely, by looking at the article.

For example, a firm making a special design of fabric for use in curtains or chair covers might register the design.

Registration

Designs may be registered and there is an appeal to the Registered Designs Appeal Tribunal if the Registrar refuses to register a particular design. Registration gives the owner of the design protection for five years and this can be extended for two further periods of five years so that the maximum period of protection is 15 years in all. The Register of Designs can be inspected on payment of a fee.

Infringement

The owner's remedies for infringement are to sue the person responsible for damages and/or an injunction, or an account of profits made from the wrongful use of the design.

Copyright

The law relating to copyright is largely contained in the Copyright Act 1956. The Act does not require the owner of a copyright to register it or to follow any formalities in respect of it. The protection is given by the 1956 Act to every original literary, dramatic, musical, and artistic work which was previously unpublished.

Ownership and duration

The author of the work is the owner of the copyright. However, it may be a term of the contract between, say, a newspaper company and its journalists that the entire copyright in the journalists' work is to belong to the newspaper company.

Under the 1956 Act protection of copyright exists in a work during the lifetime of the author of it and until the end of the period of fifty years from the end of the calendar year in which the author of the work died. The copyright then comes to an end.

Infringement

The person infringing the copyright will usually have copied from the work and an action can be brought for an injunction and/or damages or for an account of profits made from the wrongful use of the copyright work.

Trade marks

The statute law relating to trade marks is mainly contained in the Trade Marks Act 1938. The matter of trade marks would be relevant, for example, to a person who was in business as a manufacturer of fast foods of which a major product was a doughnut called 'Mr Creamy' – how could that trade mark be protected?

Types of trade marks

There are two types of trade marks – (*a*) common law or unregistered trade marks; and (*b*) registered trade marks.

A common law trade mark is any mark which has been so widely used on or in connection with a certain class of goods that it can be shown that the public recognized goods with such a mark as coming from the owner of the mark. The remedy to restrict improper use is a passing off action.

A registered trade mark is a mark registered with the Registrar on either Part A or Part B of the Register. A mark cannot be registered if it conflicts with a mark already on the Register.

If we were to register our mark 'Mr Creamy', then it would usually go on Part B of the Register because it is new. After a period of time when it was better known, it could be registered in Part A of the Register.

Infringement

As we have seen, in the case of a common law or unregistered mark, its owner will succeed in obtaining an injunction to prevent the use of it in a passing off action. (See below.)

Passing off actions are the ones most usually brought in this field because trade marks are often not registered.

Marks registered on Part A have complete protection. There is no defence to their improper use. Nobody can use the mark except the owner and an action for infringement can be brought if they do, without proving anything except Part A registration.

Part B marks are not so well protected but it is better than relying on a passing off action. In a passing off action you have to prove that the goods are known to the public but you do not have to do this with a Part B mark. However, with a Part B mark the person alleged to have been making improper use of it has a complete defence if he can show that his use of the mark was not in any way likely to mislead the consumer.

The Trade Marks (Amendment) Act 1984 extends the application of the Trade Marks Act 1938 to service marks. As we have seen, for many years those in business to supply *goods* have been able to protect their trade marks by registration.

However, those supplying a service have not been able to register. Thus well-known logos, such as the THF of Trusthouse Forte and the black horse of Lloyds Bank had protection only by passing off actions with all the cost which that involves. The 1984 Act now allows registration of service marks in the same manner as trade marks on goods.

Injurious falsehood

In our present context a person is liable for injurious (or malicious) falsehood if he makes a statement about the goods of another which is malicious and is intended to cause and does cause damage to the business of the other person.

Injurious falsehood is an aspect of defamation and where the false statement is made about another's goods it is sometimes called 'slander of goods'.

De Beers Abrasive Products Ltd v International General Electric Company of New York Ltd (1975)

De Beers made a diamond abrasive known as and marketed under the trade mark 'Debdust'. It was used for cutting concrete. International made and marketed a competing product under the trade name 'MBS-70'.

International stated in a trade pamphlet that laboratory experiments had shown that MBS-70 was superior to Debdust. De Beers alleged that the contents of the pamphlet were false and misleading. The court said that the pamphlet would amount to an actionable slander of goods if De Beers could prove the allegations and show malice on the part of International.

Passing off

Any person, company, or other organization which carries on or proposes to carry on business under a name calculated to deceive the public by confusion with the name of an existing concern, commits the civil wrong of passing off and will be restrained by injunction from doing so. Other examples more important in our context of passing off are the use of similar wrappings, identification marks, and descriptions. Thus in *Bollinger* v *Costa Brava Wine Co Ltd* (1959) the champagne producers of France objected to the use of the name 'Spanish Champagne' to describe a sparkling wine which was made in Spain and they were granted an injunction to prevent the use of that term. The remedies other than an injunction are an action for damages or for an account of profits made from wrongful use of the wrapping, mark, or description.

Confidentiality

Certain activities by employees are regarded by the law as breaches of the duty of faithful service which an employee owes to his employer. Breaches of this duty of fidelity will sometimes be prevented by the court, so that a person who retains secret processes in his memory can be restrained from using them to his employer's disadvantage *without any contract in restraint of trade*.

An employer who copies names and addresses of his employer's customers for use after leaving his employment can be restrained from using the lists *without any express restriction in his contract*.

Robb v Green (1895)

The plaintiff was a dealer in live game and eggs. The major part of his business consisted of procuring the eggs and the hatching, rearing and sale of gamebirds. His customers were numerous and for the most part were country gentlemen and their gamekeepers. The plaintiff kept a list of these customers in his order book. The defendant, who was for three years the plaintiff's manager, copied these names and addresses, and after leaving the plaintiff's employment set up in a similar business on his own and sent circulars, both to the plaintiff's customers and to their gamekeepers inviting them to do business with him. The plaintiff asked for damages and an injunction and the Court of Appeal decided that although there was no express term in the defendant's contract to restrain him from such activities, it was an implied term of the contract of service that the defendant would observe good faith towards his employer during the existence of the confidential relationship between them. The defendant's conduct was a breach of that duty of good faith in respect of which his employer was entitled to damages and an injunction.

Comment. In connection with the duty of fidelity it should be noted that it does not matter who initiates the infidelity; although in most cases the employee approaches the customer, the rule still applies even where the customers approach the employee.

Questions/activities

1. Explain the difference between real property and personal property. What kinds of personal property are there?

2. John wants to buy a house. He tells you that he has seen some advertised as 'freehold' and some as 'leasehold'.

Write a note explaining these terms to John and stating how he would be affected as a buyer in each case.

3. Explain what is meant by an easement. How does an easement differ from a profit.

Give two examples of each.

4. Anton is the owner of the Napoli restaurant. He engaged Edgar, a builder who was made redundant by Bodge Builders Ltd but has recently started up his own business, to renovate the restaurant.

On Monday, the day before Anton re-opened the restaurant to the public, he invited the Mayor, Mr Snooks and Mrs Snooks, to take a meal at the restaurant.

During the meal a large piece of plaster fell from the false ceiling which Edgar had installed. It fell on the Mayor's table, injuring both him and Mrs Snooks.

Several pieces of plaster hit and injured a local press photographer, Archie, who had got into the restaurant uninvited through a side door. Archie was hiding behind a rubber plant in the hope of getting some exclusive pictures of the new restaurant.

Advise Mr and Mrs Snooks and Archie.

5. If you had registered a patent and a design, for how long would registration protect you, and what remedies would you have if someone infringed your rights?

6. Jane's father has died. He left her by his will the copyright in a very successful novel which he wrote five years before his death. For how long will the publishers pay royalties to Jane?

7. Distinguish a trade mark from a service mark. How many of each can you see in your local shopping precinct? Make a list in two columns, one for trade and one for service marks. Compare your lists. How are trade and service marks protected?

Securities for business resources

Generally

We have already given some consideration to the methods of financing business organizations (see p. 43). We have noted the advantage of forming a limited company because of the ability within the company structure to issue *share capital*. If required share capital can be issued with a variety of different rights in terms, for example, of voting. It can be preference with a fixed dividend and/or ordinary on which dividend will be paid only if and when distributable profits are made.

However, in other forms of business organization, for example the sole trader and the partnership, it is also necessary, as it is in the company structure, to consider the raising of *loan capital* and the method by which some sort of security, over and above the contractual promise of the borrower to repay the loan, can be given.

As regards loan capital, a company has a great advantage in that it can give a floating charge over its assets to a substantial lender, e.g. a bank. Partnerships and sole traders cannot do this because they are subject to bills of sale legislation which in effect stops it. A sole trader or a firm can only mortgage its business premises and fixed plant and give personal guarantees from the sole proprietor or the partners. Sole traders and partners can also mortgage their own private property. These forms of security are also quite common in the private limited company where directors will normally be asked to give guarantees of the company's major debts and mortgage their private property to secure, for example, bank lending to the company. All of this makes something of a mockery of limited liability so far as directors of private companies are concerned.

We shall now consider these securities in more detail.

Charges

A charge is a type of security by which a person who borrows money gives the lender rights over his (the borrower's) assets to support the duty of the borrower to repay what is owed under the contract of loan. The lender thus has two rights

(1) to sue the borrower on the contract of loan; and
(2) to sell the assets which the borrower has charged in order to recover what is owed to him but no more. Any surplus on sale, less the costs of selling the property, must be returned to the borrower. The charge may be fixed or floating.

A mortgage, which will be considered below, is a term most often used to mean a fixed charge over land. However, the term 'mortgage' may be used to describe any type of fixed (but not a floating) charge over any item of land or other property such as a mortgage by a shareholder who uses his shares, which are personal property, as security for a loan.

Fixed charges

A fixed legal charge can be given over *identified property* belonging to the borrower. This property may be either real property, e.g. land and buildings, or personal property, e.g. machinery and equipment.

If real property is being used there is no need for the borrower to transfer his ownership in the land to the lender. The Law of Property Act 1925 allows the lender who has taken the fixed legal charge over, say, land and buildings, to sell it on his own without any assistance from the borrower, even though the lender has not taken a transfer of the ownership from the borrower by what is called a conveyance.

If personal property, such as machinery and equipment, were to be used as security, the borrower would have to transfer, by a method called assignment, the ownership in the machinery and equipment to the lender. Unless this was done the lender could not give a good title to a buyer of the machinery and equipment if he decided to sell it which he would want to do if the borrower did not repay the loan.

The great benefit of the fixed legal charge is that once it has been given the lender can sell the property charged by himself. The contract of loan will of course end his right to do this once the loan has been repaid.

Floating charges

(*a*) *Generally.* This is a charge which is not attached to any particular asset when the charge is made. Instead it applies to the assets of the borrower as they are at the time the charge crystallizes, as it will do if the borrower fails to make repayment of the loan as agreed.

The borrower is in the meantime free to sell the assets he has and any new assets which his business acquires are available to be sold by the lender if they were in the ownership of the borrower when the charge crystallized. When the charge crystallizes it becomes in effect a fixed charge over the assets which the borrower then has. The lender can then sell them to recoup his loan.

(*b*) *Floating charges restricted to companies.* In theory, a floating charge could be used by a sole trader or partnership but because of legislation relating to bills of sale such a charge is not viable except in the case where the borrower is a company.

A floating charge gives the lender an interest in the personal property, e.g. stock in trade, of the borrower, and yet those goods are left in the borrower's possession. This may make him appear more creditworthy to another trader who sees the borrower's assets but does not realize that these are already charged to secure a loan.

If such a charge is to be valid there must be the registration of a bill of sale listing the items charged,

e.g. the stock, in the Bills of Sale Registry. The floating charge does not lend itself to the listing of the property charged in this way because its essential feature is that the assets charged are always changing. If the borrower sold a tin of beans from his stock he would have to amend the bill of sale; if he bought four dozen jars of jam it would also have to be amended. The Bills of Sale Acts do not apply to charges given by companies and so companies do not have to follow this particular registration procedure. However, as we have seen, the registration procedures of the Companies Act 1985 must be carried out.

Guarantees

Generally

If a bank lends money to a business it will normally want, in addition to a charge over the assets, a guarantee from the sole trader or partner, or the directors of the company. These persons promise to meet the business debt from their personal resources if the business cannot.

Partners' and directors' bank guarantees are usually joint and several. This means that any partner or director is obliged to pay the whole debt and may then sue his co-partners or co-directors for a contribution. The nature of this liability has already been explained on p. 63 (as have the formalities necessary for a guarantee (see p. 169)).

Guarantees can be open, that is to cover whatever figure a loan or overdraft may reach, or be limited to a fixed amount.

Independent advice

A special problem has arisen in business law in relation to personal guarantees of business borrowing. A personal guarantee may be unenforceable by the lender because of undue influence, e.g. by a husband over his wife where she has entered into a guarantee of a business loan with her husband. Sometimes, also, the guarantor (i.e. the person who gives the guarantee) has not been liable on it because he or she has successfully claimed that there was no full understanding of the commitment being made.

Because of this a lender should now insist, especially where a wife or older parent is guaranteeing or joining in a guarantee of the liabilities of the business controlled by the husband or child, that the guarantor obtains legal advice independent of the lender. The lawyer who gives the independent advice should act as a witness to the guarantor's signature on the guarantee and confirm that he has fully explained to the guarantor the nature and content of the guarantee. An appropriate form of words appears in the box below.

Signed, sealed, and delivered by the said Joseph Jones in my presence after the contents of this guarantee had been fully explained by me to him.

Signed *John Adam*

Solicitor

Liens

Although a lien is of a different nature to a charge over property, its effect is somewhat the same.

A lien is a right to keep possession of an item of personal property as a form of security until the actual owner of that property has paid a debt owed by him to the person who is keeping possession of the item. It is therefore a sort of security for that debt. The seller's right to a lien in sale of goods was explained in Chapter 11.

General liens

General liens cover all the liabilities of the owner of the item to the person keeping possession of it. For example, a solicitor has a lien over all the papers of his client which are in his possession, even though his client may have paid him for working on some of them but not on others.

Particular liens

These are more common than general liens. They give a right to retain an item until all liabilities of the owner *in regard to that item only* have been settled.

Accountants have at least a particular lien for unpaid fees over any books, files, and papers delivered to them by clients and also over other documents which come into their possession while acting for clients.

(*Woodworth* v *Conroy* (1976).)

It would appear that there can be no lien over the books of a company client by an accountant since these are in many cases to be available for inspection by members and sometimes the public.

It is useful for professional persons to have this lien because if a client wants to go, say, to another accountant without paying his bill to a previous one, this will be made more difficult if the first accountant is exercising his rights to retain the client's books and papers.

General and particular liens can be created by the judiciary applying common law. They do not allow those who exercise the lien to sell the property retained and they cease when the item to which the lien relates leaves the possession of the creditor and, obviously, also when the debt or liability is paid or met.

Pledge

Generally

A pledge differs from a lien because the items to be used as the security are handed to the lender with the idea that they are to be used as security for a loan.

The items over which a lien is exercised are handed to a person, for example with the idea that he will do work on them. It is only later when the work is done and the debt is not paid that that person who has done the work may keep the item if it is still in his possession and, in effect, use it as security until payment is made.

Right of sale

A lien does not give the right to sell the item(s) on which the lien is being exercised. A pledge usually gives the lender a right to sell the item(s) pledged. This will be given by the contract of pledge which the lender and borrower make.

Pledge arises most usually from a contract between the lender and the borrower, rather than from the decisions of judges based on the common law.

Mortgages

Generally

A mortgage is a type of loan. It is special because the

borrower (called the mortgagor) has not just promised to repay the loan to the lender (called the mortgagee) but has given him also a charge on his (the borrower's) property. If the borrower fails, for example, to repay the loan the lender can sell the property and pay himself from the sale price. Alternatively, if the lender thinks he can get his money back from the rents, if any, which the property is producing he can ask the court for the appointment of a receiver who will collect the rents until the loan is paid off.

A person when buying a house often gets a loan in the form of a mortgage from a building society and charges the house as security.

Legal mortgages of land

If Alan Brown wishes to borrow money from the Barchester Bank by giving the bank a legal mortgage of his (Alan's) private house he will normally create a charge by way of legal mortgage over the house. This is done by means of a short deed stating that a charge on the land is created.

An example of a suitable deed for Alan Brown to sign is given in the Law of Property Act 1925. The deed may be expanded to include other matters which the borrower agrees to do, e.g. to insure the property charged, but the basic provisions are set out below. (See Fig. 17.1.) Alan Brown will then sign the deed and his signature will be witnessed.

Comment. The mortgage deed usually provides that the money is to be repaid six months after the date of the deed. However, the borrower is not expected to repay the loan by this date. It is only put in so that the lender has all his remedies from that date since he can regard himself as being owed the principal sum.

The contract of loan (or in some cases the mortgage itself) will state the time within which the loan must be repaid, but if the borrower is in breach of that arrangement the charge is fully effective for use by the lender after six months.

The above form of charge could also be used by Alan Brown to give as security any leases which he had as where he was only renting business premises under a 25-year lease and wished to give a legal mortgage of that lease.

Equitable mortgages of land

An equitable mortgage can arise where the lender and borrower do not follow the procedures set out in the section above. Where a customer wants an overdraft from the bank he may just leave the title deeds of his house with the bank. This creates an equitable mortgage. It has already been noted at p. 169 that interests in land require a written memorandum under the Law of Property Act 1925. An equitable mortgage of land is an interest in land but a written memorandum is not required in this situation because the deposit of the title deeds amounts to an act of part performance making

---

THIS LEGAL CHARGE, is made the first day of June 1986 between Alan Brown of 14 River Street, Barchester of the one part and the Barchester Bank of the other part.

WHEREAS Alan Brown is seised of the hereditaments hereby charged and described in the Schedule hereto for an estate in fee simple in possession free from encumbrances;

NOW IN CONSIDERATION, of the sum of £50 000 now paid by Barchester Bank to Alan Brown (the receipt whereof Alan Brown doth hereby acknowledge) this Deed witnesseth as follows;

1. Alan Brown hereby covenants with Barchester Bank to pay on the first day of December next the sum of £50 000 with interest thereon at the rate of 14 per cent per annum.

2. Alan Brown as beneficial owner hereby charges by way of legal mortgage All and Singular the property mentioned in the Schedule hereto with the payment to Barchester Bank of the principal money and interest hereby covenanted to be paid by Alan Brown.

Fig. 17.1 A mortgage deed.

the security enforceable in equity.

The position of the lender is not so strong where the mortgage is by deposit of title deeds. The lender cannot sell the property but must first apply to the court for an order for sale or if he thinks he can get his money back from the rents, if any, which the property is producing he can ask the court for an order appointing a receiver.

The borrower's right of redemption

Lawyers call this the 'equity of redemption', and as we have seen the mortgage deed provides when the money is to be repaid. It is usual to say 'after six months' in order that the lender's range of remedies is available after that period. Originally at common law the land used as a security became the property of the lender as soon as the date for repayment had passed unless the loan had been repaid by then, even if only a small amount was still owed. However, equity allowed and still allows the borrower the right to redeem the land and free it from its position as a security even though the contractual date for repayment has passed and even though it has not yet arrived.

If a person wants to repay a mortgage early he will normally have to give notice, say six months, that he intends to do this or be prepared to pay interest for, say, six months ahead after he has repaid the loan, so that the lender can find another investment.

Thus if A repays his loan on 30 June (ahead of time) he will probably, according to the agreement, have given notice not later than 31 December in the previous year. If not he will, according to the agreement, pay off the capital plus the interest due to date on the 30 June but also interest until 31 December next.

A mortgage is also subject to the rules of restraint of trade (see also p. 175). It may also sometimes happen that a mortgage may prevent repayment for a reasonable time as regards the rule as to equity of redemption and yet redemption may be allowed before that time because while the mortgage term lasts unreasonable restrictions are placed on the freedom of a person to pursue his trade or profession.

Thus in *Esso Petroleum Co. Ltd* v *Harper's Garage (Stourport) Ltd* (1967) (see also p. 175) an agreement not to repay a mortgage on a garage for twenty-one years was probably not an unreasonable time in terms of the equity of redemption rule. However, during that time the garage owner had to sell only Esso fuels. It was

decided that the restraint on fuel sales was unreasonable and that the mortgage could be repaid earlier, leaving the owner of the garage free to sell other fuels.

A further right of the borrower on repayment of the loan is that on redemption the property must be returned to him free of any conditions which applied while the loan was unpaid and the mortgage was in existence.

Noakes and Co. Ltd v Rice (1902)

Mr Rice wanted to buy a public house. He borrowed the money from Noakes and Co. Ltd who were brewers and owners of the pub. The brewers lent Mr Rice the money but he had to agree to sell only Noakes' beer. After Mr Rice had repaid his mortgage Noakes said he must still sell only their beer. The court decided that he was not bound to do so. During the mortgage Mr Rice was bound to sell only Noakes' beer but not after repayment of the loan.

Comment. Much depends upon the bargaining power of the parties. In mortgage arrangements between large companies what is called a collateral advantage may be allowed to continue after repayment of the loan. For example, in *Kreglinger* v *New Patagonia Meat & Cold Storage Co. Ltd* (1914) Kreglinger had lent money to New Patagonia and New Patagonia gave Kreglinger a mortgage of its property. The mortgage said that for five years New Patagonia should not sell sheepskins to anyone without offering them first to Kreglinger. New Patagonia repaid the loan after two years but the House of Lords decided that New Patagonia was still bound to offer the sheepskins first to Kreglinger.

The possibility of using the rules of restraint of trade to attack restraints during the period of the mortgage is considered above. (See *Esso Petroleum Co. Ltd* v *Harper's Garage (Stourport) Ltd* (1967).)

Consumer Credit Act

A mortgage term relating, for example, to interest, must not be an extortionate credit bargain under the Consumer Credit Act 1974. If it is the court may change the mortgage arrangements to do justice between the parties. These provisions apply to any mortgage.

The other provisions of the 1974 Act relating to loans are directed at second mortgages and apply only to loans of £15 000 or under which are *not* made by building societies, local authorities, insurance companies or friendly societies.

Mortgages of personal property

Just as land can be used as a means of securing debts so also can personal goods. There are two main ways in which this can be done –

(a) *By mortgage*. In this case the person who borrows the money retains the business assets, e.g. office equipment, but transfers the ownership of them to the lender to secure the loan.

As we have seen, this raises a problem because, since the borrower keeps the asset, those who do business with him, perhaps on credit, may be misled as to his creditworthiness, the assets displayed are owned by a lender and not by the borrower who has them.

To stop this happening the security is void and the lender cannot sell the goods mortgaged unless a bill of sale is made out and registered in the Central Office of the Supreme Court under the Bills of Sale Acts 1878–82. These bills must be re-registered every five years if they are still in operation. This Register is open to public examination and therefore those who do business with the borrower can find out whether he has mortgaged his goods.

(b) *By pledge (or pawn)*. We have already considered what a pledge or pawn is. The distinction between this and the mortgage is that in a pledge or pawn the lender takes possession of the assets which are to be used to secure his loan, though the borrower retains ownership. There is therefore no danger that the borrower will obtain credit because the assets will not be with him but with the lender until the loan is repaid.

Mortgages of choses in action

As we have seen, personal property (i.e. property other than land) is divided into two kinds known as choses in possession and choses in action. Choses in possession are goods such as jewellery and furniture which are tangible things and *can be physically used and enjoyed* by their owner. Choses in action are intangible forms of property which are *not really capable of physical use or enjoyment*. Their owner is normally compelled to bring an action at law if he wishes to enforce his rights over property of this sort. A contrast is provided by a fire

extinguisher and a fire insurance policy. The extinguisher is a *chose in possession*. If you had a fire *you could use the extinguisher* to put it out – the insurance policy would not be much use for this. However, it is a valuable piece of property because although, *as a chose in action, it has no physical use* it gives a right to require the insurance company to make good any loss caused by the fire. Other examples of choses in action are debts, patents, copyrights, trade marks, shares, negotiable instruments such as cheques, and the goodwill of a business.

It is possible to use a chose in action as security for a loan and lenders frequently take life assurance policies as security. A bank would do this in the case of an overdraft. However, shares in companies are perhaps the commonest chose in action to be used as security.

Shares can be made subject to a legal mortgage but the shares must actually be transferred to the lender and his name is in fact entered on the company's share register. An agreement is made out in which the lender agrees to retransfer the shares to the borrower when the loan is repaid.

You can also have an equitable mortgage of company shares and this is in fact often the method used. The share certificate is deposited with the lender, together with a blank transfer. This means that it is signed by the registered holder, i.e. the borrower, but the name of the person to whom the shares are to be transferred is left blank. The shares are not actually transferred, but the agreement which accompanies the loan allows the lender to sell the shares by completing the form of transfer and registering himself or someone else as the legal owner if the borrower fails to repay the loan. The shares can then be sold and transferred as required.

Questions/activities

1. Distinguish between a pledge and a lien.

2. Give a short account of ways in which mortgages of real and personal property may be created. Explain what is meant by the 'equity of redemption'.

3. Give three examples of the different ways in which goods may be used as a security for a loan.

4. Distinguish between a general and a particular lien. What sort of a lien does an accountant have? What advantage is it for an accountant to have such a lien? What is the lien over? State with reasons whether or not

it is available against a company client's books and papers.

5. Discuss the importance in securities transactions of the Bills of Sale Acts.

6. When is it important for a person giving a guarantee to be advised by an independent solicitor?

Employing labour

In this chapter we are concerned with employment law. This is based upon and deals with the relationship of employer and employee. Employment law is made up of common law and, more and more these days, of statute law passed by Parliament.

Employer and employee

Generally

It is important to know how this relationship comes into being and to distinguish it from the relationship between a person who buys the services of someone who is self-employed (often called an independent contractor).

Usually it is not difficult to decide whether A is employed by B so that the relationship of employee and employer exist between them. If A is an employee he or she will have been *selected* by B; A will usually work *full-time* for B under a degree of *supervision* for a *wage or salary*.

Of course A may still be an employee even though working *part-time*. However, a part-timer will be unable to claim the protection of employment legislation, e.g. in regard to unfair dismissal, unless the working hours are at least sixteen per week. After five years' employment this figure is reduced to eight hours.

Also, if A is an employee, B will deduct *income tax* from A's pay (if it exceeds A's allowances) under PAYE (pay as you earn) arrangements. B will also make *social security contributions* for A and will often provide a *pension scheme* which A can join. In addition, although a contract of employment (or service) need not be in writing, if A is an employee, then B must, under the Employment Protection (Consolidation) Act 1978, give A within thirteen weeks after the beginning of the employment *written particulars* of the major terms of the contract. (See further p. 271.)

The control test

In earlier times the above tests would not all have been available, particularly the deduction of income tax which, after some earlier experiments beginning in 1799, was finally brought in for good in 1842. Social security legislation and the modern deductions from pay, together with contributions from the employer, have only come in on the present scale since the Second World War.

In times past, therefore, a person, whether employed or self-employed, would simply receive money from the employer and it was less easy to distinguish one from the other.

There was, even so, a need to do so, because an employer was liable to pay damages to those injured by his employee if those injuries took place during the course of the employee's work. This is called an employer's vicarious liability and it is dealt with in greater detail later in this chapter.

A person was not vicariously liable for injury caused to others by a self-employed (or independent) contractor who was doing work for him. Obviously, then it was necessary to find a test to decide whether A was, or was not, an employee of B.

The earliest test was called 'the control test'. Since it is not normally necessary to use this test today in order to decide whether A is the employee of B because we have much more evidence of the relationship now, why should we bother with it?

The answer is that it is sometimes necessary to decide whether B, who is truly employed by A, has been temporarily transferred to another person, C, so that C (the temporary employer) and not A (the general employer) is liable vicariously for the injuries caused to a person or persons by B.

Mersey Docks and Harbour Board v Coggins & Griffiths (Liverpool) Ltd (1946)

The Board owned and hired out mobile cranes driven by skilled operators who were employees of the Board. Coggins & Griffiths, who were stevedores, hired one of the Board's cranes and an operator, Mr Newell, to unload a ship.

In the course of unloading the ship a person was injured because of Mr Newell's negligence and the court had to decide whether the Board or Coggins & Griffiths were vicariously liable along with Mr Newell for the latter's negligence. The matter was one of control because the Board was quite clearly the general employer. Actually, the answers given by Mr Newell to questions put to him by counsel in court were highly important. At one point he said: 'I take no orders from anybody'. Since he was not truly employed by Coggins & Griffiths *and* since he did not, so he said, take orders from them, there was no way in which he could be regarded as under their control. Therefore, his true employers, the Board, were vicariously liable for Mr Newell's negligence.

Comment. It is *presumed* in these cases that the general employer continues to be liable and it is up to him to satisfy the court that control has passed to a temporary employer. This is a very difficult thing to do and the temporary employer will not be liable very often, though it is a possibility.

The organization test

Later on a test called the 'organization or integration' test was brought in because the control test was not really suitable for employees who were highly skilled.

There was a possibility that even though there was a lot of general evidence of employment, such as PAYE deductions from pay, an employer would not be vicariously liable for the acts of a highly skilled employee, such as a doctor, or, really, anyone qualified and experienced and acting in a professional field, if that employer could convince the court in his defence that he did not have the necessary control of the skilled person.

This has not been possible because of the organization test put forward by Lord Denning in *Stevenson, Jordan & Harrison Ltd* v *Macdonald & Evans Ltd* (1952). He decided in that case, in effect, that an employee is a person who is integrated with others in the workplace or business, even though the employer does not have a detailed control of what he does.

Independent contractors – self-employment

The main feature here is the absence of control or meaningful supervision which can be exercised by those who buy the services of an independent contractor by means of what is called a *contract for services*.

Particular cases examined

In the majority of cases there is no difficulty in deciding whether a person is employed or self-employed. For example, factory employees, office clerical staff, and agricultural workers are clearly employees. Garage proprietors, house-builders, and dry cleaners are contractors independent of the members of the public who use them.

As we have seen, a particularly compelling example comes from a comparison between a chauffeur and a person who owns and drives his own taxi. The chauffeur is an employee; the taxi-driver is an independent contractor. Suppose, then, that Fred is employed as my chauffeur: I would have enough control over him to ask him to drive more slowly in a built-up area. In the case of the taxi-driver, I would not have (or even feel I had) the necessary control to insist on a change of speed.

Contract of service or for services – why distinguish?

First of all, because of the existence of *vicarious liability*, an employer is liable, for example, for damage caused to another by his employee's negligent acts while that employee is acting in the course of his employment, that is, doing his job, but not otherwise. (See further p. 286.)

Secondly, the *rights and remedies provided by*

employment legislation, such as the Employment Protection (Consolidation) Act 1978, are available to an employee, but not to the self-employed. We shall be looking at these rights and remedies more closely later in this chapter.

The contract of employment

Generally

The ordinary principles of the law of contract apply. So in a contract of employment there must be an offer and an acceptance, which is in effect, the agreement. There must also be an intention to create legal relations, consideration, and capacity, together with proper consent by the parties, that is, no mistake, misrepresentation, duress or undue influence. In addition, the contract must not be illegal.

However, since we have already looked at these general principles of the law of contract, it is only necessary to highlight certain matters which are of importance in the context of employment law.

Written particulars

A contract of employment does not require any written formalities and can be made orally. However, certain written particulars of it are required to be given to the employee by the Employment Protection (Consolidation) Act 1978. (See p. 247.) These particulars must be given to the employee not later than 13 weeks after the employment started.

Contents – generally

The statement must contain the following information –

(1) *The names of the employer and the employee.* A letter of engagement will usually be sent to the employee at his address. This will identify him and the letter-heading will identify the employer.

(2) *The date when the employment began.* This is important if it becomes necessary to decide what period of notice is to be given. The 1978 Act provides for certain minimum periods of notice to be given by employers. For example, they must give one week's notice after four weeks' service, two weeks' after two years' service, and so on up to twelve weeks after twelve years' service. (See further p. 314.) The date when the

job began obviously settles this point.

In addition, the length of the employment affects the period necessary to make certain claims. For example, redundancy claims require two years' continuous service *since the age of eighteen.* Unfair dismissal requires two years' of continuous service, usually with a particular employer (but see below), regardless of the age at which the service began, unless the dismissal is automatically unfair, as where it was because the employee was (or proposed to become) a member of a trade union.

(3) *Whether the employment counts as a period of continuous employment with a previous employment, and the date of commencement of the previous employment where this is so.* This is important because the rights of an employee to complain of unfair dismissal or to claim a redundancy payment, depend upon whether that employee has served the necessary period of continuous employment. This may be with one employer, but if it is with more than one employer, it must be possible to regard the employments with the various employers as continuous. Situations of continuous employment, despite a change of employer, taken from the Employment Protection (Consolidation) Act 1978, are –

(*a*) a transfer between associated employers. For example, if A is employed by B Ltd and is transferred to work for C Ltd, and B Ltd and C Ltd are subsidiaries of X PLC, then A's employment with B Ltd and C Ltd is regarded as continuous;

(*b*) a sale of the business in which the employee was employed to another person.

There are other provisions which now relate to the situation in (*b*) above and protect employees from a break in continuous employment on a change of employer. The Transfer of Undertakings (Protection of Employment) Regulations 1981 apply. The main provisions of the regulations in regard to business transfers are that employees who are employed by the old employer 'immediately before' the transfer automatically become the employees of the new employer. The new employer takes over the employment protection liabilities of the old employer but not, according to *Angus Jowett & Co.* v *NUTWG* (1985), liability to pay a protective award. A protective award is payable when an employer fails to consult with a recognized trade union when he is intending to make the workforce or some part of it redundant. (See further p. 313.) So, if A gives notice of future redundancy to his employees without proper consultation with their union, and they are still working for him when he sells the business to B, then A and not B is liable to pay the protective award.

(c) *A change in the partners where a person is employed by a partnership.* A partnership is not a separate person at law as a company is. Employees of a partnership are employed by the partners as people. So, if A works for a partnership of C and D, and D retires and is replaced by E, then A's employers have changed but his employment with C and D and C and E is regarded as continuous. Therefore, if C and E unfairly dismiss A he can make up his two years' continuous service to be able to claim by adding together his service with C and D and C and E in order to make a claim against C and E.

(d) *A succession of contracts between the same parties are regarded as continuous.* So, if A works for B as a clerk and is then promoted to a manager under a new contract, the two contract periods can be added together to make a period of continuous employment.

Contents - terms of the employment

The written particulars then go on to set out the terms of the employment. The terms which must be given are –

(1) the scale or rate of pay and the method of calculating pay where the employee is paid by commission or bonus;

(2) when the payment is made – that is weekly or monthly, and the day or date of payment;

(3) hours to be worked, e.g. 'The normal working hours are ...'. Compulsory overtime, if any, should be recorded to avoid disputes with employees who may sometimes not want to work it;

(4) holiday entitlement and provisions relating to holiday pay if the employee leaves in a particular year without taking holiday. If holiday entitlement is set out clearly it can help to avoid disputes regarding a requirement to work in what is a normal holiday period in the area or during the school holidays;

(5) sick pay and injury arrangements;

(6) whether or not there is a pension scheme;

(7) the length of notice which the employee must give and the length of notice the employee is entitled to receive. We have already said that there are minimum periods of notice required to end contracts of employment and full details of these appear on p. 314. The contract can, of course, provide for a longer period of notice but not a shorter one;

(8) the job title, which is important in dealing with redundancy cases where to justify that a dismissal is because of redundancy and is not an unfair dismissal, the employer may show that there has been a reduction in 'work of a particular type'. The job title indicates what type of work the employee does. In equal pay claims also, it may show that a man or woman is employed on 'like work'.

Contents - disciplinary rules and grievances

Disciplinary procedures deal, for example, with the number of warnings, oral or written, which will be given before suspension or dismissal. *Grievance procedures* relate to complaints in regard to any aspect of the employment with which the employee is not satisfied. The employee should be told who to complain to and any right of appeal, as it were, beyond that to, say, a more senior manager. This procedure is to be available if the employee is not satisfied with the *disciplinary decision* or for some *other grievance.*

The written particulars need not actually contain the disciplinary and grievance procedures. They can be (and often are) in a separate booklet. If so, the written particulars should refer to that booklet and the employee must have access to a copy of it.

Changes in the terms of the contract. If the terms of the contract are changed then, because of the provisions of the Employment Protection (Consolidation) Act 1978, the employee must be told *in writing* within one month of the change, either by a statement which is given to the employee to keep, or a reasonably obvious notice on, say, a well-sited notice board.

If the particulars which the employee received when he started the job referred to a document such as a handbook in which future changes in the terms of the employment were to be recorded, an employer, who includes the changes in that document within one month of the date when they were made need not give a written notice to each employee.

If the terms of the employment can be changed by a collective agreement with a trade union, the particulars should say so because if this is the case, the terms of the job can be changed *without* the employees' consent. The results of the employer's negotiations with the unions are incorporated into the contracts of the employees. In other cases, the terms of the employment cannot be changed unless the employee has agreed and if the employer introduces a variation in the contract as by, say, lowering pay, then the employer is in breach of the contract.

Failure to comply with the obligation to give written particulars

The 1978 Act provides that if an employer fails to give written particulars at the start of the employment, or fails to notify changes in the terms of the contract, the employee can go to an industrial tribunal. If a statement is given but the employee thinks it is not complete, either the employee or the employer can go to an industrial tribunal to see which of them is right.

The tribunal may make a declaration that the employee has a right to a statement and also say what should be in it. The statement as approved by the tribunal is then assumed in law to have been given by the employer to the employee and forms the basis of the contract of employment. Failure to give written particulars does not make the contract of employment unenforceable by the parties.

Health and safety

The Health and Safety at Work Act 1974 states that an employer must prepare, and revise when necessary, a statement of his policy in regard to the health and safety at work of his employees. (See further p. 291.) This must be contained in a separate document but it is often given out with the written particulars which we are now looking at. Employers with fewer than five employees are not required to give this statement.

Exemptions from the written particulars requirements

There are some situations under the 1978 Act where an employer does not have to give the written particulars. Those which may be found in the average business are –

(1) An employee who leaves his job and comes back within six months on the same terms and conditions need not be given a statement when he comes back if he had one when he was first employed.

(2) Part-time workers who work less than sixteen hours each week need not be given written particulars. However, when they have been employed for five years they must be given the written particulars unless they are then working less than eight hours a week.

(3) Employees with fully written contracts containing all the necessary terms need not be given also the written particulars.

(4) Written particulars need not be given to an employee whose job is wholly or mainly outside Great Britain.

(5) There is no need for written particulars where the employee is the husband or wife of the employer.

(6) It is not necessary to give an employee written particulars if he is employed for a specific job, e.g. to clear a backlog of office work, which is not expected to last more than three months. If it does last for more than three months the worker is entitled to written particulars.

An example of a written statement published by HMSO on behalf of the Department of Employment appears on p. 274. (Fig. 18.1.) An interpretation of that statement in terms of an actual employment appears at p. 276. (Fig. 18.2.)

Rights and duties of the parties to the contract

The duties of an employer and an employee come from common law and Acts of Parliament. They will be dealt with under the headings which follow.

Duties of an employer

To provide remuneration

In business organizations the duty of the employer to pay his employees and the rate or amount of pay is decided as follows –

(1) by the contract of employment; or

(2) by the terms of what is called a collective agreement made between a trade union and the employer. The terms of this agreement, including the part on pay, are then assumed to be part of the individual contracts of employment of the members.

The pay which the worker is to get should nearly always be definite because it is included in the written particulars which we have just dealt with and also because the Employment Protection (Consolidation)

Example of a written statement

The following gives an example of a possible form of a written statement of main terms and conditions of employment under the Employment Protection (Consolidation) Act 1978.

Part I of this statement sets out particulars of the terms and conditions which I (*name of employer*) am employing you (*name of employee*) on (*date on which statement is issued*).

Part II of this statement sets out information on disciplinary rules, whom you should contact if you wish to appeal against a disciplinary decision or to take up a grievance, and the subsequent steps to be followed in the disciplinary and grievance procedures.

Your employment with me began on (*date*) and, by virtue of paragraph 17 or 18 of Schedule 13 to the above Act or the Transfer of Undertakings (Protection of Employment) Regulations 1981, your previous employment with (*name of previous employer or employers*) counts as part of your continuous period of employment which therefore began on (*date continuous period of employment commenced*).

or

Your employment with me began on (*date*). Your employment with your previous employer does not count as part of your continuous period of employment.

Part I

(1) You are employed as a (*insert job title*).

(2) Pay will be (*insert scale or rate of remuneration, or the method of calculating remuneration and intervals at which remuneration is to be paid*).

(3) Hours of work are (*give normal hours and any other related terms and conditions*).

(4) Holidays and holiday pay (*give sufficient details to enable entitlement, including accrued holiday pay, to be precisely calculated*).

(5) Incapacity for work (*state terms and conditions relating to sickness or injury and sick pay – if none, say so*).

(6) Pensions and pension schemes (*state terms and conditions or refer to relevant handbook or other document which is reasonably accessible to the employee – if none, say so*).

(7) Amount of notice of termination to be given by:

(*a*) the employer is (*insert period*)

(*b*) the employee is (*insert period*).

Fixed-term contracts should state date of expiry instead.

Part II

(1) The disciplinary rules which apply to you in your employment are (*explain them*).

or

The disciplinary rules which apply to you in your employment can be found in (*reference should be made to a handbook or other document which is given to the employee with the main written statement and additional note, or, if that is not practicable, can be read by the employee in a place to which access can be gained without difficulty*).

(2) If you are dissatisfied with any disciplinary decision which affects you, you should appeal in the first instance to (*name of the employee to whom the appeal should be made or the position held, for example supervisor*).

(3) You should make your appeal by (*explain how appeals should be made*).

or

The way in which appeals should be made is explained in (*refer to an accompanying handbook or a document which is reasonably accessible to the employee*).

(4) If you have a grievance about your employment you should apply in the first instance to (*give the name of the employee with whom the grievance should be raised or the position held, for example personnel officer*).

(5) You should explain your grievance by (*explain how grievances are to be raised*).

or

The way in which grievances should be raised is explained in (*refer again to an accompanying handbook or, if necessary, a document which is reasonably accessible to the employee*).

(6) Subsequent steps in the firm's disciplinary and grievance procedures are (*explain them*).

or

Details of the firm's disciplinary and grievance procedures are set out in (*refer to an accompanying handbook or, if necessary, another document which is reasonably accessible to the employee*).

Note: These separate stages can of course be telescoped where, for example, the same person is the first to be approached for appeals against disciplinary decisions and for grievances, or where the method of application for both is the same.

(7) A contracting-out certificate under the Social Security Pensions Act 1975 is/is not* in force for the employment in respect of which this written statement is being issued.

*Delete as appropriate.

Fig. 18.1 An example of a written statement.

Act 1978 requires itemized pay statements. (See further p. 280.)

If there is no provision for payment in the contract – which is highly unlikely – then if the worker sued for payment the court would fix a fair rate of pay for the job by taking evidence as to what rates of pay were usual in the type of work being done.

To give holidays and holiday pay

The rights and duties of the parties here depend upon what the contract of employment says or what the terms of a collective agreement with the union are. Again, there should be no doubt about holidays and holiday pay because the 1978 Act states that this information is to be given to the employee in the written particulars.

To provide sick pay

Entitlement to sick pay must be dealt with by the written particulars. An employer has *no general duty to provide sick pay from his own funds*. There is a *statutory duty* under the 1978 Act to pay an employee who goes sick during the statutory period of notice and is not able to work out all or part of the notice.

Employers are required to provide what is called *statutory sick pay* on behalf of the government. The law is to be found, in the main, in the Social Security and Housing Benefit Act 1982 and the Social Security Act 1985. It is not necessary in a book of this nature to go into details in regard to the statutory sick pay scheme but the main principles are that when an employee falls sick he or she gets a weekly amount from the employer and not from the Department of Health and Social Security. The employer recovers the amount paid as statutory sick pay from his overall liability for employers' National Insurance contributions.

This goes on for twenty-eight weeks and since the vast majority of employees are not sick for anything like as long as this, employee sickness benefit is, in effect, now paid by the employer. It is not possible to avoid the statutory sick pay provisions and any clause in a contract of employment which sets out to do this is void.

To provide pay during suspension

(1) *On medical grounds.* Under the Employment Protection (Consolidation) Act 1978 an employee who has had at least four weeks' continuous service with his employer and who is suspended from work, for example, under the Health and Safety at Work Act 1974, normally on the advice of an Employment Medical Advisor, not because he is ill but because he might become ill if he continues at work, since he is currently engaged on an industrial process which involves a potential hazard to his health – is entitled to be paid his normal wages while he is suspended for up to twenty-six weeks. This could occur, for example, where there was a leak of radioactivity at the workplace.

An employee may complain to an industrial tribunal under the 1978 Act if his employer has not paid him what he is entitled to during a period of suspension and the tribunal may order the employer to pay the employee the money which he should have had.

(2) *On disciplinary grounds.* Suppose an employee takes a day off without permission, in order to go to a football match. His employer decides to suspend him for a further day without pay: is this legal? Well, there is no implied right to suspend an employee for disciplinary reasons without pay. In practice, if the employer wants a power to suspend it must be made an express term of the contract which is agreed to by the employee and be in the written particulars of the job. If so, it will be justified and the employee will have to accept it.

Maternity provision

(1) *For ante-natal care.* Under the Employment Protection (Consolidation) Act 1978, as amended by the Employment Act 1980, a pregnant employee who has, on her doctor's advice, made an appointment to get ante-natal care must have time off to keep it and she must also be paid. The employer can ask for proof of the appointment in the form, for example, of an appointment card. The employer who does not give the employee these rights can be taken to a tribunal by the employee but this must normally be during the three

To Ms Jane Doe,
350, Elton Road,
Manchester M62 10AS

The following particulars are given to you pursuant to the Employment Protection (Consolidation) Act 1978

1. The parties are as follows:

Name and address of Employer:

Michael Snooks Ltd,
520 London Square
Manchester M42 145A

Name and address of employee:

Jane Doe
350, Elton Road
Manchester M62 10AS

2. The date when your employment began was: 2 February 1987

Your employment with John Bloggs Ltd from whom Michael Snooks Ltd purchased the business and which began on 3 February 1986 counts as part of your period of continuous employment with Michael Snooks Ltd. No employment with a previous employer counts as part of your period of continuous employment.

3. The following are the particulars of the terms of your employment

as at ___9 March 1987___

(a) You are employed at _520 London Square, Manchester M62 145A_

as _a Shorthand - Typist_

(b) The rate of your remuneration is _£150_ per _week_

(c) Your remuneration is paid at weekly intervals

(d) Your normal working hours are from _9.30a.m_ to _5p.m_

Mondays to Fridays inclusive

(e) (i) You are entitled to ___two weeks___ holiday with pay after _one_ completed year of service and to _three weeks_ holiday with pay every year after _two_ completed years of service.

These holidays are to be taken at a time convenient to the employer between _1st May_ and _30 October_ in each year. If an employee's employment terminates before all holiday accrued due has been taken, the employee is entitled to payment in lieu thereof on leaving the said

Fig. 18.2 Contract of employment.

employment. You are also entitled to the customary holidays with pay, i.e. New Year's Day, Good Friday, Easter Monday, May Day, Spring Bank Holiday, Late Summer Bank Holiday, Christmas Day and Boxing Day.

(ii) Regulations as to payment while absent during sickness or injury are available for inspection during normal working hours

in the office of the Secretary/PA to the Personnel Manager

(iii) There is no pension shceme applicable to you.

(f)   The length of notice which you are obliged to give to end your contract of employment is _One week_ and the length of notice you are entitled to receive unless your conduct is such that you may be summarily dismissed is as follows:—

(i) One week if your period of continuous employment is less than two years.

(ii) One week's notice for each year of continuous employment if your period of continuous employment is two years or more but less than twelve years: and

(iii) Twelve weeks if your period of continuous employment is twelve years or more.

(g)   *NOTE*

If you are not satisfied with any disciplinary decision relating to you or seek redress of any grievance relating to your employment you can apply in the first place to _the person in charge of the typing pool_

Details of the procedure available and to be followed in connection with your employment are _posted in the staff room_

Dated _ninth_ day of _March_ 19_87_

Signed

Sarah Snooks

Company Secretary

Comment

The employee should be required to sign the employer's copy in the following way

'I have received and read a copy of the above particulars which are correct in all respects.'

Signed _Jane Doe_

Date _9 March 1987_

months following the employer's refusal. Compensation may be given to the employee. Part-time employees are entitled to this time off and it does not make any difference how many hours they work each week.

(2) *For statutory maternity pay.* The Social Security Act 1986 made major alterations to the maternity payments scheme. Prior to the Act a woman who qualified received maternity pay from which was deducted the state maternity allowance. Maternity pay was then recouped by the employer from the Maternity Pay Fund..

(a) *As regards the amount and time for which it is paid*, under the Social Security Act of 1986 statutory maternity pay (SMP) is payable through the employer who recoups it from National Insurance contributions (as for statutory sick pay). To qualify the woman must have worked for her present employer for at least six months. If so, she is entitled to a payment at the lowest rate of statutory sick pay (at present £32.85 per week) for 18 weeks. Women who have been with the employer for two years or more will receive SMP of 90 per cent of earnings for the first six weeks of the maternity leave. Thirteen weeks of the leave must be taken to cover the period of six weeks before the baby is due and seven weeks after it is born. Women may choose when to take the other five weeks.

(b) *As regards time limits*, if an employer fails to make a payment, the employee can complain to a tribunal, normally within three months of the last day on which she was entitled to that pay. The tribunal can order the employer to pay what is due. If he will not, or cannot (as where he is insolvent), the employee may apply to the Department of Employment for payment. If the Department of Employment makes the payment it may recover from the employer as by proving in the insolvency.

(3) *The right to return to work.* The employee must comply with certain formalities in order that she may have the right to return to work. These are that she must give her employer at least twenty-one days written notice before her absence begins –

(a) giving the reason why she will be absent and the expected week of confinement; and

(b) of her intention to return to work if this is what she is going to do.

The employer may require the employee to produce a medical certificate giving the expected date of confinement.

Although a woman gives notice of her intention to return to work she is not forced to do so. This leaves the employer in a state of some uncertainty. The 1978 Act, as amended by the Employment Act 1980, allows the employer to check what the situation is. The employer is allowed to make a request for information from the employee. The employer cannot do this until seven weeks have passed from the beginning of the week of confinement. The employer's request must be in writing and will ask the employee to confirm her intention to return.

An employee intending to return must confirm the fact in writing within fourteen days of receiving the request or as soon as reasonably practicable, otherwise the right to return is lost. However, confirmation does not oblige the employee to return.

In order actually to get back to work, the woman must give written notice to the employer at least twenty-one days before the notified date of return, that date being not later than twenty-nine weeks after the beginning of the week in which the birth occurred.

The return to work can be postponed by either the employer or the employee by up to four weeks from the date notified. The employer can postpone it for any reason so long as those reasons are notified to the employee. The employee can only postpone if she is ill and cannot work and has a medical certificate to that effect.

If there is, for example, industrial action, so that the woman cannot return on the date notified, then she may return when the interruption is over or as soon as is reasonably practicable afterwards.

If the employee carries out all the formalities for return to work but the employer refuses to allow her to return, she will be regarded as dismissed and the employer will have to show that this was not unfair dismissal. (See further p. 304.)

If, because of a reorganization in the firm during the woman's absence, her job is no longer available, the employer must offer her suitable alternative employment. If there is such employment and it is not offered to her she can claim unfair dismissal. If no such work is available she is redundant and can claim a redundancy payment. If she refuses to take suitable alternative work she will have no claim on the employer.

Small employers are specially protected because they cannot easily cope with a long absence by an employee. So, if there are not more than five employees counted together with those of an 'associated employer' (e.g. in a holding and subsidiary company situation you would have to count the employees in the holding company together with those of the subsidiary company in deciding whether the figure was five or less), at the time when the employee left, and it is not reasonably practicable for the employer to take the employee back or to offer alternative work, then the employer is not liable if he does not take the employee back.

To make payments during lay-off – guarantee payments

(1) *Lay-off.* To avoid difficulty the right of the employer to lay off employees without pay because of lack of work should be made an express term of the contract of employment. However, even if the employer has given himself that right in the contract he must still comply with the provisions of the 1978 Act in the matter and cannot have clauses in the contract which are worse for the employee than the basic statutory rights which provide for guarantee payments.

(2) *Guarantee payments.* The 1978 Act provides that employees with four weeks or more of continuous service are entitled to a guarantee payment up to a maximum sum, which is currently £10.90 per day, if they are not provided with work on a normal working day. This does not apply if the failure of the employer to provide work is because of industrial action or if the employee has been offered suitable alternative work but has refused it.

An employee can only receive a payment for five workless days during any period of three months. The effect of this is that in order to get payment for a day of lay-off the three months before that day of lay-off must be looked at to see whether the employee has already received the maximum five days' guarantee pay. If the lay-off was, for example, on 20 June and the worker had been paid for lay-offs on 5 June, 27 May, 21 May, 4 April, and 2 April, he would not be entitled to a payment but he would for a lay-off on 3 July.

An employee can go to a tribunal if the employer fails to pay all or part of a guarantee payment which the employee should have had. The tribunal can order the employer to pay it. The employee must apply to the tribunal within three months of the day on which the payment should have been made.

To pay during statutory time off

The 1978 Act gives employees certain rights to time off work (see also p. 283). In *two* cases the employee is also entitled to be paid during the time off. These situations are dealt with here as part of the law relating to the right to be paid. They are –

(1) *Time off for carrying out union duties.* An employer must allow an employee, who is an official of an independent trade union which is recognized by the employer, to take time off during working hours to carry out the duties of a trade union official if those duties are concerned with industrial relations between the employer and his employees. For these purposes an independent trade union is a union which is not dominated or controlled by the employer and is not liable to interference by the employer as some staff associations may be.

Time off must also be given for union officials to take training in aspects of industrial relations which are relevant to the carrying out of their duties and in addition are approved by the Trades Union Congress or by the independent union of which the employee is an official. The employee is entitled to be paid his normal hourly rate.

If there is a breach by the employer of this duty the employee may complain to a tribunal which may declare the employee's rights in its order, so that the employer may carry them out, and may also award money compensation.

(2) *Redundant employees.* An employee who has been continuously employed by his employer for at least two years and who is given notice of dismissal because of redundancy has a right before the period of his notice expires to reasonable time off during working hours so that he can look for another job or make arrangements for training for future employment.

While absent the employee is entitled to be paid but not more than two-fifths of a week's pay in respect of the whole period of notice. If an employer is in breach of the above provisions, the employee can complain to a tribunal within three months but the tribunal's compensation is limited to two-fifths of a week's pay.

Itemized pay statements

Under the Employment Protection (Consolidation) Act 1978 an employer must give his employees an itemized pay statement. Before these provisions came into force an employer could simply state the amount of take-home pay with no details of how it had been arrived at.

Under the Act the employee must receive a statement at the time of or before receiving his pay, showing gross pay and take-home pay and the variable deductions, e.g. income tax, which make up the difference between the two figures. Details of how it is paid must also be given, e.g. is it contained in the pay packet or has it been credited to a bank account?

Fixed deductions, e.g. savings, need not be itemized every pay day. If the employer gives the employee a separate statement setting out the fixed deductions he may simply show a lump sum representing these in the weekly/monthly pay statement. This fixed deduction statement must be updated in writing if it is changed and in any case it must be re-issued every twelve months.

If the employer does not comply with the pay statement requirements the employee can complain to a tribunal which will make a declaration of the law

that a statement should have been given and as to what it should have included. The employer must comply with this declaration. In addition, the tribunal may order the employer to give back to the employee any deductions which were made from the employee's pay and which were not notified to him during the thirteen weeks before the date of the application by the employee to the tribunal.

Method of payment and deductions from pay

Under the Wages Act 1986 employees no longer have a right to be paid in cash. The Truck Acts 1831–1940, which used to give this right, were repealed by the 1986 Act. Payment may still, of course, be made in cash, but an employer can if he wishes pay the employee, for example, by cheque or by crediting the employee's bank account.

Deductions from pay are unlawful unless they are:

(1) authorized by Act of Parliament, such as income tax and National Insurance deductions; or

(2) contained in a written contract of employment; in these cases deductions from the wages of workers in the retail trade, e.g. petrol station cashiers, for stock and cash shortages are limited to 10 per cent of the gross wages.

These provisions are enforceable by the employee against the employer in industrial tribunals.

Equal pay

The Equal Pay Act 1970 (EPA) (as amended by the Sex Discrimination Act 1975 (SDA) and the Equal Pay (Amendment) Regulations 1983), implies a term called an equality clause into contracts of service. This clause means that a man or a woman must be given contractual terms not less favourable than those given to an employee of the opposite sex when they are each employed –

(1) *on like work*, in the same employment; or

(2) *on work rated as equivalent* in the same employment, e.g. by a job evaluation scheme; or

(3) *on work which is in terms of demands made on the worker*, under such headings as effort, skill and decision making *of equal value* to that of a worker in the same employment.

As regards the relationship between the EPA and the SDA, the EPA covers not only matters concerning wages and salaries, but also other terms in the contract of service, such as sick pay, holiday pay and unequal working hours. Other forms of sex discrimination in employment, such as discrimination in recruitment techniques, are covered by the SDA (see further p. 300).

Application of the Equal Pay Act. The Act applies to all forms of full and part-time work. There are no exemptions for small firms or in respect of people who have only recently taken up the employment, though the Act does not apply, for example, to those who do their work wholly outside Great Britain.

The Act applies to discrimination against men but in practice claims are normally made by women. We shall from now on consider the law on the basis of a claim by a woman.

Main provisions of the Equal Pay Act. These are as follows –

(1) *If a woman is engaged in the same or broadly similar work as a man* and both work for the same or an associated employer (see below), the woman is entitled to the same rate of pay and other terms of employment as the man.

The comparison can be made with a previous holder of the same job. In *Macarthys* v *Smith* (1980) the Employment Appeal Tribunal decided that Mrs Smith, a stockroom manageress, was entitled to pay which was equal to that of a previous manager of the stockroom, a Mr McCullough. However, the EAT did say that tribunals must be cautious in making such comparisons unless the interval between the two employments is reasonably short and there have not been changes in economic circumstances.

The term 'broadly similar work' means that although there may be some differences between the work of the man and the woman, these are not of sufficient practical importance to give rise to what the EPA calls a 'material difference'.

Capper Pass v Lawton (1976)

A female cook who worked a 40-hour week preparing lunches for the directors of Capper was paid a lower rate than two male assistant chefs who worked a 45-hour week preparing some 350 meals a day in Capper's works canteen. The female cook claimed that by reason of the EPA (as amended) she should be paid at the same rate as the assistant chefs since she was employed on work of a broadly similar nature.

It was held by the EAT that if the work done by a female applicant was of a broadly similar nature to that done by a male colleague it should be regarded as being like work for the purposes of the EPA unless there were some practical differences of detail between the two types of job. In this case the EAT decided that the work done by the female cook was broadly similar to the work of the assistant chefs and that the differences of detail were not of practical importance in relation to the terms and conditions of employment. Therefore the female cook was entitled to be paid at the same rate as her male colleagues.

Comment. An interesting contrast is provided by *Navy, Army and Airforce Institutes* v *Varley* (1977). Miss Varley worked as a Grade E clerical worker in the accounts office of NAAFI in Nottingham. NAAFI conceded that her work was like that of a Grade E male clerical worker employed in NAAFI's London office. However, the Grade E workers in Nottingham worked a 37-hour week, while the male Grade E clerical workers in the London office worked a 36½-hour week. Miss Varley applied to an industrial tribunal under the EPA for a declaration that she was less favourably treated as regards hours worked than the male clerical workers in London and that her contract term as to hours should be altered so as to reduce it to 36½ hours a week. The industrial tribunal granted that declaration but NAAFI appealed to the EAT which held that the variation in hours was genuinely due to a material difference other than the difference of sex. It was due to a real difference in that the male employees worked in London where there was a custom to work shorter hours. Accordingly, NAAFI's appeal was allowed and Miss Varley was held not to be entitled to the declaration. The judge said that the variation between her contract and the men's contracts was due really to the fact that she worked in Nottingham and they worked in London.

Another common example of a sensible material difference occurs where, for example, employee A is a new entrant of twenty-one and employee B is a long-serving employee of fifty, and there is a system of service increments, then it is reasonable to pay B more than A though both are employed on like work. Obviously, however, it is not enough to say that because at the present time men are on average paid more than women this is a material difference justifying paying a woman less in a particular job. This was decided in *Clay Cross*

(*Quarry Services*) *Ltd* v *Fletcher* (1979).

(2) *If the job which one woman does has been given the same value as a man's job under a job evaluation scheme*, then the woman is entitled to the same rate of pay and other terms of employment as a man.

(3) *Equal value.* If the job which a woman does is in terms of the demands made upon her, for instance under such headings as effort, skill and decision-making, is of equal value to that of a man in the same employment, then the woman is entitled to the same pay and other contractual terms as the man.

A complaint may be made to a tribunal on the grounds of equal value even if the two jobs have been regarded as unequal in a job evaluation study. However, there must be reasonable grounds to show that the study was itself discriminatory on the grounds of sex.

When a complaint about equal value is made, the tribunal can commission a report from an expert on the matter of value. The report of the expert goes to the tribunal and copies go to the parties. Although the report will obviously be extremely important in the decision which the tribunal makes, it is not in any way bound by it and can disregard it.

It is important to note that having decided that a woman is of equal value to a man a tribunal will not necessarily allow a claim for equal pay. It seems that the Equal Pay (Amendment) Regulations 1983 require a tribunal to look at the conditions of 'equal value' employees across the board.

In *Hayward* v *Cammell Laird Shipbuilders Ltd* (1986) a qualified canteen cook, Miss Julie Hayward, who had convinced a tribunal that she was of equal value with male painters, joiners and thermal heating engineers and therefore entitled to equal pay, was told by the Employment Appeal Tribunal that she could not isolate the term about pay. The EAT asked the Tribunal to look at the case again. Although Miss Hayward's pay was not equal, her employers claimed that she had better sickness benefit than the men and also paid meal breaks and extra holidays which they did not have. So it might be possible to say that she was, looked at overall, treated as well.

Associated employers. Comparison of contracts of service for equality purposes is usually made with people who work at the same place. However, comparison can be made with people who work at different places so long as the employer is the same or is an associated employer. As regards an associated employer, this would be the case with a group of companies. Thus if H PLC has two subsidiaries, A Ltd and B Ltd, workers in A Ltd could compare themselves with workers in B Ltd, and workers in B Ltd with those in A Ltd, and workers in A Ltd and B Ltd could compare themselves with workers in H PLC. Workers in H PLC could, of course, compare themselves with workers in A Ltd and B Ltd.

Reference to an industrial tribunal. A complaint of unequal treatment under the EPA may be made to a tribunal at any time while the person who wants to complain is still doing the job or within six months after it came to an end. There is no power to extend the time.

Employer's duty to provide work

There is, in general, no duty at common law for an employer to provide work. If the employer still pays the agreed wages or salary the employee cannot regard the employer as in breach of contract. The employee has no right to sue for damages for wrongful dismissal but must accept his pay. The main authority for this is *Collier* v *Sunday Referee* (1940) where Mr Justice Asquith said: 'If I pay my cook her wages she cannot complain if I take all my meals out'.

There are some exceptions at common law. For example, a salesman who is paid by commission must be allowed to work in order to earn that commission and if he is not his employer is in breach of contract and can be sued for damages. This is also the case with actors and actresses because they need to keep a public image which requires occasional public performances.

Employee's property

An employer has in fact no duty to protect his employee's property.

Deyong v Shenburn (1946)

The plaintiff entered into a contract of employment with the defendant under which the plaintiff was to act the dame in a pantomime for three weeks. Rehearsals took place at a theatre and on the second day the plaintiff had stolen from his dressing room his overcoat as well as two shawls and a pair of shoes forming part of his theatrical equipment. In the county court the judge found that the defendant had been negligent in failing to provide a lock on the dressing room door and having no-one at the stage door during the morning of the particular rehearsal day to prevent the entry of unauthorized persons. However, the county court judge decided that the defendant was under no duty to protect the clothing. The plaintiff appealed to the Court of Appeal which also decided that the defendant was not liable. The Court of Appeal accepted that if there was an accident at work caused by the employer's negligence, then in an action for personal injury the employee could also include damage to his clothing if there had been any. In addition, if in such an accident the employee's clothes were, say, torn off his back but he suffered no personal injury, then it would seem that he could be entitled to recover damages in respect of the loss of his clothes. However, outside of this an employer has no duty to protect the property of his employee.

Comment. This decision was also applied in the later case of *Edwards* v *West Herts Group Hospital Management Committee* (1957) where the plaintiff, a resident house physician at the defendants' hospital, had some articles of clothing and personal affects stolen from his bedroom at the hostel where he was required to live. He brought an action for breach of an implied duty under his contract of employment to protect his property. His action was dismissed in the county court and his appeal to the Court of Appeal was also dismissed on the basis that there was no such contractual duty in respect of property.

Employee's indemnity
An employer is bound to indemnify (that is, make good) any expenses, losses and liabilities incurred by an employee while carrying out his duties.

Re Famatina Development Corporation Ltd (1974)
A company employed a consulting engineer to make a report on its activities. The written report contained matters which the managing director alleged were a libel upon him and he brought an action against the engineer in respect of this on the basis of the publication of the report to the directors of the company, all of whom had received a copy. The managing director's action failed but the engineer incurred costs in defending the claim, not all of which he could recover and he now sought to recover them from the company.

The Court of Appeal decided that the comments made in the report were within the scope of the engineer's employment. His terms of engagement required him to report fully and frankly and in the circumstances he was entitled to the indemnity.

Comment. There is no duty to indemnify an employee against liability for his own negligence. Thus, if by negligence an employee injures a third party in the course of employment and the third party sues the employee, the employer is not required to indemnify the employee and indeed, if the employer is sued as vicariously liable (see further p. 286) he has a right to an indemnity against the employer. This was decided in *Lister* v *Romford Ice and Cold Storage Ltd* (1957), though the action is unlikely to be brought because it upsets industrial relations.

Trade union membership and activities
Under the Employment Protection (Consolidation) Act 1978 employers have a duty not to take action against employees just because they are members of, or take part in at an appropriate time, the activities of a trade union which is independent of the employer. According to the decision in *Post Office* v *Union of Post Office Workers* (1974) this includes activities on the employer's premises.

If action is taken against employees they may complain to a tribunal which can award money compensation or make an order saying what the trade union rights of the employee are so that the employer can grant them in the future. If the employee has been dismissed then the unfair dismissal remedies apply. (See further p. 317.)

Time off work
Under the 1978 Act employees have a right to time off work in certain circumstances. Sometimes they are also entitled to pay as in the case of trade union officials and also redundant employees who are looking for work or wanting to arrange training for another job. These cases have already been looked at as part of the law relating to pay. (See p. 279.) However, there are two other cases in which employees are entitled to time off but the employer is not under a duty to pay wages or salary for it. These are as follows –

(1) *Trade union activities.* An employee who is a member of an independent trade union which the employer recognizes is entitled to reasonable time off for trade union activities. The Advisory, Conciliation, and Arbitration Service (ACAS), a statutory body set up by the Employment Protection Act 1975 to promote, for example, the improvement of industrial relations, has published a *Code of Practice 3* which

gives guidance on the time off which an employer should allow.

(2) *Public duties.* Employers also have a duty to allow employees who hold certain public positions and offices reasonable time off to carry out the duties which go along with them. Details are given in the 1978 Act which covers such offices as magistrate, member of a local authority, member of an industrial tribunal, and member of certain health, education, water and river authorities.

Complaints in regard to failure to give time off under (1) and (2) above may be taken to an industrial tribunal. In general the complaint must be made within three months of the date when the failure to give time off occurred. An industrial tribunal may make an order declaring the rights of the employee so that these can be observed by the employer and may also award money compensation to be paid by the employer where there is injury to the employee, e.g. hurt feelings.

Testimonials and references

There is no law which requires an employer to give a reference or testimonial to an employee or to answer questions or enquiries which a prospective employer may ask him. This was decided in *Carroll v Bird* (1800). However, if an employer does give a reference or testimonial, either orally or in writing, which is false, he commits a criminal offence under the Servants' Characters Act 1792. The employer may also be liable in civil law to pay damages to certain persons as follows.

(1) *To a subsequent employer*, who suffers loss because of a false statement *known* to the former employer to be untrue (*Foster v Charles* (1830)), or made *negligently* without reasonable grounds for believing the statement to be true, because there is probably a duty of care between an employer and a prospective employer. (*Hedley Byrne & Co. Ltd v Heller & Partners Ltd* (1963).)

The Rehabilitation of Offenders Act 1974 is also relevant here. The provisions of the Act are an attempt to give effect to the principle that when a person convicted of crime has been successfully living it down and has avoided further crime, his efforts at rehabilitation should not be prejudiced by the unwarranted disclosure of the earlier conviction.

The Act therefore prevents any liability arising from failure by an employee to disclose what is called a spent conviction to a prospective employer. For example, the Act removes the need to disclose convictions *resulting in a fine* recorded more than five years before the date of the reference or testimonial.

Sentences of imprisonment for life or of imprisonment for a term exceeding thirty months are not capable of rehabilitation. The rehabilitation period for a prison sentence exceeding six months but not exceeding thirty months is ten years, and for a term not exceeding six months it is seven years or, as we have seen, if the sentence was a fine, it is five years.

If an employer does refer to a spent conviction in a testimonial or reference the employee may sue him for *libel* in the case of a written testimonial or reference, or *slander* where the testimonial or reference is spoken. The defence of justification, i.e. that the statement that there was a conviction is true, will be a defence for the employer only if he can show that he acted without malice.

While discussing the 1974 Act it is worth noting that it makes provision for questions by employers relating to a person's previous convictions to be treated as not applying to spent convictions.

The Act also provides that a spent conviction or any failure to disclose a spent conviction shall not be a proper ground for dismissing or excluding a person from any office, profession, or occupation, or employment, or for prejudicing him in any way in any occupation or employment.

However, the Rehabilitation of Offenders Act 1974 (Exceptions) (Amendment) Order 1986 (SI 1986/ 1249), allows those who employ persons who will have contact with those under eighteen to ask, for example, questions designed to reveal even spent convictions, particularly any with a sexual connotation.

(2) *To the former employee*, for libel or slander if things have been stated in a testimonial or reference which damage the employee's reputation. However, the employer has the defence of qualified privilege, as it is called, so that he can speak his mind about the employee and so in order to get damages the employee would have to prove that the employer made the statement out of malice, as where there was evidence that the employer had a history of unreasonable bad treatment of the employee.

Finally, an employee who maliciously defaces his own reference or testimonial commits a criminal offence under the Servants' Characters Act 1792.

Non-contractual duties of the employer

Before leaving the contractual duties of the employer, it should be noted that he has other duties in regard to the health, safety, and welfare of his employees. These are based mainly on the common law of tort and statutes such as the Health and Safety at Work Act 1974 and the Factories Act 1961. These duties will be considered later.

Duties of an employee

To use reasonable skill and care in the work

The *common law* provides that an employee who claims to have a particular skill or skills but shows himself to be incompetent may be dismissed without notice. His employer can also raise the matter of the incompetence of the employee if the employer is sued under *statute law*. i.e. the Employment Protection (Consolidation) Act 1978 for unfair dismissal (see further p. 304).

The common law also requires unskilled employees to take reasonable care in carrying out the job. However, they may be dismissed only if there is a serious breach of this implied term of the contract.

To carry out lawful and reasonable instructions

The law implies a term into a contract of employment which requires the employee to obey the lawful and reasonable instructions of his employer. However, an employee is not bound to carry out illegal acts. In *Gregory* v *Ford* (1951) one of the decisions of the court was that an employee could not be required to drive a vehicle which was not insured so as to satisfy the law set out in what is now the Road Traffic Act 1972. If the employee does refuse he is not in breach of his contract.

The duty to give faithful service (or the duty of fidelity)

This is an implied term of a contract of employment. Certain activities of employees are regarded by the law as breaches of the duty to give faithful service. Thus, as we have seen, an employee who while employed copies the names and addresses of his employer's customers for use after leaving the employment can be prevented from using the information. (*Robb* v *Green* (1895); see also p. 260.)

However, the implied term relating to fidelity does not apply once the contract of employment has come to an end. Therefore, a former employee cannot be prevented under this implied term from encouraging customers of his former employer to do business with him, though he can be prevented from using actual lists of customers which he made whilst still employed. If an employer (A) wants to stop an employee (B) from trying to win over his, A's, *customers*, then the contract of employment between A and B must contain an *express* clause in restraint of trade preventing this. Such a clause must, as we have seen, be reasonable in time and area (see also p. 175).

A former employee can, however, be prevented by the court from using his former employer's *trade secrets* or *confidential information* without a clause in the contract about restraint of trade.

Confidential information

It is an implied term of a contract of service that the employee must not disclose *trade secrets*, e.g. a special way of making glass as in *Forster & Sons Ltd* v *Suggett* (1918), or *confidential information* acquired during employment. There is no need for an express clause in the contract.

However, the use by an employee of knowledge of trade secrets and information cannot be prevented if it is just part of the total job experience. An employee cannot be prevented from using what he could not help but learn from doing the job.

Printers & Finishers v Holloway (No. 2) (1964)

The plaintiffs brought an action against Holloway, their former works manager, and others, including Vita-tex Ltd, into whose employment Holloway had subsequently entered. They claimed an injunction against Holloway and the other defendants, based, as regards Holloway, on an alleged breach of an implied term in his contract of service with the plaintiffs that he should not disclose or make improper use of confidential information relating to the plaintiffs' trade secrets. Holloway's contract did not contain an express covenant relating to non-disclosure of trade secrets.

The plaintiffs were flock printers and had built up their own fund of 'know-how' in this field. The action against Vita-tex arose because Holloway had, on one occasion, taken a Mr James, who was an employee of Vita-tex Ltd round the plaintiffs' factory. Mr James' visit took place in the evening and followed a chance meeting between himself and

Holloway. However, the plant was working and James did see a number of processes. It also appeared that Holloway had, during his employment, made copies of certain of the plaintiffs' documentary material and had taken these copies away with him when he left their employment. The plaintiffs wanted an injunction to prevent the use or disclosure of the material contained in the copies of documents made by Holloway.

The court held that the plaintiffs were entitled to an injunction against Holloway so far as the documentary material was concerned, although there was no express term in his contract regarding non-disclosure of secrets.

However, the court would not grant an injunction restraining Holloway from putting at the disposal of Vita-tex Ltd his memory of particular features of the plaintiffs plant and processes. He was under no express contract not to do so and the Court would not extend its jurisdiction to restrain breaches of confidence in this instance. Holloway's knowledge of the plaintiffs' trade secrets was not readily separable from his general knowledge of flock printing.

An injunction was granted restraining Vita-tex Ltd from making use of the information acquired by Mr James on his visit.

Vicarious liability

Because of this principle of the law an employer is liable for damage caused to another person by his employee, *while the employee was carrying out his work* (or while he was in the course of employment, as it is called). The principle applies whether the injury was to an outsider or to a fellow-employee (see further p. 290). The employer is liable even though he was not in any way at fault and this rule, which seems at first sight to be unfair to the employer, is based upon *law* and *policy*.

So far as the law is concerned, employer and employee are regarded as *associated parties* in the business in which both are engaged. If the amount of work increases so that the owner of a business cannot do it all with his own hands he must employ other hands and is in law responsible for the damage done by those hands as he would be for damage done by his own.

The point of policy is to provide the injured person with a defendant who is likely to be able to pay any damages which the court may award. An employer and the business generally profit from the employee's work

and it is perhaps not entirely unreasonable that the employer should compensate those who are injured by the employee. The employer will normally insure against the risk of liability and of course the cost of that insurance is represented in the price at which the goods or services of the business are sold. Thus, in the end, the injured person is compensated by those members of the public who buy the goods or services.

It is worth noting here that under the Employers' Liability (Compulsory Insurance) Act 1969 an employer *must insure* himself in respect of injuries caused by his employees to fellow employees, but insurance is *not compulsory* (though highly advisable) in respect of injuries to outsiders.

Finally, it should be noted that the employee who actually caused the injury is always liable personally along with the employer, but of course the prime defendant is the employer because he has either insurance or other funds which the employee probably does not have.

The course of employment

Whether an employee was or was not acting in the course of employment when he brought about the injury for which the person injured wants to make the employer liable is a matter for the court to decide in each case. The decision is sometimes a difficult one to make and we may all from time to time disagree with a decision made by a judge in a particular case.

However, the following analysis of the cases gives some idea of the way in which the courts have dealt with this most important aspect of employers' liability.

(1) *Acts outside of the contractual duties.* If the employee is engaged on a private matter personal to him the employer will not be liable for injuries caused by the employee during this time.

Britt *v* Galmoye & Nevill (1928)

Nevill was employed by Galmoye as a van driver. Nevill wanted to take a friend to the theatre after he had finished work and Galmoye lent Nevill his private motor car for this purpose. Nevill, by negligence, injured Britt and Britt's action against Galmoye was based upon vicarious liability so that it was necessary to deal with the matter of course of employment. The court decided that as the journey was not on Galmoye's business and Galmoye was not in control, he was not liable for Nevill's act.

Comment. Britt's case is a rather obvious example of an act outside of the contract of service. However, sometimes the court is called upon to make a more difficult decision. In particular it should be noted that an employee does not make his employer liable by doing some act which is of benefit to the employer during the course of what is basically an outside activity. For example, in *Rayner v Mitchell* (1877) a van man employed by a brewer took, without permission, a van from his employer's stables in order to deliver a child's coffin at the home of a relative. While he was returning the van to the stables he picked up some empty beer barrels and was afterwards involved in an accident which injured Rayner. Rayner sued the van man's employer and it was held that the employer was not liable. The journey itself was unauthorized and was not converted into an authorized journey merely because the employee performed some small act for the benefit of his employer during the course of it.

(2) *Unauthorized ways of performing the contractual duties.* The employer may be liable in spite of the fact that the employee was acting improperly if the act was, even so, part of his contractual duties.

Century Insurance Co v Northern Ireland Road Transport Board (1942)

The driver of a petrol tanker was engaged in transferring petrol to an underground tank when he lit a cigarette and threw the match to the floor. This caused a fire and an explosion which did great damage, and the question of the liability of the Board, his employer, for that damage, arose. The court decided that the employer was liable for the driver's negligence. His negligence was not independent of the contract of service but was a negligent way of discharging his actual duties under that contract of service.

(3) *Acts which the employer has forbidden the employee to do.* Just because an employer has told his employee not to do a particular act does not always excuse the employer from vicarious liability if the employee causes damage when doing the forbidden act. There are two sorts of cases, as follows.

(a) *Where the act itself is forbidden.*

Rand (Joseph) Ltd v Craig (1919)

The defendants' employees were taking rubbish from a site and depositing it on the defendants'

dump. They were working on a bonus scheme related to the number of loads per day which they dumped. The defendants had strictly forbidden their employees to tip the rubbish elsewhere than on the authorized dump. However, some of the employees deposited their loads on the plaintiff's property which was nearer. The defendants were sued on the basis that they were vicariously liable in trespass, the plaintiffs arguing that the employees had general authority to cart and tip rubbish. The court decided that the defendants were not liable. The employees were employed to cart the rubbish from one definite place to another definite place. Shooting the rubbish on to the plaintiff's premises was a totally wrongful act not directly arising out of the duties that they were employed to perform.

Comment. A contrast is provided by *Rose v Plenty* (1976). Leslie Rose, aged thirteen, liked helping Mr Plenty, a milkman, to deliver the milk. Co-operative Retail Services Ltd, who employed Mr Plenty, expressly forbad their milkmen to take boys on their floats or to get boys to help them deliver the milk. On one occasion, while helping Mr Plenty, Leslie was sitting in the front of the float when his leg caught under the wheel. The accident was caused partly by Mr Plenty's negligence. The court decided that Mr Plenty had been acting in the course of his employment so that his employers were liable to compensate Leslie Rose for his injuries. There is really quite a difference in the facts of this case and those in *Rand*. Leslie Rose's presence on the milk float was connected with the delivery of the milk which was a reason connected with the employment and this seems to be why the court decided as it did.

(b) *Where the employer's instruction relates only to the way in which the contractual duty is to be done.* Obviously, perhaps, an employer cannot avoid liability by saying to his employees: 'do your job in such a way as not to injure anyone'.

Limpus v London General Omnibus Co. (1862)

The plaintiff's bus was overturned when the driver of the defendants' bus drove across it so as to be first at a bus stop to take all the passengers who were waiting. The defendants' driver admitted that the act was intentional and arose out of bad feeling between the two drivers. The defendants had issued strict instructions to their drivers that they were not to obstruct other omnibuses. The court decided that the defendants were liable. Their driver was acting within the scope of his employment at the time of the collision, and it did not matter that the defendants had expressly forbidden him to act as he did.

(4) *Employee's fraudulent acts.* At first the courts would not make an employer liable for the fraudulent acts of his employee. Gradually, however, they began to accept that the employer could be liable, first in cases where the employee's fraud was committed for the employer's benefit, and later even to cases where the fraud was carried out by the employee entirely for his own ends, as the following case shows.

Lloyd v Grace, Smith & Co. (1912)
Smith was a Liverpool solicitor and Lloyd was a widow who owned two properties at Ellesmore Port and had also lent money on mortgage. She was not satisfied with the income from these investments and she went to see Smith's managing clerk, Sandles, for advice. He told her to sell the properties and call in the mortgages, and re-invest the proceeds. At his request she signed two deeds which, unknown to her, transferred the properties and the mortgage to him. Sandles then mortgaged the properties and transferred the other mortgages for money and paid a private debt with the proceeds. The court decided that the firm of solicitors was vicariously liable for Sandles' fraudulent acts. An employer could be vicariously liable for a tort committed by an employee entirely for his own ends.

Comment. This decision seems to contain at least some public policy and to be based on the principle that since someone must be the loser by reason of the fraud of the employee, it is more reasonable that the employer who engages and puts trust and confidence in the fraudulent employee should be the loser rather than an outsider.

(5) *Employee's criminal acts.* An employer may even be vicariously liable for a criminal act by his employee. The criminal act may be regarded as in the course of employment so that the employer will be liable at civil law for any loss or damage caused by the employee's criminal act.

Morris v C W Martin & Sons Ltd (1965)
The plaintiff sent a mink stole to a furrier for the purpose of cleaning. With the plaintiff's consent the furrier gave it to the defendants to clean. While it was in the possession of the defendants the fur was stolen by a person called Morrisey, who had been employed by the defendants for a few weeks only, though they had no grounds to suspect that he was dishonest. The plaintiff sued the defendants for damages for the tort of conversion. The county court judge held that the act of Morrisey, who had removed the stole by wrapping it around his body, was beyond the scope of his employment.

The Court of Appeal, however, decided that the defendants were liable to the plaintiff because Morrisey had been entrusted with the stole in the course of his employment.

Comment. The above rule applies only in circumstances where the employee is entrusted with, or put in charge of, the goods by his employer.

The mere fact that the employee's employment gives him the opportunity to steal goods is not enough. Thus in *Leesh River Tea Co.* v *British India Steam Navigation Co.* (1966) a person employed to unload tea from a ship stole a brass cover plate from the hold of the ship while he was unloading the tea and the court decided that he was not acting in the course of his employment on the grounds that his job had nothing to do with the cover plate.

Perhaps if the plate had been stolen by someone who was sent to clean it, then that person would have been acting within the course of employment and his employer might well have been liable.

(6) *Corporations and the ultra vires rule.* Where the employer is a corporation there are further difficulties as regards the corporation's vicarious liability, because the act which the employee does when he causes injury may be beyond the corporation's powers (or *ultra vires*), i.e. beyond the scope of what its constitution says it can do. This constitution may, as we have seen, be a statute, as with the Coal Board, or a charter, as with a professional body, such as the Institute of Chartered Secretaries and Administrators, or the objects clause of the memorandum in the case of a registered company. It is necessary, therefore, to distinguish between those acts of employees which are within the company's powers (*intra vires*) and outside its powers (*ultra vires*).

(*a*) *Intra vires activities.* If an employee of a corporation injures someone by negligence while acting in the course of his employment in an *intra vires* activity, then the corporation is liable. Although it has been said that any wrongful act committed on behalf of a corporation must be *ultra vires* since the corporation has no authority in its constitution to commit wrongful acts, this view has not been accepted by the courts. Therefore, a corporation can have liability in law without capacity in law.

A corporation is liable, therefore, under the rule of vicarious liability, for injuries caused by its employees on *intra vires* activities. Thus a bus company which is, obviously, authorized by its memorandum to run buses, will be liable if an employee injures a pedestrian while driving a bus along its route.

(*b*) *Ultra vires activities.* A corporation will not be liable if one of its employees gets involved in an act which is *ultra vires* the corporation unless he has *express authority* from management to do the act.

Poulton v London & South Western Railway Co. (1867)

The plaintiff was arrested by a station master for non-payment of carriage in respect of his horse. The defendants, who were the employers of the station master, had power to detain passengers for non-payment of their own fare, but for no other reason. The court decided that since there was no express authorization of the arrest by the defendants, the station master was acting outside the scope of his employment and the defendants were not liable for the wrongful arrest.

Comment. A contrast is provided by *Campbell* v *Paddington Borough Council* (1911). The members of the Council had passed a resolution authorizing the erection of a stand in Burwood Place, London in order that members of the Council could view the funeral procession of King Edward VII passing along the Edgware Road. The plaintiff, who had premises in Burwood Place, often let them so that people could view public processions passing along the Edgware Road. The Council's stand obstructed the view of the funeral procession from the plaintiff's house and she could not let the premises for that purpose. The court decided that the Council was liable. The fact that the erection of the stand was probably *ultra vires*, since there was no specific power in the Council's charter to put one up, did not matter. There had been authorization by the Council resolution.

Employer's defences

There are three main defences which an employer may

have if he is sued under the rule of vicarious liability. These are set out below.

(1) *An exclusion clause in a contract or notice.* Because of the Unfair Contract Terms Act 1977, an employer, like other people, cannot exclude or reduce his liability for *death or bodily injury* caused by his own negligence or that of his employees. As regards other types of damage, such as damage to property, an exemption clause in a contract or a notice will apply to exclude or reduce the liability, but only if the court thinks that it is *reasonable* that this should happen.

Thus, in the case of a dry-cleaning contract, if by the negligence of employees cleaning material is not properly removed so that the owner of the clothing contracts a skin disease, to which he is not especially susceptible, no exclusion clause in the contract for cleaning or in a notice in the shop can remove or restrict the employer's liability for this bodily harm.

However, if the clothing is, by reason of an employee's negligence, merely damaged and there is no resulting physical injury, then an exclusion clause or notice might operate to remove or restrict the liability of the employer if the judge thought it was reasonable for it to do so in the circumstances.

Although the Act gives no criteria for what is reasonable and it is a matter to be decided by the judge in each case, it would be generally true to say that the device of an exclusion clause in a contract or notice has lost a lot of its force as an employer's defence. (See further p. 204.)

(2) *Voluntary assumption of risk.* This defence is also referred to as *volenti non fit injuria* (to one who is willing no harm is done). This defence is most often tried in employment cases when employees sue their employers for injuries received at work. We will have a look at these cases later in this chapter. However, the defence is available to an employer when an outsider sues him on the basis of vicarious liability for injury caused by his employees.

Cutler v United Dairies (London) Ltd (1923)

The defendants' employee left the defendants' horse and van, two wheels only being properly chained, while he delivered milk. The horse, being startled by the noise coming from a river steamer, bolted down the road and into a meadow. It stopped in the meadow and was followed there by the employee who, being in an excited state, began to shout for help. The plaintiff, who had seen all of this, went to the employee's assistance and tried to hold the horse's head. The horse lunged and the plaintiff was injured. The plaintiff sued the defendants alleging negligence because apparently the horse was given to bolting and should not have been used on a milk round at all.

The court decided that in the circumstances the plaintiff voluntarily and freely assumed the risk. This was not an attempt to stop a runaway horse so that there was no sense of urgency to require the plaintiff to act as he did. He therefore knew of the risk and had had time to consider it and by implication must have agreed to incur it.

Comment. A different situation arises in what are known as the *rescue cases*. In these the plaintiff is injured while trying to save life or property which has been put in danger by the defendant's negligence. If the intervention is a reasonable thing to do for the saving of life or property then this does not constitute an assumption of risk, nor does the defence of contributory negligence (see below) apply. Cutler, of course, was not effecting a rescue.

(3) *Contributory negligence.* Sometimes when an injury occurs the person injured and the person causing the injury have both been negligent. In such a situation liability can be divided between the person injured and the person causing the injury.

The person injured can still claim damages but under the Law Reform (Contributory Negligence) Act 1945 they will be reduced according to how much the court thinks he was to blame. Thus if the court thinks that A who has been injured by B's negligence is entitled to £1000 but is 60 per cent to blame for the injury, it will deduct £600 from A's damages so that he will get only £400.

Again, this defence is most often used where an employee is suing his employer for injuries received at work and the employer claims that the employee was partly to blame and his damages should be reduced. This situation has yet to be looked at. However, an employee, A, who was sued as vicariously liable for injuries caused by employee B to a person who was not an employee, C, could, in the right circumstances, claim that the damages given to C should be reduced because of C's contributory negligence.

Employer's liability for injuries to his employees

In addition to the duties of an employer under the contract of service with which we have been dealing so far, an employee who is injured at work by a negligent act will want to sue his employer for damages. Under the Employers' Liability (Compulsory Insurance) Act 1969 an employer *must* insure himself in respect of liability for injuries caused to his employee where these arise from a negligent act.

These employee claims are brought on the basis of negligence by the employer and, because of the decision of the House of Lords in *Wilsons and Clyde Coal Co. v English* (1938), the employer's duties towards his employees, i.e. the duty to take care which he owes them, can be set out under the headings which appear below.

Safe plant, appliances, and premises
An employer has a duty to *provide* and *maintain* suitable plant, appliances, and premises.

Lovell v Blundells and Crompton & Co. Ltd (1944)
Lovell was told by the defendants, who were his employers, to carry out an overhaul of a ship's boiler tubes. He could not reach some of the tubes so he got some planks for himself and from them he made up his own staging. The planks were unsound and collapsed, injuring Lovell. The defendants had not provided any form of staging, nor had they laid down any system of working.

The court decided that the employers were liable in negligence. They had failed to supply plant in a situation where there was an obvious requirement for it.

Comment. Having supplied plant, an employer will be liable if the employee is injured by it by reason of the employer's failure to inspect and maintain it and remedy defects. Thus, in *Baker v James Bros and Sons Ltd* (1921) Baker, who was a commercial traveller employed by the defendant, had to travel in a particular district taking orders and for this purpose the defendant supplied him with a car. The starting gear was defective and Baker complained to the defendants several times about this but nothing was done. On one occasion when Baker was out taking orders he was badly injured while trying to start the car with the starting handle. The court decided that

Baker was entitled to damages. His employers had failed to maintain the car as they should. In the circumstances Baker could not be regarded as having consented to run the risk of injury, nor could he be regarded as guilty of contributory negligence.

The Employer's Liability (Defective Equipment) Act 1969 puts liability on an employer who provides defective equipment to an employee which causes that employee injury. The employer's liability is strict, which means that he is liable even though he was not himself negligent, as where the injury was caused by the negligence of the organization which made the equipment. Where the defect in the equipment is the fault of the manufacturer, the employer, having been sued for damages by the employee, can himself sue the manufacturer to recover from him any damages awarded to the employee. The employee can also sue the manufacturer direct if he chooses to do so.

Safe system of work

An employer is required to set up a safe way of working. It is also the duty of an employer to enforce the safe system having once set it up. Thus where an employee may suffer damage to his eyes by flying sparks, as in welding, the employer must provide goggles or a face guard and introduce a system of supervision to ensure, as far as he can, that the protective equipment is being used by the relevant work force.

Employer's defences

Contributory negligence. Contributory negligence is available as a defence to an employer in a claim brought against him by an employee who says he has been injured because of his employer's negligence.

Cakebread v Hopping Brothers (Whetstone) Ltd (1947)

The employers of the plaintiff, who was engaged in a woodworking factory, had failed to see that the guard on a circular saw was properly adjusted and the plaintiff, who worked the saw, was injured as a result. However, it appeared that the plaintiff did not like working the machine with the guard properly adjusted and he had arranged with the foreman that the saw should be operated with an improperly adjusted guard. The court decided that the employer was in breach of his duty of care, but also that the plaintiff had failed to exercise the care of a prudent

employee for his own safety and reduced his damages by 50 per cent.

Assumption of risk by the employee. This is unlikely to provide the employer with a successful defence these days since it is now the law that just because an employee *knows* of the risk he cannot for that reason be regarded as having *consented* to it.

Smith v Baker & Sons (1891)

Smith was employed by Baker & Sons to drill holes in some rock in a railway cutting. A crane, operated by fellow employees, often swung heavy stones over Smith's head while he was working on the rock face. Both Smith and his employers realized that there was a risk that the stones might fall, but the crane was nevertheless operated without any warning being given at the moment that it began to swing the stones over Smith's head. Smith was injured by a stone which fell from the crane because of the negligent strapping of the load.

The court decided that Smith had not voluntarily undertaken the risk of his employers' negligence and that his knowledge of the danger did not prevent him recovering damages.

Fatal accidents

If, as a result of the employer's negligence, an employee is killed in the course of his employment the personal representatives of the deceased have a claim on behalf of the estate under the Law Reform (Miscellaneous Provisions) Act 1934 (as amended by the Administration of Justice Act 1982). In addition, under the Fatal Accidents Act 1976 (as amended by the Administration of Justice Act 1982), certain dependent relatives, e.g. husband or wife and children are entitled to claim in a personal capacity if they were dependent on the deceased for their living expenses.

Health and safety at work

This part of the chapter will consider those provisions of the law which deal with the health, safety, and welfare of persons at work, and also the legal controls over industry in regard to the use of dangerous substances and emissions of noxious and/or offensive substances into the atmosphere.

Health and Safety at Work Act 1974

Generally

The 1974 Act states that it is the duty of every employer to ensure, so far as it is reasonably practicable, the health, safety and welfare at work of all his employees.

As regards the health and safety of employees, there is, of course, a duty on the employer *at common law* in respect of this. An employee may, as we have seen, be given damages in a *civil* action against his employer if he suffers injury because his employer does not concern himself properly with the health and safety of his employees.

However, the difference here is that failure to comply with the 1974 Act is a *crime* and can result in an employer receiving a prison sentence of up to two years and/or a fine of unlimited amount. It can therefore be enforced through the state by means of inspectors and does not depend upon an employee bringing a civil claim.

It should also be noted that the 1974 Act applies to *all* places of work and not just to factories.

Particular duties

The 1974 Act states that in addition to the *general and broad duty* set out above an employer's duty extends *in particular* to the following matters.

(1) An employer must ensure the *provision* and *maintenance* of plant and systems of work that are, so far as is reasonably practicable, safe and without risks to health.

There is, of course, a similar duty at common law but, as we have seen, failure to comply with the 1974 Act is a crime, so that an employer could be prosecuted for failing to maintain, e.g. an electric drill which flew apart and injured an employee, though it should be noted that the Act could be enforced if there was a failure by the employer to maintain equipment *even though no accident had occurred.*

(2) An employer must make arrangements to ensure, so far as is reasonably practicable, safety and absence of risks to health in the use, handling, storage and transport of articles and substances.

The 1974 Act states that 'article for use at work' means any plant designed for use or operation by persons at work. 'Substance' is defined as any natural or artificial substance, whether in solid or liquid form, or in the form of a gas or vapour.

So, care must be taken to prevent, e.g. the irritant effect of caustic soda, or the use of solvents without subsequent washing to remove oil and grease from the skin. This is one of the most important causes of skin disease in industry, i.e. dermatitis, which is the commonest of all occupational diseases.

(3) An employer must provide such information, instruction, training, and supervision as is necessary to ensure, so far as is reasonably practicable, the health and safety at work of his employees.

The Health and Safety Inspectorate (see p. 296) will want to see arrangements which a business has made for safety training generally. In some cases it is a criminal offence to allow persons to work machinery when they have not had sufficient training. An example is provided by woodworking machinery which can cause horrendous injuries to operators who are not trained in its use.

(4) An employer must, so far as is reasonably practicable, in regard to any place of work under his control, *maintain it* in a good condition so that it is safe and without risks to health. He must also provide and maintain *means of getting to and away from* the place of work which are safe and without risks.

Thus items such as stairways used by persons to get to their work must be properly maintained and safe and without risks.

(5) An employer must provide and maintain a working environment for his employees which is, so far as is reasonably practicable, safe, without risks to health, adequate as regards facilities and arrangements for the welfare of employees at work. As regards welfare, this means the provision of proper toilet facilities, canteens, heating, lighting, and ventilation.

The duties set out in (1) to (5) above are wide-ranging. They apply in factories, on oil rigs, and even to the employer of a bread roundsman who is, e.g. required to work in a van with a leaky exhaust, which is a risk to the roundsman's health.

Statements of policy

The 1974 Act makes it the duty of every employer *to prepare* and as often as may be appropriate, *revise*, a written statement of his general policy towards the health and safety at work of his employees and the organization and arrangements which are in operation for carrying out the policy. He must bring the statement and any revision of it to the notice of all his employees.

Employers with fewer than five employees need not do this. Others are liable to be prosecuted if there is no statement or if it is defective in the sense that it is not an adequate guide to procedures, in that it does not say who is responsible for what in the safety area and safety training, and so on. An employer who fails to comply with the arrangements which he has put into his statement may also be prosecuted.

As regards policy, this seems only to require a statement that it is the policy of the organization to concern itself at all times with the health and safety of its employees. There must, of course, be an organization to deal with health and safety, and this requires the appointment, e.g. of safety committees, safety representatives, and possibly a safety officer.

The statement should deal with possible hazards and dangerous occurrences at the workplace and should explain to employees how they can avoid accidents arising from them. The statement may simply be displayed on notice boards, but it is better practice to give a copy of the statement to each employee.

Under the 1974 Act the Secretary of State for Trade and Industry may make regulations under which the annual reports of company directors must contain information regarding arrangements in force during the year relating to the health, safety and welfare of employees. At the time of writing no such regulations have been made.

Duties of employers and the self-employed to persons who are not their employees – generally

The 1974 Act makes it the duty of every employer to carry on his business in such a way as to make sure, so far as is reasonably practicable, that persons who are *not* his employees but who might be affected by the conduct of the business are not exposed to risks to their health or safety. The Act places this duty also on self-employed persons.

The provisions cover a wide variety of people, including customers in a shop, people who occupy the premises next door, and even members of the public who pass the workplace. The Act makes it a criminal offence for which the person at fault can be prosecuted, whether anyone is injured or not, to run a business *negligently* or to create a *nuisance*.

Thus, if a customer in a shop trips over a trailing wire left by a maintenance man there is the possibility of an action by the customer for damages for negligence, and the possibility, also, of a prosecution under the 1974 Act. In a similar way, excess noise or vibration from premises on which the business is conducted may result in an action by a person who occupies premises next door for nuisance and there is also the possibility of a prosecution under the 1974 Act.

Statements

The 1974 Act gives the Trade Secretary power to make rules by means of delegated legislation (see also p. 14), so as to make it the duty of every employer and every self-employed person to give, to people who are not his employees but who may be affected by the way he conducts his business, *information* about those aspects of the business he is running which might affect their health or safety. This might mean telling those who come on to the business premises how to avoid accidents. At the time of writing no rules have been made.

Duties of employers and the self-employed to non-employees – premises

Under the 1974 Act certain duties are imposed upon employers and the self-employed in regard to people who are not employees but who come on to their business (not domestic) premises. The duty is to make sure, so far as is reasonably practicable, that the premises and the means of getting in and out of them and any plant or substance on the premises, are safe and without risk to health. The Act also puts these duties upon a landlord who is letting business premises. Failure to comply with these duties may lead to prosecution.

Once again, a wide variety of people is covered, such as window-cleaners and painters, the employees of contractors maintaining lifts or installing central heating. The actual employer owes the duties of an employer to these people, also, and must, for example, set up a safe system of working. However, the occupier of the premises owes the duties we have been looking at in regard to injuries received from defects in the premises or plant or a substance on them. Obviously, the occupier can assume that the employees of contractors will take proper steps, as trained people, to avoid the risks which are usually associated with the job.

Duties in regard to harmful emissions in the atmosphere

The 1974 Act allows the Trade and Industry Secretary to control by regulations the emission into the atmosphere from premises of noxious or offensive substances and for making harmless and inoffensive such substances as may be emitted. The provisions are concerned only with air pollution. Other forms of pollution, such as the discharge of effluent into rivers, are not controlled by them.

General duties of those who make, import, or supply articles of equipment or substances, or who erect or install equipment

This part of the 1974 Act creates the following duties –

(1) to ensure, so far as is reasonably practicable, that the article, e.g. a machine, is so designed and constructed as to be safe and without risks to health when properly used or, in the case of a substance, e.g. cyanide, is safe and without risk to health when properly used.

(2) To carry out or arrange for the carrying out of such testing and examination as may be necessary for the performance of the duty laid down in (1) above.

(3) To take such steps as may be necessary to make sure that there is available as regards the use of the article or substance at work adequate information about the use for which it is designed or made and has been tested, and about any conditions necessary to make sure that when the article or substance is put to that use it will be safe and without risk to health.

All forms of supply are included and this part of the 1974 Act covers the supplying by way of sale, leasing, hire or hire purchase.

As regards the installation and erection of equipment, the 1974 Act provides that it is the duty of any person who erects or installs any article for use at work in any premises where the article is to be used by people at work to make sure, as far as is reasonably practicable, that nothing about the way in which it is erected or installed makes it unsafe or a risk to health when properly used.

Research, examination and testing

This part of the Act makes it the duty of any person who undertakes the design or manufacture of an article for use at work or the manufacture of a substance for use at work to carry out or arrange for the carrying out of any necessary research with a view to the discovery, and, so far as is reasonably practicable, the elimination or minimization of any risks to health or safety to which the design, article or substance may give rise.

There is no need to repeat any testing, examination or research which has been done by someone else if it is reasonable to rely on the results of another's testing, examination or research. For example, those who lease goods are not required to go again through the manufacturer's testing, examination and research programmes.

If you design, manufacture, import or supply an article to someone else's specification or request then the Act says that if you have a *written undertaking* as part of the documentation of the contract from that person to take specified steps sufficient to ensure, so far as is reasonably practicable, that the article will be safe and without risk to health when properly used, then the written undertaking will relieve the designer, manufacturer, importer or supplier of liability to such an extent as is reasonable having regard to the terms of the undertaking.

General duties of employees at work

It is the duty of every employee while at work –

(1) to take reasonable care for the health and safety of himself and of other persons who may be affected by his acts or omissions at work; and

(2) as regards any duty or requirement put upon his employer or any other person by the relevant Acts of Parliament to co-operate with him so far as is necessary to enable that duty or requirement to be carried out or complied with.

Furthermore, the 1974 Act provides that no person shall intentionally or recklessly interfere with, or misuse anything provided in the interests of health, safety, or welfare.

These are useful sections which could enable an employer to enforce his safety policies. Some workers are reluctant to use safety equipment, such as machine guards, because they feel it slows them down or prevents the most efficient operation of the machine in terms of its production. If the employee's wages depend, because of the system of payment, upon his production, then it is even more difficult to gain his acceptance of safety devices which might affect production.

In this connection it should be noted that an employee's consent to a dangerous practice, or his willing participation in it, is no defence for an employer who is prosecuted under the Act.

Duty not to charge employees for things done or provided by the employer by law

The 1974 Act states that no employer shall levy or permit to be levied on any employee of his any charge in respect of anything done or provided by the employer as a result of the provisions of an Act of Parliament or Statutory Instrument. This would apply, for example, to personal protective clothing which an employer was required to provide by law. For example in workplaces where there is a noise hazard from a woodworking machine, ear protectors must be provided and the employee must not be charged for them. The employee, in turn, must treat them properly and not misuse them.

The statutory duties and civil liability

The 1974 Act states that failure to comply with any of the duties considered above shall not be construed as conferring a right of action in civil proceedings. Thus the Act creates no new civil liability.

However, the ordinary action for negligence at common law remains available. If there is an action by an employee at common law, say for injuries received at work by what he alleges to be the employer's negligence, the employee can plead that the employer has been convicted under the Act and where this is so the employee's claim is near certain to succeed. So where the employer has infringed the Act and this has caused injury to the employee, the Act is a relevant part of establishing the employee's case for damages at civil law.

The Health and Safety Commission and the Health and Safety Executive

The 1974 Act establishes the above bodies and describes their powers. Briefly, the Commission is concerned to make codes of practice, assist and encourage research and the availability of information and training, to recommend to government areas in which new regulations are required and what they should be and, as we shall see below, to conduct inquiries.

The Executive is required, through its inspectors, to enforce the provisions of the Act throughout the country by covering all industries.

Investigations and inquiries

If there is, for example, a serious accident on a particular employer's premises, then this part of the Act may be brought into effect. It provides that whenever there has been any accident, occurrence, situation, or other matter of any sort which the Commission thinks it necessary or expedient to investigate, which includes the situation where new regulations might be required, the Commission may –

(1) direct the Executive to investigate and report; or

(2) authorize another person, e.g. someone with particular expertise, to investigate and report; or

(3) direct an inquiry to be held if the Secretary of State agrees.

There is a provision that normally the inquiry is to be held in public and regulations made dealing with the conduct of inquiries include provisions giving the person conducting the inquiry powers of entry and inspection of premises, the power to summon witnesses to give evidence or produce documents, and the power to take evidence on oath and require the making of declarations as to the truth of statements made.

The Act also provides that the Commission may publish the report of the inquiry or part of it as it thinks fit.

Other enforcement

The investigations and inquiries referred to above are, of course, a form of enforcement but in the main enforcement is through the powers conferred on the Commission and the Inspectorate.

The Commission

The Commission has the following general duties –

(1) to assist and encourage health and safety measures;

(2) to make arrangements for the carrying out of research, the publication of the results of research, and the provision of training and information in connection with these purposes, and to encourage provision of training and research in the publication of information by others;

(3) to make arrangements for an information and advisory service;

(4) to submit recommendations for new regulations;

(5) to direct the holding of investigations and inquiries.

The Inspectorate and its major powers

Under the 1974 Act inspectors are given power to serve improvement notices and prohibition notices.

(1) *Improvement notices.* The Act provides that if an inspector is of the opinion that a person is contravening one or more of the statutory provisions relating to health and safety or has done so in the past and the circumstances suggest he is likely to do so again, then he may serve an improvement notice on him requiring the person concerned to put matters right within the period stated in the notice.

(2) *Prohibition notices.* The Act also provides that if an inspector is of the opinion that activities as they are carried on or are about to be carried on involve a risk of serious personal injury, then the inspector may serve a prohibition notice on the person who controls the activities. The notice must give the inspector's reasons for thinking that the activity is unsafe. When the notice has been served the activity must cease immediately. It should be noted that improvement and prohibition orders may be issued in respect of offences under the provisions of, e.g. the Factories Act 1961, and the Offices, Shops, and Railway Premises Act 1963. They have, for example, been served in regard to service lifts (sometimes called dumb waiters) in restaurants, which can be overworked and not properly maintained; they have also been served in respect of dangerous staircases leading to kitchens in a restaurant, resulting in the restaurant being closed until the staircase has been put into good order.

(3) *Appeal against improvement or prohibition notice.* There are rights of appeal against improvement and prohibition notices. The appeal is to an industrial tribunal. An improvement notice is suspended until the appeal is heard or withdrawn and things can go on as before. A prohibition notice is not automatically suspended but may be if the person making the appeal asks for suspension and the tribunal so directs. Suspension is from the date of the tribunal's direction.

There is a right of appeal from the tribunal to the Employment Appeal Tribunal, both against the making of either notice or against a refusal to suspend a prohibition notice.

(4) *Power to deal with cause of imminent danger.* Under the 1974 Act an inspector has power to enter premises and remove from them any article which he has reasonable cause to believe is a cause of imminent danger of serious personal injury and cause it to be made harmless, whether by destruction or in some other way. This part of the 1974 Act requires the inspector to make a report giving his reasons for taking the article and to give a copy to a responsible person at the premises from which the article was removed and to the owner if the two are not the same, as where the owner has let his premises for industrial use.

(5) *Actions against inspectors – indemnity.* It is possible to bring at common law an action for damages against an inspector who negligently issues an improvement, or more particularly, a prohibition, notice which causes loss to the person against whom it is issued. If the inspector loses his case then the Executive is given power under the 1974 Act to indemnify him (i.e. make good) any damages, costs or expenses which he incurs.

(6) *Obtaining of information.* The Act carries provisions under which the Commission or the Executive can obtain information which is needed for the discharge of their duties by the serving of a notice requiring the person concerned to supply that information within a specified time.

Offences due to the fault of another person

The Act provides that if an offence under the Act was the fault of some other person that other person is guilty of the offence and may be charged and convicted of it whether or not proceedings are taken against anyone else who is responsible.

The effect of this provision is that, for example, an executive of a company or other business organization may be prosecuted rather than the company or other organization where the Act was infringed because the executive himself was at fault. However, before blame can be passed on in this way the company or other organization should have a very good system to ensure, for example, safety, which the executive did not in practice operate.

Offences by bodies corporate

This part of the Act also imposes potential liability upon the executive of a company but not because the person concerned was *directly* involved in a failure, for example, to operate a safety system, under the above provision, but where the offence was committed with his consent, connivance or neglect.

In effect the section will enable members of boards, managers and company secretaries to be prosecuted where nothing has been done by management to prevent the commission of an offence under the Act or where with knowledge of its commission management has consented to, for example, a dangerous practice being carried on, or has connived at its being carried on, as where a blind eye has been turned on the wrongful activity.

Codes of practice

Reference has already been made to certain ACAS codes of practice issued under the EPCA 1978. However, codes of practice may also be issued in the field of health and safety by the Health and Safety Commission, and in particular, the Commission has issued a Code and Guidance Notes relating to Safety Committees.

Some general matters

The Act applies to agricultural workers on farms and agricultural holdings and to employees, e.g. lorry drivers, while working abroad. Part II of the Act is concerned with the Employment Medical Advisory Service and in particular paragraph 8 of the Third Schedule to the Act allows regulations to be made to require the making of arrangements for securing the health of persons at work, including arrangements for medical examinations and health surveys.

Part III of the Act (see now the Building Act 1984) is concerned with building regulations and seeks to secure the health, safety, and welfare, and convenience of persons in or about buildings, and of others who may be affected by the buildings or other matters concerned with buildings. It is of interest mainly to builders, architects, and surveyors and has not been dealt with here. In particular, however, the Act is concerned with the types of materials and components used and this is designed in particular to have effect on the 'towering inferno' problems in terms of fire which may result when certain materials are used in a building.

The Factories Act 1961

This Act, which also forms part of the law relating to health and safety at work will now be considered. Some of the more important safety provisions of the Factories Act 1961 are given below.

Fencing

The general rule under the Act is that every dangerous part of any machinery shall be securely fenced so that it is safe to persons employed or working on the premises. These provisions which were previously contained in the Factories Act of 1937, are the basis of many claims for damages by workpeople against their employers, so it is important to have at least a basic understanding of the provisions.

According to Lord Reid in *John Summers & Sons Ltd* v *Frost* (1955) a part of machinery is dangerous if it is a *reasonably foreseeable cause of injury* to anybody acting in a way in which a human being may be reasonably expected to act in circumstances which may reasonably be expected to occur. This definition was accepted and affirmed again by the House of Lords in *Close* v *Steel Company of Wales Ltd* (1961).

An illustration of this foreseeability test is given below.

Smith v Chesterfield & District Co-operative Society Ltd (1953)

The plaintiff worked a rolling machine which rolled puff pastry. The machine was fitted with a guard to prevent the operator from having access to the rollers, though there was a three-inch gap at the bottom of the guard. On one occasion the plaintiff, acting contrary to instructions, pushed her hand under the guard to press some dough back into the machine and was injured when her fingers came into contact with the rollers. She claimed damages from the defendants, her employers, on the basis that they were in breach of what is now the Factories Act 1961.

The Court of Appeal decided that the conduct of the plaintiff, unreasonable as it was, was reasonably foreseeable by the defendants, and, as the guard which was provided was such that the plaintiff could put her hand beneath it and so come into contact with the rollers, the rollers of the machine were not securely fenced within the meaning of the Factories Act. Therefore the defendants were in breach of their duty under the Act. However, it was also held that the plaintiff could not recover the whole of the damages because of her contributory negligence and the damages were in fact reduced by 60 per cent.

Comment. The case shows that an employer will not be absolved from liability simply because the employee is ignoring instructions, though in such a case damages will normally be reduced on the basis of contributory negligence. In this connection the judgment of Lord Goddard, C. J., is helpful, particularly where he said: 'It has been said that the provisions of the Factories Act regarding fencing are not meant only to prevent accidents to careful workmen. It is recognized that people in factories are not always careful, but, on the contrary, they are often thoughtless and sometimes they do things deliberately which they ought not to do and which involve themselves in injury. Fencing is intended to protect the careless and the ignorant as well as the careful and the well-instructed.'

Floors, passages and stairs

Under the 1961 Act all floors, stairs, passages and gangways must be of sound construction, properly maintained and, so far as is reasonably practicable, kept free from any obstruction and free from any substance which is likely to cause persons to slip. A number of cases have been brought under this part of the Act: the two which follow provide some illustration of its application.

Dorman Long (Steel) v Bell (1964)

Two heavy metal plates were put temporarily on the floor of a factory. The plates became slippery when a layer of dust collected on them and Mr Bell, who was employed on maintenance work at night, stepped on them whilst making his way to the place where he had to work. He slipped on the plates, injured himself, and sued Dorman's, his employers, for damages based on a breach of the Factories Act. The House of Lords decided that Mr Bell's action succeeded.

Latimer v AEC Ltd (1953)

Mr Latimer was a milling machine operator employed by AEC at their works in Southall, Middlesex. The works were about fifteen acres in extent and some 4000 people were employed there. Because of an extraordinarily heavy rainstorm the factory became flooded and the floodwater mixed with oil used for cooling the machines. When the water had drained away there was a slippery film of oil left on the surface of the floor. The employer spread sawdust on the floor but because a very large area was involved and the flood was unprecedented, there was not enough sawdust to cover the whole floor. Mr Latimer slipped on part of the floor which was not treated and was injured. He then brought a claim for damages against his employers for breach of the Factories Act. The

House of Lords decided that the employers were not in breach of their duty. The Act was concerned with the general condition and soundness of construction of the floor and did not relate to what the court called 'a transient and exceptional condition'. In addition, the employers had taken every reasonable step to avoid danger and were not liable for negligence at common law either.

Comment. It should be noted that an employer who is found not to have infringed the Factories Act may still be liable at common law for allowing an unsafe system of work to operate, but in this case AEC were not in breach of that common law duty either.

The Offices, Shops, and Railway Premises Act 1963

The provisions relating to railway premises are rather specialized and this part of the book will be confined to offices and shops.

Generally

Office premises includes a building or part of a building, the sole or principal use of which is for office purposes. The expression 'office purposes' includes the functions of administration, handling of money, telephone operating and clerical work, such as writing, book-keeping, filing, sorting papers, typing duplicating, machine calculating, drawing and the preparation of material for publication. Premises which are used along with the office premises are also included, such as dining rooms, washrooms, strongrooms, storage rooms and approaches and exits.

As regards shop premises, these include shops in the usual sense of the word and also all buildings or parts of them which are used for the retail trade, warehouses in the occupation of wholesalers, buildings where the public is invited to deliver goods for repair or other treatment and open fuel storage premises such as coal depots. There are some exceptions, notably, premises where no one is employed except the husband, wife, parent, grandparent, son, daughter, grandchild, brother or sister of the employer. This, of course, exempts many retail shops run by families.

Health, safety and welfare provisions

Under the Act all premises, furniture, furnishings, and fittings must be kept clean. In addition, rooms in which people work must not be overcrowded and effective provision must be made for securing and maintaining a reasonable temperature in rooms where persons are employed other than for short periods. If the work being done does not involve serious physical effort a temperature not less than 16°C (60.8°F) after the first hour is reasonable. The Act also requires that a thermometer be provided in a conspicuous place on each floor of the premises. There are some exceptions such as rooms in which goods are stored which would deteriorate at 16°C. However, employees who work in such rooms must be provided with convenient, accessible and effective means of warming themselves.

The Act also provides that every room in which persons are employed must be adequately ventilated and supplied with fresh or artificially purified air, and there must also be suitable sufficient lighting, either natural or artificial, in all parts of the premises.

Under the Act suitable and sufficient sanitary conveniences must be provided. These must be kept clean and be properly maintained, lit and ventilated. Regulations which have been made under the Act provide that where there are male and female employees separate lavatories shall be provided for each sex.

Also, suitable and sufficient washing facilities must be provided. This includes a supply of clean, running, hot and cold (or warm) water, soap, and clean towels or other suitable means of drying.

There is also a provision that an adequate supply of wholesome drinking water be made available. If the supply is not piped it must be contained in suitable vessels and must be renewed daily. If water is supplied other than by jet a supply of disposable drinking vessels must be available and, if washable, non-disposable vessels are used there must be a supply of clean water in which to rinse them.

A further requirement is that suitable and sufficient provision be made for clothing which is not worn while at work and, so far as is reasonably practicable, arrangements must be made for drying the clothing.

Where reasonable opportunities exist for sitting during working hours the Act provides that suitable sitting facilities are to be made available and the Act also says that those who sit to do their work must be provided with a seat together with a footrest if, for example, an employee is short-legged and cannot support his or her feet comfortably without one.

As regards floors, passages, and stairs, these must, under the Act, be of sound construction, properly maintained and kept free from obstruction and slippery substances. Handrails must be provided on stairways and where a stairway is open on both sides there must be two handrails and both sides must be guarded to prevent persons slipping between the rails and the steps. In addition, all openings in floors must be fenced except where the nature of the work makes such fencing impracticable.

As regards the fencing of machinery, the Act provides that dangerous parts of machinery must be fenced unless the machine is as safe without a fence as it would be with one. Furthermore, no person under eighteen may clean any machinery if this exposes him or her to the risk of injury; the Act goes on to provide that no person shall work dangerous machinery unless he or she has received sufficient training or is under adequate supervision by someone with a thorough knowledge and experience of the machine.

The Act also deals with heavy work and provides that persons shall not be required to lift, carry or move loads which are so heavy as to be likely to cause injury to them.

The Act also deals with first aid provisions and states that all premises to which the Act applies must have a first aid box or cupboard readily accessible and containing only first aid requisites or appliances. Where there are more than 150 workers there must be one box for each 150 workers or fraction thereof.

As regards fires, the Act states that all premises covered by the Act must be provided with means of escape in case of fire.

Specific and detailed legal requirements relating to fire safety at work are laid down in the Fire Precautions Act 1971 and regulations which have been made under it. These replace and extend the various precaution provisions in the Factories Act 1961 and in the Offices, Shops, and Railway Premises Act 1963.

In particular, regulations made under the 1971 Act make compulsory the inspection and issue of a fire certificate in respect of most workplaces where more than twenty people are employed or more than ten persons are employed at any one time elsewhere than on the ground floor.

Applications for a fire certificate must be made to the local fire authority on forms available from it. The detailed requirements for such a certificate are really beyond the scope of a book of this nature and will not be considered further.

Discrimination on grounds of sex, marital status or race

In recruitment and selection of employees

The relevant provisions of the Sex Discrimination Acts 1975 and 1986 and the Race Relations Act 1976 are set out below.

Offers of employment

It is unlawful for a person in relation to an employment by him at a place in England, Wales or Scotland to discriminate against men or women on grounds of sex, marital status, colour, race, nationality or ethnic or national origins:

(a) in the arrangements he makes for the purpose of deciding who should be offered the job; or

(b) in the terms on which the job is offered; or

(c) by refusing or deliberately omitting to offer the job.

'Arrangements' is a wide expression covering a range of recruitment techniques, e.g., asking an employment agency to send only white applicants, or male applicants. Discrimination by employment agencies themselves is also covered.

As regards the terms of the contract of employment, it is unlawful to discriminate against an employee on the grounds listed above in terms of the employment which is given to him or the terms of access to opportunities for promotion, transfer or training, or to any other benefit, facilities, or services, or subjecting him to any other detriment. Thus it is unlawful to discriminate in regard to matters such as privileged loans, and mortgages by banks and building societies, and discounts on holidays given to employees of travel firms.

A person who takes on workers supplied by a third party, rather than employing them himself, is obliged by the Acts not to discriminate in the treatment of them or in the work they are allowed to do. This means that temporary staff supplied by an agency are covered by the anti-discrimination provisions.

The anti-discrimination provisions are also extended to partnerships as regards failure to offer a partnership, or the terms on which it is offered including benefits, facilities and services. The provision regarding race (but not sex) discrimination applies only to firms of six or more partners, although there is a power in the legislation to reduce this number. The provision as it stands will allow race (but not sex) discrimination in the majority of medical practices but not, for example, in the major accounting and law firms.

Exceptions

There are some circumstances in which it is lawful to discriminate and these will now be considered.

(1) *Genuine occupational qualification.* So far as sex discrimination is concerned, an employer may confine a job to a man where male sex is a 'genuine occupational qualification' (GOQ) for a particular job. This could arise, for example, for reasons of physiology as in modelling male clothes, or authenticity in entertainment, as where a part calls for an actor and not an actress. Sometimes a man will be required for reasons of decency or privacy, such as an attendant in a men's lavatory. Sometimes, too, where the job involves work outside the United Kingdom in a country whose laws and customs would make it difficult for a woman to carry out the job, being a male may be a GOQ. As regards marital status, it may be reasonable to discriminate in favour of a man or a woman where the job is one of two held by a married couple, as where a woman is a housekeeper living in with her husband who is employed as a gardener.

There are, of course, a number of situations where female sex would be a GOQ for a certain type of job as the following case illustrates.

Sisley v Britannia Security Systems (1983)

The defendants employed women to work in a security control station. The plaintiff, a man, applied for a vacant job but was refused employment. It appeared that the women worked twelve-hour shifts with rest periods and that beds were provided for their use during such breaks. The women undressed to their underwear during these rest breaks. The plaintiff complained that by advertising for women the defendants were contravening the Sex Discrimination Act 1975. The defendants pleaded genuine occupational qualification, i.e. that women were required because of the removal of the uniform during rest periods was incidental to the employment.

The Employment Appeal Tribunal accepted that

defence. The defence of preservation of decency was, in the circumstances, a good one. It was reasonably incidental to the women's work that they should remove their clothing during rest periods.

As regards race, it is lawful to discriminate where there is a GOQ for the job as, for example, in the employment of a West Indian social worker or probation officer to deal with problems relating to young West Indians. Other instances are dramatic performances or other entertainment, artists or photographic models and employment in places serving food or drink to be purchased and *consumed* on the premises by the public. Thus being Chinese is a GOQ for employment in a Chinese restaurant, but not necessarily in a 'takeaway'.

(2) *Other major exceptions.* These are as follows –

(a) *private households.* Race discrimination is not unlawful where the employment is in a private household. Sex and marital discrimination is now unlawful even in private households. (Sex Discrimination Act 1986.) However, the 1986 Act provides that sex discrimination may take place where the job is likely to involve the holder of it doing his work or living in a private house and needs to be held by a man because objection might reasonably be taken to allowing the degree of physical or social contact with a person living in the house or acquiring the knowledge of intimate details of such a person's life.

(b) *Work outside Great Britain.* Discrimination legislation does not apply to work which is done wholly or mainly outside Great Britain. However, it does apply to work on a British ship, aircraft, or hovercraft unless the work is wholly outside Great Britain. The Court of Appeal decided in *Haughton* v *Olau Line (UK) Ltd* (1986) that an industrial tribunal had no jurisdiction to hear a claim for unlawful discrimination contrary to the Sex Discrimination Act 1975 where the case was brought by a woman who was employed by an English company on a German registered ship which operated mainly outside British territorial waters. Her employment was not 'at an establishment within Great Britain' as the 1975 Act requires.

(c) *Special cases.* The anti-discriminatory rules apply to Crown appointments but the provisions regarding sex discrimination do not apply to the armed forces. Women are also still prevented by the

Mines and Quarries Act 1954 from being employed in a job where the duties ordinarily require the employee to spend a significant amount of time below ground in an active mine. In general terms, service with the police is covered by anti-discrimination provisions, as is service in HM Prisons. Furthermore, the legal barriers to men becoming midwives have been removed.

Types of discrimination

There are two forms of discrimination as follows –

(1) *Direct discrimination,* which occurs where an employer or prospective employer treats a person less favourably than another on grounds of sex, race, or marital status, as where an employer refuses, on grounds of sex or race, to grant a suitably qualified person an interview for a job. In addition, the segregation of workers once in employment on the grounds of sex or race is also unlawful direct discrimination.

Examples are provided by the following cases –

Coleman v Skyrail Oceanic Ltd (1981)

The plaintiff, Coleman, who was a female booking clerk for Skyrail, a travel agency, was dismissed after she married an employee of a rival agency. Skyrail feared that there might be leaks of information about charter flights and had assumed that her dismissal was not unreasonable since the husband was the breadwinner. The Employment Appeal Tribunal decided that the dismissal was reasonable on the basis that the husband was the breadwinner. However, there was an appeal to the Court of Appeal which decided that those provisions of the Sex Discrimination Act which dealt with direct discrimination and dismissal on grounds of sex had been infringed. The assumptions that husbands were breadwinners and wives were not was based on sex and was discriminatory. The plaintiff's injury to her feelings was compensated by an award of £100 damages.

Comment. The plaintiff was also held to be unfairly dismissed having received no warning that she would be dismissed on marriage. The additional and discriminatory reason regarding the breadwinner cost the employer a further £100.

Johnson v Timber Tailors (Midlands) (1978)

When the plaintiff, a black Jamaican, applied for a job with the defendants as a wood machinist the defendants' works manager told him that he would be contacted in a couple of days to let him know whether or not he had been successful. Mr Johnson was not contacted and after a number of unsuccessful attempts to get in touch with the works manager, was told that the vacancy had been filled. Another advertisement for wood machinists appeared in the paper on the same night as Mr Johnson was told that the vacancy had been filled. Nevertheless, Mr Johnson applied again for the job and was told that the vacancy was filled. About a week later he applied again and was again told that the job had been filled although a further advertisement had appeared for the job on that day. An industrial tribunal decided that the evidence established that Mr Johnson had been discriminated against on the grounds of race.

(2) *Indirect discrimination*, as where an employer has applied requirements or conditions to a job but the ability of some persons to comply because of sex, marital status, or race is considerably smaller and cannot be justified.

Examples are provided by the following cases.

Price v The Civil Service Commission (1977)

The Civil Service required candidates for the position of executive officer to be between seventeen-and-one-half and twenty-eight years. Belinda Price complained that this age bar constituted indirect sex discrimination against women because women between those ages were more likely than men to be temporarily out of the labour market having children or caring for children at home. The Employment Appeal Tribunal decided that the age bar was indirect discrimination against women. The court held that the words 'can comply' in the legislation must not be construed narrowly. It could be said that any female applicant could comply with the condition in the sense that she was not obliged to marry or have children, or to look after them – indeed, she might find someone else to look after them or, as a last resort, put them into care. If the legislation was construed in that way it was no doubt right to say that any female applicant could comply with the condition. However, in the view of the court, to construe the legislation in that way appeared to be wholly out of sympathy with the spirit and intention of the Act. A person should not be deemed to be able to do something merely because it was theoretically possible; it was necessary to decide whether it was possible for a person to do so in practice as distinct from theory.

Bohon-Mitchell v Council of Legal Education (1978)

The plaintiff, an overseas student, complained of discrimination in regard to a requirement of the defendants that a student would have to undergo a twenty-one month course, as opposed to a diploma of one year, to complete the academic stage of training for the Bar where he did not have a UK or Irish Republic university degree. This rule was regarded by an industrial tribunal to be discriminatory because the proportion of persons not from the UK or Irish Republic who could comply was considerably smaller than persons from the UK or Irish Republic who could and the rule was not justifiable on other grounds. The plaintiff satisfied the tribunal that there had been indirect discrimination.

Comment. The other side of the coin is illustrated by *Panesar* v *Nestle Co. Ltd* (1980) where an orthodox Sikh who naturally wore a beard which was required by his religion, applied for a job in the defendants' chocolate factory. He was refused employment because the defendants applied a strict rule under which no beards or excessively long hair were allowed on the grounds of hygiene. The plaintiff made a complaint of indirect discrimination but the defendants said that the rule was justified. The Court of Appeal decided that as the defendants had supported their rule with scientific evidence there was in fact no discrimination.

Remedies

Allegations of discrimination may be the subject of a complaint to an industrial tribunal which may, among other things, award monetary compensation.

In addition, the Equal Opportunities Commission, which is responsible for keeping under review the working of sex discrimination legislation, including equal pay, and the Commission for Racial Equality, which has a similar function in terms of racial discrimination, may carry out formal investigations into firms where discrimination is alleged and may issue non-discrimination notices requiring the employer to comply with the relevant legislation.

The employer may appeal to an industrial tribunal within six weeks of service of the notice. If there is no appeal, or the industrial tribunal confirms the notice, then the employer must comply with it; if he does not the relevant Commission may ask the county court for an injunction which, if granted, will make an employer who ignores it in contempt of court and he may be fined and/or imprisoned for that offence.

The Commissions are also required to enter non-discrimination notices which have become final in a Register. Copies of the Register are kept in Manchester (Equal Opportunities Commission) and in London (Commission for Racial Equality), and are available for inspection to any person on payment of a fee and copies may also be obtained.

Relationship between the Sex Discrimination Act and the Equal Pay Act

The two Acts do not overlap. Complaints of discrimination in regard to pay and other non-monetary matters governed by the contract of employment, such as hours of work, are dealt with under the Equal Pay Act and complaints of discrimination in regard, e.g. to access to jobs, are dealt with under the Sex Discrimination Act. A complaint to an industrial tribunal need not be based from the beginning on one Act or the other. A tribunal is empowered to make a decision under whichever Act turns out to be relevant when all the facts are before it.

Discriminatory advertisements for employees

The sex discrimination and racial discrimination legislation make it unlawful to place advertisements for employees which are discriminatory unless they relate to a recognized exceptional case, as where, for example, there is a GOQ. Thus job descriptions such as 'waiter', 'salesgirl', 'stewardess' or 'girl friday' have largely disappeared from our newspapers and one now finds the descriptions 'waiter/waitress' or the expression 'male/female' as indicating that both sexes are eligible for employment. However, one still sees advertisements which are clearly intended to attract female applicants which, nevertheless, remain within the law, e.g. 'publishing director requires sophisticated PA/secretary with style and charm who can remain cool under pressure'.

Before legislation relating to discrimination came into force, advertisements in the UK were discriminatory mainly as regards sex, but obviously an advertisement which said 'Chinese only' would be unlawful unless there was a GOQ as, for example, there would be where the advertisement was for a waiter in a Chinese restaurant.

As regards sanctions, the placing of discriminatory advertisements may lead to the issue of a non-discrimination notice by the appropriate Commission; this, if not complied with, may lead to proceedings being taken by the Commission in an industrial tribunal. If the industrial tribunal accepts the contention of discrimination and yet the advertiser does not comply but continues to advertise in a discriminatory way, the Commission may take proceedings in the county court for, amongst other things, an injunction. If this is not complied with the advertiser is in contempt of court and may be punished by a fine or imprisonment unless he complies.

In addition, it is a criminal offence to place a discriminatory advertisement and those who do so may be tried by magistrates and are subject to a fine. The person who publishes the advertisement, e.g. a newspaper proprietor, also commits a criminal offence. However, he may not know precisely that the advertisement is discriminatory. For example, without a knowledge of the advertiser's business, he cannot really know whether there is a GOQ or not. Accordingly, he is given a defence to any criminal charge if he can show that in publishing the advertisement –

(*a*) he relied on a statement by the person placing it to the effect that it was not unlawful and on the face of it might come within one of the exceptional cases; and

(*b*) it was reasonable for him to rely on that statement.

Discrimination once in employment

We have already considered the law relating to discrimination in formation of the contract, i.e. in recruitment and selection, and in terms of remuneration, i.e. equal pay. Discrimination on termination of the contract will be dealt with later when we look at discriminatory dismissal. Here we are concerned with discrimination in the treatment of employees during the course of the contract of employment.

Discrimination on the grounds of sex or race. Under the sex and race discrimination legislation it is unlawful to discriminate against a person on grounds of sex or race as regards opportunities for promotion, training, or transfer to other positions, or in the provision of benefits, facilities, or services, or by dismissal or by any other disadvantages.

However, as we have seen, the law allows women to receive special treatment when they are pregnant and there is no discrimination where the sex or racial status of the employee is a genuine occupational qualification.

There are some exemptions in special cases; for example, the armed forces are not covered.

There is also an exemption in respect of discriminatory training. An employer or a body responsible for training may provide training exclusively applicable to persons of a particular sex or racial group where the purpose is to enable them to take up work in situations where that sex or racial group is under-represented, but there may not be discrimination in terms of recruitment for such work. Trade unions may also take special action to attract members of particular sexual or racial groups into membership or to office in the union where there is under-representation.

As regards enforcement, if an unlawful act of discrimination is committed by an employee such as a personnel officer, the employer is held responsible for the act along with the employee unless the employer can show that he took all reasonable steps to prevent the employee from discriminating. If he can do this, only the employee is responsible.

Individual employees who believe that they have been discriminated against may make a complaint to an industrial tribunal within three months of the act complained of. It is then the duty of a conciliation officer to see whether the complaint can be settled without going to a tribunal. If, however, the tribunal hears the complaint, it may make an order declaring the rights of the employer and the employee in regard to the complaint, the intention being that both parties will abide by the order for the future.

The tribunal may also give the employee monetary compensation and may additionally recommend that the employer take, within a specified period, action appearing to the tribunal to be practicable for the purpose of obviating or reducing discrimination.

Discrimination against married persons

The anti-discriminatory provisions outlined in the previous section are applied also to discrimination against married persons. An employer must not treat a married person of either sex, on the ground of his or her marital status, less favourably than he treats or would treat an unmarried person of the same sex; e.g. there must not be a marriage bar attached to a particular employment, unless, of course, there is a GOQ.

Victimization in employment

Under the sex and racial discrimination legislation it is unlawful to treat a person less favourably than another because that person asserted rights under the equal pay or other anti-discriminatory legislation relating to sex or race or has helped another person to assert such rights or has given information to the Equal Opportunities Commission or the Commission for Racial Equality, or it is thought that he or she might do so.

Termination of the contract of employment

Unfair dismissal

Generally

Before a person can ask an industrial tribunal to consider a claim that another has unfairly dismissed him or her it is once again essential to establish that the relationship of employer and employee exists between them. In this connection the Employment Protection (Consolidation) Act 1978 provides that an employee is a person who works under a contract of service or apprenticeship, written or oral, express or implied.

An example of a case where a person failed in an unfair dismissal claim because he was unable to show that he was an employee is given below.

Massey v Crown Life Insurance Co. (1978)

Mr Massey was employed by Crown Life as the manager of their Ilford branch from 1971 to 1973, the company paying him wages and deducting tax. In 1973, on the advice of his accountant, Mr Massey registered a business name of J R Massey and Associates and with that new name entered into an agreement with Crown Life under which he carried out the same duties as before but as a self-employed person. The Inland Revenue were content that he should change to be taxed under Schedule D as a self-employed person. His employment was terminated and he claimed to have been unfairly dismissed. The Court of Appeal decided that being self-employed he could not be unfairly dismissed.

In addition to showing that he is an employee the claimant must satisfy an *age requirement*. The unfair dismissal provisions do not apply to the dismissal of an employee from any employment if the employee has on or before the effective date of termination attained the age which, in the undertaking in which he is employed, was the normal retiring age for an employee holding the position which he held, or, for both men and women age sixty-five. (Sex Discrimination Act 1986.)

However, such persons are not excluded where the dismissal is automatically unfair, e.g. for taking part in trade union activities. (See further p. 308.)

As regards the period of employment, the unfair dismissal provisions do not apply to the dismissal of an employee from any employment if the employee has not completed one year's continuous employment ending with the effective date of termination of employment unless the dismissal is automatically unfair. For those who started work on or after 1 October 1980 the total length of employment must exceed two years provided that during that period there were no more than twenty employees in the same firm, together with any associated employer. Again, this does not apply if the dismissal is automatically unfair and, clearly, companies within a group are associated employers. Those who started work on or after 1 June 1985 must also complete at least two years' service regardless of the size of the firm unless the dismissal is automatically unfair.

In addition, the 1978 Act states that no account should be taken of employment during any period when the hours of employment are normally less than sixteen hours per week. After five years' employment the figure is reduced to eight hours. Again, the requirement of having worked sixteen or eight hours, as the case may be, does not apply to dismissals which are automatically unfair.

As regards persons ordinarily employed outside Great Britain, the 1978 Act states that an employee has no protection against unfair dismissal if he is engaged in work wholly or mainly outside Great Britain.

The following are also ineligible and cannot claim:

(1) Those on fixed contracts of two years or more if they have agreed in writing, either in the contract or during its duration to forgo the right to compensation. If the contract was made on or after 1 October 1980 the period of the fixed term is reduced to one year.

(2) Those who at the date of their dismissal were taking part in a strike or other industrial action and others involved were not dismissed (or, if they were, had re-employment offered to them within the three months of their dismissal) if they do not claim within six months of their dismissal. For example, A, B, and C are on strike. Their employer dismisses them. After two months he offers to re-engage B and C. A may complain of unfair dismissal for another four months. If he fails to do so or the offer to re-engage B and C is made six or more months after their dismissal A cannot claim.

(3) Women who are dismissed because of pregnancy if they have not been employed for two years prior to the eleventh week before the expected week of confinement.

(4) Certain other categories are excluded by the 1978 Act, e.g. members of the armed forces and of the police.

Dismissal – meaning of

An employee cannot claim unfair dismissal unless there has first been a dismissal recognized by law. We may consider the matter under the following headings:

(1) *Actual dismissal*. This does not normally give rise to problems since most employees recognize the words of an actual dismissal, whether given orally or in writing.

A typical letter of dismissal appears below.

Dear Mr Bloggs,

I am sorry that you do not have the necessary aptitude to deal with the work which we have allocated to you. I hope that you will be able to find other work elsewhere which is more in your line. As you will recall from your interview this morning, the company will not require your services after the 31st of this month.

---

(2) *Constructive dismissal*. This occurs where it is the employee who leaves the job but he is compelled to do so by the conduct of the employer. In general terms the employer's conduct must be a fundamental breach so that it can be regarded as a repudiation of the contract. Thus, if a male employer were sexually to assault his female secretary then this would be a fundamental breach entitling her to leave and sue for her loss on the basis of constructive dismissal.

(3) *Fixed term contracts*. When a fixed term contract expires and is not renewed there is a dismissal. However, where a contract is for two years or more the

employee may have waived his right to complain of unfair dismissal. If the contract is made on or after 1 October 1980 the period of the fixed term is reduced to one year.

Dismissal - grounds for

If an employer is going to escape liability for unfair dismissal he must show that he acted *reasonably* and, indeed, the 1978 Act requires the employer to give his reasons for dismissal to the employee in writing.

It should be remembered that the question whether a dismissal is fair or not is a matter of *fact* for the particular tribunal hearing the case and one cannot predict without absolute accuracy what a particular tribunal will do on the facts of a particular case. Basically, when all is said and done, the ultimate question for a tribunal is: 'Was the dismissal fair and reasonable' in fact.

The Employment Act 1980 amended the Employment Protection (Consolidation) Act of 1978 by including in the test of reasonableness required in determining whether a dismissal was a fair, the 'size and administrative resources of the employer's undertaking'. This was included as a result of fear that the unfair dismissal laws were placing undue burdens on small firms and causing them not to engage new workers. The 1980 Act also removed the burden of proof from the employer in showing reasonableness so that there is now no 'presumption of guilt' on the employer and the tribunal is left to decide whether or not the employer acted reasonably.

(1) *Reasons justifying dismissal.* These are as follows –

(a) *Lack of capability.* This would usually arise at the beginning of employment where it becomes clear at an early stage that the employee cannot do the job in terms of lack of skill or mental or physical health. It should be remembered that the longer a person is in employment the more difficult it is to establish lack of capability.

By way of illustration we can consider the case of *Alidair* v *Taylor* (1977). The pilot of an aircraft had made a faulty landing which damaged the aircraft. There was a board of inquiry which found that the faulty landing was due to a lack of flying knowledge on the part of the pilot who was dismissed from his employment. It was decided that the employee had

not been unfairly dismissed, the tribunal taking the view that where, as in this case, one failure to reach a high degree of skill could have serious consequences, an instant dismissal could be justified.

(b) *Conduct.* This is always a difficult matter to deal with and much will depend upon the circumstances of the case. However, incompetence and neglect are relevant, as are disobedience and misconduct, e.g. by assaulting fellow employees. Immorality and habitual drunkenness could also be brought under this heading and, so, it seems, can dress where this can be shown to effect adversely the way in which the contract of service is performed.

Boychuk v H J Symonds (Holdings) Ltd (1977)

Miss B was employed by S Ltd as an accounts audit clerk but her duties involved contact with the public from time to time. Miss B insisted on wearing badges which proclaimed the fact that she was a lesbian and from May 1976 she wore one or other of the following: (a) a lesbian symbol consisting of two circles with crosses (indicating women) joined together; (b) badges with the legends 'Gays against fascism' and 'Gay power'; (c) a badge with the legend 'Gay switchboard' with a telephone number on it and the words 'Information service for homosexual men and women'; (d) a badge with the word 'Dyke', indicating to the initiated that she was a lesbian.

These were eventually superseded by a white badge with the words 'Lesbians ignite' written in large letters on it. Nothing much had happened in regard to the wearing of the earlier badges but when she began wearing the 'Lesbians ignite' badge there were discussions about it between her and her employer. She was told she must remove it – which she was not willing to do – and if she did not she would be dismissed. She would not remove the badge and was dismissed on 16 August 1976 and then made a claim for compensation for unfair dismissal.

No complaint was made regarding the manner of her dismissal in terms, e.g. of proper warning. The straight question was whether her employers were entitled to dismiss her because she insisted on wearing the badge. An industrial tribunal had decided that in all the circumstances the dismissal was fair because it was within an employer's discretion to instruct an employee not to wear a particular badge or symbol which could cause offence to customers and fellow-employees. Miss B appealed to the Employment Appeal Tribunal which dismissed her appeal and said that her dismissal was fair. The EAT said that there was no question of Miss B having been dismissed because she was lesbian or because of anything to do with her private life or private behaviour. Such a case would be entirely different and raise different questions. This was only a case where she had been dismissed because of her conduct at work. That, the EAT said, must be clearly understood.

Comment. The decision does not mean that an employer by a foolish or unreasonable judgment of what could be expected to be offensive could impose some unreasonable restriction on an employee. However, the decision does mean that a reasonable employer, who is, after all, ultimately responsible for the interests of the business, is allowed to decide what, upon reflection or mature consideration, could be offensive to customers and fellow employees, and he need not wait to see whether the business would in fact be damaged before he takes steps in the matter.

(*c*) *Redundancy.* Genuine redundancy is a defence. Where a person is redundant his employer cannot be expected to continue the employment, although there are safeguards in the matter of *unfair selection for redundancy* (see p. 308).

(*d*) *Failure to join a trade union.* A dismissal for failure to join a trade union will be fair if it is the practice in accordance with the union membership for employees of the same class to belong to one (or more) independent trade unions, and the only (or principal) reason for the dismissal was that the employee ceased to be a member of, or refused to join, or proposed to refuse to join or remain a member of the union, in accordance with the union agreement, provided the union membership agreement has been approved by ballot and that a ballot has been held within five years of the notice of dismissal. The ballot must have been approved by not less than 80 per cent of all those entitled to vote and in some cases the percentage can be 85 per cent.

Dismissal for failure to belong to a trade union will, however, become unfair, even though there has been a proper ballot for a closed shop if –

(*i*) the employee has an objection to being a member of the union on grounds of conscience or other deeply held personal conviction. Thus in *Saggers* v *British Railways Board* (1977) the

Employment Appeal Tribunal decided that, in considering whether an employee's refusal to join a trade union was because of a genuine objection on the grounds of religious belief, the industrial tribunal should have regard not only to the general creed of the religious sect (in this case Jehovah's Witnesses) to which the employee belonged, but also to his personal beliefs. In this case it appeared that the Jehovah's Witnesses did not object to their members joining trade unions, but it was held by the EAT that it was not enough for an industrial tribunal to base its decision on this. The tribunal should look at the personal beliefs of the employee concerned and as he had objected on religious grounds that was enough; or

(*ii*) the employee holds qualifications necessary for the job which are subject to a code of practice which precludes him from taking part in industrial action, including strikes, and he is expelled from, or refused membership of, the union because of that code. This is particularly important in regard to the medical and nursing professions in the Health Service; or

(*iii*) he has been unreasonably expelled or excluded from the union and a tribunal has decided that that is so.

(*e*) *Statutory restriction placed on employer or employee.* If, for example, the employer's business was found to be dangerous and was closed down under Act of Parliament or ministerial order, the employees would not be unfairly dismissed. Furthermore, a lorry driver who was banned from driving for twelve months could be dismissed fairly.

(*f*) *Some other substantial reasons.* An employer may on a wide variety of grounds which are not specified by legislation satisfy an industrial tribunal that a dismissal was fair and reasonable.

Crime and suspicion of crime may be brought under this head, though if dismissal is based on suspicion of crime, the suspicion must be reasonable and in all cases the employee must be told that dismissal is contemplated and in the light of this information be allowed to give explanations and make representations against dismissal.

Where an employee has been charged with theft from the employer and is awaiting trial, the best course of action is to suspend rather than dismiss him, pending the verdict. Investigations which the employer must make, as part of establishing a fair dismissal, could be regarded as an interference with the course of justice. It is best, therefore, not to make them, but to suspend the employee.

The matter of fair or unfair dismissal depends also upon the terms of the contract. If the difficulty is that a particular employee is refusing to do work which involves him, say, spending nights away from home, then his dismissal is likely to be regarded as fair if there is an *express term* in his contract requiring this. Of course, the nature of the job may require it, as in the case of a long-distance lorry driver – where such a term would be implied, if not expressed.

Employees who are in breach of contract are likely to be regarded as fairly dismissed. However, this is not an invariable rule. Thus a long-distance lorry driver who refused to take on a particular trip because his wife was ill and he had to look after the children would be unfairly dismissed (if dismissal took place) even though he was, strictly speaking, in breach of his contract.

(2) *Grievance and disciplinary procedures* are usually part of the contract. The employer must comply with them if he wishes to avoid liability. If a series of oral and written warnings is laid down, the procedure should be observed. However, reasonableness will always prevail. Thus if an employee commits an armed robbery on his employer's premises he could, and would, be dismissed quite fairly without going through a warning procedure. There would be no need to tell him that if he robbed the premises again he was in danger of losing his job!

(3) *Employee's contributory fault.* This can reduce the compensation payable to the employee by such percentage as the tribunal thinks fit. Suppose an employee is often late for work and one morning, his employer who can stand it no more, sacks him. The dismissal is likely to be unfair in view of the lack of warning, but a tribunal would very probably reduce the worker's compensation to take account of the fact situation.

Principles of natural justice also apply; it is necessary to let the worker state his case before a decision to dismiss is taken. Furthermore, reasonable inquiry must be made to find the truth of the matter before reaching a decision. Failure to do this will tend to make the dismissal unfair.

(4) *Unacceptable reasons for dismissal.* These are as follows –

(a) *dismissal in connection with trade unions.* If the only (or principal) reason for the dismissal is as set out below, the dismissal will be automatically unfair –

(i) because the employee was, or proposed to become, a member of an independent trade union; or

(ii) because he had taken part, or proposed to take part in the activities of an independent trade union at an appropriate time;

(iii) because he was not a member of any trade union nor of a particular one. Alternatively, that he had refused or had proposed to refuse to join or remain a member of a trade union or a particular one – *unless* (in which case dismissal will be fair) there is a properly ballotted closed shop – *unless* (in which case dismissal will become unfair) the employee has an objection to being a member of the union on the grounds of conscience or other deeply held personal conviction (see *Saggers* v *British Railways Board* (1977) p. 307) or, the employee holds qualifications necessary for his job which are subject to a code of practice which prevents him from taking part in industrial action, including strikes, and he is expelled from or refused membership of the union because of that code. As we have seen, this is particularly important in the Health Service; or he has been unreasonably expelled or excluded from the union and a tribunal has declared his expulsion to be unreasonable.

(b) *Unfair selection for redundancy.* An employee dismissed for redundancy may complain that he has been unfairly dismissed if he is of the opinion that he has been unfairly selected for redundancy, as where the employer has selected him because he is a member of a trade union or takes part in trade union activities, or where the employer has disregarded redundancy selection arrangements based, for example, on 'last in, first out'. Ideally, all employers should have proper redundancy agreements on the lines set out in the Department of Employment booklet *Dealing with Redundancies*.

However, even though there is in existence an agreed redundancy procedure, the employer may defend himself by showing a 'special reason' for departing from that procedure, e.g. because the person selected for redundancy lacks the skill and versatility of a junior employee who is retained.

There is, since the decision of the Employment Appeal Tribunal in *Williams* v *Compair Maxam* (1982), an overall standard of fairness also in redundancy arrangements. The standards laid down in the case require the giving of maximum notice; consultation with unions, if any; the taking of the views of more than one person as to who should be dismissed; a requirement to follow any laid down procedure, i.e. last in, first out; and finally, an effort to find the employees concerned alternative employment within the organization. However, the EAT stated in *Meikle* v *McPhail* (*Charleston Arms*) (1983) that these guidelines would be applied less rigidly to the smaller business.

(*c*) *Strikes.* If an employee is dismissed during a strike, an industrial tribunal has no power to hear an application for unfair dismissal by that person and in consequence the question whether the dismissal is fair or unfair never arises. However, a tribunal can hear a claim in regard to dismissal during a strike where other employees involved in the strike were not dismissed or, if they were dismissed, were afterwards offered re-engagement by the employer but the person making the claim was not.

(*d*) *Dismissal of pregnant employee.* A woman who is dismissed because she is pregnant will be treated as having been unfairly dismissed unless certain circumstances apply, for example that she is unable to do her job and cannot be offered, or has refused suitable alternative work. Even in these cases where the dismissal would be regarded as fair, the woman is nevertheless entitled to maternity pay and may claim re-instatement after confinement.

Refusal to take a woman back after pregnancy is also unfair dismissal. However, if at the start of the absence due to pregnancy there are five employees or less (including those employed by an associated company) the employer may show that it is not reasonably practical to offer the worker her old job back or another one substantially similar in terms and there is no unfair dismissal. In larger firms than this, as we have seen above, the employee's rights can be curtailed only if the employer can show that it is not reasonably practical to give the old job back and that a suitable alternative has been offered and unreasonably refused. Failure by the employer to comply with the obligations placed on him by law

can result in the employee obtaining an order that she be taken back or, if this is refused or is not practical, an order for compensation on the grounds of unfair dismissal.

(*e*) *Pressure on employer to dismiss unfairly.* It is no defence for an employer to say that pressure was put upon him to dismiss an employee unfairly. So, if other workers put pressure on an employer to dismiss a non-union member so as, for example, to obtain a closed shop, the employer will have no defence to a claim for compensation for the dismissal if he gives in to that pressure. If an employer alleges that he was pressurized into dismissing an employee and that pressure was brought on him by a trade union or other person by the calling, organizing, procuring, or financing of industrial action, including a strike, or by the threat of such things, and the reason for the pressure was that the employee was not a member of the trade union, then the employer can join the trade union or other person as a party to the proceedings if he is sued by the dismissed worker for unfair dismissal. If the tribunal awards compensation it can order that a person joined as a party to the proceedings should pay such amount of it as is just and equitable, and if necessary this can be a complete indemnity so that the employer will recover all the damages awarded against him from the union.

(*f*) *Transfer of business.* The Transfer of Undertakings (Protection of Employment) Regulations 1981 apply to transfers of businesses which take place on or after 1 May 1982. Under the regulations, if a business or part of it is transferred and an employee is dismissed because of this, the dismissal will be treated as automatically unfair. However, the person concerned is not entitled to the extra compensation given to other cases of automatically unfair dismissal. (See p. 271.)

If the old employer dismissed before transfer, or the new employer dismissed after the transfer, either will have a defence if he can prove that the dismissal was for 'economic, technical, or organizational' reasons requiring a change in the workforce and that the dismissal was reasonable in all the circumstances of the case.

Meikle v McPhail (Charleston Arms) (1983)

After contracting to take over a public house and its employees, the new management decided that economies were essential and dismissed the barmaid. She complained to an industrial tribunal on the grounds of unfair dismissal. Her case was based upon the fact that the 1981 Regulations state that a dismissal is to be treated as unfair if the transfer of a business or a reason connected with it, is the reason or principal reason for the dismissal. The pub's new management defended the claim under another provision in the 1981 Regulations which states that a dismissal following a transfer of business is not to be regarded as automatically unfair where there was, as in this case, an economic reason for making changes in the workforce. If there is such a reason, unfairness must be established on grounds other than the mere transfer of the business.

The Employment Appeal Tribunal decided that the reason for dismissal was an economic one under the Regulations and that the management had acted reasonably in the circumstances so that the barmaid's claim failed.

Unfair dismissal and frustration of contract

In cases appearing before industrial tribunals there is a certain interplay between the common law rules of frustration of contract (see p. 315) and the statutory provisions relating to unfair dismissal. At common law a contract of service is frustrated by incapacity, e.g. sickness, if that incapacity makes the contract substantially impossible of performance at a particularly vital time, or by a term of imprisonment (see *Hare* v *Murphy Bros* (1974) (p. 178)). If a contract has been so frustrated then a complaint of unfair dismissal is not available because the contract has been discharged on other grounds, i.e. by frustration. Thus termination of a contract of service by frustration prevents a claim for unfair dismissal.

Remedies for unfair dismissal

These are as follows –

(1) *Conciliation.* An industrial tribunal will not hear a complaint until a conciliation officer has had a chance to see whether he can help. A copy of the complaint made to the industrial tribunal is sent to the conciliation officer and if he is unable to settle the complaint, nothing said by employer or employee during the process of conciliation will be admissible in evidence before the tribunal.

(2) *Other remedies.* An employee who has been dismissed may –

(a) seek reinstatement or re-engagement; or

(b) claim compensation.

The power to order (a) above is discretionary and in practice rarely exercised. However, reinstatement means taken back by the employer on exactly the same terms and seniority as before; re-engagement is being taken back but on different terms.

(3) *Calculation of compensation.* The compensation for unfair dismissal is in four parts as follows –

(a) *the basic award* (maximum: dismissals before 1 April 1987 £4560: thereafter £4740). This award is computed as a redundancy payment (see p. 313 before reading on) except that there is no maximum age limit. Contributory fault of the employee is taken into account. *Example*: Fred, a thirty-five year old lorry driver employed for ten years earning £120 per week (take home £100) is unfairly dismissed. He did his best to get a comparable job but did not in fact obtain one until two weeks after the tribunal hearing. Fred had a history of lateness for work and his contributory fault is assessed at 25 per cent.

Fred's basic award. Fred is in category 22 years of age but under forty-one for redundancy purposes which allows one week's pay for every year of service.

$$10 \times £120 \quad £1200$$
$$\text{Less: } 25\% \quad \underline{300}$$
$$\underline{£900} \quad = \text{ basic award}$$

If Fred's dismissal had been automatically unfair, e.g. for union membership, the minimum award is £2300. This may be reduced for contributory fault.

(b) *Compensatory award.* (Maximum: £8500). This consists of –

(i) estimated loss of wages, net of tax and other deductions to the date of the hearing less any money earned between date of dismissal and the hearing;

(ii) estimated future losses;

(iii) loss of any benefits such as pension rights and expenses;

(iv) loss of statutory rights. It is rare to get an award under this heading but it can be given for loss of minimum notice entitlement. For example, Fred has been continuously employed for ten years. He was entitled to ten weeks' notice which he did not get. He now has a new job but it will take him time to build up that entitlement again. A tribunal can award something for this. Once again contributory fault is taken into account.

Fred's compensatory award

	£	£
The loss up to the hearing	10 × £100	1000	
Loss up to time of getting new job	2 × £100	200	
		1200	
Less: 25%		300	
			900
Loss of statutory rights: a nominal figure of		100	
Less: 25%		25	
			75
			975

Fred's total award is therefore

Basic	900
Compensatory	975
	1875

If Fred has lost anything else, e.g. use of firm's van at weekends and or pension rights, these would be added to the compensatory award subject to a 25 per cent discount for contributory fault.

(c) *Additional award.* This is available in addition to the above where an employer fails to comply with an order for reinstatement or re-engagement unless it was not practicable for him to do so.

(*i*) If the original dismissal was unlawful under the Race Relations Act or Sex Discrimination Act, it is not less than twenty-six weeks' pay nor more than fifty-two weeks' pay with a maximum of £158 per week, and an overall maximum of £8500.

(*ii*) In other cases (not where dismissal is automatically unfair, see below), it is not less than thirteen weeks' pay nor more than twenty-six weeks' pay calculated as in (*i*) above.

(d) *A special award.* This is payable where the dismissal is automatically unfair and the employee has asked for reinstatement or re-engagement but the tribunal has refused to make such an order. It can make a special award instead. The compensation is a week's pay but without limit as to amount, multiplied by 104 weeks with a minimum amount of £11 500 and a maximum of £23 000. However, if a tribunal does make an order for reinstatement or re-engagement and the employer does not comply but cannot show that it was reasonably impracticable for him to do so, the compensation is increased to a week's pay (no limit) multiplied by 156 with a minimum of £17 250 and no maximum. In all cases

a deduction will be made for contributory fault, if any, of the employee.

Any unemployment or supplementary benefits received by the employee are deducted from any award made by a tribunal. However, the employer must pay the amount(s) in question direct to the DHSS.

(4) *Time limits.* A claim for compensation against an employer must reach the tribunal within three months of the date of termination of employment. The period in regard to dismissal in connection with a strike or other industrial action is six months. A worker can claim while working out his notice but no award can be made until employment ends.

A tribunal can hear a claim after three months if the employee can prove that:

(*a*) it was not reasonably practicable for him to claim within three months;

(*b*) he did so as soon as he could in the circumstances.

Discriminatory dismissal

In addition to legislation relating to unfair dismissal generally, the Sex Discrimination Act 1975 and the Race Relations Act 1976 deal with complaints to industrial tribunals for dismissal on the grounds of sex, marital status, or race. The nature and scope of these provisions has already been considered and it is only necessary to add here that there are provisions in the Employment Protection (Consolidation) Act 1978 which prevent double compensation being paid, once under sex discrimination legislation or race discrimination legislation, and once under the general unfair dismissal provisions of the 1978 Act.

Redundancy

The Employment Protection (Consolidation) Act 1978 gives an employee a right to compensation by way of a redundancy payment if he is dismissed because of a redundancy.

Meaning of redundancy

Under the 1978 Act redundancy is *presumed* to occur where the services of employees are dispensed with because the employer ceases, or intends to cease carrying on business, or to carry on business at the place where the employee was employed, or does not require so many employees to do work of a certain kind. Employees who have been laid off or kept on short time without pay for four consecutive weeks (or for six weeks in a period of thirteen weeks) are entitled to end their employment and to seek a redundancy payment if there is no reasonable prospect that normal working will be resumed.

Eligibility

In general terms, all those employed under a contract of service as employees are entitled to redundancy pay, including a person employed by his/her spouse. Furthermore, a volunteer for redundancy is not debarred from claiming. However, certain persons are excluded by statute or circumstances. The main categories are listed below –

(*a*) a domestic servant in a private household who is a close relative of the employer. The definition of 'close relative' for this purpose is father, mother, grandfather, grandmother, stepfather, stepmother, son, daughter, grandson, granddaughter, stepson, stepdaughter, brother, sister, half-brother, or half-sister;

(*b*) an employee who has not completed at least two years of continuous service since reaching the age of eighteen;

(*c*) male employees of sixty-five years or over (sixty for women);

(*d*) part-time workers who normally work less than sixteen hours per week. After five years' employment the figure is reduced to eight hours;

(*e*) where in the case of a fixed term contract of two years or more the employee has agreed in writing in the contract or at any stage of the contract to forgo his right to claim redundancy payment;

(*f*) employees who normally work outside Great Britain under their contract;

(*g*) workers on strike can generally be dismissed by their employers without liability to make a redundancy payment. This applies even though the employer was short of work at the time of the strike so that a redundancy situation did exist. Where the strike takes place after a redundancy notice has been given, the employee concerned may still get part or all of his redundancy pay by applying to a tribunal which has a power under the Employment Protection (Consolidation) Act 1978 to make an award which is 'just and

equitable', the amount being arrived at by the tribunal.

An employee who accepts an offer of suitable alternative employment with his employer is not entitled to a redundancy payment. Where a new offer is made, there is a trial period of four weeks following the making of the offer, during which the employer or the employee may end the contract while retaining all rights and liabilities under redundancy legislation. An employee who unreasonably refuses an offer of alternative employment is not entitled to a redundancy payment.

Fuller v Stephanie Bowman (1977)

F was employed as a secretary at SB's premises which were situated in Mayfair. These premises attracted a very high rent and rates so SB moved their offices to Soho. These premises were situated over a sex shop and F refused the offer of renewed employment at the same salary and she later brought a claim before an industrial tribunal for a redundancy payment. The tribunal decided that the question of unreasonableness was a matter of fact for the tribunal and F's refusal to work over the sex shop was unreasonable so that she was not entitled to a redundancy payment.

In addition, it should be noted that in *North East Coast Ship Repairers* v *Secretary of State for Employment* (1978) the Employment Appeal Tribunal decided that an apprentice who, having completed the period of his apprenticeship, finds that the firm cannot provide him with work is not entitled to redundancy payment. This case has relevance for trainees and others completing contracts in order to obtain relevant practical experience.

As regards time limits, the employee must make a written claim to the employer or to an industrial tribunal within six months from the end of the employment. If the employee does not do this an industrial tribunal may extend the time for a further six months, making twelve months in all, but not longer, from the actual date of termination of the employment, provided that it can be shown that it is just and equitable having regard to the reasons put forward by the employee for late application and to all relevant circumstances.

Amount of redundancy payment

Those aged 41 to 65 (60 women) receive 1½ weeks' pay

(up to a maximum of £158 per week) for each year of service up to a maximum of 20 years. In other age groups the above provisions apply except that the week's pay changes, i.e. for those aged at least 22, but under 41, it is one week's pay, and for those of at least 18, but under 22, it is half a week's pay.

For example, a man of 52 who is made redundant having been continuously employed for 18 years and earning £120 per week as gross salary at the time of his redundancy would be entitled to a redundancy payment as follows.

34 to 41 years = 7 years at one week's pay	=	7 weeks
41 to 52 years = 11 years at one and a half week's pay	=	16½ weeks
		23½ weeks

It follows, therefore, that the redundancy payment would be 23½ weeks × £120 = £2820.

Employees over 64 (59 for women) have their redundancy payment reduced progressively so that for each complete month by which the age exceeds 64 (or 59) on the Saturday of the week on which the contract ends, the normal entitlement is reduced by 1/12th. Thus a man aged 64 years and three months would have 3/12th of the award deducted. Complaints by employees in respect of the right to redundancy payment or questions as to its amount, may, as we have seen, be made to an industrial tribunal which will make a declaration as to the employee's rights which form the basis on which payment can be recovered from the employer.

Rebates for employers
It should be noted that employers of 10 or more persons who have made a redundancy payment can no longer claim a rebate from government funds.

Procedure for handling redundancies
A good starting point is to ask for voluntary redundancies. If this does not provide enough persons then any agreed formula must be followed, e.g. last in, first out. If there is no agreed procedure the employer must decide after considering the pros and cons in each case. Everyone should, as far as possible, be allowed to express their views, e.g. through elected representatives, if any. An attempt to relocate a redundant worker should be considered. Failure to do so can result in a finding of unfair dismissal unless, of course, there was

no chance of finding suitable alternative work.

Selecting, say, a white single girl, or a West Indian single man to go, rather than a married white man with two children and a mortgage might appear to be humane. However, unless the decision is made on the basis of competence, experience, reliability, and so on, the dismissal is likely to be unfair and also a breach of the Sex Discrimination Act 1975 and/or the Race Relations Act 1976.

Under the Employment Protection Act 1975 where an employer proposes to dismiss as redundant any employee where there is an independent trade union recognized by that employer in regard to the class of the employee concerned, the employer has a duty to consult with representatives of that union. In particular, where a hundred or more workers are to be dismissed within ninety days or less, the employer must consult at least ninety days before the first dismissal takes place. If the proposal is to dismiss ten or more workers within thirty days at one establishment he must consult at least thirty days before the first dismissal.

Failure to do this gives the union(s) a right to go to a tribunal which, unless it finds that the employer could not reasonably consult because of circumstances, may make a declaration of non-compliance and possibly *protective awards*. These are awards of remuneration for a protected period for those employees dismissed without proper consultation. The maximum period where a hundred or more workers are dismissed is ninety days; ten or more, thirty days; less than ten, twenty-eight days.

The employer must also inform the Department of Employment if dismissing a hundred or more employees within ninety days or less, or ten or more within thirty days or less. The DoE must be informed of this intention at least ninety days or 30 days respectively, before the first dismissal is to take place. There is no need to notify if it is proposed to make less than ten employees redundant. Failure to notify can mean a fine on conviction by the court. Notification to the DoE applies whether or not there is a recognized trade union.

General standards of fairness for redundancy were laid down by the Employment Appeal Tribunal in *Williams* v *Compair Maxam* (1982). These were the giving of maximum notice; consultation with unions, if any; the taking of the views of more than one person as to who should be dismissed; the requirement to follow any laid down procedure, e.g. last in, first out; and, finally, an effort to find the employees concerned alternative employment within the organization. It should be noted that in *Meikle* v *McPhail* (*Charleston Arms*) (1983) the Employment Appeal Tribunal stated that these guidelines would be applied less rigidly to the smaller business.

Collective agreements on redundancy. The Secretary of State may, on the application of the employer and the unions involved, make an order modifying the requirements of redundancy pay legislation if he is satisfied that there is a collective agreement which makes satisfactory alternative arrangements for dealing with redundancy. The provisions of the agreement must be 'on the whole at least as favourable' as the statutory provisions, and must include, in particular, arrangements allowing an employee to go to an independent arbitration or to make a complaint to an industrial tribunal.

Other methods of termination of contract of service

Having considered the termination of the contract by unfair or discriminatory dismissal or redundancy, we must now turn to other ways in which the contract of service may be brought to an end. These are set out below.

By notice

A contract of service can be brought to an end by either party giving notice to the other, although, where the employer gives notice, even in accordance with the contract of service or under the statutory provisions of the Employment Protection (Consolidation) Act 1978, he may still face a claim for unfair dismissal or a redundancy payment.

The most important practical aspect is the length of notice to be given by the parties, in particular the employer. The 1978 Act contains statutory provisions in regard to *minimum* periods of notice and the only relevance of the express provisions of a particular contract of service on the matter are that a contract may provide for longer periods of notice than does the Act. Under the 1978 Act an employee is entitled to one week's notice after employment for one month or more; after two years' service the minimum entitlement is increased to two weeks, and for each year of service

after that it is increased by one week up to a maximum of twelve weeks' notice after twelve years' service.

An employee, once he has been employed for one month or more, must give his employer one week's notice and the period of one week's notice applies for the duration of the contract so far as the employee is concerned, no matter how long he has served the employer.

Breach of the provisions relating to minimum periods of notice do not involve an employer in any penalty, but the rights conferred by the 1978 Act will be taken into account in assessing the employer's liability for breach of contract. Thus an employer who has dismissed his employee without due notice is generally liable for the wages due to the employee for the appropriate period of notice at the contract rate.

It should be noted that the 1978 Act provisions regarding minimum periods of notice do not affect the common law rights of an employer to dismiss an employee at once without notice for misconduct, e.g. disobedience, neglect, or drunkenness. (See p. 306.)

In practice a contract of service is often terminated by a payment instead of notice and this is allowed by the 1978 Act.

By agreement

As in any other contract the parties to a contract of employment may end the contract by agreement. Thus if employer and employee agree to new terms and conditions on, e.g. a promotion of the employee, the old agreement is discharged and a new one takes over.

An employee could agree to be 'bought off' by his employer under an agreement to discharge the existing contract of service. In this connection it should be noted that discharge of a contract of service by agreement is not a 'dismissal' for the purposes, e.g. of an unfair dismissal claim, but should a claim for unfair dismissal be brought by an employee who has been 'bought off' the tribunal concerned will want to see evidence of a genuine and fair agreement by employer and employee and may allow a claim of unfair dismissal if the discharging agreement is one-sided and biased in favour of the employer.

By passage of time

In the case of a fixed term contract, as where an employee is engaged for, say, three years, the contract will terminate at the end of the three years though there may be provisions for notice within that period.

By frustration

A contract of service can, as we have already seen, be discharged by frustration – which could be incapacity, such as illness. However, other events can bring about the discharge of a contract of service by frustration, e.g. a term of imprisonment, as in *Hare* v *Murphy Bros* (1975) (see p. 178).

Furthermore, death of either employer or employee will discharge the contract by frustration from the date of the death so that, for example, the personal representatives of the employer are not required to continue with the contract. However, the employee has a claim for wages or salary due at the date of death.

Under the 1978 Act claims for unfair dismissal arising before the employer's death survive and may be brought after the death of the employer against his estate. Furthermore, the death of a human employer is usually regarded as a 'dismissal' for redundancy purposes and the employee may make a claim against the employer's estate.

If the employee is re-engaged or the personal representatives renew his contract within eight weeks of the employer's death, the employee is not regarded as having been dismissed. Where an offer of renewal or re-engagement is refused on reasonable grounds by the employee, then he is entitled to a redundancy payment. If he unreasonably refuses to renew his contract or accept a suitable offer of re-engagement he is not entitled to such a payment.

Partnership dissolution

A person who is employed by a partnership which is dissolved is regarded as dismissed on dissolution of the firm. Under the 1978 Act this is regarded as having occurred because of redundancy.

The dismissal is also regarded as wrongful at common law and there may be a claim by the employee for damages but these will be nominal only if the partnership business continues and the continuing partners offer new employment on the old terms. (*Brace* v *Calder* (1895); see p. 181.)

A partnership is dissolved whenever one partner dies or becomes bankrupt or leaves the firm for any reason.

Of course, if a firm or sole trader sells the business as a going concern, employees are transferred to the new employer automatically under the Transfer of Under-takings (Protection of Employment) Regulations 1981.

Appointment of an administrator

As we have seen, the object of administration orders is to allow a company to be put on a profitable basis if possible, or at least disposed of more profitably than would be the case if other forms of insolvency proceedings, such as liquidation, were used. On the appointment of an administrator the company's executive and other directors are not dismissed but their powers of management are exercisable only if the administrator consents. He also has power to dismiss and appoint directors.

Since an administrator is made an agent of the company by the court under the administration order, employees are not automatically dismissed. In addition, an administrator is not taken to have adopted a contract of employment by reason of anything done or omitted to be done within fourteen days after his appointment. This provision, which is also applied to an administrative receiver (see below), is to correct a possible unfairness which existed under the previous law before the coming into force of the present insolvency provisions, which are contained in the Insolvency Act of 1986. In earlier times an administrator or administrative receiver would have been able to take the services of an employee of the company for some weeks and then say 'your contract is with the company: the company is insolvent and I do not intend to pay you'. Thus the employee might work for some time without any right to pay. Under the provisions of the Insolvency Act 1986 if an administrator or an administrative receiver allows an employee of the company to contribute his services and says nothing to him for more than fourteen days about his contract of employment, then he is deemed to have adopted it and he cannot refuse to pay for those services.

If, of course, an administrator or administrative receiver dismisses an employee, that employee can make a claim for a redundancy payment.

Appointment of an administrative receiver

As we have seen, where a company has borrowed money and given security for the loan by charging its assets under a debenture, the debenture holders may, if, e.g. they are not paid interest on the loan, appoint a receiver and manager, now referred to as an administrative receiver. The most common appointment is by a bank in respect of an overdraft or loan facility to a company.

If the administrative receiver is appointed under the terms of the debenture he is, under the Insolvency Act 1986, an agent of the company and where this is so employees of the company are not dismissed on his appointment and their employment is continuous for the purposes of employment legislation. Employees are, however, dismissed if the administrative receiver sells the undertaking or where continuance of the employees' contracts would be inconsistent with the appointment of a receiver as could be the case in regard to the contract of a managing director. However, even a managing director may not be regarded as dismissed where the receiver has a part-time appointment, as was the case in *Griffiths* v *Secretary of State for Social Services* (1973).

If the appointment is made by the court then the receiver is not the agent of the company but an officer of the court and his appointment terminates the contracts of all employees and the continuity of their employment ceases and they have a claim for a redundancy payment. The receiver may, of course, continue the employment by offering what are in effect new contracts, but where this is so there is a break in the continuity in the employment for the purposes of employment legislation. The employees are now employed by the receiver and not by the company to which he has been appointed.

Company liquidation

There are three possibilities, as follows –

(1) *A compulsory winding up*. Here the court orders the winding up of the company, usually on the petition of a creditor because it cannot pay his debt. The making of a compulsory winding up order by the court may have the following effects according to the circumstances of the case –

(a) where the company's business ceases the winding up order will operate as a wrongful dismissal of employees;

(b) where the liquidator continues the business he may be regarded as an agent of the company so that the employment continues or, alternatively, the court may regard the appointment of the liquidator as a giving of notice to the employee who then works out that notice under the liquidator. It is, however,

the better view that employees may, if they so choose, regard themselves as dismissed because the company has ceased to employ them, the new contract being with the liquidator.

(2) *A voluntary winding up*. This commences on the resolution of the members and if the company's business ceases there is a dismissal of employees. If the company's business continues the position would appear to be as set out in (1)(b) above.

Bankruptcy

The bankruptcy of a human employer, or indeed of the employee, does not automatically discharge the contract of service, though it will if there is a term to that effect in the agreement. Thus, the employment can continue, though in practical terms it may be impossible to pay employees' wages; in this case they will be discharged and be able to make a claim for redundancy payment and also in the bankruptcy for wages accrued due (in regard to which they have a preferential claim in the bankruptcy).

A trustee in bankruptcy cannot insist that an employee should continue in service because the contract is one of a personal nature. The bankruptcy of an employee will not normally affect the contract of service unless there is a term to that effect in the contract. Company directors provide a special case since the articles of most companies provide for termination of the office on becoming bankrupt (see p. 143).

Wrongful and summary dismissal at common law

The claim at common law for wrongful dismissal is based on a general principle of the law of contract, i.e. wrongful repudiation of the contract of service by the employer.

The common law action has, of course, been largely taken over by the statutory provisions relating to unfair dismissal and a common law claim is only likely to be brought by an employee who has a fixed term contract at a high salary. Thus a company director who has a fixed term contract for, say, three years at a salary of £50 000 per annum might, if wrongfully dismissed, find it more profitable in terms of damages obtainable to sue at common law for breach of contract. The employer, however, may be able to resist the claim where the employee was guilty, e.g. of misconduct, disobedience or immorality.

In other cases where the contract of service is not for a fixed term, there is no claim for damages at common law provided the employer gives proper notice or pays wages instead of notice, though in such a case the employee has at least potentially, a claim for unfair dismissal which he could pursue. Again, the employer may resist a claim for unfair dismissal on the basis of misconduct, disobedience or immorality; we have already given some consideration to these matters in the context of statutory unfair dismissal.

Rights and remedies on dismissal

These are as follows.

Written statement of reasons for dismissal

At common law an employer is not required to give his employee any reasons for dismissal. However, the Employment Protection (Consolidation) Act 1978 provides that where an employee is dismissed, with or without notice, or by failure to renew a contract for a fixed term, he must be provided by his employer on request, within fourteen days of that request, with a written statement giving particulars of the reasons for his dismissal. This provision applies only to employees who have been continuously employed for a period of six months. The written statement is admissible in evidence in any proceedings relating to the dismissal and if an employer refuses to give a written statement the employee may complain to an industrial tribunal. If the tribunal upholds the complaint it may make a declaration as to what it finds the employer's reasons were for dismissing the employee and must make an award of two weeks' pay without limit as to amount to the employee.

Employer's insolvency

If the employer is bankrupt or dies insolvent, or where the employer is a company and is in liquidation, the unpaid wages of an employee have priority as to payment but only to a maximum of £800 and limited to services rendered during the period of four months before the commencement of the insolvency. Any balance over £800 or four months ranks as an ordinary debt. Also preferential is accrued holiday remuneration payable to an employee on the termination of his employment before or because of the insolvency.

The 1978 Act adds to the above preferential debts by including in the list sums owed in respect of statutory guarantee payments, guaranteed payments during statutory time off, remuneration on suspension for medical grounds, or remuneration under a protective award given because of failure to consult properly on redundancy. Statutory sick pay under the Social Security and Housing Benefits Act of 1982 is also a preferential debt.

It should also be noted that under the 1978 Act an employee may, in the case of his employer's insolvency, make a claim on the Redundancy Fund rather than relying on the preferential payments procedure set out above. If the employee is paid from the Redundancy Fund the Secretary of State for Employment may then claim in the employer's insolvency for the amount paid out of the Redundancy Fund; the claim is preferential to the extent that the employee paid would have been.

The limits of the employee's claim on the Redundancy Fund are as follows –

(*a*) Arrears of pay for a period not exceeding eight weeks with a maximum of £158 per week.

(*b*) Holiday pay with a limit of six weeks and a financial limit of £158 per week.

(*c*) Payments instead of notice at a rate not exceeding £158 per week.

(*d*) Payments outstanding in regard to an award by an industrial tribunal of compensation for unfair dismissal.

(*e*) Reimbursement of any fee or premium paid by an apprentice or articled clerk.

There is no qualifying period before an employee becomes eligible and virtually all people in employment are entitled.

It should also be noted that claims on the Redundancy Fund will not normally be admitted if the liquidator or trustee in bankruptcy can satisfy the Secretary of State that the preferential payments will be paid from funds available in the insolvency and without undue delay.

Damages for wrongful dismissal

These are covered by common law rules and will be looked at in the context of a fixed term contract which has been wrongfully repudiated by the employer before the term has expired. The damages will be the amount of money which the employee would have earned under the contract less the amount of money which he could reasonably have expected to earn elsewhere. Arrears of pay for work done prior to dismissal, if any, are also included.

A general principle of the common law, which is that a plaintiff suing for breach of contract must mitigate his loss, applies and reference should be made at this point to the case of *Brace* v *Calder* (1895) (see p. 181).

Damages for loss of benefits other than salary may be included, e.g. a rent-free house, provided these were rights given in the contract of service. There is no claim for discretionary benefits which an employer may or may not give, such as discretionary bonuses.

It should also be noted that, since damages for wrongful dismissal normally involve an assessment of lost salary, a deduction for income tax must be made before the plaintiff receives his award. (*Beach* v *Reed Corrugated Cases Ltd* (1965).)

Furthermore, sums which the employer would have had to deduct from salary for social security contributions and any unemployment benefit received by the employee will also go to reduce damages. In addition, sums which the employee has received by way of redundancy payments also go to reduce the damages (*Stocks* v *Magna Merchants Ltd* (1973)), and so, it would seem, on the basis of the above case, do amounts received by the employee in respect of a claim for unfair dismissal. The deduction of these sums seems wrong in that they are rewards for past services rather than compensation for loss of a job.

The equitable remedy of specific performance and injunction

A decree of specific performance is, as we have seen, an order of the court and constitutes an express instruction to a party to a contract to perform the actual obligations which he undertook under its terms. If the person who is subject to the order fails to comply with it, he is in contempt of court and potentially liable to be fined or imprisoned. For all practical purposes the remedy is not given to enforce performance of a contract of service, largely because the court cannot supervise that its order is being carried out. A judge would have to attend the place of work on a regular basis to see that the parties were implementing the contract.

An injunction is, as we have seen, an order of the court whereby an individual is required to refrain from the further doing of the act complained of. Again, a person who is subject to such an order and fails to comply with it is in contempt of court and the consequences set out above follow from the contempt. An injunction may be used to prevent many wrongful acts, e.g. the torts of trespass and nuisance, but in the context of contract the remedy will be granted to enforce a negative stipulation in a contract in a situation where it would be unjust to confine the plaintiff to damages. In a proper case an injunction may be used as an indirect method of enforcing a contract for personal services, such as a contract of employment; but in that case a clear negative stipulation is required. Reference should be made to *Warner Brothers* v *Nelson* (1937) at p. 182 as an illustration of the application of the negative stipulation rule.

In this connection it should also be noted that the Trade Union and Labour Relations Act 1974 provides that no court shall by way of specific performance or an injunction compel an employee to do any work or attend any place for the doing of any work. Thus the Act is in line with the judicial approach to specific performance, but to some extent out of line with the judicial approach to the granting of an injunction. Thus the availability of an injunction in cases involving contracts of service is subject to the provisions of the 1974 Act. Although the matter has not been worked out by the courts, it would seem that, on general principles, the granting of an injunction in the context of a contract of employment is no longer possible since statute law prevails over decisions of the judiciary – but the matter is not beyond doubt.

Employee's breach of contract

An employer may sue his employees for damages for breach of the contract of service by the employee. Such claims are potentially available for, e.g. damage to the employer's property, as where machinery is damaged by negligent operation, as was the case in *Baster* v *London and County Printing Works* (1899), or for refusal to work resulting in damage by lost production, as was the case in *National Coal Board* v *Galley* (1958). Such claims are rare and impractical because of the fact that the employee will not, in most cases, be able to meet the claim, and also, perhaps more importantly, because they lead to industrial unrest. In these circumstances we do not pursue the matter further here.

Questions/activities

1. How is the relationship of employer and worker established?

2. In connection with the provisions for maternity leave and statutory maternity pay –

(a) what is the maximum leave entitlement?

(b) what is the amount of maternity pay?

(c) for how long must the claimant have been continuously employed?

3. Des and Eric are both employed by a bus company. Des is a bus driver and Eric a conductor. Eric has always nursed an ambition to be a driver and Des has, on occasion, let Eric drive a bus around the depot before other employees turned up for work. Last week, while Eric was having a drive around the yard, he struck Des who was riding his motor bike around the yard at 60 mph.

Discuss the liability of Eric and the bus company in regard to the injuries suffered by Des.

4. Monty signalled to a van driver of Python Ltd to stop and asked him to take him to the Grotty Towers Hotel. The hotel was some five miles away from the route which the driver would usually take in the course of his duties, but he nevertheless agreed to give Monty a lift to the hotel. When the driver had deviated a quarter mile from his authorized route he carelessly collided with another vehicle and Monty was injured.

As company secretary of Python Ltd you have received a letter from a firm of solicitors representing Monty threatening legal action against Python Ltd. Your managing director asks you to draft a memorandum for him on the legal aspects of the case.

Draft the memorandum.

5. You have recently been appointed the company secretary of Foundry Ltd. The following problems emerge at the first board meeting.

(a) The board is concerned as to whether they are taking appropriate steps to communicate with the employees as to how the company is fulfilling its obligations under the Health and Safety at Work Act.

You are asked to write an explanatory memorandum for the next board meeting as to the legal requirements and indicate the steps which the company should be taking.

(b) It appears that Foundry Ltd employs 100 women and 50 men in an area where there are a large number of immigrant families. The managing director appears to have paid little or no attention to sex, race and equal pay legislation. The board, which is concerned about this, asks for an explanatory memorandum, again for the next board meeting, summarizing the main provisions of the relevant legislation and setting out procedures which the company should adopt to ensure that the law is complied with.

6. John is one of the employees of a firm in which you are a partner. He suffers badly from arthritis. He has been employed for ten years. However, he has had a number of absences of two to three weeks' duration over the past three years.

John is employed as a shop assistant and the manager of the shop has just informed you that John has now been off work for eight weeks with arthritis and is still not fit to come back to work. The manager wants to write to John telling him that he is dismissed.

Prepare a note for your next partnership meeting as to the legal position if John is dismissed.

7. Alan worked for ten years for Pleasant Ltd. They were taken over eighteen months ago by Aggressive Ltd and Alan continued his job. He has found the management of Aggressive Ltd to be very difficult and domineering. Amongst other things, they have asked him to work in the stores issuing and accounting for equipment issued to Aggressive's employees. Alan feels that he has not been trained to do this and has given in his notice.

Advise him as to his rights.

8. The company of which you are secretary makes components for cars. Business has fallen off lately and the board has decided that it will have to dismiss 120 employees during the next five weeks. Write an explanatory memorandum to the board regarding any legal requirements there may be in terms of –

(a) notification of the redundancies;

(b) selection of employees for redundancy;

(c) amounts of compensation that may be involved.

General Index